"Stuart's work interests me very much. He handles this subject well."

> —*Don J. Briel (1947–2018), founder of the Center for Catholic Studies at the University of St. Thomas, St. Paul, Minn.*

"If I had to summarize the overall impression that Joseph Stuart's work has left on me, it would be this: I'm convinced—now more than ever—that Dawson is a scholar of enduring influence. There are serious implications here for the fields of sociology, psychology, and history so often absent from our sociological considerations in late modernity."

> —*Garrett Potts, Religious Studies, University of South Florida*

"Joseph Stuart has produced a timely and deeply researched study of the originality of Christopher Dawson's achievement. He shows that the basis of Dawson's 'cultural mind' was an extraordinary integration of thought that gave rise to a new synthesis of understanding based on the blending of spiritual insights and the modern social sciences."

> —*Karl Schmude, Co-founder of Campion College, Sydney, Australia*

CHRISTOPHER DAWSON

CHRISTOPHER DAWSON

A Cultural Mind in the Age of the Great War

JOSEPH T. STUART

The Catholic University of America Press
Washington, D.C.

Epigraph is from Hayden White, review of *Les Moines
Blanc: Histoire de l'Ordre Cistercien* by Louis J. Lekai,
Speculum 34, no. 2 (April 1959): 308.

Design and composition by Kachergis Book Design

Library of Congress Cataloging-in-Publication Data
Names: Stuart, Joseph T., author.
Title: Christopher Dawson : a cultural mind in the age of
the Great War / Joseph T. Stuart.
Description: Washington, D.C. : The Catholic University
of America Press, [2022] | Identifiers: LCCN 2022006582
(print) | LCCN 2022006583 (ebook) | ISBN 9780813234571
(paperback) | ISBN 9780813234588 (ebook)
Subjects: LCSH: Dawson, Christopher, 1889–1970—
Criticism and interpretation. | Dawson, Christopher,
1889–1970. | Historians—Great Britain—Biography. |
Christian civilization. | Christianity and culture. |
Civilization, Western. | World War, 1914–1918—
Influence. | Catholic historians—Biography.
Classification: LCC CB18.D38 S78 2022 (print) |
LCC CB18.D38 (ebook) | DDC 907/.2024 [B]—dc23/
eng/20220210
LC record available at https://lccn.loc.gov/2022006582
LC ebook record available at https://lccn.loc.
gov/2022006583

Dedicated to my mentors
James Gaston,
Annette Kirk,
James McMillan, and
Owen Dudley Edwards,
who made it possible.

And to my beloved wife,
Barbara Ann Stuart, who
supported it.

"No historian worthy of the name is only a historian."—*Hayden White*

CONTENTS

ACKNOWLEDGMENTS

This book is the result of over twenty years of researching and teaching the work of Christopher Dawson (1889–1970), the British historian of culture. The influence of James Gaston, my inspiring undergraduate professor who first introduced me to the work of Dawson, pervades this whole volume. He once counselled me to find wise and intelligent mentors and to beat a path to their door. With the help of Annette Kirk and Jeff Nelson, I found such mentors in my doctoral advisors James McMillan and Owen Dudley Edwards at the University of Edinburgh. I am incredibly grateful for the formation provided by these two men in my work on Dawson. The School of History, Classics, and Archaeology at the University of Edinburgh granted me several scholarships for which I am very grateful. To the H. B. Earhart Foundation and my sponsor, Vigen Guroian, I owe more than words can express. I am much indebted to the staff of the National Library of Scotland for all its help over the years, and to Ann Kenne, Head of Special Collections at the University of St. Thomas, the home of the Dawson papers. The Russell Kirk Center provided me grants, a home, and opportunities for discussion. Finally, I am so grateful to all those at the University of Mary, where I teach, who contribute to a flourishing life of the mind there. I thank Amanda Reeve at the University of Mary's Welder Library for tirelessly tracking down hundreds of resources for me, and Patrick McCloskey, editor-in-chief of the *360 Review*, for all the ways he worked with me to improve my writing style. I am grateful for a John T. Ford Award to help me present my views on the relationship between Dawson and John Henry Newman's educational thought at the Newman Association of America Conference in 2018.

I am also grateful to those who provided hospitality to me on various research trips, including Maria and Giacomo Mazzi, Ken and

Acknowledgments

Christine Cox, Maura and Ian Shanley, Robert and Maria O'Brien, Stratford and Leonie Caldecott, Rev. Michael Kelly, and the Catholic seminary of St. Paul, Minnesota. Magdalen Goffin (1925–2015), the daughter of E. I. Watkin (Dawson's close friend) and Fellow of the Royal Society of Literature, invited me to her sixteenth-century cottage and detached library in the English countryside west of Tunbridge Wells. There, I was able to examine Watkin's diary about his visit to the Dawson home in Yorkshire. I will never forget walking through the beautiful pasture with Magdalen behind her home, talking of many things. I was able to go to Yorkshire due to the generous hospitality of Maureen Fraser and her husband, who live in a partition of the former Dawson home, Hartlington Hall. They hosted me for a couple of days to experience first-hand Dawson's place and region that so profoundly shaped his views of culture. Through the help of Goffin and Fraser, I was able to publish the section of Watkin's diary about his 1911 visit to Hartlington ("Yorkshire Days in Edwardian England: E. I. Watkin's Diary and his Friendship with Christopher Dawson," introduction and notes by Joseph T. Stuart, *Yorkshire Archaeological Journal* LXXXIV [2012]: 205–23).

I thank Matthew Gerlach for his conversation and inspiration over the years. I am particularly grateful for the opportunity to assist him in launching the Catholic Studies program at the University of Mary in 2010. Based largely on the example of Don J. Briel's pioneering Catholic Studies program at the University of St. Thomas, and on the Humanities and Catholic Culture program at the Franciscan University of Steubenville, the curriculum and course development work with Gerlach over five years, along with student interaction, formed a fruitful matrix for this book to germinate. The current director, Scott Cleveland, and the Catholic Studies Fellows have continued to give me opportunities to share my work on Dawson and develop my pedagogical approach.

A big thanks also to all those who provided critical feedback, discussion, and assistance on both the dissertation stage and the book stage of this project, including (in no particular order) John Lukacs, John Rodden, Rev. Fergus Kerr, Tom Devine, John Morrill, Chad Litton, Daniel Davy, Sebastien Renault, Edward King, Fae Presley, Lee Trepanier, R. Jared Staudt, Denis and Sara Kitzinger, Karl Schmude, Bradley

Birzer, Julie Yarwood, Ann Brodeur, Donald Bungum, Garrett Potts, Michon Matthiesen, Michael Milburn, Jeremy Skrzypek, Ivan Jankovic, and several anonymous reviewers. Over many meals together in Edinburgh and Rome, Robert di Pede first alerted me to a critical "logic of charity" by which one penetrates beneath the surface of an author's texts through identifying implicit questions and categories; thank you to him. Julian Scott, Dawson's grandson and literary executor, has remained a friend, a resource, and a helpful critic for many years; I am so grateful for his encouragement. The remarkable educator and general editor of the *Works of Christopher Dawson* series at the Catholic University of America (CUA) Press, Don J. Briel (1947–2018), before he passed away, supplied critical suggestions for Dawson's thought on education. He also invited me to write the introduction to Dawson's *Gods of Revolution*, reprinted by CUA Press in 2015—a great honor. Correspondence with Gail Porter Mandell, Emerita Bruno P. Schlesinger Chair in Humanistic Studies at St. Mary's College, helped me understand how the Christian Culture program there, inspired by Dawson's ideas, evolved over the years. University of Mary students Amelia Kumpel ('19), Juliana Gagliardi ('19), Brendan Thorp ('19), MaryGrace Franz ('20), Jordan L. Grant ('20), and Peter Collart ('21) helped with the bibliography and appendices. Thank you to all—especially Annie Roufs ('21) and James Gillis ('24), who helped with the index.

Any mistakes herein are my responsibility alone.

I am grateful to *The Political Science Reviewer* (XLI, no. 2 [2017]: 303–34) for permission to republish large sections from my article "Christopher Dawson and Political Religion"; chapter 6 is closely based on it.

Stephen Little first saw merit to publishing this book, and his encouragement got the ball rolling. Trevor Lipscombe and his team at the Catholic University of America Press have been incredible publishers to work with, and I am so grateful for their guidance of this project through to completion.

My beloved wife Barbara is my strongest supporter and critic. Her encouragement and suggestions sustained me as this book took shape. She challenged me amid our young family life to find a way to write in little spaces of time. Thank you.

ABBREVIATIONS

Abbreviations

REFERENCE WORKS

ODNB *Oxford Dictionary of National Biography* (2004), online edition (http://www.oxforddnb.com)

OED *Oxford English Dictionary* (1989), online edition (http://www.oed.com)

CHRISTOPHER
DAWSON

Introduction

And the first step in the transformation of culture is a change in the
pattern of culture within the mind, for this is the seed out of which
there spring new forms of life which ultimately change the social way
of life and thus create a new culture.

—Christopher Dawson

British historian Christopher Dawson (1889–1970)[1] has been called
one of the foremost Catholic thinkers of modern times.[2] Many of his
books have been republished.[3] When Dawson retired from Harvard
University in 1962, Pope John XXIII sent his Apostolic blessing by
telegram. Dawson's work has been favorably compared with theologian Joseph Ratzinger[4] and philosophers R. G. Collingwood and Eric
Voegelin,[5] and his comparative religion studies have been cited as a

Christopher Dawson, "The Outlook for Christian Culture Today," *Cross Currents* 5 (Spring 1955): 131.

1. The author of more than twenty books, Dawson was an independent scholar. He served as assistant lecturer in the History of Culture, University College, Exeter (1925), Forwood Lecturer in the Philosophy of Religion, University of Liverpool (1934), Gifford Lecturer at the University of Edinburgh (1947 to 1949), and as Professor of Roman Catholic Studies at Harvard University (1958 to 1962). He was elected Fellow of the British Academy in 1943 and edited the *Dublin Review* during the Second World War.

2. James Likoudis, "Christopher Dawson, Historian of Christian Divisions and Prophet of Christian Unity," *The Catholic Social Science Review* 11 (2006): 385.

3. The Catholic University of America Press has released *Progress and Religion* (2001), *Medieval Essays* (2002), *The Making of Europe* (2003), *Enquiries into Religion and Culture* (2009), *Understanding Europe* (2009), *The Crisis of Western Education* (2010), *The Judgment of the Nations* (2011), *The Age of the Gods* (2012), *The Movement of World Revolution* (2013), *Religion and Culture* (2013), and *The Gods of Revolution* (2015). ISI Books, Ignatius, and Cluny Media have republished books by Dawson, too, as well as St. Austin in Britain, Ediciones Encuentro in Spain, and É Realizações Editora in Brazil.

4. R. Jared Staudt, "'Religion and Culture' and 'Faith and Renewal of Society' in Christopher Dawson and Pope Benedict XVI," *Logos* 16, no. 1 (Winter 2013): 31–69.

5. Philip I. Mitchell, "Civilizational Sickness and the Suspended Middle: R. G. Collingworth, Christopher Dawson, and Historical Judgment," *Logos* 21, no. 3 (Summer 2018): 85–113; Lee Trepanier, "Culture and History in Eric Voegelin and Christopher Dawson," *Political Science Reviewer* 41, no. 2 (December 2017): 211–42.

Introduction

refutation to New Atheism.[6] Dawson has also been recognized as arguably the greatest British sociologist of the early twentieth century, an important figure in returning religion to the agenda of Western historiography, an indirect influence on postmodernist historiographical concerns, a "first rank" metahistorian and world historian of the twentieth century, and an authority on intercivilizational interaction.[7]

Dawson's ideas about religion and culture have inspired educational institutions in the English-speaking world and academic programs in the spirit of *Ex Corde Ecclesiae* (1990), the apostolic constitution by Pope John Paul II directed at Catholic colleges and universities.[8] John Paul defined "culture" as a way of life, like Dawson did, and used it to describe the mission of the New Evangelization: "A faith that does not become culture is not fully accepted, not entirely thought out, not faithfully lived."[9] Dawson was one of the most prominent Catholics to

6. Gerald J. Russello, introduction, in *Religion and Culture*, by Christopher Dawson (1948; Washington D.C.: The Catholic University of America Press, 2013).

7. Garrett Potts and Stephen P. Turner, "Making Sense of Christopher Dawson," in *The History of Sociology in Britain: New Research and Revaluation*, ed. Plamena Panayotova (Cam: Palgrave Macmillan, 2019), 103; Jay D. Green, *Christian Historiography: Five Rival Versions* (Waco, Tex.: Baylor University Press, 2015), 18–19; Herman Paul, "Metahistory: Notes towards a Genealogy," *Práticas da História* 1, no. 1 (2015): 17–31; Paul Costello, *World Historians and Their Goals: Twentieth-Century Answers to Modernism* (DeKalb: Northern Illinois University Press, 1993), 153; and Stephen G. Carter, "Christopher Dawson and Ayatollah Khatami and 'The Dialogue of Civilizations': A Christian-Muslim Conversation," *Islam and Christian-Muslim Relations* 18, no. 3 (July 2007): 403–20.

8. For example, Dawson's influence can be found in (1) educational institutions such as the International Institute for Culture (Philadelphia), the G. K. Chesterton Institute (Seton Hall University, New Jersey), the Christopher Dawson Centre for Cultural Studies (Hobart, Tasmania), and the Christopher Dawson Society for Philosophy and Culture (Perth, Australia); and (2) academic programs such as Catholic Studies at the University of St. Thomas (St. Paul, Minnesota), the University of Mary (Bismarck, North Dakota), Aquinas College (Grand Rapids, Michigan), the Franciscan University of Steubenville (the Humanities and Catholic Culture program), and in the very founding of Campion College (Sydney, Australia). The Catholic Studies Center at the University of St. Thomas acquired the Christopher Dawson library and manuscript collection in 1998. At St. Thomas, and in other places, Dawson's cultural mind has conspired with the legacy of John Henry Newman to inspire educational renewal *ex corde ecclesiae* ("from the heart of the Church") through the work of James Gaston, Karl Schmude, Don J. Briel, and others. See, for example, R. Jared Staudt, ed., *The University and the Church: Don J. Briel's Essays on Education* (Providence, R.I.: Cluny Media, 2019).

9. Pope John Paul II, "Address to the Italian National Congress of the Ecclesial Movement for Cultural Commitment," January 16, 1982; cf. *L'Osservatore Romano*, English edition, June 28, 1982, 7; "The New Evangelization and Culture," Mother of the Americas Institute: A Think Tank for the New Evangelization, https://mainstitute.org/tutorials/new-evangelization-and-culture (accessed November 19, 2019).

engage the social sciences and this idea of culture before the concept found a place in the Catholic Church's magisterial teaching during and after the Second Vatican Council.[10]

Culture is essential to human life because it helps people adapt to their environments, yet it is a frustratingly vague concept. Despite its common use to designate the arts, it is one of the most complex English words. Few people, even social scientists, agree on its meaning.[11] Dawson often defined culture simply as the common way of life of a people, including their vision of reality. Understood in this way, he constructed his historical narratives around cultures rather than around states, civilizations, or institutional churches, which other historians of his day often assumed as their organizing principles.

Dawson's modest description of culture as a common way of life is significant not only because it indicates one of Dawson's central interests but also because it shaped *the way he looked at the world*. In studying world cultures, he developed what I call a "cultural mind" by which he attempted to "see things whole"—analogous to an "aesthetic mind"[12] or a "scientific mind"[13] perceiving reality in terms of beauty or scientific reason. Dawson perceived human reality in terms of cultural reason. In this context, "cultural," as an adjective in "cultural reason"

10. Staudt, "'Religion and Culture' and 'Faith and Renewal of Society' in Christopher Dawson and Pope Benedict XVI," 31. Tracy Rowland argued that one reason for confusion after the Second Vatican Council was lack of clarity on the meaning of culture as used in *Gaudium et spes*; the document neglected approaches like those found in Dawson's work. See Tracey Rowland, *Culture and the Thomist Tradition: After Vatican II* (New York: Routledge, 2003), 22, 28.

11. Christian Smith, "The Conceptual Incoherence of 'Culture' in American Sociology," *The American Sociologist* 47, no. 4 (2016): 388–415. Smith wrote: "Despite the fact that 'culture' is a basic and essential concept in social science, especially sociology and anthropology, what that term denotes remains uncertain" (388).

12. An aesthetic mind perceives reality in terms of beauty of form and splendor, pulling the human person in a movement of love toward objects, other people, or the source of beauty itself. See W. David O. Taylor, "Beauty as Love: Hans Urs von Balthasar's Theological Aesthetics," *Transpositions* (2012), http://www.transpositions.co.uk/beauty-as-love-hans-urs-von-balthasars-theological-aesthetics/.

13. A scientific mind "questions everything around it," seeking underlying patterns and relations in reality that bind "the parts of the whole together." It "finds beauty" in both complexity and simplicity. "It conceptualizes the seemingly random information around it to follow a more elegant framework. It constantly seeks to reason out everything it is exposed to, to find the story behind the events that led to this particular moment." This description of the scientific mind is from Quora, the online question-and-answer forum (blog entry by Joshy Antony). See "What is a Scientific Mind?" https://www.quora.com/What-is-a-scientific-mind (accessed January 5, 2020). The cultural mind is an all-embracing paradigm of thinking like this.

Introduction

or "cultural mind" means, most broadly, "relating to the ideas, customs, and social behavior of a society." Dawson possessed the kind of mind that looks at the world through the lens of culture, connecting ideas and social ways of life. He denied "noncultural starting points of inquiry."[14]

Dawson's cultural mind is a particular application in the social sciences of what John Henry Newman (1801–1890) referred to as the "philosophical habit" of mind or "culture of mind"—the "power of viewing many things at once as one whole" and their interrelations.[15] Newman deeply influenced Dawson.[16] Dawson effectively instantiated Newman's interdisciplinary "philosophical habit" of mind in a particular way, unavailable in Newman's own time because Dawson later accessed the new conception of culture as a social way of life that emerged from anthropology during the early twentieth century.

Dawson's contemporaries found his cultural mind so significant that hundreds of book reviews about his work appeared. Many thinkers critically engaged it, including historians (William H. McNeill and R. H. Tawney),[17] philosophers (C. E. M. Joad and Etienne Gilson),[18] novelists (Aldous Huxley and Vera Brittain),[19] journalists (Barbara Ward and Douglas Woodruff),[20] foreign scholars (Jacques Le Goff and Louis Halphen),[21]

14. Russell Hittinger, "Christopher Dawson: A View from the Social Sciences," in *The Catholic Writer*, vol. 2, ed. Ralph McInerny, *Proceedings of the Wethersfield Institute* (San Francisco: Ignatius, 1991), 36.

15. John Henry Newman, *The Idea of a University* (1873; Tacoma, Wash.: Cluny Media, 2016), 84, 107, 108.

16. Not only did Dawson attend the same Oxford college (Trinity) as Newman, but Newman's conversion to Catholicism influenced his own conversion. Dawson later published a study of Newman's Anglican background; and he interpreted some of Newman's ideas on education in ways that would help inspire educational renewal movements (see chapter 8 and the conclusion).

17. William H. McNeill, review of *Dynamics of World History*, *Journal of Modern History* XXIX (1957): 257–58; R. H. Tawney, "Tract for the Times," review of *The Judgment of the Nations*, *Manchester Guardian*, March 24, 1943, 3.

18. C. E. M. Joad, "Forward to Christendom," review of *The Judgment of the Nations*, *New Statesman and Nation*, August 28, 1943, 141–42; Bradley J. Birzer, *Sanctifying the World: The Augustinian Life and Mind of Christopher Dawson* (Front Royal, Va.: Christendom Press, 2007), 4.

19. Aldous Huxley, "Light on the Dark Ages," review of *The Making of Europe*, *Spectator*, August 20, 1932, 235; Vera Brittain, "Modern Europe Adrift," review of *Progress and Religion*, *Time and Tide*, May 17, 1929, 592–93.

20. Barbara Ward, review of *The Movement of World Revolution*, *New York Times*, March 29, 1959, BR 7; Douglas Woodruff, "Christopher Dawson," *Tablet*, June 6, 1970, 558–59.

21. See fn. 121 in this introduction.

poets (Rachel Annand Taylor and T. S. Eliot),[22] archeologists (C. Daryll Forde and V. Gordon Childe),[23] Catholic theologians (Bernard Lonergan and Thomas Merton),[24] non-Catholic theologians (V. A. Demant and Reinhold Niebuhr),[25] sociologists (Robert E. Park and Karl Mannheim),[26] and educationalists (Justus George Lawler and Eugene Kevane),[27] among many others. Many readers admired Dawson's erudition along with the clear and crisp style of his books. "The greatest living authority on culture is Christopher Dawson," the Anglican Bishop George Bell testified before the British Parliament in 1949.[28]

But there have been plenty of critics, too. The Marxist historian Christopher Hill (1912–2003), erroneously assuming Dawson was dead, wrote in 1957: "The late Mr. Dawson was not a great historian: he was a diligent Roman Catholic publicist with a considerable and genuine interest in history."[29] The Cambridge Protestant historian Herbert Butter-

22. Rachel Annand Taylor, review of *Progress and Religion, Sociological Review* XXII (1930): 52–65; T. S. Eliot, *Notes towards the Definition of Culture* (New York: Harcourt, Brace, 1949), preface.

23. C. Daryll Forde, review of *The Age of the Gods, American Anthropologist*, new series, XXXIV, no. 2 (1932): 340–41; V. Gordon Childe, review of *The Age of the Gods, Antiquity* II (December 1928): 485–86.

24. Arthur Kennedy, "Christopher Dawson's Influence on Bernard Longergan's Project of 'Introducing History into Theology,'" *Logos* 15, no. 2 (Spring 2012): 138–64; Birzer, *Sanctifying the World*, 5.

25. V. A. Demant, *Theology of Society: More Essays in Christian Polity* (London: Faber & Faber, 1947), 187; Reinhold Niebuhr, "What's a Mote to One Is a Beam to Another," review of *The Historic Reality of Christian Culture, New York Times*, March 13, 1960, BR 18.

26. Robert E. Park, review of *Enquiries into Religion and Culture, American Journal of Sociology* XLI (1935): 109–11. Karl Mannheim viewed Dawson as a fellow sociologist, and they interacted through their membership in the Moot. See Potts and Turner, "Making Sense of Christopher Dawson," in *The History of Sociology in Britain: New Research and Revaluation*.

27. Justus George Lawler, "*The Crisis of Western Education* [2]," review of *The Crisis of Western Education, Harvard Educational Review* 32, no. 1 (1962): 214–20; Eugene Kevane, "Christopher Dawson and Study of Christian Culture," *Catholic Educational Review* 57, no. 1 (1959): 447–62.

28. Bishop George Bell, "The Work of UNESCO," in *George Bell: House of Lords Speeches and Correspondence with Rudolf Hess*, ed. Peter Raina (Oxford: Peter Lang, 2009), 114.

29. Christopher Hill, "The Church, Marx and History," review of *Dynamics of World History*, *Spectator*, September 20, 1957, 370. With Chestertonian humor, Dawson wrote a response letter headlined "Manalive": "Sir,—my attention has just been drawn to the article in your current issue by Mr. Christopher Hill on 'The Church, Marx and History' in which he states that 'the late Mr. Dawson was not a great historian.' I do not wish to assert that I am 'great,' but I do most emphatically deny that I am 'late'!" Dawson could not resist a little revenge, as he continued: "and I feel doubtful whether a writer who is unable to discover the truth in a contemporary matter of fact which is easily ascertainable is competent to survey the vast field which he has embraced in his article." Hill responded a few weeks later apologizing for any embarrassment caused; he said that he assumed the author was dead because the book in question seemed like a definitive collection that was put together by someone else. See Christopher Dawson, *Spectator*, September 27,

field (1900–1979) characterized Dawson's modern history as weak, and the American world historian William H. McNeill (1917–2016) thought Dawson failed to reconcile sociology with his Catholicism.[30] Joan Keating, in a very insightful dissertation, thought that Dawson's conservatism, criticism of urban culture, and romanticized view of poverty and rural life betrayed the views of a "sheltered upper class man of his era."[31] More recently, Catholic writer John Zmirak attacked Dawson's noncapitalist economic perspective as "radically wrong."[32] In the following chapters and the conclusion, I respond to these critiques.

The Argument

How did Dawson think about culture, and why does it matter? Those are the questions I hope to answer. Dawson studied world cultures as common ways of life that develop through interaction with their environments and each other. In so doing, I argue, he acquired a "cultural mind," by which he attempted to push beyond the specialization of modern knowledge to "see things whole," to account for both visible and invisible forces in the synchronic structures of cultures and in their diachronic evolution. This rich, meaningful, and multilayered approach to culture is the key to his work and his relevance. Through it, he created an integrated response to the cultural fragmentation of the Age of the Great War, which I define as lasting from 1914 to 1991, when the Soviet Union—spawned by the Russian Revolution in 1917—disintegrated. The purpose of this book is to excavate the frame of Dawson's cultural mind in order to demonstrate how it not only reconciles intellectualist and behaviorist approaches to culture but also provides a synthesis helpful in thinking about the relationship between religion and politics, reforming education as enculturation, coordinating spe-

1957, 398, letter to the editor; Christopher Hill, *Spectator*, October 11, 1957, 479, letter to the editor.

30. Herbert Butterfield, "Religion's Part in History," review of *The Dividing of Christendom*; *The Gods of Revolution*, *Times Literary Supplement* (July 28, 1972): 882; McNeill, review of Dawson 258.

31. Joan E. Keating, "Roman Catholics, Christian Democracy and the British Labour Movement, 1910–1960" (PhD diss., University of Manchester, 1992), 128, 135, 136.

32. John Zmirak, "Christopher Dawson's Economic Blindness," April 14, 2014, https://isi .org/intercollegiate-review/christopher-dawsons-economic-blindness/. See my response, Joseph T. Stuart, "Bourgeois or Baroque?" September 28, 2017, https://voegelinview.com/bourgeois-or-baroque/.

cialized research, and constructing a more meaningful cultural history today.

Through published sources and archival research in both Britain and the United States, I support these claims by demonstrating in part 1 of the book how Dawson formed his cultural mind by practicing an interdisciplinary science of culture (in the fields of anthropology, sociology, history, and comparative religion). In part 2, I show how he applied his cultural thinking to problems in politics and education.

Dawson's cultural mind linked the "science of culture" in its fullest sense to the Catholic intellectual tradition[33] for the first time in the English-speaking world. This is "science" as an ordered body of knowlege and/or wisdom based on either casual explanation (*erklären*) or interpretive understanding (*verstehen*) (or both together). Dawson was interested in not only the nature and structure of culture, cultural morphology, and comparative study of cultures but also in culture as a moral and symbolic sphere of meaning. Dawson's cultural mind coordinated two "modes" of the science of culture, bringing into conversation two traditions of cultural understanding—what I call the "socio-historical" mode (emerging out of Émile Durkheim, Max Weber, and the new field of anthropology rising to prominence around the time of the Great War) and the "humanistic" mode (inhabiting a deep Western etymology back to classical roots in "cultivation" and "worship").[34] The socio-historical tradition of cultural understanding priori-

33. Most broadly, the two-thousand-year-old Catholic intellectual tradition has sought to connect faith and reason, faith and life, and faith and culture. Dawson's work helped make the idea of culture more prominent in this tradition. See *The Catholic Intellectual Tradition: A Conversation at Boston College*, The Church in the 21st Century Center, Boston College, 2010, https://dlib.bc.edu/islandora/object/bc-ir:101053/datastream/PDF/view; Robert Royal, *A Deeper Vision: The Catholic Intellectual Tradition in the Twentieth Century* (San Francisco: Ignatius, 2015), 361–74; and Joseph T. Stuart, "Catholic Studies and the Science of Culture," in *Renewal of Catholic Higher Education: Essays on Catholic Studies in Honor of Don J. Briel*, ed. Matthew T. Gerlach (Bismarck, N.D.: University of Mary Press, 2017), 182–99.

34. Dawson did not use these labels "socio-historical" and "humanistic," but the distinction is apparent throughout his work. Occasionally, he wrote directly about the difference between the anthropological idea of cultures (plural) and the "old unitary conception which is deeply rooted in our educational traditions [the humanistic conception of culture]." To the average educated person, he continued, "culture is still regarded as an absolute. Civilization is one: men may be more cultured or less cultured, but in so far as they are cultured, they are all walking along the same high road which leads to the same goal. The idea that there are a number of different roads leading, perhaps, in opposite directions, still remains a difficult idea to assimilate." See

tizes empirical, descriptive accounts of cultures (plural) as diverse ways of life, and the humanistic tradition prioritizes prescriptive, normative accounts of culture (singular) oriented toward authentic human development, narration, and interpretation of myth. When studying the highest spiritual and intellectual values of culture, the two uses of the concept "become almost indistinguishable," Dawson wrote: "i.e., classical culture in the humanist sense is part of the study of Graeco-Roman culture in the sociological or anthropological [socio-historical] sense." This created great complications, he concluded, "but then the study of higher cultures is inevitably a complicated matter."[35]

In other words, because a culture is a moral order, it can be both a comparative object of knowledge and an embedded sphere of rival loves. Dawson's cultural mind passed back and forth between modes depending on the problem at hand because the science of culture necessitated either a descriptive mode ("this is how cultures *are*"—the socio-historical) or a prescriptive mode ("this is how culture *should be*"—the humanistic). Detached investigation *and* combative commitment to what it means to be human marked the two poles of Dawson's cultural writing, which he brought together. This distinguished him from those cultural theorists who claim to sidestep the question of truth and its relevance to our own culture today.[36]

By holding these two perspectives together in tension, Dawson espoused a moderate cultural relativism. One studied culture *from somewhere*, from within a culture, its own traditions and ways of expressing truth, goodness, and beauty, different from others. Thus, one may say, according to the socio-historical view, there is not one culture but

Christopher Dawson, *The Historic Reality of Christian Culture: A Way to the Renewal of Human Life* (London: Routledge & Kegan Paul, 1960), 60.

35. Christopher Dawson, *The Crisis of Western Education* (1961; Washington, D.C.: The Catholic University of America Press, 2010), 114.

36. "Value judgments about what is sane, rational, 'true,' or otherwise should have no place in the study of cultural meaning." See David G. Robertson, "Conspiracy Theories and the Study of Alternative and Emergent Religions," *Nova Religio: The Journal of Alternative and Emergent Religions* 19, no. 2 (2015): 12. However, Christian Smith, a contemporary sociologist, wrote: "I argue that the most adequate approach to theorizing human culture must be a normative one that conceives of humans as moral, believing animals and human social life as consisting of moral orders that constitute and direct social action." See Christian Smith, *Moral, Believing Animals: Human Personhood and Culture* (New York: Oxford University Press, 2003), 7.

many cultures in the world, each with its own way of life and its own world of values. Yet according to the humanistic view, one may also criticize harmful cultural practices at home and abroad. Cultures do not stand completely alone as independent value systems. They live by their own norms, but they also nestle around a common humanity expressed through natural law or human rights. This fruitful and unappreciated polarity in Dawson's work between socio-historical commitment to cultural relativity and humanistic commitment to universals has never been fully recognized.

In addition, because he saw culture as simultaneously spiritual and material, Dawson studied it using interdisciplinary cooperation. This enabled him to transcend specialization and allowed him to enter more deeply into the truths each discipline held, revealing the roots of the cultural crisis he faced in his time, the Age of the Great War. He employed his bedrock theological and philosophical principles to draw out the best of modern scholarship. In this way, his faith worked as a sort of "engine that makes perception operate," as Flannery O'Connor (1925–1964) put it, in his simultaneous appreciation of the transcendent in human life *and* commitment to empirical reality.[37]

Four Rules of the Cultural Mind

Dawson's cultural mind operated within either mode of the science of culture according to a "logic of interdisciplinarity"[38] involving four implicit rules: intellectual architecture, boundary thinking, intellectual bridges, and intellectual asceticism. Rules guide conduct in a sphere of activity—in this case, Dawson's activity in the disciplines of knowledge he engaged, creating much of the richness and continued relevance of his work.

(1) "INTELLECTUAL ARCHITECTURE," the first rule of cultural mind, refers to the mental structures or categories Dawson built up

---

37. Flannery O'Connor, *Mystery and Manners*, ed. Sally and Robert Fitzgerald (New York: Farrar, Straus & Giroux, 1969), 109.

38. Andrew Barry, Georgina Born, and Gisa Weszkalnys, "Logics of Interdisciplinarity," *Economy and Society* 37, no. 1 (2008): 20–49.

within himself during years of study and observation that helped him classify and locate new knowledge and relate it back to the whole. Each bit of knowledge had its proper place in his cultural mind, according to this rule. For example, Louis A. Schuster visited Dawson in the early 1950s and remembered crawling with him on hands and knees up and down between rows of books on the floor of the study. "I think each row represented a different century," he noted concerning the historian's method of study:

Books on architecture, painting, sculpture, literature, economics, philosophy, theology, history—seemingly juxtaposed at random. He opened and fondled quite a few explaining how valuable each one was because of a certain well written chapter, or this insight, or this interesting new primary evidence stuck away in a footnote on page 391 etc.

I remember squatting across the centuries from him as he pulled up another book and asked me whether I had noticed the difference between the baroque churches in Spain and those in Austria and by implication the cultural differences at work in either case. He insisted I go to Austria on my next vacation and visit especially this and that. And so it went all afternoon until my head was spinning and popping lights like a pinball machine.[39]

Dawson studied culture both diachronically, in terms of long chronological eras, and synchronically, within those eras in terms of the widest possible variety of perspectives. Every discipline could seemingly tell him something about human life in the past. "Christopher Dawson may be seen as discovering the possibilities for unity among the many intellectual disciplines of our time," one commentator wrote.[40]

Newman wrote in his *The Idea of a University* (1852) about the mind's energetic action upon new ideas and facts rushing in upon it. By a "formative power," the mind reduces to order and meaning the matter of our learning. A cultivated intellect digests what it receives into the substance of one's previous state of thought through comparison and systemization. Thus, a truly great intellect is not one simply full of facts, Newman wrote. Rather, it is one that takes a "connected view of old and new, past

39. Louis A. Schuster to Christina Scott, December 25, 1984, STAC, box 1, folder "General Correspondence 1985–2000."
40. James Ambrose Raftis, "The Development of Christopher Dawson's Thought," *The Chesterton Review* IX (1983): 132.

and present, far and near, and which has an insight into the influence of all these one on another: without which there is no whole and no centre."[41] Dawson's connected view was his "intellectual architecture." Accordingly, Dawson sought "a new conception of history" by studying the past "not as an inorganic mass of isolated events, but as the manifestation of the growth and mutual interaction of living cultural wholes."[42]

The architecture of Dawson's mind was founded on the unity of truth as accessed through many disciplines of knowledge. Culture is so complex that no single formal object[43] sufficiently makes it intelligible. That is why it is an inherently interdisciplinary subject, as any serious humanistic project must be. Reviewers noted how Dawson's drive to understand the "whole pattern of the past"[44] led him to a "pluralist"[45] methodology that attempted to give simultaneous recognition to many perspectives through the various disciplines. In Dawson's case, however, interdisciplinary research integrating theoretical frameworks of two or more fields led to *transdisciplinary* thinking: when one transcends two or more disciplinary approaches to form a completely new holistic way of addressing particular problems. It is this transdisciplinary approach that I have labelled his cultural mind. As one reviewer wrote, "That is the really essential quality of Mr. Dawson's work: an opening up of frontiers, a broad integration of isolated disciplines in the crucible of a humane and passionate mind, an unfreezing of cold abstractions into the human realities: love, enthusiasm, faith, anger, death. It is no mean achievement; and we can all, scholars and amateurs, sceptics and believers, derive great benefit from it."[46]

If reality can be fully understood only when one uses all the pos-

41. Newman, *The Idea of a University*, 106.

42. Christopher Dawson, *The Age of the Gods* (1928; Washington, D.C.: The Catholic University of America Press, 2012), xxi.

43. In the technical language of philosophy, the subject matter of a science is called the *material object*. The point of view from which it is studied is called the *formal object*. If the material object of Dawson's science of culture was culture, the formal object shifted according to the mode (humanistic or socio-historical) he employed or the question he asked. Aware of the limits of his own field of history, Dawson tried to utilize multiple formal objects when writing about culture due to its complexity.

44. Crane Brinton, review of *Dynamics of World History*, *Speculum* XXXIII (1958): 273.

45. Brinton, review of *Dynamics of World History*, 273; Hayden White, "Religion, Culture and Western Civilization in Christopher Dawson's Idea of History," *English Miscellany* IX (1958): 253.

46. Peter Morris Green, "God and History," review of *The Dynamics of World History*, *Times Literary Supplement*, December 27, 1957, 782.

sibilities made available by reason,[47] then one must study objects of knowledge in history with "patient and impartial investigation," letting that object determine which methods to employ in understanding it. Thus, Dawson's intellectual architecture worked against—in his words—the "lust for simplification,"[48] whereby a single method is applied indiscriminately, and parts are mistaken for wholes. As philosopher J. S. Mill wrote, "Every truth which men of narrow capacity are in earnest about is sure to be asserted, inculcated, and in many ways even acted on, as if no other truth existed in the world, or at all events none that could limit or qualify the first."[49] Such simplification plays a part in ideological constructions of reality—as in evolutionary naturalism,[50] fundamentalist creationism,[51] or economic or management "science" today in their mechanistic views of the human person that might appear as neutral descriptions of how the world is but, in fact, propel moral and political visions of how the world should be.[52]

The lust for simplification particularly overshadowed the years following the Great War, as Dawson was maturing as a scholar. When world leaders gathered at Versailles in 1919, for example, they chose to focus on a single cause of the war and blame Germany. They lacked the ability or the courage to utilize an intellectual architecture needed to handle complex causality and acknowledge that others also shared blame for the war. Their simplification led to horrible consequences in the psyche of the German people. The Treaty of Versailles, Dawson wrote, "failed to establish European order," and Europe thereby became "the focus of international disorder" for decades afterward.[53]

Simplification troubled other areas of life in the early twentieth century. Sociologists reduced culture to external human practices or to in-

---

47. Marco Bregni, "The Facts Speak for Themselves," *Traces* XI, no. 4 (2009): 19.

48. Christopher Dawson, *Enquiries into Religion and Culture* (Washington, D.C.: The Catholic University of America Press, 2009), xx.

49. J. S. Mill, *On Liberty* (1859; Indianapolis, Ind.: Hackett, 1978), 49.

50. Thomas Nagel, *Mind and Cosmos: Why the Materialist Neo-Darwinian Conception of Nature Is Almost Certainly False* (New York: Oxford, 2012).

51. Joel Cracraft, "The Scientific Response to Creationism," *Science, Technology, & Human Values* 7, no. 40 (1982): 79–85.

52. Jason Blakely, *We Built Reality: How Social Science Infiltrated Culture, Politics, and Power* (New York: Oxford University Press, 2020), 43

53. Christopher Dawson, *Understanding Europe* (1952; Washington, D.C.: The Catholic University of America Press, 2009), 38, 39.

ternal beliefs, historians reduced it to politics, politicians reduced it to money or class or race, and educationalists reduced it to specialization or—sometimes in American Catholic colleges—to Thomistic philosophy. Fissiparous specialization obscured reality and spawned ideological constructions that created new problems even as they tried to solve other ones. A largely one-sided notion of culture reduced human life to either its material or spiritual dimension. This problem—implicit in many of the figures Dawson critically engaged, as seen throughout the following chapters—resulted from a lack of intellectual architecture.

In summary, rule one of Dawson's cultural mind was attempting to view a given problem in light of the whole picture and to put everything in its right place.

(2) "BOUNDARY THINKING," the second rule of Dawson's "logic of interdisciplinarity," emerged out of his childhood. Dawson was born at Hay-on-Wye in a twelfth-century castle marking the permeable boundary between two worlds—one of the Welsh farmers who came down to the town on market-days, the other of the English-speaking town itself. Hay-on-Wye was nestled between two geographical regions: "I can remember I was conscious of the co-existence of two worlds—the rich Herefordshire countryside and the poor and wild Welsh hills of Radnor Forest to the North and the Black Mountain which rose immediately behind Hay to the South."[54] Different kinds of cultural influences met and mingled there on the border between England and Wales, shaping young Dawson's mind.

Boundaries denote ownership and signify who has responsibility for what. In relationships, protective and porous boundaries mark where one person ends and the other begins. It takes courage to respect and maintain personal boundaries, but they protect one's status as a free agent and make authentic interaction with others possible. Something like this is true for cultural interaction as well.[55]

However, when people think of boundaries today, they often imagine "walls" barring outside influence. They might jettison the whole

54. Christopher Dawson, "Memories of a Victorian Childhood," in Christina Scott, *A Historian and His World: A Life of Christopher Dawson* (1984; New Brunswick, N.J.: Transaction, 1992), 224.

55. Henry Cloud and John Townsend, *Boundaries in Marriage: Understanding the Choices that Make or Break Loving Relationships* (Grand Rapids, Mich.: Zondervan, 1999), 18, 20, 23, 24, 28.

idea of boundaries because they seem selfish or inherently conflict-
ual—as in colonialism, nationalism, and racial discrimination.

While those evils are real enough, *cultural boundaries*, even more
than political boundaries, can also give positive meaning to people's
lives, as the anthropologist Ira Bashkow wrote. They do not contain so
much as they demarcate or differentiate. Cultural boundaries "are less
like barriers than they are like thresholds or frontiers that mark the
movement across them and even create the motivation for relationship with what lies beyond." In fact, it is at those cultural boundaries,
those places where different cultures meet, "that people feel the distinctions of culture most acutely, since these are so often relevant to
navigating their complex social landscape."[56] For Bashkow, as for Dawson, one might conceive of boundaries as cultural distinctions that are
plural and permeable. Dawson was interested in the process of cultural
change through migration and cultural interaction across boundaries,
in the borderlands of history.

For example, in his book *The Making of Europe* (1932), a work for-
mally introduced later, Dawson used his socio-historical view of culture to emphasize the diversity and complexity of cultural interactions
across borders in Egypt and the Byzantine Empire during the early centuries of the Christian era. In Ptolemaic and Roman Egypt, the country
peoples of the Nile River Valley retained their old cultural and religious
traditions that had persisted from time immemorial under the shad-
ows of the pyramids, even as cities such as Alexandria developed as
brilliant centers of the foreign Hellenistic culture of the age. These two
currents of civilization ran alongside each other—one rural, the other
urban; one old Egypt, the other new Egypt; one national, the other imperial. But the conversion of Egypt to Christianity changed all this. "It
destroyed the religious barriers which kept the native population artificially segregated in a world of its own and brought them into contact
with the rest of the population of the Empire," Dawson wrote. Archaic
Egyptian culture ended. This happened not due to the destruction of
the political basis of society but due to the collapse of the religious ba-

56. Ira Bashkow, "A Neo-Boasian Conception of Cultural Boundaries," *American Anthropologist* CVI (2004): 450, 453.

sis of society with the coming of Christianity. "The ultimate barriers between peoples are not those of race or language or region," Dawson commented elsewhere, "but those differences of spiritual outlook and tradition . . . there is a different conception of reality, different moral and aesthetic standards, in a word, a different inner world." Some traditions of old Egyptian culture persisted, however, while the church naturally took the place of the old state religion in representing the nation. As the Roman rulers had usurped the pharaohs, so now the new Christian patriarchs of Egypt took their place as the all-powerful leaders of the nation—at least until the coming of Islam.[57]

Dawson's account of the borderlands of Christian culture and the old pagan culture of Egypt helped him explain how the Egyptian patriarch acquired such an absolute power over the church and the wider society there. The patriarch was like a Christian pharaoh of Alexandria, raising that city to great prominence in early Christianity. As in today's borderlands history and in cultural history's interest in cultural frontiers, encounters, and translations, Dawson focused on regions of cultural mixing because they are unstable. They are places of change, their "boundaries" passing-through places for caravans of trade and ideas. In the borderlands of history, in the porous boundaries between old Egypt and new Egypt, for example, historians can discern the new directions of whole peoples and ages.[58]

Attention to cultural boundaries translated into Dawson's respect for disciplinary boundaries. Here, his boundary thinking supported his intellectual architecture: it meant acknowledging the "logics"[59] or forms of reasoning appropriate to each discipline. Whereas intellectual architecture made sure everything was in its right place considering the whole problem, boundary thinking protected the integrity of each discipline and acknowledged its limits. In a letter to Christian ecumen-

57. Christopher Dawson, *The Making of Europe: An Introduction to the History of European Unity* (1932; Washington, D.C.: The Catholic University of America Press, 2003), 119; Christopher Dawson, *Progress and Religion: An Historical Enquiry* (1929; Washington, D. C.: The Catholic University of America Press, 2001), 67.

58. Pekka Hämäläinen and Samuel Truett, "On Borderlands," *Journal of American History* 98, no. 2 (September 2011): 338; Peter Burke, *What Is Cultural History?* (Cambridge: Polity, 2008), 118–23.

59. Mark Bevir, *The Logic of the History of Ideas* (Cambridge: Cambridge University Press, 1999), 2.

ist J. H. Oldham (1874–1969), Dawson complained about the tendency for the practitioners of one discipline to "regard their own methods as complete and exhaustive." Again, here is the problem of simplification. Such totalizing claims made cooperation between kindred sciences impossible, he thought.

Thus if we exclude from the start the theologian's claim to study eternal super-temporal truths and values, we are denying the basic conditions of his thinking, in fact denying the existence of theology, so that there is no place left for any co-operation. I cannot myself see why the sociologist should not admit in principle the existence of elements which cannot be resolved in purely sociological terms, though he naturally claims to extend the area of sociological explanation to its furthest possible limits.[60]

Dawson accused sociologist Émile Durkheim (1858–1917), for example, of explaining the origin of religion solely in terms of social consciousness—thus collapsing the former into the latter and nullifying metaphysical boundaries. "This is not a scientific explanation," he wrote, "but an amalgamation of religion and society by means of an illegitimate substitution of one category for another."[61] Durkheim broke the boundary-thinking rule in this case. Those sociologists who sought to go beyond studying actual societies to aim at the reconstruction of society based on a new religious ideal, such as the American sociologist Charles Ellwood (1873–1946) in *The Reconstruction of Religion* (1922), also violated boundary thinking. Their "theological sociologies," Dawson thought, were "vitiated by an inherent confusion of method."[62]

"The fact is that all 'simple' explanations are unsatisfactory and irreconcilable with scientific sociology," Dawson wrote. Social phenomena cannot be reduced to either material or spiritual causes.

60. Dawson to Oldham, no date, E-JHOP, box 9, folder 3. The letter, labeled "Confidential," was likely written around 1940, based on its archival context.
61. Christopher Dawson, "Sociology as a Science," in *Dynamics of World History*, ed. John J. Mulloy (1956; Wilmington, Del.: ISI Books, 2002), 27.
62. Dawson, "Sociology as a Science," 29. Ellwood's violation of the boundary-thinking rule: "Social science must find its completion in social religion. These two should become but different aspects of one fundamental attitude in all normal, educated minds." See Charles Ellwood, *The Reconstruction of Religion: A Sociological View* (New York: Macmillan, 1922), x–xi.

As [Vilfredo] Pareto has shown, the essential requirement of sociological method is to abandon the idea of a one-sided relation of causal dependence between the different factors and view the social process as the result of a complex series of interdependent factors. Material environment, social organization and spiritual culture all help to condition social phenomena, and we cannot explain the social process by one of them alone, and still less explain one of the three as the cause and origin of the other two.[63]

A confusion of method arises in which the thinker attempts to "explain the whole by one of its parts, or to reduce his knowledge of the whole to his knowledge of one of its parts."[64] Without boundary thinking, a limited kind of knowledge is used to make a total claim, unsettling "the boundary lines between science and science," Newman wrote, disturbing their action and destroying the "harmony which binds them together." This is a violation of reason that may reflect ignorance or pride, or it may be committed by someone with an agenda wanting to use a field of knowledge as a weapon. If practitioners do not understand the limits of their disciplines, how do they know when they are practicing them? What questions are relevant to them? What evidence is relevant to a problem?[65]

Such illegitimate disciplinary border-crossings resulted from a "naïve confusion of thought," Dawson believed. The "aspects of reality that are revealed in religion, philosophy, and art may be no less true and no less ultimate than the knowledge that is derived from physical science," he wrote in 1927: "Only their method of approach is different; for they conceive reality in terms of substance, quality, and value, whereas science views the world exclusively in terms of quantitative relations." In addition, theology and physical science have their own formal principles. They are not mere functions of society but have their own ends, which transcend the social category—a strike against sociological simplification. In addition, while the sociologist is justified in studying religious beliefs in their influence on society, the theolo-

---

63. Dawson, "Sociology as a Science," 27, 28. Vilfredo Pareto (1848–1923) was an Italian industrialist, sociologist, economist, and philosopher.

64. Étienne Gilson, *The Unity of Philosophical Experience* (1937; San Francisco: Ignatius, 1964), 105, 250.

65. Newman, *The Idea of a University*, 83; Wm. Oliver Martin, *The Order and Integration of Knowledge* (Ann Arbor: University of Michigan Press, 1957), 4–5, 7–8.

gian "does not judge his belief or theory in terms of social value, but in terms of religious truth." Nevertheless, just as the sociologist needs the theologian to fully account for the spiritual elements in the social process, the theologian needs the sociologist in order to recognize the social and economic elements in religious phenomena.[66] Thus, by using the boundary-thinking rule, Dawson intended to guide analytical methods of approach to knowledge of culture.

In addition to this cultural and epistemological boundary thinking, Dawson also recognized important boundaries in the political realm. He warned of social idealism and its tendency to confuse religion and politics, as in the case of socialism, which directly appealed to social conscience and religious hopes. On the other hand, the tradition of conservative thought and politics found in Samuel Johnson (1709–1784), Lord Shaftesbury (1801–1885), Joseph de Maistre (1753–1821), and Prince Metternich (1773–1859), for example, recognized the "essential distinction of political from religious action" and the limits of political influence.[67] Recognizing such boundaries between religion and politics as porous "foyers" could help solidify group identity and at the same time facilitate interaction between church and state. Church and state do not necessarily conflict, Dawson thought, but can cooperate toward practical goals according to their respective expertise.[68] Respecting boundaries made mutual influence across boundaries possible.

(3) "INTELLECTUAL BRIDGES," the third rule of Dawson's cultural mind, connected seemingly divergent things together, whereas boundary thinking distinguished between them. "Bridge building" helped construct intellectual architecture. The image of a "bridge" was deeply rooted in Dawson's earliest literary memory. He recalled a poem his mother used to repeat. He never discovered the name of the author or the title of the poem, he recorded, but it was about, "Bran the Bless-

66. Christopher Dawson, "The Crisis of the West," *Dublin Review* CLXXXI (1927): 274–75; Dawson, "Sociology as a Science," 28, 31, 32. On the theologian's need of the sociologist: "Most of the great schisms and heresies in the history of the Christian church have their roots in social or national antipathies, and if this had been clearly recognized by the theologians the history of Christianity would have been a very different one" (32). See also R. Jared Staudt, "Christopher Dawson on Theology and the Social Sciences," *Logos* 12, no. 3 (Summer 2009): 91–111.
67. Dawson, "Conservatism," a lecture written in June 1932, STA, box 3, folder 38, pp. 5, 6.
68. Dawson, "Comments on Middleton Murry's Paper," no date, E-JHOP, box 14, folder 4.

ed, the mythical ancestor of the Holy Families of Wales—the story of the Lodestone river and the saying 'He who will be chief, let him be a bridge.'"[69]

This image shaped the way Dawson perceived his deep mission: to connect divergent realities in a world fragmented by the Great War and resulting political ideologies. In his practical work during the Second World War with the Sword of the Spirit movement, for example (see chapter 7), Dawson sought to bridge different interest groups. He primarily had a national and European cultural program in mind, not an ecclesiastical or political one. In his 1940 editorial note printed in the first two issues of the Catholic journal the *Dublin Review*, Dawson wrote that "the need for organs of opinion which are not tied to a political party or confined to specialist studies is greater than ever before."[70] During the previous twenty years, he thought, the great obstacle to the preservation of the common values and traditions of Western culture had been the division of writers, politicians, and economists into two camps—"Left" and "Right." This gave a partisan character to all intellectual activity and left no room for common action. Further, this division obscured the real issues. "The revolutionary forces which inspire the two rival extremisms of the Left and the Right are both alike the enemies of Europe, and they have far more in common with each other than with either the conservative or democratic elements in Western society."[71] Because Dawson was concerned that political powers, including in Britain, would use religion as a tool for psychological domination, one had to watch carefully both sides of the political spectrum, he thought, for "overconcentration [sic] on the danger from one side may give the other its opportunity."[72] In response, his cultural program as editor of the *Dublin Review* tried to make that journal into an exchange not only between Right and Left but also between

---

69. Dawson, "Memories of a Victorian Childhood," 225. This proverb came not from a poem but from the *Mabinogion*, a collection of prose stories collated from medieval manuscripts of Welsh mythology. Brân the Blessed appears in the second branch of this collection. He was a giant and a Welsh king of Britain. During an invasion of Ireland to rescue his abused sister, he laid himself down as a bridge across a river so that his army could cross.

70. Christopher Dawson, "Editorial Note," *Dublin Review* CCVII (October 1940): 129.

71. Dawson, "Editorial Note," 130–31.

72. Dawson, "Supplementary Comments," E-JHOP, box 14, folder 4.

Introduction

British, French, and German writers from a variety of affiliations and disciplines during the Second World War. Following the rules of bridge building and "intellectual asceticism" (see rule 4) helped him abstain from superficial entanglements in political ideologies and realize the dangers inherent in them.

Dawson also viewed religion and culture as bridges. In his first series of Gifford Lectures published in 1948, he wrote about how the historic function of religion had been the "building of a bridge between the two worlds" of reason and science, on the one hand, and the psyche and religious experience, on the other. He thought it was only by cooperation of these two spheres that the world of culture had come into existence. He sharpened the comparison with simile: religion is "like a bridge between two worlds by means of which the order of culture is brought into conscious relation with the transcendent reality of spiritual being." One could see this even in Buddhism, which seemed to turn away from the world, in its strong institutional tradition of monasticism and influence on literature, both of which bridged religion and culture.[73]

In addition, the third rule of Dawson's cultural mind created disciplinary bridges supporting intellectual architecture. He wrote in a letter to an American correspondent, "I find it very difficult to understand the principle of the delimitation between sociology and anthropology. . . . As I see it, the study of primitive societies is called anthropology, that of modern societies is sociology and that of the literate societies of the past is called history: and yet all are really parts of the same subject. And I think the concept of culture provides the bridge between all three."[74] All three fields, along with comparative religion, played key roles in the science of culture forming Dawson's cultural mind.

Dawson's bridge-building humanism[75] served as the archetype for

---

73. Dawson, *Religion and Culture*, 16, 76, 149.

74. Dawson to John J. Mulloy, July 1, 1954, STA, box 10, folder 13, "Dawson to Mulloy Correspondence 1954–1958."

75. Dawson's humanism put the human person at the center of cultural analysis. It resembled that of other humanists of the day such as Irving Babbitt, T. E. Hulme, Nicholas Berdyaev, and T. S. Eliot. Like Dawson, these men espoused a nuanced view of the human person as more than physical matter. This was very different than the antisupernatural humanism that emerged with the 1933 *Humanist Manifesto*.

his entire science of culture. It is the nature of the human being, Dawson thought, to bridge the gap between spirit and matter. Humans as composite beings make up human cultures, so cultures, too, serve as bridges between different kinds of reality. According to rule 3, then, Dawson's cultural mind constantly sought to draw diverse fragments of the world together, to bridge whole disciplines, from art to economics and theology—connecting them in new ways to link distant regions of intellectual architecture together.

(4) "INTELLECTUAL ASCETICISM," the fourth rule of the cultural mind, connected factual fastidiousness, ideological restraint, and English reserve to clear writing. There is a story about his Harvard professorship (1958–1962) in which Dawson visited Bishop John Wright (1909–1979) in Pittsburgh. The bishop had a gardener who loved impressing visiting scholars with his erudition. This gardener politely approached Dawson and told him that in one of his famed books, the footnotes did not match the text due to the use of a different translation of scripture. Dawson rushed up stairs and searched through versions of the Bible. He eventually came down and said the man was quite correct, while everyone enjoyed a good laugh.

On another occasion, in his Minister's Institute speech given before the Harvard Divinity School in 1959 entitled "What Is a Christian Civilization?" Dawson said to his audience that he used words such as "Christian," "culture," and "civilization" descriptively, without implying value judgments.[76] In this way, emphasizing the socio-historical view of culture, Dawson the historian shared with the scientist the ideal of patient and impartial investigation of what lies within his or her field. This ideal made him a sort of "intellectual ascetic," as one reviewer noted.[77]

Dawson's acquaintances remembered his encyclopedic mind. The publisher Maisie Ward wrote that, "Letters to Dawson from an expert in Indian religions treat him as a fellow expert; from an expert on the history of the Irish in the United States, as an equal in that field also."

76. Christopher Dawson, "What Is a Christian Civilization?" Minister's Institute, Harvard Divinity School, January 29, 1959, recorded on a compact disc copy, HDA, bMS 613, box 9.

77. Huxley, "Light on the Dark Ages," 235. The story of the gardener is found in Scott, *A Historian and His World*, 193.

Introduction

She recounted: "From Chinese dynasties to American Indians, from prehistory to the Oxford Movement, from Virgil to the latest novel or even 'Western,' Christopher can talk of anything although you can also find him plunged in an almost unbreakable silence and impervious to the people and things around."[78]

Yet for all his erudition, "clarity and charity" suffused his writings, as the Canadian-born historian of modern Europe, Geoffrey Bruun (1898–1988), put it in the *New York Times*.[79] Dawson refrained from writing simply for fellow intellectuals, seeking instead to make the fruits of his specialized scholarship accessible to a general audience. Thus, he strove for concision and careful generalization without "showing off" how much he knew. He did not write in the service of triumphalist Catholicism or pedantry or political ideology. When engaging contemporary crises, such as during the Second World War, editing the *Dublin Review*, or advocating for Catholic educational reform in the United States, Dawson took a broad cultural and ecumenical approach. No wonder Dawson's poet-friend David Jones noted after a dinner conversation: "O dear, it's nice to talk to someone whose brain is the right kind—that's what one sighs for—the disagreements don't matter—but the temper—the kind—the sort of thing that a chap regards as significant—that's what one wants—and that is hard to come by."[80] Even from the ranks of the American progressive intelligentsia came high praise for Dawson's mellowness, urbanity, and tolerance.[81] These qualities resulted from Dawson's intellectual asceticism.

The following chapters show how these four rules formed Dawson's cultural mind and how he applied them. Rules one and three governed the synthetic impulse in Dawson's thought. Rule two grounded him in analytical penetration. Rule four made the communication of his ideas fair-minded and accessible.

78. Maisie Ward, *Unfinished Business* (New York: Sheed & Ward, 1964), 117–18.

79. Geoffrey Bruun, "Why Civilizations Rise and Decline," review of *Dynamics of World History*, *New York Times*, January 25, 1959, BR 26.

80. Jones to Harman Grisewood, June 1, 1942, in René Hague, ed., *Dai Greatcoat: A Self-Portrait of David Jones in His Letters* (London: Faber & Faber, 1980), 119.

81. Harry Elmer Barnes, review of *Dynamics of World History*, *American Historical Review* LXIII (1957): 78, 79.

Methods and Assumptions

Three rich biographies of Dawson already exist,[82] and at least two
other full-length studies.[83] Scholarship has advanced understanding
of him as a Catholic scholar[84] and his location within the context of
the early twentieth-century English Catholic intellectual community.[85]
Now the task is to broaden Dawson studies by situating him in the wider landscape of modern history and assessing his relevance by examining how he formed and applied his cultural mind. That is why this
book is not a biography or summary of his many books. Rather, it is a
"biographical study" that looks through Dawson's life and work at the
world around him, to see how his cultural mind interacted with it. The
approach is like books on other significant intellectual figures in which
the authors do not simply narrate the lives of their subjects but seek to
use them as windows onto a wider mental world. In this way, these authors focus and historicize a whole way of thinking through thematic
chapters arranged loosely in chronological order.[86]

There is danger in studying a figure of the past one admires, but
there are also advantages in a sympathetic understanding of such a figure. To a scholar, however, veneration can threaten honest appraisal.
One should view the past as much as possible in its own terms. Dawson

82. Scott, *A Historian and His World*; Birzer, *Sanctifying the World*; and Karl Schmude, *Christopher Dawson: A Biographical Introduction* (Hobart, Tasmania: Christopher Dawson Centre for Cultural Studies, 2014). Based on interviews, memories, unpublished letters, and family documents, see also Julian Scott, "The Life and Times of Christopher Dawson," *The Political Science Reviewer* 41, no. 2 (December 2017): 141–63.

83. John Thornhill, *The Road all Peoples Travel: Christopher Dawson's Interpretation of Cultural Developments that Ultimately Produced our Western Civilization* (self-pub., FeedARead.com, 2018); Daniel A. Connor, *The Relation between Religion and Culture: A Synthesis of the Writings of Christopher Dawson* (1952; Providence, R.I.: Cluny Media, 2019).

84. Adam Schwartz, *The Third Spring: G. K. Chesterton, Graham Greene, Christopher Dawson, and David Jones* (Washington, D.C.: The Catholic University of America Press, 2005); Birzer, *Sanctifying the World*; Patrick Allitt, *Catholic Converts: British and American Intellectuals Turn to Rome* (Ithaca, N.Y.: Cornell University Press, 1997); and Stratford Caldecott and John Morrill, eds., *Eternity in Time: Christopher Dawson and the Catholic Idea of History* (Edinburgh: T&T Clark, 1997).

85. James R. Lothian, *The Making and Unmaking of the English Catholic Intellectual Community, 1910–1950* (Notre Dame, Ind.: University of Notre Dame Press, 2009).

86. Examples of other "biographical studies" include Matthew Stanley, *Practical Mystic: Re-
ligion, Science, and A. S. Eddington* (Chicago: University of Chicago Press, 2007); Peter J. Stanlis, *Robert Frost: The Poet as Philosopher* (Wilmington, Del.: ISI Books, 2007); and Massimo Mazzotti, *The World of Maria Gaetana Agnesi, Mathematician of God* (Baltimore: Johns Hopkins University Press, 2007).

viewed reality through a Christian lens, and so does this study of him, but an "ethics of reception," as historian John Rodden called it, should discipline one's admiration and perspective. Rodden studied the ways political writers on both the Left and the Right, for example, appropriated the literary reputation of George Orwell (1903–1950). Without such discipline, Rodden warned, it is too easy for writers to identify so strongly with a subject they project their own needs and aspirations on him or her.[87]

At times, Dawson studies have lacked this discipline. Emphasis on Dawson as an "anti-modern rebel"[88] needs to be balanced with the facts that Dawson was spiritually close to the Catholic modernist Friedrich von Hügel (1852–1925), was an early pioneer in the ecumenical movement, and worked all his life to convince his readers of the importance of modern disciplines such as anthropology for the historical study of religion and culture. Polemical tendencies by some who wrote about Dawson's work were noticed in the 1980s when Adrian Hastings, author of *A History of English Christianity* (1986), wrote to Christina Scott, Dawson's daughter and biographer: "How *truly* absurd that American Catholic sectaries should be adopting your father as their patron saint."[89] In his view, Dawson's thought was far too layered and profound to attach him to narrow agendas, and appropriating him to polemics betrays the universality of his message. In his own day, commentators admired Dawson as someone who possessed a "mastery" over voluminous historical material and who opened up exciting new horizons of research.[90]

Embracing these warning markers as guides through the book,

87. John Rodden, *Every Intellectual's Big Brother: George Orwell's Literary Siblings* (Austin: University of Texas Press, 2006), 181, 182.

88. Adam Schwartz, "'I Thought the Church and I Wanted the Same Thing': Opposition to Twentieth-Century Liturgical Change in the Thought of Graham Greene, Christopher Dawson, and David Jones," *Logos* I (1998): 48. However, Schwartz himself later pointed out the danger of labeling thinkers, making them seem glib. See Adam Schwartz, "Sitting Still with Christopher Dawson," review of *Eternity in Time: Christopher Dawson and the Catholic Idea of History*, *Touchstone*, March/April 1999, 48.

89. Hastings to Scott, October 5, 1986, STAC, box 1, folder "Correspondence with Adrian Hastings."

90. Gervase Mathew, "Religion in History," review of *Religion and the Rise of Western Culture*, *Times Literary Supplement*, April 7, 1950, vii; Fernando Cervantes, "Progress and Tradition: Christopher Dawson and Contemporary Thought," *Logos* II (Spring 1999): 106.

this biographical study utilizes the insights of two intellectual historians to excavate Dawson's cultural mind and to assess its relevance—those of R. G. Collingwood (1889–1943) and Quentin Skinner (b. 1940). Collingwood, author of the famous *Idea of History* (1946), directed excavations at archaeological sites as a young man. He realized what he learned from the site depended on what specific questions he asked. One learned nothing when simply trying to "see what one could find" in an open-ended manner. Is that black material peat moss or occupation-soil bearing the imprint of humans? Are those just loose stones or a ruined wall? He came to see questions as much a part of knowledge as their answers. This held for texts, as well. One could not simply read them to understand them. One also needed to uncover, through historical research, the original questions motivating them. This historical reconstruction of questions served as the basis for Collingwood's "logic of question and answer" as an historically responsible approach to texts.[91] Historical enquiry reveals the "situatedness of all enquiry," wrote philosopher Alasdair MacIntyre (also influenced by Collingwood)—the relation of standards of truth and judgment to specific times and places.[92] Such historical enquiry will allow the reader to see the deep patterns and relevance of Dawson's cultural mind.

Relevance consists of more than simply tracing one's own thinking to earlier figures. Intellectual historians must translate between historical periods through patient "eavesdropping" on the conversations of the past, coming to understand them as one learns a language.[93] This allows the past to illuminate the present by revealing a wider range of possibilities. Quentin Skinner, former Regius Professor of History at Cambridge, described how the value of studying intellectual history consists in the exciting possibility of a "dialogue between philosophical analysis and historical evidence." This makes the study of past belief and thought "relevant" not because "crude 'lessons' can

---

91. R. G. Collingwood, *An Autobiography* (1939; Oxford: Clarendon, 1978), 24, 26-27, 30–31, 37, 39.

92. Alasdair MacIntyre, *After Virtue: A Study in Moral Theory*, 3rd ed. (Notre Dame, Ind.: University of Notre Dame Press, 2007), xii.

93. John W. Burrow, "Intellectual History in English Academic Life: Reflections on a Revolution," in *Advances in Intellectual History*, ed. Richard Whatmore and Brian Young (Houndmills: Palgrave Macmillan, 2006), 21–23.

be picked out of them but because the history itself can provide a lesson in self-knowledge."[94] The "relevance" of past beliefs, Skinner stated elsewhere, is found precisely in their alien character: "The kind of enquiry I am describing offers us an additional means of reflecting on what we believe, and thus of strengthening our present beliefs by way of testing them against alternative possibilities, or else of improving them if we come to recognize that the alternatives are both possible and desirable."[95] By linking past and present to deep human questions, intellectual history helps make the past meaningful to each new generation.

Interpreting the Context

The reconstruction of questions leads one into the historical context of Dawson's life and work—what I call "the Age of the Great War." One must look here for the nuances of his cultural mind. As an intellectual and cultural historian, I try to interpret the Great War (1914–1918) as a whole, to understand its meaning for those at the time as well as for us today in the twenty-first century. From my perspective, it was not simply a military event but a major spiritual rupture, the "original sin"[96] of the twentieth century, and the font of later wars, political religions, and shifting values. The Age of the Great War lasted beyond 1918 and even beyond 1945, to at least 1991, when the Soviet Union, spawned by the Great War, dissolved. One could make a case for legacies of 1914 reaching into our own times through the rise of the United States to global dominance (making the world "safe for democracy," an idea from the Great War), the continued effects on cultural fragmentation and family breakdown of the sexual revolution that began during the 1920s and continues into the twenty-first century, and through ideological

94. Quentin Skinner, "Meaning and Understanding in the History of Ideas," in *Visions of Politics*, vol. 1 (Cambridge: Cambridge University Press, 2002), 87, 89. This chapter is a revised version of an article that originally appeared under the same title in *History and Theory* 8 (1969): 3–53.

95. Quentin Skinner, "Interpretation and the Understanding of Speech Acts," in *Visions of Politics*, vol. 1, 126–27. This chapter is an adapted version of Skinner's final section of "Reply to My Critics" in *Meaning and Context: Quentin Skinner and his Critics*, ed. James Tully (Cambridge: Polity Press 1988), 259–88.

96. Simon Schama, "Flaubert in the Trenches," *The New Yorker*, April 1, 1996, 97.

infiltration from fascism, Nazism, and communism into the radical-ized Islam that now plagues the world.[97] The problems exposed in the twentieth century of secularization and new corresponding forms of sacralization still haunt us. This is why Dawson's works continue to live beyond their immediate historical context to speak to us still.

The scholars Bradley J. Birzer and Jacob D. Rhein have argued that Dawson interpreted his context in the manner of Augustine (354–430). He read Augustine's *The City of God* along with Edward Gibbon's *The Decline and Fall of the Roman Empire* in the years just before the Great War broke out in 1914 and returned to those two great classics through-out his life. They gave him a sense of déjà vu because the Age of the Great War was not the first "decline of the West" on record. The sacking of Rome in 410 profoundly revealed the fragility of civilization in Augus-tine's time, just as the European civil war of 1914, the global pandemic of 1918, and economic depression did in Dawson's time. The streets of Rome were "filled with dead bodies, which remained without burial during the general consternation," Gibbon wrote, just as the streets of Warsaw and the concentration camps were in the twentieth century. Augustine responded to this collapse of the human order as a scholar, a social theorist, and a Christian, just as Dawson later did.[98]

Rhein studied the marginalia in Dawson's Latin and English copies of *The City of God* kept in the Christopher Dawson Collection at the University of St. Thomas to see how he read it. He found that Dawson highlighted passages in both copies with blunt pencil, especially those connected to providence, time, and human nature. Dawson seemed attracted to two major aspects of Augustine's view of human beings: they are *social by nature* and they are *moved by love*, Rhein wrote. Every human society finds its organizing principle in a common will oriented toward common objects of love. Those objects ultimately reduce to the "City of Man" (love of self) and the "City of God" (love of God). Just as

---

97. Joseph T. Stuart, "The War to Start All Wars: The Great War & Its 100-Year Legacy," *360 Review*, Summer/Fall 2019, 22–29; Joseph T. Stuart, "North Dakota and the Cultural History of the Great War," *North Dakota History* 83, no. 2 (2018): 3–17; and Ivan Jankovic, "Monstrous Modernity: Western Roots of Islamic Radicalism," *360 Review*, Summer/Fall 2019, 78–89.

98. Birzer, *Sanctifying the World*; Jacob D. Rhein, "How Dawson Read *The City of God*," *Logos* 17, no. 1 (Winter 2014): 36–62; and Edward Gibbon, *The Decline and Fall of the Roman Empire*, ch. 31, https://www.ourcivilisation.com/smartboard/shop/gibbone/rome/volume1/chap31.htm.

Introduction

the Roman Empire did at certain stages in its history, Europe ran out of spiritual and moral capital in 1914 (the "love of God") even in the very midst of the greatest material prosperity she had ever known. In his own age, Augustine "looked beyond the aimless and bloody chaos of history to the world of eternal realities," Dawson wrote, "from which the world of sense derives all the significance which it possesses." Dawson translated this insight of Augustine's into twentieth-century terms of the modern social sciences, maturing about the time of the Great War: "A society which has lost its religion becomes sooner or later a society which has lost its culture."[99] Dawson wrote this not as a pious statement but as an anthropological one.

Birzer and Rhein are surely correct in their assessment of Dawson's Augustinian interpretation of the Age of the Great War. I argue that he also responded in terms of his cultural mind. This was because the Great War's meaning partly resided in the questions it churned up about cultural identity, cultural change and interaction, and the relation of religion to culture. In 1916, Pope Benedict XV, maintaining the Vatican's neutrality, called the conflict the "suicide of civilized Europe."[100] Contemporaries experienced it as so traumatic they questioned much of their cultural inheritance (in the humanistic sense). "Culture" itself seemed in crisis, possibly dying, but certainly changing—creating a mental environment conducive to analyzing Western and world cultures (plural) through the social sciences maturing around this time.

Dawson was twenty-four years old when the war started in August 1914. He had left behind his youthful Anglicanism and agnosticism and entered the Catholic Church that January. His mind matured during the years of fighting and during the ten years afterward. Too sickly to physically participate in the conflict, he became emotionally and spiritually embroiled in it along with his entire generation, caught up in the questions of meaning it raised. He wrote in his personal notebook some-

99. Rhein, "How Dawson Read *The City of God*," 42, 46; Christopher Dawson, "St. Augustine and His Age," in *Enquiries into Religion and Culture*, 184; Dawson, *Progress and Religion*, 180.

100. Pope Benedict XV, "Lenten Letter to Cardinal-Vicar Pompilj," cited in Agnes de Dreuzy, *The Holy See and the Emergence of the Modern Middle East: Benedict XV's Diplomacy in Greater Syria (1914–1922)* (Washington, D.C.: The Catholic University of America Press, 2016), 20. Dreuzy cited *Al Tremendo Conflitto* (March 4, 1916), *Acta Apostolicae Sedis* 8 (1916): 59.

time during the mid-1920s that, "All the events of the last years have convinced me what a fragile thing civilisation is & how near we are to losing the whole inheritance which our age might have enjoyed."[101] This heightened sensitivity drew him to the new anthropological conception of culture as a common way of life emerging at the time. It sent him delving into books stacked three rows deep on his shelves in the late hours of the sleepless nights he often suffered. Throughout his life, he sought answers to large questions. If cultures can decline, how do they? What factors explain why religion sometimes acts as a unitive and conservative force in cultures and at other times as a socially disruptive force? What does it mean to think holistically about cultures? How can Europe preserve its cultural inheritance in the face of nationalism, intellectual fragmentation, and the expansion of politics? Why are political religions spreading so widely after the Great War? What can we do to resist them? In response to the forces of national assimilation among Catholics in the United States, unleashed by the Great War into full-blown desire for Catholic identification with American culture by the 1960s, what would it look like to rethink education in order to better transmit the deeper and wider inheritance of Christian culture in the American context? These were some of the important questions from the Age of the Great War driving the various stages of Dawson's work to which he applied the rules of his cultural mind. "It is not possible to discuss the modern situation either from the point of view of religion or politics without using the word 'culture,'" Dawson wrote in 1942.[102]

Outline of Chapters

Part 1 of this book shows how Dawson's cultural mind formed through practicing the science of culture in the Age of the Great War. This science involved holism in anthropology, (chapter 1), analysis of synchronic cultural components (Ideas, Folk, Work, and Place) in sociology (chapter 2), diachronic study of cultural change in history

101. Christopher Dawson's Notebook, STA, box 9, folder 18, "Notebook 1922–1925 Philosophy."
102. Christopher Dawson, *The Judgment of the Nations* (1942; Washington, D.C.: The Catholic University of America Press, 2011), 63.

Introduction

(chapter 3), reconsideration of historical objects of knowledge, methodology, and epistemological assumptions (chapter 4), and comparative religion as providing an important hermeneutical key and explanatory principle of culture study (chapter 5). Part 2 studies Dawson's application of cultural mind in politics and education. One could choose other areas in which he applied it, such as in European or American cultural criticism, but I chose these two because of the large volume of Dawson's writings on them, and because of my own interests.

Chapter 1 explains how Dawson entered the Age of the Great War armed with a deep sense of mission to write the history of culture. In that lifelong pursuit, he ultimately sought cultural self-knowledge and renewal by joining an older humanistic (prescriptive) view of culture with the socio-historical (descriptive) perspective maturing among anthropologists during the 1920s. Together, these two traditions of cultural understanding would inform Dawson's idea of culture.

Dawson's holistic idea of culture had a strong analytical basis. British sociology of the early twentieth century (chapter 2) gave him the scientific categories needed to study the material life of human beings organized into societies. He brought together the conflicting perspectives of biological sociologists in Edinburgh with idealist sociologists in London. Analysis of culture, in Dawson's view, depended on a methodology informed by both the material and spiritual hemispheres of human nature. This dual perspecptive, in turn, affected the way he approached sociology through the rules of his cultural mind in order to avoid both reductionism and medievalism.

The next three chapters (3 through 5) continue to show the historical-contextual root of Dawson's cultural mind in a particular field of study and then reflect back on how he engaged that field. Chapter 3 shows how Dawson's cultural morphology integrated cyclical views of cultural change patterned on nature with intellectualist views of development, making for the possibility of authentic human progress. He utilized insights of German historicism to attack both rationalist and extreme relativist views of history prevalent during the 1920s. Chapter 4 again looks at history, this time from a more disciplinary, methodological viewpoint, arguing Dawson's attempt to study culture as a whole helped him solve three major problems afflicting the field in the first half of the twentieth century: too much focus on politics, an impoverished epistemology (*sola* empiricism) that neglected many kinds of historical sources, and a failure to relate religion to history.

The heart of the book is chapter 5, about comparative religion, because it makes a case for one of Dawson's main arguments: that religion plays a central role in cultural unity and development and is thus key to interpreting and explaining world cultures. Religion is not a purely private experience of the transcendent, on the one hand, or the result of the "collective consciousness" of society, on the other. Rather, religion connected the vertical and horizontal dimensions of human life. Thus, Dawson defended the irreducibility of religious experience from reductionist thinkers such as James Frazer, Sigmund Freud, and Émile Durkheim. At the same time, inspired by Friedrich von Hügel, Dawson held religion to be a field of tension involving personal experience along with intellectualism and institutionalism. Different historic "ideal types" such as prophet, priest, and king serve as channels through which religion shapes culture in world history. Thus, religion played an important role in what Dawson called the "culture-process" by which different factors affect cultural change. A truly scientific comparative religion, Dawson believed, must bridge the particular cultural artifacts of a people studied by the social sciences with the universal orientation of theology and philosophy. Dawson's cultural mind connected "particular" and "universal" and thereby revealed how he held religion to be the "key of history"—even in modernity.

Chapters 6 through 8 demonstrate how Dawson applied his cultural mind to contemporary problems in politics and education. Chapter 6 tests Dawson's idea from chapter 5 that religion is intimately and inevitably linked to culture even in a secular age. I explain Dawson's argument that the "expansion of politics" after the Great War was a result of "political religions" that made politics the highest expression of values. The liberal attempt to separate religion from culture in the nineteenth century created a "spiritual vacuum" that could not last: Lenin, Mussolini, and Hitler manipulated the spiritually volatile atmosphere of Europe to create their all-embracing political systems. The privatization of the transcendent emptied out the inside of Europe's public squares and left them ripe for colonization by political religion. Thus, secularization is unstable and, in fact, fosters conditions conducive to the sacralization of temporal realities.

I argue in chapter 7 that Dawson's cultural mind shaped the constructive response he made to the expansion of politics through his leadership in the Sword of the Spirit movement seeking to unite British Christians in the war effort in 1940. He defended the independence of the church; the liberal ideal of personal and political freedom; the conservative ideal of society based on the cooperation of complementary institutions and voluntary associations, not class warfare; and the claims of culture against the claims of politics. In all of this, Dawson approached political questions only *after* explaining their cultural roots, giving him a broad-mindedness that usually avoided ideological dichotomy.

As professor of Catholic Studies at Harvard University (from 1958 to 1962), Dawson's career reached its pinnacle as he advocated for holistic study of Christian culture (chapter 8). "In order to free the mind from its dependence on the conformist patterns of modern secular society," Dawson wrote at the time, "it is necessary to view the cultural situation as a whole and to see the Christian way of life not as a number of isolated precepts imposed by ecclesiastical authority, but as a cosmos of spiritual relations embracing heaven and earth and uniting the order of social and moral life with the order of divine grace."[103] The education undergirding the continuity of Western civilization was not merely a transmission of texts and ideas. It was the handing on of a way of life. He challenged American colleges and universities to create programs and avenues for students to encounter an organic study of actual, historical Christian cultures in all their dimensions—from liturgy to theology, philosophy, economics, literature, art, and social customs. Grounding classes and curricula in the living reality of Christian culture, he believed, would help students understand Western civilization from the inside out, so to speak. It would combat the centrifugal tendencies of competing specialisms in modern education and resist over-intellectualization and ideological rigidity. Chapter 8 explains why Dawson made his case for educational reform in the United States

103. Dawson, *The Crisis of Western Education*, 115.

and why Catholic critics there attacked his ideas. Despite criticism, however, Dawson's work inspired new ventures in educational reform during his own time (at St. Mary's college in Notre Dame, Indiana, for example) and, as the conclusion to the book indicates, in the twenty-first century as well.

The appendixes are based on pedagogical interpretations and applications of Dawson's work in the classroom. They are referred to throughout the text.

Dawson's Books

The present work is not about Dawson's books but rather about his mind. However, some awareness of his overall work is necessary to comprehend the argument, so I will summarize here. Dawson was prolific: he produced more than twenty books and hundreds of articles and book reviews. From the time he started writing during the Great War, he planned to create a five-volume series on the world history of culture called *The Life of Civilizations*, starting with ancient history and moving forward to the modern world. This never happened. He did publish the first volume (*The Age of the Gods*, 1928) and the third (*The Making of Europe*, 1932), as well as his introduction to the series (*Progress and Religion*, 1929), but the other volumes never came together. Nevertheless, the rest of his writings made up much of the ground he would have covered. A main concern of all these works was to show the intimate sociological relationship between religion and culture. Religion, he held, has functioned as a central dynamic in cultural life throughout history, and to understand the people of the past, one must identify the highest allegiances that moved them in addition to the material factors shaping their lives. His works can be organized into four major categories:

1. THE DYNAMICS OF WORLD HISTORY. Never in his career did Dawson write a work of national history. Due to the global implications of the clash of nationalisms in the Great War, he and a few other historians of the 1920s rejected the nation as an object of historical study. They experimented with alternatives, such as civilizations, cities,

and cultures, and they created a true "world history" for the first time. It studied global patterns of the past from ancient to contemporary times, as well as the causes and significance of historical change. Dawson stood among the front ranks of the new world historians, which included H. G. Wells (1866–1946), Oswald Spengler (1880–1936), and Arnold Toynbee (1889–1975), but with a difference.[104]

Dawson did not create encyclopedic or speculative world history. Rather, in seven books,[105] he focused on actual, historical cultures that make up civilizations ("super-cultures") and on the *dynamics* of world history. Thus, "the essential basis of the study of history must be, not just a comparative study of the higher civilizations but a study of their constituent cultures," he wrote, "and here we must follow, not the grand synoptic method of the philosophers of history, but the more laborious and meticulous scientific techniques of the social anthropologists."[106] In these multiple works, the socio-historical mode of Dawson's science of culture took on mature form.

The Age of the Gods (1928), his first book, examined the history and culture of ancient Europe and Asia. It demonstrated how the rise of civilizations followed not only the grooves of geology but also the paths of the gods and included analysis of primary sources such as theoretical works, archeological discoveries, literature, legal codes, liturgical texts, and the visual arts. Drawing from the work of ancient historians and anthropologists, his meticulous attention to facts led to bold interpretations.[107]

104. Costello, *World Historians and Their Goals*, 4. Chapter 6 of Costello's book is about Dawson.

105. *The Age of the Gods* (1928), *Progress and Religion* (1929), *Enquiries into Religion and Culture* (1933), *Religion and Culture* (1948), *Dynamics of World History* (1956), *The Movement of World Revolution* (1959), and *Religion and World History* (1975).

106. Christopher Dawson, "Arnold Toynbee and the Study of History," in *Dynamics of World History*, 417.

107. James Hitchcock, "Christopher Dawson," *The American Scholar* 62, no. 1 (Winter 1993): 111, 117. Dawson's Oxford tutor, Ernest Barker, recommended his first book to the publisher John Murray. He praised Dawson's "union of solid scholarship and philosophic grasp," and said, "What Mr. Dawson has written is no ordinary 'Outline of History.' It is based on archaeological and sociological study: it is original in its treatment and its suggestions." See Barker's letter to Murray, March 29, 1927, NLS. Murray wrote to Dawson on May 9, 1927 (NLS): "We have given careful consideration to your manuscript. . . . I am sorry to say that the sale for books of the kind is not what it used to be, for, since the War, much less attention is paid by the general public to serious books; but yours seems to us so good in every way that we hope its merit may help it to success."

One such interpretation was the central place of religion in the rise of the first civilizations. Historians since Dawson's time agree that the discovery of agriculture ten thousand years ago led to civilization and the greatest change to ever affect human life. They do not agree, however, on *how* farming was discovered. Did happenstance and the right environmental conditions in the Fertile Crescent lead to the first domestication of plants and animals there, which then led to civilization and finally to organized religion? Or did wonder at nature and the primitive cult of the Earth Mother lead to the discovery of domestication, settlement, and then civilization? In other words, did religion come before or after organized social life? Did humans create religion, or did religion, so to speak, create them and form their ways of life from the earliest times? Perhaps different answers to these foundational questions apply to different locations and times, and no conclusive answers may ever be known. Maybe there was no single, primary cause of civilization. What is certain, though, is that the different emphases of these questions brush up against the mystery of what it means to be human.

In facing questions such as these, Dawson drew from recent archeological discoveries at the Sumerian city of Ur (1922), the tomb of Tutankhamun (1922), and the Indus Valley civilization (1924) to interpret religion as a likely gateway to agriculture and the rise of civilization. Dawson acknowledged the necessary environmental conditions in the Fertile Crescent for the earliest discovery of agriculture there, especially the presence of easily domesticated plants and animals (wild wheat, barley, goats, pigs, sheep, and oxen). The brilliant, Pulitzer Prize–winning *Guns, Germs, and Steel: The Fates of Human Societies* (1997), by geographer Jared Diamond, explained the rise of civilization exclusively in terms of such environmental factors as these.[108] Unlike Diamond's

108. Jared Diamond, *Guns, Germs, and Steel: The Fates of Human Societies* (1997; New York: W. W. Norton, 1999), 25. Diamond is not a geographical determinist, however. He admits of cultural factors and the influences of individuals upon later history unrelated to the natural environment. For example, he cites the Greco-Judeo-Christian tradition of critical empirical inquiry as a factor in the rise of Europe to dominance in modern history (410, 417–418). Dawson would have greatly appreciated much of Diamond's work, I think. I do not fully agree with the stark contrast drawn between Diamond and Dawson in Clement A. Mulloy, "The Impact of the West on World History: The Contrasting Methods and Views of Jared Diamond and Christopher Dawson," *Catholic Social Science Review* 15 (2010): 137–52.

powerful—if one-sided—argument, Dawson's cultural mind integrated environmental factors with the religious side of the question.

In Dawson's view, ancient humans conceived of themselves as entirely dependent on divine power, manifested in the fruitfulness of the earth. "It was only by obedience to the laws of the Great Mother and by an imitation of her mysteries that man could learn to participate in her gifts. Thus, every agricultural operation was a religious rite or a sacramental act through which divine powers were brought into activity," he wrote. Is it possible that agriculture and the domestication of animals "originated in Western Asia by the religious observation and ritual imitation of the processes of Nature; that animals were first tamed as sacred animals, dedicated to the Mother Goddess, and that the utilitarian development of the discovery was a secondary consequence." It seems the earliest agriculture grew up around shrines of the Mother Goddess, he wrote, which became economic centers and germs of future cities. Organized religion therefore preceded the rise of civilization, at least in some places.[109]

An archeological excavation of an ancient temple at Göbekli Tepe in southern Turkey (which began in 1994) suggests Dawson's bold interpretation may be correct. This is the oldest known monumental architecture anywhere in the world, from around 9,000 B.C. It was designated a UNESCO World Heritage Site in 2018. Recent DNA analysis has shown the closest wild relative of modern wheat grows within sixty miles of the site, suggesting this may have been a place where wheat was first domesticated. It seems to have been built by hunter-gatherers. Lead archeologist Klaus Schmidt (1953–2014) speculated that organized religion could have come *before* the rise of agriculture. The need to provide for many worshippers may have led to the gathering of wild cereals and then the discovery of food production. "Twenty years ago everyone believed civilization was driven by ecological forces," Schmidt noted in 2011. "I think what we are learning is that civilization is a product of the human mind."[110]

In a sense, then, one could say: first the temple, then the city, or first

109. Dawson, *The Age of the Gods*, 78, 80, 81.
110. Charles C. Mann, "Birth of Religion: The World's First Temple," *National Geographic* 219, no. 6 (June 2011): 57, 58.

religious vision, then material embodiment. To be sure, multiple causes led to the rise of civilizations, and many temples arose along *with* their cities. But religion may have played a stronger role in rousing people to common action than some scholars have thought. As humans gathered around their sacred sites, they learned to observe and measure the heavens. The need for ritual sacrifice timed rhythmically to the seasons opened the door to mathematics, astronomy, and calendrical science. Religion powered progress—not as the only factor but certainly as a key one. Dawson's dynamics of world history implied that multiple levels of human consciousness were at work in human history—a theme explored in chapter 5.

According to reviewers of *The Age of the Gods*, Dawson achieved the difficult feat of combining synthesis and analysis. One anonymous writer praised his restrained generalizations and refusal to push the evidence further than it was worth. The reviewer called Dawson an "archæological judge," contrasting him with those polemical "archæological advocates" like James Frazer (1854–1941), who supported his own "pet thesis."[111] This view of Dawson as a careful "judge" of evidence also appeared in a review by the archeologist and anthropologist C. Daryll Forde (1902–1973), who in 1945 founded the department of anthropology at University College London. While he thought that many points in Dawson's general thesis were open to criticism, "the author is to be congratulated on his skillful and conscientious use of the archaeological material. . . . The discussion of religious life and spiritual culture is allowed to develop from direct consideration of the archaeological evidence."[112] This was the intellectual asceticism rule of his cultural mind in action.

In Dawson's view of the past, the dynamics of world history were powered by material forces pushing up against spiritual and intellectual ones. While the formation of human cultures resembled the adaptation of an animal or plant species to its environment, the role of reason meant no uniform laws of biological development determined their trajectory. Human spiritual creativity was and is a factor in how

111. "The Age of the Gods," review of *The Age of the Gods*, *Dublin Review* CLXXXII (April 1928): 286, 287, 289.
112. Forde, review of *The Age of the Gods*, 340.

cultures relate to nature and to each other, coalescing into civilizations during the course of world history. Sometimes those cultures amalgamated, and sometimes they retained their own identity within a larger whole. Either way, the religious factor played an important role in their interaction and development.[113]

2. THE MAKING OF EUROPE. The second major theme of Dawson's publications was the history and identity of Europe as a "society of peoples."[114] He took up the challenge of communicating the continuity of European history in six books,[115] which led him to support the economic and political project of European unity after World War II—a movement that became the European Union. (Several of the architects of this project were devout Catholics who believed in the ideal of European unity—such as Robert Schumann (1886–1963), Alcide de Gaspari (1881–1954), and Konrad Adenauer (1876–1967)).

Dawson viewed the making of Europe in a non-Eurocentric way— that is, as a vast case study in the dynamics of world history, not as if only European values and perspectives mattered. His approach exemplified cultural morphology, by which diverse human peoples interacted with each other in the evolution of a new civilization, including the Byzantine Empire and Muslim Spain. The four main cultural influences in *The Making of Europe*, as he titled his 1932 book, however, were Greece, Rome, the native peoples who provided the raw materials of Europe, and Christianity, with its ecclesiastical organization and spiritual influence permeating the "dough" of those raw materials. Christianity's transformation of the classical world and its native successor peoples are striking examples, Dawson wrote, of how historical development can change course due to the intervention of new spiritual forces. "History is not to be explained as a closed order in which each

113. However, too great an identification between religion and culture could be fatal to both and lock them in a mummified stagnation, stultifying social development at a certain level—as eventually happened in ancient Egypt and throughout much of the ancient world.

114. Dawson, *Understanding Europe*, xvii.

115. *The Making of Europe* (1932), *Religion and the Rise of Western Culture* (1950), *Understanding Europe* (1952), *Medieval Essays* (1954), *The Dividing of Christendom* (1965), and *The Formation of Christendom* (1967). For an excellent summary, see Khalil M. Habib, "Christianity and Western Civilization: An Introduction to Christopher Dawson's *Religion and the Rise of Western Culture*," *The Political Science Reviewer* 41, no. 2 (2017): 164–89.

stage is the inevitable and logical result of that which has gone before."
There is a mysterious element due not only to chance or individual genius but also to the "creative power of spiritual forces."[116]

The advantage of studying the European story and its relation to
Christianity is the wide availability of sources compared to the rise of
other civilizations. The world religions are like great rivers that flow
through history watering the historical landscape of the world cultures, but usually their origins are obscure, Dawson wrote. In the case
of Christianity, much is known about its historical environment. The
letters of its founders still exist, for example, allowing historians to
work back to the beginning. In fact, an abundance of existing material
for the study of every aspect of European civilization sometimes ob-
scures the picture of the whole.[117]

Different specializations developed in response to these riches. The
scientific historian, interested in the criticism of documents in political and economic history, for a long time worked apart from the ecclesiastical historian, interested in the development of the institutional
churches. This separation meant the "vital subject of the creative interaction of religion and culture in the life of Western society has been left
out and almost forgotten, since from its nature it has no place in the
organized scheme of specialized disciplines," Dawson wrote. He sought
to bridge various specializations by integrating political, economic,
and social history with the history of art, monasticism, education, and
intellectual and spiritual life in the making of Europe.[118]

Dawson believed the age stretching from the Desert Fathers to the
Cluniac Reform of the eleventh century was of the greatest importance
for understanding how European civilization took shape. Though less
externally impressive than the High Middle Age or the Renaissance,
he thought it the most sociologically interesting period of European
history because "it created not this or that manifestation of culture,
but the very culture itself—the root and ground of all the subsequent

116. Dawson, <i>The Making of Europe</i>, 33.
117. Christopher Dawson, <i>Religion and the Rise of Western Culture</i> (1950; New York: Image Books, 1991), 12.
118. Dawson, <i>Religion and the Rise of Western Culture</i>, 12–13.

cultural achievements."[119] Europe *became* Europe in this age through the work of outstanding figures such as St. Benedict (c. 480–c. 543) and St. Boniface (c. 675–754) as well as the forgotten monks who copied ancient manuscripts or labored silently to bring Christ, agriculture, and learning to the peoples of the northern forests, laying the foundations of Europe. This activity was hidden. It was an internal, organic process in which new cultures formed as subsidiary wholes within the larger unity of European civilization. Enlightened philosophers of the eighteenth century and secular nationalists of the nineteenth despised this period as one of barbarism and superstition. It was precisely the taming of those forces by Christianity, however, that made this so-called Dark Age relevant to the new Dark Age of the twentieth century, when barbarism had reasserted itself through the machine gun and European self-destruction.[120]

The Making of Europe established Dawson as a respected historian. It was praised in both the academic and popular periodicals. Henry Moss, whose own *Birth of the Middle Ages, 395–814* would be published in 1935, wrote of Dawson's "mastery of the material" in *History*, the journal of the Historical Association. H. A. L. Fisher, whose *History of Europe* would also be published in 1935, remarked that Dawson was a "real historian" with "unusual learning" and a "freshness and independence of judgment." Aldous Huxley called the book "quite admirable" in the *Spectator* and praised his erudition and sober and cautious generalizations. In the *American Historical Review*, the book was hailed as an "outstanding piece of work," and the French medieval specialist Louis Halphen applauded "ce livre remarquable" as one of the best introductions to the historical background of modern Europe. Halphen helped secure a French translation of the book, which was then approved by Augustin Fliche as "brillant." The French translation was reprinted in 1960 with a preface by the great medievalist Jacques Le Goff. The German edition received attention, too.[121]

119. Dawson, *The Making of Europe*, 3.

120. Dawson, *Religion and the Rise of Western Culture*, 24–25.

121. H. St. L. B. Moss, review of *The Making of Europe*, *History* XVIII (October 1933): 251; H. A. L. Fisher, "European Unity," review of *The Making of Europe*, *English Review* LV (1932): 98; Huxley, "Light on the Dark Ages," 235; James Edward Gillespie, review of *The Making of Europe*, *American Historical Review* 38, no. 4 (July 1933): 785; Louis Halphen, review of *The Making of Europe*, *Revue*

The making of Europe had global implications in modern history for good and for ill. It released forces that transformed the world beginning around 1500 through geographical expansion, religious fragmentation, and scientific discovery. Dawson termed these forces "the movement of world revolution" in a book by that title. They established the world hegemony of European civilization by the nineteenth century through not only global trade, communication and transportation networks, and the worldwide missionary movement but also through colonization and imperialism, slavery, and economic exploitation, he acknowledged. By the mid-twentieth century, he recognized, with the rise of the United States and Russia, Europe "can no longer hope to play a dominant political role, either for good or evil."[122]

Here, Dawson engaged the "rise of the West" master narrative that has been attacked by historians today for its use to justify Western domination. The story has buttressed the myth of "Eurocentrism"—the idea that Europe and Western culture enjoy a "permanent superiority" over others, which historian Robert B. Marks criticized. This myth, said Marks, holds all that is good and innovative starts in Europe and is universally applicable; the West alone makes history, and the rest of the world responds. Marks proposed instead a truly global perspective on the making of the modern world in which non-Western parts of the Earth also played important roles. Instead of the seeming inevitability of the "rise of the West," this new story shows how Europe's dominance rested on a series of accidents (e.g., coal deposits in Britain in the Industrial Revolution) and conjunctures (e.g., Chinese demand for silver during the Early Modern period, which fueled European trade using newfound supplies of the precious metal in the New World). These ingredients would create a non-Eurocentric narrative of the rise of Europe.[123]

Dawson went some way in these directions. It is true his account

historique CLXXI (1933): 407; Augustin Fliche, *Le Moyen Age* VII (1936): 142; and W. Kölmel, *Stimmen der Zeit* CXXX (1936).

122. Christopher Dawson, *The Movement of World Revolution* (1959; Washington, D.C.: The Catholic University of America Press, 2013), 15.

123. Robert S. Marks, *The Origins of the Modern World: A Global and Environmental Narrative from the Fifteenth to the Twenty-First Century*, 4th ed. (Lanham, Md.: Rowman & Littlefield, 2020), 9, 10.

of the rise of the modern world now seems dated in places, and he occasionally fell into the "Europe acted, and the rest responded" model,
as when he wrote: "What we need is a new historical analysis of the
whole process of world change, tracing the movement from West to
East." This was partly due to the lack of research available on other
parts of the world in his day. As Marks acknowledged in 2020, his own
book "could not have been written without the vast amount of scholarship published in English on Asia, Africa, and Latin America, which
provides the basis for a non-Eurocentric narrative."[124]

Nevertheless, Dawson agreed historians had given too much attention to the political history of the West and neglected the "all-important
question of the relation of Europe to the outer world." While he neglected some of the accidents and conjunctures Marks later covered,
he did attempt to view non-Western actors on their own terms in the
making of the modern world. For example, the discovery of Sanskrit
literature in the nineteenth century "had a profound effect on European thought, especially in Germany and France," he wrote. In addition,
he recognized the "heroic figures" resisting Western imperialism in the
nineteenth century. However, they "were doomed to inevitable defeat
because they did not possess the techniques and the scientific organization of the civilization that they resisted," he noted. This movement
of resistance and cultural recovery outside the West he termed "oriental nationalism." Paradoxically, it was largely a product of Western influence: all the triumphs of oriental nationalism, he wrote, "have been
the work of men of Western education, who were able to use the ideas
and knowledge of the West in the service of their own peoples." Even
Marxism partly owed its appeal in Asia to values of "humanity" and the
"rights of man" originating in the West. He concluded that "the movement of world change that was inaugurated in Western Europe several
centuries ago has now been so fully assimilated by the East that it is
being carried forward by the very forces that are most overtly hostile
to the West." In the end, Dawson wrote, to understand this movement
of world revolution one needed not only the help of Western historians
to trace its origins in the European past but also the help of oriental-

124. Marks, *The Origins of the Modern World*, 16; Dawson, *The Movement of World Revolution*, 17.

ists "who can appreciate the part of the non-European cultures and understand their reactions to the impact of modern civilization." Both perspectives were needed.[125]

Such a project had to involve a vast interdisciplinary study. The expansion of Europe into "Western civilization," Dawson argued, for good and for ill, was not due simply to imperialistic aggression and material exploitation. Other civilizations throughout world history had manifested aggression and exploitation, too, but they did not transform the world. Rather, he concluded, European civilization became the source of global ferment because changing the world emerged as an integral part of its cultural ideal. Europeans did not worship timeless perfection but rather a spirit that strives to incorporate itself into humanity and to transform societies. This outward-oriented energy exploded through individual initiative, competition between groups, and European aptitude for institutionalization—as in the globe-trotting Jesuits, international joint-stock companies, and the rise of the modern state. All of this deeply shaped the rise of the modern world.

Dawson's penchant for ideas and cultural explanation set him apart from environmental historians like Marks today and place him closer to an economic historian like Niall Ferguson, who also credits religion as part of the explanation for the rise—and possible decline—of the West in modern history. "Religions matter," Ferguson wrote, and Christianity matters, in particular because it offers the kind of common moral foundation needed to support vibrant economic life. Despite the passing dominance of Europe by the second half of the twentieth century, Dawson argued, the study of European history retains its importance—an understanding that Ferguson, too, seems to share. Dawson wrote that "Europe was the original source of the movement of change in which the whole world is now involved, and it is in European history that we find the key to the understanding of the ideologies which divide the modern world."[126]

On a side note, in 2002, a scholar of the Chinese Academy of Social

125. Dawson, *The Movement of World Revolution*, 6, 9, 10, 11, 13, 17.

126. Dawon, *The Movement of World Revolution*, 7, 16; Dawson, *Religion and the Rise of Western Culture*, 15, 17; and Niall Ferguson, *Civilization: The West and the Rest* (New York: Penguin, 2011), 264, 287.

Introduction

Sciences—who requested anonymity—substantiated Dawson's religious interpretation of the movement of world revolution. He reported to a group of Americans touring Beijing about investigating with his colleagues what accounted for the preeminence of the West all over the world. Was it better guns? Politics? Economics? In reality, "we have realized that the heart of your culture is your religion: Christianity. That is why the West has been so powerful. The Christian moral foundation of social and cultural life was what made possible the emergence of capitalism and then the successful transition to democratic politics. We don't have any doubt about this."[127] This view from outside the West suggests Dawson's interpretation of the significance of the religious dynamic involved in the making of Europe and modern history may have something to it.

3. HISTORICAL MOMENTS: THE FRENCH REVOLUTION. This third theme of Dawson's corpus examined specific historical moments rather than vast distances of time and space. There are three books in this category: *The Spirit of the Oxford Movement* (1933), *The Mongol Mission* (1955), and *The Gods of Revolution* (1972). In the first, he focused on the Anglo-Catholic stage of the Oxford Movement as the background to the life of John Henry Newman. This was a significant example of the possibility of religious renewal by reversing secularization and its cultural consequences in the modern world. In *The Mongol Mission*, he edited and wrote an introduction for a collection of letters by Franciscan missionaries to Mongolia and China in the thirteenth and fourteenth centuries as an example of cultural interaction on the world stage. *The Gods of Revolution* linked his thoughts on religion and culture in ancient and medieval history to the modern world.

The Gods of Revolution appeared posthumously, but Dawson wrote most of it in the mid-to-late 1930s.[128] It showed how the "religion of hu-

127. David Aikman, *Jesus in Beijing: How Christianity is Transforming China and Changing the Global Balance of Power* (Washington, D.C.: Regnery, 2003), 5.
128. Christina Scott wrote in her biography that Dawson "had started to write a book on the French Revolution, when at the beginning of 1936 he had a serious illness." See Scott, *A Historian and His World*, 127. In a footnote, she remarked that this was posthumously published as *The Gods of Revolution*. Thus, Dawson wrote some if not much of this book in the 1930s, though he made some changes later; the last chapter, for example, mentioned the Second World War.

manity" preached by secular prophets such as Jean-Jacques Rousseau
and Thomas Paine tried to replace Christianity with a substitute religion during the French Revolution. The sixty pages at the middle of the
book contained the most concentrated writing of Dawson's career. He
kept himself within the confines of twenty years, the 1780s and 1790s,
relating the events, people, and ideas of the French Revolution. Other
than his *Spirit of the Oxford Movement*, also devoted to a twenty-year
span (the 1830s and 1840s), this was his most sustained treatment of a
narrow historical period.

It received modest praise by reviewers. M. J. Sydenham of Carleton
University, author of *The French Revolution* (1965), thought the first
part on European thought from the Reformation to the Enlightenment
"brilliant" and the whole a sound overview of a complex history. While
written without recent economic and sociological studies, the book
was nevertheless founded on thorough knowledge of contemporary
writings and on a "remarkably perceptive appreciation of the interaction of social change with political and religious convictions." The central argument, Sydenham thought, was that church and state of the *ancien régime* became so interdependent that political change inevitably
implied a "new and greater Reformation." While this political change
had profound implications, the revolution remained fundamentally a
spiritual conflict, "the outcome of which is still unresolved." This argument, Sydenham thought, was overstated and unoriginal. For example,
when Dawson suggested the French Revolution was not merely a political but also a "spiritual revolution," like the Reformation, Alexis de
Tocqueville had already made that comparison in his *The Ancien Régime and the French Revolution* (1856). However, Dawson developed his
argument more deeply than did the Frenchman. Sydenham conclud-

---

Scott recorded: "In 1938 Frank Sheed was anxiously pressing Christopher to finish his book on the
French Revolution but he was to be disappointed for by this time he [Dawson] had turned again
to solving the problems of the day in a successor to *Religion and the Modern State* entitled *Beyond
Politics*" (131). *The Gods of Revolution* was to be originally entitled *The European Revolution*, as is
found in the Dawson archive at the University of St. Thomas (box 3, folders 27–34). Manuscripts
of eight chapters are stored there. Several of the chapters appeared as articles during the 1950s,
but the fact that the (incomplete) bibliography in the 1972 publication refers to no scholarship
more recent than 1935 is additional evidence that the composition of the book largely took place
during the 1930s.

ed that despite its lack of originality, Dawson's work was nevertheless well-written and well-balanced.[129]

One of Dawson's overall points about modern history is that even in secularizing societies, spiritual forces tend to infiltrate through the back door to fill their spiritual needs. In this way, they propel people into ultimate allegiance to ideas or utopian political dreams. "Every living culture must possess some spiritual dynamic, which provides the energy necessary for that sustained social effort which is civilization," Dawson wrote. "Normally this dynamic is supplied by a religion, but in exceptional circumstances the religious impulse may disguise itself under philosophical or political forms."[130] Unable to express itself fully through traditional channels, the religious impulse has emerged in modern history as attachment to the "secularized sacred" in those political religions of fascism, communism, and Nazism, anthropologist Scott Atran wrote. Influences from these Western movements infiltrated the Islamic world to inspire a new breed of "devoted actors"[131] committed in the twenty-first century to uncompromising, sacralized political causes. This reality suggests Dawson's diagnosis of the exceptional circumstances of modernity may possess continued relevance.

4. PROPHETIC SOCIOLOGY. This category has seven books in which Dawson addressed contemporary problems—*sub specie aeternitatis*.[132] He wrote from a broadminded, Christian perspective open to engagement with ideas coming from any direction. Writing just over a decade after the end of the Great War, he noted how the destructive and negative tendencies of modern culture had destroyed valuable traditions of the past. However, "they have also swept away many of the inherited prejudices and fixed forms of thought which isolated the Catholic tradition from vital contact with the realities of modern

129. M. J. Sydenham, review of *The Gods of Revolution, Canadian Historical Review* LIV (1973): 434–35.

130. Dawson, *Progress and Religion*, 3–4.

131. Scott Atran, "The Devoted Actor: Unconditional Commitment and Intractable Conflict Across Cultures," *Current Anthropology* 57, no. 13 (June 2016): 194.

132. *Christianity and the New Age* (1931), *The Modern Dilemma: The Problem of European Unity* (1932), *Religion and the Modern State* (1935), *Beyond Politics* (1939), *The Judgement of the Nations* (1942), *The Historic Reality of Christian Culture* (1960), and *The Crisis of Western Education* (1961).

life."[133] Dawson opposed nostalgia and desired to help reestablish such vital contact between faith and modern life.

In this regard, the social thinker Russell Hittinger once noted that Dawson stood in the classical tradition of pre-statistical sociology derived from Max Weber and Émile Durkheim, who deeply pondered the relationship between religion and modernity. They worked on the borders of disciplines such as history, cultural anthropology, and philosophy. In addition, Dawson also operated out of that slightly older tradition of "prophetic sociology" (Hittinger's phrase) of Alexis de Tocqueville (1805–1859) and Henry Adams (1838–1918). This was an "investigation of social data that leads not so much to scientific generalizations as to a moral or religious vision. Here I am only paraphrasing Dawson's own characterization of Tocqueville, with whom he closely identified," Hittinger wrote.[134]

As Tocqueville stated in his great study of the French Revolution, "My aim has been to compose a picture which was strictly accurate but which, at the same time, might be instructive." Tocqueville's mind, like Dawson's, linked research to wisdom. Based on descriptive factual investigation (socio-historical mode), Tocqueville arrived at prescriptive judgments (humanistic mode) intended to guide contemporary ways of life. Tocqueville also wrote in *Democracy and America* that he contemplated the development of equality in history under a "kind of religious awe." It was a "providential fact" and an "irresistible revolution." Tocqueville and Dawson believed examining historical particulars could lead to universal principles of human social existence. They did not simply record facts: rather, they reflected on their profound meaning in their causes and their consequences. They judged them and then tested their judgments against more facts. This linked past and present, allowing one to live more fully in the present and choose more prudently for the future.[135]

---

133. Christopher Dawson and T. F. Burns, eds., *Essays on Religion and Culture*, vol. 1 (1931; Providence, R.I.: Cluny Media, 2019), iii.

134. Hittinger, "Christopher Dawson: A View from the Social Sciences," 33, 34. For Dawson's appreciation for Tocqueville, see Christopher Dawson, "The Problem of Metahistory," in *Dynamics of World History*, edited by John J. Mulloy, 303–10 (1957; Wilmington, Del.: ISI Books, 2002).

135. Alexis de Tocqueville, *The Ancien Régime and the Revolution* (1856; New York: Penguin Books, 2008), xix, 11; Delba Winthrop, "Tocqueville's *Old Regime*: Political History," *Review of*

In this way, porous boundaries between description and prescription, fact and value, defined Dawson's prophetic sociology. He thought one should view the social sciences as closer to the methods and interpretive style of the humanities than of the hard sciences—a suggestion unpopular in some circles today but one taken up by social scientist Jason Blakely: "Should a future, more interpretively sensitive social science deploy a new style, one that is historically sensitive, locates and identifies the voice of the author, allows others voices to speak, and is not afraid to avow a cultural perspective?" Blakely asked. Yes, it should. Social science "must be read again and in a way that does not itself participate in the popular culture of scientism"—which Blakely defined as granting undue authority to scientific methods.[136] Dawson's cultural mind consistently worked against such simplification not by rejecting the scientific side of the social sciences but by attempting to put it in its proper place and in relation to humanistic perspectives.

These four categories of Dawson's work—the dynamics of world history, the making of Europe, his interest in particular historical moments such as the French Revolution, and his prophetic sociology—began to emerge when, as an historian, he gave serious attention to anthropology and sociology in the 1920s, the subjects of chapters 1 and 2.

Politics 43, no. 1 (1981): 88–89; and Alexis de Tocqueville, *Democracy in America*, vol. 1 (New York: Vintage Books, 1972), 6.

136. Blakely, *We Built Reality*, xiii, 125, 126.

Part 1

FORMATION OF A CULTURAL MIND

Chapter 1

The Culture Idea and the Great War

[The Great War] broke out and robbed the world of its beauties. It destroyed not only the beauty of the countrysides through which it passed and works of art which it met with on its path but it also shattered our pride in the achievements of our culture.

—Sigmund Freud

The war presumably marks the end of an age no less decisively than did the wars of the French Revolution.

—Christopher Dawson

Cultures are the medium through which human life is made whole.

—Jason Blakely

Two seminal moments in the life of Christopher Dawson occurred in Rome. The first happened during Holy Week of 1909 when the nineteen-year-old Englishman toured the ancient city with a party of pilgrims organized by the mother of his friend, the future Catholic writer Edward Ingram Watkin (1888–1981). The old city—before Mussolini's transformative urban planning—felt hemmed-in, premodern, and radically foreign. Dawson fell in love with it. Rome came as a revelation to him. The Anglican Oxford student suddenly realized that developing

Sigmund Freud, "On Transience" (1915), quoted in Alan Kramer, *Dynamic of Destruction: Culture and Mass Killing in the First World War* (Oxford: Oxford University Press, 2007), 257; Christopher Dawson, "The Passing of Industrialism," *Sociological Review* XII (1920): 6; Blakely, *We Built Reality*, 124.

simultaneously with the post-Reformation English Protestant culture was the culture of the Catholic Reformation. In it, he discovered the art of the Baroque, which became a life-long joy to him, and it led him later to the literature of St. Theresa of Avila (1515–1582) and St. John of the Cross (1542–1591). He went on expeditions outside the city, visited monasteries and churches, and attended an audience with Pope Pius X (1835–1914).[1]

He also visited the ancient church of Santa Maria in Aracoeli, where he awakened to the purpose of his life. The church stands on the summit of the Capitol above the Roman Forum, the heart of ancient republican and imperial Rome where triumphal marches, commerce, elections, and public speeches once took place. One of the most important temples of ancient Rome, that of Juno, sat atop the Capitoline Hill, and it was here the Christians built Santa Maria in Aracoeli out of the ruins. At the time of Dawson's visit, working-class tenements crowded around the church.

Dawson sat on the very steps where he knew Edward Gibbon (1737–1794) had conceived of his most famous work, *Decline and Fall of the Roman Empire*. Gibbon wrote: "It was at Rome, on the 15th of October 1764, as I sat musing amidst the ruins of the Capitol, while the bare-footed fryars were singing vespers in the temple of Jupiter, that the idea of writing the decline and fall of the city first started to my mind."[2] At the time, Dawson's enthusiasm for Gibbon was matched only by his love of Augustine's *City of God*. The pagan roots of Christianity impressed him as he sat there on the steps up to the church. Its very architecture revealed the dynamic collision of two cultures, classical and Christian. "Classical columns, mosaic pavements and the marble tombs of Roman dignitaries are reminders of that earlier pagan civilization," Dawson's biographer wrote, "while medieval and Renaissance Rome is represented by the baroque high altar, the great gilded ceiling commemorating the victory of Lepanto and Pinturicchio's frescoes depicting the life of St Bernadino of Siena." Here, Dawson suddenly perceived the power of religion to transform the dying classical civilization into a new world of

1. Scott, *A Historian and His World*, 48.
2. Edward Gibbon, *Memoirs of My Life and Writings* (1796), Project Gutenberg, http://www.gutenberg.org/ files/6031/ 6031-h/6031-h.htm.

Christian culture. Sitting on the steps of Santa Maria, he first conceived of writing a history of culture. In his journal later that year, he referred to a vow "made at Easter in the Ara Coeli" and stated that he had since "had great light on the way it may be carried out. However unfit I may be, I believe it is God's will I should attempt it."[3]

Armed with this sense of calling, young Dawson returned to Oxford and plunged into what he would later call the "apostolate of study."[4] During his life, he would bear witness to the historical reality of Christian culture and its continued relevance in the modern world through writing and advocating for educational reform in the United States. He labored for decades at the intersection of anthropology, sociology, history, comparative religion, and Christian thought—ranging across millennia and the peoples of the world—in order to develop a cultural language his contemporaries might understand.

The second pivotal moment also happened in Rome, this time to Dawson's future wife, Valery Mills, and had deep implications for them both. She first met Christopher at a party in Oxford just after his return from Rome. She was tall, dark, and beautiful, and Christopher kept secret a picture of her dressed as Joan of Arc for a pageant. By 1912, Valery lived with her mother in Florence, where she sang in churches and studied Italian art and architecture. She was fascinated by the shy Christopher Dawson back in England, the "walking encyclopaedia," as she called him, and she knew he was in love with her. But in Florence, she was caught up with dances, parties, and flirtations.

Then, on a visit to Rome, she attended an audience with Pope Pius X. He looked earnestly at each person, and he looked at Valery twice. She never forgot the way he looked at her, and she experienced a change of heart. When she returned to Oxford in the summer of 1913, Christopher proposed and she no longer had any hesitation to accept, even though both sides of the family were against the match. Valery's mother thought Christopher too sickly, and his mother thought marrying a Catholic was an act of desertion. In fact, it was Valery who propelled his eventual conversion to Catholicism—along with the influ-

.

---

3. Scott, *A Historian and His World*, 49.

4. Christopher Dawson, "Future of Christian Culture," *Commonweal*, March 19, 1954, 598.

ence of his Catholic friend Watkin; the external remnants of Christian culture still present in the Oxford colleges; his study of scripture, the church fathers, and the Oxford Movement; and John Henry Newman's *Apologia Pro Vita Sua.* "Like Newman his approach to Catholicism was through history," Dawson's biographer wrote.[5]

After their marriage in 1916, Valery took a strong lead in the Dawson household and shielded her ethereal husband from the material shocks of life. Her love and devotion made the development of Dawson's cultural mind possible. Cardinal Richard Cushing, Archbishop of Boston, awarded her an honorary doctorate from Regis College in 1962. In his citation, the cardinal wrote: "Without the light and sweetness and strength which Valery Mary Dawson brought to the labors of her husband, some of the world's most enlightened scholarship would never have come to exist." One of their children (Christina Scott) and one of their grandchildren (Julian Scott) would keep alive this life's work through a biography and website into the twenty-first century.[6]

The purpose of this chapter is to explain what happened after these two transformative moments. Living through the tragedy of the Great War with the people of his generation transformed Dawson's awareness of the formative humanistic cultural traditions that had shaped their lives. The world before the war seemed afterward as a foreign land with different values. The cultural crisis heightened by the conflict deepened his sense of chronological fracture as much as his sense of vocation, and it propelled him to bridge past and present (as an historian) and engage modern thought (as a cultural theorist) with new sets of questions informed partly by the new field of anthropology. Ultimately, Dawson sought for cultural self-knowledge and renewal by joining an older humanistic (prescriptive) view of culture with the socio-historical (descriptive) perspective emerging among anthropologists during the 1920s. Dawson's cultural mind moved between these two traditions of cultural understanding that constituted the science of culture he practiced.

5. Scott, *A Historian and His World*, 63.

6. Scott, *A Historian and His World*, 50–51, 59–60, quoted on 202. Julian Scott has created the website http://www.christopherdawson.org.uk/ to promote the work of Christopher Dawson to a wider audience.

Humanistic Cultural Traditions

Two years after their fortuitous Roman pilgrimage together, E. I. Watkin stepped from the Yorkshire Dales Railway car in Grassington, England, on a visit to Hartlington Hall, the home of his friend Christopher. It was August 7, 1911, and both young men had just graduated from Oxford. Christopher met him in a horse-drawn carriage, and together they drove six-and-a-half miles along the high road with glorious views out over the valley of the River Wharfe. According to his diary, Watkin delighted to see the green hills of Yorkshire, as well as the stone cottages of the small village of Burnsall and its one-thousand-year-old church, St. Wilfrid's.

Christopher's father came out to meet them from Hartlington Hall less than a mile from Burnsall. Hartlington was a Yorkshire manor house built of grey stone with gables and mullioned windows. Watkin was shown to his room, oak-panelled and tapestried. He had stayed there before and loved its peacefulness. The room had a view out across the valley to the grassy hills beyond. Above the fireplace hung a plaque of the Madonna and Child and a little crucifix. Christopher took him up into a tower where the family had an oratory that was ideal for prayer. "The more I see of the Dawsons and their house," Watkin wrote in his diary that evening before bed, "the more delightful they are. The house is full of books of all sorts and kinds, including a collection of mystical and other theological books worthy of a monastery. The whole family love books and are definitely Christian to a degree rare today." He added: "Oh that they were also Catholics."[7] The two friends enjoyed a lovely view of the full moon just above the slope of the hill before turning in for the night.

Watkin recorded each day of his two-week visit in his diary. He described conversations with Dawson walking through the beautiful Yorkshire Dales, arguing with his friend on the terrace outside Hartlington Hall about books and ideas, swimming naked in the River Dibb, writing letters, his thoughts on art, and the Dawson family and their home. The reader of Watkin's diary comes to understand the deep

---

7. E. I. Watkin, diary entry, August 7, 1911, in Joseph T. Stuart, "Yorkshire Days in Edwardian England: E. I. Watkin's Diary and his Friendship with Christopher Dawson," *Yorkshire Archaeological Journal* 84, no. 1 (2012): 213.

sense of continuity with the past and the stability of ancient traditions of land, family, and faith shaping Dawson's life. The future historian was imbued in a humanistic tradition of culture as a hierarchy of values embedded in stories passed down from generation to generation.

Some of the books the young friends loved and argued over—as recorded by Watkin—included Dante's *Inferno*, John Ruskin's *Modern Painters*, and Kenelm Digby's *The Broad Stone of Honour, or Rules for the Gentlemen of England*. They considered Dante the world's perfect poet. They loved Ruskin for his ideals of truth to nature and beauty, though Watkin expressed dismay at his anti-Catholic bias. Digby, the Victorian writer, defined chivalry as that "general spirit or state of mind which disposes men to heroic and generous actions, and keeps them conversant with all that is beautiful and sublime in the intellectual and moral world."[8] This chivalric conception of humanistic culture continued to influence the educated classes right up to 1914 and even afterward. (In 1912, for example, the final actions of the men who stayed behind on the Titanic to make room for women and children in the lifeboats were portrayed as "gentlemanly" and "honorable."[9]) This was a world in which values appeared stable. Books such as these supported common understandings of Chivalry, Glory, and Honor—keywords among educated British classes that inspired thousands to volunteer for the trenches in the Great War.

The humanistic sense of culture so apparent in young Dawson's world reached back to the word's Latin roots in *cultus*: "worship," "tending," or "cultivating." In addition to cultic practices, then, the oldest idea of culture really rests on a metaphor: the tending of natural growth, taking care of it toward authentic development. The idea of tending natural growth was applied to the human mind, so that by the seventeenth century, "culture" (in English) referred to the improvement and refinement of the mind, manners, and faculties of the person by education and training.[10] The humanistic tradition, therefore, is rooted

8. Kenelm Digby, *Godefridus* (London: Bernard Quaritch, 1877), 109.

9. Mark Girouard, *The Return of Camelot: Chivalry and the English Gentleman* (New Haven, Conn.: Yale, 1981), 3–5.

10. OED, "culture," senses 2, 3, and 4; Raymond Williams, *Culture & Society: 1780–1950* (1958; New York: Columbia University Press, 1983), 335.

in the leisure-space created by worship, whereby people can cultivate their humanity in truth, goodness, and beauty.[11]

Near the end of his visit, Watkin recorded in his diary that, "Both this night and last I saw from my bedroom window over the opposite hill two bright planets, Mars and Saturn close together." He finished his entry for the day with these words: "Col. Dawson, who is something of an astrologer, tells me that this conjunction of Mars (war) and Saturn (pestilence) in Aries signifies war followed by pestilence for Britain, France, Germany and Bassania (S. Russia). This is a curious coincidence when relations are so strained between Britain and Germany."[12] Relations were indeed strained: all during the summer of 1911, tension had mounted over the Agadir Crisis. When the German gunboat *Panther* arrived in the Moroccan port city of Agadir, the British feared that the Germans would establish a naval base on the Atlantic. The Great War would erupt only three Augusts later as the seminal event of the twentieth century and of Dawson's life.

The Great War of Cultures

France, Britain, and Russia (with the United States and Italy joining later) fought against Germany, the Austro-Hungarian Empire, and the Ottoman Empire from 1914 to 1918. Both Dawson and Watkin escaped military service due to medical reasons. Nevertheless, the two friends did not share the same views of the war. Watkin opposed it and expressed dismay at the many Catholic leaders in England who supported it wholeheartedly, ignoring Pope Benedict XV's calls for peace. He was scandalized how the churches acted as recruiting agents during the conflict. Dawson, the son of a professional soldier, supported England's participation in the war.[13]

11. Josef Pieper, *Leisure the Basis of Culture* (1952; San Francisco: Ignatius, 2009), 71, 72. On his first page, Pieper included the following epigraph from Plato: "But the gods, taking pity on man, born to work, laid down the succession of recurring Feasts to restore them from their fatigue and gave them the Muses, and Apollo their leader, and Dionysus, as companions in their Feasts, so that nourishing themselves in festive companionship with the gods, they should again stand upright and erect." This is from Plato, *Laws*, book 2.

12. Watkin, diary entry, August 14, 1911, in Stuart, "Yorkshire Days in Edwardian England: E. I. Watkin's Diary and his Friendship with Christopher Dawson," 222.

13. Magdalen Goffin, *The Watkin Path, An Approach to Belief: The Life of E. I. Watkin* (Brighton: Sussex Academic Press, 2006), 93, 98.

Formation

Despite their differences, when Christopher and Valery married on August 9, 1916, Watkin and his new wife Helena were the only nonfamily guests at the Dawson wedding. The ceremony occurred the day after British forces launched a fresh assault on the Somme across "Death Valley." On August 10, a silent documentary film played in London called *The Battle of the Somme*. It showed actual footage of the detonation of the huge mine that inaugurated the attack. This was the most graphic portrayal of trench warfare yet seen by the public, and the film sold approximately twenty million tickets in Britain in two months.[14] Dawson wrote in one of his first publications: "The present war must make clear to everybody the enormous increase of power in the modern State—power not only in the matter of material resources, but also in the complete subordination of the individual to the society."[15]

Christopher and Valery lived in London during the final year of the war. He worked for the Admiralty Intelligence Department at the Hertford House in a section dealing with history and ethnology. She volunteered for the Catholic Women's League, sending parcels to the front or writing letters to the bereaved relations of dead soldiers. Valery remembered shaking with fear at night as they listened to the German Zeppelins flying over the city. Then the terrible influenza pandemic hit, a flu virus mutated by abnormal trench conditions.[16] The disease killed tens of millions worldwide. The elder Dawson's prediction in 1911 of coming war and pestilence proved correct. Young Dawson and his wife were staying at an inn when he caught it. They could hear workmen hammering together coffins in the yard outside meant for the many people who did not survive the affliction.

World War I was called the "Great War" because both sides fought for a great cause: to defend their own cultural values. But twenty million deaths and nightmarish trench conditions destroyed not only many of those values but also bodies and souls. The legacy of the Great War involved replacing much of civilization with brutalization. Trau-

14. Martin Gilbert, *The Somme: Heroism and Horror in the First World War* (New York: Henry Holt, 2006), 148–50.

15. Christopher Dawson, "The Catholic Tradition and the Modern State," *Catholic Review* (1916): 24.

16. Carol R. Byerly, *Fever of War: The Influenza Epidemic in the U.S. Army during World War I* (New York: New York University Press, 2005), 4, 8.

ma, on both an individual and group level, created spiritual vulnerabilities and additional opportunities for evil to gain entrance into souls.[17] The war inaugurated a proclivity toward more evil in subsequent generations, and so its legacy has haunted the world ever since through the loss of innocence that occurred. In addition, the war spread the logic of mobilization that pushed efficiency as the highest value, creating a new ideal of "man the worker" with a mind of metal and wheels, an ideal that eroded the humanistic values of Dawson's time.

Before the war, for example, many people believed in "progress," never doubting the idea that science and technology increase human happiness and improve society. "The word *machine* was not yet invariably coupled with the word *gun*," Paul Fussell noted.[18] After years of bloody conflict, however, people wondered if it had been worth it. They mourned loved ones but, as historian Modris Eksteins noted, avoided thinking about the object for which they had died. What did the war really mean? The empty answer to that question propelled people into hedonism and narcissism during the 1920s.[19] Evading the tough questions about the meaning of the war's suffering and what is ultimately worth living for, many people threw themselves into frenetic activity, pleasure, and addiction to try to fill the void. In Germany, the Great War was lost, and everything seemed permitted, especially widespread drug use. Elsewhere, the war had been won, yet there, everything also seemed permitted. The Flappers and the Bright Young Things of London flouted conventional behavior and sexual norms. A profound spiritual crisis descended on the postwar decade.

Some who fell into disillusion stopped believing in the goodness of life. Dorothy Day, for example, an American Catholic social activist, recalled that her veteran husband was "obsessed by the war" during the 1920s. He did not believe in bringing a child into such a world. They eventually separated because he refused to empathize with her turn toward God.[20]

17. Chad Ripperger, "The Sixth Generation," *Latin Mass*, Summer 2012, 34–38.

18. Paul Fussell, *The Great War and Modern Memory* (1975; New York: Oxford University Press, 2000), 24.

19. Modris Eksteins, *Rites of Spring: The Great War and the Birth of the Modern Age* (Toronto: Lester & Orpen Dennys, 1989), 254–56.

20. Dorothy Day, *The Long Loneliness* (1952; New York: HarperOne, 1980), 136.

Formation

Many people found it difficult after the war to respect authority and tradition. Henry de Man, a Belgian trench mortar officer, wrote in 1919 about the loss of "human modesty" in himself, which is the fundamental attitude of mind required by every religion. "I find it very hard to bow my head to any living human being or to any of their works. This kind of modesty has been *shelled* out of me."[21] He predicted an increase in the number of people who, even if spiritually oriented after the war, would not belong to any organized church.

Millions of men artificially massed together during the war lost their innocence in other ways. Because soldiers were separated from their women, they frequented prostitutes—the number of whom increased four-fold in Brussels, for example. Venereal disease spread to tens of thousands of soldiers, even though the war popularized condoms. As traditional authority and relationships broke down, an historic shift in human sexual beliefs and practices also altered the language of morality to the language of public health. The conflict contributed to changing sexual mores in the first wave of the Sexual Revolution during the 1920s.

Henry de Man, the Belgian trench mortar officer mentioned above, visited Paris on military leave after a particularly horrendous spell at the front. Wandering around the city, he came across the program for a classical concert by a renowned symphony orchestra and decided to attend. For the previous two years, he had heard only soldiers' songs and ragtime improvisations. De Man listened to several hours of Bach, Beethoven, and Mozart (ironically, all Germanic composers). "I could have wept for delight in feeling like a human being again," he wrote. "It was as though I had suddenly been relieved of the armour which had become identified with myself for two long years."

After the concert, however, he felt confused, weakened somehow. He realized that it did no good for a soldier to cultivate musical beauty. His job was to kill Germans in order to win the war. The less he was a human being, he wrote, the better he would be suited for that job— "and there was no other job worth doing until the war was won." So, he resolved to avoid concerts on his next leave and spend his money

21. Henry de Man, *The Remaking of a Mind: A Soldier's Thoughts on War and Reconstruction* (New York: Charles Scribner's Sons, 1919), 211.

on a good dinner with a big bottle of wine to make up for months of poor meals. In that way, he believed he would gather strength for the struggle ahead.[22]

Besides the loss of innocence, a second major legacy of the total war effort was the "logic of mobilization." It emptied souls of beauty and goodness, filling them instead with frenetic activity and mechanistic efficiency. The mobilization of entire societies toward a single goal squelched the full humanity of its citizens. Governments sought to control even time itself in order to conserve coal during the war by enforcing daylight savings time, starting in 1916. The war popularized the wearing of wristwatches, synchronized to make coordinated bombardments more effective. Modern life would subsequently run according to the movement of clocks.

It is difficult to reverse the logic of total war and mobilization once it is accepted. The "moral situation is damnable," British captain John Crombie wrote to his mother in 1917: "We can only beat Germany by assuming her mentality, by recognizing the State as the Supreme God whose behests as to military efficiency must be obeyed, whether or no they run counter to Christianity and morality. We call their use of gas inhuman, but we have to adopt it ourselves; we think their policy of organizing the individual life contrary to the precepts of freedom, but we have to adopt it ourselves."[23] The logic of the Great War affected everyone, winners and losers alike.

Mobilization of whole societies, their military, industry, media, churches and, ultimately, souls for total war meant total work. Not only did total work often involve Sundays and cause church attendance to decline, it also changed the conception of the human being and the meaning of existence. Man, the worker, emerged as the image of a new, total way of life. The National Socialist German Workers' Party (the Nazi Party) took up this new utilitarian conception of the human person. Human beings can create their own meaning, their own values—if they work hard enough. *Arbeit macht frei*—"work sets you free" read the sign above the gates of Auschwitz.

---

22. de Man, *The Remaking of a Mind*, 209–10.

23. John Crombie to his mother, March 2, 1917, in *World War I & European Society: A Sourcebook*, ed. Marilyn Shevin-Coetzee and Frans Coetzee (Lexington, Mass.: D. C. Heath, 1995), 201.

Formation

If people do not work hard enough, they lose their meaning. In Germany, a controversial 1920 book was published titled *Allowing the Destruction of Life Unworthy of Life* by Alfred Hoche (a professor of medicine) and Rudolf Binding (a professor of law). So many patients had died of starvation and disease in German psychiatric hospitals during the Great War, due to lack of resources, that people pondered new questions: If healthy soldiers can give their lives for their country, should not sick people give their lives too, to ease the burden on the state? Should not the state help them end their lives, thereby saving resources? Should we build houses and tanks or feed imbeciles? One must earn the right to life. The "worthless life" in psychiatric institutions can have no sense of value, wrote Hoche and Binding. Their destruction, they believed, is not only tolerable but even humane.[24] This transvaluation of values that stemmed from the logic of the Great War led to euthanasia and, later, to the Final Solution in Nazi Germany during World War II. The Great War made the unthinkable thinkable, attacking the intrinsic goodness of human dignity. Something terrible, irreversible, and overwhelming had emerged from that world conflict of 1914 into the very heart of the twentieth century.

"What a helplessness this [war] will make afterwards," the German-language poet Rainer Maria Rilke wrote in 1915, "when all the accepted orthodox concepts are taken off the pedestals upon which they have been exhibited, and the bewildered survivors will want to attach themselves again to the abandoned laws of innermost being." Other literary artists jotted down similar insights. "Things fall apart; the centre cannot hold," W. B. Yeats wrote in 1920. Cultural continuities fragmented in a "heap of broken images," T.S. Eliot penned in 1922, like the shattered stained-glass windows of Reims cathedral, shelled by the Germans at the start of the war.[25]

This crisis seemed to unmoor the present from the past. Dawson wrote in his short memoir after the Second World War that, "those of

24. Karl Binding and Alfred Hoche, *Allowing the Destruction of Life Unworthy of Life: Its Measure and Form*, trans. Christina Modak (1920; Greenwood, Wisc.: Suzeteo Enterprises, 2015), 2, 15.

25. Rainer Maria Rilke to Ellen Delp, October 10, 1915, in *Wartime Letters of Rainer Maria Rilke*, trans. M. D. Herter Norton (New York: W. W. Norton, 1940), 48; W. B. Yeats, "The Second Coming," line 3, 1920; and T. S. Eliot, "The Waste Land," line 22, 1922. Both poems can be found at https://www.poetryfoundation.org/.

us who remember the world before the wars have witnessed a change in human consciousness far greater than we have realized, and what we are remembering is not the Victorian age but a whole series of ages—a river of immemorial time which has suddenly dried up and become lost in the seismic cleft that has opened between the present and the past."[26] Similarly, in a letter to his friends on his eightieth birthday, the historian Arnold Toynbee wrote that for him and others of his generation, August 1914 marked a dividing line between two ages of history. "Looking back from 1969 to the fifteen or twenty years before 1914, I am amazed at the degree to which my generation's expectations have been falsified."[27]

Anthropology and the Problem of the Human

Shell shock led to culture shock. The Great War signalled a crisis of humanity that would overshadow the next century. "It was the War, and still more the subsequent period of confusion and disillusionment which made the average man realise how fragile a thing our civilisation is, and how insecure are the foundations on which the elaborate edifice of the modern world-order rests," Dawson wrote.[28] In response, some proposed utopian politics of the Right or Left, others religious revival, a planned economy, world government, or eugenics programs.[29] Dawson saw the crisis of the modern world as the result of the denial of spiritual reality, the loss of contact between religion and culture, the loss of the humanist tradition, the loss of intellectual unity in ramifying disciplines, and the loss of "biological equilibrium between human society and its natural environment."[30] Instead of turning to theology, philosophy, or literature, however, as did many Christian thinkers in response to this crisis,[31] Dawson threw himself into the newly emerging

26. Dawson, "Memories of a Victorian Childhood," in Scott, *A Historian and His World*, 239.

27. Arnold Toynbee to friends, March 30, 1969, BL, box 59 "80th Birthday Book."

28. Christopher Dawson, "Progress and Decay in Ancient and Modern Civilisation," *Sociological Review* XVI (1924): 1, 2.

29. Richard Overy, *The Morbid Age: Britain Between the Wars* (London: Allen Lane, 2009), 4.

30. Christopher Dawson, "The End of an Age," *Criterion* IX, no. 1 (April 1930): 386–401; Dawson, "The Crisis of the West," 261–77; and Dawson, *Progress and Religion*, quoted on 164, 169, 180.

31. Robert Royal, *A Deeper Vision: The Catholic Intellectual Tradition in the Twentieth Century* (San Francisco: Ignatius, 2015).

social sciences. Anthropology studied human cultures in their structure and development. If Western cultures were in trouble, as seemed so clear during this time, perhaps studying *other* cultures could shed light on the nature of the problem back home.

In the English language, the story of this new socio-historical view of culture begins in 1871, when the founder of cultural anthropology, Edward Tylor (1832–1917), published his book *Primitive Culture*. It joined ethnographic research with the traditional humanistic view of culture as universal and represented an important transition in the culture idea because it conceived of culture as something that all people have, not just Europeans (though he still thought of European culture as representing the highest development). His definition of culture as a "complex whole" would be one of his most enduring contributions to anthropology. One should study, according to Tylor, the "knowledge, belief, art, morals, law, custom, and any other capabilities and habits acquired by man as a member of society" *together* in order to make culture intelligble.[32] This powerful, synthetic insight encouraged the rise of an empirical science of culture in the early twentieth century that Dawson's cultural mind relied on heavily.

The full anthropological concept of culture did not emerge in the English-speaking world, however, until the force of German thought made itself felt during the two decades before the Great War. The German thinker Johan Gottfried Herder (1744–1803) spoke of "cultures" in reference to the unique collective *Volk*, or organic people of a particular place united in language, institutions, arts, and literature. Each Volk possessed its own, unique culture, and all were equal before God. German historiography picked up this idea of the Volk as a dynamic whole and made it a central object of study.[33] This focus unleashed a wave of scholarly activity in *historicism*, a complex concept with three different meanings.[34] Here it means a theory of historical knowledge that

32. Edward Tylor, *Primitive Culture*, vol. 1 (1871; New York: Harper & Row, 1958), 1.

33. Ernst Breisach, *Historiography: Ancient, Medieval, and Modern*, 3rd ed. (Chicago: University of Chicago Press, 2007), 222–23.

34. Georg G. Iggers, "Historicism: The History and Meaning of the Term," *Journal of the History of Ideas* 56, no. 1 (1995): 129. Iggers described these three meanings: "A number of writings have dealt with the so-called 'crisis of historicism' in the context of the late nineteenth and the early twentieth centuries. Here historicism has come to be identified with relativism and loss of

essentially created the discipline of history in nineteenth-century Germany. Historicism affirmed the possibility of real understanding of the past and that all phenomena of past life "had to be grasped in terms of unique entities (such as persons, cultures, or nations)."[35] Cultures should be interpreted on their own terms and not judged by other cultures or outside, abstract ideals—as the French had attempted to impose on German people under Napoleon. The unfolding of cultures was totally unique and possessed no universal aim.

Under this influence, later anthropologists in the English-speaking world rejected Tylor's idea of studying the universal development of culture according to a "law of stages" as false universalism, favoring instead the German approach of studying unique cultures on their own terms. This approach came to early twentieth-century American anthropology through the German transplant Franz Boas (1858–1942) who had been influenced by historicism in his studies back home. The universal "culture" of Tylor became plural, as Boas spoke of *cultures*.

Boas contributed four major ideas to modern anthropology. First, historical particularism meant cultures develop along their own, unique paths depending on the historical influences that affect them, not according to any predetermined progressive movement, as Tylor had argued. Second, building on these historical considerations, ethnologists needed to observe cultural dynamics through field work. In other words, both diachronic and synchronic perspectives needed to inform the science of culture Boas proposed. Third, one should consider cultures on their own terms, without judgment by external standards (cultural relativism). Fourth, culture is holistic. One can only understand individual cultural traits considering the context of other cultural elements. Ethnographers—those doing anthropological field work—must spend enough time among a people to understand how the different elements of the culture relate to each other. Only "by un-

---

faith in the values of modem Western culture. This relativism has been considered a permanent aspect of intellectual life under the conditions of the modem world. A very different literature has identified historicism more narrowly with the historiographical outlook and practices of nineteenth- and, to an extent, twentieth-century scholarship in the human sciences. Finally, the term 'New Historicism' has been used recently in a still different context by literary and cultural critics in America" (129). I adopt here the second definition of Iggers.

35. Breisach, *Historiography: Ancient, Medieval, and Modern*, 325.

derstanding the whole body of cultural features could the ethnographer see the significance of the individual parts," philosopher of social science Mark Risjord commented.[36] These intellectual breakthroughs came into view just before the Great War. In fact, the plural of the word "culture" began to appear with regularity in the first generation of Franz Boas's students in the United States around 1910 or 1911.[37]

The war itself was a well-known turning point for anthropology. When the British Association for the Advancement of Science (BAAS) met in Melbourne, Australia, in August of 1914, the Great War broke out, putting the German attendees in an awkward position. The conference included leading figures in British anthropology, such as W. H. R. Rivers, whose later studies during the war on shell shock proved that all peoples can degenerate. (Dawson would use his work on Melanesia to show how anthropology and history cooperate toward understanding cultural development.[38]) The BAAS meeting proceeded normally at first, and the attitude toward the German participants remained friendly. This mood did not last, however, and as war nationalism heated up, several German attendees were arrested or had to escape from the conference.

One of those arrested was Bronisław Malinowski (1884–1942), a Polish subject of the Austrian Empire deeply influenced by Rivers during the years he (Malinowski) had lived in Britain. He was forced to remain in Australia as an "enemy alien" during the war, unable to return home.

36. Garrick Bailey and James Peoples, *Essentials of Cultural Anthropology*, 3rd ed. (Belmont, Calif.: Wadsworth Cengage Learning, 2014), 86; Franz Boas, "The Methods of Ethnology," *American Anthropologist* 22, no. 4 (October-December, 1920): 316, 317; and Mark W. Risjord, "Ethnography and Culture," in *Philosophy of Anthropology and Sociology*, ed. Stephen P. Turner and Mark W. Risjord (Amsterdam: North-Holland, 2007), 404.

37. George W. Stocking, "Franz Boas and the Culture Concept in Historial Perspective," *American Anthropologist* (new series) 68, no. 4 (August 1966): 871; Robert H. Lowie, *Culture and Ethnology* (1917; New York: Basic Books, 1966), 5.

38. Dawson, *Progress and Religion*, 49–50. The 1898 Cambridge Anthropological Expedition to Torres Straits (Melanesia), in which Rivers participated, provided a significant example of island research that aided anthropology's transition into a field science. While the "island model" of anthropological study has been shown to assume too much isolation between peoples, the biogeographical rationale of this expedition "was fundamentally sound and its findings significant" for demonstrating the importance of environment, biology, and history in culture formation, proving that Dawson, at least in this instance, possessed a good sense for utilizing high quality anthropological research in his own work. See Henrika Kuklick, "Islands in the Pacific: Darwinian Biogeography and British Anthropology," *American Ethnologist* 23, no. 3 (August 1996): 611, 613, 623–24, 626.

Significantly, however, the Australian government gave him funds to do ethnographic work in the Trobriand Islands studying indigenous culture. This research, done while under "house arrest," allowed him to publish *Argonauts of the Western Pacific* in 1922 in England. Anthropologists have "drawn some very important conclusions on the origin of human customs, beliefs and institutions," Malinowski wrote, "on the history of cultures, and their spread and contact; on the laws of human behaviour in society, and of the human mind."[39] The book helped launch modern anthropology in England, just as Dawson was maturing intellectually during his early thirties.

As the fieldwork methodology of Boas and Malinowski came to be known and anthropology professionalized after the war, the concept of culture gained a new status as a theoretical entity with explanatory power over human action and thought.[40] It percolated into Dawson's thought through the publications of Boas's students Alfred Kroeber (1876–1960), Clark Wissler (1870–1947), and R. H. Lowie (1883–1957), as the bibliographies of Dawson's first two books attest.

"Culture" is criticized today as overemphasizing the unity of a people while neglecting diversity and relationships of power.[41] However, social scientists continue to use it.[42] Anthropologist Eric Wolf (1923–1999) believed the concept of culture remains serviceable because it brings together sectors of life otherwise at risk of disconnection. "It is precisely the shapeless, all-encompassing quality of the concept that allows us to draw together . . . material relations to the world, social organization, and configurations of ideas. Using 'culture,' therefore, we

---

39. Bronislaw Malinowski, *Argonauts of the Western Pacific: An Account of Native Enterprise and Adventure in the Archipelagoes of Melanesian New Guinea* (London: George Routledge & Sons, 1922), xv.

40. Risjord, "Ethnography and Culture," in *Philosophy of Anthropology and Sociology*, 402, 407.

41. Stanley R. Barrett, Sean Stokholm, and Jeanette Burke, "The Idea of Power and the Power of Ideas: A Review Essay," *American Anthropologist* 103, no. 2 (2001): 468, 477; Burke, *What Is Cultural History?* 25; and John Monaghan and Peter Just, *Social & Cultural Anthropology: A Very Short Introduction* (Oxford: Oxford University Press, 2000), 34, 48.

42. Bailey and Peoples, *Essentials of Cultural Anthropology*, 21–22. For example, economic historian Joel Mokyr remarked that, "For quite a few years now, economists have become increasingly open to the idea that long-term economic change cannot be seriously analyzed without some concept of 'culture' and some idea of how it changes and why these changes matter." See Joel Mokyr, *A Culture of Growth: The Origins of the Modern Economy* (Princeton, N.J.: Princeton University Press, 2017), 7.

can bring together what might otherwise be kept separate."[43] *Bringing together what might otherwise be kept separate*: this synthetic impulse in anthropology, dating back to Tylor, made the idea of culture as the common way of life of a people the discipline's most significant contribution to modern thought in the twentieth century.

Three major reasons help explain why it gained currency after the Great War, ending up as the central concept of Dawson's work. The first was simply the wealth of ethnographic material that had accumulated since the nineteenth century and the urgency scholars felt to gather it, to organize it, and to preserve it as native cultures around the world experienced the impact of globalization.

The second reason the anthropological idea of culture spread may have been the Great War itself. As the American anthropologist Clark Wissler (a student of Boas) noted, the immense rationalization of social phenomena that accompanied the mobilization of entire societies for total war turned everyone's attention to human societies as *wholes*, and the term "culture" could be used helpfully to represent those wholes. In addition, the threat of the war to cultural artefacts (e.g., the destruction of the medieval Cloth Hall in Ypres and Rheims Cathedral) and the corresponding fight to defend one's culture from the "dynamic of destruction"[44] created the necessary conditions for culture consciousness to emerge. "For the first time in the history of the world men began to think in terms of culture and, so, little by little we are evolving a conception of culture rights," Wissler noted in 1923—a conception one gains only by viewing culture as a whole. The dignity of each culture must be respected, he wrote. The Great War turned all eyes to culture as a common way of life of a people. The notion "found its way into the average vocabulary, thus furnishing the basis for a serious inquiry into the nature of the phenomenon" during the 1920s, Wissler proscribed.[45] Dawson took up this new challenge to unpack "cultures."

Thirdly, and most profoundly, the rapid changes in British culture

43. Barrett, Stokholm, and Burke, "The Idea of Power and the Power of Ideas: A Review Essay." Eric Wolf is quoted on p. 469 of this article, and the authors referenced Wolf's *Envisioning Power: Ideologies of Dominance and Crisis* (Berkley: University of California Press, 1999), 288.
44. Kramer, *Dynamic of Destruction*, 5.
45. Clark Wissler, *Man and Culture* (New York: Thomas Y. Crowell, 1923), 327, 334.

after the war created a widespread sense of cultural alienation. Previously, nineteenth-century British intellectuals such as Tylor or theologian John Henry Newman, reassured on every side by the visible evidence of European wealth and world dominion, thought of European civilization as the height of cultural development. They had inherited a humanistic, hierarchical sense of values by which they evaluated the rest of the world.[46] This intellectual environment was not friendly to the emergence of a relativistic, socio-historical concept of culture. This new concept "requires a certain attitude toward the values of one's own culture"—a certain distance and personal disengagement. Its historical emergence involved, if not disillusion, "at least a rejection of contemporary values and an alienation from contemporary society" that Tylor, Newman, and others simply did not feel in the nineteenth century.[47] As Herodotus wrote long ago about the military clash between Persian and Egyptian culture in 525 B.C.: "If you ask people to select from all possible customs the ones that are best, they will examine the matter and choose their own—for everyone considers the religion and ways of his own people far the finest."[48] The Great War undermined some of this attachment to European and national cultural superiority, thereby creating just that sense of widespread alienation needed to open up more space in which people more easily gained enough critical distance from their humanistic values to appreciate *other* cultures for their own sakes. Appreciation of other cultures as different could then reflect back self-knowledge about one's own culture and even about human nature itself, giving one a more catholic view of the world. Perhaps this was why Dawson wrote that the cultural destruction of the

46. Newman wrote he would have "nothing to do with ethnology." Thus, because he and others of his generation lacked a sense of cultural relativism, he characterized Western civilization as Civilization in the universal sense, with a capital "C." Western civilization is "so distinctive and luminous in its character, so imperial in its extent, so imposing in its duration, and so utterly without rival upon the face of the earth, that the association may fitly assume to itself the title of 'Human Society,' and its civilization the abstract term 'Civilization,'" he noted. See John Henry Newman, *The Idea of a University* (1873; Tacoma, Wash.: Cluny Media, 2016), 189. Due to the rise of anthropology to prominence during the Age of the Great War, this older, absolute notion of Western civilization largely disappeared.

47. George W. Stocking, "Matthew Arnold, E. B. Tylor, and the Uses of Invention," *American Anthropologist* (new series) 65, no. 4 (August 1963): 795.

48. Herodotus, *The Essential Herodotus*, trans. William A. Johnson (New York: Oxford University Press, 2017), 106.

Great War as not all negative. It also destroyed "inherited prejudices and fixed forms of thought" that had isolated the Catholic tradition from vital contact with the realities of modern life (as quoted in the introduction).

Dawson was one of the people who absorbed the new "culture consciousness." Along with Wissler and other anthropologists, he upheld the need for detached, scientific understanding of cultures. This did not imply simply amassing cultural facts, however. One could sense the reality of a culture "or even form an idea of its character," as Wissler noted, by first examining its unifying elements. It is "a core of ideas and beliefs, actuating a people and in a large measure controlling their career, that forms the backbone, or at least the unifying element, in the culture-complex," Wissler noted.[49] Dawson agreed. By studying the ideas, values, and religion of a people, one could make intelligible to some degree the heart of their culture. Yet Dawson was aware of the dangers of scientific detachment from culture. It altered one's relation to it. "Happy is the people that is without a history," Dawson wrote, "and thrice happy is the people without a sociology, for as long as we possess a living culture we are unconscious of it, and it is only when we are in danger of losing it or when it is already dead that we begin to realise its existence and to study it scientifically."[50]

The scientific study of culture as an anthropological concept gained widespread acceptance at exactly the moment of humanistic cultural decay and change after the Great War. Dawson adopted the former in his effort to shore up the latter. Using the same word to describe humanistic values and anthropological insights could cause confusion—as when speaking of a "man of culture," Wissler wrote. Used in this way, culture "means superiority; but this use has little in common with its meaning when applied to a people as a whole, for in history and social science we speak of the mode of life of this or that people as their culture," Wissler continued.[51] Despite the risk of ambiguity in confusing humanistic and socio-historical meanings, Dawson made these two meanings of the culture idea the foundation of his work.

49. Wissler, *Man and Culture*, 2–3.
50. Dawson, *Enquiries into Religion and Culture*, xvii.
51. Wissler, *Man and Culture*, 1.

One finds evidence of the anthropological view of culture in Dawson as early as 1924. He wrote that "any sound science of social progress must concern itself first and last with the concrete historical and individual cultures and not with the achievements of civilization in the abstract." This is a remarkable sentence, for the word "cultures" appears in the plural. The historical particularism of this anthropological idea of culture had only recently appeared on the intellectual landscape of the Western world. He continued:

For a culture is essentially a growth, and it is a whole. . . . It is a living body from the simple and instinctive life of the shepherd, the fisherman and the tiller of the soil up to the highest achievements of the artist and the philosopher. The man of genius is not an absolute and unrelated phenomenon in society. . . . He is, in an even more intimate sense than the ordinary man, the product of a society and a culture. Science and philosophy are social products just as much as language is. . . . A great culture sets it seal on a man, on all that he is, and all that he does, from his speech and gesture to his vision of reality and his ideals of conduct, and the more living it is, the deeper is the imprint. . . . Hence every culture develops its own types of man, and norms of existence and conduct, and we can trace the curve of the growth and decline of cultural life by the vitality of these characteristic types and institutions as well as by the art and literature in which the soul of the culture finds expression.[52]

There is much of Dawson's characteristic ways of thinking in this quotation. One notes his historical particularism, his cultural relativism, and his organic conception of a culture uniting the life of the peasant to the highest achievements of art and philosophy. He was interested in the factors supporting cultural vitality and development. He manifested the "anthropological spirit," which tried to understand cultures from within their own universe of values.

Dawson adopted all these ideas in his own work—a highly unusual move for a Catholic scholar working in the interwar period, since many at the time perceived anthropology as having an anti-faith bias. "Christopher Dawson's writing . . . is to be respected as the work of a powerful, dedicated pioneer," anthropologist Mary Douglas (1921–2007) wrote

---

52. Dawson, "Progress and Decay in Ancient and Modern Civilisation," 3.

Formation

in her introduction to a reprint edition of one of Dawson's books.[53] Most of the British founders of the field were agnostic rationalists. Malinowski, for example, considered his childhood Catholicism a "noble lie." The Oxford anthropologist E. E. Evans-Pritchard (1902–1973) once noted that, "Almost all the leading anthropologists of my own generation would, I believe, hold that religious faith is total illusion." They believed religion was a superstition to be explained. Evans-Pritchard, however, converted to Catholicism in 1944 and befriended Dawson since they both lived in Oxford during that decade.[54]

Culture as a Moral Order

Dawson interpreted the findings of anthropology in a way compatible with Catholicism. He built a bridge between faith and reason by connecting humanistic and socio-historical (anthropological) conceptions of culture. The basis of that connection was his idea of human nature, sketched out in one of his first essays. Man "is neither flesh nor spirit, but a compound of both," he wrote. "It is his function to be a bridge between two worlds, the world of sense and the world of spirit, each real, each good, but each essentially different." Man's nature is "open on either side to impressions and is capable of a twofold activity, and his whole destiny depends on the proper co-ordination of the two elements in his nature." This was his message right after the Great War when spiritualist societies spread widely throughout British society in stark contrast to the Marxian and Freudian materialism that also gained currency. Dawson differentiated between but also integrated spirit and matter as the basis for his worldview.

He wrote that Catholicism claims a new power has entered the world capable not only of reconciling human nature to itself but of making man a new creation. Human beings are capable of cooperating with the New Man, Jesus Christ, in the work of renewal affecting the

53. Dawson, *Progress and Religion*, xxii.
54. Timothy Larsen, *The Slain God: Anthropologists and the Christian Faith* (Oxford: Oxford University Press, 2014), quoted on 9 and 10. Curiously, the British anthropologist Mary Douglas herself was a Catholic, and another British anthropologist, Victor Turner, converted to Catholicism in 1958.

{ 72 }

entire natural order. Thus, "The supernatural is not the contradiction of nature," Dawson wrote, "but its restoration and crown, and every faculty of man, whether high or low, is destined to have its share in his new supernatural life." By coordinating the two sides of human nature, therefore, "Christianity creates the motive power—spiritual will—on which all true progress must ultimately rest." Without a spiritual foundation, the development of science, industry, and political organization "only extends the range of human suffering, and the possibilities of social disorder," so evident in the Great War.[55] In a culture without higher spiritual ends and the will to pursue them, therefore, its common life fragments because of various and contradictory impulses of animal instinct.

Yet mastering instinct is the very task of culture. "For human culture is not instinctive," Dawson wrote. "It [culture] has to be conquered by a continuous moral effort, which involves repression of natural instinct and the subordination and sacrifice of the individual impulse to the social purpose." The hedonist believes one can follow instinct and maintain the achievements of culture. "It is the lesson of history," however, "that the higher the achievement of a culture the greater is the moral effort and the stricter is the social discipline that it demands." Culture can be fragile in this sense, he wrote after the Second World War: "the delicate balance of its [culture's] social structure is overthrown as soon as its spiritual limits are broken and its individual members lose faith in the validity and efficiency of its moral order."[56] That loss of faith happened to Western culture as early as the 1920s, leading to transvaluation.

The Great War detached young people from their homes and massed them together in new ways—girls in munitions factories and men in the military camps.[57] Sexual intimacy was elusive for many

---

55. Christopher Dawson, "The Nature and Destiny of Man," in *Enquiries into Religion and Culture*, 256, 269, 281, 282. This essay was first published as Christopher Dawson, "The Nature and Destiny of Man," in *God and the Supernatural: A Catholic Statement of the Christian Faith*, ed. Father Cuthbert (London: Longmans, Green, 1920), 84–118.

56. Christopher Dawson, "Christianity and Sex," in *Enquiries into Religion and Culture*, 225; Christopher Dawson, *The Formation of Christendom* (New York: Sheed & Ward, 1967), 46.

57. Martin Pugh, *We Danced all Night: A Social History of Britain Between the Wars* (London: Vintage Books, 2008), 2.

during the war. Because of this, Marie Stopes's message in *Married Love* (1918) that contraception made intercourse more enjoyable sold thousands of copies as soldiers returned home.[58] A special committee of the National Council of Public Morals declared this a "revolution" comparable to the discovery of steam power. Individuals had to decide whether to use birth control or not, but they warned that it could easily undermine personal responsibility.[59] The radical American literacy critic Victor Francis Calverton (1900–1940) noted with approval that: "Pirouetting to the rhythm of the tango, ravaged by the contortions of the Charleston, or, cigarette in hand, shimmeying to the music of the masses, the New Woman and the New Morality have made their theatric debut upon the modern scene." This was the first stage of the sexual revolution.[60]

Dawson thought writers such as Calverton seemed "entirely reckless of the social consequences of their theories."[61] Their new morality, he noted, consisted simply in emancipating sex from all social restrictions. New moralists across the Western world, from the United States to Russia, were attempting to detach civilization from its roots in nature and tradition. They justified hedonism and the romantic ideals of emotional freedom in terms of anthropological data about wide variation in sexual practices within the human cultures of the world.

Dawson believed anthropological evidence pointed the other way, however. "The whole tendency of modern anthropology," he wrote, "has been to discredit the old views regarding primitive promiscuity and sexual communism, and to emphasise the importance and universality of marriage." There has never been a presocial stage of human life before family structures when sexual relations were open and "free." Whether social organization is matrilineal and patrilineal, whether morality is strict or loose, the regulation of sexual relations is an essential condition for culture. Thus, while the structure of families is shaped by culture, the family itself is not a product of culture but rather (he

58. Juliet Nicolson, *The Great Silence: Britain from the Shadow of the First World War to the Dawn of the Jazz Age* (New York: Grove, 2009), 8, 123–26.

59. *The Ethics of Birth Control*, (London: Macmillan, 1926), 22.

60. V. F. Calverton, *The Bankruptcy of Marriage* (New Work: Macaulay, 1928), 11.

61. Dawson, "Christianity and Sex," 221.

quoted from anthropologist Bronisław Malinowski) the "starting point of all human organisation" and the "cradle of nascent culture."[62]

Of all the changes affecting modern civilization, this breakdown of traditional morality surrounding sex and family was "undoubtedly the most important," Dawson wrote. To the modern girl, he worried, marriage and motherhood would increasingly appear not as a condition of her wider life, as they did for her grandmother, but as the sacrifice of her independence and her career. The traditional and Catholic view of the family rests not simply on revelation but also on natural law. Marriage is a spiritual union of husband and wife as well as an organic union expressing the socially oriented, biological purpose of sex—a fact confirmed by anthropology, in Dawson's view. If sex became separated from its biological and social functions, then a hedonism resulted that reduced sexual life to an "emotional thrill only." This individualistic reduction of sex would undermine the family as (historically) the cradle of humanistic culture and as (socially) the semiautonomous and permanent bulwark against the power of the state. The state would take the place of the family as the guardian and educator of children, and the life of the individual citizen would be controlled from cradle to grave—as was already happening in Russia with its reorganization of marriage and family.[63]

Dawson's pluralistic methodology, grounded in his differentiated conception of the human person, utilized socio-historical cultural perspectives on other cultures toward humanistic ends within his own culture. As Dawson sometimes integrated these two traditions of cultural understanding, he tried to answer different kinds of questions from both points of view: not only about how religion has shaped exotic cultures remote in time and place but also about how it *should* shape our own, Western cultures in the present; not only about how Christians have viewed politics in different times and places but about how they *should* view it here and now, in particular, cultural contexts;

62. Dawson, "Christianity and Sex," 223; Bronisław Malinowski, *Sex and Repression in Savage Society* (London: Kegan Paul, Trench, Trubner, 1927), 184, 185.

63. Dawson, "Christianity and Sex," 215, 217–20, 224, 230, 235. Dawson's cultural approach to sex and family have been connected to the twenty-first century: see Edward Short, "Christopher Dawson and the Embattled Family," *Human Life Review* 43, no. 4 (Fall 2017): 49–58.

not only about what kinds of educational ideals have prevailed in the past, but about what principles *should* inform a humane education in the present. It was Dawson's destiny to imbricate these descriptive and prescriptive approaches to culture. Shaped by two pivotal moments in Rome, just before the outbreak of global conflict, Dawson's integration of cultural perspectives toward a holistic understanding created the uniqueness of his work. Yet was it possible to do this without violating his own rule of boundary thinking? The tendency toward synthesis in Dawson's cultural mind was counterbalanced by his encounter with British sociology during the 1920s. This deepened his commitment to analysis, differentiation, and empirical knowledge.

Chapter 2

Sociology

The problem of sociology is probably the most vital scientific issue of our time, for if we admit the impossibility of creating a scientific sociology we are confessing the failure of science to comprehend society and human culture.

—Christopher Dawson (1934)

Cultural analysis was a counterweight to the anthropological impulse toward synthesis in Dawson's science of culture. Social scientists to this day remain uncertain and divided over how exactly to go about cultural analysis. They often separate intellectualist from behavioralist approaches in mutually incompatible ways, reducing culture to ideas in people's heads or to practices people perform.[1] Dawson joined these two sides together. Because *human beings* make human cultures, Dawson considered a comprehensive analytical agenda top priority in the science of culture, and British sociology of the 1920s pointed the way forward. Dawson's openness to modern, scientific sociology was unusual for most Catholic intellectuals of the early twentieth century, who often focused on fields like literature, philosophy, or theology.[2]

Due to his friendship with members of the Sociological Society in Britain, his sociological research, his articles in *Sociological Review*, and his early books, Dawson came to see himself as competent[3] in sociology

---

Christopher Dawson, "Sociology as a Science," 14.

1. Smith, "The Conceptual Incoherence of 'Culture' in American Sociology," 400.

2. Hittinger, "Christopher Dawson: A View from the Social Sciences," 31, 32.

3. Dawson was not trained in the field, however; there were few opportunities for academic training in sociology during the early twentieth century, especially in Britain. He was trained in history and agricultural economics at Oxford.

Formation

and was viewed as so by others. For example, applying for the vacant
Chair of the Philosophy and History of Religion at Leeds University in
1933, he wrote to Alexander Farquharson, a friend at the Sociological
Society: "Personally I think it is very desirable that they [the committee
members for the appointment] should have someone who is prepared
to treat the subject on sociological lines & not in a purely abstract theological or philosophical way, & from this point of view I think I should
do as well as any one, considering the comparatively small number of
workers in the field."[4] Despite support from several eminent scholars, he
did not obtain the position, possibly because of his Catholicism.[5]

Nevertheless, one of the most influential figures in early sociology
in the United States, Robert E. Park (1864–1944), recognized Dawson as
a fellow sociologist in his review of Dawson's *Enquiries into Religion and
Culture* (1933). The essays therein, Park wrote, focused on the social function of religion and were "at once historical and sociological." Dawson
was fascinated by cultural change in general and the role of religion in
the rise and decline of culture, in particular, the American noted. In addition, the German sociologist Karl Mannheim (1893–1947), who helped
found the sociology of knowledge, also accepted Dawson as a fellow sociologist. He even tried to solicit a book from Dawson for his new Routledge Library of Sociology and Social Reconstruction series in 1942.[6]

In this chapter, I show how sociology played a lead role in Dawson's science of culture. Building on the influence of Patrick Geddes
(1854–1932), Victor Branford (1863–1930), and other members of the
British Sociological Society right after the Great War, he arrived at a
mature palette of analytical categories for the scientific study of culture: Folk (F), Work (W), and Place (P), together representing the external side of culture (including human action) and Ideas (I) referring

4. Dawson to Farquharson, January 27, 1933, KA-AF, folder "Christopher Dawson Letters."
5. Scott, *A Historian and His World*, 110. The chair went to E. O. James (1888–1972), an anthropologist in the field of comparative religion. According to Scott's biography, Dawson received
support for the position from Ernest Barker, his tutor at Oxford and then professor of political
science at Cambridge. Barker wrote in his recommendation letter: "I always knew that in intellectual power, he [Dawson] stood alone among all the men I had ever taught." However, the selection
committee members had known Nonconformist and anti-Catholic views (109–10).
6. Robert E. Park, review of *Enquiries into Religion and Culture, American Journal of Sociology* XLI (1935): 109; Potts and Turner, "Making Sense of Christopher Dawson," 105. The American
sociologist Thomas F. O'Dea (1915–74) also referenced Dawson's work in his *Sociology of Religion*
(Englewood Cliffs, N.J.: Prentice Hall, 1966).

{ 78 }

to both ideas and spiritual vision in a particular society, the inner side of culture. These internal/external dimensions of culture (I/FWP) were meant to cover the full range of social phenomena among the peoples of the world. One needed to approach them empirically in order to understand how their mutual influence on one another powered the "culture-process," as Dawson called it. Cultural analysis, Dawson held, would contribute toward understanding the structures of cultures, how they change, and what contributes to cultural stability in a time of crisis (like the 1920s).

I will also show how Dawson, in pursuing a responsible scientific sociology that could adequately deal with religion, sidestepped the "Christian sociology" of the time imbued with nostalgic medievalism, the speculative and idealist sociology of L. T. Hobhouse (1864–1929), and the psychological reduction of religion in the "subjective sociology" of the Sociological Society. In their place, Dawson integrated a robust conception of the spiritual side of human nature—open to the transcendent—into the biological sociology of Geddes and Branford. In this way, he tried to coordinate the material limits and the spiritual freedom of individuals within human cultures.

Despite his reputation as a sociologist between the wars, Dawson has not been remembered as such. In fact, British sociology in general during the early twentieth century has been described as a failed enterprise.[7] This view, however, is changing. Not only are scholars realizing the richness of British social theory during that time, they are also counting Dawson as a significant contributor. He advanced a sophisticated theory of how cultural diffusion of technologies, customs, and ideas works among populations encountering each other.[8] Scholars Garrett Potts and Stephen P. Turner have even claimed Dawson was the greatest product of early-twentieth-century British sociology. He is "a sociological classic and major historian, and the person whose influence as a public intellectual has been the greatest and most enduring" among early twentieth-century British sociologists.[9] While only

7. Reba N. Soffer, "Why Do Disciplines Fail? The Strange Case of British Sociology," *English Historical Review* XCVII (1982): 767–802.

8. John Scott, *British Social Theory: Recovering Lost Traditions Before 1950* (London: SAGE, 2018), 135.

9. Potts and Turner, "Making Sense of Christopher Dawson," 103.

Geddes's town planning ideas are still studied today,[10] Dawson's reputation as a sociologist is coming back. That is perhaps partly because
he engaged the classic sociological tradition on religion and modernity
(including Durkheim and Weber, figures taken up in later chapters),
whereas Geddes did not. In addition, the sound insights of the environmental sociology developed by Le Play and Geddes, which Dawson adopted, give staying power to Dawson's work, even as American sociology has been reviving serious interest in "culture" over the last couple
of decades. One practicing sociologist, Christian Smith, has recently
referenced Dawson in this regard.[11]

Christopher Dawson and British Sociology

In Germany, France, and the United States, sociology rose to academic prominence by the early twentieth century for the study of
modern societies. A "whole new world has been opened to us," Dawson
wrote. Resources for "understanding human development and its social processes have been immeasurably increased."[12]

In Britain, however, few academic sociologists appeared. Instead,
sociology took on a more popularized form in works of social criticism:
The Superstition of Divorce (G. K. Chesterton), *Womanhood at the Cross-
roads* (Edith Gell), and *Life in a Madhouse* (Ernest Parley). These books
all appeared under the heading for new books in sociology in the *Times
Literary Supplement* in 1920. Sociology was a particular way of thinking
or imagining that sought to understand human beings in the context of
their social, economic, and moral environments. Concerned with practical problems and social renewal, it emerged from largely nonacadem-
ic sources in Britain,[13] with the exception of L. T. Hobhouse, the liberal

10. John Scott and Ray Bromley, *Envisioning Sociology: Victor Branford, Patrick Geddes, and
the Quest for Social Reconstruction* (New York: State University of New York Press, 2013), 126, 209.

11. Christian Smith, *Moral, Believing Animals: Human Personhood and Culture* (New York: Oxford University Press, 2003), 77.

12. Dawson, "Sociology as a Science," 15.

13. C. Wright Mills, *The Sociological Imagination* (New York: Oxford University Press, 1959),
19; Soffer, "Why Do Disciplines Fail? The Strange Case of British Sociology," 768; and Lawrence
Goldman, "Victorian Social Science: From Singular to Plural," in *The Organisation of Knowledge
in Victorian Britain*, ed. Martin Daunton (Oxford: Oxford University Press, 2005), 87–88. The book
titles appeared under the heading for new books in sociology in the *Times Literary Supplement*,
February 5, 1920, 91.

political theorist and idealist sociologist, who was appointed Martin White Professor of Sociology at the London School of Economics in 1907. He founded and edited (from 1908 to 1910) the *Sociological Review*. His influence would extend throughout British academia but did not affect Dawson much.

Part of the slow-start problem for academic sociology in Britain was disagreement over the nature of the field. If sociology is a science, what are its facts? Three men arrived at the Sociological Society in the decade before the Great War with different answers to that question.

The first was the English eugenicist Francis Galton (1822–1911), half-cousin of Charles Darwin (1809–1882), who pushed a racial sociology based on hereditary biology and the belief that society suffered from biological instability. Pushing the use of questionnaires and statistics, adherents of racial sociology sought to control population growth for the betterment of the race and nation. This view of sociology had little discernible influence on Dawson, and its credibility later tanked as the results of Nazi racial hygiene became known by midcentury.

The second was L. T. Hobhouse. He and other idealists of the "ethical sociology" tradition in London-based groups such as the Charity Organization Society and the Christian Social Union were partly inspired by the British idealist philosophical tradition of T. H. Green (1836–1882). While Hobhouse appreciated that human societies develop within material environments, he viewed the social world as a network of communicating individual minds who circulate ideas and meanings. Central to this social "mind" were the "rules" making up major social institutions—the normative principles (hence "ethical sociology") regulating social interaction.[14] Hobhouse maintained a clear distinction between man and animal, stressing the rational mind and the ability for self-improvement. He had a very different vision than either Galton or Geddes, for Hobhouse stressed the importance of human agency in social development as well as the independence of sociology from biology. Thus, when he was chosen for the chair of sociology at the London School of Economics instead of the other two men, it signaled a shift in British sociology away from biology in the

14. Scott and Bromley, *Envisioning Sociology*, 21.

long run.[15] While Dawson rejected this one-sided idealist sociology, he would retain Hobhouse's confidence in reason as an original and creative force in human societies, albeit open to the transcendent.

The third figure was the Scottish biologist and geographer Patrick Geddes, who founded a distinctive environmental sociology that deeply influenced Dawson. Along with his supporter, the businessman Victor Branford, Geddes formed a collaborative circle of friends sharing an intellectual vision. They based their movement at Outlook Tower in Edinburgh, and after 1920, at Le Play House in London. Geddes located human beings firmly within their physical environments, which he closely observed, studied, and worked to improve. His motto was "vivendo discimus"—we learn by living. He and Branford pursued a master vision of sociology uniting all the social sciences (anthropology, economics, and geography) with psychology. This integration would aid social reconstruction through local initiatives, not sweeping government programs; civics, town planning, and spiritual (inner) renewal would also play a part.

Geddes and Branford were among the first social thinkers to notice the inherently global character of human activity. "Social life cannot be understood as purely localized in its region," as Scott and Bromley summarized their insights, "but must be seen as embedded in natural and transnational interchanges that fundamentally affect it." Immediately after the Great War, Geddes and Branford hoped to capture the war spirit of public effort toward a common goal, recast as social reconstruction through the aid of sociology. "There must be some vision, clear yet moving, of a better future," they believed.[16] It was just then Dawson encountered their work.

Perhaps it was through his mentor at Oxford, Ernest Barker (1874–1960), who was involved in the Sociological Society, that Dawson was drawn into their orbit. However it happened, this was Dawson's first intellectual association since his Oxford days. He credited it as vital to

15. Chris Renwick, *British Sociology's Lost Biological Roots: A History of Futures Past* (New York: Palgrave Macmillan, 2012), 10; R. J. Halliday, "The Sociological Movement, the Sociological Society and the Genesis of Academic Sociology in Britain," *Sociological Review* (new series) XVI (1968): 379.

16. Scott and Bromley, *Envisioning Sociology*, 92, 214; Victor Branford and Patrick Geddes, *The Coming Polity: A Study in Reconstruction* (London: Williams and Norgate, 1917), xiii–xiv.

his early writing and teaching career[17]—even though Patrick Geddes moved to India in 1919 to oversee urban planning there. Dawson greatly admired Victor Branford, who boiled over with energy and ideas. Branford exuded joy in approaching a subject from many different sides and took over editing the *Sociological Review* from 1917 until about the time of his death in 1930. He praised Dawson's first book, *Progress and Religion* (1929), which was based on much of the research Dawson had tested among his sociological friends. Dawson, in turn, wrote a glowing memorial for Branford after his death in 1930.[18]

The *Sociological Review* and the Sociological Society provided the first serious outlet for Dawson's ideas. He contributed twelve articles to the *Review*,[19] many of them later republished in books, and thirteen book reviews.[20] He wrote about industrialism, class conflict, urban re-

17. Birzer, *Sanctifying the World*, 44.

18. Victor Branford, review of *Progress and Religion*, *Sociological Review* XXI (1929): 361–62; Christopher Dawson, "He Gave.... His Whole Self," *Sociological Review* XXIV (1932): 24.

19. (1) "The Passing of Industrialism," *Sociological Review* XII (1920). This piece was later published in Dawson's *Enquiries into Religion and Culture*, at the end of which Dawson added a note: "This essay was written during the war and first printed in 1920. The crisis of modern industrialism has taken a very different form to that which I then predicted. Nevertheless, and partly for this very reason, I think the essay still retains sufficient interest and actuality to justify its inclusion in the present volume" (63). (2) Christopher Dawson, "On the Development of Sociology in Relation to the Theory of Progress," *Sociological Review* XIII (1921). It was later published in Dawson's *Dynamics of World History* as "Sociology and the Theory of Progress." (3) Christopher Dawson, "The Life of Civilisations," *Sociological Review* XIV (1922). (4) Christopher Dawson, "Herr Spengler and the Life of Civilisations," *Sociological Review* XIV (1922). It was later published with additional material as "Oswald Spengler and the Life of Civilizations" in *Dynamics of World History*. (5) Christopher Dawson and Alexander Farquharson, "The Beginnings of Rome," *Sociological Review* XV (1923). (6) Christopher Dawson, "A Scheme of British Culture Periods, and of their Relation to European Cultural Developments," *Sociological Review* XVI (1924). (7) Christopher Dawson, "Progress and Decay in Ancient and Modern Civilisation," *Sociological Review* XVI (1924). Part of this article was incorporated into Dawson's *Progress and Religion* and was republished in *Dynamics of World History*. (8) Christopher Dawson, "Religion and Primitive Culture," *Sociological Review* XVII (1925). (9) Christopher Dawson, "Civilisation and Morals; or, The Ethical Basis of Social Progress," *Sociological Review* XVII (1925). This piece was later published in Dawson's *Enquiries into Religion and Culture* and in *Dynamics of World History*. (10) Christopher Dawson, "Mystery of China," *Sociological Review* XIX (1927). It was later published in *Enquiries into Religion and Culture*. (11) Christopher Dawson, "European Democracy and the New Economic Forces," *Sociological Review* XXII (1930). (12) Christopher Dawson, "Prevision in Religion," *Sociological Review* XXVI (1934). This was a paper read at the International Sociological Congress at Geneva in October 1933 as a contribution to the discussion of the general topic of Prevision in Sociology. It was later republished in *Dynamics of World History*.

20. Dawson reviewed the following books for the *Sociological Review*: (1) *The History of Social Development*, by Dr. F. Müller-Lyer and trans. E. C. and H. A. Lake (1920) (XIII, 1921, 116–17); (2) *The New Calendar of Great Men*, eds. Frederick Harrison, S. H. Swinny, and F. S. Marvin (1920)

newal, the "co-operative" state, immigration, progress, primitive societies, religion, changes in contemporary Chinese society, Arabic thought, the Dravidian element in Indian culture, race,[21] and the structures and development of culture—all from a sociological point of view. Dawson also contributed to the Conference on Some Living Religions within the Empire held in 1924 at the Imperial Institute in London, partly sponsored by the Sociological Society. Dawson delivered a paper entitled "Religion and the Life of Civilization" on the connection between religion and the development of peoples throughout history.[22] All of this writing and presenting, along with his sociological friendships, not only sustained his lonely occupation as independent scholar during the 1920s but also laid much of the foundation of his cultural mind.

Others connected to the Sociological Society included the American writer and social reformer Lewis Mumford (1895–1990) when he lived in London in 1920; Alexander Farquharson, a schoolteacher, civil servant, and founder-member of the Sociological Society; Carr Saunders (1886–1966), who was a sociologist and academic administrator educated in biology and also directed the London School of Economics from 1937 to 1965; Morris Ginsberg (1889–1970), a British sociologist

---

(XIII, 1921, 179–81); (3) *Illustrations of the History of Medieval Thought and Learning*, by Reginald Lane Poole (2nd ed., 1920) (XIV, 1922, 148–49; (4) *Arabic Thought and its Place in History*, by De Lacy O'Leary (1922) (XIV, 1922, 237–38); (5) *Die Berliner Romantik*, by Josef Nadler (1921) (XV, 1923, 166–67); (6) *The Hellenistic Age*, by J. B. Bury et al. (1924) (XVI, 1924, 361); (7) *The Dravidian Element in Indian Culture*, by Gilbert Slater (1924) (XVI, 1924, 364–65); (8) *The Children of the Sun: A Study in the Early History of Civilization*, by W. J. Perry (1924) (XVI, 1924, 158–61); (9) *Small Houses of the Late Georgian Period: 1750–1820*, vol. 1, by Stanley C. Ramsey (1919), vol. 2, by Ramsey and J. D. M. Hervey (1923) (XVI, 1924, 76); (10) *Primitive Religion*, by Robert H. Lowie (1925) (XVIII, 1926, 258–59); (11) *Danses et Légendes de la Chine Ancienne*, by Marcel Grant, 2 vols. (1927) (XIX, 1927, 260–61); (12) *Whither Mankind? A Panorama of Modern Civilization*, ed. C. A. Beard (1928) (XXI, 1929, 256–57); (13) *Der Übergang vom Feudalen zum Bürgerlichen Weltbild*, by Franz Borkenau (1934) (XXVI, 1934, 414–15).

21. Dawson thought of "race" not so much as the result of a predetermined racial inheritance but as the product of long-term cultural development in a particular place—see *Religion and Culture*, 35–36.

22. Christopher Dawson, "Religion and the Life of Civilization," in *Religions of the Empire: A Conference on Some Living Religions with the Empire*, ed. William Loftus Hare (New York: Macmillan, 1925). The conference on religion was organized in connection with the Empire Exhibition of 1924. The first part of the conference focused on the Oriental religions of the empire and the second part on the "psychology and sociology of religion," in which a "series of papers was read by specialists who expounded the religious process and its mode and purpose as it operated in their sphere of observation" (*Religions of the Empire*, 4). Dawson's paper was also published in *The Quarterly Review* CCXLIC (1925): 98–115.

who played a (later) central role in the development of the discipline, and who was influenced by Hobhouse, served as editor of the *Sociological Review* in the 1930s, and interacted with the group around Geddes; and architect Stanley C. Ramsey (1882–1968), a member of the Sociological Society and author of *Small Houses of the Late Georgian Period: 1750–1820* (1924). Dawson reviewed Ramsey's book with high praise, for the author judged that "architecture is not merely a question of styles and individuals, but that it rests on deep social foundations, or rather that it is the vital expression of a great society."[23]

Surviving correspondence suggests an even closer relationship with several of these figures than Dawson's biographers have hitherto portrayed. His colleagues esteemed him, and he, them. They thought of Dawson as a fellow sociological thinker. In 1924, Mumford wrote to Geddes: "All of us, Farquharson, Dawson, Ramsey, and the rest, would profit a good deal if you and Branford would put your heads together for a turn to discuss the *strategy* of our sociological attack."[24] Farquharson wrote to Dawson in 1933 encouraging him to give a paper at the up-coming International Sociological Congress in Geneva: "You already know of the new arrangements for the *Sociological Review* which will commence from January next: the *Review* from thenceforward being in the control of an Editorial Board consisting of Ginsberg, Carr Saunders and myself." Farquharson continued: "All three of us are unanimous in wishing that [the January issue] should contain a contribution by yourself [Dawson] as one of the very few people who can claim outstanding importance in the English sociological world." This was high praise indeed. Carr Saunders, Farquharson continued, "speaks in the warmest terms of the value of your work, and of its importance in non-catholic circles."[25] Dawson did not go to Geneva, but his paper was read there

23. Christopher Dawson, review of *Small Houses of the Late Georgian Period: 1750–1820*, *Sociological Review* XVI (1924): 76.

24. Lewis Mumford to Patrick Geddes, January 5, 1924, in Frank G. Novak, Jr., ed., *Lewis Mumford and Patrick Geddes: The Correspondence* (London: Routledge, 1995), 189. Mumford corresponded with Geddes between 1917 and 1932. Mumford himself wrote to Dawson in 1924: "Dear Mr. Dawson: I follow your writing with so much pleasure and profit that I cannot forbear to write you at last and make my acknowledgements. Your synopsis in the April number of the review is a masterly bit of work" (May 8, 1924, STA, box 15, folder 58, "Mumford, Lewis"). The "synopsis" Mumford referred to was Dawson, "A Scheme of British Culture Periods, and of their Relation to European Cultural Developments."

25. Farquharson to Dawson, July 27, 1933, KA-AF, folder "Dawson, C. Lectures and Letters."

by someone else and published in the *Sociological Review* as "Prevision in Religion" (1934), explicating the connection between sociology and the study of religion.[26] Several months later, Farquharson wrote to Dawson: "We had a meeting of the Editorial Board of the *Review* yesterday, and a very keen discussion upon your sociology of which I shall tell you more when we meet."[27] Dawson was viewed as a fellow traveler.

More than this, the letters reveal friendships. In a correspondence just after Branford's death in June 1930, Geddes wrote to Dawson that, "I'd value a day or two with you! & particularly to talk over those long views of *history* we have each been seeking (I'd come to Exeter for a week-end in early autumn, if you have time?)" He concluded, "Pardon my thus troubling you—& with so long a letter! but you are one of the few in the Society to whom I can look for criticism & counsel!"[28] Farquharson and Dawson coauthored a two-part article on the city of Rome in 1923.[29] Two years later, Dawson wrote to Farquharson from Dawlish, Devonshire: "Do you think it will be possible to pay us a visit before long? . . . I am so very anxious to see you again."[30] In another letter, working on the recent history of sociology, Dawson asked: "Have you come across anything new on sociology of late? The great problem to me is to explain the development of sociology after Herbert Spencer, up to then there is a continuous tradition, afterwards everything becomes confused (until at least one gets Geddes & Branford taking up the old tradition of Comte)."[31]

Farquharson helped the historian gain his first teaching post in 1925 as part-time lecturer in the History of Culture at Exeter University, then University College of the South West. He wrote to the principal, H. J. Hetherington, introducing Dawson as "one of my most valued colleagues among the group interested in the *Sociological Review* and also

26. Dawson, "Prevision in Religion."
27. Farquharson to Dawson, October 3, 1933, KA-AF, folder "Christopher Dawson Letters."
28. Geddes to Dawson, August 4, 1930, STA, box 15, folder 135, pp. 2, 3.
29. Dawson and Farquharson, "The Beginnings of Rome."
30. Dawson to Farquharson, April 25, 1925, KA-AF, folder "Christopher Dawson Letters."
31. Dawson to Farquharson, December 24 (n.d.), KA-AF, folder "Christopher Dawson Letters." Dawson only partly managed to resolve this conundrum about the history of sociology in the first decade of the twentieth century. In his chapter on sociology for *Progress and Religion*, published in 1929 just after he wrote these letters, he described the tendency in the early twentieth century to "dethrone the intellect." Sociology emphasized the nonrational side of life, as "manifested in crowd psychology and 'herd instinct,' and still more in the vitalist social theory of George Sorel, the philosopher of Syndicalism." See Dawson, *Progress and Religion*, 29.

a great friend." He described him as "a life-long specialist in historical studies," adding: "Working closely with him, as I have done, I have had convincing proof of his sound scholarship and remarkable range of knowledge; indeed I do not know anyone who has quite the same clear and broad view of civilization in its historical development." On the basis of this recommendation, a post was created for Dawson.[32]

Ironically, this new position may have played a role in drawing Dawson away from the Sociological Society, as Geddes remarked in a letter to Mumford: "I don't think Spengler was sent to *Sociological Review* for review, but I'm asking Branford. Certainly Dawson would do a thoughtful critique—but somehow he seems to be dropping out of *Review*, whether too busy with his History Chair at Exeter (a new start), or having altered his views & diverged from us, as a good Catholic may not unnaturally do, though we are not so unsympathetic as may appear."[33] (Dawson did address the work of Oswald Spengler, as discussed in the next chapter.) By the late 1920s, Dawson was indeed starting to drift toward more Catholic circles and noticing the alarming political developments on the continent, so his interests (though not his commitment to sociological principles) did begin to shift.

Nevertheless, though Geddes died in 1932, Farquharson and Dawson remained close through the years. While not a religious person, Farquharson remained deeply interested in religion as an object of study, so the two men had much in common. In 1932, Dawson wrote to Farquharson complaining of his inability to obtain recent literature in sociology. "The London Library is very deficient there, & the Times Book Club won't buy sociological books on the ground that they are 'not of general interest.' Alas! Too true."[34] In 1945, Farquharson wrote to Dawson after the latter was forced out of his position as editor of *Dublin Review* the year before. This happened due to the machinations of the Catholic fascist sympathizer Douglas F. Jerrold (1893–1964), who hated the way Dawson included essays by Catholics with "left-wing"

---

32. Scott, *A Historian and His World*, 75.

33. Geddes to Mumford, February 12, 1927, in Novak, *Lewis Mumford and Patrick Geddes: The Correspondence*, 259. Geddes must have been referring to the new English translation of Oswald Spengler's *Decline of the West* in 1926, for Dawson had already reviewed the first volume of the German edition in 1922; see Dawson, "Herr Spengler and the Life of Civilisations."

34. Dawson to Farguharson, April 19, 1932, KA-AF, folder "Christopher Dawson Letters."

politics. Farquharson sincerely regretted the change. "I have read the Review regularly and with care during your editorship and cannot easily find words to say how much I have admired your conduct of the periodical and how greatly I have gained by studying it," he wrote. "Under your guidance the Review was taking a notable place as an organ of sociological discussion. Were your policy to be followed for a generation I believe that the cause of Catholic thought and scholarship in this country would be assisted in an outstanding degree."[35] Such was the Scotsman's generosity of mind and his respect for Dawson.

Folk, Work, and Place (FWP): Environmental Sociology

Geddes and his colleagues pushed an environmental sociology that examined human societies in their relation to natural environments. Geddes was a charismatic leader whose energetic presence impressed strong intellectual influence on others. As a teacher, he tended to attract those seeking answers to fundamental questions, Scott and Bromley noted. His synthetic vision inspired disciples who believed they had discovered "the truth" and had an almost religious obligation to bring it to others.[36] In the long run, this tendency worked against Geddes' legacy because his disciples failed to develop arguments necessary to ensure his academic standing. Dawson, however, did not look to Geddes for answers to fundamental metaphysical questions, so he possessed the distance necessary to evaluate and adopt ideas from Geddes that could actually forward sociological analysis.

Geddes was born in Scotland, where his father was an Elder in the Free Kirk and gave his son a strict religious upbringing. Losing his faith to an agnosticism about ultimate religious truths, Geddes would retain an enthusiasm for the sociological importance of spiritual values. He also retained from his childhood a love of books and the countryside, acquired during many rambles with his father through rural Scotland that led to life-long interests in natural history, gardening, and field observation. He went to London to study under the biologist Thomas

35. Farquharson to Dawson, February 5, 1945, STA, box 14, folder 127, "Farquharson, Alexander and Dormea."

36. Scott and Bromley, *Envisioning Sociology*, 210.

Henry Huxley (1825–1895), and while there, travelled to France, where he encountered the pregnant ideas of sociologist and engineer Frédéric Le Play (1806–1882).

Le Play wrote his great work *Les ouvriers européens, étude sur les travaux, la vie domestique et la condition morale* (1855) as a social study of European workers and their family structures from Russia to England. Based on direct observation, he analyzed social structure ("Family") in terms of adaptation to economic life ("Work") and the natural environment ("Place"). He desired to understand the basis of stability and peace in human societies, and during his travels in 1837 to inspect the Donetz coalfield (modern Ukraine) he found himself on the steppes among a society very unlike his own. "My eyes," he wrote, "were suddenly opened to the true meaning of history and of contemporary facts." He saw for the first time what the complexity of Western society disguised, wrote a biographer: "that every occupation leads to the development of a certain type of family, which adapts to the nature of the given occupation. Around this family type spring up religious, moral and ethical ideals which become part of the soul of a nation and make it what it is," Herbertson summarized.[37]

This discovery led Le Play to an important methodological insight: "My path was clear," he wrote, "from the moment I perceived that in Social Science there was nothing to invent."[38] In other words, do not turn sociology into philosophy, as other nineteenth-century sociologists did[39]: rather, observe social life first-hand. Le Play, Dawson summarized, was a man of faith and of facts (Le Play returned to the practice of his Catholic faith toward the end of his life). He studied working families not second hand, "through statistics and blue-books, but by the direct observation of their way of life and by a meticulous study of their family budgets, which he used as a basis for the quantitative analysis of the facts of family life. Le Play's method of social analysis

37. Dorothy Herbertson, *The Life of Frédéric Le Play*, ed. Victor Branford and Alexander Farquharson (Ledbury: Le Play House, 1950), 48.

38. Herbertson, *The Life of Frédéric Le Play*, 106.

39. For example, Auguste Comte (1798–1857) and Herbert Spencer (1820–1903). Dawson contrasted these two "social philosophers" with Le Play, who "had no general philosophy to serve" in his attempt to observe the actual conditions of social life. See Dawson, "Sociology and the Theory of Progress," in *Dynamics of World History*, 37–39.

affords an insight into just those fundamental social realities which so often escape the notice of the historian and the student of politics."[40] For Le Play, human labor shaped the natural environment into a *mode of life*,[41] which prefigured Dawson's simple anthropological definition of "culture" as a "common way of life—a particular adjustment of man to his natural surroundings and his economic needs."[42] Thus, "The first thoroughly objective study of human life in relation to its geographical environment and its economic functions," Dawson wrote, "was due to a man [Le Play] who knew nothing of anthropology and had little sympathy with earlier sociological theories."[43]

Geddes brought the news of the Le Play school of thought to Scotland. Le Play's empirical approach to sociology "interested Geddes intensively—he saw it as the mission to which he wanted to devote his life."[44] Accordingly, Geddes started Outlook Tower in 1892 in Edinburgh as a civic observatory, sociology "laboratory," and museum dedicated to the Le Playist perspective, and he organized Edinburgh Summer Schools in the 1890s that brought in speakers versed in Le Play's ideas. His sociology of "civics" ultimately embraced humanistic ends: to train young people through community action to cherish their environment for the benefit of future generations. Geddes himself had personally overseen the renovation of historic buildings on the upper Royal Mile in Edinburgh, providing places for students from different disciplinary backgrounds to live together in community.[45] His empirical sociological views, rooted in Le Play, described how human societies actually work but also gave insight into how they *should* work, laying the basis for practical social reconstruction.

40. Dawson, "Sociology as a Science," 23; Dawson, *Progress and Religion*, 51.

41. Herbertson, *The Life of Frédéric Le Play*, 111.

42. Dawson, *The Age of the Gods*, xxiv.

43. Dawson, *Progress and Religion*, 51. Philippe Périer, coeditor of the *International Review of Sociology*, agreed with Dawson's assessment. Périer remarked in his foreword to Michael Brooke's biography of Le Play that, "Le Play should justly be recognized as the first person to have developed a scientific method for the observation of social facts, and to have personally applied this method for twenty-five years in almost every country of Europe." See Michael Z. Brooke, *Le Play: Engineer and Social Scientist: The Life and Work of Frédéric Le Play* (London: Longman, 1970), vii. Le Play did not use the word "sociologist," however, for he was suspicious of Comte.

44. "Geddes, Patrick (1854–1932)," entry by Helen Meller, ODNB.

45. Roy M. Pinkerton and William J. Windram, *Mylne's Court: Three Hundred Years of Lawnmarket Heritage* (Edinburgh: University of Edinburgh Information Office, 1983), chap. 8.

Geddes and Branford modified Le Play's "Family" to the broader category of "Folk." Thus, "Folk, Work, Place" (FWP), adopted from Le Play and handed on to Dawson, served as fundamental categories of his cultural analysis (see appendix A). Dawson used them to help explain everything from the rise of the sacred cities of ancient Sumer to the sociological factors in the age of Reformation and the development of twentieth-century political religions. Recent scholars have, in effect, used them to describe how a generic "place" (lower-case) can become a more emotionally rich sense of "Place" (upper-case) through a certain allure of the built environment that draws people and new businesses to a location.[46] Dawson's innovation to the FWP formula, described later, was to add a fourth category of Ideas (I), opening up new possibilities beyond simply naturalist teleology.

The magic of FWP was its grounding in basic biology. If life results from organisms (O) functioning (F) in their environments (E), as Geddes and Branford believed, then life = OFE. OFE for plants and animals = FWP for people (Organism/Folk, Function/Work, and Environment/Place). Thus, the FWP formula provided a way to relate biology and sociology.[47]

In this way, Dawson wrote, Le Play's method of study was "more biological and more in harmony with the spirit of Darwin himself than any of the ambitious evolutionary theories or writers like Herbert Spencer or Lewis Morgan." In fact, for Dawson, "the process of the development of a culture has a considerable analogy to that of a biological species or subspecies. A new biological type arises in response to the requirements of the environment, normally perhaps as the result of the segregation of a *community* in a new or changing environment."[48] Culture results from intimate communion of human beings with their

---

46. Colleen Layton, Tawny Pruitt, and Kim Cekola, eds., *The Economics of Place: The Value of Building Communities Around People* (Ann Arbor, Mich.: Michigan Municipal League, 2011), 41.

47. This fact was appreciated by practicing biologists as well. J. Arthur Thomson (1861–1933), expert on soft corrals and friend of Patrick Geddes, wrote: "Fundamental in Biology is the Organism-Function-Environment relation, the three sides of the prism of life. The living creature, its activities, and its surroundings must be considered together; they form an inseparable trinity. If Biology has any contributions to make to Sociology it must make them within these three co-ordinates, which become in Sociology—Folk, Work, Place: or Famille, Travail, Lieu." See J. Arthur Thomson, "Biological Contributions to Sociology," *Sociological Review* XV (1923): 85.

48. Dawson, *Progress and Religion*, 52.

environment. "In every direction, the natural character of the region determines the modes in which a culture will express itself, and these in turn react upon the character of the culture itself."[49] Place shapes F and W, that is, P → FW.

Geddes and Branford defined "region" as a particular unity of FWP. A region was a socially transformed "place." The adjective *regional* referred "to all those features that comprise the spirit of a place: all the customs, values, and cultural traditions associated with a specific locality," Scott and Bromley wrote. Regional analysis, for Geddes and Branford, began in scientific description of the geology and physical geography of a place (P). This is the sphere in which humans act and which conditions the patterns of work available (W). "Technology and the mode of production are always and necessarily located in a particular environment, and the material conditions within that place constrain the choices that can be made about occupations and forms of labor," Scott and Bromley summarized. Work turns environmental resources toward human purposes. Work conditions activity, institutions, and the whole social way of life (F). Work patterns shape distinct communities with particular institutions, customs, and laws, and this "rustic process" is supplemented by the parallel "civic process" in towns and cities. Urban centers are the foci of their regions. They link local ideas and products to the wider world and more universal values.[50]

The FWP formula was (and still is) useful shorthand for analyzing cultures in any time and place. In Geddes's vision, it related the social sciences (anthropology, economics, and geography) to each other under the overall coordination of sociology, helping to form intellectual architecture. In a letter to Dawson, Lewis Mumford found FWP "highly useful as a check to keep one from leaving out data that ... less rigorous categories might let one neglect."[51] They acted as a constant reminder of the need of multicausal explanations of social phenomena.

The analytical power of FWP shaped not only Dawson's study of

49. Dawson, *Progress and Religion*, 55.

50. Scott and Bromley, *Envisioning Sociology*, 83.

51. Mumford to Dawson, n.d., STA, box 15, folder 58, "Mumford, Lewis"; Scott and Bromley, *Envisioning Sociology*, 84–87.

historic cultures but also his criticism of the maladaptation of modern cultures to their environments and basic biological needs. The first consideration for a society, he wrote, is not to maintain the volume of its industrial production or even the "standard of life" but rather the quality of its population, "and that cannot be secured by the mere expenditure of money on the so-called 'social services,' but only by the preservation of the natural foundations of society: the family and the land." True social renewal, Dawson argued—which Le Play had also argued before him—involved studying these foundations of society (family and land) beneath commerce and industry. The "economic mechanism" had to be adapted to the needs of the social organism. Science and technology should serve both rural life and urban industry, and a better balance between rural and urban England should be sought in order to strengthen the whole structure of the social organism. That involved a more even distribution of social leadership and noneconomic resources between the city and the countryside.[52] A false relationship to environment would, in the long run, undermine modern civilization:

No civilization, however advanced, can afford to neglect these ultimate foundations in the life of nature and the natural region on which its social welfare depends, for even the highest achievements of science and art and economic organization are powerless to avert decay, if the vital functions of the social organism become impaired. Apparent progress is often accompanied by a process of social degeneration or decomposition, which destroys the stability of a civilization, but, as Le Play insisted, this process in not an inevitable one. However far the process of degeneration has gone, there is always a possibility of regeneration, if society recovers its functional equilibrium and restores its lost contacts with the life of nature.[53]

In this way, FWP could function not only as a methodological tool to study human societies as they are but also as a way to advocate programmatically for social reform. This dual descriptive/prescriptive ap-

---

52. Christopher Dawson, "The World Crisis and the English Tradition," in *Dynamics of World History*, 234–36. See Frédéric Le Play, "Social Reform in France (1864)," in *Critics of the Enlightenment: Readings in the French Counter-Revolutionary Tradition*, ed. Christopher O. Blum (Wilmington, Del.: ISI Books, 2004), 197–256.

53. Dawson, *Progress and Religion*, 62.

proach to culture, present in both Le Play's and Geddes's work, also constantly informed Dawson's work, and by it, he could avoid environmental determinism while recognizing the overwhelming importance of material factors in human culture.

"Christian Sociology"

How did Dawson relate the biological categories FWP to *culture as a common intellectual and spiritual vision*? There were at least four models available for how one might connect them. The first was "Christian sociology," a movement of social thought that overlapped with the Social Gospel movement in the United States and Christian Socialism in Britain. Christian sociology proclaimed the kingdom of God as an ideal by which to express Christian faith in social forms,[54] and it made a significant contribution to British sociology as a whole. In fact, many Anglican clergy saw sociology as a kind of applied Christianity and supported it enthusiastically.[55]

One element of Christian sociology was "medievalism,"[56] a nostalgia for an integrated medieval social order that arose around 1850 to describe appeals by (largely non-Catholic) social critics such as John Ruskin (1819–1900) and William Morris (1834–1896) to an idealized and ahistorical idea of the Middle Ages in criticizing modern industrial civilization.[57]

By the early twentieth century, British writers and political figures

54. Stephen P. Turner, "Religion and British Sociology: The Power and Necessity of the Spiritual," in *The Palgrave Handbook of Sociology in Britain*, ed. John Holmwood and John Scott (New York: Palgrave Macmillan, 2014), 107–9.

55. John D. Brewer, "Sociology and Theology Reconsidered: Religious Sociology and the Sociology of Religion in Britain," *History of the Human Sciences* XX (2007): 8, 16. Brewer defined "religious sociology" as sociology in support of the ethical tenets of faith (8). See also Brian Taylor, "The Anglican Clergy and the Early Development of British Sociology," *Sociological Review* XLII (1994): 438–51. Some lay Roman Catholics in Britain also wrote of a "Catholic sociology"; see Michael de la Bédoyère, "An Introduction to Catholic Sociology," *Dublin Review* CXCIII (1933): 31–45; J. Arthur O'Connor, "The Issues of Catholic Sociology," *Dublin Review* CXCIV (1934): 101–16.

56. For a survey of medievalism in English literature and graphic arts from the eighteenth through the twentieth century, see Michael Alexander, *Medievalism: The Middle Ages in Modern England* (New Haven, Conn.: Yale University Press, 2007).

57. Peter C. Grosvenor, "The British Anti-Moderns and the Medievalist Appeal of European Fascism," *The Chesterton Review* XXV (February/May 1999): 104.

such as Hilaire Belloc (1870–1953),[58] A. J. Penty (1875–1937),[59] R. H. Tawney (1880–1962),[60] Saunders Lewis (1893–1985),[61] and Oswald Mosley (1896–1980)[62] embraced the antimodernism inherent in medievalist social criticism. They perceived an organic unity in medieval life between peoples, economics, places, and religion and held up medieval institutions such as the monastery and the guild as examples of working communal societies promising healthy alternatives to modern individualism.[63]

For example, in *The Return of Christendom* (1922), various Anglican writers imagined an ideal relation between faith and the cultural order, inspired by medieval precedents. Maurice B. Reckitt (1884–1980), a leading Anglo-Catholic and Christian socialist writer, wrote about the fragmented instability of life after the Great War, arguing that in response to that malaise, the "ideals and even the achievements of Medievælism, for all their enormous imperfections, offer us a pattern so inspiring, an example so unique."[64] A Christian social order, "Christendom," became a central theme in his work editing the quarterly journal of Christian sociology *Christendom* from 1931 to 1950. In his 1937 encyclical *Divini Redemptoris*, Pope Pius XI wrote that under the influence of the church there arose during the Middle Ages "prodigious charitable organizations, great guilds of artisans and workingmen of every type. These guilds, ridiculed as 'medieval' by the liberalism of the last century, are today claiming the admiration of our contemporaries in many countries who are endeavoring to revive them in some modern form."[65]

Despite the fruitfulness of some of these interwar movements, Christian sociology, especially in its medievalist brand, did not at-

---

58. "Mr. Belloc on the Middle Ages," *Tablet*, February 4, 1922, 22.

59. Penty wrote *Towards a Christian Sociology* (1923) and then supported the British fascist movement in the 1930s.

60. R. H. Tawney, *The Acquisitive Society* (London: G. Bell & Sons, 1921), 231–32.

61. Lewis was a devout Catholic and founder of Welsh nationalism.

62. Mosley was a nonpracticing Anglican who founded the British Union of Fascists.

63. Raymond Williams, *Culture and Society 1780–1950* (London: Chatto & Windus, 1958), 19.

64. M. B. Reckitt, "The Idea of Christendom in Relation to Modern Society," in *The Return of Christendom* (New York: Macmillan, 1922), 26–27.

65. Pope Pius XI, *Divini Redemptoris* (1937), §37, http://www.va/holy_father/pius_xi/encyclicals/documents/hf_p-xi_enc_19031937_divini-redemptoris_en.html.

tract Dawson as a model for relating religion and sociology. The group
around him, the Sociological Society, insisted "Christian sociology"
was a contradiction in terms, for a science cannot be founded on religion.[66] Other than the case of theology (a science founded on divinely
revealed facts), Dawson agreed with this assessment.

There were specific problems with the medievalism that suffused
Christian sociology. Ernest Barker (Dawson's mentor at Oxford) distinguished between the "actual Middle Ages" and the "idealized Middle
Ages" of William Morris, Hilaire Belloc, and G. K. Chesterton. The ideal,
Barker, wrote, "moves the mind and stirs the spirit of men, but the motion and the stirring are those not of the Middle Ages themselves, but
rather of a certain antiquarian idealism—an inverted Utopianism, as it
were, leading men to find the Utopia, or Nowhere, of the future in what
one may call a Never Was of the past."[67] Raymond Williams agreed:
the trouble with historical nostalgia is that the "organic community"
is always gone. Each generation of social critics laments the passing of
the community in the previous generation, which had also made the
same criticism—and so on.[68] Dawson did not think it easy or always
helpful to judge the present in terms of the past. "One might suppose,
perhaps, that the historian would be more inclined than the journalist
or the man of affairs to judge the present situation in terms of the past,"
he wrote. "As a matter of fact, the case is just the reverse—it is only
the trained mind that can recognize the new factors in a situation, the
change of social direction which characterises a new period."[69]

Medievalism has been mistakenly attributed to Dawson.[70] In reality, he warned against it in his introduction to *The Making of Europe*.
While some historians,[71] he noted, used the past in support of the

66. Turner, "Religion and British Sociology," 117.

67. F. J. C. Hearnshaw, ed., *Mediæval Contributions to Modern Civilization* (New York: Barnes & Noble, 1921). See Barker's preface, 6.

68. Williams, *Culture and Society 1780–1950*, vii, 259–60. See also William Stafford, "This Once Happy Country: Nostalgia for Pre-Modern Society," in *The Imagined Past: History and Nostalgia*, ed. Christopher and Malcolm Chase Shaw (Manchester: Manchester University Press, 1989).

69. Dawson, "European Democracy and the New Economic Forces," 32.

70. Charles Taylor, *A Secular Age* (Cambridge, Mass.: Belknap/Harvard University Press, 2007), 733.

71. For example, the classical scholar and historian J. B. Bury (1861–1927), presented in the next chapter.

modern age to justify their conception of progress, others used history "as a weapon *against* the modern age, either on account of a romantic idealisation of the past, or in the interests of religious or national propaganda." The danger of falsifying history in the interest of apologetics was particularly serious for the Catholic historian of the Middle Ages, Dawson wrote, particularly since the romantic revival first brought in the conception of the Middle Ages as the social expression of Catholic ideals in the nineteenth century. "In the past this was not so, and Catholic historians, like Fleury, often tended to err in the opposite direction by adopting the current prejudices of the post-Renaissance period against the 'Gothic' barbarism and ignorance of the Dark Ages." He continued: "But for the last century and more there has certainly been a tendency among Catholic writers to make history a department of apologetics and to idealise medieaval culture in order to exalt their religious ideals. Actually this way of writing history defeats its own ends, since as soon as the reader becomes suspicious of the impartiality of the historian he discounts the truth of everything that he reads."[72] The idealization of medieval history for religious or social purposes could undermine itself and work against the very causes it served. Indeed, the Dominican priest Paul Foster, who met Dawson while studying at the Dominican House of Studies in Oxford during the 1940s, once asked Dawson if he planned a medieval sequel to *The Making of Europe*. "He replied," Foster remembered, "decisively, No. Catholics were too obsessed with the Middle Ages and should devote their attention to modern influences—the French Revolution, for instance—which had contributed so much to the problems of the day."[73] Christian sociology and medievalism were out.

Idealist Sociology

The second option for relating ideas and values to sociological analysis presented itself in the work of London sociologist L. T. Hobhouse. Described starkly as a man who, outside his tight circle of friends,

72. Dawson, *The Making of Europe*, 4, 5.
73. Paul Foster, "The Making of Europe," *The Chesterton Review* IX (May 1983): 141.

"showed limited interest in people, while remaining passionate about humanity,"[74] Hobhouse devoted his life to the relationship between social evolution and progress and believed in both firmly. One of his last students remembered: "I always had the idea that he concealed a wholly irrational (i.e., non-amenable to rational analysis) 'Belief' behind his brilliancy of analysis and interpretation. Otherwise, it is hard to explain his dynamic. But what that 'Belief' was is difficult to say. It was wholly in the efficacy and ultimate rule of harmony, achieved through sympathetic reason; and to that extent it was a belief in man's salvation in Man"[75]—his secular faith.

Hobhouse believed that sociology suffered from too close a relationship with biology. Unlike Geddes, he thought any social science that tried to explain human institutions solely in terms of physical environment misunderstood the nature of social development, which is best understood in terms of human rationality. Sociology should focus on the interaction of human minds, he wrote in 1924.[76] For him, the environment did not determine social structure as though humanity was merely "wax to its seal." The environment did not make the art and institutions of men; such phenomena proceeded from their energy and will. Rather, the environment determines "the lines on which human energy can succeed" and decides "what experiments and tentative beginnings will ripen into institutions."[77] For Hobhouse and his colleagues, any social science that tried to explain human beings and their institutions solely in terms of family type, occupation, and natural environment (FWP) "had mistaken the nature of man's evolution and misunderstood social development. Human institutions were best

74. "Hobhouse, Leonard Trelawny (1864–1929)," entry by Michael Freeden, ODNB.

75. J. A. Hobson and Morris Ginsberg, *L. T. Hobhouse: His Life and Work* (1924; London: Routledge/Thoemmes, 1996), quoted on 84 (the student is not named). Hobhouse was heavily influenced by Comte and positivism and had almost a religious humanitarianism (100–101). Hobhouse believed that people could create their own religion, and that his (Hobhouse's) understanding of development and purpose, if sound, provided the answers to the meaning of life; see L. T. Hobhouse, *Development and Purpose: An Essay towards a Philosophy of Evolution*, revised ed. (1913; London: Macmillan, 1927), 485–86.

76. L. T. Hobhouse, *Social Development: Its Nature and Conditions* (London: George Allen & Unwin, 1924), 7, 11; Halliday, "The Sociological Movement, the Sociological Society and the Genesis of Academic Sociology in Britain," 386–87.

77. Hobhouse, *Social Development: Its Nature and Conditions*, 7.

viewed as the products of rational thought and common purposes."[78] Geddes and his friends denied the uniqueness of human beings by linking them too closely to the rest of nature, Hobhouse believed.

For Hobhouse, "Mind" was the moving force of all development. It was not simply a part of nature, but capable of actually directing evolution as a self-conscious force, regulating its own life and controlling its own development toward social cooperation through mastery of the physical and psychological conditions of existence. He believed that the self-conscious Mind was like a god, finite and emergent, the culmination of evolution, at which point, evolution could itself be directed. Ruling over the chaos of biological struggle for existence, it was the organizing principle of evolution. This meant that, "Human evolution . . . is the work of man—the product of the being who evolves. Man does not stand outside his own growth and plan it. He becomes aware of its possibilities as he grows, and, if we are right, there comes a stage when conception of the perfected growth seizes upon him, and makes him intelligently work towards it."[79]

For Dawson, Hobhouse's sociology was too speculative. His ideas lacked the empirical grounding of Geddesian sociology, and Dawson rejected them on that basis. However, Dawson did share Hobhouse's concern for human reason and not subsuming the human person into the material world.

Subjective Sociology

The third analytical model, found in Geddes's own work, tried to coordinate "objective sociology" (FWP) with "subjective sociology" (psychology "Ps"). In effect, his FWP formula became PsFWP. With this, Geddes believed, he could more fully account for the mental and spir-

78. Halliday, "The Sociological Movement, the Sociological Society and the Genesis of Academic Sociology in Britain," 386, 387.

79. Randall C. Morris, "Whitehead and the New Liberals on Social Progress," *Journal of the History of Ideas* LI (1990): 86–87; Stefan Collini, *Liberalism and Sociology: L. T. Hobhouse and Political Argument in England, 1880–1914* (Cambridge: Cambridge University Press, 1979), chap. 5; W. Warren Wagar, *Good Tidings: The Belief in Progress from Darwin to Marcuse* (Bloomington: Indiana University Press, 1972), 53; Hobhouse, *Development and Purpose*, xviii, xxii, xxv, xxix, xxxiv; Hobhouse, *Social Development*, 335, 339–40, 343; and L. T. Hobhouse, *Mind in Evolution*, 3rd ed. (1901; London: Macmillan, 1926), 436. The quotation comes from *Mind in Evolution*, 439.

itual side of human life through theology, ethics, and art (see appendix B). Geddes recognized the same problem Dawson did: one must combine descriptive socio-historical with normative humanistic perspectives to fully account for human communities. Values give direction to life and must find a place in sociology, and some sociologists still share this concern in the twenty-first century.[80]

Geddes did not, however, conceive of spiritual reality as its own, independent principle, metaphysically distinct from physical reality. Hence, it lacked causal force. Perhaps that was why, to those associated with the *Sociological Review* who readily accepted the coordination of material life by Le Play's formula FWP, Geddes's account of the psychological and spiritual side of life (as emergent out of biology) remained unconvincing.[81]

The problem was that within the Sociological Society, religion held an ambiguous place. Geddes and Branford were not religious in any conventional sense, but since they were rationalists of a Comtean[82] strain, they maintained the importance of religious values for social

80. Christian Smith wrote in 2007: "In what follows I argue that the most adequate approach to theorizing human culture must be a normative one that conceives of humans as moral, believing animals and human social life as consisting of moral orders that constitute and direct social action." See Smith, *Moral, Believing Animals: Human Personhood and Culture*, 7.

81. Patrick Geddes and J. Arthur Thomson, *Biology* (London: Williams & Northgate, 1925), 223, 229, 231–32; Scott and Bromley, *Envisioning Sociology*, 81, 100–101. Geddes's attempt to relate biology and psychology was not utilized by other writers in the *Review*. In 1924, Mumford wrote to Dawson: "I myself have never made any intelligible advance with the squares [of Geddes's graphical formula of the psychological side of life] devoted to sense-experience-feeling in their inter-relations" (May 8, 1924, STA, box 15, folder 58, "Mumford, Lewis").

82. Auguste Comte founded the modern discipline of sociology in France. He recognized a need for social reconstruction based on scientific principles after the French Revolution. He saw sociology as the master science that would integrate all the other sciences and relate their findings in a comprehensive whole. He formulated the modern approach of *positivism*, the philosophical theory that certain ("positive") knowledge only comes through sense knowledge as interpreted by reason and logic. Metaphysics and theology are rejected because their claims cannot be verified through sense knowledge. Without them, Comte sought to fill the spiritual void of society with his Religion of Humanity, a secular religion complete with beliefs and rituals. This system deeply influenced secular humanists later, including members of the British Sociological Society around Dawson. Comte recognized that social progress depended on spiritual unity in society, and Dawson respected him for this, despite his disagreement with Comte's move to replace theology with sociology. In "order to construct a genuine sociology," Dawson wrote, summarizing Comte's views, "the study of social institutions must go hand in hand with the study of the intellectual and spiritual forces which give unity to the particular age and society in question." Dawson's entire lifework, and his later educational proposals for the study of Christian culture, would build on that insight of Comte's. See Dawson, "Sociology and the Theory of Progress," 39.

unity. They interacted with evangelicals, Christian socialists, Eastern religious ideas, Theosophy, and spiritualism.[83] Desire for unity over dualism, however, led to a certain natural monism closed in on itself, even though they and other writers for the *Sociological Review* used the language of religion and spirituality.

In 1920, for example, a certain George Sandeman reviewed a book by Geddes and speculated that if formal religion died in the modern world, sociology might replace it. Perhaps the notion of the Ideal City could function as a viable modern religion, containing enough potency in it to coordinate all the fragments of modern life into a higher unity. Sociology could play a pseudo-religious role in teaching people about an Ideal City in *this* world.[84] Some of the members of the Sociological Society saw themselves as medieval friars on a modern (secular) mission.[85] Alexander Farquharson wondered: if we see in human life the same vital, biological functions of other living organisms, "how are we to account for the whole of civilization and culture—politics, religion, and art?"[86] That was *the* question, indeed, and no one in the Sociological Society knew quite how to answer it.

In a letter to Dawson toward the end of his life, Geddes wrote: "I've long had contacts with highly religious people . . . enough to feel something at least of religious values, & this need of them; but have written little—not ready to!"[87] Sadly, after the death of his son on the Western Front and his wife in 1917, Geddes's formula FWP became a kind of obsession for him (an "agnostic substitute for prayer," according to Lewis Mumford), especially as he constantly tried to rework it and extend it in new directions.[88] The difference between Dawson and Geddes worked itself out in their conceptions of the relationship between so-

83. Scott and Bromley, *Envisioning Sociology*, 49–51.

84. George Sandeman, "A Gardener of Paradise," review of *Town Planning Towards City Development, Sociological Review* XII (1920): 58–63. On p. 58, the editor noted that for George Sandeman, religion, life, and thought should not be separated.

85. S. K. Ratcliffe, "S. H. Swinny," *Sociological Review* XV (1923): 274–77.

86. Alexander Farquharson, "The Oxford Conference on the Correlation of the Social Sciences: An Appreciation of the Discussions, with abstracts of the papers read," *Sociological Review* XV (1923): 49.

87. Geddes to Dawson, August 4, 1930, STA, box 15, folder 135, p. 3.

88. This was Lewis Mumford's critique; see "The Geddesian Gambit" (appendix 3) in Novak, *Lewis Mumford and Patrick Geddes: The Correspondence*, 363, 365–66.

ciology and religion: Dawson saw them as two metaphysically distinct, interrelated spheres, whereas Geddes collapsed religion into sociology. Hobhouse put mind over matter in his vision of social reconstruction; Geddes put matter over mind. They failed to offer a complete palette of categories needed to analyze culture.

Dawson's Fourth Category of Cultural Analysis: Ideas

Dawson proposed connecting the biological categories FWP not to Christian sociology, idealist sociology, or subjective sociology but to a conception of mind and soul expansive enough to make vital contact with realities both above mind (transcendent) and below mind (physical). Dawson effectively modified the Geddes formula to I/FWP—with "I" (Ideas) serving as a broader category than Geddes's "Ps" (psychology)(see appendix C). The slash mark in this formula I/FWP is my representation of Dawson's moderate dualism in distinguishing between spirit and matter as metaphysically different but interrelated orders of being. Dawson integrated FWP and I in a kind vital union "like that of the human organism."[89] He explained: "the intellectual element in culture is consubstantial with its material substratum, in the same way that the mind of the individual is consubstantial with his body. But just as the individual mind infuses the body, so too is the intellectual element the soul and the formative principle of a culture," Dawson wrote, utilizing Aristotelian terms.[90]

The ways these factors all influence each other at any given time is the "culture-process," an important concept to Dawson that generalized the rustic and civic processes of Geddes and Branford described earlier. The cultural-process describes how when one element of culture changes, the other elements change, too. For example, if a people change environments by moving to a new place (e.g., British people migrating to Australia, $P_1 \rightarrow P_2$) or change religions (e.g., Arabic tribes converting to Islam, $I_1 \rightarrow I_2$), then the rest of the culture will feel the effects of the change; that is, $P_1 \rightarrow P_2 = I_2/F_2W_2P_2$ and $I_1 \rightarrow I_2 = I_2/F_2W_2$

89. Dawson, "Sociology as a Science," 33.
90. Dawson, *Progress and Religion*, 67.

P_2, the subscripts referring to the modified culture in the new place (P_2) or according to the new ideas (I_2) and the arrow signifying change. Changes in F and W may result in similar kinds of cultural effects, as in the adoption of new social customs (e.g., late-nineteenth-century Japanese elites dressing in Western clothing, $F_1 \rightarrow F_2$) or technology (e.g., Native American tribes adopting firearms, $W_1 \rightarrow W_2$) changing cultures. These are all examples of the culture-process at work in history.

For Dawson, the intellect "is the active and creative element in culture, since it emancipates man from the purely biological laws which govern the development of animal species, and enables him to accumulate a growing capital of knowledge and social experience, which gives him a progressive control over his material environment."[91] It is not simply emergent out of biology, as Geddes held, but includes its own principles of "rational technique" in analyzing the world and openness to the sources of inspiration above itself. The most vital changes in human life come from within as the profoundest example of cultural process, often through the action of the exceptional person, the seer, the teacher, the creative mind.[92] There is a great religion behind every great civilization. "The spiritual faith and ideals of a man or a society—their ultimate attitude toward life—colour all their thought and action and make them what they are," Dawson wrote in his first article for *Sociological Review*.[93] Thus, like Hobhouse, he thought the greatest agent of progress is the human mind. Unlike the idealist Englishman, however, Dawson showed how progress of the mind must be in harmony with natural regions and social vitality—the FWP of the biologically oriented Scotsman Geddes. Figuratively speaking, Dawson's cultural mind built a bridge from Edinburgh to London.

Sociology in Dawson's Cultural Mind

C. Wright Mills described a certain "sociological imagination" commonly belonging to serious novelists, journalists, and social critics. It joins hitherto isolated facts, especially by connecting the personal to

91. Dawson, *Progress and Religion*, 67.
92. Dawson, *Progress and Religion*, 66, 176.
93. Dawson, "The Passing of Industrialism," 16.

the social. It aids reflective people in accessing an ocean of information and forming useful summaries and syntheses that can make sense of the world inside and outside of them. The sociological imagination is the "capacity to shift from one perspective to another—from the political to the psychological; from examination of a single family to comparative assessment of the national budgets of the world; from the theological school to the military establishment; from considerations of an oil industry to studies of contemporary poetry." To be aware of the idea of social structure and to use it to understand linkages between personal milieu and those structures—that is to possess the sociological imagination.[94]

Dawson cultivated such an imagination with the help of his analytical categories I/FWP, and this formula was the basis of his intellectual architecture. As such, it was an important component of the science of culture defining the parameters of his cultural mind. His mind shifted from one viewpoint to another—from theology (I) to economics (W), from sociology (F) to geography (P), in studying culture. He was sensitive to how different elements of human life affect each other and how that culture-process powers history and forms the human person.

In shifting perspectives, he applied boundary thinking to the relationship between theology and sociology. In 1933, Dawson asked Farquharson: "I wonder if my paper for the soc. congress [International Congress of Sociology in Geneva] seemed to you to help to establish the limits of the soc. [sociological] and theological provinces?"[95] Dawson argued that Catholics needed to carefully work out the relation between theology and sociology. In notes for a 1934 lecture, he typed: "Need for Catholic study of sociology, since the main assault on Christianity has based itself on sociological theories (Rousseau, Comte, Marx and others)."[96] In that same year, Dawson also wrote "Sociology as a Science" as a chapter for a book entitled *Science Today: The Scientific Outlook on World Problems Explained by Leading Exponents of Modern*

94. Mills, *The Sociological Imagination*, 5, 7, 8, 10–11, 14. The extended quotation is on p. 7.
95. Dawson to Farquharson, October 28, 1933, KA-AF, folder "Christopher Dawson Letters."
96. Synopsis of Paper to be read by Mr. Christopher Dawson at the Linnean Society's Hall on June 19th at 8 p.m. on "The Place of Sociology in Catholic Thought," KA-AF, folder "Dawson, C. Lectures and Letters."

Scientific Thought.[97] Dawson argued that if a culture is not merely a community of people, work, and place but above all a community of thought, then—building on the work of Patrick Geddes and Victor Branford—the "problem of sociology" was fundamentally one of "intellectual jurisdiction," of coordinating the study of both material factors *and* spiritual factors (see appendix C).

The great temptation for the sociologist was simplification, confusing sociology with other disciplines and wading blindly into the deep waters of ethics and metaphysics, Dawson also noted in that chapter: "Thus the efforts of the Encyclopaedists, the St. Simonians and the Positivists result in the creation of a theory of society which was at the same time a philosophy of history, a system of moral philosophy and a non-theological substitute for religion." Some sociologists, such as Hobhouse, had confused their discipline with ethical idealism, on the one hand, or with the hard sciences, on the other. While it was true that a certain "biological" method was central to sociology, as Le Play, Geddes, and Branford had shown, it was impossible to explain society by reference to material factors alone.

Spiritual and intellectual realities, Dawson continued, had to be interpreted *from their own viewpoint* through their own disciplines of theology and philosophy, not simply as derivatives of something else— while also keeping in mind the influence of social context on them.

The intrusion of these qualitatively distinct categories or orders of being [material and spiritual] into the sociological field is a great stumbling-block in the social sciences. The natural scientist has a completely homogeneous material in the material phenomena that he investigates; so also has the philosopher in the region of ideas; but the sociologist has to deal impartially with material and spiritual factors, with things and ideas, with moral and economic values, with all the multifarious experience of the two-sided nature of man.

---

97. Christopher Dawson, "Sociology as a Science," in *Science Today: The Scientific Outlook on World Problems Explained by Leading Exponents of Modern Scientific Thought*, ed. J. G. Crowther and Sir J. Arthur Thomson (London: Eyre & Spottiswoode, 1934). This essay later appeared in *The Dynamics of World History*, 13–33—the version cited here.

This meant one could not usurp the functions of theology or philosophy as a sociologist, but that sociology had to recognize at once "the determination of natural conditions and the freedom of spiritual forces" in the culture-process—a principle that Geddes and Branford also already acknowledged in their own way, though with an inadequate conception of the spiritual, from Dawson's point of view.[98]

If sociologists needed an intellectual architecture respecting theology, philosophy, and science as possessing their own ends, and not as mere functions of society, so, too, philosophers and theologians needed an intellectual architecture capable of incorporating the contributions of sociologists. "We cannot understand an idea unless we understand its historical and social foundations," Dawson wrote. Theologians had consistently failed to recognize the social and economic elements in religious phenomena. "Most of the great schisms and heresies in the history of the Christian church," Dawson penned insightfully, "have their roots in social or national antipathies, and if this had been clearly recognized by the theologians the history of Christianity would have been a very different one."[99] In order to see the world aright, theologians and other Christian thinkers need the social sciences.

The primary task of sociology, Dawson wrote, is to study the social structure of a people, but this structure rests on the foundation of geographical environment and economic function, on the one hand, and is "the foundation of a spiritual superstructure which embodies the higher cultural values,"[100] on the other. Hence, I/FWP, with "F" serving as the middle ground between higher and lower realities from nonsentient to supernatural being.

As sociologists, Dawson wrote, "we have to accept the existence of this independent order of spiritual truths and values and to study their influence on social action." Does society require a religious foundation? What is the actual working religion of a particular society? How does religion affect the social process? How far do material and social factors affect religious beliefs, values, and philosophy? These are all valid sociological questions, "but the objective intellectual validity or spiri-

98. Dawson, "Sociology as a Science," 16, 24, 25, 33.
99. Dawson, "Sociology as a Science," 28, 31, 32.
100. Dawson, "Sociology as a Science," 25.

tual value of religious doctrines and philosophical theories lies entirely outside our province," he noted.[101]

In all of this, Dawson's humanistic concerns ultimately oriented his sociological interests toward cultural understanding and renewal rather than scientific generalizations for their own sake. For example, on the question of educational reform in Christian colleges and universities, he wrote in 1955:

The central problem of the Catholic educationalist is a sociological one: how to make students culturally conscious of their religion; otherwise they will be divided personalities—with a Christian faith and a pagan culture which contradict one another. . . . Thus the sociological problem of Christian culture is also the psychological problem of integration and spiritual health. I am convinced that this is the key issue."[102]

The sociological roots of Dawson's educational ideals will be explored further in chapter 8.

Ultimately, the limitation of I/FWP was that it failed to account for the *time* factor of development and change affecting cultures. As an evolutionary biologist, Geddes was fully aware of the importance of time in any theory of living organisms, but he could not capture it graphically in the FWP formula. He tried to locate the principle of historical development in a mystical life-force,[103] but that was too unscientific for Dawson. Sociology had to ally forces with history for a more complete (synchronic *and* diachronic) science of culture. The danger was that false theories of history could easily obscure the true conditions of cultural development.

101. Dawson, "Sociology as a Science," 30.
102. Christopher Dawson, "Problems of Christian Culture," *Commonweal*, April 15, 1955, 36.
103. Geddes and Thomson, *Biology*, 236; Helen Meller, *Patrick Geddes: Social Evolutionist and City Planner* (London and New York: Routledge, 1990), 314. Geddes corresponded with the French philosopher Henri Bergson (1859–1941), famous for his theories of "emergent evolution."

Chapter 3

History (I)

*There are, in fact, two movements in history; one of which is due . . . to
the life process of an individual people in contact with a definite geographical environment, while the other is common to a number of different peoples and results from intellectual and religious interaction
and synthesis. . . . Only by taking account of both these movements
is it possible to understand the history of human development, and
to explain the existence of that real element of continuity and integration in history which alone can justify a belief in human progress.*
—Christopher Dawson (1929)

Before Dawson, British sociology did not account in a satisfactory way for the problem of change and progress of cultures in history.
We started to see a solution to this problem in Dawson's idea of the
"culture-process" in the last chapter. As described, this referred to the
observation that when one element of culture changed, then the other elements changed as well. But how does this process actually work
in history? What are the true conditions of cultural development, and
what is the meaning of such changes? Are they blind cycles of evolution, or steps in the upward progress of humankind? Wrestling with
such questions was important for Dawson, because only in that way
could he correctly judge lines of causality in the past, weighing and lo-
cating facts according to an overall metanarrative of time.

In the brilliant introduction to his first book, *Age of the Gods* (1928),
Dawson took up the problem of change and progress of cultures in history. Despite the tendency toward fixation of cultures in unchanging

Dawson, *Progress and Religion*, 46.

forms in world history, he wrote, it is "impossible to deny the reality and importance of cultural progress." He continued:

This progress is not, however, as the philosophers of the eighteenth century believed, a continuous and uniform movement, common to the whole human race, and as universal and necessary as a law of nature. It is rather an exceptional condition, due to a number of distinct causes, which often operate irregularly and spasmodically. Just as civilisation itself is not a single whole, but a generalization from a number of historic cultures each with its own limited life, so Progress is an abstract idea derived from a simplification of the multiple and heterogeneous changes through which the historic societies have passed.

Dawson set aside the idea of a single, uniform law of progress because he thought it necessary to distinguish between five main types of social change in which the culture-process fully manifested its diachronic dimension. Cultures change through (1) adaptation to an environment (as in the case of native adaptation to environments in Australia thousands of years ago); (2) a people moving into a new environment (as in the case of the British colonizers of Australia in the nineteenth century) or the old environment changes; (3) two different cultures coming into contact, often through war (as in the case of cultural symbiosis between Akkadian and Sumerian culture in ancient Mesopotamia); (4) one culture adopting an element of material culture from another (as in the case of firearms among Native Americans); and (5) a culture modifying its way of life due to the acquisition of new knowledge or a new vision of reality (as in the transformation of ancient civilization by Christianity or of Arabian tribes by Islam).

Notice that type number 3 also includes type number 2 for at least one of the two different peoples coming into contact. Two different cultures coming into contact "is the most typical and important of all the causes of culture change, since it sets up an organic process of fusion and change, which transforms both the people and the culture, and produces a new cultural entity in a comparatively short space of time."

Number 4 is a comparatively superficial kind of change compared to number 3, "but it is of great importance as showing the close interdependence of cultures." Metal, weapons, irrigation, animals, germs—

all have passed in history from one people to the next. "But it is re-markable how often such external change leads not to social progress," Dawson noted, "but to social decay. As a rule, to be progressive change must come from within."

Herein lies the importance of the fifth type of cultural change. The first four types could give an impression of determinism without space for spiritual and intellectual freedom, because, Dawson said, "it might be thought that if the highest products of a culture are the flowers of a social organism that has had its roots in particular geographical and ethnological circumstances, no permanent and objective progress will be achieved and the greatest works of art and thought will simply re-produce in a more sophisticated form the results of the past experi-ence of the organism." But thanks to the existence of "Reason," which Dawson capitalized in this context, there is the possibility of acquiring new powers and a new conception of reality. There is a "continual en-largement of the field of experience, and, thanks to Reason, the new does not simply replace the old, but is compared and combined with it." Reason is a creative power that organizes the "raw material of life" into the "ordered cosmos of an intelligible world."

The influence of the psychological factor extends beyond reason to religious vision: "Every religion embodies an attitude to life and a con-ception of reality, and any change in these brings with it a change in the whole character of the culture." Thus, he concluded, "the prophet and the religious reformer, in whom a new view of life—a new *revelation*—becomes explicit, is perhaps the greatest of all agents of social change, even though he is himself the product of social causes and the vehicle of an ancient cultural tradition."[1]

In this chapter, I argue that Dawson's simple and ingenious outline of cultural morphology integrated cyclical views of cultural change patterned on the cycles of nature with intellectualist views of develop-ment, both making possibile authentic human progress. In this way, he addressed a problem felt acutely during the 1920s. The Great War had killed and maimed millions of soldiers and civilians, fragmenting lives and cultures. In notes handwritten sometime during the conflict, Daw-

1. Dawson, *The Age of the Gods*, xxvi–xxx.

son mused on the "radical change brought about by the war." Even an inconclusive peace, he thought, "could not bring back the old state of things. We are irrevocably committed to a new age and new systems." "It is impossible," he continued, "to foresee what the future may bring, it may be disaster, it may be renewed life. What is possible and necessary is to take stock of the factors of the new situation and see as far as possible what alternatives are before this new age."[2] One of these new factors was that the Great War helped make human progress itself into a philosophical and historical problem.

Two views about progress dominated the 1920s, that of the "rationalists" and that of the "declinists." False theories of history embedded in both these views obscured the conditions of true human development. The rationalists believed in the idea of progress as the "continuous and uniform movement" upward that Dawson critiqued earlier. As I argue elsewhere, the war did not make a significant difference to their views.[3] Leading British rationalists such as historian J. B. Bury (1861–1927), author of *The Idea of Progress* (1920), were members of the older generation of thinkers born in the 1860s. They held tightly to their fundamental idealist assumptions about historical change conceived in terms of secular human progress. Traditional religions, they thought or implied, impeded human progress, which is secured by the spread of reason and science alone. The idea of progress itself functioned something like a religion for some rationalists. The then-agnostic classical scholar Gilbert Murray (1866–1957) wrote in 1922: "And as to Progress, it is no doubt a real fact. To many of us it is a truth that lies somewhere near the roots of our religion."[4]

The declinist view, on the other hand, held that progress was an illusion, and this would play an important role in the cultural pessimism of later twentieth-century phenomena such as the Frankfurt School,

2. Christopher Dawson's reflections on "Social Reconstruction & the War," STA, box 4, folder 111.

3. Joseph T. Stuart, "The Question of Human Progress in Britain after the Great War," *Britain and the World* I (2008): 53–78. Here I examine the work of celebrity rationalist Joseph McCabe (1867–1955), the sociologist L. T. Hobhouse (discussed in chapter 2), the historical thinkers F. S. Marvin (1863–1943) and H. G. Wells (1866-1946), and the academic historian J. B. Bury. See also Joseph Stuart, "Christopher Dawson and the Idea of Progress," *Logos* 14, no. 4 (2011): 74–91.

4. Gilbert Murray, "Religio Grammatici: The Religion of a 'Man of Letters,'" in *Essays and Addresses* (London: George Allen & Unwin, 1922), 19.

the philosophy of Michel Foucault (1926–1984), multiculturalism, and radical environmentalism.[5] The Great War did much to create fertile ground for the idea of decline. Even in Britain, which had "won" the war, criticism of the idea of progress increased after 1918 because the war and its aftermath raised some difficult questions about social and historical development. In his 1920 Romanes Lecture, W. R. Inge (1860–1954), dean of St. Paul's Cathedral, condemned the idea of progress as a "superstition." The idea of progress "has begun to lose its hold on the mind of society," Dawson wrote, "because the phase of civilization of which it was characteristic is already beginning to pass away." Disillusion flourished among some British intellectuals, arising out of the collision between the events of the war and the public language and ideas used for over a century to celebrate the idea of progress.[6] On the continent, this movement flourished more broadly. *The Decline of the West* by Oswald Spengler (discussed later in this chapter) created an entire historical philosophy based on the rise and fall of natural cycles, thus negating the idea of progress and promoting radical relativism of all values.

For Dawson, the rationalists rightly pointed to human reason as an indispensable factor in human progress, but they tended to narrow their conception of reason by their exclusion of religion—warping their view of history and neglecting the foundation of natural environment in human life. They overemphasized the role of ideas and adopted a too-universal conception of culture. By contrast, the declinists such as Spengler rightly emphasized the place of natural cycles in human existence and the plurality of cultures, but they neglected the role of reason, falling into an irrational cultural relativism that failed to account for the reality of permanent things discovered through cultural interaction and continuity in history that alone provide the groundwork for believing in human progress. Dawson brought these two views into conversation in his account of cultural change and development.

---

5. Arthur Herman, *The Idea of Decline in Western History* (New York: Free Press, 1997).

6. Dawson, *Progress and Religion*, 16, 71; W. R. Inge, "The Idea of Progress," in *Outspoken Essays* (London: Longmans, Green, 1922), 163; Fussell, *The Great War and Modern Memory*, 169.

The Idea of Progress: Dawson and the Rationalist J. B. Bury

Despite the pessimism present in Europe after the Great War, the idea of progress continued to hold a powerful sway over many minds, not without good reason. Dawson wrote in 1929 that, "Today, to the average European, and still more to the average American, Progress consists in the spread of the new urban-mechanical civilization: it means more cinemas, motor-cars for all, wireless installations, more elaborate methods of killing people, purchase on the hire system, preserved foods and picture papers." Derivative senses of the word "progress" proliferated in British business and manufacturing language for years during and after the war: examples include "progress committee" (from 1914), "progress clerk" (1921—a person who pushed forward work through various stages until it was ready for delivery), "progress department" (1925), "progress manager" (1925), and "progress report" (1929).[7]

As a philosophy of history, the idea of progress also survived beyond the Great War in various rationalists such as Irishman J. B. Bury, the eminent classicist and historian of the late Roman and Byzantine empires. Bury's 1920 book *The Idea of Progress* argued that "civilization has moved, is moving, and will move in a desirable direction."[8] It appeared in the bibliography of Dawson's own *Progress and Religion*.

Another of Bury's books, *History of Freedom of Thought* for the Home University Library in 1914, was intended for a popular audience, and its table of contents is indicative of the rationalist interpretation of history: after the introductory chapter, chapter 2 is called "Reason Free (Greece and Rome)," chapter 3 "Reason in Prison (the Middle Ages)," chapter 4 "Prospect of Deliverance (the Renaissance and the Reformation)," and chapter 7 "The Progress of Rationalism (Nineteenth Century)." Though Bury produced the excellent 1905 work *Life of Saint Patrick*, the chapter titles of this 1914 book clearly show Bury's assumptions about reason, progress, the "dark" Middle Ages, and the obscurantism of religion.

Denigration of the Middle Ages first began in the Renaissance, when humanist scholars championed classical learning against that of

---

7. Dawson, *Progress and Religion*, 17; OED, "progress," sb., sense 7.

8. J. B. Bury, *The Idea of Progress: An Inquiry into its Origin and Growth* (London: Macmillan, 1920), 2.

the intervening centuries. Then, during the eighteenth century, French Enlightenment thinkers such as Voltaire (1694–1778) and Jean le Rond d'Alembert (1717–1783) helped create a progressive narrative of the rise of science that had been held back by the Catholic Church. John William Draper (1811–1882), Thomas Huxley (1825–1895), and Andrew Dickson White (1832–1918) brought this theme to English-speakers during the nineteenth century, as in White's *History of the Warfare of Science with Theology in Christendom* (1896), giving it intellectual respectability and linking it to the kind of rationalism still prevalent in Dawson's day.

Dawson noted that in the *History of the Freedom of Thought*, even "so distinguished an historian as the late J. B. Bury could still describe medieval thought under the rubric *Reason in Prison.*" This was because "the book in question was written with a pronounced rationalistic bias, and as a rule even those who regard medieval metaphysics as of purely historical interest, nevertheless recognize, like Prof. Whitehead, that the European mind received from medieval scholasticism that fundamental training in rational thought on which all its later achievements are dependent." In *Progress and Religion* and his later work, Dawson refuted the rationalist narrative of the history of science and drew from an alternative view that emerged in the early twentieth century in the work of Pierre Duhem (1861–1916), George Sarton (1884–1956), and Alfred North Whitehead (1861–1947). Duhem had stumbled across largely unread medieval manuscripts that suggested medieval science had been "sophisticated, highly regarded, and essential to later developments," Dawson noted, a view supported by leading scholars today. Modern science rests on the foundations built by Christian thinkers and institutions in the medieval and early modern periods, and thus Dawson used the history of medieval science to subtly undermine rationalist history and its secularist conception of progress.[9]

9. The quotations in this paragraph come from Christopher Dawson, *Medieval Essays* (1954; Washington, D.C.: The Catholic University of America Press, 2002), 119. For an account of this subject that substantiates Dawson's views of the significance of medieval thought for later European history, see James Hannam, *The Genesis of Science: How the Christian Middle Ages Launched the Scientific Revolution* (Washington, D.C.: Regnery, 2011). *Le système du monde de Platon à Copernie* (1913–1917) by French physicist and historian Pierre Duhem, and *Science and the Modern World* (1925) by English mathematician and philosopher Alfred North Whitehead appeared in the bibliography of *Progress and Religion*. The work of Belgian-American chemist and historian George Sarton appeared from 1927 to 1948 as his three-volume *Introduction to the History of*

Bury's conception of progress overlapped with the way he viewed his work as an historian. He was regarded by the British historical profession as the "prototype of an objective and impartial scholar"[10] and viewed history as a science. This supported his idea that progress meant the increase of knowledge through research. Human life would become more logical and less subject to contingencies as command over nature grew, he argued. The "march of science is continuous, systematic, and imperturbable."[11] Bury stated that since accurate knowledge of the past was crucial for making sound decisions in the present and future, a true understanding of history was needed—sounding like Hobhouse as discussed in chapter 2—for "moulding our evolution." Bury continued: "It is therefore of supreme moment that the history which is taught should be true; and that can be attained only through the discovery, collection, classification, and interpretation of facts—through scientific research." The purpose of historical research was the progressive accumulation of knowledge until, someday in the future, historical truth would emerge.[12] Progress would be assured by research and reason.

After the Second World War, a major international reevaluation of the Bury thesis commenced, stressing the importance of the Christian theological and historical background to the idea of progress.[13] These were points Dawson had already made in *Progress and Religion*. The main lines of attack proceeded against Bury's idealism and his antireligious bias.

The idealism of rationalist thinkers such as Bury overestimated

---

Science, which covered the ancient and medieval worlds. Dawson referred to Sarton in his essay on medieval science in his 1934 work *Medieval Religion*, republished in 1954 and 2002 as *Medieval Essays*, the version used here.

10. Doris S. Goldstein, "J. B. Bury's Philosophy of History: A Reappraisal," *American Historical Review* LXXXII (1977): 911.

11. J. B. Bury, "Cleopatra's Nose," in *Selected Essays of J. B. Bury*, ed. Harold Temperley (Cambridge: Cambridge University Press, 1930), 69. This essay was first published in the *R.P.A. Annual* (1916): 16–23.

12. J. B. Bury, *An Inaugural Lecture, Delivered in the Divinity School Cambridge on January 26, 1903* (Cambridge: Cambridge University Press, 1903), 23, 24, 31–32; Goldstein, "J. B. Bury's Philosophy of History: A Reappraisal," 906.

13. W. Warren Wagar, "Modern Views of the Origins of the Idea of Progress," *Journal of the History of Ideas* XXVIII (1967): 63–64. See Karl Löwith, *Meaning in History* (Chicago: University of Chicago Press, 1949); Reinhold Niebuhr, *Faith and History: A Comparison of Christian and Modern Views of History* (London: Nisbet, 1949); John Baillie, *The Belief in Progress* (London: Oxford University Press, 1950); and Emil Brunner, *Eternal Hope*, trans. Harold Knight (London: Lutterworth, 1954).

the place of ideas in history, treating them almost as gods. Historian H. G. Wells did this when he wrote, "Human history is in essence a history of ideas." For Bury, "Ideas rule the world."[14] If Marxists tended to reduce the historical process to material factors, Dawson wrote, then rationalist idealism tended to the opposite extreme, for it is

marked by a belief in an absolute Law of Progress and an unlimited faith in the power of reason to transform society. Concepts such as Liberty, Science, Reason and Justice are conceived, not as abstract ideas, but as real forces which determine the movement of culture, and social progress itself, instead of being regarded as a phenomenon that requires explanation, is treated as itself the efficient cause of social change.[15]

The idea of progress, a fortuitous discovery of the modern world, was the ultimate principle for Bury, on the basis of which he viewed the rest of history. Dawson commented on the eighteenth-century rationalist philosophers who "hypostatized human reason into a principle of world development."[16] This was precisely what the later believers in progress did—and with increased insistence after the Great War— because they desired so strongly to find an ultimate universal ideal to inspire action in the service of social renewal. Ideas, for them, were self-creative abstractions. The philosopher and classical scholar John Alexander Smith (1863–1939) published "Progress as an Ideal of Action" in 1916. He asserted several times as a self-sufficient axiom "that what is or can be an ideal of action for us must be wholly and solely of our own making, the very thought of it self-begotten in our mind, every step to its actual existence the self-created deed of our own will."[17] For Bury and other rationalists of the day, the intrinsic goodness of the self-created idea of progress seemed to guarantee a new and continually improving human community.

Bury warned against treating ideas in this way, writing that from

14. Bury, *The Idea of Progress*, 1; H. G. Wells, *The Outline of History: Being a Plain History of Life and Mankind* (London: George Newnes, 1920), 748.

15. Christopher Dawson, "Sociology as a Science," in *Science Today: The Scientific Outlook on World Problems Explained by Leading Exponents of Modern Scientific Thought*, ed. J. G. Crowther and Sir J. Arthur Thomson (London: Eyre & Spottiswoode, 1934), 165.

16. Dawson, *Progress and Religion*, 26, 31.

17. J. A. Smith, "Progress as an Ideal of Action," in *Progress and History*, ed. F. S. Marvin (London: Oxford University Press, 1916), 301.

the "scientific point of view," such ideas as progress or nationality had no existence outside the minds of individuals.[18] But in practice, he treated progress as a thing-in-itself, an "it" in his book; he wrote of those who "did not hit upon" it or of the "obstacles to its appearance" that did not fall away until the sixteenth century. British intellectual historian Quentin Skinner has recently warned of the dangers of the "histories of ideas" and their tendency to hypostasize an idea or doctrine into an entity. He specifically criticized Bury by pointing out that "ideas presuppose agents." How did people come to espouse the idea of progress in the first place? How did history *before* the eighteenth century relate to the idea of progress? Bury did not say. He left the impression that the idea of progress created itself when certain barriers, such as religion, fell away.[19]

Dawson approached ideas as inhabiting human beings living in socio-historical cultures. He attacked a history of ideas that left no room for the contribution of the biologist and the anthropologist. Indeed, every culture rests on a foundation of geographical environment and social inheritance, which conditions its highest activities, Dawson wrote: "The change of culture is not simply a change of thought, it is above all a change of life."[20] Dawson's attitude toward the nature of ideas was well-expressed by a phrase of the American sociologist Charles Ellwood: "our ideas, ideals, and values must be so expanded that they include, and give adequate recognition to, the material conditions of life."[21] For Dawson, abstract ideas and human reason were not world forces or ultimate determinants; *thought* always took place within a context, a common discourse of the times and a general belief about reality. Therefore, historical study should focus not so much on ideas but on culture, on ideas-in-context, on rational human beings existing in an environment and oriented toward the world and each other by way of their fundamental beliefs.

Dawson agreed with Bury on the importance of science for human

18. J. B. Bury, "Darwinism and History," in *Selected Essays of J. B. Bury*, 33–34.
19. Quentin Skinner, *Regarding Method*, vol. 1 (Cambridge: Cambridge University Press, 2002), 62; Bury, *The Idea of Progress*, 7.
20. Dawson, *Progress and Religion*, 45.
21. Charles A. Ellwood, "The Social Problem and the Present War," *Sociological Review* VIII (1915): 12.

development. However, "It is in vain that we look to science for a power which will unite and guide the divided forces of European society. Science provides, not a moral dynamic, but an intellectual technique," Dawson wrote.[22] Religion, on the other hand, could provide a moral dynamic. It had historically played an essential role in human progress—even in the formation of the idea of progress itself, something that Bury completely overlooked.

Anticipating arguments developed two years later by the American historian Carl Becker (1873–1945),[23] Dawson wrote that while:

the philosophers of the 18th century attempted to substitute their new rationalist doctrines for the ancient faith of Christendom, they were in reality simply abstracting from it those elements which had entered so deeply into their own thought that they no longer recognized their origin. . . . Above all this was the case with the idea of Progress, for while the new philosophy had no place for the supernaturalism of the Christian eschatology, it could not divest itself of the Christian teleological conception of life. Thus the belief in the moral perfectibility and the indefinite progress of the human race took the place of the Christian faith in the life of the world to come, as the final goal of human effort.[24]

The rise of the idea of progress was related to the secularization of positive Christian beliefs. The first man identified by both Bury and Dawson to have formulated the idea of progress—the Abbé de St. Pierre (1658–1743)—was a radical Catholic priest, Dawson pointed out.[25] The

22. Dawson, *Progress and Religion*, 176.

23. See his 1931 Storrs Lectures given at the School of Law, Yale University, and published as Carl L. Becker, *The Heavenly City of the Eighteenth-Century Philosophers* (New Haven, Conn.: Yale University Press, 1932). Becker's thesis was that "the *Philosophes* were nearer the Middle Ages, less emancipated from the preconceptions of medieval Christian thought, than they quite realized or we have commonly supposed" (29). I am not the first to link Becker and Dawson and the significance of their new perspective on the eighteenth century—see Wagar, "Modern Views of the Origins of the Idea of Progress," 62–63. Becker's thesis attracted much attention and debate; see Wagar's article, just mentioned, and, most famously, Peter Gay, "Carl Becker's Heavenly City," in *Carl Becker's Heavenly City Revisited*, ed. Raymond O. Rockwood (Ithaca, N.Y.: Cornell University Press, 1958): 27–51.

24. Dawson, *Progress and Religion*, 149. See also Christopher Dawson, "Christianity and the Idea of Progress," *Dublin Review* CLXXX (1927): 28. Dawson believed the "Religion of Progress" found its fulfilment in Christianity because the progressive spiritualization of human nature through Christianity is the necessary complement to the progressive intellectualization of nature that is the work of modern science. The future of human progress depends on the coordination of these two processes. See Dawson, *Progress and Religion*, 189–190.

25. Dawson, *Progress and Religion*, 150.

sources of the eighteenth-century idea of progress were not only reason and science but also the Christian teleological conception of reality.

Dawson's immersion in Christian teleology owed much to Augustine, a major source of personal and historical inspiration in his life and work. In one of the two essays he wrote for the 1930 *Monument to St. Augustine*, Dawson noted that the Greeks tended to value only the eternal, that which does not change, and those aspects of history independent of time, such as the ideal character of the hero or the polis. Augustine, by contrast, perceived the value of time and development. While Bury saw in Augustine a lack of interest in temporality, that was not the case, Dawson argued. Augustine, in fact, showed how to connect eternity and time, for while he looked beyond the "aimless and bloody chaos of history" to the unchanging reality of God, he believed at the same time that divine providence ordered the messy history of human beings toward his purposes. Rather than subscribe to the theory of eternal recurrence, the cycles of endless time characteristic of the ancient world, Augustine drew out the implication already present in Christianity, founded not on mythologies but on a sacred history, that time has an absolute beginning and travels toward an absolute end. Time is not a revolving image of the eternally moving heavenly bodies, as the Greeks thought. The measure of time cannot be in things, because things constantly change. One cannot measure change against change; one needs an absolute point of reference to measure change, to know if progress is happening. If not in things, the measure of time must be found in the soul, Augustine thought; therefore, time is *spiritual extension*. "Thus the past is the soul's remembrance, the future is its expectation, and the present is its attention." This new view of time was one of Augustine's greatest achievements and really made him the "first man in the world to discover the meaning of time," Dawson noted. This discovery implied a new view of history: it is a creative process; it does not repeat itself meaninglessly. The past does not die, for it can pass on as an inheritance. Thus, progress is possible, "since the life of society and of humanity itself possesses continuity and the capacity for spiritual growth no less than the life of the individual."[26]

26. Bury, *The Idea of Progress*, 21; Christopher Dawson, "St. Augustine and His Age," in *Enquiries*

Formation

In *Progress and Religion*, Dawson contrasted this Augustinian vision with the pessimistic and cyclical conceptions of reality in Greek philosophy and the Indian Upanishads. The Judeo-Christian tradition uniquely valued history over metaphysical speculation. Even the rationalist Bury recognized this distinction between Greek and Christian thought. While the philosophers of Greece and India meditated on the illusory cosmic process, the prophets of Israel affirmed purpose in history. Christianity grew out of this radically historical-centric view of reality and based itself not on a mythological figure or abstract cosmic principles but on a historic person, Jesus Christ. His incarnation was a unique event, not a recurrent one, and by it, "the Absolute and the Finite, the Eternal and the Temporal, God and the World were no longer conceived as two exclusive and opposed orders of being standing over against one another in mutual isolation. The two orders interpenetrated one another, and even the lower world of matter and sense was capable of becoming the vehicle of the divine life," Dawson wrote. Eternity entered into time. This transcendent valuation of the material order and the call for "progressive transformation of human nature" implanted a new conception of reality vis-à-vis that of the ancient world, one that revolutionized the whole development of the West after Christianity took root there from the East. This teleological, transformative view of the soul and of the world ultimately lay behind the very idea of progress claimed by Bury and the eighteenth-century rationalists as their own, *contra* religion. The loss of such theological optimism could have dire consequences, Dawson warned. "When once we abandon the theological doctrine of Creation, which is common both to orthodox Christianity and to the philosophic Deism which is derived from it, we are left with an eternal cosmic process, which does not admit of ultimate and absolute progress," he concluded.[27]

---

into Religion and Culture, 184, 186, 207–8. It appears Bury agreed with Dawson's interpretation of Greek views on time, at least in one essay: "The most eminent of the ancient historians were pragmatical; that is, they regarded history as an instructress in statesmanship, or in the art of war, or in morals. Their record reached back such a short way, their experience was so brief, that they never attained to the conception of continuous process, or realized the significance of time; and they never viewed the history of human societies as a phenomenon to be investigated for its own sake." See Bury, "Darwinism and History," 23–24.

27. Dawson, *Progress and Religion*, 124, 129, 172.

In addition to warping of the history of the Middle Ages and of science, overemphasizing the role of ideas in history, and denigrating the importance of "theological optimism" in the teleological conception of time, the rationalists suffered from fideism in their assertion of progress as the cause and purpose of cultural development. While Bury and others paid homage to empirical science, "they remained Cartesians in their hearts," Dawson wrote, for they retained their faith even after the Great War in "human reason as an infallible authority," neglecting other factors.[28] Their faith in the idea of progress obscured real analysis of historical cultures and their relationship to nature and each other as the basis for understanding the authentic conditions of cultural development in history.

The Idea of Decline: Dawson and the Relativist Oswald Spengler

The rationalists' intellectual shortcomings contributed to the appeal of Spengler's nature-based analogy for cultural development. His *Decline of the West* created an entire historical philosophy based on negating the idea of progress. The work was conceived before 1914 and worked out fully by 1917, but it was postwar conditions that impelled people to read it, leading to the printing of tens of thousands of copies. Spengler sought to create a true German philosophy of historical development in response to profound questions: What is deeper than politics and unifies our knowledge of history? What moves history forward? Does world history present to the seeing-eye certain large trends? Spengler concluded that all the cultures of the world are independent, natural growths. Their historical trajectories are determined by the patterns of growth and decay that affect all organic beings; thus, he said, progress is an illusion. While a civilization could progress for a while, inevitably, it would decline, just as all organisms grow and then eventually die. Everything changes, including the basic principles of reason and morality embedded in Western civilization. Cultural pessimism led to cultural relativism.

Dawson paid keen attention to Spengler, engaging his insights into

28. Dawson, *Progress and Religion*, 21.

the natural cycles affecting human culture without embracing his radical relativism. To understand Dawson's appreciation and criticism of Spengler, it is necessary to examine Spengler's intellectual context in German historicism, which held that a culture develops in an organic process without outside influence.

Among other meanings, historicism refers to the philosophy of history developed in nineteenth-century Germany. The new discipline of history strove to acquire knowledge of the "universal through immersion in the particular."[29] This view assumed a coherence behind the world one could discover through research. This exciting realization sent historians scurrying to newly opened archives to examine documents. They rediscovered their national pasts and the wonder of ages previously ignored due to a classical bias, such as the medieval age.

Early historicism, as interpreted by German historian Leopold von Ranke (1795–1886), for example, affirmed the ultimate unity of life in God, but at the same time—in the description of historian Ernst Breisach—stressed that one must understand the past in terms of "unique entities" (such as persons, cultures, or nations). One should look for the universal *in* the particular ("history recognizes something infinite in every existence," wrote Ranke). At the same time, because all values arise within an historical context, one should interpret cultures on their own terms and not judge them by other cultures or outside, abstract ideals—such as natural law, human rights, or the French ideal of progress that viewed history as the universal story of increasing scientific rationality.[30]

Dawson appreciated some of the insights of historicism, as seen in his criticism of the Enlightenment historian Edward Gibbon. He praised Gibbon's "architectonic power" of ordering a shapeless mass

29. Georg G. Iggers, "Historicism: The History and Meaning of the Term," *Journal of the History of Ideas* 56, no. 1 (1995): 131.

30. Breisach, *Historiography: Ancient, Medieval, and Modern*, 325; Leopold von Ranke, "On the Character of Historical Science," in *The Theory and Practice of History*, ed. Geog G. Iggers (1830s; New York: Routledge, 2011), 11; Georg C. Iggers, *The German Conception of History: The National Tradition of Historical Thought from Herder to the Present*, rev. ed. (1968; Middletown, Conn.: Wesleyan University Press, 1983), 5, 10. Ranke continued (on the same page): "It is not necessary for us to prove at length that the eternal dwells in the individual. This is the religious foundation on which our efforts rest. We believe that there is nothing without God, and nothing lives except through God."

of historical data, as well as his ability to identify himself so intimately with his subject of Rome. Gibbon's great weakness, however, was his lack of understanding of the religious forces that shaped Byzantine and Western culture, and his too-unitary conception of culture. He could not grasp the mechanisms of cultural change because he was so much influenced by the static rationalist idealism that judged the past by classical and Enlightenment standards of perfection. By contrast, Dawson wrote, "History deals with particular cultures rather than with world civilization;" thus the historian should—according to the tenets of historicism—"desire to appreciate every culture for its own sake" without attempting to judge, for example, the "civilization of the Yucatan by the standards of modern England."[31]

As fruitful as early historicism was, by the end of the nineteenth century, partly due to the secularization of the European mind and the loss of transcendent reference points, this movement led to a crisis in historicism. This involved the uncertain status of general statements about human beings and the moral neutrality resulting from the exclusive commitment to the contextual nature of all values, Breisach wrote. If everything has a history, and therefore history is the only guide to an understanding of things human (this was a kind of reductionism), radical relativism ensues. By 1914, commitment to the ethical autonomy of cultures and states tragically encouraged thinking about politics, international relations, and warfare outside the framework of natural law. Dawson did not embrace this historical reductionism because it not only made impossible comparative generalizations between cultures, it also denied other ways of knowing truth besides historical methods, violating the rules of intellectual architecture and boundary thinking.[32]

Dawson's personal contact with this immensely fruitful, but at the same time deeply problematic, line of thought began during a visit to Germany with his father as a young man in the summer of 1908. Exploring together the churches, monasteries, and art galleries of Bruges, Cologne, and Strasbourg, they ended up in Baden-Baden in the Black

31. Christopher Dawson, "Edward Gibbon and the Fall of Rome," in *Dynamics of World History*, 347–48, 362–64. Quotation on p. 362.

32. Breisach, *Historiography*, 222–23, 325–27.

Formation

Forest, where Dawson was to spend some months learning German, Dawson's biographer recounted. He "struggled unsuccessfully with German, and although he mastered it sufficiently so that he was able to read Goethe, Hegel, Troeltsch and later Spengler, he never learnt to speak it satisfactorily." Dawson became disenchanted with the Germans and their language (philology was never one of his interests). "'This country is most dreadful' he wrote to his sister from Baden 'it is really like the state of society in *Lord of the World*.' (This was Robert Hugh Benson's startling novel about the end of the world.) 'People get on so very well without religion. They do not seem bigoted like English "undenominationlists" but they examine Christianity as if it was a kind of beetle. It is all as different as if one was living among Chinese.'"[33] Despite his doubts as a young man of twenty, Dawson eventually came to greatly admire German culture. He wrote as a mature scholar of the central importance of Germany to understanding Europe as a whole. Indeed, the "very existence of Europe as an international society" depended on solving the problem of Germany's relations to societies and peoples around it.[34]

The influence of historicism on Dawson can be traced through four German scholars, in particular. The Protestant theologian and church historian Adolf von Harnack (1851–1930) was a leading historian of the early church who profoundly influenced general historical scholarship. Along with Ernst Troeltsch (1865–1923), a preeminent Protestant theologian interested in the relationship between religion and society, Harnack was a leading proponent of a liberal Protestantism that sought to shift focus away from dogma to Christianity as an historical religion. Harnack's *Lehrbuch der Dogmengeschichte* first appeared in 1885, and in a seven-volume English translation in 1899 as *History of Dogma*. Ironically, this Protestant historian influenced Dawson's conversion to Catholicism, because in his vast survey of history, Harnack inadvertently demonstrated the Church of Rome as the only one to stand in the unbroken tradition from the Apostles.[35] Certainly, Harnack's wide vision over hundreds of years of history impressed Dawson, for he referred to

33. Christina Scott, *A Historian and His World*, 39–40.
34. Christopher Dawson, *Understanding Europe*, 53.
35. Scott, *A Historian and His World*, 63.

this multivolume work several times in *Progress and Religion*. Some-times, he adopted its interpretations, as of medieval scholasticism as the foundation of European scientific thought. Most significant-ly, Harnack sought to show how dogmas (rational explanations of an unchanging divine revelation) arose and were influenced by changing historical circumstances of different times. He sought to purify Christi-anity by interpreting eternity in terms of time, to historicize what had appeared to early-church and medieval theologians as unchanging dogma. This became possible, he wrote, only with the "great spiritual revolution" of the beginning of the nineteenth century, when scholars reacted against seeing dogma as a static or rationalist system above history and therefore without a history. Only in his own age could the idea of development "obtain its proper place" and the history of dogma reach maturity, Harnack wrote. When Harnack described historicism in this way, he sought to relate all things to change and historical con-text, even apparently unchanging things, in order to bring greater un-derstanding to the unchanging itself.[36]

Troeltsch sought to relate eternity to time as well, but here the cri-sis in historicism became evident. Historian Georg Iggers pointed out the self-contradiction within historicism in basing a positive faith in a meaningful universe on historical relativism. The mistake was in trying to found knowledge of true values only on history. In the *Social Teach-ings of the Christian Churches* (1912), a book Dawson admired for its historical and sociological approaches to religion, Troeltsch combined socio-historical questions about *how* the social teaching of the church-es had, in fact, developed in time and place with humanistic ones about what *should* be the basis of this teaching in the modern world. To do this, he surveyed the relation between Christianity and the socio-logical development of the ancient, medieval, Reformation, and mod-ern eras. This sweeping examination of religion in historical relation to culture exemplified a key historicist nexus: the attempt to examine the unchanging through the changing particularities of history. He looked to the science of history as a kind of magisterium from whose mouth

36. Adolf Harnack, *History of Dogma*, vol. 1 (Boston: Roberts Brothers, 1897), 32–33; Dawson, *Progress and Religion*, 136. Dawson referenced the English translation of *History of Dogma*, vol. 6, 25.

he hoped for certain norms. Since his youth, he had directed his desire for knowledge toward history. Despite his opposition to historicism in its relativistic and pessimistic mode, however, Troeltsch failed to find the certainty he looked for because—in Iggers' words—he "wished to have his cake and eat it, too; to see in history the only key to knowledge and to value, and yet be assured of absolute, transcendent values. This could only be done on the basis of faith." Committed to the historical approach alone, Troeltsch could never effectively assuage his doubts and suspicions that all is meaningless flux, even as he remained a committed Christian.[37] Troeltsch lacked the intellectual architecture of a fully developed cultural mind.

If Dawson admired Troeltsch's historicist approach to religion as far as it would go, Dawson was willing to connect to other ways of knowing truth than merely history. If one relies only on history, Dawson wrote, then it is impossible to transcend the sphere of relativity. Only in the realms of religion and metaphysics (faith *and* reason) can one find truths that claim absolute and eternal validity. Troeltsch's quip, "History has to be overcome by history" did not work. For Dawson, reason is not simply "tradition-dependent," as philosopher John Knasas put it, but also "tradition-initiating" through its encounter with *being* (here Dawson was indebted to Thomas Aquinas). Because Dawson retained allegiance to reason as a universal power capable of making being intelligible, his attempt to write within the historicist nexus of eternity-in-time did not necessarily undermine itself. For example, he linked time to eternity in *Progress and Religion*—"progress" referring to change and "religion" to a reality subject to change but connected to an unchanging, transcendent realm. Studying one in light of the other would become a central thrust of Dawson's historicist approach to culture, for to write well about culture as both spiritual and material, he had to be able to relate the unchanging to the changing. His mind would pass from one to the other—as French philosopher A. G. Sertil-

37. Ernst Troeltsch, *The Social Teaching of the Christian Churches*, vol. 1, trans. Olive Wyon (1912; Louisville, Ky.: Westminster/John Knox, 1992), 24, 34; Iggers, *The German Conception of History*, 13, 176, 189–90, 195; Scott, *A Historian and His World*, 72; and Jeffrey Kinlaw, "Troeltsch and the Problem of Theological Normativity," in *The Anthem Companion to Ernst Troeltsch*, ed. Christopher Adair-Toteff (London: Anthem, 2018), 105, 107.

langes (1863–1948) put it, in an "alternating movement" from the particular fact in time to God and back again to the benefit of both. In that
paradox of the immutable and the mutable, Dawson's history of culture
resided. German historicism desired to operate in this place, too, but
as its commitment to the transcendent and to natural law waned, the
task became impossible. It took the terrible calamities of Nazism and
the Second World War to force a serious rethinking of historicism within Germany.[38]

The work of sociologist Max Weber (1864–1920), Troeltsch's brilliant
friend, had a less profound influence on Dawson, but it also demonstrated how religion played a dynamic role in social development.
Dawson appreciated Weber's *Die protestantische Ethik und der Geist des
Kapitalismus* (1905), translated into English in 1930 as *The Protestant
Ethic and the Spirit of Capitalism*.[39] In particular, he pointed to Weber's
socio-historical method as a fine example of how to "understand the
beliefs of the past as a means to understanding its history" from the
inside out. In this way, Weber was one of the first modern exponents of
"a sociology that understands" (*verstehende Soziologie*), Dawson wrote,
which sought to create a social science not on the model of the physical sciences (seeking general laws) but one investigating the origin and
structure of particular historical complexes. In order to do this, Weber
tried to avoid monocausal explanations of the role of religion in history. Weber noted: "The modern man is in general, even with the best
will, unable to give religious ideas a significance for culture and national character which they deserve. But it is, of course, not my aim to substitute for a one-sided materialistic an equally one-sided spiritualistic

38. Christopher Dawson, "The Kingdom of God and History," in *Dynamics of World History*,
286–87; Iggers, *The German Conception of History*, 13; John F. X. Knasas, "Tracey Rowland's 'Augustinian Thomist' Interpretation of Culture," *Angelicum* 86, no. 1 (2009): 697; and A. G. Sertillanges,
The Intellectual Life: Its Spirit, Conditions, Methods (1921; Washington, D.C.: The Catholic University
of America Press, 1998), 33. The Troeltsch quotation comes from Christian Polke, "Troeltsch's Personalism," in *The Anthem Companion to Ernst Troeltsch*, 72. Polke cites *Der Historismus und seine
Probleme. Erstes Buch: Das logische Problem der Geschichtsphilosophie*, ed. F. W. Graf (1922; Berlin:
Walter De Gruyter, 2008), 1098.

39. First published in the *Archiv für Sozialwissenschaft und Sozialpolitik*, vols. XX and XXI,
1904–1905; republished in 1920; first translated into English in 1930 as *The Protestant Ethic and
the Spirit of Capitalism*. For Dawson's appreciation, see Dawson, *Progress and Religion*, 159. R. H.
Tawney, in his *Religion and the Rise of Capitalism* (1926), was known as the "English face" of the
Weber thesis.

causal interpretation of culture and of history." Dawson's intellectual architecture shared this concern for avoiding reduction and simplification of all kinds. For example, Dawson noted how in *The Protestant Ethic* "the development of Capitalism is not to be explained as a purely economic process, but has its spiritual roots in a new religious attitude towards industry and saving that grew up in Protestant Europe after the Reformation. On the other hand, there are other phenomena which seem at first sight to be purely religious and yet have their basis in economic or social causes."[40] In order to explain human actions, change, and the rise of institutions in history, one cannot resort to one kind of cause; causation can proceed in both directions: spiritual to material and material to spiritual effects (I→FWP, FWP→I, as described in the culture-process in chapter 2).

Dawson admired Troeltsch and Weber for their *history*, not their philosophy, for with Weber, the underlying relativism within the historicist milieu emerged into plain view. It is apparent in Harnack and Troeltsch, too, but they still believed in God and Christianity as transcendent reference points giving meaning to the endless flux of change. Other scholars without these anchors (like Weber), however, searched in vain for an absolute point of reference to ground historical truth. If rationalism itself was an "historical concept" for Weber, how can reason transcend the constant flux of time? And so for Weber, the social sciences could show only how actions occurred and what values guided them, but could do no more. The entirety of the human condition could not be known.[41] Overemphasizing the epistemological priority of history and the social sciences without grounding in universal truths subsumed all of reality under the dominance of change and relativity.

This is precisely the position in which Oswald Spengler found him-

---

40. Dawson, "Sociology as a Science," 31; Max Weber, *The Protestant Ethic and the Spirit of Capitalism*, trans. Talcott Parsons (1904–1905; Mineola, N.Y.: Dover, 2003), 183. For more on *Verstehen*, the German word for "understanding," see Daniel L. Pals, *Eight Theories of Religion*, 2nd ed. (Oxford: Oxford University Press, 2006), 153–55. The principle of *Verstehen* was that one cannot understand the actions of human beings as one understands happenings in nature. Behavior could not be explained only in terms of external causes; internally held ideas and felt emotional states played roles as well. For Weber, "social values or beliefs acquire reality only insofar as they gain assent in the minds of individuals" (155 in Pals).

41. Breisach, *Historiography: Ancient, Medieval, and Modern*, 283; Weber, *The Protestant Ethic and the Spirit of Capitalism*, 78.

self. In his *Decline of the West*, the relativizing tendency of German historicism reached its radical conclusion, and Dawson wrote extensively
about it in *Sociological Review* and in his second chapter of *Progress
and Religion*. Harnack and Weber dismissed the book, but it powerfully influenced younger thinkers such as Ludwig Wittgenstein, Thomas
Mann, Martin Heidegger,[42] and Dawson himself. Spengler viewed the
idea of progress as an illusion. He was deeply influenced by German
philosopher Friedrich Nietzsche (1844–1900), who had historicized ethics and attacked the Enlightenment view of progressive historical development in his 1887 *Genealogy of Morals*. Spengler's denial of ultimate
human progress corresponded with an extreme relativism: "There are
no eternal truths," he wrote, and: "Here there is nothing constant, nothing universal." History alone can interpret reality, for all knowledge is
historically relative and an expression of one specific existence and one
only, he claimed.

Rather than one linear world history of ancient-medieval-modern
viewed from the perspective of the West, Spengler tried to account for
the incredible diversity of the world's past and the drama of a number
of cultures, "each springing with a primitive strength from the soil of a
mother-region to which it remains firmly bound throughout its whole
life-cycle." Each culture shaped its people and possessed its own idea,
passion, life, will, feeling, and death. The cultures of the world "bloom
and age as the oaks and the pines." Spengler spoke of ripening and decaying, preferring biological terms to abstract ones. Reacting against a
too humanistic conception of culture, he wrote that, "There is not *one*
sculpture, *one* painting, *one* mathematics, *one* physics, but many," each
one self-contained, just as a plant species bears fruit in its growth and
then declines. "These Cultures . . . grow with the same superb aimlessness as the flowers of the field." This inevitable natural process ensured
that the future of the West would not be a "limitless tending upwards"
toward our highest ideals but a "single phenomenon of history," which
covered a few centuries. This historical change of epoch, of growing
and declining, is the single idea that has only to be stated clearly to
become indisputable, and with it, one can resolve all those separate

---

42. Herman, *The Idea of Decline in Western History*, 244, 336.

problems of religion, philosophy, economics, and politics. Viewing world history in this way, he concluded ominously in his second volume of 1922, prepares the way for the triumph of the will-to-power and the coming Caesarism that *"will* be accomplished with the individual or against him."[43]

Without embracing the Nietzschean will to power or the radical relativism found in Spengler, Dawson did hold that culture deeply shapes even science, philosophy, and religion. For example, decades before philosopher of science Thomas Khun made the point in his *Structure of Scientific Revolutions* (1962), Dawson argued against the idea of *one* history of science. While the truths of the natural world are themselves not relative, science "takes a different form in every culture, Babylonian, Greek, Moslem and Christian, and until a culture has created a scientific ideal that is in harmony with its own spirit, it cannot bear scientific fruit." Different cultures produced different conceptions of the *purpose* of science (its ideals)—contemplative in ancient Greek culture, magical in medieval Muslim culture, and applied (practical) in medieval and especially modern Western culture.[44]

Like science, philosophy involves unchanging truth. At the same time, however, "A philosophy is itself one of the most elaborate of culture constructs," Dawson wrote to his American correspondent John J. Mulloy in 1955. It is the highest and the most abstract manifestation of a culture, he said, but in no way did he deny truth. "The fact is that every culture," Dawson wrote to Mulloy a few months earlier, "even the lowest, is concerned with objective truths and values." Culture is man's response to reality. It is not a law unto itself, he wrote, nor does it create its own reality; "what it creates is a social approach to reality, a collaboration or coordination between human activities and psychological experience and the real world in which man lives." Religion, too, is culturally conditioned, but it is the only sphere of activity that by its nature seeks to transcend the sphere of culture and "to achieve relations with a supernatural reality," Dawson wrote in a memorandum to Mulloy.[45]

43. Oswald Spengler, *The Decline of the West*, abridged ed. (1918, 1922; New York: Modern Library, 1962), 12, 17–19, 30–31, 415.
44. Dawson, *Medieval Essays*, 137–39.
45. Christopher Dawson to John J. Mulloy, August 31, 1955, NDA, box 1, folder 15, "The Dynamics

Even as Dawson appreciated the insights of German historicism into culture-study, he pointed out the obvious weaknesses of its extreme forms. Without any connection to the transcendent, the only absolute that was left in Spengler's vision was power. This was because, in Dawson's view, "Unless men believe that they have an all-powerful ally outside time, they will invariably abandon the ideal of a supernatural or anti-natural moral progress, and make the best of the world as they find it, conforming themselves to the law of self-interest and self-preservation which governs the rest of nature."[46] Spengler's views not only left no room for unchanging principles but they also denied the possibility of real progress. Evolutionary changes resulted in nothing more than blind cycles of cultures revolving from birth to death with no ultimate ethical or rational meaning. The law of destiny rather than of causality prevailed. The roots of historical change lay not in reason but in biology, in the blood of a people, Spengler thought. Cultural development owes nothing to reason in its deepest sense or to a tradition that lies beyond the experience of one people.

Yet, this view of history as nothing but blind cycles of isolated cultures is demonstrably false, as Dawson's attention to permeable cultural boundaries and intellectual interaction proved. For example, drawing from the anthropological work of W. H. R. Rivers, the English ethnologist and psychiatrist introduced in chapter 1, Dawson described how isolated cultures, such as those of Melanesia, adapted to their environments and then stagnated without change or advance until new external influences of ideas or tools arrived through interaction with other peoples, leading to a process of evolution and limited progress. The formation of a culture is not merely an historical phenomenon but also a biological one that resembles the formation of a new species. "This process of social evolution is the true explanation of the cyclical character of the life of cultures which is the foundation of Herr Spengler's philosophy," Dawson wrote. If a culture fails to adapt to adverse climatic conditions, as in the case of the Greenland Vikings and per-

of Culture Change," p. 42; Christopher Dawson to John J. Mulloy, June 16, 1955, NDA, box 1, folder 15, "The Dynamics of Culture Change," p. 42; Christopher Dawson, memorandum, letter to John J. Mulloy, September 13, 1955, NDA box 1, folder 15, "The Dynamics of Culture Change," p. 44.

46. Dawson, *Progress and Religion*, 28.

haps of the Mayans as well, it fades away or collapses. Most often, however, a culture declines as it is absorbed into the life of a conquering people.[47] Using historicist insights, Dawson exposed the fallacies of historicist philosophy: while autonomous cultures can take shape as worlds of meaning unto themselves, they can also interact with each other and help each other penetrate to truth, goodness, and beauty—however partial. In Dawson's conception of cultural boundaries as not merely barriers but also thresholds, the power of human reason in history to compare and synthesize different cultural traditions proved fatal to Spengler's conception of autonomous historical development of disconnected cultures. For example, Dawson wrote, to understand early Islamic culture, one had to consider the influence not only of the Arabs but also the Byzantine, Syro-Egyptian culture of the Levant that influenced Islam from the beginning. Further, the cultures of Sassania, Persia, the Turks, the Berbers and other Africans, and possibly Bactrian Greeks, all contributed to medieval Islamic civilization. There was no such thing as "Islamic culture" as an autonomous thing in itself unfolding according to its destiny in Spengler's life-cycle formula. The whole network of intellectual and spiritual influences in the creation of Islamic civilization readmitted the principle of causality that Spengler had thought to eliminate. This situation provided opportunities for historical and rational analysis not only of the process of cultural change and development but of other truths, too.[48]

The Meaning of Cultural Change

Progress and Religion provided a bridge between the two models of historical change prevalent during the 1920s, declinist and progressive. "There are, in fact, two movements in history," Dawson wrote. One of them is due to the "life process of an individual people in contact with a definite geographical environment, while the other is common to a number of different peoples and results from intellectual and religious interaction and synthesis." Attempting to explain history in terms of

47. Dawson, *Progress and Religion*, 56–58.
48. Dawson, *Progress and Religion*, 40–42.

only one of these factors is "doomed to failure."[49] One must consider both of them in order to understand cultural morphology. True progess occurred not simply through scientific and technological advancement but in communion with deeper truths of human nature and the cycles of natural environments.

These dual truths about human progress meant that to judge the permanence and strength of a culture, one must look first not to the abstract rationality of its institutions but to what Dawson called its "inner vitality." The strength of its institutions is in their connection to the living traditions of the people and their intimate connection to a particular natural region. A superficial and abstract progress can actually indicate the vital decline of a culture, as in Western Asia after Alexander the Great and during the Roman period. There, rulers built municipal institutions such as theatres, gymnasia, and schools of rhetoric that destroyed local traditions of culture but did not turn the Asians into Greeks or Romans. "The same thing may be true of representative institutions, universal education, a daily press and all the other insignia of modern civilization," Dawson wrote. If an institution such as representative government does not possess a living relation to its society, it may be set aside, as recently in Italy, Dawson commented in 1929, where it was set aside for a more primitive system (fascism) that was "more deeply rooted in the political traditions of the people." Change must be the spontaneous expression of a society for it to progress; when the internal vital development of a society ceases, "change means death."[50]

For example, the glorious Greek world in the age of Pericles suggested the future of humanity was assured, Dawson wrote. Art, science, and democracy flourished in a hundred free cities. At the very moment when the barbarians were turning to the Greeks for true learning, their whole culture shriveled, turning on itself in hatred and war. "When Hellenic science was in full flower, the life of the Hellenic world withered from below, and underneath the surface brilliance of philosophy and literature the sources of life of the people were drying up." The strength of their life in the regional and agrarian foundations of the cit-

49. Dawson, *Progress and Religion*, 46.
50. Dawson, *Progress and Religion*, 58–59.

izen farmer and family religion faded as the Greeks increasingly moved from the land to the towns. Slaves cultivated the farms and the citizen class fought each other or emigrated to distant cities. Hellenic civilization lost the highly differentiated life of the free city-states to become a formless cosmopolitan society without roots in the past or a particular region, Dawson wrote; "Hence the degradation of the Greek type." Yet, throughout this period of vital decline, the intellectual achievements of the Greeks spread far and wide. If intellectual progress can coexist for a time with vital decline from within, then the optimistic assumptions of the idea of progress lose their validity. "The fate of the Hellenic world is a warning to us that the higher and the more intellectually advanced civilizations of the West may be inferior in point of survival value to the more rudimentary Oriental cultures," explained Dawson. That is because there is a great difference between cultural stagnation (as in ancient China and Egypt) and cultural dissolution, as in the case of ancient Greece and Rome. "The cultures of China and Egypt survived for thousands of years because they preserved their foundations intact. By their fixed and hieratic ordering of social relations they gave to the simplest and humblest functions all the consecration of religion and tradition." Greece and Rome, however, "neglected the roots of their life in a premature concentration on power or wealth." They paid for their conquest of the world with the degeneration of their own social organs.[51]

The rawness and ugliness of modern European culture, he concluded, are signs of "biological inferiority," of a false relation to the environment. "No civilization, however advanced," Dawson wrote, "can afford to neglect these ultimate foundations in the life of nature and the natural region on which its social welfare depends, for even the highest achievements of science and art and economic organization are powerless to avert decay, if the vital functions of the social organism become impaired." Material conditions of life played an intimate, supporting role in the intellectual and spiritual progress of a people:

We do not regard the dependence of an artist on his material as a sign of weakness and lack of skill. On the contrary, the greater the artist, the more

51. Dawson, *Progress and Religion*, 59–61.

fully does he enter into his material, and the more completely does his work conform itself to the qualities of the medium in which it is embodied. In the same way the conformity of a culture to its natural environment is no sign of barbarism. The more a culture advances, the more fully does it express itself in and through its material conditions, and the more intimate is the co-operation between man and nature.[52]

If human reason made real the possibility of human progress, it had to be a reason connected to realities both higher and lower than itself, to the transcendent but also to the body, to the earth, to the humble nature of things that sometimes proved to be stumbling blocks to the rationalist enamored with abstractions. Ideas need to be viewed in relation to material conditions in order to counter the "urban distaste for the concrete" (in F. Scott Fitzgerald's phrase) prevalent in rationalism.[53]

Through his critique of the rationalist and the relativist accounts of history, Dawson attempted to supply a new history for a new age, an environmental, sociological, and religious account of history as potentially degenerating *and* progressing in different ways, depending on factors both inside and outside human control. Dawson combined both descriptive and prescriptive modes of cultural inquiry, which was all very different than the empiricist historical writing of the time focused on documents and politics. His interdisciplinary history of culture constituted a fundamental challenge to the British historiography of his day.

52. Dawson, *Progress and Religion*, 54, 62.
53. F. Scott Fitzgerald, *The Great Gatsby* (1925; Oxford: Oxford University Press, 1998), 41.

Chapter 4

History (II)

The unfortunate peculiarity of the history of man is, that although its separate parts have been examined with considerable ability, hardly any one has attempted to combine them into a whole, and ascertain the way in which they are connected with each other.

—H. T. Buckle (1857)

History played a central role in Dawson's lifelong project to make culture intelligible. It offered depth of understanding, showed how a culture's fluid identity changes over time, and traced how cultures interact with other cultures to become themselves. At the same time, Dawson's cultural mind shaped the way he practiced history. It did so in three, interrelated ways that I will examine in the context of early twentieth-century historiography:

First, because Dawson focused on culture as an historian, he avoided the tendency of British historians of his day to use the *nation* as the basic collective entity of their work, privileging politics as the fundamental object of knowledge in the field. In addition, his focus on culture led him to oppose the simplificiation of *internationalism* in the new world history that emerged after the Great War.

H. T. Buckle, *History of Civilization in England*, vol. 1 (London: J. W. Parker & Son, 1857), 3–4. The quotation continues: "Hence the singular spectacle of one historian being ignorant of political economy; another knowing nothing of law; another nothing of ecclesiastical affairs and changes of opinion; another neglecting the philosophy of statistics, and another physical science: although these topics are the most essential of all, inasmuch as they comprise the principal circumstances by which the temper and character of mankind have been affected, and in which they are displayed. These important pursuits being, however, cultivated, some by one man, and some by another, have been isolated rather than united: the aid which might be derived from analogy and from mutual illustration has been lost; and no disposition has been shown to concentrate them upon history, of which they are, properly speaking, the necessary components" (4).

Second, Dawson's focus on culture gave his historical writing a more expansive epistemology than is generally found in the historiography of his day. This allowed him to draw from a wide variety of evidence, not just documents, in ways comparable to parallel historiographical developments on the European continent, particularly among the French historians associated with the *Annales* school. The Great War entrenched many British historians—called "modernists"—more firmly in their commitment to a specialized, empiricist, and political history rooted in documents. Dawson rejected these priorities for history because of his interest in culture and refused to accept the assumptions of British empiricism in historical writing that prided itself on an "objectivity" understood as philosophical neutrality in front of bare facts. While upholding the importance of facts in historical research, he proposed epistemological renovations in his history of culture that opened up space for the historian to select and communicate facts in response to meaningful questions and in accordance with a unifying vision that gave them significance in light of particular traditions. These concerns predated by several decades similar ideas in postmodernism for recasting history as constructed narrative rather than "scientific knowledge."

In Dawson's case, this unifying vision was theological humanism: his view of the human and natural worlds as fundamentally good and knowable because they participate in the image of God, providing the third way in which his cultural mind shaped the way he practiced history. With his neglect of nation in favor of culture, and his postempiricist epistemological perspective, his religious vision functioned differently in relation to his historical writing than the Catholicism of other British historians, such as Lord Acton or Hilaire Belloc, because it was filtered through his socio-historical/humanistic science of culture. Within those parameters, he helped pioneer a much broader interdisciplinary history by interpreting religions not only as institutional churches but also as spiritual forces in history that operate both inside and outside churches in the wider world of culture. His sacramental faith interpreted history *sub specie aeternitatis* (under the aspect of eternity) in attempting to reconcile the classic historicist nexus of the particular and the universal through his concept of culture, thus creating a foundation for the rapprochement of ecclesiastical historiography and other forms of academic historical writing.

National Historiography in the Age of the Great War

Dawson's focus on culture as an historian put him at odds with mainstream British historiography in terms of both its object of study (the nation) and its epistemology (empiricism). Since the time of Thucydides, historians have focused on political and military events by narrating the deeds of great men. A broad social and cultural history only began to emerge during the Enlightenment, but this was marginalized in the nineteenth century. The cult of the nation in Germany, for example, developed around the time of the Wars of Liberation against the French conqueror Napoleon. Resisting the universal reason and empire represented by the French, the Germans adopted the particularistic and exclusive idea of "nation" as the basis for collective life as well as historical study. Benedict Anderson argued that nationality or nation-ness, as well as nationalism, are a particular kind of cultural artefact that emerged toward the end of the eighteenth century as the older sacral culture of Christendom declined. Before that time, people conceived social groups as "centripetal and hierarchical, rather than boundary-oriented and horizontal." Religiously imagined communities gave way to politically imagined communities—"imagined" because no one ever met all the members of the national community—thus, it primarily had to live in their minds.[1]

The rise of the nation meant that political history held the high ground, including in German historicism. While this focus opened up vast new sources in state archives for historians to draw from and inspired the rise of the first professional historical journals, it also distracted scholars and the wider public from both lesser and greater unities than the nation in the human past. Massive public demonstrations of nationalist sentiments played an important role in determining Europe's fate during the summer of 1914, historian Modris Eksteins ar-

---

1. Benedict Anderson, *Imagined Communities: Reflections on the Origin and Spread of Nationalism* (1983; London: Verso, 1991), 6–7, 15–16.

gued. The idealism of the nation excluded other ideals from the minds of Europeans, and historians held some blame for this. Dawson wrote in 1928 that, "During the last two centuries the history of Europe has been given an almost exclusively national interpretation. And since the unit is a political one, the method of interpretation has tended to be political also, so that history has often sunk to the level of political propaganda. . . . This state of things was one of the great predisposing causes of the late War."[2] Historiography has consequences.

Individual historians in France, England, Germany, and the United States tried to pursue alternative histories of religion, society, economics, and culture, while sociologists such as Émile Durkheim saw history as merely an auxiliary to the real science of society that he practiced. Historians who worked on other kinds of history looked "nonprofessional," however, so nonpolitical history was excluded from the discipline.[3] Dawson was part of this rebel movement because he sought to write interdisciplinary history, one focused on culture rather than politics—anticipating the "cultural turn" in later twentieth-century historiography.

He did so within the context of the Great War's ambiguous effects on European historical thinking, for it both narrowed it and opened up new opportunities. While the period from 1890 to 1914 did see a broadening of historical interest beyond politics, the outbreak of war interrupted this trend for many historians because they felt a patriotic duty to subordinate their scholarship to serve the war effort, as through the Committee of Public Information set up by President Woodrow Wilson (1856–1924). Further, the prewar international cooperation of historians broke down, poignantly demonstrated by the rupture of friendship between the Belgian medievalist Henri Pirenne (1862–1935) and the German Karl Lamprecht (1856–1915), an ardent supporter of the German cause. When Lamprecht sought to visit Pirenne, the Belgian slammed the door in front of him. Pirenne embodied the ambiguity of the Great War and historiography, for while he opposed inviting Ger-

---

2. Dawson, *The Age of the Gods*, xii–xiii; Modris Eksteins, *Rites of Spring: The Great War and the Birth of the Modern Age* (Toronto: Lester & Orpen Dennys, 1989), 56.

3. Peter Burke, *The French Historical Revolution: The Annales School, 1929–89* (Stanford, Calif.: Stanford University Press, 1990), 6–9.

mans to international history conferences well into the 1920s, he nevertheless influenced the broadening of history by his "extraordinary combination of erudition and analytical imagination, patriotism and cosmopolitanism, devotion to the past and present-mindedness," historian Carole Fink recounted. Pirenne championed comparative history as the antidote for the ways that the Great War had undermined the scholarly basis of history as a discipline.[4]

The Great War also created new opportunities for historical thought. Pirenne wrote his great *History of Europe* while in German captivity, separated from archives and libraries, largely from memory, leading him to forgo standard chronological narrative to examine the larger picture of European social and economic developments. Furthermore, some younger historians such as Marc Bloch (1886–1944) in France, enthused by the work of Pirenne and amazed by the mass mobilization of troops and new technologies, sought to push the field beyond the traditional preoccupation with politics, war, and great leaders. They wanted to supplement simple narrative with analytical frameworks to make history more complex, more accurate, and more human. They had encountered the social sciences before the war, and afterward, they took up new academic positions in which they continued to lay the foundations of a robust social and cultural history.[5]

In the case of Bloch, the war actually created the conditions under which these new developments took shape, because the peace settlement brought the University of Strasbourg under French control in 1918. The new French faculty who entered the institution around the same time, replacing the German professors, contributed to an innovative academic environment. In this way, Bloch took up a position in medieval history and met his friend Lucien Febvre (1878–1956) there in 1920. Out of the interdisciplinary conversations between these two men and their colleagues formed one of the most influential schools of historiography of the twentieth century known as the "*Annales* school," named after their journal *Annales d'histoire économique et so-*

---

4. Carole Fink, *Marc Bloch: A Life in History* (Cambridge: Cambridge University Press, 1989), 106; Georg G. Iggers and Q. Edward Wang, *A Global History of Modern Historiography* (Harlow: Pearson/Longman, 2008), 174.

5. Fink, *Marc Bloch: A Life in History*, 104–5.

ciale. Bloch's great 1924 book *Les Rois Thaumaturges* (*The Royal Touch*) sought to replace narrative-based history with problem-based history. He tried to fit chronology to the problem under consideration, in this case the problem of how people could believe for centuries that kings could cure the skin disease scrofula by touching the sick. This reevaluation of the sacred nature of European monarchy gave a long-term perspective to centuries of political history, set against a wide cultural background—the *longue durée*, typical of the *Annales*. Second, Bloch's book sought to understand the psychology of belief and thus provided an early example of historical sociology and anthropology. As Febvre prescribed, "At the frontiers [of disciplines], astride the frontiers, with one foot on each side, that is where the historian has to work." Third, the book concerned itself with comparative history.[6]

Dawson's own views on the tasks of history reflected these characteristics of *Annales* history. He, too, would seek to fit chronology to historical problems rather than the other way around, examine the relationship between religion and culture, and write comparative history beyond the nation-state according to long-term views of the past. He praised French historiography in general, and Bloch in particular, for strong sociological concerns, especially in Bloch's *Feudal Society*.[7] Dawson's book *The Making of Europe* treated the entirety of early medieval Europe as a sociological case-study in the relation between religion and culture. In this way, Bloch, Dawson, and others attempted to create a new kind of history in the two decades after the Great War.

In Dawson's England, however, many obstacles resisted this movement to broaden history, even well into the 1960s, not least because of the entrenched "whig" historiography and because of the strong tradition of empiricism and the methodological individualism that assumed entities such as "society" or "culture" are fictitious, while individuals alone exist.[8] Whig historians dominated the Oxford of Dawson's college years. These were not the political "Whigs" who helped found the nineteenth-century Liberal Party but rather a concatenation of au-

6. Burke, *The French Historical Revolution*, 17–19; Lucian Febvre, "A New Kind of History," in *A New Kind of History: From the Writings of Febvre*, ed. Peter Burke (1949; London: Routledge and Kegan Paul, 1973), 31.

7. Dawson, "The Problem of Metahistory," 307.

8. Burke, *The French Historical Revolution*, 97.

thors known as the "whig historians" for their common interpretation of English national history, including Thomas Babington Macaulay (1800–1859) and the Anglican bishop of Oxford William Stubbs (1825–1901), who was regarded as the greatest English historian of his age, known especially for his three-volume *Constitutional History of England* (1878). The growth of the English constitution, Stubbs argued, was due to factors such as the "national character" and "the institutions of the people."[9] Its enemies were Catholicism and absolute monarchs or dictators. Whig historians believed in a continuity of institutions and practices from Anglo-Saxon times that had shaped the unique, freedom-loving character of the English nation. Parliament, Protestantism, and empire revealed an inner progress in English history toward limited government and a global civilizing mission. Whig history was a master narrative determining the subjects and the meaning of English history.[10]

The Great War did not destroy this whig tradition of British historiography, but it did modify it. This is seen, for example, in the work of G. M. Trevelyan, Regius Professor of Modern History at Cambridge (1927–1940). Trevelyan, in company with philosopher Bertrand Russell (1872–1970), historian Lord David Cecil (1902–1986), and Christopher Dawson, contributed to a BBC series in 1948 on *The Ideas and Beliefs of the Victorians*. He served with an ambulance unit on the Italian front from 1915 until the end of the war, and it had a devastating effect on him. "A great war necessarily has a profound effect on the policy and philosophy of the nation engaged in it," Trevelyan noted in 1920. "It is curiously different," he wrote to his mother in 1921, "living before the war and after it. The certainty of permanence has gone." There was disillusion over the old creed of liberalism and progress. Never again would he write with the ardent optimism of his prewar books on Guiseppe Garibaldi, the Italian political leader. The Liberal Party eventually gave way to the Labour Party—a catastrophe in Trevelyan's eyes.[11]

9. William Stubbs, *The Constitutional History of England: In Its Origin and Development*, 6th ed., vol. 1 (Oxford: Clarendon, 1903), 1.

10. Michael Bentley, *Modernizing England's Past: English Historiography in the Age of Modernism 1870–1970* (Cambridge: Cambridge University Press, 2005), 6, 19–20.

11. G. M. Trevelyan, *The War and the European Revolution in Relation to History* (London: University of London Press, 1920), 27; David Cannadine, *G. M. Trevelyan: A Life in History* (London:

Against a background of new and powerful governments rising on the continent after the Great War, Trevelyan's belief in English exceptionalism only grew, so that after 1918, he focused more intensely on national historical writing than ever and sought a new identity as the "national historian."[12] But he also believed nationalistic history could be dangerous: "If wrongly studied it [history] may end in filling the streets with blood, and the countryside with trenches and bursting shell," he wrote. "The war of 1870 was ascribed by some to the historical writings of Thiers, and the greater catastrophe of our own era [the Great War] to those of Treitschke. There was probably an element of truth in these charges. But, if rightly taught, the annals of mankind cultivate a more intelligent patriotism that respects the claims of others."[13] In this way, Trevelyan wrote a liberal national history, recognizably in the whig tradition, that was not narrow, unfair, or nationalistic. His one-volume *History of England* (1926), which he resolved to write during the Great War as an offering of thanks to the English people, replaced J. R. Green's *Short History of the English People* (1874) as the definitive account of the English past during the interwar years. He was committed to surmounting the specialized research of his day in order to communicate a national, political history of parliamentary government and religious toleration to the public. His account stressed the unique British virtues of liberty, stability, and order—which seemed so scarce on the continent at that time.[14]

Dawson admired the literary style and broad appeal of the whig historians, but he differed greatly from their assumptions about progress, Protestantism, and the nation. Unlike Trevelyan, Dawson never wrote from a national perspective—none of his own book titles ever

---

Penguin Books, 1992), 87, 88. Cannadine cites a letter from Trevelyan to his mother, Lady Caroline Trevelyan, dated October 1921, in the Sir George Otto Trevelyan manuscripts. Trevelyan wrote *Garibaldi's Defence of the Roman Republic* (1907), *Garibaldi and the Thousand* (1909), and *Garibaldi and the Making of Italy* (1911).

12. Cannadine, *G. M. Trevelyan*, 75, 90, 109, 114, 120.

13. G. M. Trevelyan, "The Present Position of History," in *Clio, A Muse, and other Essays* (London: Longmans, 1930), 178. Louis-Adolphe Thiers (1797–1877) was a French politician and historian who wrote the very popular, ten-volume *Histoire de la Revolution française* (1823–1827). Heinrich Gotthard von Treitschke (1834–1896) was a nationalist German historian and political writer whose great work was the five-volume *Deutsche Geschichte im 19. Jahrhundert*, published in 1879–1894.

14. Cannadine, *G. M. Trevelyan*, 126–27.

contained the word "England" or "Britain." The closest he came was his *Spirit of the Oxford Movement* (1933), which examined an aspect of English religious culture of the 1830s and 1840s, a short essay on "The World Crisis and the English Tradition,"[15] and a lengthy essay on the English poet William Langland in *The English Way* (1933), edited by Maisie Ward. In this essay, Dawson's imbrication of history and literature showed how he normally contextualized national histories within a larger, cultural context:

The fourteenth century was . . . the age of the Great Schism and the Black Death and the Hundred Years' War, but it was also the age of Dante and Petrarch, of St. Catherine and St. Bridget, of Tauler and Suso and Ruysbroeck, an age of poets and mystics and saints. It was the breakdown of the universal theocratic order of mediaeval Christendom and the rise of political nationalism and religious division, and at the same time it witnessed the passing of the old agrarian and feudal society and the rise of capitalism and urban industrialism.[16]

In this passage, Dawson passed over a wide landscape and placed its inhabitants in their spiritual, social, economic, European, and military contexts—all as a concise background to help understand the Englishman William Langland. Though Dawson wrote on European and worldwide themes and had lived and studied abroad as a young man (Switzerland, Sweden, Italy, Germany), he was thoroughly English in his sentiments, religion, and manner of life, like Trevelyan. Like him, Dawson wrote as an Englishman, but seldom about England.

Alternatives to National Historiography

If the Great War challenged Trevelyan to rethink the writing of national history, it prompted others to reconceive the very foundations of history. For some people, the Great War undermined the construction of historical narratives based on the nation state. What kinds of

15. Christopher Dawson, "The World Crisis and the English Tradition," *English Review* LVI (1933): 248–60.
16. Christopher Dawson, "William Langland (1333–?1399): *The Vision of Piers Plowman*," in *The English Way: Studies in English Sanctity from St. Bede to Newman*, ed. Maisie Ward (London: Sheed & Ward, 1933), 160–61.

communities, other than the nation, could historians see as meaningful objects of study after the Great War? Some decided on the world community, leading to the rise of world history. For example, Arnold Toynbee, author of the twelve-volume global panorama *A Study of History* (1934–1961), wrote that, "In 1915 and 1916, about half the number of my school fellows were killed. . . . The longer I live, the greater grows my grief and indignation at the wicked cutting-short of all those lives. I do not want my grandchildren and great-grandchildren to have the same fate. The writing of this book has been one of my responses to the challenge that has been presented to me by the senseless criminality of human affairs."[17] In his final volume, he described the transformation of his historical thinking after 1918 as he discovered a new object of knowledge other than the nation: "I then duly rejected the self-regarding hallucination of mistaking the England of my time for the culmination of history," he wrote. "I found that England, taken by itself, was not, in fact, an 'intelligible field of study' either in my time or at any earlier date since the time when such a thing as England had first become discernible on the political map. I therefore went in search of the minimum unit, of which England is a part, that might be found intelligible if treated as being self-contained, and I found this in the Western Civilization,"[18] he explained, leading him to the discovery of other civilizations. Civilizations, then, were the subjects of his famous work.

Along with Dawson, British historians Arnold Toynbee, H. G. Wells, and Eileen Power played major roles in the rise of world history after the Great War. World history had tremendous appeal to the public in the twentieth century in Paul Costello's view partly because many moderns lost their connection to meaningful entities larger than themselves. Mountains of information distracted them from a wider vision of the world, and they found themselves unable to come to terms with fundamental issues, so world history sought to heal some of these con-

---

17. Arnold Toynbee, *A Study of History*, rev. ed. (London: Oxford University Press, 1972), 11.

18. Arnold Toynbee, *Reconsiderations* (London: Oxford University Press, 1961), 12: 162. Toynbee admired Dawson's work on world history and referenced him forty-four times in this final volume of his *Study of History*. He also wrote the introduction to Christopher Dawson, *The Gods of Revolution* (London: Sidgwick & Jackson, 1972).

cerns by studying patterns of the whole.[19] It also sought to replace nationalism with *internationalism,* as in the best-selling *Outline of History* (1920) by H. G. Wells. Education in world history, he thought, would prepare people to accept the fact that their true nationality is mankind, not their nation state, and to work toward world government.[20] Eileen Power (1889–1940), who knew both Wells and Toynbee, agreed. She wrote an introduction to world history during the 1930s, a book of twenty-eight chapters, though it was never published. Greatly affected by the national experience of the Great War, in 1921, she wrote an essay called, "The Teaching of History and World Peace." An answer to the international problem, she wrote, was a different historical pedagogy focused on life in communities not based on class or nation. Her BBC broadcasts and her books such as *Medieval English Nunneries* (1922), *Medieval People* (1924), and *Boys & Girls of History* (1926) proclaimed her emphasis on ordinary human lives in an international setting.

Eileen Power's first-rate history books notwithstanding, crediting internationalism as an antidote to nationalism risked oversimplification, Dawson pointed out. As an abstraction with few historical roots and little respect for real cultural boundaries and differences in traditions, internationalism as an ideology could make as weak a basis for foreign policy as it could for historical writing.[21] The League of Nations and the international movement failed, Dawson wrote in the midst of the Second World War, because they reduced nations to ideological collectives and failed to understand them sociologically, as parts of the larger community of European culture. "The modern tendency for every State or group of States to identify itself with one of the rival types of political ideology is as fatal to any kind of world order as were the religious wars of the past. . . . The true basis of international life is to be found not in ideological unity, but in a community of culture." Dawson quoted from Edmund Burke's *Letters on the Regicide Peace* (1796) in which Burke described this community of culture as the

19. Paul Costello, *World Historians and Their Goals: Twentieth-Century Answers to Modernism* (DeKalb: Northern Illinois University Press, 1993), 4.
20. H. G. Wells, *The Outline of History: Being a Plain History of Life and Mankind* (London: George Newnes, 1920), 2, 750, 752.
21. Dawson, *The Making of Europe*, 9–10.

"similitude throughout Europe of religion, laws and manners." As with an extended family made up of different individuals—Dawson quoted Burke again: "Nothing is so strong a tie of amity between nation and nation as correspondence in laws, customs, manners and habits of life. They are obligations written in the heart."[22] Only through communion in the wider European society of peoples had the different national cultures "attained their actual form," Dawson wrote.[23] Their very diversity expressed a greater whole. Burke's "habits of life" (culture) were the true basis of European unity, not an abstracted and oversimplified internationalism. Dawson's boundary thinking showed the importance of respecting the historical roots and permeable boundaries of different cultures, nations, and peoples that made up larger unities.

Dawson critiqued the syncretism found within internationalism that ignored the importance of boundaries. He wrote a critical essay on *A Study of History* in 1955 and described Toynbee's division of world history into distinct and autonomous civilizations culminating in the emergence of the higher world religions. This philosophy of history essentially reduced the past to religion, and this would no more convince theologians than it did historians, Dawson thought. Toynbee's theological syncretism, the unifying principle of his work, not only oversimplified religion from an historical point of view but also confused disciplinary boundaries. One can test historical claims by historical criteria, but religion "transcends the sphere of history and is not amendable to empirical study." When one actually examines the world religions theologically, and not just with the methods of history, one sees that they are "neither identical nor convergent."[24] Dawson's clear differentiation of history and theology worked against the simplification inherent in Toynbee's work.

He singled out for particular criticism Toynbee's focus on *civilization* as the central object of historical knowledge. This tended to ignore the cultural components of civilizations and exaggerate the gulf

---

22. Dawson, *The Judgment of the Nations*, 57, 58, 59.

23. Dawson, *The Making of Europe*, 9.

24. Christopher Dawson, "Arnold Toynbee and the Study of History," in *Dynamics of World History*, 410–13. This was originally published in *International Affairs* XXXI (April 1955): 149–59 under the title "Toynbee's Study of History: The Place of Civilizations in History."

between them and undeveloped cultures. One cannot disregard the existence of neighboring and related peoples when studying a civilization—even across national borders, Dawson argued, as in comparing Mexican culture with Pueblo culture of the southwestern United States when trying to understand the wider civilization of Latin America.[25]

In reality, a civilization is a far more complex phenomenon than philosophers of history have realized. Dawson wrote in his essay on Toynbee:

The higher civilizations usually represent a fusion of at least two independent traditions of culture. . . . Hence I do not believe it is possible to study the high civilizations satisfactorily until we have succeeded in analyzing their different cultural components. In other words, the essential basis of the study of history must be, not just a comparative study of the higher civilizations, but a study of their constituent cultures, and here we must follow, not the grand synoptic method of the philosophers of history, but the more laborious and meticulous scientific technique of the social anthropologists.

Dawson adopted the microscope of the anthropologists before picking up the telescope of the world historian. He argued that *culture* should form the essential basis of historical study rather than civilization because a civilization is usually a "super-culture" that absorbs less advanced cultures and unites them in an extended field of communication that is really an intercultural society. "My fundamental criticism of Toynbee's great work," he concluded his essay, "is that it is too telescopic and that a true science of human cultures must be based on a more microscopic technique of anthropological and historical research."[26]

Thus, in his search for an alternative to national historical writing, shared with other British world historians of the 1920s and 1930s, Dawson attempted to avoid the oversimplification embedded in their motives (the internationalist cause) and their methods (too philosophical and telescopic). He did this by arguing that the socio-historical conception of culture emerging from anthropology after the Great War should take precedence over nation or civilization in the study of history. Socio-historical cultures are both narrower and wider, and reach

25. Dawson, "Arnold Toynbee and the Study of History," 416–17.
26. Dawson, "Arnold Toynbee and the Study of History," 417, 418.

deeper, in their influence on human history than the state. Cultures are the fundamental social realities "on which all the other social phenomena are dependent."[27] He maintained his focus on culture throughout his historiography.

Epistemological Renovations in Dawson's History of Culture

Dawson's focus on culture rather than nation or civilization in his historiography meant that he regularly handled facts and evidence differently than other historians of the time. He preferred question-led to source-led historiography, substituted a broader concept of scientific historiography for the typical Anglo-American understanding, and rethought the role of facts, generalization, objectivity, and imagination in historical writing.

Reba Soffer explained how in the English universities of the late nineteenth and early twentieth centuries, most people viewed history as a liberal art with the humanistic purpose of training morally upright leaders and instilling them with national confidence. The universities imparted to their students a largely homogenous interpretive scheme in which the study of history simply contributed to reinforcing a national narrative. Economic, social, and scientific developments held importance in so far as they exemplified the endurance of national values, as in J. R. Green's *A Short History of the English People*. For Green, historical facts made sense in so far as they contributed to an understanding of the political history of the nation. "Teachers and writers of history believed themselves to be objective because they rigorously tested evidence," Soffer wrote. "But the effect of their teaching and writing was a coherent narrative sequence or a completed series of documents that provided evidence for their national faith."[28]

It was challenging to think outside the assumptions of this national whig historiography, as Dawson found out as an Oxford undergraduate from 1908 to 1911. The history program there educated students

---

27. Dawson, "Sociology as a Science," 20.

28. Reba N. Soffer, *Discipline and Power: The University, History, and the Making of an English Elite, 1870–1930* (Stanford, Calif.: Stanford University Press, 1994), 5, 8, 34, 42, 210; J. R. Green, *A Short History of the English People*, rev. ed. (1874; New York: American Book, n.d.), xviii.

in English constitutional and political history, with some reading in political science and economics. The tradition of teaching history as a liberal art (rather than a science) thrived still, but it was a narrow interpretation of "liberal art" that neglected other important dimensions of a liberal education. For example, students would learn humane judgment by studying examples of honorable and dishonorable values, but they lacked training in scepticism and interdisciplinary thinking. Dawson reported later in life that he had gotten little out of his Oxford education. He had "little interest in the set history syllabus—Stubbs on Constitutional History, Oman on the Normans and the like," one of his biographers wrote. "He therefore devoted his time to following his own course of reading and studies which were mainly in the field of the philosophy of history and religion."[29] The teaching of history at Oxford lacked those connections with other disciplines that could open up historical study to self-critique and nonpolitical questions about culture that so interested Dawson—connections that he exemplified in his later writing and proposed in his educational reforms (chapter 8).

Meanwhile, there was a growing movement at Oxford to incorporate more training in research into the history program. This occurred amidst a general debate over the nature of the undergraduate history degree: should it be a liberal education, a general training of the mind? Or should the history curriculum focus on teaching research methods to undergraduates? At Oxford, the eminent historian Charles Firth (1857–1936) strongly proposed the latter model. He wanted students to receive training in historical research methods that would enable them to eventually add to the general fund of historical knowledge. Firth only partially succeeded in convincing the university to reform its curriculum because the old ideal of the university serving primarily as an institution of education for public service (rather than research) held out, as it did at Cambridge.[30]

This emphasis on the critical and impartial skills of scholarship served Dawson well later in life, and he remained grateful for his ini-

29. Soffer, *Discipline and Power*, 209–210; Scott, *A Historian and His World*, 44–45.
30. Peter Slee, *Learning and a Liberal Education: The Study of Modern History in the Universities of Oxford, Cambridge and Manchester 1800–1914* (Manchester: Manchester University Press, 1986), 91–92, 103–4, 149, 163–64.

tiation into them at Oxford. This occurred through his contact with scholars such as his tutor Ernest Barker, also from the north of England. While professors at Oxford gave leisurely public lectures and focused on research, tutors served in the colleges working closely with students and trying to keep up with developments in their fields. Barker's field was mainly political science (in the whig tradition), but he was widely educated, having received Firsts (highest academic honors) in both Greats[31] and Modern History a decade before his young student arrived at Oxford. Barker initiated Dawson into medieval studies and encouraged his wide range of reading, reflecting the ease with which Barker moved from ancient to modern history. The classics provided the unity among all the humanities at this time, serving as a common background or language that made it easy for classically educated tutors such as Barker and others to cross disciplinary boundaries. "The result was a general fellowship of learning," Barker remembered, and "no great gulf between faculty." He trained his students through weekly essays and conversation to work together in the common search for truth—"the truth of historical facts and of 'the things that had actually happened.'" That search for truth led him into some unusual directions, such as when, shortly after Dawson graduated, Barker published a short book on the rise of the English representative system in the thirteenth century. The medieval church, Barker argued, "supplied both the idea of representation and its rules of procedure," and the Dominican Order, through its convocations, modelled and supported the spread of the principle of representation in English society. One needed to understand this movement toward political representation in England against the backdrop of medieval history as a whole, he wrote. In this way, Dawson saw in his mentor a tradition of broad education and interest in religion as an historian. Barker recalled later in life that young Dawson was "the most philosophically minded of any of my pupils in history." He stood in the company of a Lord Acton or a Baron von Hügel, Barker wrote, and "the academic world has never yet understood, or at any rate recognized, his [Dawson's] quality."[32]

31. This is the nickname for the *Literae humaniores* undergraduate degree at Oxford, which is an interdisciplinary study of classical culture.
32. Julia Stapleton, *Englishness and the Study of Politics: The Social and Political Thought of*

Firth's emphasis on the professionalization of history at Oxford involved practicing it more as a science with systematic methods than viewing it as a humane formation of future national leaders—the very tension between socio-historical and humanistic perspectives Dawson strove to integrate. The trend toward "scientific" history was inaugurated in the nineteenth century, the "age of archives," or the "documentary age," as Acton called it, when new historical sources in national archives became available for the first time. Trained by Ignaz von Döllinger (1799–1890), the foremost Roman Catholic church historian in Germany, Acton toured various archives on the continent in the 1860s, helped found the *English Historical Review* in 1886, and ended up as Regius Professor of Modern History at Cambridge. His rise to prominence owed much to his mastery of the piles of new facts found in documents and the archives.

Nineteenth-century historians' excitement over *facts* reveals something important about their world view. The concept of fact, historian Barbara J. Shapiro has argued, emerged in early-modern English legal practice, where it went on to influence a host of other intellectual fields (including history) and played a central role in the development of English empiricism. If one possesses the facts, then one grasps the event, as in a court of law, this view held. The past should not be imagined so much as *observed* through facts the way a scientist observes facts. Systematic archival research methods for ascertaining the truth of facts in the age of archives naturally began to embody an empiricist approach to knowledge that privileged politics because research mainly unearthed political facts. Acton wrote: "For the science of politics is the one science that is deposited by the stream of history, like grains of gold in the sand of a river." Imagination and interpretation faded in importance as this scientific ideal powerfully attracted historians.[33]

This empiricist ideal often involved trying to maintain a philosoph-

Ernest Barker (Cambridge: Cambridge University Press, 1994), 33; Ernest Barker, *Age and Youth: Memories of Three Universities & Father of the Man* (London: Oxford University Press, 1953), 17, 56–57, 59–60; and Ernest Barker, *The Dominican Order and Convocation: A Study of the Growth of Representation in the Church During the Thirteenth Century* (Oxford: Clarendon, 1913), 3, 72–75.

33. Lord Acton, *A Lecture on the Study of History* (London and New York: Macmillan, 1895), 3, 19; Bentley, *Modernizing England's Past*, 12–13, 15; and Barbara Shapiro, *A Culture of Fact: England, 1550–1720* (Ithaca, N.Y.: Cornell University Press, 2000), 3.

ically neutral objectivity in front of the facts. On this basis, for example, Acton planned the *Cambridge Modern History*, writing in an 1898
letter to contributors: "Our scheme requires that nothing shall reveal
the country, the religion, or the party to which the writers belong." This
neutrality was essential "not only on the ground that impartiality is the
character of legitimate history, but because the work is carried on by
men acting together for no other object than the increase of accurate
knowledge." History would become "independent of historians," he
observed in his inaugural lecture as Regius Professor. This was a view
largely shared by J. B. Bury, famous for his book on the idea of progress,
as discussed in the last chapter. In 1903, Bury advocated "scrupulously
exact conformity to facts" in order to present readers with "untaint-
ed and unpainted truth." True history "can be attained only through
the discovery, collection, classification, and interpretation of facts—
through scientific research," he declared in his own inaugural lecture
as Regius Professor. While Bury was regarded by the British historical
profession as the model of an objective and impartial scholar, he did
recognize that complete freedom from bias was neither possible nor
desirable. In a letter at the end of his life, Bury said that personal vision
was important for great history, and that without bias, the historian
will produce "colourless and dull work."[34] Nevertheless, the scientific
ideal of objectivity underpinned most of Bury's writing.

By contrast, Trevelyan dissented from this movement to view history as a science. His purpose, as a good whig, was to awaken the historical imagination in the general reader.[35] Historical imagination would
draw people to the heroes of the past and to the national virtues. In his
1913 essay "Clio, A Muse," Trevelyan argued against Bury's characterization of history as a science of facts. To Trevelyan, history was only
partly a matter of fact because facts were useless unless they produced

34. Lord Acton, "Letter to Contributors to the *Cambridge Modern History*," in *Essays in the Liberal Interpretation of History*, ed. William H. McNeill (Chicago and London: University of Chicago Press, 1967), 397; Acton, *A Lecture on the Study of History*, 18, 19; Bury, *An Inaugural Lecture, Delivered in the Divinity School Cambridge on January 26, 1903*, 11, 24; Goldstein, "J. B. Bury's Philosophy of History: A Reappraisal," , 896–919; and J. B. Bury, "A Letter on the Writing of History," in *Selected Essays of J. B. Bury*, 70.

35. G. M. Trevelyan, "Clio, A Muse," in *Clio, A Muse, and other Essays*, 152; Cannadine, *G. M. Trevelyan*, 126–27.

a new state of mind in the reader. The past could not be accessed in its totality, so it had to be *imagined*, not "observed" as the empiricists insisted. The true historical tradition of England was not the scientific conception of history, which he blamed on German influence, but the native literary tradition that had thrived since the day of his own great-uncle, Thomas Babington Macaulay (1800–1859), Whig politician and also an historian.[36]

Nevertheless, research methods and an empiricist philosophy of knowledge coalesced to create a new scientific historiography (also called modernist historiography) that ran parallel to Trevelyan's whig tradition. Dawson stood outside both of them, even as they influenced his education in critical methods at Oxford (empiricist tradition) and his creative desire to write a history that would communicate with a wide audience (whig tradition).

British empiricist historiography would dominate the British historical profession until the 1970s. By 1900, its key tenets were: (1) the rigorous examination of historical evidence, verified by references; (2) impartial research, devoid of *a priori* beliefs and prejudices; and (3) an inductive method of reasoning, from the particular to the general. The theory of knowledge implied by these principles suggested the past existed independently of the mind and was both observable and verifiable, and it was possible to be objective because the truth of an historical account rested simply upon its correspondence to the facts (Acton's "grains of gold"). These methods and outlook formed the authoritative magisterium of British history by imposing consensus about making truth-claims and certifying facts from within the rapidly professionalizing discipline of history.[37]

The Great War accentuated the professionalization of a more empiricist and specialized history. Britain "won" the Great War, so historians could retain their belief in the objectivity of their profession and that impartial research could help govern the new world emerging after the Treaty of Versailles. This strong commitment to the ob-

36. Trevelyan, "Clio, A Muse," 145, 148, 152, 163, 169.

37. Anna Green and Kathleen Troup, *The Houses of History: A Critical Reader in Twentieth-Century History and Theory* (Manchester: Manchester University Press, 1999), 3; Bentley, *Modernizing England's Past*, 216.

jectivity of history and the "ultimate arbitrating power of documents" led to the founding of new scholarly journals devoted to "scientific," research-based historical writing; to new institutions, such as the Institute of Historical Research (1921); and to the search for as many documents as possible relating to the origins of the war. Multivolume histories of the war and editions of foreign policy papers poured off the presses. Prominent British historians, such as Harold Temperley (1879–1939) and G. P. Gooch (1873–1968), deeply influenced by the assumptions and methods of empiricist historiography and working with masses of newly available archive material after the war, turned to diplomatic history to help explain the contours of the world emerging in the 1920s and 1930s.[38]

In this "source-led" history, scholars would try to advance the discipline by hunting for "new material" not used by other historians rather than by asking new and more penetrating questions. Sources, rather than questions, led the way. The field of history during the 1920s set its path toward the ever-more-minute and specialized search for an "unused" piece of the past, Bentley noted, and periods of history should be short so that primary sources could be mastered. Some of these tendencies appeared in the work of one of the great British empiricist historians of the interwar years, Lewis Namier (1888–1960). His *Structure of Politics at the Accession of George III* (1929) examined only a few years of history in minute detail to expose the financial and family connections of politicians of that era. This miniaturist approach revolutionized the study of history in Britain, for it showed historians how to use the mass of raw material constantly increasing around them rather than despair in front of it. While Namier could also write essays summing up the vast sweep of the past, he struggled to express the results of his research as a whole. "Namierization" could lead historians to easily fall into the almost bottomless depths of research and find themselves unable to communicate it in any meaningful way, Atkinson noted. Such historians would—in the words of R. H. Tawney—"make a darkness, and call it research." The overwhelming amount of the

38. Bentley, *Modernizing England's Past*, 204–7; Richard J. Evans, *Cosmopolitan Islanders: British Historians and the European Continent* (Cambridge: Cambridge University Press, 2009), 110–20.

sources of history could easily flood-out any meaningful questions one might ask about the past.[39]

The British empiricist tradition of historiography, focused on documents and the objectivity of historical knowledge, held great authority in the twentieth century. However, Dawson and those around him approached history in a different way because they held a more expansive epistemology of historical knowledge, one less bound to documents. The American historian and sociologist Lewis Mumford wrote to Dawson in 1924:

Do you find any movement setting in towards the history of culture and civilization, outside the Le Play House group in England? Things are coming very slowly in America; for our historians are still exercizing a sort of gymnastic rigor in dealing with the Document, as they have been taught to do by the French and German archivists, and they are slow to see that their narrow interpretation of the "document" leaves them ignorant of a great deal of unwritten history that has nevertheless left its imprint.[40]

Like Mumford, Dawson thought of the history of culture as a much broader enterprise than empiricist historiography's commitment to critical study of documents, as important as that is for the field. As Chesterton wrote in 1924: "The neglected side of English history does not consist of little things which the learned obscurely conceal, but rather of large things which the learned frequently ignore. Much of it can be learned, not only without any prodigy of book-learning, but practically without any books. It can be learned from large and obvious things, like the size of Gothic churches or the style of classical country houses."[41] Dawson vigorously agreed, for his intellectual architecture was built on his studies in archeology, art, technology, geography, cultural artifacts, theology, literature, and the principles of biology and human nature. Out of all these kinds of evidence, and more, and with the empiricist *and* nonempiricist epistemologies implied

39. B. J. Atkinson, "Historiography," in *The Twentieth-Century Mind: History, Ideas, and Literature in Britain*, ed. C. B. Cox and A. E. Dyson (Oxford: Oxford University Press, 1972), 63; Bentley, *Modernizing England's Past*, 15, 199–200, 207; and R. H. Tawney, "The Study of Economic History," *Economica* XIII (1933): 19.

40. Mumford to Dawson, May 24, 1924, STA, box 15, folder 58, "Mumford, Lewis."

41. G. K. Chesterton, *A Short History of England* (London: Chatto & Windus, 1924), v.

by the methods needed to understand them, he wrote his history of culture.

Dawson's history of culture departed from the epistemology of the dominant British historiographical tradition because it originated out of a different conception of "science." In the languages of the continent, Iggers observed, "*Wissenschaft* (German), *science* (French), *scienza* (Italian), *ciencia* (Spanish), or *nauk* (Russian) denote a systematic approach to any sphere of knowledge, including the humanities, guided by methods of investigation accepted by a community of scholars." British (and American) historians, however, commonly held images of the natural sciences in their minds when they used the word "science." For example, Albert Pollard called for the founding of a "historical laboratory" in 1920, which later became the Institute of Historical Research in London. He wrote that, "the real historian has learnt from the real man of science that patient, original, and minute investigation is the only sure foundation of truth." This meant that if historians observed the facts objectively ("value-free") and arrange them properly, they would reveal their inner connections.[42]

This Anglo-American tendency to privilege the natural sciences undermined real understanding of historical objects, however, because those objects have an inner life. One could easily, in the words of philosopher Edmund Husserl (1859–1938), "take for *true being* what is actually a *method*."[43] In other words, enthusiasm over the methods of the natural sciences could lead scholars to see only those objects for which that method held good, ignoring or denying the existence of those objects not amenable to it. This confusion, rampant in the social sciences, led to the reduction of sociological or historical explanation to a materialist "simple" explanation of causal dependence, Dawson pointed out.[44]

---

42. Hayden White, "Collingwood and Toynbee: Transitions in English Historical Thought," *English Miscellany* VIII (1957): 151; Georg G. Iggers, *Historiography in the Twentieth Century: From Scientific Objectivity to the Postmodern Challenge* (Hanover, Conn.: Wesleyan University Press, 1997), 17; and A. F. Pollard, "A School of Historical Research," *Contemporary Review* CXVIII (1920): 507, 513.

43. Edmund Husserl, *The Crisis of European Sciences and Transcendental Phenomenology*, trans. David Carr (1936; Evanston, Ill.: Northwestern University Press, 1970), 51.

44. Dawson, "Sociology as a Science," 25.

Formation

Dawson's answer to this reductionism was boundary thinking. This involved acknowledging the limitations of disciplines and the appropriate correspondence between method and the object of knowledge. Physical science, Dawson wrote, "does not reveal the intrinsic nature of things, but deals simply with their quantitative relations and variations. Instead of giving an exhaustive causal explanation of reality, it offers a translation of reality into mathematical symbols or imagery. . . . Science provides, not a moral dynamic, but an intellectual technique."[45] In addition, "science" cannot create a universal philosophy, for there are only particular sciences. When studying human society scientifically, one must beware of the sin of simplification, that is, treating one factor as the cause of all the rest. This merely creates false analogies. The physical sciences are distinct (and therefore limited) modes of human thought existing *within* the mind of the human person and hence within history. They cannot serve as the only tool of the thinker.

Dawson's historicist view of physical science meant that his history of culture was based on different assumptions than those of the empiricists, especially concerning *facts*, *generalization*, *objectivity*, and *imagination*. Isolated facts of history were not, per se, historical. They could not speak for themselves or arrange themselves with other facts. To become truly historical, Dawson thought, facts had to be set in relation to (1) a social tradition and (2) the synthetic power of the mind of the historian. "Hence the essence of history is not to be found in facts but in traditions," he wrote. "The pure fact is not as such historical. It only becomes historical when it can be brought into relation with a social tradition so that it is seen as part of an organic whole." He gave an example:

A visitor from another planet who witnessed the Battle of Hastings would possess far greater knowledge of the facts than any modern historian, yet this knowledge would not be historical for lack of any tradition to which it could be related; whereas the child who says "William the Conqueror 1066" has already made this atom of knowledge an historical fact by relating it to a national tradition and placing it in the time-series of Christian culture.

45. Dawson, *Progress and Religion*, 174, 176.

Simply viewing the facts of an historical situation tells one little; relating them to a tradition, however, to a story over time about significance and change, locates them in their proper perspective. But not just any tradition: one had to interpret facts *in their own tradition* and not impose on them anachronistically by applying the values of a later time to them. The historical thinker must relate "historical facts to the social tradition to which they belong" and use "the spiritual beliefs and the moral and intellectual values of that tradition as the key to their interpretation."[46]

The relating of facts to traditions requires generalization—something empiricist historiography tends to dampen. For example, H. A. L. Fisher (1865–1940) wrote in the preface to his *History of Europe*, "Men wiser and more learned than I have discerned in history a plot, a rhythm, a predetermined pattern. These harmonies are concealed from me. I can see only . . . one great fact with respect to which, since it is unique, there can be no generalizations." Historians should rest content with "little truths," in a metaphysical sense. Naturally, Fisher went on in his book to make all sorts of generalizations about the Athenian empire, polytheism, and political strife partially based on implicit metaphysical assumptions. One cannot write history without generalization. Empiricism risks cutting people off from the "rich reward of engrossing, life-commanding truths," because it tends to separate history from the wider unity of knowledge and to deeper human meaning that helps make the field something more than merely fact-collecting.[47]

Dawson sought to make careful generalizations open to just such "engrossing, life-commanding truths" because he believed the universal is present in the particular. Medievalist Glenn Olsen, calling Dawson a "brilliant generalist," noted that his approach to culture stemmed from the Romantic (and historicist) idea that each age possessed its own "spirit." At the same time, in the spirit of Tocqueville and Ranke, Dawson looked for the universal truth in the specific event. These aims prompted Dawson to treat cultures as wholes connected to meaningful truths and linked history to the unity of knowledge. In this way, the

---

46. Christopher Dawson, "The Kingdom of God and History," in *Dynamics of World History*, 285–86.

47. H. A. L. Fisher, *A History of Europe* (London: Edward Arnold, 1936), v; R. R. Reno, "Thinking Critically about Critical Thinking," *First Things*, June-July 2011, 7.

idea of culture, in all of its complexity, provided impetus toward gener-alization, and Dawson often pulled this off well. Writer Aldous Huxley (1894–1963), for example, commented on Dawson's *Making of Europe*, writing that Dawson "generalizes with a sobriety and a caution worthy of the highest praise." His readers do not stumble on any of the "meta-physical hypotheses" that have excited German historians.[48]

Nevertheless, certain difficulties surround the Romantic-inspired idealism toward unity and generalization, Olsen observed. The typical temptation of cultural history is overgeneralization, "a kind of fudging" in which the historian "goes beyond his evidence." It was no wonder, he continued, that British empiricists regarded the Germanic tendency toward generalization with suspicion. One should not "co-opt every-thing under forms more general than what actually characterizes the people of a society, failing to acknowledge the great variations between individuals," Olsen wrote.[49]

Some reviewers did note certain overgeneralizations in Dawson's work. For example, one criticized his underestimation of the temporal interests of the twelfth-century papacy. Another noted that contempo-rary scholarship does not support Dawson's interpretation of the bish-ops of Merovingian and Carolingian Gaul as chosen by their people for their suitability. This interpretation may appear correct when reading documents at face value, the reviewer noted; however, current schol-arship has stressed the precarious and politically motivated nature of episcopal rule at the time. This is to say Dawson may have idealized too much the Frankish-papal alliance. The historian Peter Brown, while re-ferring to Dawson as "deeply humane and learned," noted that he may have made a "premature attempt" to ascribe the unity of early medieval Europe to a "single, pre-eminent center" in Rome. In reality, the "unity" of Western Christendom was like a geodesic dome more than a great tent upheld by a single tent-pole fixed in Rome.[50] While Dawson did

48. Glenn W. Olsen, "Why We Need Christopher Dawson," *Communio* 35 (Spring 2008): 132, 133; Aldous Huxley, "Light on the Dark Ages," review of *The Making of Europe*, *Spectator*, August 20, 1932, 235.

49. Olsen, "Why We Need Christopher Dawson," 135, 136.

50. John Francis O'Doherty, review of *Medieval Religion*, *Irish Ecclesiastical Record* XLIV (1934): 555; Alexander Murray, introduction, in *The Making of Europe*, by Christopher Dawson, xxvii–xxviii; and Peter Brown, *The Rise of Western Christendom: Triumph and Diversity, A.D. 200–1000* (Oxford: Blackwell, 2003), 5, 14, 16.

stray sometimes in his generalizations about cultural unity, his interest in cultural boundaries and places of cultural pluralism as the dynamic centers of historical change countered this tendency.

Concerning objectivity, Dawson held that one must never impose one's own assumptions on the past. In that sense, historians should strive for objective scholarship, but they should not strive for an impossible philosophical neutrality in front of bare facts. The agenda of the philosophic neutrality movement that gained ground in nineteenth-century comparative religious study, for example, proved to be impracticable, he wrote in *Religion and Culture*. Both the comparative method and the concept of evolutionary development used in comparative religion "involved judgments of value which had philosophical implications." Critical and scientific thinking does not give one a privileged view from nowhere, Dawson believed, but exists within a cultural context. "For the idea that the historian or the sociologist is in a privileged position, from which he can study any and every culture and religion in Olympian detachment, is really an absurdity and the source of countless errors," Dawson wrote. The desire of the modern historian to "transcend the tradition of his own society and to see history as one and universal" was, in fact, impossible, because "such a universal history does not exist. There is as yet no history of humanity, since humanity is not an organized society with a common tradition or a common social consciousness."[51]

Pretending to such neutral objectivity could actually promote a negative bias against nonempirical disciplines. In commenting on the work of Hungarian-born sociologist Karl Mannheim (1893–1947), Dawson wrote to his Protestant friend J. H. Oldham (1874–1969), formerly secretary of the International Missionary Council, probably around 1940, that, "I am doubtful whether the scientific impartiality, which Mannheim rightly demands for the sociologist, does not often in fact conceal a negative and exclusive attitude to theology and metaphysics, which makes co-operation [between sociology and theology] impossible."[52]

51. Dawson, *The Historic Reality of Christian Culture*, 77; Dawson, *Religion and Culture*, 12; and Dawson, "The Kingdom of God and History," 286.
52. Dawson to Oldham, no date, E-JHOP, box 9, folder 3. Mannheim was a Jewish, Hungarian-born sociologist involved in Oldham's discussion group called the Moot, which Dawson was also part of for a short time—see chapter 7.

Instead, one must try to understand human realities from within their own frames of reference, including religious frames of reference. "The more learned and conscientious a historian is," Dawson wrote, "the more conscious he is of the relativity of his own knowledge, and the more ready he is to treat the culture that he is studying as an end in itself, an autonomous world which follows its own laws and owes no allegiance to the standards and ideals of another civilization." History deals with civilizations and cultures rather than civilization in an absolute sense, he continued, "with the development of particular societies and not with the progress of humanity."[53] At the same time, each civilization or culture, within its own framework, also exists *sub specie aeternitatis*.

Instead of "Olympian detachment" that pretended to view the past "objectively" and without assumptions, Dawson recognized the importance of imaginative vision in history. Mastery of facts and methods of empiricist historiography could not alone create a great work. The historian also needs a penetrating insight and synthetic imagination to link facts into a meaningful narrative. Dawson wrote:

> The academic historian is perfectly right in insisting on the importance of the techniques of historical criticism and research. But the mastery of these techniques will not produce great history, any more than a mastery of metrical technique will produce great poetry. For this something more is necessary—intuitive understanding, creative imagination, and finally a universal vision transcending the relative limitations of a particular field of historical study. The experience of the great historians such as Tocqueville and Ranke leads me to believe that a universal metahistorical vision of this kind, partaking more of the nature of religious contemplation than of scientific generalization, lies very close to the sources of their creative power.[54]

Dawson highlighted the value of critical research methods but also the necessity of intuition, imagination, and what he called "universal vision" in comprehending and communicating history.

His attention in this extended quotation to Tocqueville and Ranke is revealing of Dawson's own view of history. Tocqueville wrote in *Democracy in America:* "It is not necessary that God himself should speak

53. Dawson, "The Kingdom of God and History," 286.
54. Dawson, "The Problem of Metahistory," 309–10.

in order that we may discover the unquestionable signs of his will. It is enough to ascertain what is the habitual course of nature and the constant tendency of events." This vision lay close to the source of Tocqueville's "creative power," Dawson noted. If one compares Tocqueville with other historians of his time, such as François Mignet (1796–1884) or Adolphe Thiers (1797–1877), who wrote more conventional narratives of political history, one is forced to admit that Tocqueville was the greater historian because he was more profound. He was more profound because of the breadth of his spiritual vision.[55]

Leopold von Ranke, mentioned in the previous chapter in connection to historicism, wrote a massive corpus of scholarship, including *Die Römischen Päpste* (1834–1836). He was misunderstood in the English-speaking world by those who failed to read him in the context of German idealism. He was characterized as a positivist aiming for a purely factual account of the past "wie es eigentlich gewesen," often translated as "how it actually was." Georg Iggers argued this phrase should instead be translated as "how it essentially was."[56] The mere assembly of facts is not "history," for historical events are only partially visible. Besides documentary analysis, one must employ intuition and contemplation of wholes in order to choose among the most representative facts. By these dual sets of methodologies, one will illustrate how things "essentially" were, penetrating to the inner causal nexus among events and ideas within their own contexts.

Ranke believed history and the cultural sciences differ from the physical sciences by their focus on human values and intentions. "I am of the opinion," Ranke wrote, "that historical science at its best is both called upon and able to rise in its own way from the investigation and contemplation of the particular to a general view of events and to the recognition of their objectively existing relatedness."[57] Interested in style as much as the science of research, Ranke composed his works as wholes, and only then did he go back to add his reference notes. In ad-

---

55. Dawson, "The Problem of Metahistory," 308–9; Alexis de Tocqueville, *Democracy in America*, vol. 1 (New York: Vintage Books, 1972), 7.

56. Leopold von Ranke, "Preface to the First Edition of *Histories of the Latin and Germanic Peoples*," in *The Theory and Practice of History*, ed. Georg G. Iggers (1824; New York: Routledge, 2011), 86; Georg G. Iggers, introduction, in *The Theory and Practice of History*, xiv.

57. Ranke, "On the Relations of History and Philosophy," in *The Theory and Practice of History*, 6.

dition, later (empiricist) historians believed that Ranke would critically examine sources free from the biases of received tradition. However, he wrote as a Lutheran infused with German idealism and situated in the midst of political struggles. Like Tocqueville, he thought that history testifies to God: "In all of history God dwells, lives, can be recognized. Every deed gives testimony of Him, every moment preaches His name, but most of all, it seems to me, does so the connectedness of History." This faith that facts contain a connection to something beyond them animated early German historicism. Behind Ranke's willingness to immerse himself in the chaos of data and events that the historical record contained was his belief that an accurate and compelling narrative could nevertheless emerge from a coherent vision.[58]

That belief, that commitment to a vision, served as Ranke's "pre-archival mind," to borrow a phrase from historian Michael Bentley: the universal quality Ranke brought *to* his research. For Dawson, the work of great historians like Tocqueville and Ranke was a constant conversation between *a priori* beliefs and *a posteriori* evidential experience. Dawson viewed historical reason as the coordination of a faith or a vision (prearchival beliefs, judgments, assumptions, and insights) *with* empirical facts. This reasoning began not from a view from nowhere but from real questions emerging out of the historian's fundamental assumptions about reality in his or her present. These questions propelled the historical mind to interpret the facts discovered through critical and technical skills. The questions began in self-knowledge, for as literary theorist Hayden White (1928–2018) later wrote: "Knowledge is a product of a wrestling not only with the 'facts' but with one's self."[59]

---

58. Hayden White, *Metahistory: The Historical Imagination in Nineteenth-Century Europe* (Baltimore: Johns Hopkins University Press, 1973), 190; Christopher Shannon and Christopher O. Blum, *The Past as Pilgrimage: Narrative, Tradition and the Renewal of Catholic History* (Front Royal, Va.: Christendom Press, 2014), 39; and Anthony Grafton, "How the Historian Found His Muse: Ranke's Path to the Footnote," in *The Modern Historiography Reader: Western Sources*, ed. Adam Budd (New York: Routledge, 2009), 179. The quotation from Ranke about God is from Ranke, "Letter to Heinrich," in *The Theory and Practice of History*, 4.

59. White, *Metahistory*, 192; Michael Bentley, *Modern Historiography: An Introduction* (London: Routledge, 1999), 41.

Religious Faith and Dawson's History of Culture

When Dawson "wrestled with himself," he chose not to separate faith from facts any more than Tocqueville or Ranke had. The way he maintained that connection set him apart not only from the main camp of British historians in the early twentieth century but also from the religious historians, who primarily wrote *ecclesiastical historiography* concerned with the institutional church and its hierarchy, theology, morality, liturgy, and discipline.[60] Like political history during the nineteenth century, European ecclesiastical history developed in response to the opening of archives and the study of documents. In England, the great figures of ecclesiastical history were members of the Church of England,[61] though significant Catholic figures wrote, too.[62] These historians equated "religion" with "institutional church."

Dawson sought to write a new kind of history that departed not only from the nation as the basic object of study in secular history but also from empiricist assumptions and from the institutional church as the basic object of study in religious history. He wanted to study religion not so much as an institution but as a cultural force that could manifest itself inside or outside of churches. To do this, he made use of the social sciences and comparative religion to investigate the role of religion in human culture and cultural change in world history.

Dawson's concept of culture helped him to connect religion and other elements of the historical world so often fragmented into specialized fields by researches, to show their relations and mutual influence.

60. John Alzog, *Manual of Universal Church History*, trans. F. J. Pabisch and Thos. S. Byrne, vol. 1 (Cincinnati, Ohio: Robert Clarke, 1874), 7–9.

61. For example, William Stubbs (1825–1901), bishop of Oxford. His *Councils and Ecclesiastical Documents Covering the History of the Anglo-Saxon Church* (1878) provided a foundation for William Bright (1824–1901), Regius Professor of Ecclesiastical History at Oxford, in his *Chapters of Early English Church History* (1878), which was concerned with the conversion of England to the Christian faith and the great figures in that development, such as St. Columba and St. Aidan.

62. Such as John Lingard (1771–1851), a priest, who published his *Antiquities of the Anglo-Saxon Church* in 1806; Francis Gasquet (1846–1929), cardinal and prior of the Downside Benedictine community, who published his two-volume *Henry VIII and the English Monasteries* in 1888–1889; Philip Hughes, a priest, who published vol. 1 of his *History of the Church* in 1934; and David Mathew (1902–1975), bishop auxiliary of Westminster during the Second World War, who published his *Catholicism in England 1535–1935, Portrait of a Minority: Its Culture and Tradition* in 1936.

Formation

In 1932, Dawson wrote in the introduction to his *Making of Europe* that, "This [book] is not a history of the Church or a history of Christianity; it is a history of a culture."[63] In 1950, he explained what he had been trying to accomplish for decades:

On the one side, the scientific historian has concentrated his researches on the criticism of sources and documents; on the other, the student of Christianity has devoted himself to the history of dogma and ecclesiastical institutions, with the result that we have a number of highly developed separate studies—political history, constitutional history, and economic history, on the one side, and ecclesiastical history, the history of dogma, and liturgiology on the other. But the vital subject of the creative interaction of religion and culture in the life of Western society has been left out and almost forgotten, since from its nature it has no place in the organized scheme of specialized disciplines.[64]

Dawson proposed cultural history as a bridge between ecclesiastical history and other forms of academic history. Because he considered culture as both secular and religious, linked in a common way of life, this concept could serve as a shared space between too-often mutually exclusive histories.

This attention to the creative interaction of religion and culture differentiated him from other British Catholic historians such as Lord Acton and Hilaire Belloc. Dawson's faith shaped his historiography through the intellectual architecture and boundary thinking of his cultural mind, concerned with the unity and differentiation of knowledge. By contrast, Acton tended to separate his faith and history, while Belloc suffocated his history with his faith.

Ironically, Acton profoundly influenced not later Catholic historians but *non-Catholic* historians of the early twentieth century such as G. P. Gooch and George Trevelyan, whereas it was Belloc's ideas that often inspired the English Catholic intellectual community that flourished between the world wars. Neither Acton nor Belloc was great for a particular work of history, but both were great for the same reason: the character of their historical minds, Acton for his erudition and Belloc

63. Dawson, *The Making of Europe*, 7.
64. Dawson, *Religion and the Rise of Western Culture*, 12–13.

for his historical imagination and sensitivity to historical perspective.

But their approach to *facts* was problematic from a Dawsonian perspective. Acton's commitment to neutralist objectivity has already been discussed. Döllinger trained him as a scientific, critical historian and taught him to hate absolutism and love truth, but Acton's love of truth meant almost exclusively *historical* truth. Because he refused "to see style as an integral part of a written document," Acton loved facts over interpretation and imagination.[65] This meant that he would not write until he saw *all* the sources for a subject. This, along with his sense of isolation, made it difficult for him to express the results of his research as a whole (as in the case of Namier) or even to produce a book at all. He is known rather for his published articles, scattered lectures, vast erudition, and posthumous collections such as *Lectures on Modern History* (1906) and *The History of Freedom and other Essays* (1907).

If Acton overvalued facts, Belloc undervalued them. He consciously strove to communicate history with literary style. *The Path to Rome* (1902) secured Belloc's literary reputation, and during the Edwardian era, he acquired a public literary personality as a lover of beer, wine, songs, walking, and sailing. *Robespierre* (1901) revealed Belloc's séance-like approach to history: "Very often I have sat alone at evening before a fire of logs in a room near the Rue St. Honoré, and tried to call up for myself the great men who from that air challenged necessity, and, within the screen of their armies, created the modern world." Belloc continued:

In the attempt to fix exactly an historic figure, it is necessary first to make the physical environment reappear. In the great phrase of Michelet such history must be 'a resurrection,' and there is no resurrection without the resurrection of the flesh. In the second place, it is necessary to admit laborious and dusty discussion, not only of disputed events, but of the inner workings of a mind.[66]

Belloc later explained "resurrection of the flesh" in the *Dublin Review*. He brought into an historical portrait of a person or an event of the

---

65. Seamus F. Deane, "Lord Acton and Edmund Burke," *Journal of the History of Ideas* XXXIII (1972): 334.

66. Hilaire Belloc, *Robespierre: A Study* (1901; London: Nisbet, 1927), xiii, xv–xvi.

past the numerous living details such as time of day, landscape, weather, bodily movement (walking, running), physical location in relation to buildings or other people, timing of events, physical appearance and moods, geographical location, etc. This was important because "*when you have presented the mere physical picture so vividly and so truly, a great number of false judgements, a whole series of moral actions in the men concerned, which bias might presuppose, are seen to be impossible.*" Belloc emphasized the physical context because this framed and limited "the subjective part of history in such a manner as to subject the relation of motive and of human actions to much the same standard as they receive from our daily sight and hearing and touch of contemporary things."[67] He sought to make the past living, to approach it from a broad engagement with life in the present, and to show that the facts of history were not just present in archives but also in past people and their environments, which the imagination could reconstruct.

Historical thinking demanded three kinds of accuracy, according to Belloc: (1) the general atmosphere of an event (Belloc's "resurrection of the flesh" idea), (2) statements of motive and direction in action: accuracy in the relation of one statement to those around it (i.e., context and spirit of a text or person), and (3) statements of dates, wording of documents, etc. Belloc admitted that "no one writing history to-day" had been guiltier than himself of trespassing against the third principle. However, he considered the first two types of accuracy as far more important: "Accuracy in general atmosphere and accuracy in relation of one statement to another can only be judged by a man already possessed of a full knowledge of the subject; whereas accuracy in positive detail such as dates can be settled by reference to a few admitted authorities, or in the last resort to documents, and the statements are of their nature things which any man can judge for himself."[68] But, one could question Belloc, is not "full knowledge of the subject" related significantly to said "positive detail?" Is not the essence of a subject seen *through* accurate facts, as Ranke might say?

---

67. Hilaire Belloc, "On a Method of Writing History," *Dublin Review* CXLIX (1911): 143, 152. Emphasis in the original.

68. Hilaire Belloc, "Professor Bury's *History of Freedom of Thought*," *Dublin Review* CLIV (1914): 156–58.

Because Belloc clearly distinguished between empirical facts and their interpretation, he understood the power of "subversive stories" in ways that Acton did not and worked to counteract them. The "anti-Catholic bias of history is a matter curiously missed by most modern Catholics," Belloc wrote. He fought to set the record straight, especially in the case of rationalists such as Edward Gibbon, H. G. Wells, and J. B. Bury. In contrast to Dawson's assessement of Gibbon, Gibbon's attack on Christianity was poor history, Belloc thought, because it did not "weigh" its opponent accurately in regard to the actual historical significance the church had for the formation of Europe.[69] Such a perspective exerted a subtly powerful secularizing influence, and Belloc would certainly have agreed with philosopher Russell Hittinger's assessment: without having to address theology, Gibbon had subtly advanced an apology against Christianity by simply rendering it a "a relatively minor, though unfortunate, chapter in the history and development of Western culture." Most people "care little for metaphysical debate, but they are willing to entertain a new story." The subversive story "consists in [an] invitation to take a novel view of history; and . . . it does not so much ask for a consent to carefully worked-out philosophical premises, but calls for a conversion of perspective."[70] Belloc thought the same about H. G. Wells's *Outline of History* and Bury's *History of Freedom*. Facts or literal statements could be "true," but they could also convey the exact opposite of historical truth depending on the aim or tone of the narrative that embeds those facts or statements. The real task of the historian was to strive for accuracy in the three areas outlined above and to write a properly proportioned narrative. "This does not mean that a man cannot write history unless he is a Catholic," Belloc wrote, "but it does mean that he cannot write the history of Europe unless he knows what the Faith is, and puts it where it

69. Hilaire Belloc, "A Page of Gibbon," *Dublin Review* CLIX (1916): 362, 363; Hilaire Belloc, "The Entry into the Dark Ages," review of *The Cambridge Mediaeval History*, vol. I, *Dublin Review* CLI (1912): 359.

70. Russell Hittinger, "The Two Cities and the Modern World: A Dawsonian Assessment," *Modern Age* XXVIII (1984): 193–94; Russell Hittinger, "The Metahistorical Vision of Christopher Dawson," in *The Dynamic Character of Christian Culture*, ed. Peter J. Cataldo (New York: University Press of America, 1984), 7–8. Dawson was very aware of the power of historical narratives to shape fundamental views of reality; see chapter 5, "Communism and the Christian Interpretation of History," in his *Religion and the Modern State*.

should be, at the centre of our system."[71] In this way, Belloc's history became a branch of apologetics.[72] While Dawson shared Belloc's disdain for rationalist history, he admired him more as a poet than as an historian because he considered Belloc's historical views unreliable and he did not share his triumphant Catholicism. Europe was not always "the Faith," as Belloc thought, and his views of facts and historical accuracy, while insightful, were flawed.[73]

If Belloc sometimes overemphasized the claims of faith upon his historical writing, Acton underemphasized them. There is no doubt, however, that Acton's Catholicism was real. As a young scholar, he published a Catholic journal, *The Rambler*, hoping to influence Catholic intellectual life, worshipped and married as a Catholic, and wanted his children to be educated as Catholics. He practiced his faith until the end of his life, but he also took an unfavorable view of the exercise of church authority in the past to such an extent that his mind became vulnerable to the secularizing influences of his age. This intellectual trajectory began when, in the course of his archival tours, he became aware of the efforts of other Catholic historians to further the interests of their church. With wit, dry humor, and immense learning, he sought to expose the truth of the past about the corruption of power, so that Catholic people would not commit the sin of persecution again—as in his article "The Massacre of St. Bartholomew" (1869).[74] He thought that dedication to the truth could never be ultimately detrimental to the church.

The later Acton, however, began to hold ideas that sat only loosely with Catholic tradition, such as hatred of the hierarchy, loss of faith in authority, and preoccupation with moral truth to the neglect of doctrinal truth. He lost intellectual sympathy with John Henry Newman, who remained largely unmoved by the nineteenth-century cult of progress.

71. Belloc, "The Entry into the Dark Ages," 359, 361; Belloc, "Professor Bury's *History of Freedom of Thought*," 160, 167.

72. James R. Lothian, *The Making and Unmaking of the English Catholic Intellectual Community, 1910–1950* (Notre Dame, Ind.: University of Notre Dame Press, 2009), 43–50.

73. Scott, *A Historian and His World*, 71, 96.

74. Lord Acton, "The Massacre of St. Bartholomew," in *Essays in the Study and Writing of History*, ed. J. Rufus Fears, vol. 2 of *Selected Writings of Lord Acton* (Indianapolis, Ind.: LibertyClassics, 1986), 198–240.

Owen Chadwick remarked that the Acton of the 1860s could not have
affected the British mind like the Acton of the 1880s and 1890s, "despite
the total absence of any published work which changed anyone's historical view about any particular event." Acton believed it the vocation
of the historian to mix historical apprehension with ethical axioms,
which led him to absorb contemporary assumptions about the pure
benevolence of liberalism and progress. These ideals gave his historical
mind shape and wide influence.[75]

Acton's commitment to neutralist objectivity separated his supernatural faith from his history. Thus, contemporary assumptions
increasingly influenced his historical vision, and he came to think of
truth in exclusively historical terms. In Chadwick's opinion, Acton
thought "a person's attitude to history and his philosophy of life and
morality are not two different attitudes but are the same."[76] Ranke ultimately made a similar kind of historical recuctionism in which, Iggers
pointed out, especially in his idealistic theory of the state: "not philosophy but history is the true guide to value."[77] Similarly, Acton held that
"history is the true demonstration of Religion."[78] He had little sympathy
for philosophy, so, for him, scientific history became the master discipline, and his idea of progress as advance in knowledge and freedom
became the interpretive framework of reality.[79] Such an exalted view
of history threatened to push the discipline beyond its limitations, beyond its place as a distinct discipline among others. Butterfield once
wrote, "The historian, like other specialists, easily imagines that his
own pocket of thinking is the whole universe of thought." He continued:
"It would seem that the decline of religion gives undue power to history
in the shaping of men's mind . . . and multitudes of young students have
even come to the study of technical history in the expectation that it
would help them to shape their fundamental views about life. It is an

75. Owen Chadwick, *Acton and History* (Cambridge: Cambridge University Press, 1998), 65,
124, 126, 187, 189, 192–99, 202–3. The young Acton had, in fact, previoulsy criticized writing history
as the story of progress—see Lord Acton, "Review of Philp's *History of Progress in Great Britain*," in
Essays in the Study and Writing of History, 31–33.

76. Chadwick, *Acton and History*, 211.

77. Iggers, introduction, in *The Theory and Practice of History*, xxxi.

78. Acton, *A Lecture on the Study of History*, 32.

79. Lionel Kochan, *Acton on History* (Port Washington, N.Y.: Kennikat, 1954), 115, 119.

expectation that is often disappointed."[80] History alone cannot explain the fundamental problems of life, and Acton did not seem to be aware of how close he had drifted to a secular worldview.

Acton's lack of a cultural mind for integrating multiple disciplines and retaining critical sensitivity to cultural assumptions of his own day meant he succumbed to some of those assumptions. He failed to work out a "unified intellectual framework for his life's work," MacDougall noted; "His *magnum opus*, a History of Liberty, could never be written until he had resolved the conflict between his Catholicism and his Liberalism on the one hand, and his Liberalism and History on the other."[81] His aversion to philosophy, however, made such reconciliation impossible. He wrestled with facts but not enough with himself.

Dawson, on the other hand, was more philosophically orientated than Acton. He was able to work out a synthesis of empirical disciplines such as anthropology, sociology, history, and comparative religion with nonempirical fields such as theology and philosophy to create a coherent cultural vision. This gave a fundamental unity to his work as a whole, based on understanding the limits of each discipline and their places in the unity of knowledge. Despite Acton's lack of intellectual architecture and boundary thinking rules of the cultural mind, his failure to reconcile faith and reason, and his interpretation of history in terms of the theory of progress, these weaknesses did not destroy the value of Acton's work. If one is "a good historian, as Acton was, your preconceived metahistorical idea will not destroy the value of the historical research which has been motivated by it," Dawson noted.[82]

Unlike Acton, Belloc did not succumb to the secularizing influences of his day. His faith remained in constant touch with his thought due to its nature. In the year of Belloc's birth, the Franco-Prussian war broke out, and Pope Pius IX (who reigned from 1846 to 1878) declared the doctrine of papal infallibility. Both events greatly shaped Belloc's life, a biographer noted: first by forcing his family to flee France and instilling in him a dislike of Germany, and second by encouraging Belloc in

80. Herbert Butterfield, *Man on His Past: The Study of the History of Historical Scholarship* (1955; Boston: Beacon, 1960), 18, 30–31.
81. Hugh A. MacDougall, *The Acton-Newman Relations: The Dilemma of Christian Liberalism* (New York: Fordham University Press, 1962), 184.
82. Dawson, "The Problem of Metahistory," 304–5.

ultramontane views on theology and church politics. The claim of infallible authority persuaded Belloc of Catholicism's uniqueness and divine origin. The very element of Catholicism that repelled Acton attracted Belloc. The authority of the institutional church was important to him, though he disagreed with the position of neutrality taken by Pope Benedict XV (who reigned from 1914 to 1922) during the Great War. In addition, Belloc's faith seemed steeped in the intellectual, with little emotion, as in his criticisms of Blaise Pascal's "emotional" faith in *Characters of the Reformation*. In the opinion of a biographer, Belloc did not possess "personal religion." He could not understand the idea of "union with God" in the mystics like St. John of the Cross and St. Theresa, though he was moved by personal holiness and the ritual of Benediction.[83]

Belloc's strong sense of religion as object, as institution, as church, meant that his religious history focused on great political and ecclesiastical churchmen of the past, as in *Richelieu* (1929). He focused on institutional religion so exclusively that he sometimes smothered other realities of history: "The Faith is Europe and Europe is the Faith," he wrote.[84] Dawson argued in a much more nuanced fashion that the making of Europe resulted from the interaction of four major forces: the Greek intellectual and artistic tradition, the Roman Empire and its ideal of unity, the native or "barbarian" peoples who provided the raw materials of Europe, and Christianity with its ecclesiastical organization and spiritual influence. Dawson's nontriumphalist faith, very different than Belloc's, more easily supported wide, ecumenical views and protected the proper autonomy of the secular order.

Nevertheless, Belloc did possess more of an intellectual architecture than did Acton, even though he was inferior to him simply as a historian. Belloc criticized using history to make a philosophical point, because this could easily make for poor history. "The character which is not obtainable by man is an historically certain philosophy," he wrote in 1914, rebutting the central contradiction within German historicism. "We cannot, merely as historians, solve the problem of the universe and

83. A. N. Wilson, *Hilaire Belloc* (1984; London: Gibson Square Books, 2003), 3, 20, 257, 258, 259; Hilaire Belloc, *Characters of the Reformation* (London: Sheed & Ward, 1936), 303–312.

84. Hilaire Belloc, *Europe and the Faith* (London: Constable, 1920), 3, 5; John P. McCarthy, "Hilaire Belloc and Catholic History," *Thought* LXVII (1992): 65.

be certain that the religion or philosophy which we take for granted in our work is the true one. That is a matter not of human science but of Faith." If the general outline of reality is wrong, if people make an "original and general error" at the beginning of their thinking about human life and history, no amount of detailed historical knowledge piled into such a scheme can possibility fix that original error. Dawson agreed, for he wrote that "if we rely on history alone we can never hope to transcend the sphere of relativity; it is only in religion and metaphysics that we can find truths that claim absolute and eternal validity."[85] Like Dawson, Belloc recognized a clear difference between *historical* thinking and *philosophical* or *theological* thinking and how those differences related to historiography.

Dawson's integration of faith and reason, in light of a more robust grasp of the unity and differentiation of knowledge, pushed him into a more interdisciplinary path marked out by the rules of his cultural mind. In this way, he showed himself in the tradition of Newman, whereas both Acton and Belloc had an aversion to Newman.[86] Dawson's attachment to the unity of knowledge and boundary thinking kept history and faith in their proper places, respecting the methods of both.

Unlike the bracketed Christian faith of Acton or the triumphalist faith of Belloc, Dawson's *sacramental* faith operated to expand and deepen both his historical writing and his cultural mind. He held that it may be impossible for a non-Christian to fully understand the Christian view of history, for Christian revelation is essentially historical in nature. Far from creating a narrow and sectarian historical vision, however, the Christian faith possessed resources that could help the historian see reality in its fullness in ways accessible to a universal audience by placing the particular in intimate relation to the universal—as

85. Belloc, "Professor Bury's *History of Freedom of Thought*," 156; Belloc, "The Entry into the Dark Ages," 367; and Dawson, "The Kingdom of God and History," 286–87.

86. Acton fell out with Newman in disagreements over the papacy, and Belloc, who had attended Newman's Oratory school in Birmingham as a young man, thought him too remote a figure and too much of a don. Belloc preferred the political and social radicalism of Henry Cardinal Manning (1808–1892) to Newman's more theological and spiritual orientation, as Lothian wrote (Lothian, *The Making and Unmaking of the English Catholic Intellectual Community, 1910–1950*, 8, 10–11).

Ranke himself had attempted. For example, if the Incarnation of Christ is the basis of time, as it already is for the Gregorian calendar, the most widely used international calendar in the world, then there is the possibility of an underlying spiritual unity behind the entire historic process. There is an order and a significance behind the apparently disconnected chaos of world history. This order allows one to interpret history *sub specie aeternitatis*, which means that the humble details of history gain a significance and a dignity in their connection to God—the classic historicist nexus. As historians lost their supernatural faith and their metaphysics, the particular and the universal came apart or realigned according to worldly faiths ("false universals") like Acton's history of freedom. But Dawson retained a sacramental and humble faith that the true progress of history is a mystery and that the seemingly smallest events have great significance. Beneath the surface-world of cause and effect, hidden spiritual forces and the laws of being operate.[87]

For example, to the ordinary educated person looking at the world in A.D. 33, the attempts of the Roman government "to solve the economic crisis by a policy of free credit to producers must have seemed far more promising that the doings of the obscure group of Jewish fanatics in an upper chamber at Jerusalem." Nevertheless, Dawson wrote, "there is no doubt today which was the most important and which availed most to alter the lot of humanity." Even the non-Christian historian had to agree that the entire Roman world of power and wealth and culture and corruption sank in a flood of ruin and that the other world, the one of apostles and martyrs, survived and laid the foundations for a new civilization. Beneath the surface of history, hidden spiritual forces move. This is a matter of historical perspective, and one

87. Dawson, "The Kingdom of God and History," 288, 299; Christopher Dawson, "The Christian View of History," in *Dynamics of World History*, 247–248; and Christopher Dawson, "History and the Christian Revelation," in *Dynamics of World History*, 269. Hayden White attacked Dawson for believing it was difficult for a non-Christian to understand the full meaning of subjects such as the Christian Middle Ages. Dawson meant, White wrote, that there is "a truth available in the historical documents which requires not human understanding, historical ability, but a special epistemological dispensation." Thus, Dawson held an "anti-historical view." Dawson might have somewhat agreed, I think, for he did not reduce all knowledge to history. See White, "Religion, Culture and Western Civilization in Christopher Dawson's Idea of History," fn. 67. Other believing historians, too, have noticed their unique, internal link to the religious past in a way that is almost autobiographical. See Jay D. Green, *Christian Historiography: Five Rival Versions* (Waco, Tex.: Baylor University Press, 2015), 32.

open to Christian or non-Christian: the world is ruled by powers that it does not know. Those who seem to be the "makers of history are in reality its creatures," Dawson wrote. The seemingly smallest events can have the greatest of significance, he observed in *Progress and Religion*, such as when Mohammad saw human life as transitory as the beat of a gnat's wing in comparison with the Divine Unity in the cave of Mount Hira, an experience that has transformed the entire way of life of whole peoples ever since.[88]

Historian Dermot Quinn commented that by looking for meaning beyond the local and the particular, the Christian historical vision finds meaning *in* the local. He wrote that for Dawson, "sacred history" had to respect the dignity of little truths if it intended to claim respect for greater ones. "By honoring sources it honors itself," Quinn noted. Unlike Belloc, Christian faith grounded Dawson's commitment to the empirical facts of history. Jesus Christ, after all, became a "little fact," a baby in a manger in Bethlehem. Dawson's sacramental vision helped him to see the historical past in a way that respected the truth of that past, even in the humble statement of dates and wording of documents that Belloc sometimes treated lightly. Dawson wrote that the Incarnation does not destroy or supersede nature. "It is analogous and complementary to it, since it restores and extends man's natural function as the bond of union between the material and the spiritual worlds." Grace builds on nature, and the humble details of history must form the foundation of any Christian view of history that is worth anything at all.[89]

Dawson's faith connected his mind intimately to both material and spiritual reality. While he viewed the past as subject to social, economic, and geographic determinations (FWP), the spiritual and intellectual dimension of history (I) made him attentive to the freedom of individuals and the contingency of events. History is not a "closed order" in which each stage is inevitably caused by the previous one. "There is in

88. Dawson, "History and the Christian Revelation," 270–71; Dawson, "The Kingdom of God and History," 299; and Dawson, *Progress and Religion*, 68.

89. Dermot Quinn, introduction, in *Dynamics of World History*, xxv; Dermot Quinn, "Christopher Dawson and Historical Imagination," *The Chesterton Review* XXVI, no. 4 (2000): 476; and Dawson, *Progress and Religion*, 138.

it always a mysterious and inexplicable element, due not only to the influence of chance or the initiative of the individual genius, but also to the creative power of spiritual forces."[90] Therefore, understanding Christianity "involves a good deal more than the study of ecclesiastical history in the traditional sense," he wrote.

It involves the study of two different processes which act simultaneously on mankind in the course of time. On the one hand, there is the process of culture formation and change, which is the subject of anthropology, history and allied disciplines; and on the other there is the process of revelation and the action of divine grace which has created a spiritual society and a sacred history . . . studied only as a part of theology.[91]

Ecclesiastical history had to come into relation to material sources outside itself in order to avoid exclusive identification with the history of religious institutions and their theologies. The sociological and cultural function of religion, in general, had to join with the specific history of Christianity and its institutions.[92]

As an example of this broadened ecclesiastical history, Dawson wrote about the decay of the Roman Empire, which created a social and spiritual vacuum attracting many kinds of spiritual forces:

The mystery religions of Asia Minor spread westwards in the same way as Christianity itself, and the religion of Mithras accompanied the Roman armies to the Danube and the Rhine and the British frontier. The Egyptian worship of Isis and the Syrian cults of Adonis and Atargatis, Hadad of Baalbek, and the Sun-God of Emesa, followed the rising tide of Syrian trade and migration to the West, while in the oriental underworld new religions, like Manichaeanism, were coming into existence."

The essential historical question was: how had Christianity survived in such an environment? Here is where Dawson connected his sense of religion as both spiritual force in society *and* institution: "If Christianity had been merely one among the oriental sects and mystery religions of the Roman Empire it must inevitably have been drawn into this orien-

---

90. Dawson, *The Making of Europe*, 33.
91. Dawson, *The Formation of Christendom*, 18.
92. Hittinger, "The Metahistorical Vision of Christopher Dawson," 8, 9.

tal syncretism. It survived because it possessed a system of ecclesiastical organization and a principle of social authority that distinguished it from all the other religious bodies of the age."[93] In this way, Dawson combined his broad understanding of religion as spiritual and social force with religion as institution, allowing him to widen ecclesiastical history and connect it to a wider history of culture in ways that Acton and Belloc did not do.

Dawson thought literary historians, not ecclesiastical historians, had done the best work toward a new and broader religious history. "With all his faults," he commented, the rationalist literary critic Charles Augustin Sainte-Beuve (1804–1869) was a "real religious historian" when he wrote his *Port Royal* (1837–1859). That work, a study of the Jansenist abbey of Port-Royal-des-Champs, near Paris, greatly influenced French thought on history, in particular, religious history. Sainte-Beuve and his associates, such as historians Hippolyte Taine (1828–1893) and Ernest Renan (1823–1892), sought a new kind of history, one less preoccupied with politics and more concerned with reconstructing the whole, vanished life of a time, from its ideas to its habits and fashions based on new sources and new methods. These French men of letters prefigured some of the concerns of the *Annales* in the twentieth century.[94]

In his own day, Dawson pointed to the admirable work of the American intellectual historian and atheist Perry Miller (1905–1963), whose *New England Mind: The Seventeenth Century* appeared in 1939. Miller broke down his study of puritanism into a synchronic anatomy of cultural themes and a diachronic narrative of change, just as Dawson himself did in his culture-study. Miller, too, sought to understand the modern world through examination of a major movement of the Western intellect, puritanism, and to view it as a "living force" that shaped fundamental concepts of modern culture. He viewed puritanism as an expression of a "recurrent spiritual answer to interrogations eternally posed by human existence," but within the context of "peculiar accidents of time

93. Dawson, *The Making of Europe*, 33, 37, 38.

94. Jonathan Dewald, "'À la Table de Magny': Nineteenth-Century French Men of Letters and the Sources of Modern Historical Thought," *American Historical Review* 108, no. 4 (2003): 1020, 1027; Christopher Dawson, *The Dividing of Christendom* (Garden City, N.Y.: Image Books, 1965), 16.

and place." By this, he, like Dawson, entered into the historicist nexus of the eternal and the contingent.[95] While personal religious faith might aid this kind of history, it was not absolutely necessary.

On the Catholic side, Dawson pointed to the great work of Henri Bremond (1865–1933), a French historian and theological modernist who published his twelve-volume *Histoire litteraire du sentiment religieux en France depuis la fin des Guerres de Religion jusqu'à nos jours* in the years from 1916 to 1936. Influenced by Sainte-Beuve, John Henry Newman, and Baron Friedrich von Hügel, Bremond lectured at Strasbourg during the early 1920s, where his concern for historical psychology influenced Lucien Febvre's work on the Reformation, as the *Annales* movement took shape. Bremond drew from a wide variety of printed sources with the intent—in his first volume—of studying the "inner life of French Catholicism during the seventeenth century." Bremond's historicist purpose involved studying those who exerted an influence and in whom "there has been, so to speak, an incarnation of some particular aspect of the religious genius of the epoch." To make that genius intelligible, his method compared writers and saints, for he saw these figures as complementary to each other and as evidence for the connection of faith and the intellect to life and human will in the period under consideration. Religious treatises needed to be tested against biographies to keep them in touch with reality, and *thought* needed to be viewed in relation to the active life of people striving for holiness in the broader culture to live out the Christian faith. This corresponded with Dawson's own sociological method of studying "I" in relation to "FWP," as discussed in chapter 2.

Like Bremond's work, Dawson's history focused on this connection of faith and life. Dawson wrote about how the rule of St. Benedict (c. 480–c. 547), for example, and the subsequent modification of monastic life and wider European history through the efforts of great active figures such as St. Boniface (c. 675–754) first made Germany a "living member of the European society." Studying the connection between the ideals and rules in Benedict's document to changing ways of life in suc-

95. Perry Miller, *The New England Mind: The Seventeenth Century* (1939; Cambridge, Mass.: Harvard University Press, 1954), vii–viii, 4; Dawson, *The Dividing of Christendom*, 16.

ceeding centuries made culture intelligible because it revealed *how* the religious vision of a people modified their common lives over time. This connection of belief or thought to the wider culture pervaded Dawson's historiography, and not only in a Christian context. It was a universal method he used to examine any culture.[96]

For the rapprochement of ecclesiastical and other forms of historiography to happen, ecclesiastical historians had to lose their apologetical edge. Unlike Belloc, the star Oxford debater, Dawson was not a controversialist. He sought to understand the past on its own terms: "it is impossible to understand the past unless we understand the things for which the men of the past cared most."[97] One must attempt to view the past through the eyes of those who lived there. That was true objectivity. In his introduction to *The Making of Europe* (1932), he wrote: "If I have written at length on these matters [religion], it is not to prove a theological point or to justify a religious point of view, but to explain the past."[98] Acton and the best traditions of "scientific history" would have agreed with this purpose, which is why Dawson drew the admiration of contemporary British historians such as H. A. L. Fisher. In his review of *The Making of Europe*, Fisher noted that, "Mr. Dawson is a real historian. We have seldom read a book by a young writer so remarkable by reason of its combination of unusual learning with a firm grasp of general lines and principles, and a freshness and independence of judgment."[99] Further, from the great Cambridge historian and Catholic monk David Knowles came an immense respect, as when he wrote in an obituary for Dawson that, "to those who were young, or not so old, in the late 1920s and the 1930s he [Dawson] will always remain as a master."[100] Dawson's vision of connecting religion and culture in his historiography drew applause from those inside and outside Catholicism.

Nonecclesiastical history also had to develop by opening itself up to

96. Dawson, *The Dividing of Christendom*, 16; Henri Bremond, *A Literary History of Religious Thought in France: From the Wars of Religion Down to Our Own Times*, trans. K. L. Montgomery, vol. 1 (1916; London: Society for Promoting Christian Knowledge, 1928), v–vi, xi, xiv, xv–xvi; Dawson, *The Making of Europe*, 184, 190; and Burke, *The French Historical Revolution*, 16–17.

97. Dawson, *The Making of Europe*, 7.

98. Dawson, *The Making of Europe*, 7.

99. Fisher, "European Unity," 97–98.

100. David Knowles, "Christopher Dawson," obituary, *Tablet*, June 6, 1970, 558.

the spiritual dimension of human life. Historian Fritz Wagner noticed in the 1960s that under the impact of twentieth-century catastrophes and their consequences, the tasks to be done by what he called "secular history" and church history were converging. Those tasks involved making descriptive, objective history more meaningful to a wounded present. Since the Great War, he wrote, attention to *meaning* and "ultimate things" had increased in the world of historical writing, thanks to metahistorians such as Oswald Spengler and Arnold Toynbee and sociologists such as Pitirim Sorokin (1889–1968). The era of the world wars brought a "heightened consciousness of a problematic existence." Political and "objective" history was failing to address the kinds of questions people were asking. Why did millions of men die in the trenches? Why did the world wars happen? What meaning did they have? How can we avoid another war? How can we avoid the use of science for destructive purposes? The more that traditional political history declined, "the sooner the determining factors of religious life may find their way back into secular historiography," Wagner predicted. "Faced with the difficult task of the elucidation of being, the interpretation of meaning, the existential diagnosis . . . historians, at least within our civilization, will find themselves more and more dependent upon one another."[101] The founding of the journal *History and Theory* (1960) confirmed the increasingly strong link between the two words of its title and the increasing attention to philosophical contemplation in relation to empirical facts. Wagner thought that the separated disciplines of church and secular history had a "transcendental point of reference" which could be of great importance in the future.[102] This "transcendental point of reference" was the series of questions arising in *both* fields of history—secular and ecclesiastical—about meaning in human life. Common questions could point toward cooperation and even convergence of perspectives—*sub specie aeternitatis*.

Dawson realized, like Wagner, that the way totalitarian regimes used historical myths as the basis of their social unity revealed some-

---

101. Fritz Wagner, "Church History and Secular History as Reflected by Newton and His Time," *History and Theory* VIII (1969): 98, 99, 100–101, 109. This article was translated from *Saeculum* XVII (1966): 193–204.

102. Wagner, "Church History and Secular History as Reflected by Newton and His Time," 97.

thing important about history. The practice of history does not consist simply in the laborious accumulation of facts. It has a "direct bearing on the fate of modern society," he wrote.[103] The answer was not retrenchment into empiricist historiography, on the one hand, or into apologetical church history, on the other, but rather acceptance of the fact that history has a real bearing on the common good. The common good of particular human communities included Wagner's "transcendental point of reference," that locus of shared questions and hence of cooperation between distinct disciplines of knowledge. By departing from the national, empiricist, and ecclesiastical traditions of British historiography, Dawson's history of culture attempted to coordinate history with other disciplines because reality is a complex whole. He oriented historical specialization away from periods and disciplinary boundaries toward specialization around key problems, especially the causes of cultural change and their implications for the fate of modern societies. His interdisciplinary and comparative approach did not necessitate mastery of all fields but did demand functional competence in several fields beyond history—including comparative religion.

103. Dawson, *Religion and the Rise of Western Culture*, 13.

Chapter 5

Comparative Religion

Religion is the key of history. We cannot understand the inner form of a society unless we understand its religion. We cannot understand its cultural achievements unless we understand the religious beliefs that lie behind them. In all ages the first creative works of a culture are due to a religious inspiration and dedicated to a religious end. The temples of the gods are the most enduring works of man. Religion stands at the threshold of all the great literatures of the world. Philosophy is its offspring and is a child which constantly returns to its parent.
—Christopher Dawson (1948)

Dawson advocated the convergence of secular and ecclesiastical historiography based on shared questions and problems illuminating the relationship between religion and culture. Comparative religion examines this relationship. This is the field of study concerned with systematic investigation of world religions. Dawson was competent in comparative religion and engaged the major religious theorists of his day to gather the fragments of truth in their work into a wider whole. All religion, he wrote, "is based on the recognition of a superhuman Reality of which man is somehow conscious and toward which he must in some way orientate his life."[1] Dawson defended the irreducibility of religious experience from reductionist thinkers such as James Frazer, Sigmund Freud, and Émile Durkheim. At the same time, inspired by Friedrich von Hügel, Dawson held religion to be a field of tension involving personal experience and intellectualism along with institutionalism (the social

Christopher Dawson, *Religion and Culture*, 37–38.
1. Dawson, *Religion and Culture*, 18.

dimension). Different historical "ideal types," such as prophet, priest, and king, serve as channels through which these various elements of religion connect to culture in world history. Through them, religion played an important role in the "culture-process" (introduced in chapter 2) by which different factors affect cultural structures and change. A fully scientific approach to comparative religion, Dawson believed, should attempt to link the particular cultural artifacts of a people studied by the social sciences to the universal orientation of theology and philosophy. If anthropology supplied the principle of cultural holism in Dawson's science of culture, sociology the elements of cultural analysis, and history the basis of cultural morphology, then comparative religion provided a hermeneutical key in uncovering cultural meaning in spiritual experience and explanatory principles in analyzing the culture-process in intellectual and institutional developments.

Dawson showed his contemporaries that the historic function of religion is to bridge between the human world and the realm of the gods, so to speak, and even between different levels of human consciousness. Joining the vertical dimension of religion (connecting to the transcendent) to the horizontal dimension of religion (connecting to culture) mattered to Dawson because he believed this relationship had fractured in the modern world. "To the English mind religion is essentially a private matter, a question of personal opinion," he wrote in 1931.[2] The Great War had only increased this subjectivist tendency. Spiritualism went through a revival during and after the Great War as more and more bereaved people wondered, "Where are our dead?"[3] Thereby, one could be spiritual without being religious in the full sense of the word. The Belgian trench mortar officer Henry de Man, quoted in chapter 1, wrote about how the war had caused him to lose some of the human modesty required as a fundamental attitude of mind by any church. "This kind of modesty has been *shelled* out of me," he wrote.

2. Christopher Dawson, introduction, in *The Necessity of Politics*, by Carl Schmitt (London: Sheed & Ward, 1931), 10.

3. J. M. Winter, "Spiritualism and the First World War," in *Religion and Irreligion in Victorian Society*, ed. R. W. Davis and R. J. Halmstadter (London: Routledge, 1992); S. W. Sykes, "Theology," in *The Twentieth-Century Mind: History, Ideas, and Literature in Britain*, ed. C. B. Cox and A. E. Dyson (Oxford: Oxford University Press, 1972); and Sir Arthur Conan Doyle, "My Religion," in *My Religion* (London: Hutchinson, 1925), 31.

His spiritual attitude had become "too big for the size of any church or chapel." His conception of religion lost all attachment to an institutional reality outside himself—a common experience by the early twentieth century, it seems. A book titled *My Religion*, a collection of *Daily Express* articles on that subject, was published in England in 1925. In it, the English novelist Hugh Walpole (1884–1941) wrote, "Religion has become in these post-war days so individual a thing that no one is afraid of speaking of it." He thought personal religious experience alone held validity. "It seems to me," Walpole continued, "that in general the people of our time are passing from rather blind obedience to dogmatic teaching to an active demand for some freer, more individual, spiritual life."[4] The English philosopher and mathematician Alfred North Whitehead aptly summarized this whole tendency in his *Religion in the Making* (1926): "Religion is what the individual does with his own solitariness."[5]

Religion had been separated from culture, Dawson diagnosed. This parting of the "inner world of the moral consciousness from the outer world of economics and politics," he interpreted, "is the true cause of the spiritual tension and the economic disorder of modern society."[6] The religious experience of the modern person lay on one side of a chasm, and rational science, philosophy, and the social order lay on the other—not only skewing the view of modern people about the historic importance of religion in past human societies but also frustrating the spiritual aspirations of present human societies.

Therefore, Dawson believed a renewed and deepened science of comparative religion that revealed the function of religion in historical world cultures would go some way toward helping his twentieth-century contemporaries reimagine the place of religion in modern life. He noted, "We cannot understand the inner form of a society unless we understand its religion."[7]

4. Hugh Walpole, "My Religion," in *My Religion*, 13, 15, 17; de Man, *The Remaking of a Mind*, 211.

5. Alfred North Whitehead, *Religion in the Making* (New York: Macmillan, 1926), 16. Furthermore, Whitehead wrote, the primary religious virtue is personal sincerity, for "religion in its decay sinks back into sociability" (15, 23). "Collective enthusiasms, revivals, institutions, churches, rituals, bibles, codes of behaviour, are the trappings of religion, its passing forms. . . . Religion is beyond all this" (17).

6. Christopher Dawson, "The Problem of Wealth," *Spectator*, October 17, 1931, 486.

7. Dawson, *Religion and Culture*, 37.

Formation

In order to make this case, Dawson engaged the field of comparative religion from the start of his career as part-time lecturer in the History of Culture course at Exeter University during the 1920s. His lectures there made up the content of his first books. Dawson's pursuit of comparative religion exhibited a certain intellectual boldness, anthropologist Mary Douglas commented in her introduction to the 2001 edition of *Progress and Religion*, for at the time, that field of study (like anthropology) was regularly used to attack Christianity as superstitious. Undaunted, Dawson's leadership in this area inspired others, such as Bede Griffiths (1906–1993), a British-born Benedictine monk. Griffiths became a leading figure in dialogue between Christianity and Hinduism through the Christian Ashram Movement in India that attempted to combine Christian faith with the *ashram* (Hindu monastery).[8] Dawson was known for his participation in ecumenical groups,[9] his wide religious views, and his sympathetic approach to non-Western cultures. His comparative religion came to a climax in his Gifford Lectures of 1947 to 1949.

The Gifford Lectures

The Gifford Lectures are one of the great British institutions, an "unparalleled exhibition of modern thinking about God."[10] Since their inauguration in 1888, the lectures take place at different Scottish universities in St. Andrews, Aberdeen, Glasgow, and Edinburgh. They continue to connect Britain to the international world of scientific and religious thought today. Dawson was neither the only historian to give the lectures[11] nor the first Catholic to do so.[12] He built on the dis-

8. Scott, *A Historian and His World*, 176–77; Bede Griffiths, *The Golden String* (London: Harvill, 1954), 150–51; and Dawson, *Progress and Religion*, xxi–xxii.

9. Such as the Moot and the Sword of the Spirit movement—see chapter 7.

10. Larry Witham, *The Measure of God: Our Century-Long Struggle to Reconcile Science & Religion* (San Francisco: HarperSanFrancisco, 2005), 5.

11. The others were Albert Schweitzer (1934–1935), Arnold Toynbee, and Herbert Butterfield (1965–1967).

12. Friedrich von Hügel was invited to the University of Edinburgh for the years 1924 to 1926 but could not deliver his lectures due to ill health. The French neoscholastic philosopher and historian of philosophy Etienne Gilson (1884–1978) became the first Catholic to deliver the lectures when he spoke at Aberdeen in 1931 and 1932 (published as *L'Esprit de la philosophie medievale* in 1932).

tinguished legacies of William James, Friedrich von Hügel, and James Frazer, also chosen to deliver their lectures in the Scottish capital of Edinburgh. Dawson's lectures consisted of two published volumes: *Religion and Culture* (series I, 1948) and *Religion and the Rise of Western Culture* (series II, 1950). Dawson wrote gratefully that "it is only thanks to some exceptional foundation like that of the Gifford Lectures that it is possible to find an opportunity to bring [religion and culture] into relation with academic studies."[13]

Dawson argued in his first lecture series that (1) religion should be treated as its own category of human experience, not reduced to something else, and (2) religion has played a key role in cultural identity and development throughout world history. He backed up these claims by appealing to testimony from world cultures concerning human dependence on unseen powers and by sketching a picture of the specialized social organs through which such powers have shaped the common way of life of a people: the prophetic type (the seer), the priestly type (the ritual specialist), and the kingly type (the lawgiver). Dawson's purpose was to challenge the religious theorists of his day such as Frazer, Durkheim, and Freud. who reduced religion to fear, social forces, and neurosis, respectively, in order to alert his contemporaries to the need for bridging the gap between secularized, scientific civilization without a soul, on the one hand, and individualized faith without a body, on the other. The "fruitful collaboration of religion and culture has from the beginning been the normal condition of human society," wrote a reviewer for the *Spectator*, summarizing Dawson's argument. "Even to have framed the question lucidly is no small service."[14]

In his second lecture series, Dawson ventured into the topic of Christian culture, which he had avoided earlier, not because it lay outside the scope of the Gifford Lectures, he wrote, but because it is "the culture to which we all in some sense belong, and therefore it is impossible for us to study it in the same way as the cultures of the remote past."[15] As an historical religion, Christianity had, like other religions,

13. Dawson, *Religion and the Rise of Western Culture*, 13.
14. Keith Guthrie, "The Modern Dilemma," review of *Religion and Culture*, *Spectator*, December 10, 1948, 786.
15. Dawson, *Religion and the Rise of Western Culture*, 11.

influenced the social ways of life of various peoples in creative and dynamic ways. This happened in the formative period of Western civilization during the early medieval centuries, which Dawson viewed as a vast case study in the themes of comparative religion developed in his first series of lectures. Dawson has long been recognized "as one of the most significant of living English historians," a reviewer of the second series wrote in the *Times Literary Supplement*. "The steady and consistent development of historiography in England increasingly throws into relief the importance of his particular contribution."[16] Prominent historians reviewed the second series in other journals, too.[17] Chapter 8 will explore the theme of Christian culture in Dawson's work. The present chapter is largely concerned with his first series of lectures and other writings on non-Christian world religions.

The Scottish judge Lord Adam Gifford (1820–1887) founded the lectures through his will. He believed that "nothing but good can result from free discussion." He set up an £80,000 endowment to fund recurring lectureships (open to the public) for the purpose of "Promoting, Advancing, Teaching, and Diffusing the Study of Natural Theology," or the "Knowledge of God." The lecturers could be of any denomination or no denomination at all, provided only that they be "reverent men, true thinkers, sincere lovers of and earnest inquirers after truth." By "natural theology" he meant the "knowledge of God" treated as a "strictly natural science . . . just as astronomy or chemistry is."[18]

This kind of natural theology rose to prominence during the Enlightenment. Examples included the Boyle Lectures established in 1692 and theologian William Paley's landmark work *Natural Theology* (1802), which Charles Darwin (1809–1882) read at Cambridge and later rejected. These accounts focused on the observable world and assumed that

---

16. Gervase Mathew, "Religion in History," review of *Religion and the Rise of Western Culture*, *Times Literary Supplement*, April 7, 1950, vii. Mathew was an "Inkling," that is, one who sometimes participated in the literary discussion group around J. R. R. Tolkien.

17. F. M. Powicke, review of *Religion and the Rise of Western Culture*, *Journal of Ecclesiastical History* II (1951): 109–12; H. R. Trevor-Roper, review of *Religion and the Rise of Western Culture*, *New Statesman and Nation*, March 11, 1950, 276–77.

18. Adam Gifford, extracts from his will, dated August 21, 1885, published in the *Edinburgh University Calendar, 1888–1889*, 493–97, E-UA, Da36. Quotations are on pp. 494–96. Lord Gifford's will was published in Stanley L. Jaki, *Lord Gifford and His Lectures: A Centenary Retrospect* (Edinburgh: Scottish Academic Press, 1986), 66–76.

the scientific study of nature might provide evidence for God's existence and attributes.

This approach to religion faded during the nineteenth century, however, due to the flood of new knowledge about diverse religious practices around the globe. "The abstract *a priori* constructions of eighteenth-century rationalism faded before the rich and complex realities of man's actual religious experience," Dawson wrote. In these exciting discoveries, the new science of comparative religion had its beginnings. Dawson noted how coparative religion "led men to pay attention to the more obscure and non-rational aspects of religion which the theologians of the Enlightenment had despised and neglected."[19]

By the late nineteenth century, the new field of comparative religion had replaced natural theology as the only recognized scientific approach to religious questions. It aimed at the study of facts in human religious development, Dawson wrote, while refraining from theological and philosophical judgments. "This attitude was determined, on the one hand, by an ideal of scientific objectivity borrowed from the physical sciences and, on the other, by the practical necessity of establishing a neutral territory on which orientalists, missionaries, anthropologists and psychologists could co-operate harmoniously."[20]

All these specialized fields produced a wealth of material about religion, but their program of philosophical neutrality denied any "criterion by which to judge the intrinsic value and significance of the religious phenomenon," Dawson noted. Comparative religion replaced the objective science of the existence of God with exotic descriptions of human behavior and belief. "But the new science suffered from the same fundamental weakness as the old Natural Theology" of the eighteenth century, Dawson judged. "Both of them were equally rationalistic and reduced the deepest problems of human consciousness to superficialities." The natural theology of the Enlightenment reduced the living God of the Christian tradition to the "celestial engineer of the cosmic mechanism," while comparative religion "created a museum of dead cults and anthropological curiosities."[21] The profound depths of reli-

19. Dawson, *Religion and Culture*, 10, 11.
20. Dawson, *Religion and Culture*, 12.
21. Dawson, *Religion and Culture*, 13.

gious experience and mystery were ignored. Following from these earlier precedents, various kinds of reductionism characterized religious theorists during the twentieth century, eliminating the vertical dimension of religion altogether in favor of the horizontal. Dawson vigorously engaged these theorists and sought to acknowledge their strengths and expose their weaknesses.

Defending the Irreducibility of Religious Experience

By the early twentieth century, reductionism claimed some of the most celebrated intellects of the age in reducing religion to a purely natural phenomenon.[22] Freud, Durkheim, and Frazer, for example, tried to explain the origin of religion as something other than that credited by the believer. The faith-filled person may *think* religion puts him or her in contact with the spiritual world, but in reality, religion is a manifestation of illusion, the social bond, or attempts to deal with mysterious natural forces. "Reduction" in this case did not mean simply a form of explanation, a relating of two independent phenomena to a common category, which is, after all, a cardinal principle of all science. Reductionist thinkers, by contrast, pursued the more ambitious agenda of explaining an entire realm of data (religion) as belonging to another realm (psychology, society, mythology, etc.)—a violation of boundary thinking, to Dawson's cultural mind.[23] The simplicity of universal explanations of religion in terms of something else, however, undoubtedly contributed to popular appeal.

One reductionist whose work Dawson engaged was James Frazer (1854–1941). He was a British social anthropologist, classical scholar, and secularist who helped establish the intellectual consensus of the early twentieth century concerning the reductive origins of religion. Religion was a matter of beliefs arising from the mind of individuals as they struggled to explain the world and control nature, he argued.

---

22. Daniel L. Pals, *Eight Theories of Religion*, 2nd ed. (Oxford: Oxford University Press, 2006), 149; Daniel L. Pals, "Reductionism and Belief: An Appraisal of Recent Attacks on the Doctrine of Irreducible Religion," *Journal of Religion* LXVI (1986): 18.

23. Daniel L. Pals, "Is Religion a *Sui Generis* Phenomenon?" *Journal of the American Academy of Religion* LV (1987): 261–62.

Frazer's *Golden Bough* (single-volume edition, 1922) was, in England, "almost the bible of the 1920s: the book of religion par excellence."[24] This fascinating book of comparative anthropology and mythology exerted a huge influence, especially through literary figures such as T. S. Eliot (1888–1965) and D. H. Lawrence (1885–1930).[25] Frazer essentially created "primitive religion" as a subject of popular interest. Christianity appeared to sink into a jungle of irrational myths that had grown up throughout world history. The medieval literary scholar and later popular Christian writer C. S. Lewis (1898–1963) left his childhood faith partly due to Frazer. Dawson, however, arrived at the opposite conclusion. The comparative study of religion did not have to lead to relativism; it could also help one realize more clearly the "unique character of the spiritual dynamism of Christianity," he wrote in a letter to an American correspondent.[26]

Despite Frazer's reductionism, Dawson was deeply affected by Frazer's anthropological approach to religion. Writing about Frazer's impact on Dawson and others, literary historian John Vickery commented that, "Among the most erudite and interesting" of studies designed to introduce common readers to the earliest sources of culture in the 1920s, "were Christopher Dawson's *Age of the Gods* and *Progress and Religion*." He continued:

A historian of strong Roman Catholic convictions, Dawson analyzes and speculates on the relations between religion and culture. Though critical of some of the views of evolutionary anthropologists such as Frazer, he nevertheless is deeply indebted to *The Golden Bough* for many of his ideas. This is most clearly seen through his interest in the connections of primitive art

24. Adrian Hastings, *A History of English Christianity: 1920–1990*, 3rd ed. (1986; London: SCM, 1991), 223. The many editions of *The Golden Bough* sold in the tens of thousands of copies. Frazer thought of himself as a true servant of the facts; religion was a necessary stage in mental evolution, but one based on false premises. Religion had been superseded by the new worldview of the sciences. While Frazer treated Christianity very subtly, in Robert Ackerman's opinion, "In truth he was engaged all the while in a covert campaign against religion in general and Christianity in particular and may perhaps be seen, along with H. G. Wells, as the most important exponent of secularism in the twentieth century." See the James Frazer entry by Robert Ackerman, ODNB.

25. John B. Vickery, *The Literary Impact of The Golden Bough* (Princeton, N.J.: Princeton University Press, 1973).

26. Christopher Dawson to John J. Mulloy, June 11, 1955, NDA, box 1, folder 15, "The Dynamics of Culture Change," p. 31; Hastings, *A History of English Christianity: 1920–1990*, 236.

and ritual, the importance of the individual for religious development, the religious significance of taboos on the priest-king, and the ritual drama as also an economic agricultural cycle.[27]

Frazer alerted Dawson not only to the important connections between primitive art and ritual but also to the role of individuals in religious development. Dawson was intrigued by Frazer, whose works appeared in the bibliographies of both books mentioned by Vickery. In a letter to Victor Branford at the *Sociological Review* Dawson wrote: "If you should want Frazer's new book 'The Worship of Nature' reviewed, I would be delighted to do it."[28]

In *Progress and Religion* and in his Gifford Lectures, however, Dawson criticized Frazer's projection of modern rationalism back onto the primitive pattern (a criticism also made by Dawson's contemporary, the analytic philosopher Ludwig Wittgenstein, similarly fascinated by Frazer's book[29]). Ritualism and magic did not arise from an early form of scientific positivism, Dawson argued, but from a primitive type of religious experience—"the ecstasy of the Shaman lies behind the stereotyped formulae of the magician, just as the religious experience of a Buddha or a Mohammad lies behind the developed ritualism of modern Buddhism and Islam."[30] Empty yourself, the religiously wise of the past said; then the spirits will come to you. "The religious magic of the primitive hunter is not a technique for the control of subhuman nature, but a means of communion with divine powers," Dawson wrote.[31]

Dawson rejected Frazer's metaphysical assumptions. He adopted instead the nonreductionist methodological principle of taking seriously those who, like Muhammad, for example, claimed authentic contact with the supernatural through religious experience. Dawson adopted this principle as best illuminating the otherwise inexplica-

27. Vickery, *The Literary Impact of The Golden Bough*, 102, 103.
28. Dawson to Branford, May 9 (n.d.) (the letter was written from Dawlish, Devon), KA-VB, folder "Branford Correspondence." Frazer's *The Worship of Nature* (1926) was given as his Gifford Lectures at Edinburgh from 1923 to 1925. No review by Dawson has been found, but he was clearly interested in Frazer.
29. Fergus Kerr, *Theology after Wittgenstein* (Oxford: Basil Blackwell, 1986), 159–61.
30. Dawson, *Progress and Religion*, 87.
31. Dawson, *Religion and Culture*, 103.

ble development and growth of Islam, which appealed to the spiritual needs of millions. Whatever other cultural and psychological factors may have contributed to Muhammad's experience, one could not simply reduce it to those factors without violating boundary thinking.

What was this "religious experience" Dawson claimed lay partly behind religious developments in history? He responded to Frazer utilizing insights from William James, Rudolf Otto, and his own personal interest in mysticism. The psychologist and philosopher William James (1842–1910) published his *Varieties of Religious Experience* in 1902. This book became a key text for the study of religion in the twentieth century and an important influence on Dawson's approach to comparative religion. The significance of James was that he applied his "radical empiricism"[32] to those people he called religious "geniuses" of "exalted emotional sensitivity" who witnessed in their writings to the "original experiences" that shape the "spiritual inwardness" of religion—such as George Fox (founder of the Quakers) or Theresa of Avila (Catholic mystic), as well as obscure people, such as a certain Stephen H. Bradley, whose conversion due to a Methodist revival was recorded in a rare American pamphlet in 1830. These varieties of religious experience revealed unsuspected depths or layers of the human psyche.

An important motive behind James's attention to such religious experience may very well have been the desire to demonstrate the admissibility of religious belief in the modern world against those who asserted that religion was a thing of the past.[33] In fact, James noted that the inability to believe may be intellectual in origin. Within such people:

Their religious faculties may be checked in their natural tendency to expand, by beliefs about the world that are inhibitive, the pessimistic and materialistic beliefs, for example, within which so many good souls, who in former times would have freely indulged their religious propensities, find themselves nowadays, as it were, frozen; or the agnostic vetoes upon faith as something

---

32. William James, *The Will to Believe: And Other Essays in Popular Philosophy* (London: Longmans, Green, 1896), vii–viii. "I say 'empiricism,' because it is contented to regard its most assured conclusions concerning matters of fact as hypotheses liable to modification in the course of future experience; and I say 'radical,' because it treats the doctrine of monism itself as an hypothesis" (vii).

33. Charles Taylor, *Varieties of Religion Today: William James Revisited* (Cambridge, Mass.: Harvard University Press, 2002), 42–43.

weak and shameful, under which so many of us today lie cowering, afraid to use our instincts. In many persons such inhibitions are never overcome. To the end of their days they refuse to believe, their personal energy never gets to its religious centre, and the latter remains inactive in perpetuity.[34]

James revealed deeper levels of human psychology that the modern world had forgotten in its quest to amplify conscious reason.

Dawson shared James's concern about the limitations of modern, rationalized culture and his fascination with accounts of religious experience. "The influence of the exceptional man—we may even say of the genius—whether as organizer, teacher, or seer, is to be observed among savages no less than in advanced civilizations," Dawson wrote, utilizing Jamesian language. Both men attempted to consider such experience from a nonreductionist viewpoint, through the eyes of the protagonists. Only by making a "provisional acceptance" of religion's "internal spiritual autonomy" can one understand religion at all, even as it is molded by the influences of environment and social function, Dawson posited.[35] He believed James defined an immensely fruitful, empirical approach to the study of personal religious experience, but one that was ultimately incomplete as the basis for comparative religion.

Like William James, Rudolf Otto (1869–1937), a German theologian and historian of religion, took keen interest in the unique character of religious experience in his book *Das Heilige* (1917, translated in 1923 as *The Idea of the Holy*). Drawing on James's work, Otto's book appeared during the travail of the Great War. It quickly passed through many editions and translations. *The Idea of the Holy* became a key text in twentieth-century religious theory because of its assertive defense of a distinctly religious experience, entirely of its own kind, as a protest against the dominant reductionisms of the age.[36] Whereas James proceeded empirically to investigate religious experience, Otto developed a more categorical argument partly inspired by German philosopher Immanuel Kant (1724–1804).

---

34. William James, *The Varieties of Religious Experience* (New York: Random House Modern Library, 1902), 201.

35. Dawson, *Progress and Religion*, 66; Dawson, *Religion and Culture*, 16–17.

36. Daniel L. Pals, *Introducing Religion: Readings from the Classic Theorists* (Oxford: Oxford University Press, 2009), 207.

As a devout Protestant and interested in world religions, Otto argued there existed an irreducible category of "the holy" (or the sacred) *to* which subjective feelings pointed through a kind of awareness.[37] The holy was not the same thing as moral goodness. It reached beyond the ethical dimension to the *numinous*, a term coined by Otto and derived from the Latin *numen* meaning "arousing spiritual or religious emotion; mysterious or awe-inspiring." The numinous induced a feeling of dependency. In the *mysterium fascinans*, the numinous is experienced as fascinating, ravishing, and compelling. In the *mysterium tremendum*, the numinous is experienced as "overpoweringness," suprarational, awe-inspiring and powerful mystery.[38] The primary fact in this religious experience of the numinous is not the feeling but the encounter with the wholly other beyond rationalistic categories.

This "wholly other" was not something people in a thoroughly rationalized and secularized culture could easily comprehend. For them, the human mind is the highest spiritual reality; "there is no transcendent order except the order of culture," as Dawson characterized their view. The religious attitude to transcendence, pervasive among human cultures, is, however, "closely bound up with that sense of the Holy or the Numinous of which Rudolf Otto has written," Dawson noted. It is an *a priori* category that "issues from the deepest foundation of cognitive apprehension which the soul possesses," Dawson quoted Otto, and has "its independent roots in the hidden depths of the spirit."[39] There is an irreducible element of religious experience.

A third influence on Dawson's approach to religious experience was his own studies in mysticism, defined as the experience of union with the divine through contemplation and self-surrender. The early decades of the century witnessed something of a revival of interest in the subject. Even the agnostic Max Weber took an interest in it.[40] The first serious book on mysticism in Britain was Baron Friedrich von Hügel's two-volume work, *The Mystical Element in Religion as Studied in Saint*

37. John W. Harvey, translator's preface, in *The Idea of the Holy*, by Rudolf Otto, trans. John W. Harvey, 2nd ed. (1923; Oxford: Oxford University Press, 1958), xvi–xvii.

38. Otto, *The Idea of the Holy*, 3, 11, 19, 23, 31.

39. Dawson, *Religion and Culture*, 28–29, quoted on p. 29. See Otto, *The Idea of the Holy*, 36.

40. Christopher Adair-Toteff, "Max Weber's Mysticism," *Archives Européennes de Sociologie* XLIII (2002): 339–53.

Catherine of Genoa and Her Friends (1908), which would have a lasting influence on Dawson (discussed later).

Dawson's interest in mysticism emerged during these early years of the twentieth century, as evidenced by his letters to his sister Gwendoline[41] and a surviving manuscript. In 1909, twenty-year-old Dawson wrote an unpublished, handwritten essay on mysticism: "From the earliest times there has been a tendency to use the word [mysticism] very loosely . . . it is now commonly used to describe anything that is obscure, mysterious or unreasonable." Dawson thought "it may not be impossible to describe what cannot be satisfactorily defined. . . . I think that it would be generally agreed that the province of mysticism is spiritual experience: all that the spirit can feel and know without the use of the senses and the reason is mystical." He also wrote: "Mysticism is simply Natural Theology translated from the bare knowledge of the Reason, to the living experience of the Spirit and the Emotions."[42] His Gifford Lectures thirty years later would again take up this theme of mysticism's role in natural theology.

"From the time that I was thirteen or fourteen," Dawson wrote, "I had come to know the lives of the Catholic saints and the writings of the mediæval Catholic mystics, and they made so strong an impression on my mind that I felt that there must be something lacking in any theory of life which left no room for these higher types of character and experience."[43] It seems that his encounters with the lives of the saints gave him an instinctual resistance to theories of religion he would encounter later in life that tried to reduce religion to something else. The mystics opened a real and irreducible world to him and helped pull him out of a youthful agnostic phase (before arriving at Oxford in 1908).

The mature Dawson was even interested in non-Christian mysticism. During the 1910s and especially the 1920s, a host of books ap-

41. Gwendoline Dawson, a very mystical woman, never married and became an Anglican missionary in Africa and worked in England supporting missionary causes (interview by the author with Julian Scott, Christopher Dawson's grandson and literary executor, in London, June 9, 2009). Dawson's letters to her indicate that his interest in mysticism dates from the 1910s and are in the JSC.
42. Dawson, "On Mysticism," STA, box 4, folder 9 (undated essay). Dawson's biographer put the date of this essay at around 1909. (Scott, *A Historian and His World*, 56).
43. Christopher Dawson, "Why I Am a Catholic," *Catholic Times*, May 21, 1926, 11.

peared in France and Britain on Islamic mysticism. Dawson reviewed many of these in 1930, drawing attention to the close relationship between the great poets and the literary expression of spiritual experience among the Persians, the Arabs, and the Turks.[44] Dawson's interest in the mystical and transcendent aspects of religion remained with him throughout life as a basis of his own personal faith.[45]

In summary, the "element of transcendence is a primordial element of human experience," Dawson wrote. "Man is born into a world that he has not made, that he cannot understand and on which his existence is dependent." These facts compel human beings to grope toward mystery. Dawson remarked on how the mere existence of religious experience breaks down the exclusive claim of the rational consciousness to represent the totality of knowledge. In fact, in many world cultures, this knowledge-through-religious-experience constitutes *real knowledge* in its highest form. The idea of the universe as sealed off from the intrusion of any higher order of being is quite rare in human history.[46]

When the *mysterium tremendum* manifesting in the universe is worshipped in itself, Dawson wrote, drawing from Otto's terminology, one finds the typical religious developments of paganism and the worship of nature. "But when the God of Nature, the transcendent power which creates and governs the world is identified with the God of the Soul, the transcendent spiritual Being, the presence of which is obscurely felt in the profoundest states of human consciousness, then the basis exists for a higher type of development, such as we find in the historic world religions,"[47] Dawson noted. Comparative religion must not only look outward at the universe to understand religion but also inward—to the deepest levels of human consciousness.

---

44. Christopher Dawson, "Islamic Mysticism," *Dublin Review* CLXXXVI (1930): 34–61. Dawson's article was highly praised in a response; see NA, review of "Islamic Mysticism," *Sufi Quarterly* VI, no. 1 (1930): 62–65.

45. Scott, *A Historian and His World*, 45.

46. Dawson, *Religion and Culture*, 21, 24, 26, 29.

47. Dawson, *Religion and Culture*, 27.

Levels of Consciousness

The psychology of religion consists of the application of psychological methods and interpretive frameworks to the diverse contents of religious traditions. Inaugurated by William James, it was taken up by psychologist Sigmund Freud (1856–1939). While he appreciated James, Dawson attacked the rationalism at the base of Freud's work even as he adopted a modified form of the "unconscious mind" Freud popularized. Freud relied heavily on Frazer (as well as Durkheim) but approached religion by assuming a similarity between primitive psychology and the neurotic psychology of individuals contemporary to his day. Thus, he believed he could unlock the secrets of the primitive origin and universal development of religion out of unconscious wishes, fears, and guilt.[48] His most direct writing on religion was in *The Future of an Illusion* (1927, translated in 1928). He specifically compared the development of humanity out of its early religious needs to the development of the individual person out of the neuroses and father complexes of childhood. Religion involved both "obsessional restrictions" and a system of "wishful illusions." Religious ideas "are not precipitates of experience or end results of thinking: they are illusions, fulfillments of the oldest, strongest and most urgent wishes of mankind," he wrote.[49] These emerged out of the "unconscious," the part of the mind existing beneath conscious awareness, including memories, urges, and conflicts, often of a sexual nature. Freud believed the contents of the unconscious exert powerful influence over behavior and desires.

Dawson held the discovery of the unconscious to be the greatest contribution of psychology to the study of religion. By it one can understand much about the unexplored territories of the soul that have been so important for religious experience: "the world of dream and vision; the world of symbol and myth; and the unconscious forces of sublimation and repression that control the moral aspects of the per-

48. Sigmund Freud, "Totem and Taboo," in Sigmund Freud, *The Basic Writings of Sigmund Freud*, trans. A. A. Brill (New York: Modern Library, 1938), 807, 918.

49. Sigmund Freud, "The Future of an Illusion," in Pals, *Introducing Religion*, 84, 85, 87. Freud's reductionist empiricism is evident here: "But scientific work is the only road which can lead us to a knowledge of reality outside ourselves. It is once again merely an illusion to expect anything from intuition and introspection" (85).

sonality."[50] Modern psychology, he noted, has illuminated the ways in which human behavior is never entirely the product of rational motives and enlightened self-interest, as nineteenth-century thinkers tended to believe. One cannot simplify the concept of "mind," the "I" in the Geddes-Le Play formula, entirely to the sphere of rational consciousness. One cannot starve the emotions and ignore the existence of unconscious forces in psychological life. If one overlooks other levels of consciousness in favor of the rational, one produces an internal schism in personality and culture that is ultimately disastrous, Dawson wrote. "Sooner or later the forces that have been ignored and repressed take their revenge and destroy the rational unity of the personality and the culture by their violent eruption into the sphere of consciousness," he diagnosed—as in the succession of revolutions and wars ripping through the twentieth century. The new secular culture has "proved unable to control the sub-rational forces which are always present beneath the surface of culture," Dawson observed.[51]

The rationalism of psychologists such as Freud led them to "concentrate their attention on a single aspect of the unconscious—the repression of the sexual impulses—and to neglect the rest," Dawson wrote. They wanted a "rational" principle from which they could deduce certain conclusions, but it was impossible to understand "social problems in terms of the Freudian dualism between unconscious impulse and rational consciousness." Freud inverted the true relation, for he derived the "sociological structure from a pre-existent psychological complex instead of *vice versa*."[52]

---

50. Christopher Dawson, "Religion," in *Chamber's Encyclopedia* (London: George Newnes, 1950), 593. Drawing from the medieval Arab Muslim historian Ibn Khaldun, Dawson distinguished three kinds of dreams that correspond to the three human psychological levels (subrational, ratio, and intellectus—see appendix C): "There is the confused and meaningless dream which is due to the uncontrolled activity of the mind working on the forms that are stored in its memory without any deeper background of spiritual apprehension; secondly there is the symbolic dream, in which the sensible image has a symbolic value or analogous relation to some higher spiritual idea which can be discovered by analysis and interpretation; and finally there is the true dream which carries immediate conviction in a flash of spiritual knowledge and which therefore is more akin in its nature to genuine prophetic inspiration than anything else in man's normal experience." See Dawson, *Religion and Culture*, 58–59.

51. Dawson, *The Historic Reality of Christian Culture*, 91, 92.

52. Christopher Dawson, "Christianity and Sex," in *Enquiries into Religion and Culture*, 224; Dawson, *The Historic Reality of Christian Culture*, 91, 92.

Formation

The problem was partly that Freud focused on only two levels of human consciousness, whereas Dawson believed human life involved three psychological levels, not two:

There is first the sub-rational life of unconscious instinct and impulse which plays such a large part in human life, especially the life of the masses. Secondly there is the level of conscious voluntary effort and rational activity which is the sphere of culture, *par excellence*. And finally there is the super-rational level of spiritual experience, which is the sphere not only of religion but of the highest creative forces of cultural achievement—the intuitions of the artist, the poet and the philosopher—and also of certain forms of scientific intuition which seem to transcend the sphere of rational calculation and research.[53]

It is this third level that Dawson identified as the center of unity for the human being and for human society. In this quotation, he unveiled his vision of the intellectual side of human culture (see appendix C). The problem was that modernity privileged the second sphere of conscious intellectual effort (*ratio*) alone. This level of culture "has grown until it has subjugated the world of nature and pushed back the frontiers of the superhuman spiritual world beyond the boundaries of consciousness."[54] It seemed to him the power of active reason had vanquished both the higher and the lower realms of psychological reality.

However, the fact that modern rationalists have invested most of their attention and activity in the "region which can be explored by human reason and controlled by human will" does not change its limits. Such rationalists are in contact only with the "artificially lit and hygienically conditioned City of Man" and so are living on a relatively superficial level of existence and consciousness, Dawson wrote. The primitive peoples, on the other hand, in their weakness and ignorance, are "nearer to the basic realities of human existence" and remind the modern rationalist of deeper truths of life. Many modern writers on anthropology and primitive thought, Dawson observed, assumed religion is a secondary phenomenon and that "man's earliest attitude to reality was a kind of empirical materialism." This was untrue. "The whole mentality of

53. Dawson, *The Historic Reality of Christian Culture*, 92.
54. Dawson, *Religion and Culture*, 20.

primitive man is religious," Dawson rebutted. Humans are rational animals who can recognize they are limited internally by the conditions
of their consciousnesses and externally by their dependence on nonhu-
man forces that transcend their animal existence, he wrote. "No man
can succeed in life alone," Dawson quoted a Native American, "and he
cannot get the help he needs from men."[55] Dawson regularly employed
representates from world religions to chasten Western rationalists.

The problem in the modern world, Dawson thought, was the disintegration of these three levels of consciousness (the subrational, the
rational, and the superrational) into unrelated realms. "The world of
reason has become more arid and spiritually void," he noted, "and the
world of the soul has lost the consecrated ways by which it expresses
itself in the world of culture and has been left at the mercy of the forces
of darkness which are the negative and destructive aspects of the Unconscious." When the prophets are silent, when those figures long respected in human history for their connection to the deepest level of
human consciousness cease channeling the divine realm into the human realm, "the way to the lower depths is still open and man's frustrat-
ed spiritual powers will find their outlet in the unlimited will to power
and destruction." One could think here of twenty-first century violent
Islamism or radical social activism in the West. Modern intellectuals,
having cut themselves off from the superrational, have failed to provide
a unitive "I," a vision for the people which could unite modern society.
Consequently, Dawson wrote, "they have proved unable to resist the
non-moral, inhuman and irrational forces which are destroying the humanist not less than the Christian traditions of Western culture."[56]

This divorce between the levels of consciousness, between science
and spirit, is "abnormal, unnatural and morbid," Dawson wrote. The
world of human culture came into existence through the cooperation
of the higher and lower psyche. In fact, it was in the sphere of religion
that advance in learning and study first took place in human civilizations. It was there the idea of systematic scientific knowledge first
arose—as in mathematics, astronomy, and the science of calendars,

---

55. Dawson, *Religion and Culture*, 21; Dawson, *Progress and Religion*, 70, 71, quoted on 82.
56. Dawson, *Religion and Culture*, 15, 65, 83.

all oriented toward harmonizing the natural and ritual cycles of the ancient world which shaped the lives of both commoners and elites.[57] Religion created a bridge across the ranges of human psychology as well as human classes.

On this basis, Dawson rejected Freud's idea of religion as mass delusion, escapism, and an illusory substitute for reality. The more deeply one peers into the hidden life of the psyche, Dawson thought, the more disposed one becomes to recognizing the "reality and creativity of the spiritual forces which manifest themselves in the religious experience of the human race."[58] If Freud was right, he wrote, "it would be useless to look to religion as a source of spiritual power; on the contrary, it would be a source of weakness, a kind of collective neurosis which perverts and saps social energy." Yet one could not reconcile such a view with the facts of history. "For religion has undoubtedly been one of the greatest motive powers in human history. It seems to have increased collective energy rather than diminishing it, and whenever humanity has been on the move, religion has been like the pillar of fire and the cloud that went before the Israelites in their desert journeyings."[59] Religion appears often as an impetuous force in history rather than mere escapism from reality.

Thus, the tasks of comparative religion included demonstrating how "the vital relation has been maintained between the depths of the Unconscious and the surface of the social order," and how religion asserts its "internal spiritual autonomy," on the one hand, and "how it is moulded and conditioned by the influences of environment and social function," on the other.[60]

Religion as a Field of Tensions

If religious experience were the only determinative and ultimate reality of religion, Dawson would have been unable to establish its im-

---

57. Dawson, *Religion and Culture*, 32.

58. Dawson, *Religion and Culture*, 14.

59. Dawson, *The Judgment of the Nations*, 87. Dawson cited *Civilization, War and Death: Selections from the Work of Sigmund Freud*, trans. John Richman (London: Hogarth, 1939), 34.

60. Dawson, *Religion and Culture*, 16–17.

portance as the "key of history," to use his phrase. For religion to be that key, it cannot be merely a private experience but must also connect to public realities. Dawson labored to demonstrate how religious figures of the past consistently tried to create a bridge from the psyche to the social order. Religion touched on multiple elements of human life beside personal experience, including the rational order and the social order. It was a field of tensions.

This multiple-elements-of-religion idea was communicated to Dawson mainly by Friedrich von Hügel, one of the great philosophers and theologians of the early twentieth century who first inspired Dawson's interest in comparative religion from his Oxford years (1908 to 1911) onward.[61] A devoted Roman Catholic, von Hügel's spirituality was deeply incarnational, devoted to the church and science as sacred and secular means to spiritual purification and the growth of personality. Von Hügel cultivated an active interest in entomology, geology, biblical criticism, literature, history, philosophy, and the arts.[62] Abbot Cuthbert Butler (1858–1934) of Downside Abbey remembered on their walks together he and von Hügel would stop to make a visit to the Blessed Sacrament, "and there I would watch him sitting, the great deep eyes fixed on the Tabernacle, the whole being wrapt in an absorption of prayer, devotion, contemplation. Those who have not seen him so know only half the man."[63]

Von Hügel's greatest work was *The Mystical Element of Religion as Studied in St. Catherine of Genoa and Her Friends* (1908). In it, von Hügel introduced one of his greatest contributions to the study of religion, his "Three Elements of Religion" typology: (1) religion as experience (intuition, feeling, mystical); (2) religion as thought (question and argument, system, truth); and (3) religion as institution (external, authoritative, historical, traditional, communal). These elements were often found separated from each other among religious theorists, but von Hügel brought together. Amidst his rigorous historical-critical examination

61. Scott, *A Historian and His World*, 45. In a letter to his sister Gwendoline from 96 Holywell, Oxford, dated November 17, 1910, Dawson mentioned that a speaker from "the Pusey House is coming to read us a paper on von Hügel" (JSC).

62. James Luther Adams, "The Sacred and the Secular: Friedrich von Hügel," in *The Prophethood of All Believers*, ed. George K. Beach (Boston: Beacon, 1986), 69.

63. Abbot Butler, "Friedrich von Hügel," *Tablet*, February 14, 1925, 202.

of the life of the Italian mystic Catherine of Genoa (1447–1510) and her friends, von Hügel concluded that one never finds any one of these three elements without a trace of the others.

He thought it challenging, however, to hold together in one's religious life mysticism, intellectualism, and institutionalism. Enthused about one element, believers might suppress the others due to their longing for simplification in religion. On their own, mysticism tended toward subjectivism, intellectualism toward rationalism, and institutionalism toward superstition and routinization. For example, one who discovered the emotional-experiential side of religion would be tempted, von Hügel thought, to "sweep aside both the external, as so much oppressive ballast; and the intellectual, as so much hair-splitting or rationalism." And if such a person succeeded in sweeping aside those other elements of religion, "a shifting subjectivity, and all but incurable tyranny of mood and fancy," would result; "fanaticism is in full sight." In other words, in a healthy religious personality, each element needed to supplement, purify, and stimulate the other, protecting a one-sided religion from itself. The "cross" of religious existence meant the creative acceptance of the balance, tension, and friction of these elements *together*.[64]

Von Hügel experienced this cross personally. It cost him much to maintain an integrated understanding of religion in an age that sought to separate the personal from the intellectual and the institutional. After all, two of his close friends[65] had just found themselves excommunicated by the institutional church as modernists when *The Mystical*

---

64. Baron Friedrich von Hügel, *The Mystical Element of Religion as Studied in Saint Catherine of Genoa and Her Friends*, vol. 1 (1908; London: J. M. Dent & Sons, 1961), 44, 51–53, 55, 59, 61, 72, 82.

65. Von Hügel's biblical criticism drew him into close association with Alfred Loisy (1857–1940) and George Tyrrell (1861–1909), putting him at the center of the modernist controversy. Modernism attacked the intellectualism of scholastic theology and favored contemporary biblical criticism. It was condemned by Pope Pius X in his decree *Lamentabili* (1907) and his encyclical *Pascendi* (1907). In 1907, Tyrrell was excommunicated; Loisy was excommunicated in 1908, but von Hügel was not. Schoeck wrote, "Doubtless this was due in large part to his social position and to the great respect in which he was held by so many scholars and notables outside the Roman Catholic church. Von Hügel, however, did not modify his views or his essential position. . . . He remained publicly faithful to free scientific and historical investigation, and staunchly loyal to friends who suffered under the ecclesiastical censures." See the Friedrich von Hügel entry by R. J. Schoeck, ODNB. See also Lawrence F. Barmann, "The Modernist as Mystic," in *Catholicism Contending with Modernity: Roman Catholic Modernism and Anti-Modernism in Historical Context*, ed. Darrell Jodock (Cambridge: Cambridge University Press, 2000), 215–47.

Element appeared in print in 1908. Von Hügel, however, maintained a delicate position between acknowledging contemporary efforts to re-think the faith and the legitimate right of authority to determine what pertains to the Christian faith. In his opinion, the modernist movement failed not only because of clumsy church authority but also because of failures within the movement itself.[66] Remarkably, von Hügel main-tained his love for the historical and institutional church. In a letter to his friend Norman Kemp Smith (1872–1958), the Scottish philoso-pher, he urged Smith to join a "clearly avowed and regularly practiced traditional, institutional, religion." "For myself," von Hügel explained, "such definite appurtenance has cost me much, all my life. Yet I am more than ever penetrated by the simply *immense* debt I owe (I mean, also just *qua* philosopher of religion) to such appurtenance."[67] Many did not share von Hügel's ability to bridge inner and outer religion—like William James, as noted below. Von Hügel's whole personality, however, worked to integrate all three elements of religion in his life and work.

Dawson's Oxford tutor, Ernest Barker, greatly impressed by his stu-dent, later complimented Dawson "as being a man and a scholar of the same sort of quality as Acton and von Hügel."[68] Indeed, von Hügel's typology of religion shaped the structure of Dawson's own work on the subject—though von Hügel remained ever the philosopher of religion, while Dawson pursued the social sciences. Nevertheless, like von Hü-gel, Dawson's cultural mind viewed religion from multiple points of view. One could not simply reduce it to *either* inner reality (mysticism and intellectualism) *or* to outer institutionalism because, in truth, the phenomenon of religion contained both.[69]

66. Lawrence F. Barmann, *Baron Friedrich von Hügel and the Modernist Crisis in England* (Cambridge: Cambridge University Press, 1972), 246, 247.

67. Von Hügel to Smith, July 1, 1919, SAA, papers of Fredrich von Hügel, MS. 30420/4. Em-phasis was von Hügel's. This letter can also be found in Lawrence F. Barmann, ed., *The Letters of Baron von Hügel and Professor Norman Kemp Smith* (New York: Fordham University Press, 1981), 37.

68. Ernest Barker, letter of recommendation backing Dawson for a position at Leeds Univer-sity, quoted in Scott, *A Historian and His World*, 110.

69. For obvious examples of von Hügel's influence on Dawson, see the latter's account of the importance of the "institutional element in Buddhism," despite the Buddhist teaching on the unreality of reality, and his characterization of the "intellectualism" of the Indian religious tradi-tion. He did not cite von Hügel in these instances, but the way he contrasted different elements or sides of religion (here, and other places in his work) strongly suggests the connection. See

This was why even James and Otto, so useful for establishing the irreducible category of religious experience, failed to offer a complete model for comparative religion, Dawson thought. They did not approach their subject as a field of tensions. For example, James defined religion as: "*the feelings, acts, and experiences of individual men in their solitude, so far as they apprehend themselves to stand in relation to whatever they may consider the divine*" (James's emphasis). He specifically divided institutional religion and systematic theology from "personal religion pure and simple"—the very three elements von Hügel (and Dawson) sought to hold together. This was because behind James lay that tradition of "inner religion" of Emanuel Swedenborg (1688–1772), represented in Henry James Sr., his father. William James did not want his readers to associate "religion" with "church," which he thought for many of them implied "hypocrisy and tyranny and meanness and tenacity of superstition" and justified their being "down" on religion altogether.[70]

In fact, Friedrich von Hügel gently criticized James on this very point in a letter to him, objecting to his separation of religious experience from its "institutional-historical occasions and environment and from the analytic and speculative activity of the mind."[71] Such a focus on the personal and the private in religion led James to—in the words of one scholar summarizing von Hügel's critique— "abandon his [James's] inductive, concrete *a posteriori* method and to exhibit a reductive *a priori* conception that neglects corporate religious experience with its institutional influences, disciplines, and responsibilities."[72] Even Freud criticized James on this point: "If the truth of

---

Dawson, *Religion and Culture*, 76, 78. See also Dawson's somewhat negative comparison of Ronald Knox's *Enthusiasm* with von Hügel's *Mystical Element of Religion* in Christopher Dawson, "Religious Enthusiasm," review of *Enthusiasm*, *Month* (new series) V (1951): 7–14.

70. James, *The Varieties of Religious Experience*, 4, 8, 31–32, 327–28.

71. Von Hügel to James, May 10, 1909. The letter and commentary are found in James Luther Adams, "Letter from Friedrich von Hügel to William James," *Downside Review* XCVIII (1980): 214–36. See p. 230 for the quotation. During the 1960s, the Unitarian theologian James Luther Adams discovered this letter in the Houghton Library at Harvard University. The letter had remained tucked for decades in a copy of von Hügel's two-volume book *The Mystical Element of Religion* (1908), which he had autographed and sent to James. Besides his criticisms, von Hügel expressed substantial indebtedness to James's famous work on mysticism, *The Varieties of Religious Experience*.

72. James Luther Adams, "Letter from Friedrich von Hügel to William James," *Journal of the*

religious doctrines is dependent on an inner experience which bears witness to that truth, what is one to do about the many people who do not have this rare experience?" What significance is this experience to others if it does not mean something in terms of reason?[73]

Viewing religion primarily in terms of religious experience is inadequate, the Lutheran theologian George Lindbeck argued, because it fails to account for the way human experience is conditioned and even made possible by language and cultural characteristics acquired prior to a religious experience.[74] Prior cultural context and language gives shape to experience; personal experience and communal culture cannot be separated. This problem plagued the individualistic theorists of religion such as James. Dawson concluded that despite his valuable insights on religion-as-experience, James failed to find a real solution to the study of religion.[75]

A similar problem seemed to shadow Otto, too, despite the German thinker's recognition of the connection between rational and nonrational elements in the historical evolution of religion. The numinous (the immense, otherworldly mystery) is conceptualized through different formulas—Jehovah, many gods, Brahman, Allah, the Tao—in order to frame a rational understanding of the divine, one scholar summarized Otto.[76] The *mysterium fascinans* is schematized according to

---

American Academy of Religion XLV (1977): 497. Ernst Troeltsch, von Hügel's friend, shared this criticism; see Adair-Toteff, "Max Weber's Mysticism," 340–41. The Canadian philosopher Charles Taylor recently wrote an appreciative book on James, but his critique paralleled that of von Hügel. James's rigorous and exclusive focus on personal religious experience failed to provide a basis for understanding collective religious life. Furthermore, Taylor questioned whether anyone can ever really have an "individual" religious experience because all experiences require a language of expression, and language is a gift from society to the individual. See Taylor, *Varieties of Religion Today*, 23–24, 26–28.

73. Mary Kay O'Neil and Salman Akhtar, eds., *On Freud's "The Future of an Illusion"* (London: Karnac Books, 2009), 34. The quotation is from Freud's text in this book.

74. George A. Lindbeck, *The Nature of Doctrine: Religion and Theology in a Postliberal Age* (Philadelphia: Westminster, 1984), 33–34; Taylor, *Varieties of Religion Today*, 27–28. "Relativism, by indiscriminately giving value to practically everything, has made 'experience' all-important. Yet, experiences, detached from any consideration of what is good or true, can lead, not to genuine freedom, but to moral or intellectual confusion, to a lowering of standards, to a loss of self-respect, and even to despair." Benedict XVI, opening address at World Youth Day, July 17, 2008, in Sydney, Australia; quoted in "The Year of Benedict," Tim Drake, *National Catholic Register*, January 4–10, 2009, 1.

75. Dawson, *Religion and Culture*, 13.

76. Pals, *Introducing Religion*, 206.

goodness and love, while the *mysterium tremendum* is schematized according to rational ideas of justice and moral will, Otto wrote. "By the continual living activity of its non-rational elements a religion is guarded from passing into 'rationalism,'" he noted. "By being steeped in and saturated with rational elements it is guarded form sinking into fanaticism or mere mysticality, or at least from persisting in these, and is qualified to become a religion for all civilized humanity."[77] Here Otto sounded much like von Hügel by conceiving of religion as a field of tension.

However, Otto wrote in *The Idea of the Holy* that, "The reader is invited to direct his mind to a moment of deeply felt religious experience, as little as possible qualified by other forms of consciousness. Whoever cannot do this, whoever knows no such moments in his experience, is requested to read no further."[78] Such a statement could easily appear to sideline intellectualism and intuitionalism. Indeed, Dawson criticized Otto on that very basis. In 1930, he wrote, "recent German writers such as Otto, Heiler, and Karl Beth tend . . . to exaggerate the mystical and intuitive character of religious experience, whether in its primitive or advanced manifestations."[79] There was a danger in isolating the experiential element of religion and its subjective meaning away from other elements. What force can it then exert in history? Religious experience constituted only one side of religion, and Dawson needed to find a way to bridge from that side of religion to the community in a way that even von Hügel did not fully develop, despite his commitment to "institutionalism." Enter French sociologist Émile Durkheim (1858–1917).

---

77. Otto, *The Idea of the Holy*, 140, 141.

78. Otto, *The Idea of the Holy*, 8.

79. Christopher Dawson, "The Dark Mirror," *Dublin Review* CLXXXVII (1930): 184–85. Lindbeck has more recently criticized Otto in the same way; see Lindbeck, *The Nature of Doctrine*, 21. Karl Beth (1872–1959), German historian of religion and Christian thinker, helped establish the Research Institute for Psychology of Religion in Vienna in 1922 and fled to the United States at the outset of the Second World War; Dawson was possibly referring to his *Frömmigkeit der Mystik und des Glaubens* (1927). Friedrich Heiler (1892–1967), was a German theologian and historian of religion; Dawson was possibly referring to *Das Gebet* (1918), Heiler's historical and phenomenological study of prayer.

Religion as a Social Phenomenon

As one of the founders of academic sociology, Durkheim was not the only factor in Dawson's bridge-building from religious experience to cultural reality: German social thinkers Ernst Troeltsch and Max Weber contributed, too. However, Durkheim's sociology of religion pointed directly at the connection between religion and culture, and Dawson more explicitly engaged his thought than that of Troeltsch or Weber.

For the Frenchman, religion was not a disease (Freud), not an attempted rationalization and propitiation of the unknown (Frazer), and not an individual experience (James and Otto). Rather, it was a natural phenomenon expressing the "collective consciousness" of society. His classic work *The Elementary Forms of Religious Life* (1912, translated in 1915) developed the functionalist theory that society shapes all forms of human thought and behavior including religion.

Durkheim shared with Dawson a critique of the tendency among modern people to relegate religion simply to the private, subjective sphere. The Frenchman noted how such people aspired "towards a religion that would consist entirely of internal and subjective states and would be freely constructed by each of us." However, this individualist view of religion could not explain the actual place of religion in history where its foundation is a defined group, Durkheim observed. Historically, all societies have religion, and one finds "no religion without a church." Here the sociologist used the word *église* (church) to refer to any religious group or institution. Even personal cults (e.g., of patron saints) were never entirely left in the hands of individuals. Communal religions teach "the individual the identity of his personal gods, what their role is, how he must enter into relationship with them, and how he must honour them." Thus, Durkheim defined religion as "*a unified system of beliefs and practices relative to sacred things, that is to say, things set apart and surrounded by prohibitions—beliefs and practices that unite its adherents in a single moral community called a church.*" He immediately continued: "The second element that takes its place in our definition [church] is therefore no less essential than the first [beliefs and practices]: demonstrating that the idea of religion is inseparable from the idea of a church suggests that religion must be something eminently collective."[80]

In this way, Durkheim opposed James's definition of religion in individualist terms, though he agreed with James concerning the objective basis of religious experience: "this unanimous feeling of believers across time cannot be purely illusory," Durkheim noted. Thus, "we allow that religious beliefs rest on a specific experience whose demonstrative value is, in a sense, not inferior to that of scientific experiments." These statements sound nonreductionist, but Durkheim ultimately held that the reality grounding religious experience did not conform to the idea believers had of it (the transcendent or the numinous, in Otto's word). According to Durkheim, that reality "which is the objective, universal, and eternal cause of those *sui generis* sensations that make up the religious experience—is society." Society developed moral forces, attached the worshiper to his cult, raised man above himself—indeed, society made the man. Durkheim did not think one could understand the religious nature of the individual prior to society, just as one could not comprehend ideas prior to the use of words and language derived from society. The individual was an abstraction. Religious experience was not independent of history; it was a product of social causes—*contra* James and Otto.[81]

Despite Durkheim's ultimately reductionist sociology of religion, Dawson drew inspiration from his functionalist approach crediting religion as a causal force in history. In a 1925 letter to his friend Alexander Farquharson of the Sociological Society, Dawson wrote: "I have been reading Durkheim in my spare time. He seems to have much more affinity with our type of sociology than Hobhouse—perhaps owing to the common tradition of all the French schools."[82] In his *Progress and Religion*, Dawson quoted key passages he appreciated:

As Durkheim has said, religion is like the womb from which come all the germs of human civilization. "Since it [religion] has been made to embrace all of reality, the physical world as well as the moral one, the forces that move

80. Émile Durkheim, *The Elementary Forms of Religious Life*, trans. Carol Cosman (1912; Oxford: Oxford University Press, 2001), 43, 45, 46.
81. Durkheim, *The Elementary Forms of Religious Life*, 66, 79, 312, 313.
82. Dawson to Farquharson, January 12, 1925, KA-AF, folder "Christopher Dawson Letters."

bodies as well as those that move minds have been conceived in a religious form. That is how the most diverse methods and practices, both those that make possible the continuation of the moral life (laws, morals and art) and those serving the material life (the material, technical and practical sciences) are directly or indirectly derived from religion." "From the moment when men have an idea that there are internal connections between things science and philosophy become possible. Religion opened the way for them."[83]

However, if religious thought had, according to Durkheim, led human beings to scientific and philosophical thought, then it could not be true, Dawson wrote, that religion was nothing more than the divinization of the social consciousness. One cannot believe this development was

a purely collective one in which the individual consciousness was entirely merged in that of the crowd. It is impossible to exclude the factor of individual thought and leadership from any stage of religious development. The influence of the exceptional man [as quoted earlier]—we might even say of the genius—whether as organizer, teacher, or seer, is to be observed among savages no less than in advanced civilizations.

Durkheim overly emphasized the social, Dawson thought. While social life is dependent on religion, "the sphere of religion is that which lies outside social control, and the primary religious instinct is that of dependence on superhuman powers." It is the very nature of religion to transcend the social category.[84]

The problem with Durkheim's thinking was that he tried to derive the whole development of religion from a single principle (society), a violation of boundary thinking. Dawson, by contrast, derived religion from the human experience of transcendence and dependence, intellectualized and institutionalized in world religious cultures. Durkheim, Dawson thought, revealed an "anti-metaphysical prejudice which has been so general during the last generation or two, and which rejects on à priori grounds any objective interpretation of religious experience."[85] Dawson had criticized Frazer and Freud on the same grounds:

83. Dawson, *Progress and Religion*, 69–70. For Dawson's quotations in a different translation, see Durkheim, *The Elementary Forms of the Religious Life*, 168, 181.
84. Dawson, *Progress and Religion*, 66, 70.
85. Dawson, "The Dark Mirror," 183, 185.

they lacked a cultural mind that could discern a multidimensional reality.

The social scientific approach to religion by Durkheim, however, represented a major intellectual advance for comparative religion over the purely psychological analyses of James and Otto. Nevertheless, Durkheim, like James and Otto, could not supply a fully scientific theory of comparative religion. His social science tended to interpret its object in a way unrecognizable by religious people themselves. Social scientists like him explained away personal religious experience, thereby reinforcing the contemporary divide between religion and culture even further. Dawson wrote, "we have a secularized scientific world culture which is a body without a soul; while on the other hand religion maintains its separate existence as a spirit without a body." "We are faced with a spiritual conflict of the most acute kind," he added, "a sort of social schizophrenia which divides the soul of society between a non-moral will to power served by inhuman techniques and a religious faith and a moral idealism which have no power to influence human life."[86] Dawson perceived acutely the religion-culture split and its significance for modern life, a chasm exacerbated by reductive religious theorists such as Durkheim, despite his best intention to connect religion to culture in his work.

So, then, how did Dawson propose to connect religion and culture and advance a more scientific theory of comparative religion? He needed to join the psychological awareness of vertical reality found in James and Otto, including lower and higher levels of the human psyche, to the horizontal function of religion Durkheim saw so clearly at work in human societies. He needed to maintain the multiple elements of religion in a vital tension.

Building Bridges

Dawson tried to resolve the many helpful insights of contradictory religious theories by looking to the reality of religion in history. Historical world cultures long agreed on the central importance of supernor-

86. Dawson, *Religion and Culture*, 166.

mal psychic experience in dreams, visions, trances, and ecstasies. These seemed to give access to the wider world of supernatural energy (called by different names in different cultures), which possessed a character of an *other* that imposes itself on the world of humans as something more powerful or more sacred, Dawson wrote. Those who intuited their own dependency on forces larger than themselves through experiences of such reality tried to reorder their way of life (FWP) according to their vision (their I)—like in the case of Muhammad's vision around the year 610 instantiating itself in the Islamic way of life, or in that of the atheist-Jewish Harvard Business School professor Roy Schoeman, whose mystical experience in 1987 utterly changed his way of life. In addition, people with experiences such as these often became the religious leaders and the intellectual teachers of the community, like Schoeman, who left Harvard to become an evangelist explaining how Catholicism—as post-messianic Judaism—represents the fulfillment of God's revelation. Their discovery of deeper levels of consciousness had repercussions for the society at large through the witness of their testimony.[87]

Dawson wrote every historic religion, from the most primitive to the most advanced, agrees on two fundamental points: (1) divine or supernatural powers exist whose nature is mysterious, but which control the world and human life, and (2) these powers are associated with particular people, things, places, or ceremonies that act as channels or bridges of communication between the human and divine worlds. In primitive cultures, one finds the Shaman, the fetish, the holy place, and the sacred dance. In more advanced examples, one finds the prophet, the priest, the sacred king, the temple, and the sacramental liturgy. "Thus every great historic culture, viewed from within through the eyes of its members, represents a theogamy, a coming together of the divine and the human within the limits of a sacred tradition," Dawson argued.[88]

In order to exert a permanent influence on human life and behav-

---

87. "A Harvard Professor's Conversion to Catholicism," https://www.youtube.com/watch?v=EWDevlijGUI&feature=emb_logo (accessed December 14, 2019); Dawson, *Religion and Culture*, 24, 29, 30.

88. Dawson, *Religion and Culture*, 41.

ior, religions must enculturate in some form.[89] No matter how universal or spiritual, they cannot escape the necessity of clothing themselves in "institutionalism," as von Hügel would have said. Dawson devoted large sections of his Gifford Lectures to how this enculturation happens through various ideal types (in Max Weber's meaning) that he (Dawson) called "prophet," "priest," and "king." These types may never have existed in perfect form, but they nevertheless furnish a "conceptual framework into which all cases can be brought for analysis."[90] Ideal types allow one to compare across cultures and understand more deeply the sociological role of something—in this case, linking religion and culture. Prophet, priest, and king were not exclusive types, since, historically, the king might also be a priest. However, they represented distinct functions and provided a basis for a typological classification of cultures in comparative religion, Dawson wrote.[91]

These ideal types reveal how Dawson bridged disparate insights into religion as individual experience (James) of the irreducible category the "the Holy" (Otto), which is related as both cause and effect to the social order and intellectual life (Durkheim) in a tension of forces (von Hügel). By adopting a multifaceted view of religion, Dawson's account of these ideal types showed how "secular religions" could continue to dominate the modern world, where other kinds of prophets, priests, and kings channeled the organizing principles of society. In both cases—ancient and modern—they are sources of ultimate salvific knowledge leavening various world cultures. "Where there is no vision, the people perish" (Proverbs 29:18).

89. Dawson, *Religion and Culture*, 41

90. Pals, *Eight Theories of Religion*, 156. Pals contrasted Weber's ideal-type with a scientific generalization: "An ideal-type is a general concept, but it is different from what is known as a generalization in natural science. Generalizations identify a single trait or characteristic common to a group, as when we say, 'All kings have countries.' A country to rule is a kind of bare minimum qualification for a king. When we create an ideal-type of a king, however, we form almost the very opposite of a generalization. We frame a sort of purposeful exaggeration, or maximum outline, of what a ruler should be, adding to the country he rules a large set of further attributes: royal birth, male gender, rule by 'divine right,' a queen, a palace with courtiers, a crown, nobles sworn to uphold it, and so on" (155–56). For Weber's own account of the ideal-type, see Max Weber, " 'Objectivity' in the Social Sciences and Social Policy," in *Philosophy of the Social Sciences: A Reader*, ed. Maurice Natanson (New York: Random House, 1963). This essay originally appeared in the *Archiv für Sozialwissenschaft und Sozialpolitik*, XIX (1904): 22–87, as "Die 'Objectivität' sozialwissenschaftlicher und sozialpolitisher Erkenntnis."

91. Dawson, *Religion and Culture*, 50.

Dawson started with the prophet as the most important type from the purely religious point of view because this figure connected to the deepest levels of human consciousness. This type has also been characteristic of both the most primitive and most advanced forms of religion, Dawson noted. It covered the whole range of religious experience and spiritual achievement, "from the saint and the mystic through the visionary and the dreamer down to the medium and the diviner." The prophetic type was the interpreter of the divine world. "He is the man who dares to confront the perils of the unknown; who beholds in dreams and visions the mysteries which are veiled from common eyes, who hears the voices of spirits, and who in ecstasy and trance utters inspired oracles and warnings which guide chiefs and people in hours of decision"[92]—for example when Emperor Diocletian consulted the Oracle of Delphi (a sort of institutionalized prophetic voice) in 302 before launching his persecution of Christians.

Dawson focused on the prophetic type as particularly characteristic of Muslim culture, though he did not discount the important role of the Ulema (Muslim scholars of law and theology), too. He turned his attention to the Arab Muslim historian Ibn Khaldun (1332–1406), who wrote his great *Muqaddimah* in North Africa and based his whole theory of history on the dynamic influence of recurring prophetic movements. Khaldun wrote of those who hear spiritual speech and receive divine inspiration to instruct others in the ways of God and of salvation. These prophetic figures, for Khaldun, were consequently the ultimate sources of creative change in history and human society, "just as the soul moves the body, and the spiritual world changes the world of inanimate matter," Dawson summarized.[93]

Despite their important sociological functions, false prophets and unrestrained prophetic figures could also become threats to communities through an excess of individualism. They could act as channels of disruptive or revolutionary forces, as among the Anabaptists at Münster in 1534 or when Lenin stepped off his train in Finland Station, Petrograd, in 1917.

92. Dawson, *Religion and Culture*, 50, 52, 54.
93. Dawson, *Religion and Culture*, 56, 57.

Dawson argued the prophet's office "is counterbalanced by that of the priesthood which normally acts as the authoritative, regulating principle in religion and the institutional bond between religion and culture." In many societies, the priesthood absorbed the prophetic function and became the primary religious organ.[94]

The priesthood, as in ancient Mesopotamia or Egypt, represented the institutionalization of the more individualistic religious experience of the prophet in a stable, corporate body handing on its traditions of sacred knowledge and exercising responsibility for the religious life of the whole community as the master of sacrifice and worship. Offering something (a sacrifice) through a ritual established communion with the supernatural—or, among less advanced peoples, with the unknown and mysterious sources of life. "The most remarkable example of this specialized development of sacrificial and ritual technique is to be found in the religious culture of India," Dawson noted about the Rig Veda, the collection of religious poetry sacred to Hinduism. "Sacrifice is the navel of the universe," sang the composer of that poetry about the riddle of sacrifice holding together reality.[95] A navel connects an utterly dependent fetus to the nutrients and waste removal provided by the mother's bloodstream, which is powered by her heart, just as sacrifice in world religions, metaphorically speaking, is meant to ensure the "nutrients" needed from the gods and the "waste removal" of sin, evil, or misfortune. It expresses the religious economy of give and take along the umbilical cord of sacred rites managed by the priesthood. In many instances, the priesthood and its altars and temples stood at the very center of world historical cultures.

With their accumulated wealth, ancient temples—governed by priests—possessed archives and schools and all the apparatus of scholarship, linking religion to intellectual achievement. In Europe, as in India, the sacred language (Latin or Sanskrit, respectively) also served as the learned language. The modern European intelligentsia traced its roots back to the clergy, the medieval priesthood, and the religious or-

---

94. Dawson, *Religion and Culture*, 63, 65.

95. Dawson, *Religion and Culture*, 69; "Rig Veda," accessed December 17, 2019, https://www.milestonedocuments.com/documents/view/rig-veda/text In the Rig Veda, see 1.164 "The Riddle of Sacrifice," para. 35.

ders who created universities and possessed a quasimonopoly on higher intellectual culture for centuries, Dawson wrote.[96]

Dawson's comments on the intelligentsia are worth dwelling on. Implicitly, it seems today, the intelligentsia has largely taken over the sociological function of the traditional priesthood in moderating the ideals and rituals of blood sacrifice to the gods of Nation and Choice in modern cultures. For as writer David Foster Wallace (1962–2008) said: "Everybody worships." The only choice is *what* to worship. The compelling reason to choose Jesus Christ, or Allah, or the Four Noble Truths is that "pretty much anything else you worship will eat you alive."[97] There is an inevitability about the relation between religion and culture even in the modern world, despite concepts like "separation of church and state." Dawson's whole theory of political religions is predicated on that assumption (discussed further in chapter 6).

If the prophet was the organ of divine inspiration and the priest the organ of sacred worship and sacred science, the king was the organ of sacred power. As humans learned to participate in the mysteries of nature through irrigation and intensive agriculture, which multiplied population and wealth in the rise of ancient civilizations, it was inevitable that the king would be "regarded not merely as sacred but as himself a divine power, a god or a son of the gods, at once god and man, priest and king, the keystone which joined the arch of heaven and earth and established the harmony of the two worlds." Here Dawson used the example of Egyptian pharaohs as the epitome of this development because the Nile Valley was more conducive to centralization than the environments of the other riverine civilizations of the Ancient East. The whole life of the people was seen as dependent on the pharaoh. His relationship with the divine maintained regular Nile flooding and the rhythm of planting and harvesting. Thus, he embodied the divine power that ruled that land.[98]

In the religious history of culture, the king represented a divine mandate that separated him from other people. He had received the

---

96. Dawson, *Religion and Culture*, 80.

97. David Foster Wallace, "2005 Kenyon Commencement Address," May 21, 2005, https://web.ics.purdue.edu/~drkelly/DFWKenyonAddress2005.pdf.

98. Dawson, *Religion and Culture*, 89, 90.

gift of leadership, akin to the gift of prophesy with a certain superhuman quality, such as a "sudden outburst of energy" or "some incalculable decisive act," Dawson wrote.[99] Awareness of such sacred, energetic leadership has become so remote from the religious traditions of the West, he noted, that the German writer Johann Wolfgang von Goethe (1749–1832) stood alone among modern thinkers in his sympathetic understanding of it. Goethe wrote of a secret power in the universe, a kind of destiny drawing out many threads of the web that future years must complete, inexplicable by reason; this power he called the *daemonic*, meaning "inspired as if by a spirit or a genius." The daemonic nature manifested an unlimited power of action and unrest. Dawson quoted Goethe: "It [the daemonic] was not divine, for it seemed unreasonable; not human, for it lacked understanding; not angelic, for it often displayed malicious joy. It was like chance, for it pointed to no consequence; it resembled providence, for it indicated connexion and unity." The daemonic could manifest through world historical events; one sometimes saw it in artists (particularly musicians) and even animals, Goethe thought. Yet, "This daemonic character appears in its most dreadful form when it stands out dominatingly in some *Man*. Such are not always the most remarkable men either in spiritual quality or natural talents and they seldom have any goodness of heart to recommend them. But an incredible force goes forth from them and they exercise an incredible power over all creatures."[100] Goethe thought Napoleon an example of the daemonic man in the highest degree. "It is unnecessary to point out what dangerous possibilities are involved in this concept so far as modern political life is concerned," Dawson concluded.[101]

Religion and Culture

Due to the actions of figures such as prophets, priests, and kings, a two-way structural relation formed between religion and culture

99. Dawson, Religion and Culture, 85.

100. Dawson, *Religion and Culture*, quoted on 85–86. Dawson quoted from Goethe's *Dichtung und Wahrheit* (Werke, ed. Cotta XXV), 124, 126. See also Johann P. Eckermann, *Conversations of Goethe with Eckermann and Soret*, vol. 2, trans. John Oxenford (London: Smith, Elder, 1850), 355–56, 359–60.

101. Dawson, *Religion and Culture*, 86.

throughout world history. That relation might only be observable through large-scale study of a whole civilizations over many centuries, Dawson held. On the one side of this relation, the social way of life influences the approach to religion, and on the other side, the religious vision influences the way of life. In terms of the Geddes-Le Play formula, Ideas/Folk, Work, Place: I → FWP and FWP → I,[102] which Dawson called the culture-process. For example, religion consecrates (influences) folk or the social bond by linking groups of people around generational lines, as in aboriginal Australian totemic systems. It consecrates work through the ritual cycle of the agricultural year, with prayers at sprouting and harvesting time, as in the Sumerian *Farmer's Almanac* (c. 1,700 B.C.). It consecrates place through holy places, as at Delphi among the Greeks, or the Buddhist pilgrimage sites of the Gangetic Plain, the ancient sacred city, or the Jewish Holy Land. These consecrations of F, W, and P, often visible through the actions of prophetic, priestly, or kingly figures, are the main avenues by which religion finds social expression and takes on sociological form, Dawson wrote. Spiritual changes induce modifications of ways of life, and changes to the ways of life bring about a new religious attitude. This culture-process has played a strong role in the rise of new or modified cultures, which then may be transmitted to other societies and change them too.[103]

Demonstrating his ingenious combination of synthesis and nuance, Dawson cited the spread of Buddhism as a prime example of the two-way culture-process in action. The following extended quotation is worth following closely:

Buddhism was emphatically a way of life, which created communities and institutions and had a more far-reaching influence on the culture of Eastern and Southern Asia than any other movement. Even to-day [1948] the Buddhist theocracy of Tibet is the most complete and imposing example of a purely religious culture existing in the modern world. And this is a remarkably interesting case, since it shows how a highly specialized way of life

102. Read this as: "Ideas influence Folk, Work, and Place" and "Folk, Work, and Place influence each other and Ideas."

103. Dawson, *Religion and Culture*, 43, 45; Dawson, "Prevision in Religion," in *Dynamics of World History*, 98–102; Christopher Dawson, "The Institutional Forms of Christian Culture," *Religion in Life* XXIV (1955): 379.

adapted to an exceptional environment can become fused with a very highly developed religious culture, which arose in an entirely different milieu and was imported ready-made into the utterly different social and geographical world of mediaeval Tibet. Not only was the extremely subtle and elaborate structure of Buddhist metaphysics transferred intact from Sanskrit to Tibetan, but it was later retransferred *en bloc* from Tibetan to Mongolian, so that the whole of Eastern Central Asia from the Himalayas to Lake Baikhal and Manchuria is dominated by this secondary derivative Buddhist culture which has its centre in the great monasteries of Lhasa and Tashi Llumpo and Urga. Thus by a strange irony of history the most aggressive warrior people of Asia—the Mongols—came to adopt a religion of non-aggression and universal compassion; and if, as seems probable, this event gradually led to a change in the character and habits of the people which contributed to the cessation of the age-long drive of the peoples of the steppes to East and West, it may be reckoned as one of the turning points in world history.

Through the culture-process, an alien religion was imported to Tibet and Mongolia where it melded with the ways of life in those places to mold and change them. At the same time, different ways of life (FWP) exerted influences on the imported Buddhism, as evidenced by the fact that the gods of the steppes became members of the Buddhist pantheon, and the Tibetan or Mongolian Lama is really part Shaman, Dawson wrote. Religion plays an important part in the culture-process even when it is difficult to determine the relative importance of spiritual and material factors in historical movements due to the extreme complexity of cultural change.[104]

Besides its role in this two-way structural relation to culture, religion also played two diachronic/functional roles in this relation. On the one hand, it served as a conservative, unifying force of cultural synthesis by preserving moral law, guarding tradition, and educating the young in wisdom—like in the case of established Anglicanism in eighteenth-century England. On the other hand, religion could take on a creative and dynamic function in times of social change. In cases such as the spread of the Ghost Dance across the American West in 1890 or the movement of Islam outward from Mecca and Medina in the early

104. Dawson, *Religion and Culture*, 45–46.

seventh century, religion served as a "revolutionary disruptive force." The process begins when the current religion and culture synthesis is viewed as discredited. Creative leaders of the new movement, spiritually alienated from the dominant culture and religion, adopt a position of extreme otherworldliness to inspire the change of which they dream. The revolutionary impulse then draws religious forces in new directions and, unintentionally, often tends toward the secularization of culture (until a new synthesis forms). Since both these unifying and dynamic functional roles of religion can be in play at the same time, "a complex culture is always a field of tension between opposing religious forces which are continually striving against one another." For example, the Anglican establishment in eighteenth-century England existed side-by-side with the nonconformist churches and sects that served as channels for the new social forces of modernity, Dawson noted. Indeed, cultures often represent fusions of many different elements.[105] In this case of eighteenth-century England, the greater freedom of religious diversity, in contrast to France, which repressed Huguenots and Jansenists, may have actually fostered greater cultural stability by allowing revolutionary forces to blow off steam. In centrally controlled France, the forces of resentment built up, combined with other causes, and then exploded in the French Revolution.

Any extremely otherworldly or revolutionary religious movement that adopts a purely critical and negative approach to culture, Dawson wrote, is a force of destruction that mobilizes against the healthiest elements in society. At the same time, the identification of religion with a particular cultural synthesis is fatal to the universal character of religious truth, he noted; "It is indeed a kind of idolatry—the subordination of an image made by man for the eternal transcendent reality." If this identification is carried far enough, he continued, "the marriage of religion and culture is equally fatal to either partner, since religion is so tied to the social order that it loses its spiritual character, and the free development of culture is restricted by the bonds of religious tradition until the social organism becomes as rigid and lifeless as a mummy."[106]

---

105. Dawson, *Religion and Culture*, 37, 45, 150–51, 154, 155, 156.
106. Dawson, *Religion and Culture*, 157–58.

Formation

Philosopher Charles Taylor wrote: "There can never be a total fusion of the faith and any particular society; and the attempt to achieve it is dangerous for the faith."[107] Otherworldliness had to coexist with worldliness—another tension in Dawson's theory of religion.

Nevertheless, Dawson has been misunderstood as viewing culture as the embodiment of religion. This was T. S. Eliot's interpretation of the relationship between religion and culture, essentially fusing "cult" with "culture.," Though Eliot overtly acknowledged Dawson's profound influence on himself, this embodiment idea was not Dawson's view. It simplified too much the fundamental dualism between faith (rooted in the transcendent) and culture (rooted in the order of nature), especially among the higher religions.[108] Religion cannot be divorced from or reduced to culture without distortion of one's view of historical developments. This distinction was a key theme of Dawson's comparative religion, as one commentator explicitly noted in a posthumous review of Dawson's *Religion and World History* (1975).[109]

Comparative Religion and Dawson's Cultural Mind

How to reconcile the vertical and horizontal dimensions of religion? How is the profound intuition of the dependence of human life on superhuman realities to be separated from the idolization of temporal conditions in a particular culture, without also being detached from its vital horizontal connection "with man's earthly, bodily existence and transferred to a plane of inhuman abstraction?" That coordination of spiritual and temporal is the vital problem on which depends the relation of religion to culture, Dawson wrote. One had to maintain the absolute transcendent spiritual claims of religion and, at the same time, guard the value of limited, historically conditioned earthly cul-

107. Charles Taylor, *A Catholic Modernity?* Marianist Award Lectures, Book 10 (Dayton, Ohio: University of Dayton, 1996), http://ecommons.udayton.edu/uscc_marianist_award/10/.

108. T. S. Eliot, *Notes towards the Definition of Culture* (New York: Harcourt, Brace, 1949), 31–32. See Dawson's response to Eliot's position in Dawson, "T. S. Eliot on the Meaning of Culture," in *Dynamics of World History*, 115. Glen Olsen also slightly misstated Dawson's view of culture in this way, it seems to me; see Glenn W. Olsen, "Why We Need Christopher Dawson," *Communio* 35 (Spring 2008): 116, 135.

109. Loyal D. Rue, review of *Religion and World History*, *Church History* 45, no. 1 (1976): 126.

tures. In addition, the cultural forms of religion (the holy social ways, work ways, and placeways), which are consecrated by a religious ideal, "must not be regarded as possessing universal religious validity," Dawson concluded.[110]

That was easier said than done, as most religious cultures (including Christian cultures) fail in some way to uphold the tension. Cultures often idolize their own forms, on the one hand, or they view their way of life as having universal moral or spiritual validity, on the other. "The result is that every conflict of cultures is seen as a conflict of different spiritual principles, in other words a conflict of religions; and it usually becomes such in fact since the differences of culture and social tradition tend to ally themselves with differences of religious doctrine."[111] Confusing cultural values and universal truths could be deadly.

In reality, Dawson believed, every social way of life may be a way to God, "so long as it recognizes its human limitations and does not attempt to force its particular historical values into the place of universal divine truths." Cultural relativity and cultural differentiation of religion ought not present difficulties to the theologian, Dawson reflected: "For in so far as a culture represents a natural way of life, it reflects a distinct aspect of reality and has its own particular truth and its own scale of values which provide a way of approach to transcendent truths and values, and opens, as it were, a new window to heaven as well as to earth." Since all things tend toward their natural end or final good, "Every way of life is therefore a potential way to God, since the life that it seeks is not confined to material satisfaction and animal activities but reaches out beyond itself towards eternal life." Therefore, the particular artifacts of each culture that so fascinate anthropologists, archeologists, and historians are not dead ends: "they are the media by which the universal good is apprehended and through which these cultures are orientated towards the good that transcends their own power and knowledge."[112]

From the Christian point of view, the Spirit of God, the Holy Spirit, moves across all cultures, Christian or not. Dawson made this point

110. Dawson, *Religion and Culture*, 159, 160.
111. Dawson, *Religion and Culture*, 160.
112. Dawson, *Religion and Culture*, 47, 162.

not in his Gifford Lectures but—most clearly—in his work for the
Sword of the Spirit movement during the Second World War (see chapter 7). "The Spirit blows through the world like wind and fire, driving
the kingdoms before it, burning up the works of man like dry grass,
but the meaning of history is found not in the wind or in the fire, but
in 'the small voice' of the Word which is never silent, but which cannot
bear fruit unless man co-operates by an act of faith and spiritual obedience."[113] This was Christian universalism understood not as Eurocentrism or Western imperialism but as the recognition that all cultures
throughout history, in all their diversity, possess within an openness to the revelation of Jesus Christ. All the positive elements of the
pre-Christian and non-Christian world find their fulfilment, Dawson
wrote, in the Kingdom of God.[114]

These observations about every way of life being potentially a way
to God take one to the heart of Dawson's cultural mind. Is "culture" a
particular arrangement of a certain people, only understandable on its

---

113. Dawson, *The Judgment of the Nations*, 104.

114. Dawson, *The Crisis of Western Education*, 125. The uniqueness of Christianity in Dawson's
comparative religion is a large subject, and I come at it only indirectly in this book. One can think
of the Jewish experience of God, and of Jesus walking the Earth, as the "religious experience"
that institutionalized and intellectualized over the centuries in the Judeo-Christian tradition.
The Jewish revelation was of an altogether different kind than the revelations of other world religions, Dawson wrote. It was a sacred marriage involving "the introduction of a divine principle
into history, not after the pagan fashion by the deification of the powers of nature but by the
association of man with God in the fulfillment of a divine mission," he noted. This "is the key to
the whole Judeo-Christian revelation" (*The Formation of Christendom* [New York: Sheed & Ward,
1967], 71). Out of its Jewish background, Christians believe Christianity "transcends the sphere of
nature and brings human life into immediate contact and communion with the divine source of
supernatural life. Christianity is at once the revelation of the inadequacy of human knowledge
and human civilization and the communication of the Divine life by which alone human nature
can be healed and restored" (*Religion and the Modern State* [New York: Sheed & Ward, 1935], 112).
As Joseph Cardinal Ratzinger wrote, the "inward readiness for the revelation of God" is written
into human cultures; God's revelation "corresponds to an inner expectation in the cultures themselves" (*Truth and Tolerance* [San Francisco: Ignatius, 2004], 195). See R. Jared Staudt, "'Religion
and Culture' and 'Faith and Renewal of Society' in Christopher Dawson and Pope Benedict XVI,"
Logos 16, no. 1 (Winter 2013): 31–69. From the Thomistic philosophical point of view, if all people
have a "Thomist intellect" (i.e., one capable of the "intellection of being"), then all people are
disposed, no matter how remotely, to the Christian message. Many roadblocks obstruct the transmission, however. "It will take much patient listening to diagnose the culture correctly in order
to understand how to begin talking with it." That is where cultural studies are so important. The
boundaries between cultures are not impenetrable, because "being cannot be eliminated from
the human heart." See John F. X. Knasas, "Tracey Rowland's 'Augustinian Thomist' Interpretation
of Culture," *Angelicum* 86, no. 1 (2009): 699, 700.

own terms? Or is it universal and normative, subject to philosophical and other forms of reasoning? Should it be studied empirically or contemplatively? An anthropologist such as Franz Boas might favor the former perspective, while the philosopher Josef Pieper, representing the humanistic understanding of culture, the latter. In reality, Dawson realized, culture encompasses both at the same time. Therein constitutes the unique strength of Dawson's thought. Understanding culture requires multiple methodologies that he attempted to bring together and not only from the social sciences. As Raymond Williams noted in his book *Keywords: A Vocabulary of Culture and Society*, the still active and complex history of the word "culture" belies any attempt to nail down one "true" meaning of the word. In fact, it is the range and overlap of the humanistic and the socio-historical modes that is significant. He wrote:

The complex of senses indicates a complex argument about the relations between general human development and a particular way of life, and between both and the works and practices of art and intelligence. Within this complex argument there are fundamentally opposed as well as effectively overlapping positions; there are also, understandably, many unresolved questions and confused answers. But these arguments and questions cannot be resolved by reducing the complexity of actual usage. [115]

Williams meant here that the relation between universal values and particular cultures is so complex that multiple traditions of thinking about culture have developed. We need both the socio-historical and the humanistic perspectives because culture is not only something outside us and empirically observable but also in us and worth defending. The universal element in the scientific study of culture cannot be reduced to the laws of nature or an abstract idea of progress. Nor can the view that culture is relative and local fully express it.

Perhaps "universal" and "particular" present a false dichotomy. One can approach reality through the universally true mathematical equation, for example, *and* through the particulars of a poem, such as William Blake's *Auguries of Innocence*, in which one can "see a World

---

115. Raymond Williams, *Keywords: A Vocabulary of Culture and Society* (London: Fontana/Croom Helm, 1976), 80–81.

in a Grain of Sand."[116] The human mind, in any time and place, can correspond to reality through the "intellection of being," grasping the essences of beings as something-there and knowable.[117] As one philosopher wrote, "Aquinas' philosophical psychology and Dawson's reflections both indicate that a sense of being is, and has been, available to ordinary people."[118] Direct religious experience, more than rational inquiry, provided the dynamic element within "primitive" cultures; this is what Dawson called the "intuition of pure being"[119] that lies at the heart of every culture—or (not Dawson's words): "at the heart of the world"[120]—the sense of the transcendent both within the human person (personalistic) and outside the human person, perceived through nature (cosmological). This experience of "being" may induce the philosophical act of *wonder*, which philosopher Josef Pieper connected to leisure as the basis of culture.[121] The apprehension of reality can pass down from generation to generation by tradition and rational inquiry, enshrined in the institutions, customs, morals, and habits of a particular culture.

In this way, culture really can be a "bearer of human and divine truths"[122]—and of goodness and beauty, too (though cultures also ex-

116. William Blake, "Auguries of Innocence," (1863), Poetry Lovers Page, http://www.poetry loverspage. com/poets/blake/to_see_world.html.

117. Knasas, "Tracey Rowland's 'Augustinian Thomist' Interpretation of Culture," 700. "Intellection" refers to the ability of the human intellect to "take in" the essence of a being it encounters—like a tree. The essence of the tree, *what it is*, ends up in the mind through a complicated process at the end of which is a concept of the tree, and this concept bears within itself the same essence that is in the tree. The concept, however, is different from the tree, since the concept refers universally to all trees, whereas the concrete tree refers to nothing beyond itself. I am paraphrasing here an email to me of January 3, 2020, from philosopher Donald Bungum, to whom I am grateful for help.

118. John F. X. Knasas, "Aquinas' Natural Law Versus Ethical and Cultural Pluralism," in *Religion and Culture in Dialogue: East and West Perspectives*, ed. Jānis Tālivaldis Ozoliņš (Switzerland: Springer, 2016), 88.

119. Dawson, *Progress and Religion*, 76.

120. Joseph T. Stuart, "At the Heart of the World: Reflections on Mandan History & Culture," *360 Review*, Spring/Summer 2017, 6–15.

121. Josef Pieper, *Leisure the Basis of Culture* (1952; San Francisco: Ignatius, 2009), 115. Here, Pieper wrote: "The innermost meaning of wonder if fulfilled in a deepened sense of mystery. It does not end in doubt, but is the awakening of the knowledge that being, *qua* being, is mysterious and inconceivable, and that it is a mystery in the full sense of the word: neither a dead end, nor a contradiction, nor even something impenetrable and dark. Rather, mystery means that a reality cannot be comprehended *because* its light is ever-flowing, unfathomable, and inexhaustible. And that is what the wonderer really experiences."

122. Dermot Quinn, "Christopher Dawson and Historical Imagination," *The Chesterton Review* XXVI, no. 4 (2000): 484.

change degrading ideas and practices). These universals can be transferred from culture to culture as a result of contact by trade, education, or war. Just because they are perceived in particular times and places does not mean they are applicable only there, and their spread from one culture to another does not necessarily imply cultural imperialism or appropriation. The current popularity of Western classical music in China—through rigorous music education, new orchestras, and aggressive marketing by music companies—shows how certain traditions can be preserved and enriched through their encounter with other cultures.[123]

This possibility of reconciling cultural relativity with theological and philosophical truth formed the basis of Dawson's comparative religion and structured the way he applied his cultural mind. Drawing together the best of the old natural theology and of the new anthropological and psychological approaches to religion, Dawson viewed comparative religion as the "indispensable link between theology and philosophy and between the world of historic religion and the domain of rational thought." One could not leave out theology, in particular, because of the nature of the object: "religion is essentially a dynamic relation between man and a non-human or superhuman Other." One of the etymological roots of "religion" derives from *ligare* ("to bind together"), to connect the human and the divine. Thus, one cannot study religion only through the human sciences. One cannot do without the higher form of knowledge concerned with the divine object itself, and that is the task of theology. Ultimately, comparative religion must do more than simply unravel the tangled web of culture. It needs the help of theology and philosophy to properly interpret the "supercultural and purely religious elements that are contained in the hieroglyphs of ritual and myth" because "the study of religion begins and ends on the theological level," Dawson noted, "and not on the level of sociology and history, indispensable as these are for the understanding of religion in culture and in human life." In this bifocal study of religion, there is "no necessary conflict between the absolutism of pure theology and the rel-

123. Joseph Kahn and Daniel J. Wakin, "Western Classical Music, Made and Loved in China," *New York Times*, April 2, 2007, http://www.nytimes.com/2007/04/02/world/asia/02iht-china .html?pagewanted=all&_r=0.

ativism of religious phenomenology; indeed the two . . . are necessary and complementary to one another."[124]

"The Key of History"

Once an intellectual bridge connected personal religious experience and the social order, built with aid from James, Otto, von Hügel, Durkheim, and the evidence of world cultures, religion could become the key of history in Dawson's thought. The "historian of civilisation must look above all for the great spiritual movements which give unity and continuity to the world-cultures," Dawson wrote. Those movements are traced in the development of art, philosophy, and religion even more than in politics and economics, which normally absorb the attention of historians, Dawson noted, as a kind of historiographical manifesto.[125] Dawson likely would have agreed with historian Wilfred McClay, who wrote that religion is the "master narrative of master narratives." One should come away from the study of religion feeling one has passed through the "eye of a massive storm, through a force of immense power for creation and destruction, and therefore of immense consequentiality, since every religion is in some way an attempt to take account of the ultimate and of our proper relationship to it," McClay wrote.[126]

Dawson was not a monocausal thinker; he did not reduce culture to cult, as noted above. Material factors always shape any human development, but he believed it is impossible to understand cultures without grasping their religious vision; hence the "key" metaphor, which he attributed to Lord Acton.[127] Without a specific reference, it appears Dawson may have borrowed it from a letter Acton wrote to Mary Gladstone (1847–1927), the daughter and secretary to Prime Minister William Gladstone (1809–1898), since their correspondence was published in 1904.[128] Acton wrote,

124. Dawson, *Religion and Culture*, 17, 34, 47; Dawson, "Religion," in *Chamber's Encyclopedia*, 593.

125. Dawson, "Cycles of Civilisation," in *Enquiries into Religion and Culture*, 58. This essay was first presented to the Sociological Society in 1922.

126. Wilfred M. McClay, "Teaching Religion in American Schools and Colleges: Some Thoughts for the 21st Century," *Historically Speaking* 3, no. 2 (2001): part 2.

127. Dawson, *Religion and the Rise of Western Culture*, 15.

128. Herbert Paul, ed., *Letters of Lord Acton to Mary Gladstone, Daughter of the Right Hon. W. E. Gladstone* (London: George Allen, 1904), 167.

All understanding of history depends on one's understanding the forces that make it, of which religious forces are the most active, and the most definite. We cannot follow all the variations of a human mind, but when we know the religious motive, that a man was an Anabaptist, an Arminian, a Deist or a Jansenist, we have the master key, we stand on known ground, we are working a sum that has been, at least partially, worked out for us, we follow a computed course, and get rid of guesses and accidents.[129]

Dawson, like Acton, believed the master key of religion unlocked the past.

This was true not only of the deep past where religioius influence was obvious. The modern age—supposedly secularized—has also been molded by the tectonic power of religious forces. For example, while acknowledging material and social causes of the French Revolution, Dawson perceived the "gods" at work, too. In 1749, Jean-Jacques Rousseau (1712–1778) walked alone to Vincennes just outside Paris to visit his friend Diderot. He suddenly experienced "a sudden flash of inspiration which revealed to him his true mission and converted him from an unsuccessful man of letters into the prophet of a new gospel," Dawson wrote. "He saw that all the ills of man and all the evils of society were due not to man's own sin or ignorance but to social injustice and the corruptions of an artificial civilization. If man could return to nature

---

129. Acton to Mary Gladstone, March 31, 1883; see J. Rufus Fears, ed., *Essays in Religion, Politics, and Morality*, vol. 3 (Indianapolis, Ind.: LibertyClassics, 1988), 503. The Scottish writer Thomas Carlyle (1795–1881) also put the point very well: "It is well said, in every sense, that a man's religion is the chief fact with regard to him. A man's, or a nation of men's. By religion I do not mean here the church-creed which he professes, the articles of faith which he will sign and, in words or otherwise, assert; not this wholly, in many cases not this at all. . . . But the thing a man does practically believe (and this is often enough *without* asserting it even to himself, much less to others); the thing a man does practically lay to heart, and know for certain, concerning his vital relations to this mysterious Universe, and his duty and destiny there, that is in all cases the primary thing for him, and creatively determines all the rest. That is his *religion*; or, it may be, his mere skepticism and *no-religion*: the manner it is in which he feels himself to be spiritually related to the Unseen World or No-World; and I say, if you tell me what that is, you tell me to a very great extent what the man is, what the kind of things he will do is. Of a man or of a nation we inquire, therefore, first of all, What religion they had? . . . Answering of this question is giving us the soul of the history of the man or nation. The thoughts they had were the parents of the actions they did; their feelings were parents of their thoughts: it was the unseen and spiritual in them that determined the outward and actual—their religion, as I say, was the great fact about them." See Thomas Carlyle, *On Heroes, Hero-Worship and the Heroic in History* (1841; London: Chapman & Hall, 1888), 2–3.

and follow the divinely inspired instinct of his own heart, all would be well."[130] Out of this religious experience, in an example of von Hügel's "mysticism" becoming "intellectualism," Rousseau began to write, and his books appealed to a deeper psychological level than contemporary Voltaire's ever could.

Thus appeared a new "religion of democracy" (Dawson also called it the "religion of humanity") touted by prophetic figures such as Rousseau and Thomas Paine (1737–1809). It provided the dynamism that transformed France and the wider world after 1789, and it happened because the religion of democracy was a spiritual force with international significance. "Without it, the Revolution might have been nothing more than a new Fronde. With it, it changed the world."[131] The Fronde was a series of civil wars throughout France from 1648 to 1653 that resulted in the weakening of local aristocracies and the emergence of absolute monarchy. It was a significant event for France but hardly for the history of the world. These wars had no larger ideological significance, no claim to universal values, no philosophical and theological basis like the French Revolution possessed in the work of Rousseau and the Declaration of the Rights of Man and of the Citizen. In short, the Fronde lacked the support of the gods that the Revolution of 1789 possessed.

The gods of revolution, the secular religion of the eighteenth century, propelled the battle of ideas amidst the streets, bookshops, cafés, salons, Masonic lodges, and Jacobin clubs of revolutionary Paris. It was not peculiar to the Jacobins, but it acquired the external organization of a sect through them, Dawson noted. They institutionalized it, bringing together all three elements of religion identified by von Hügel. The prophetic experience entered history as a powerful force, realigning the relationship between religion and culture in the modern age.

The creed of the Jacobins centered on deistic optimism for human salvation in this world, the altar of the Fatherland, abstractions

130. Christopher Dawson, *The Gods of Revolution* (1972; Washington, D.C.: The Catholic University of America Press, 2015), 32. For a more extensive treatment of the significance of Rousseau's religious experience, see Joseph T. Stuart, *Rethinking the Enlightenment: Faith in the Age of Reason* (Manchester: Sophia Institute Press, 2020), chap. 2.
131. Dawson, *The Gods of Revolution*, 31, 53, 95.

such as reason and liberty, and sacred texts such as the Declaration of the Rights of Man and of the Citizen. They sought to create a civic religion that eliminated the distinction between religion and politics that Christianity stood for, as Rousseau had demanded in his chapter on civic religion in his *Social Contract* (1762). They sought to create one, powerful spiritual-political unity (a "church," in Durkheim's sense) as had existed among the Egyptian priest-kings and the rest of the pagan ancient world. Those who followed such ideas did not know where they would lead. Nevertheless, the few years of the Revolution witnessed the rise of diverse ideological strains, from individualism to socialism, from universalism in the religion of humanity to particularism in the rise of nationalism. The fundamental perspectives of the social and political ideologies that have shaped the modern world ever since found expression in the French Revolution.[132]

Modern ideology is a symptom of the divorce between traditional religion and culture, Dawson believed. Ideology is capable of arousing genuinely religious emotions (see appendix D). The "revolutionary attitude" is "perhaps the characteristic religious attitude of modern Europe," Dawson wrote.[133]

In his analysis of the French Revolution, Dawson made an intriguing suggestion about the nexus amongst religion, culture, and politics. In contrast with much of France, where radicalism arose in reaction to the moribund unification of the Gallican Church with the state, in the Vendée region of France and in England and America, religious renewal in the eighteenth century may have helped prevent political radicalization. For in those places, respectively, Grignon de Montfort (1673–1716), John Wesley (1703–1791), and George Whitefield (1714–1770) preached to those lower classes who could have otherwise become radicalized by political agitators. These preachers turned into religious channels those forces that in much of France had nowhere to go but social and political agitation. Due to their work, "The religious conversion of the individual took the place of the political revolution of society."[134]

---

132. Dawson, *The Gods of Revolution*, 60, 74, 75, 146.

133. Dawson, *Progress and Religion*, 178.

134. Dawson, *The Gods of Revolution*, 89, 152. Elsewhere, Dawson credited this insight to Élie Halévy's *History of the English People in the Nineteenth Century*, vol. 1, *England in 1815* (1912). See

Formation

This flash of insight is difficult to prove—how does one substantiate that people did not become revolutionary for a certain reason? Nevertheless, Dawson's theory of religion and culture implied that if traditional religious expression remains strong, then one will find little room in the souls of a people for philosophical or political substitutes of ultimate meaning. If such expression is weak, then there is plenty of room. Perhaps the radicalism of the French Revolution is evidence enough that this is so.

However that may be, for Dawson, comparative religion pointed to an uncomfortable truth: that the complex relationship between religion and culture may hold as much relevance for understanding modern societies as for ancient and medieval ones. This is a point substantiated by later anthropologists, historians, and political scientists in their work on political religion, the subject of the next chapter.

Dawson's "Institutional Forms of Christian Culture," *Religion in Life: A Christian Quarterly of Opinion and Discussion* 24, no. 3 (Summer 1955): 380.

Part 2

APPLICATION OF A CULTURAL MIND

Chapter 6

The Expansion of Politics

When religion was expelled from their souls, the effect was not to cre-
ate a vacuum or a state of apathy; it was promptly, if but momentari-
ly, replaced by a host of new loyalties and secular ideals that not only
filled the void but (to begin with) fired the popular imagination.

—Alexis de Tocqueville on the
French Revolution (1856)

The defeat of Hitlerism does not mean that we have seen the last of
such movements. In our modern democratic world irrational forces
lie very near the surface, and their sudden eruption under the im-
pulse of nationalist or revolutionary ideologies is the greatest of all
the dangers that threaten the modern world.

—Christopher Dawson (1959)

In trying to understand how Dawson approached culture in the last five chapters (part 1), readers have witnessed the formation of his cultural mind and application of its four rules within anthropology, sociology, history, and comparative religion. In part 2, I demonstrate how Dawson applied his cultural mind to specifical contemporary problems in politics and education, creating a fruitful response to the cultural fragmentation of the Age of the Great War. Here, Dawson's works in "prophetic sociology" come into view, as defined in the introduction. He linked descriptive factual investigation (socio-historical view of culture) to prescriptive judgments (humanistic view of culture) intended

Alexis de Tocqueville, *The Old Régime and the French Revolution*, trans. Stuart Gilbert (1856; New York: Doubleday Anchor Books, 1955), 156. Dawson, *The Movement of World Revolution*, 112.

as normative guides for contemporary ways of life. As demonstrated in the next chapters, recent scholars and educational leaders have verified many of Dawson's investigations and judgments, which explains why his work still feels fresh and challenging even in the twenty-first century. This continued relevance suggests, ultimately, that one might detach the concept of the cultural mind from Dawson and his context and profitablity apply it to other times and places.

Chapter 5 demonstrated how Dawson considered religion an interpretive key and explanatory principle for culture. If that is the case, then this must hold for modern, secular cultures, too. How could this be, though, if "secular" culture is defined by the absence of religion? Dawson wrote that, "Every living culture must possess some spiritual dynamic, which provides the energy necessary for that sustained social effort which is civilization. Normally this dynamic is supplied by a religion, but in exceptional circumstances the religious impulse may disguise itself under philosophical or political forms."[1] Such a view is unthinkable in terms of the old ecclesiastical history, in which "religion" equals "church." As I showed in chapters 4 and 5, however, Dawson approached the past as a historian of culture and a comparative religion scholar, not as an ecclesiastical historian. His intellectual architecture was predicated on the understanding that spiritual reality is always a factor in human life. If that is so, then one would also expect to see evidence of that in a secular age—even if disguised under "philosophical or political forms," as Dawson wrote. One does, in fact, see such evidence, which led Dawson to become a pioneer in the study of "political religions," movements ascribing ultimate values to the political realm rather than the supernatural realm that take on some of the functional apparatus of religion. The historical reality of political religion is a modern case study in Dawson's understanding of the relationship between religion and culture.

Dawson contributed to the growing body of scholarship on political religion by applying his cultural mind to its nature and roots as well as to its tendency to integrate faith and life. He suggested that "the sacred" could be applied to worldly entities, including political ones (a process

1. Dawson, *Progress and Religion*, 3–4.

recent scholars call "sacralization"). The roots of this process, Dawson suggested, included (1) the legacy of the Jacobins in the French Revolution; (2) the liberal attempt to separate religion from culture in the nineteenth century, which created a "spiritual vacuum"; and (3) the trauma of the Great War, which gave opportunity to Lenin, Mussolini, and Hitler to manipulate the spiritually volatile atmosphere of Europe for their purposes. The privatization of the transcendent emptied out the inside of Europe's public squares and left them ripe for colonization by political religions. This process extended even beyond the European world, Dawson realized, for globalizing secularization broke down traditional cultures, idealized state power, and created vulnerabilities to political religion around the world. A key feature characterizing political religions was the desire to integrate faith and life. This explained a good deal of their attraction, since people need an "I" to give shape to the FWP of their lives and societies. Secularization is unstable and, in fact, fosters conditions conducive to the sacralization of temporal realities. This suggests that sacred values can really be opposed only with other sacred values.

The Expansion of Politics in the Age of the Great War

World politics shifted dramatically around the time of the Great War. Historian A. J. P. Taylor (1906–1990) wrote, "Until August 1914 a sensible, law-abiding Englishman could pass through life and hardly notice the existence of the state, beyond the post office and the policeman."[2] English people did not need passports to travel abroad; they paid modest taxes. The state largely left the adult citizen alone. During and soon after the Great War, however, this minimal relationship between citizens and their states changed. Government took on a larger scope of activity, creating new departments of shipping, labor, food, national service, and food production. Some understood this as a direct result of the war.[3] Military drafts forced citizens to serve the state; new regulations appeared for food, the press, and beer; even the clocks

2. A. J. P. Taylor, *English History: 1914–1945* (London: Book Club Associates, 1965), 1.

3. "The War Cabinent, 1917," in *British Government 1914–1953: Select Documents*, ed. G. H. L. Le May (London: Mathuen, 1955), 229; Taylor, *English History*, 76.

changed with the first implementation of daylight savings time.[4] The politicization of life increased rapidly, and Dawson called this the "expansion of Politics."[5]

This expansion was fuelled by the circumstances of war but also by the increasing tendency to express ultimate meaning through what Dawson called "pseudo-religion[s]," "public religions," or "secular religions."[6] He used these phrases more than "political religion," but this chapter will employ the latter phrase for the sake of simplicity and to relate his account to the work of other scholars who also studied secular religions manifesting themselves through politics. Political religions are ideologies promoting the "kingdom of God" on earth through the power of the state, and without God.

Dawson partly blamed the Great War for the tendency to make politics the highest expression of values. The state increasingly became a secular church that proposed itself as the key to human salvation in this world. The mobilization of entire societies during the Great War dramatically increased expectations for state involvement in peoples' lives. As four empires collapsed during, or soon after, the war (the Russian, German, Austro-Hungarian, and Ottoman), radical political movements arose in the resulting power vacuum.

The Great War "has left throughout Europe a mood of disillusionment and despair, which calls aloud for a new religion," atheist philosopher Bertrand Russell wrote after touring Russia in 1920. "Bolshevism has supplied the new religion."[7] The result was the greatest national catastrophe experienced in Europe until that time, with about ten million dead in the brutal Russian Civil War, which raged from 1917 to 1922.

In Italy, too, the Great War directly led to the rise of fascism as political militants refused to demobilize in 1918. Mussolini and his armed followers sought to preserve the meaning and purpose they had discovered during their wartime experience of camaraderie in the trenches by trying to create an all-embracing state.

4. Taylor, *English History*, 2.

5. Christopher Dawson, "The Claims of Politics," *Scrutiny* VIII, no. 2 (1939): 136. This article was reprinted in *The Political Science Reviewer* XLI, no. 2, (2017): 335–40.

6. Christopher Dawson, *Beyond Politics* (London: Sheed & Ward, 1939), 104, 105.

7. Bertrand Russell, *The Practice and Theory of Bolshevism* (London: George Allen & Unwin, 1920), 17.

In postwar Germany, hyperinflation forced many people into poverty. Vagrants proliferated, some of whom became wandering prophets predicting the end of the world and the need for a new type of man to create a new society. In this environment, Adolf Hitler resolved to go into politics, believing the people needed a common faith. The movement he led, Nazism, would, in effect, join church and state into a singular powerful force.

Also significant was Kemalism[8] in Turkey, similarly a fruit of frustration and defeat in the Great War. Dawson located it midway between communism and Nazism in its ethnic cleansing, nationalism, militarism, and suppression of religion.[9]

The historical period after the Great War midwifed the birth of startling new deities: Class (communism), State (fascism), and Race (Nazism), for which people killed on a vast and unprecedented scale. Like the ancient Aztec god Huitzilopochtli, these modern gods demanded human blood. They inspired warrior faiths that clashed in the twentieth century, causing tens of millions of deaths. Communism alone would eventually claim one hundred million lives.

The United States did not remain immune to political religion. Through the press, Americans absorbed many of the ideas, values, and propaganda associated with the war as early as its outbreak in 1914. Their membership in a wider Western civilization, made up of mutually influencing regional cultures, meant that even farm boys and small-town nurses, far from the scene of action, became emotionally and spiritual embroiled in the conflict. Americans consented to the war largely because they came to believe Germany and its allies represented a threat to national security. President Woodrow Wilson's wartime mobilization program also gave a major boost to the politicization of society through economic oversight, propaganda, political prisoners, persecution of foreigners, regulation of publications critical of the government, cultural assimilation, and intimidation of dissenters. Subsequently, the impressive results of wartime mobilization cre-

8. Kemalism, as it was implemented by Mustafa Kemal Atatürk (1881–1938), was defined by widespread political and religious reforms designed to separate the new Turkish state from its Ottoman predecessor and embrace a modern, secular national identity.

9. Dawson, *Religion and the Modern State*, 14–16.

ated the model for the welfare state and the New Deal. Theological and political progressives, who contributed to the mentality of total war for the sake of advancing "God's kingdom on earth," learned to dream of other state-led social engineering projects, such as Prohibition and eugenics. The politicization of life spread as people came to believe in the perfectibility of human society through government action and interventionist foreign policy. The American historian Michael S. Neiberg concluded: "The country's entry into the war marked the end of one era and the start of another, one whose impact we are still feeling, even if we do not always recognize it."[10]

Political religion even spread beyond the West, into the Islamic world, for example, where Hassan al-Banna (1906–1949, founder of the Muslim Brotherhood), Sayyid Qutb (1906–1966, the spiritual father of the terrorist organization Al-Qaeda), and Abul A'la al-Maududi (1903–1979, the Pakistani theorist credited for the modern conceptualization of the "Islamic state") were inspired by European political religions and totalitarian movements to transform the concept of *jihad* into violent global revolution.[11] They wanted an ideology capable of mobilizing the Muslim masses beyond the narrow bounds of traditional political quietism in Islam, creating the "mind of jihad."[12] The Great War itself "was primarily responsible for the growth of unrest in the East," Dawson wrote. The "Russian Revolution and the propaganda against Western imperialism," he continued, "which has been organized by the Soviet Government and the allied communist organization, have given unity and coherence to the activities of the various disaffected elements among the subject people and classes throughout the world."[13] It was through the spread of communism, Dawson believed, that secular ideologies first reached the masses and "imparted a revolutionary momentum to the movement of social change," of which

10. Richard M. Gamble, *The War for Righteousness: Progressive Christianity, the Great War, and the Rise of the Messianic Nation* (Wilmington, Del.: ISI Books, 2003), 4; Joseph T. Stuart, "North Dakota and the Cultural History of the Great War," *North Dakota History* 83, no. 2 (2018): 6; and Michael S. Neiberg, *The Path to War: How the First World War Created Modern America* (New York: Oxford University Press, 2016), 7.

11. Jankovic, "Monstrous Modernity: Western Roots of Islamic Radicalism," 78–89.

12. Laurent Murawiec, *The Mind of Jihad* (New York: Cambridge University Press, 2008), 177.

13. Christopher Dawson, "The Revolt of the East and the Catholic Tradition," *Dublin Review* CLXXXIII (July 1928): 1–2.

al-Banna, Qutb, and Maududi were symptoms. Dawson's views on this movement have proven accurate, for as scholar Laurent Murawiec has shown, many Muslim leaders formed a tactical alliance with the Bolsheviks out of common hatred for Europe, and the Red Army itself became a school of terror for its many Muslim officers and soldiers.[14] In addition, the uprooting of traditional cultures by the forces of globalization since the nineteenth century (largely through Western science and technology) created unmet spiritual needs. Political religion could thus easily hijack Islam in ways that confirm Dawson's insights into the expansion of politics as a major feature of the modern age. In fact, Dawson wrote, the twentieth century witnessed the "extension to Asia and to the whole world of the revolutionary movement of change which started in Western Europe and America in the eighteenth century."[15]

What Is Political Religion?

Critical Western observers struggled to develop concepts describing this expansion of politics after the Great War. Were Russia after 1917, Italy after 1922, and Germany after 1933 dictatorships? Tyrannies? Autocracies? These regimes were perceived as something novel that traditional vocabulary could not adequately describe. New concepts were needed because these regimes sought to control human lives in unprecedented ways. Two major concepts that arose in the 1920s and 1930s were "totalitarian" and "political religion."[16]

The term totalitarian originated in 1923 among the Italian antifascist opposition, including liberals, Catholics, and socialists,[17] and it was adopted by fascists themselves. Benito Mussolini described "totalitarian" positively as the all-embracing state: "The Fascist conception of the state is all embracing; outside of it no human or spiritual values can exist, much less have value. Thus understood, Fascism is totalitarian,

14. Murawiec, *The Mind of Jihad*, 226.

15. Dawson, *The Movement of World Revolution*, 63, 73, 127.

16. Hans Maier, "Concepts for the Comparison of Dictatorships: 'Totalitarianism' and 'Political Religions,'" in *Totalitarianism and Political Religions*, ed. Hans Maier (New York: Routledge, 1996), 199–201.

17. Jens Petersen, "The History of the Concept of Totalitarianism in Italy," in *Totalitarianism and Political Religions*, 6.

and the Fascist state—a synthesis and a unit inclusive of all values—interprets, develops, and potentiates the whole life of a people."[18]

The totalitarian regimes were animated by political religions, the spirits behind the totalitarian machinery.[19] The concept of political religion describes Mussolini's idea that the state is the source of all spiritual values. Political religion sacralises entities such as nation, state, race, or class (see appendix D). Even though fascism, Nazism, and communism presented themselves as secular, advocates of the concept of political religion argue that they *functioned* as religions. While Dawson's views on totalitarianism have already been studied,[20] his approach to political religion has not.

While Dawson's writings of the 1930s were among the first sustained discussions of political religion in Britain, other European scholars also wrote of it, including Franz Werfel (1890–1945), Eric Voegelin (1901–1985), and Raymond Aron (1905–1983).[21] After the Second World War, the concept faded from scholarly attention, but since the fall of communism in western Eurasia by 1991 and the rise of fundamentalist terrorism in the early twenty-first century, the concept has returned today in the work of Michael Burleigh,[22] Emilio Gentile,[23] Hans Maier,[24] and the journal *Totalitarian Movements and Political Religions* (founded in 2000). Outside of the West, it has been applied to the Chinese Cultural Revolution[25] and Islamic terrorism.[26] A growing body of scholarship has fruitfully examined in detail the language, rituals,

18. Benito Mussolini, "The Doctrine of Fascism" (1932), Milestone Documents, http://www.milestonedocuments.com/documents/view/benito-mussolinisthe-doctrine-of-fascism/text.

19. A. James Gregor, *Totalitarianism and Political Religion: An Intellectual History* (Stanford, Calif.: Stanford University Press, 2012), 5.

20. Adam Schwartz, "Confronting the 'Totalitarian Antichrist': Christopher Dawson and Totalitarianism," *Catholic Historical Review* 89, no. 3 (July 2003): 464–88.

21. Hans Maier, "Political Religion: a Concept and its Limitations," *Totalitarian Movements and Political Religions* VIII, no. 1 (2007): 9–10.

22. Michael Burleigh, *Earthly Powers: The Clash of Religion and Politics in Europe, from the French Revolution to the Great War* (New York: HarperCollins, 2005); Michael Burleigh, *Sacred Causes: Religion and Politics, from the Great War to the War on Terror* (New York: Harper Perennial, 2008).

23. Emilio Gentile, *Politics as Religion*, trans. George Staunton (Princeton, N.J.: Princeton University Press, 2006).

24. Maier, "Political Religion: a Concept and its Limitations."

25. Zuo Jiping, "Political Religion: The Case of the Cultural Revolution in China," *Sociological Analysis* 52, no. 1 (1991): 99–110.

26. Jankovic, "Monstrous Modernity: Western Roots of Islamic Radicalism," 78–89.

and appeal of totalitarian movements in terms of political religion, which, despite its limitations as a conceptual category and tendency to overemphasize religious-psychological aspects, political scientist Hans Maier has argued, is necessary to account for the psychological and sociological appeal of twentieth-century despotic regimes.[27]

The historian Emilio Gentile argued that the idea of the numinous developed by Rudolf Otto (introduced in chapter 5) gives plausibility to the concept of political religion. The political dimension of human life can be a place of sacred experience, "as frequently occurs during times of great collective emotion such as wars or revolutions."[28] Collective experience of the *mysterium tremendum*, the fascinating, terrifying manifestation of immense, mysterious, and majestic power, can confer sacred status upon secular entities (such as nation, state, revolution, war, humanity, society, race, proletariat, liberty), as happened during and after the Great War.[29] As noted earlier, this process is called sacralization. The retreat of transcendence in the modern world leaves society to set up its own gods. This happened overtly, sociologist Émile Durkheim remarked, during the early years of the French Revolution, when secular objects, such as homeland, liberty, and reason, were transformed into sacred things.[30] They could then function as the basis of a moral community. This was the functionalist insight of Durkheim encountered earlier: religion shaped society in an all-embracing way, and vice versa. Dawson agreed. Even secular concepts like "community," "progress," and "democracy" could acquire a kind of "numinous character," giving them an emotional appeal that put them above rational criticism, he wrote.[31]

27. Maier, "Political Religion: a Concept and its Limitations," 15.

28. Emilio Gentile, "The Sacralization of Politics: Definitions, Interpretations and Reflections on the Question of Secular Religion and Totalitarianism," *Totalitarian Movements and Political Religions* I (2000): 29. Article translated by Robert Mallett.

29. Gentile, *Politics as Religion*, 10.

30. Durkheim, *The Elementary Forms of Religious Life*, 161.

31. Christopher Dawson, "Education and the State," *Commonweal*, January 25, 1957, 424. The appeal of the numinous played a role in drawing Islamic author Tawfik Hamid (born in 1961 in Egypt), for example, into political religion as a young man: "I remember feeling exhilarated at Jamaa's [an Egyptian Islamist movement considered a terrorist organization by the West] unity and vision, the singularity of purpose and fearlessness of the group displayed in the face of opposition from government and moderates. It was a feeling of raw power—the power to change the course of history and to sweep current society aside. It was, as some might say, not unlike a drug, an addiction, but it was more: Jamaa's program of religious study and their sermons spoke to my awakening interest in the divine." Tawfik eventually escaped from their influence through

Application

An example of numinous experience and the temptation to sacralise the secular comes from the memoirs of German writer Melita Maschmann (1918–2010) concerning the Nazi takeover in January 1933 and the massive demonstration in Berlin:

> On the evening of January 30 my parents took us children, my twin brother and myself, into the centre of the city. There we witnessed the torchlight procession with which the National Socialists celebrated their victory. Some of the uncanny feel of that night remains with me even today. The crashing tread of the feet, the sombre pomp of the red and black flags, the flickering torches on the faces and the songs with melodies that were at once aggressive and sentimental. . . .
>
> I longed to hurl myself into this current, to be submerged and borne along by it. . . .
>
> I was overcome with a burning desire to belong to these people for whom it was a matter of life and death.[32]

This description captures the awe, energy, and majestic power of a movement that spoke to the longing of Maschmann and many others of her generation to belong to something greater than themselves.

While Dawson did not use the term sacralization, he described it implicitly when he wrote during the 1930s about the transference of religious faith and emotion to secular objects in the political movements of his day, whether of people (Folk), labor (Work), or the fatherland (Place).[33] These sacralizations fuelled political passions by becoming absolute principles of collective action. They became sacred values, objects of "veneration and dedication, even to the point of self-sacrifice."[34]

---

his knowledge of the Bible, re-engaging critical thinking and his love of beauty. Interestingly, he commented that his wife did not join the organization; "Perhaps her father's Sufi faith granted her a stronger immunity to the group than the atheist inclinations of my own father." See Tawfik Hamid, *Inside Jihad: How Radical Islam Works, Why it Should Terrify Us, How to Defeat It* (Mountain Lake Park, Md.: Mountain Lake, 2015), 32, 36–37.

32. Melita Maschmann, "A German Teenager's Response to the Nazi Takeover in January 1933," in Robert G. Moeller, *The Nazi State and German Society: A Brief History with Documents* (Boston: Bedford/St. Martin's, 2010), 46–47. Moeller cited Maschmann's *Account Rendered: A Dossier on My Former Self*, trans. Geoffrey Strachan (London: Abelard-Schuman, 1964), 10–12, 16.

33. Christopher Dawson, "Religion in an Age of Revolution," *Tablet*, October 24, 1936, 550; Dawson, "Prevision in Religion," 103. "Prevision in Religion" originally appeared in the *Sociological Review* XXVI (1934): 41–50.

34. Gentile, "The Sacralization of Politics," 18–19.

Sacred values mobilize people to heroic action. The anthropologist Scott Atran called them "devoted actors," a theoretical framework describing the mechanisms behind their willingness to make costly sacrifices for the group in ways dissociated from likely risks. Devoted actors entering the global jihadi archipelago today, for example, are mostly young adults with little traditional religious education who convert to a radical religious vocation partly through the "appeal of a meaningful cause," Atran wrote. Violent extremism, he noted, represents the collapse of traditional cultures as young people "unmoored from millennial traditions flail about in search of a social identity that gives personal significance and glory. This is the dark side of globalization."[35]

Though perhaps obvious in the case of Islamism, some critics have wondered how an explicitly secular ideology can be a political "religion."[36] Obviously, Lenin, Mussolini, and Hitler did not establish supernatural religions but secular systems. Nevertheless, those systems did resemble Durkheim's 1912 description of religion as a *"unified system of beliefs and practices relative to sacred things, that is to say, things set apart and surrounded by prohibitions—beliefs and practices that unite its adherents in a single moral community called a church* . . . the idea of church suggests that religion must be something eminently collective."[37] In the case of the political ideologies, the "sacred things" that were "set apart" were the social *ends* that were absolute (e.g., racial purity or the classless society). Dawson wrote that the "determination to build Jerusalem, at once and on the spot, is the very force which is responsible for the intolerance and violence of the new political

35. Atran, "The Devoted Actor: Unconditional Commitment and Intractable Conflict Across Cultures," 198–99.

36. Richard J. Evans, "Nazism, Christianity and Political Religion: A Debate," *Journal of Contemporary History* 42, no. 1 (2007): 5–7.

37. Durkheim, *The Elementary Forms of Religious Life*, 46. Emilio Gentile wrote: " 'Totalitarianism' has not only an institutional significance, applicable to a system of government and a method of government, but is also indicative of a *political process* activated by a revolutionary party in order to transform the people into a harmonious collective" (emphasis in the original). See Gentile, "The Sacralization of Politics," 21. He continued: "Modernity has not eliminated the problem of religion from the consciousness of modern man. In fact, precisely because it has been a radical, overwhelming and irreversible force for change that has swept away ago-old collective beliefs and age-old, powerful institutions, modernity has created crisis and disorientation—situations which have, in turn, led to the re-emergence of the religious question, even if this has led the individual to turn not to traditional religion, but to new religions that sacralize the human" (31).

order."[38] The sacred social ends of fascism, communism, and Nazism caused them to function as political religions.

In terms of this functionalist approach, political scientist A. James Gregor (1929–2019) offered a clear test to determine that one is dealing with a political religion:

> Throughout history, one of the most important functions of religion has been to explain the ultimate origin and goal of created beings—and thereby to specifically provide codes of conduct, the grounds for moral judgment, the identification of infractions, the depiction of public purposes, as well as the prescription of individual and collective ends. When a subset of political ideologies expressly assumes such metaphysical and normative responsibilities, it can be spoken of as a "political religion."[39]

Note in this comment the assumption of "metaphysical and normative responsibilities": in other words, even if Hitler denied any supernatural purposes in Nazism, if the movement took on the metaphysical and normative functions of religion, then it is a political religion.

Evidence supports the view that Nazism did just that: the political cults, rituals, festivals, sacred spaces, sacred days, martyrs, rallies, and the moral revolution that saw the human will as the ultimate source of moral values and Hitler as the embodiment of that sacred will.[40] In a speech of April 12, 1922, Hitler told his audience that the mighty mission of the Nazi movement was to give the searching masses a new and strong belief "to which they will swear and abide by."[41] Joseph Goebbels (1897–1945), a close associate of Hitler, wrote to the future Führer in 1926:

> You gave a name to the suffering of an entire generation who were yearning for real men, for meaningful tasks. . . . What you uttered is the catechism of a new political credo amid the desperation of a collapsing, godless world. You did not fall silent. A god gave you the strength to voice our suffering. You for-

---

38. Dawson, *Religion and the Modern State*, 109.

39. Gregor, *Totalitarianism and Political Religion*, 9–10.

40. Maier, "Political Religion: a Concept and its Limitations," 7; Angela Astoria Kurtz, "God, not Caesar: Revisiting National Socialism as 'Political Religion,'" *History of European Ideas* 35, no. 2 (June 2009): 241; and Michael Burleigh, *Sacred Causes*, 94–118.

41. Adolf Hitler, "Anti-Semitic Speech," April 12, 1922, in Moeller, *The Nazi State and Germany Society*, 38. Moeller cited Louis L. Snyder, ed., *Hitler's Third Reich: A Documentary History* (Chicago: Nelson-Hall, 1981), 27–30.

mulated our torment in redemptive words, formed statements of confidence in the coming miracle.[42]

Here is the daemonic element of the "kingly type" that Dawson wrote about in his Gifford Lectures—the overwhelming power that Hitler possessed over others. In this letter, Goebbels revealed himself as a man searching for meaning so intensely that he felt compelled to use religious metaphors to describe it. Later, as Reich Minister of Propaganda, Goebbels told journalists that the purpose of propaganda was to "work on people until they are addicted to us" and that the "propagandist must be the man with the greatest knowledge of souls."[43]

Communism also intended to replace the functions of religion despite (or because of) its hostility to religion. While there was widespread endorsement of the Soviet system in British intellectual circles,[44] Dawson was influenced by continental scholars more critical of it.[45] His view that communism and Christianity were absolutely antithetical has been largely substantiated by contemporary scholarship and access to Soviet archives after 1991.[46] Communists persecuted

---

42. Ralf Georg Reuth, *Goebbels*, trans. Krishna Winston (New York: Harcourt Brace, 1993), 54. Reuth cited Joseph Goebbels, "Die Führerfrage," in *Die zweite Revolution: Briefe an Zeitgenossen* (Zwickau, 1926), 7.

43. Joseph Goebbels, "The Tasks of the Ministry for Propaganda," in Moeller, *The Nazi State and Germany Society*, 58. Moeller cited David Welch, *The Third Reich: Politics and Propaganda*, 2nd ed. (London: Routledge, 2002), 173–75.

44. Richard Overy, *The Morbid Age: Britain Between the Wars* (London: Allen Lane, 2009), 282, 288.

45. The Romanian-born René Fueloep-Miller (1891–1963) published his *Geist und Gesicht des Bolschewismus* in 1926. It was translated by F. S. Flint and D. F. Tait as *The Mind and Face of Bolshevism* (1927). Fueloep-Miller wrote that, "Anyone trained in the exact methods of thought of the West can see nothing in this Bolshevik materialism but one of those substitute religions which, since the decay of the earlier faith centred in the Church and the rise of scientific rationalism, have continually kept springing up to provide humanity with a new creed in place of the faith they have lost, and to satisfy their eternal yearning for freedom from all evil in new forms adapted to the scientific sprit of the present time." See René Fueloep-Miller, *The Mind and Face of Bolshevism* (1926; New York: Harper Torchbooks, 1965), 71. Dawson referenced this book in his article "The New Leviathan," 96. The Russian-born Waldemar Gurian (1902–1954) published his *Der Bolschewismus. Einführung in Geschichte und Lehre* in 1931. It was translated into English by Dawson's friend E. I. Watkin as *Bolshevism: Theory and Practice* (1932). It was also translated into French, Italian, and Dutch. Dawson drew from this book in his article "The Significance of Bolshevism" referenced in fn. 84. On Gurian, see Heinz Hürten, "Waldemar Gurian and the Development of the Concept of Totalitarianism," in *Totalitarianism and Political Religions*, 42–52.

46. Mattei Ion Radu, "Dawson and Communism: How Much Did He Get Right?" *The Political Science Reviewer* XLI, no. 2 (2017): 276–302.

Christianity because it was a competitor on their ground. Representative evidence from the Soviet Union includes a party directive of 1923 concerning the destruction of the religious beliefs of workers and peasants. This would require "systematic propaganda" linking religion to the interests of the ruling classes and replacing "outmoded" religious ideas with clear "scientific views of nature and human society." It would be necessary to publish easy-to-read pamphlets and leaflets, the directive said, that "answer questions about the origins of the world, of life and the essence of human relations."[47] Communists intended to take over the metaphysical and normative function of religion.

Another example of a political movement assuming metaphysical and normative responsibilities comes from Mussolini, who wrote in a 1932 article on fascism that:

The Fascist conception of life is a religious one, in which man is viewed in his immanent relation to a higher law, endowed with an objective will transcending the individual and raising him to conscious membership of a spiritual society. . . . The Fascist state is an inwardly accepted standard and rule of conduct, a discipline of the whole person; it permeates the will no less than the intellect. It stands for a principle which becomes the central motive of man as a member of civilized society, sinking deep down into his personality; it dwells in the heart of the man of action and of the thinker, of the artist and of the man of science: soul of the soul.[48]

Mussolini himself described fascism essentially as a political religion that permeates all of life to the depths of the spirit. Clearly, the concept of political religion is useful to understand the expansion of politics in Dawson's age and our own.

Roots of Political Religion

Dawson did not blame the expansion of politics on any one ideology and praise democracy as the answer. The Nazis rose to power democratically, after all. Even democratic countries did not escape his

---

47. Communist Party Directive, 1923, in Robert Weinberg and Laurie Bernstein, eds., *Revolutionary Russia: A History in Documents* (New York: Oxford University Press, 2011), 98–99.
48. Mussolini, "The Doctrine of Fascism."

prognosis; thus he predicted in 1939 the rise of a "democratic totalitarianism which would make the same universal claims on the life of the individual as the totalitarian dictatorships of the Continent."[49] While this did not fully come to pass in his time, and Dawson emphasized the benefits of democracy during the Second World War, he saw all the major political movements of his day as affected by totalitarian forces in the homogenization of mass culture through technology and state education. One could not blame one specific ideology as the source of the problem over the others. One had to go behind all of these political developments to search for their common historical roots.

The roots of political religion have been traced by political scientists and historians back to the fourteenth-century B.C. Egyptian pharaoh Akhenaton,[50] who wielded state power as the sole political and religious representative of the god Aten, and to the sixteenth-century radical Dominican friar Tommaso Campanella,[51] whose utopian *City of the Sun* greatly impressed Lenin. However, Dawson focused on the more recent roots in modern history.

The first source was among the Jacobins, the most influential political club during the Reign of Terror (1793 to 1794) in the French Revolution. As the political events of the 1930s grew more and more ominous, Dawson directed his scholarly attention toward that club. His *Gods of Revolution* was published posthumously in 1972, but much of it was written during the 1930s. Sickness, severe depression, and restless moving from rented house to rented house prevented him from finishing the book. Nevertheless, it studied the underlying psychological and religious forces that gave the revolution such world-transforming power as the first modern expressions of political religion. Robespierre (1758–1794) was the ultimate representative of a universal religion of nature that became a real national religion, like the civic religions of the ancient world. The new state cult, complete with civic festivals and churches, appropriated Christian ideas: "Like Christianity, it was a re-

---

49. Dawson, *Beyond Politics*, 3.

50. Eric Voegelin, *The Political Religions*, ed. Manfred Henningsen, trans. Virginia Ann Schildauer (London: University of Missouri Press, 2000). Originally published in 1938 in Vienna, it was quickly suppressed by authorities.

51. Burleigh, *Earthly Powers*, 17–22; Burleigh, *Sacred Causes*, 86–87.

ligion of human salvation, the salvation of the world by the power of man set free by Reason. The Cross has been replaced by the Tree of Liberty, the Grace of God by the Reason of Man, and Redemption by Revolution."[52] In the name of those ideas, the Great Terror was unleashed on all who opposed them. Because the Jacobins struggled for something more than mere political goals, their movement took on global significance. As Tocqueville had seen before Dawson,[53] the Jacobins created a powerful political religion.

Instead of finishing his book on the French Revolution in the late 1930s, Dawson turned to contemporary affairs and wrote *Beyond Politics* (1939). For that book, his studies of French eighteenth-century history proved useful:

Anyone who studies the history of the First French Republic in the light of recent political developments cannot fail to be impressed by the way in which the Jacobins anticipated practically all the characteristic features of the modern totalitarian regimes: the dictatorship of a party in the name of the community, the use of propaganda and appeals to mass emotion, as well as of violence and terrorism, the conception of revolutionary justice as a social weapon, the regulation of economic life in order to realize revolutionary ideals, and above all the attempt to enforce a uniform ideology on the whole people and the proscription and persecution of every other form of political thought.[54]

Dawson saw that the Jacobins destroyed the traditional distinction between church and state in the name of the all-embracing politico-religious community.[55] That was the outcome of the new totalitarian regimes of the early twentieth century, too. Contemporary scholars have corroborated Dawson's view of the French Revolution as the first root of twentieth-century political religion.[56] Russian revo-

---

52. Dawson, *The Gods of Revolution*, 66.
53. Alexis de Tocqueville wrote that the leaders of the French Revolution "had a fanatical faith in their vocation—that of transforming the social system, root and branch, and regenerating the whole human race. Of this passionate idealism was born what was in fact a new religion, giving rise to some of those vast changes in human conduct that religion has produced in other ages" (Tocqueville, *The Old Régime and the French Revolution*, 156).
54. Dawson, *Beyond Politics*, 71.
55. Dawson, *Beyond Politics*, 72.
56. Burleigh, *Earthly Powers*; Gentile, *Politics as Religion*, 26–29.

lutionaries, for example, distinctly recalled the French Revolution as an inspiration. Russian children were even named after Robespierre.[57] Though fascists were ambivalent toward the French Revolution and the Nazis hated it, the revolution nevertheless prepared the way for these later movements, too, by mobilizing the masses around ideological uniformity.[58]

Dawson believed that the second major root of political religion was the spiritual vacuum that developed during the late nineteenth century out of the spiritual anarchy and materialism of the age. His historical work on the nineteenth century is nowhere systematically presented. One has to glean it from articles, lectures,[59] and parts of books.[60] Perhaps this was because "few things are more difficult to understand than the mind of the immediate past."[61] However, he wrote one book focused exclusively on the nineteenth century, *The Spirit of the Oxford Movement* (1933). In it, he argued that the Oxford Movement of John Keble (1792–1866), John Henry Newman, and others was the expression of a unique moment in English history (the 1830s), when the English mind was alive to adventure and to ideas. The movement protested the spirit of the age, the utilitarianism and secularism of nineteenth-century liberalism, as well as the dominance of the English state over the Church of England, in the name of true spiritual freedom.[62]

The political religions, Dawson argued, also reacted against the spirit of the nineteenth century, when individualism and materialism rose along with the groundswell of economic development. It was an age of confidence, of progress, of exploitation, and of the ideal that government and church should get out of the way of trade and industry. In this way, material interests developed unchecked in an atmosphere

57. Burleigh, *Sacred Causes*, 51.
58. George L. Mosse, "Fascism and the French Revolution," *Journal of Contemporary History* 24, no. 1 (1989): 5–26.
59. Such as Christopher Dawson, "Religion in the Age of Revolution," *Tablet*, August 29; September 5, 12; and October 10, 24, 1936; Christopher Dawson, *The Movement Towards Christian Unity in the Nineteenth Century* (Latrobe, Pa.: Saint Vincent Archabbey, 2006). This latter source was the Wimmer Lecture for 1960.
60. Such as *Progress and Religion* and *The Movement of World Revolution*.
61. Dawson, *The Spirit of the Oxford Movement*, v.
62. Dawson, *The Spirit of the Oxford Movement*, xi, xii, 10–11.

of spiritual anarchy.[63] A kind of spiritual vacuum developed in which collective guilt, social idealism, and revolutionary movements—such as nationalism and socialism, both firmly established in the nineteenth century—could take root, destroying the religious unity and common moral values that were the basis of political and social life.

"The revolutionary attitude—and it is perhaps the characteristic religious attitude of Modern Europe—is in fact nothing but a symptom of the divorce between religion and social life," Dawson wrote.[64] The political religions of the early twentieth century arose as an attempt to "find some substitute for the lost religious foundations of society and to replace the utilitarian individualism of the liberal-capitalist State by a new spiritual community."[65] In this attempt to create new spiritual communities around ideological uniformity, the new states threatened the individual conscience and the church. They claimed the whole of life, eroding the distinction between church and state in the interest of creating a secular church-state. In this way, the political religions were a kind of anti–Oxford Movement, which had sought to renew the church by more clearly distinguishing it *from* the state in the name of spiritual freedom. The political religions wanted to collapse church and state into one great Leviathan, as Rousseau had prescribed, reverting to ancient paganism when deity and ruler were one.[66]

While Dawson did not use the phrase "spiritual vacuum" until his later work,[67] he utilized the general idea early on to help explain where political religions come from, so it is worth dwelling on this point. The force of vacuums is determined by a pressure differential between the weight of the atmosphere and the low pressure inside the vacuum. The vacuum has no attractive force of its own—the force is supplied from the outside pushing particles into the vacuum. It is the weight of the external environment that pushes its way into the emptiness. Daw-

63. Dawson, *Beyond Politics*, 75; Dawson, *Religion and the Modern State*, 1; Dawson, "The Crisis of the West," 267; and Christopher Dawson, "The Problem of Wealth," *Spectator* CXLVII (1931): 485.

64. Dawson, *Progress and Religion*, 178.

65. Dawson, *Religion and the Modern State*, 44.

66. Burleigh, *Earthly Powers*, 2, 9.

67. Dawson, *The Movement of World Revolution*, 127; Dawson, *The Crisis of Western Education*, 133.

son held that this was true of the soul, as well. The vacant soul is like a vacuum: it is an empty place into which the weight of the surrounding spiritual atmosphere tries to push itself. The ideologies and prejudices and values of the time try to force entry. The spirits of the age enter the house if they find it unoccupied. If the soul remains empty, something will eventually breach the walls and take control of it. If "nature abhors a vacuum," so, too, the soul cannot remain empty and neutral—it must have a cult (worship), a vision, and a meaning to fill it.

Viktor Frankl (1905–1997), the Austrian psychiatrist and Holocaust survivor, wrote the best-selling book *Man's Search for Meaning* and referred to an "existential vacuum." This was a widespread phenomenon of the twentieth century, though also endemic to the human condition. It had been exacerbated by the loss of traditions in the modern world, he thought. Traditions helped human beings make choices. They helped them to know what ought to be done in life. Their influence had become weak, creating the existential vacuum, and those suffering in that vacuum experienced meaninglessness and boredom.[68]

During the nineteenth and early twentieth centuries, intellectuals injected their influence into the spiritual vacuum of the age. The German philosopher Hegel (1770–1831) and his followers justified the state as a manifestation of spiritual forces, and his "religion of the state" influenced everyone from fascists to communists.[69] In the case of fascism, Dawson blamed Nietzsche, French theorist of violence George Sorel (1847–1922), Italian futurist and fascist Filippo Marinetti (1876–1944), and Italian journalist Gabriele D'Annunzio (1863–1938) as the spiritual fathers of the movement. Their theoretical justification of violence and terrorism helped transform a national movement against defeatism into a totalitarian cult of the will to power.[70]

The political religions promised social salvation. In 1924, Mussolini commissioned new lyrics for the song "Giovinezza" ("Youth"), popularized by elite Italian soldiers in the Great War, as the fascist anthem.

68. Viktor E. Frankl, *Man's Search for Meaning: An Introduction to Logotherapy* (1946; New York: Pocket Books, 1963), 61, 167–71.
69. Christopher Dawson, "The Politics of Hegel," *Dublin Review* CCXII (1943): 97, 105; Gregor, *Totalitarianism and Political Religion*, chap. 2.
70. Dawson, "The Claims of Politics," 139.

Singers swore faith to Mussolini and to "redeeming fascism."[71] This appeal to the transformation of human beings was present in socialism, too. In a 1932 lecture entitled "Conservatism," Dawson explained that the basis of the appeal of socialism was not so much political or economic as religious:

> Socialism offers men not political order but social salvation; not responsible government but a deliverance from the sense of moral guilt that oppresses modern society: or rather, the shifting of that burden from society as a whole to some abstract power such as capitalism or finance or bourgeois civilization which is endowed with the attributes of a powerful and malevolent spirit. Thus, Socialism is able to enlist all those religious emotions and impulses which no longer find an outlet through their old religious channels. The type of man who a century ago would have been a revivalist or even the founder of a new sect, today devotes himself to social and political propaganda. And this gives Socialism a spiritual power which the older political parties did not possess, though Liberalism, especially on the Continent, sometimes showed similar tendencies.[72]

Thus, socialism could appeal with great power to the spiritual vacuum created by secularization and the moral guilt associated with nineteenth-century capitalism.

The third root of political religion in Dawson's thought was the aftermath of the Great War. While the war itself was to a "great extent the product of the forces of disintegration that were already breaking up the nineteenth-century order,"[73] it, in turn, acted as a causal fac-

---

71. Fascist Anthem: "Youth," in Marla Stone, *The Fascist Revolution in Italy: A Brief History with Documents* (Boston: Bedford/St. Martin's, 2013), 68–69.

72. Christopher Dawson, lecture on "Conservatism," STA, box 3, folder 38, "Conservatism." I edited this manuscript and published it in *The Political Science Reviewer* XXXIX (2010): 232–62, quoted on 248. Viewing the appeal of socialism in religious terms was not exclusive to conservatives like Dawson. For example, the poet and historian A. L. Rowse (1903–1997), a Socialist during the interwar years, wrote the following: "One great political movement, more than any other, has the power of attracting devotion to it, and unpaid service and unquestioning loyalty like a religion; it is this power that drives the Labour Party on. . . . Of this movement, perhaps it is only certain groups, like the Independent Labour Party, the communists and the pacifists, who find in their politics a complete substation for religion. These people have found in it an idealism, which influences their lives and for good, a way of life more exacting, which demands above all the submergence of self and common-mindedness. What are these but characteristics of religion?" See *Politics and the Younger Generation* (London: Faber & Faber, 1931), 200.

73. Dawson, *Religion and the Modern State*, 1–2.

tor. The war ruined the international organization of world trade and world finance by reparation payments, war debts, inflation, tariff barriers, and unemployment. Looking back in 1935, Dawson saw the war as "directly responsible for the economic crisis from which we are suffering to-day."[74] The economic crisis of 1929 led an increasing number of people to accept the necessity of a scientifically planned economy, as in Russia's Five-Year Plan. It also fuelled the final stage of Hitler's political rise. Furthermore, with the collapse of four empires, political stability was lost, and the forces of disintegration were greatly strengthened. Dawson pointed to the revival of terrorism, religious persecution, massacres of minorities, torture, and professional assassination as evidence.[75]

In addition, Dawson argued the "spiritual results" of the Great War were just as significant as the spiritual vacuum.[76] By "spiritual results," he did not mean changes in ecclesiastical structures. Rather, Dawson thought that the conflict dealt a mortal blow to the liberal ideals of humanitarianism and optimism, while arousing dormant instincts to violence; "In a word it changed the spiritual atmosphere of Europe." While communism and the ideal of social revolution had existed since Karl Marx (1818–1883) and Friedrich Engels (1820–1895), these ideas "acquired a new significance and power of appeal in the changed atmosphere and circumstances of the world after the War"[77] because it helped create an environment in which political ideologies offering total explanations become appealing. This was one way there could be a "spiritual history" of the Great War.[78]

Others also noticed these spiritual results. As early as 1919, the British economist John Maynard Keynes (1883–1946) wrote of the situation in Russia, Austria, and Hungary, where the misery and disintegration of life were rampant. The situations there showed how in the "final catastrophe the malady of the body passes over into malady of the mind. Economic privation proceeds by easy stages . . . until the limit of hu-

74. Dawson, *Religion and the Modern State*, 2.
75. Dawson, introduction, in *The Necessity of Politics*, 19.
76. Dawson, *Religion and the Modern State*, 2.
77. Dawson, *Religion and the Modern State*, 3.
78. James F. McMillan, "Writing the Spiritual History of the First World War," in *Religie: godsdienst en geweld in de twintigste eeuw*, ed. Madelon de Keizer (Zutphen: Walburg, 2006), 47–71.

Application

man endurance is reached at last and counsels of despair and madness stir the sufferers from the lethargy which precedes the crisis." This created a dangerous environment. "The power of ideas is sovereign, and [man] listens to whatever instruction of hope, illusion, or revenge is carried to him on the air."[79] In writing this, Keynes outlined the conditions in which the political religions were even then (1919) rising.

Historians today have confirmed Dawson's instinct to examine the spiritual results of the Great War. In Germany, wandering prophets such as Ludwig Christian Haeusser (1881–1927) pandered to the mental confusion of the German people during the early 1920s. They often travelled barefoot, bearded, and long-haired, prophesying the end of the world and pointing to the need for a new type of man to create a new society.[80] There was also growing interest in occultism, spread by figures such as Guido List (1848–1919), which formed the occult roots of Nazism.[81] The brutality of total war spilled over into violence against civilians in Germany and other parts of the continent. This "became a permanent condition, in the sense that political *opponents* were regarded as deadly *enemies*," Burleigh wrote.[82] All of these material and spiritual factors created an environment in which Hitler could rise by appealing to both the economic and political needs of the people as well as to their religious and messianic hopes.

The Great War created the conditions in which Lenin, Mussolini, and Hitler could rise to power. Hans Maier wrote about the devastations following 1917: the collapse of liberalism, the self-doubt, and the "longing for a new unity and completeness that prepared the ground for the great simplifiers."[83] Dawson wrote about one of these "great simplifiers," Lenin:

The age of the Great War was an age of iron, but it gave birth to no military genius and no great statesman; its political leaders were men of paper. The one man of iron that the age produced arose from the most unlikely quarter that it is possible to conceive—from among the fanatics and revolutionary

79. Keynes, *The Economic Consequences of the Peace*, 249, 250, 251.
80. Burleigh, *Sacred Causes*, 20–22.
81. Roy H. Schoeman, *Salvation Is from the Jews: The Role of Judaism in Salvation History from Abraham to the Second Coming* (San Francisco: Ignatius, 2003), 195, 205, 207.
82. Burleigh, *Sacred Causes*, 8. Burleigh cites Horst Möller, *Europa zwischen den Weltkriegen* (Munich: R. Oldenbourg, 1998), 122.
83. Maier, "Political Religion: a Concept and its Limitations," 15.

agitators who wandered about the watering places of Switzerland and Germany conspiring ineffectually and arguing with one another.[84]

Aided by the Germans, Lenin was able to enter Russia in 1917 and immediately take a leading role in the Bolshevik movement. Ever since the United States declared war on Germany on April 6, 1917, it was imperative for the Germans to knock Russia out of the war. Consequently, the Germans, who clearly saw the power and importance of Lenin's personality, sought to help the antiwar movement in Russia flourish by facilitating Lenin's return across Europe and funding the Bolshevik party.[85]

The spiritual results of the conflict appeared dramatically in Italy, too. Mussolini fought in the Great War and received severe wounds before his disillusion and break with socialism by 1919. His experience of trench warfare and the brotherhood of radicalized soldiers it produced led him to see this group as a powerful political force, historian Marla Stone commented. Mussolini recalled the marks of the war on his soul in his dictated autobiography: the suffering, the dead, the disillusion, and the betrayal. All of this gave him force and concentration after the war. He wanted to revive the Italian nation through a "wholly new political conception, adequate to the living reality of the 20th century," Mussolini wrote. Thus, he helped found the fascist movement out of veteran, revolutionary, and nationalist groups as a heroic cohesive force that would stop the forces of dissolution. Taking advantage of the pessimism and the political and economic chaos of the immediate postwar years, the movement was by 1922 already the most significant political force in the country.[86]

Like Mussolini, Adolf Hitler was a veteran of the Great War. While recovering from severe wounds in hospital in November of 1918, he

---

84. Christopher Dawson, "The Significance of Bolshevism," in *Enquiries into Religion and Culture*, 19.

85. Martin Gilbert, *A History of the Twentieth Century*, vol. 1 (New York: William Morrow, 1997), 446; Richard Pipes, *A Concise History of the Russian Revolution* (New York: Alfred A. Knopf, 1995), 122.

86. Gilbert, *A History of the Twentieth Century*, 546; Burleigh, *Sacred Causes*, 56–57; Dawson, *Religion and the Modern State*, 10; Benito Mussolini, *My Autobiography*, trans. Richard Washburn Child (1928; London: Hutchinson, 1939), 64–66, quoted on p. 74; and Stone, *The Fascist Revolution in Italy*, 9.

learned of the end of the war. As he recorded in *Mein Kampf* (1926), he fell into deep depression. Had everything been in vain? All the sacrifices and deaths, in vain? "I, for my part, decided to go into politics," he wrote.[87] As with Mussolini, the Great War was the authentic experience that connected him emotionally to millions of ordinary suffering people looking for new meaning.[88] Unlike in Britain, where veterans never became a separate and violent political group because they were immediately integrated into the political system,[89] the Nazi Party grew out of discontented veterans and revolutionaries (as with fascism in Italy). Hitler joined in 1920. The party stressed German racial purity, the failure of democracy and laissez-faire capitalism, and the injustices forced on Germany as a result of the Great War. In this way, too, the war created the economic and spiritual conditions that brought Hitler to power.

Integrating Faith and Life

One of the leading characteristics of political religions identified by Dawson was the desire to integrate faith and life. Ironically, in a certain way, political religions were *more* religious than average Western Christians who separated their faith from their lives. "They refuse to divide life," Dawson wrote about fascism, Nazism, and communism. "They demand that the whole of life shall be devoted and dedicated to that social end which they regard as supremely valuable."[90] This startling insight of Dawson's is confirmed by the words of Mussolini himself:

I wanted to create the impression of a complete and rigid consistence with an ideal. This was not a scheming on my part for personal gain; it was a deep need in my nature of what I believed, and I still hold on to—as my life's dedication—namely, that once a man sets up to be the expounder of an ideal or of a new school of thought he must consistently and intensively live daily life and fight battles for the doctrines that he teaches—at any cost until victory—to the end![91]

87. Adolf Hitler, *Mein Kampf*, vol. 1, last sentence of chap. 7, http://www.hitler.org/writings/Mein_Kampf/ index.html (accessed January 9, 2020).

88. Burleigh, *Sacred Causes*, 103.

89. Taylor, *English History: 1914–1945*, 163.

90. Dawson, *Beyond Politics*, 105.

91. Mussolini, *My Autobiography*, 51.

Mussolini longed to live an integrated daily life according to heroic ideals in a way analogous to the saint in the religious sphere. The political religions could likewise inspire and require the allegiance of the whole person—the traditional function of religions throughout world history.

Just as in the ancient and medieval worlds, modern humans longed to find meaning in the everyday. Unlike their ancestors, however, who often found what they looked for in traditional religion, modern people languished. Spiritually sensitive figures such as Hitler recognized this, whereas materialistic Western leaders often did not. When the first unabridged English translation of *Mein Kampf* appeared in 1939, Dawson's review appeared in the *Tablet*. He called it a "remarkably frank book." Its value to English readers, Dawson thought, was that it revealed a hidden world alien from their traditions. "The chief cause of the mistakes that have been made during the last twenty years," he wrote, "is that we have concentrated our attention on one series of [external] factors as though they were the whole of political reality and ignored the rest." And the success of National Socialism was due, he continued, to the way in which Hitler mobilized and exploited the "unseen factors."[92] In 1943 Dawson wrote:

It is not possible to face the tremendous power drive of the new totalitarian parties by purely intellectual means, by argument and logic and philosophy, nor yet by ethical idealism, nor by a quietist withdrawal into the religious life, in the static sense. For Hitler, at any rate, is very conscious of the spiritual factor in social life, he returns to it again and again in *Mein Kampf*. All his early propaganda is based on the importance of faith and the power of a few men with intense convictions to overcome all obstacles and all material difficulties. The weakness of Germany, he wrote, is not due to its lack of armaments, but its lack of arms is due to its spiritual weakness. And the secret of success was to be found not in material organisation, but in the recovery of spiritual power.[93]

---

92. Christopher Dawson, "Hitler's 'Mein Kampf'," *Tablet*, March 25, 1939, 373. Anthropologist Scott Atran, from fieldwork along the Kurdish battlefront with the Islamic State in 2015, asked: "[W]hat can be done to mobilize yearning youth to a countervailing cause? What dreams may come from current government policies that offer little beyond promises of comfort and security? People who are willing to sacrifice everything, including their lives—the totality of their self-interests—will not be lured away just by material incentives or disincentives." See Atran, "The Devoted Actor: Unconditional Commitment and Intractable Conflict Across Cultures," 201.

93. Christopher Dawson, *The Power of the Spirit* (London, 1943), 8–9. This obscure pamphlet is available in the British Library.

Hitler realized implicitly that the liberal solution of privatizing the spiritual did not work. The separation of religion and culture was unsustainable. People needed collective beliefs, and he sought to arouse them to gain power. He (and others) created an ideology that, in effect, was a political religion, transcending church and state. It combined political goals with spiritual appeal to create a monistic battering ram that "swept everything that stood in its path—the Weimar Republic, the Socialists, the Catholic Centre, the Catholic Corporative régime in Austria—and it has gone on sweeping things away ever since."[94]

It was because many Western politicians focused on merely external political factors that they misunderstood Hitler. Someone like Winston Churchill (1874–1965), however, shared Dawson's perspective on Nazism's spiritual appeal by the mid-1930s. Churchill wrote that Hitler had exorcized the spirit of despair from Germany after the Great War and was now building the "Totalitarian State" based on concentration camps and hatred of the Jews and Christians. This was "the new religion of the German peoples, namely, the worship of Germany under the symbols of the old gods of Nordic paganism."[95]

Besides Nazism, communism, too, tried to integrate faith and life. Dawson thought it attracted the discontented and the disinherited proletarian, as well as the disinterested idealist, because, "Man cannot live in a spiritual void; he needs some fixed social standards and some absolute intellectual principles. Bolshevism at least replaces the spiritual anarchy of bourgeois society by a rigid order and substitutes for the doubt and scepticism of an irresponsible intelligentsia the certitude of an absolute authority embodied in social institutions." He explained that:

Bolshevism is not a political movement that can be judged by its practical aims and achievements, nor is it an abstract theory that can be understood apart from its historical context. It differs from other contemporary movements above all by its organic unity, its fusion of theory and practice, and by the way in which its practical policy is bound up with its philosophy. In a world of relativity and skepticism it stands for absolute principles; for a

---

94. Dawson, *The Power of the Spirit*, 9. See also Dawson, "Hitler's 'Mein Kampf.'"

95. Winston Churchill, "Hitler and His Choice," in *Great Contemporaries*, ed. James W. Muller (1937; Wilmington, Del.: ISI Books, 2012), 252, 257.

creed that is incarnate in a social order and for an authority that demands the entire allegiance of the whole man.

Because communism demanded the allegiance of the whole man, it did not function as an ordinary political party. "Thus the communist system, as planned and largely created by Lenin, was a kind of *atheocracy*, a spiritual order of the most rigid and exclusive type, rather than a political order." It enforced discipline. Its members served the proletariat, the "mystical entity" and "universal church" of the Marxian believers. The populace was an "unregenerate mass," and it was the duty of communist leaders to guide and organize according to the principles of the true faith. "The communist is not a representative of the people: he is the priest of an idea," moulding the common way of life by a common creed (I→FWP).[96]

Others in Britain with very different political sympathies than Dawson also discussed communist integration of faith and life. The Irish playwright and socialist George Bernard Shaw (1856–1950) wrote that, "Russia has not only political and economic strength: she has also religious strength. The Russians have a creed in which they believe; and it is a catholic creed."[97] Describing the new civilization arising in Russia—and hinting at their own social philosophy—Sidney and Beatrice Webb included chapters in volume 2 of their book *Soviet Communism* on "The Remaking of Man," "Science the Salvation of Mankind," and "The Good Life." They specifically compared the Communist Party to a "typical religious order in the Roman Catholic Church" and highlighted its membership based on denial of private property, acceptance of a creed, passage through a probationary period, voluntary good social works, assessments of character, rendering of obedience, and periodic "cleansing" through "public inquisition."[98] A distinctive feature for them was the new way of life inaugurated by communism—the promotion, "among all its participants, what it conceives to be 'the good

96. Dawson, "The Significance of Bolshevism," 18–23.

97. George Bernard Shaw, "Fabianism in Action," *Times*, August 13, 1931, 6. He continued: "To call them religious, and the Third International a Catholic Church, seems to them a Shavian joke, as it may seem to some of our own Catholics a Shavian blasphemy."

98. Sidney Webb and Beatrice Webb, *Soviet Communism: A New Civilisation?* vol. 1 (New York: Charles Scribner's Sons, 1936), 340, 342, 345, 348, 376.

life.'"[99] G. D. H. and Margaret Cole noted that the Communist Party "has been likened to . . . the Jesuit Order," and indeed required high levels of faith, discipline, and devotion, but in the end, they denied the comparison with the Jesuits because the members were not cut off from the world or celibate.[100]

There Is Always a Sacral Project

The process of secularization, Dawson wrote, arose not from the loss of faith, "but from the loss of social interest in the world of faith." It begins the moment believers retreat into their closet and they feel that "religion is irrelevant to the common way of life and that society as such has nothing to do with the truths of faith."[101] As Hans Maier noted, however, political religion "reminds us that religion does not allow itself to be easily banished from society, and that, where this is tried, it returns in unpredictable and perverted forms."[102] Dawson's sensitivity to the place of religion in human life and history, developed through practicing in the science of culture from the 1920s through the 1940s, led him to the same conclusion: while it is important to distinguish between church and state, it is impossible to separate religion and culture, the "I" from the FWP. In a secular age, the function of traditional religion in society is simply taken over by political ideologies. The spiritual vacuum cannot last, because the drive pushing humans toward *meaning* is irresistible.

Politicians who understood how to manipulate this vacuum tapped into tremendous power. By rejecting the insights of the classical liberal tradition of limited political power reaching back to the Christian Middles Ages, they created, instead, a religion of politics, attempting to meet the deeper needs of the human person. As Dawson recognized, Mussolini, Hitler, and Lenin created systems appealing to the whole person. They sought to transcend the distinction between church and state to create an all-encompassing moral community. They sacralised

99. Webb and Webb, *Soviet Communism: A New Civilation?*, vol. 2, 807.

100. G. D. G. Cole and Margaret Cole, *A Guide to Modern Politics* (New York: Alfred A. Knopf, 1934), 187, 189, 190.

101. Christopher Dawson, "The Outlook for Christian Culture Today," *Cross Currents* 5, no. 1 (Spring 1955): 130.

102. Maier, "Political Religion: a Concept and its Limitations," 15.

worldly objects that could inspire life, sacrifice, and death in their followers, forming them into devoted actors.

Anthropologist Scott Atran, in wondering how to draw people away from violent political religion, wrote: "The science suggests that sacred values are best opposed with other sacred values that inspire devotion."[103] Dawson recognized the significance of social and economic dislocation in the attraction to violent extremism and political religion. However, the long-term solution implied by his work included not only establishing social and economic order but also social conversion toward authentic religious values, such as in the Christian tradition. This in no way meant that Dawson idealized theocracy or supported measures discriminatory against non-Christians; as shown in the next chapter, he defended pluralism and individual freedom. However, in his view, only the "dynamic vitalism" of the Spirit of God, moving across the cultures of the world, could turn human beings away from the "biological vitalism of blood and race and the old pagan vitalism of the gods of the earth."[104]

103. Atran, "The Devoted Actor," 201.
104. Dawson, *The Judgment of the Nations*, 104.

Chapter 7

The Containment of Politics

It is not possible to discuss the modern situation either from the point of view of religion or politics without using the word 'culture.'
—Christopher Dawson (1942)

The political religions that arose out of the Great War united religion and politics into a single, powerful force. In response to this dangerous combination, Dawson defended the independence of the church, the liberal ideal of personal and political freedom, the conservative ideal of society based not on class warfare but on the cooperation of complementary institutions and voluntary associations, and the claims of culture against the claims of politics. He also defended the remnants of Christian culture in Britain as a source of strength against totalitarianism and political religion, a move he shared with various Conservative politicians of the time. Dawson, the shy, often depressed, bookish man who had been too sickly to fight in the Great War, did more than just write against totalitarian ideologies: he actively worked against them by attending an international conference in Rome, by participating in a highbrow discussion group called the Moot, and by his work for the Sword of the Spirit movement that sought to rally Christians behind the British and American cause in the Second World War. By then, Dawson thought the only way to combat the political religions was to face a war on two fronts: military combat and the inner fight to defend the souls of people from colonization by the totalitarian spiritual atmosphere. If Britain became totalitarian at home in order

Dawson, *The Judgment of the Nations*, 63.

to defeat totalitarianism abroad, the war could be lost in victory as well as defeat.[1] The "moral situation is damnable," the British captain John Crombie wrote to his mother during the Great War; "we can only beat Germany by assuming her mentality."[2] The danger of that mentality reached into the Second World War as well, Dawson recognized. Only by fighting a two-front war, the outer and the inner, could true human freedom survive in democratic countries. Social renewal ultimately depended on religious renewal. Ecumenism based on common social action was an important concern of the Sword of the Spirit since Dawson blamed Christian disunity for the secularization that contributed to the rise of political religion in the first place. Dawson's efforts in that movement suggested ways forward for Catholics to participate in pluralist democracies even as the Sword and its ecumenism collapsed after the immediate German threat to Britain subsided by 1942.

During all of this, Dawson gave up some of the scholarly detachment of his earlier years to stand *for* something and not merely against. He revealed himself as a partisan in the battle of rival loves and in the struggle for the containment of politics and the defense of the freedom of culture. Dawson applied his cultural mind in the defense of those traditions he believed most worth protecting. He did all of this not on his own but in the context of the wider British culture that maintained—almost alone in interwar Europe—heroic stability.

British Politics between the World Wars

The Liberal Party collapsed after the Great War, and the socialist British Labour Party rose to power by 1924. The British Union of Fascists and the Communist Party of Great Britain also gained momentum. Dawson worried that as the country seemed to abandon liberal politics, the Right would turn toward dictatorship and the Left toward Marxism, endangering the very existence of the Parliamentary system.[3] Many people in Britain were, in fact, attracted to continental political ideologies because of the widespread fear after the Great War

---

1. Dawson, *The Judgment of the Nations*, 10
2. Crombie to his mother, March 2, 1917, in *World War I & European Society*, 201.
3. Dawson, *Religion and the Modern State*, 30.

that civilization itself was collapsing—an alarmist view that Dawson himself held.[4] And yet, it did not collapse, at least in Britain, as political order and liberty held. How did British leaders, in general, and Dawson, in particular, contain or limit politics over against the "expansion of politics" so prevalent at the time?

Dawson credited the toughness and resilience of the (unwritten) British constitution compared to others in Europe. While the same forces that had destroyed parliamentarism and liberal democracy on the continent were present in Britain, they were weaker. British culture supported a governing class with a tradition of political good sense, as well as a party system largely in agreement about essentials, which meant British leaders could cooperate in defense of the national interest and the social order.[5]

Contemporary historians have confirmed Dawson's interpretation of British stability even as they have broadened it. First, Britain's geographical situation as an island isolated her from continental developments. The country did not suffer the invasion and devastation of the Great War, immigration was more difficult, and there was a continuity of political institutions across the multiple nations of Britain.[6]

Second, Britain won the Great War, and her people rallied around her political and economic systems, despite criticism of both from intellectuals and writers. Enfranchisement of adult males and most women over age thirty by the Representation of the People Act (1918), as well as four million new homes built during the 1920s and 1930s, drew more people than ever into the British property-owning democracy. Before the Great War, renting rather than buying one's home made economic sense to most families. Afterward, however, the rate of owner-occupancy rose dramatically through building societies that made easy mortgages available for families to buy new homes featuring electricity and indoor lavatories. Both Conservative and Labour politicians encouraged this trend, and as the electorate expanded after the

---

4. Richard Overy, *The Morbid Age: Britain Between the Wars* (London: Allen Lane, 2009), 19, 270.

5. Dawson, *Religion and the Modern State*, 26.

6. Andrew Thorpe, ed., *The Failure of Political Extremism in Inter-War Britain* (Exeter: University of Exeter, 1989), 9.

Great War and the threat of foreign revolutionary ideologies increased, politicians looked for ways to stabilize the British system by encouraging voter loyalty to the system rather than desire to change it.[7]

Third, the strategy of the British monarchy between the wars helped defuse political radicalism. King George V (who reigned from 1910 to 1936) was an ordinary man who spoke without a posh accent. While the German, Russian, Austrian, Greek, and Spanish monarchies collapsed during the interwar years, the British monarchy remained popular. George V raised the monarchy above partisan politics and resisted the temptation to link it with the hereditary aristocracy, as when he allowed the Liberals to reduce the powers of the peers in 1910 and 1911. Instead, he attached the monarchy firmly to the common welfare of the people. The royal family devoted themselves to charitable work: visiting unemployment centers, hospitals, and even a trade union; supporting the Girl Guides, the Boys' Welfare Association, and the Industrial Welfare Society. The king gave a radio broadcast on Christmas Day 1932 linking people directly with the monarchy for the first time. George V also helped integrate the new Labour Party into the British system, defusing its revolutionary tendencies. This was notable since he hated socialism and feared Bolshevik influence spreading as unemployment and strikes rocked the country immediately after the Great War. Nevertheless, Labour politicians were invited to Princess Mary's wedding in 1922, and the king invited Ramsay MacDonald (1866–1937) to form the first Labour government in 1924. By showing this confidence in MacDonald, the King helped integrate Labour and its working-class supporters into the British political system.[8] Thanks to George V, British people saw no contradiction between monarchy and democracy.[9]

Fourth, general patriotism and attachment to the parliamentary system remained high among British politicians and even intellectuals. Despite the existence of fascist and communist movements in Britain, as well as expectations of the death of liberalism by some Brit-

---

7. Martin Pugh, *We Danced All Night: A Social History of Britain Between the Wars* (London: Vintage Books, 2008), 58, 63–67, 71.

8. Pugh, *We Danced All Night*, 365–66, 368–73.

9. Winston Churchill, "King George V," in *Great Contemporaries*, ed. James W. Muller (1936; Wilmington, Del.: ISI Books, 2012), 315–16.

Application

ish writers,[10] there was a growing effort during the 1930s to reassert the political center as a real alternative to the political extremes. This movement united politicians from the Conservative and Labour parties around core elements of the liberal democratic tradition,[11] recast to emphasize preservation of liberal political culture, political moderation, and English identity against foreign ideologies of political extremism. Conservatives such as Stanley Baldwin (1867–1947) and socialists such as Clement Attlee (1883–1967) and George Orwell defended the liberal achievements of English culture during these years. The English countryside and its ideals of variety, individuality, and privacy were upheld as a "powerful symbolic foil to the barbarism and uniformity represented by totalitarian systems and creeds," one historian wrote. Liberal thinkers such as G. M. Trevelyan, E. M. Forster (1879–1970), and Ernest Barker distinguished "between the political and the spiritual realm—the only true realm of individuality, freedom, originality, and choice." Dawson, too, defended the distinction between the political and the spiritual, as well as the traditional English party system, based on moderation and toleration of minorities. Because of the efforts of politicians and intellectuals such as these, the rhetoric of English liberty was strengthened rather than undermined by the totalitarian challenge.[12]

Conservatives played an important role in this political center by attempting to conserve English political traditions against revolutionary idealism. The Conservatives dominated the British political landscape from the 1920s to the 1940s.[13] Conservative politicians and prime ministers such as Stanley Baldwin, Lord Halifax (1881–1959), and Winston Churchill resisted totalitarianism and defended British freedom partly by appealing to Christian ideals of human dignity and freedom. Baldwin understood the military and ideological threats of the fascist

10. Stephen Spender, *Forward from Liberalism* (London: Victor Gollancz, 1937).

11. Overy, *The Morbid Age: Britain Between the Wars*, 298; Andrew Thorpe, "'The Only Effective Bulwark Against Reaction and Revolution': Labour and the Frustration of the Extreme Left," in *The Failure of Political Extremism in Inter-War Britain*, 11–27.

12. Julia Stapleton, "Resisting the Centre at the Extremes: 'English' Liberalism in the Political Thought of Interwar Britain," *British Journal of Politics and International Relations* 1, no. 3 (1999): 271–74, 283, 288.

13. They led the nation in 1922 and from 1924 to 1929, then led coalition governments from 1931 to 1940 and from 1940 to 1945.

and communist regimes as manifestations of a deeper spiritual crisis. Britain faced not just an external but also an internal threat because ideas could spread rapidly between countries and undermine the spiritual basis of democracy, a reality Dawson also clearly perceived. Baldwin defended democracy against dictatorship and insisted that Christian faith was the ultimate source and safeguard of freedom. Even the secular-minded Winston Churchill repeatedly invoked Christian rhetoric as the Second World War drew neigh, as he drew on the most powerful language then available to strengthen the country's moral resolve. In addition, national days of prayer were held from 1938 through 1940.[14]

It is in this context of resistance to totalitarianism, patriotic defense of English national identity and institutions, and firm adherence to spiritual freedom that Dawson's political position can be understood. There were serious problems, he acknowledged, and in the mid-1930s, he censured the Conservative and Liberal parties in Britain for failing to advance even a modicum of social philosophy that could compete with that of socialism. He criticized the national government for not being truly national and advocated recovering the traditional two-party, parliamentary system. He also recognized the centralizing tendencies of the 1930s working against any recovery of that system.[15]

Nevertheless, he wrote that, "Britain is, in fact, almost the only country in Europe which has met the world crisis successfully by constitutional means, and consequently it is the only great country in which the parliamentary system is still practically unchallenged."[16] During the post–Great War period, political parties on the continent came to resemble those in France during the revolution of the 1790s, defining themselves in terms of ideological oppositions. That situation contrasted with the traditional English party system in which the parties did not, save at rare moments, stand for any well-defined body of ideas. They adapted to situations and represented dominant social and economic interests. They competed, but not to the death; they es-

14. Philip Williamson, "Christian Conservatives and the Totalitarian Challenge, 1933–40," *English Historical Review* CXV (2000): 607–9, 616–17, 628.

15. Christopher Dawson, "The Future of National Government," *Dublin Review* CXCVI (1935): 244–46.

16. Dawson, "The Future of National Government," 237.

Application

sentially sought to cooperate in the service of the nation. They were limited organizations that did not pose as the exclusive organs of the nation—as in totalitarian regimes. Personal freedom and political liberty depended on the preservation of these limitations.[17] The English parliamentary system rested on the agreement to differ.[18] Hence, political moderation, compromise, and toleration were essential to the English constitution.

Despite his criticism of liberalism for separating religion and culture in the name of "freedom," a division that had contributed to the rise of the political religions in the first place, Dawson looked kindly upon it. He distinguished between the liberal *tradition*, which possessed deep roots in the Christian Middle Ages; the modern liberal *ideology*, which owed as much to France as to England; and "liberal" as a *political party name*. There had been many varieties of liberalism, such that it could appear conservative in one country and revolutionary in another.[19] Therefore, it was "useless to discuss liberalism in the abstract unless one bears in mind the concrete social and historical background of the different forms of liberalism." Dawson saw the deep-rooted liberal tradition supporting the personal, political, and spiritual freedom of the citizen as key to reorienting Western society away from totalitarianism.[20] That tradition, reaching back in part to the Magna Carta and beyond, advocated the ideals of citizenship, the value of the individual, limited government, humanitarianism, and family independence.[21]

17. Dawson, *Beyond Politics*, 38, 45, 55.

18. Dawson, *Religion and the Modern State*, 28.

19. Dawson, *The Judgment of the Nations*, 57–59. Winston Churchill nicely summarized this liberal tradition in his 1946 "Iron Curtain" speech: "We must never cease to proclaim in fearless tones the great principles of freedom and the rights of man which are the joint inheritance of the English-speaking world and which through Magna Carta, the Bill of Rights, the Habeas Corpus, trial by jury, and the English common law find their most famous expression in the American Declaration of Independence" (https://www.milestonedocuments.com/documents/view/winston-churchillsthe-sinews-of-peace/text). This liberal tradition flourished in places more geographically isolated from others, and thus secure—like Britain and the United States. Due to proximity to Europe, however, this liberal tradition even influenced regimes such as the Ottoman Empire. Looking to the example of the West, the Ottomans proclaimed the Tanzimat decree (1839) respecting civil liberties and limited government and reaffirming certain primal values of Islam, like private property. See Mustafa Akyol, *Islam without Extremes: A Muslim Case for Liberty* (New York: W. W. Norton, 2011), 147–48.

20. Dawson, *The Judgment of the Nations*, 61, 70.

21. Dawson, *The Judgment of the Nations*, 127; Russell Hittinger, "Christopher Dawson on

{ 270 }

For the sake of the liberal tradition, Dawson argued, it was essential to defend two key freedoms: that of freedom of association, which had always characterized the free citizen community, and that of freedom of vocation, which is the condition for personal responsibility. Only when the freedom of association is informed by the spirit of vocation (as in a profession with a distinguished tradition of service) can the liberal tradition make man's freedom fruitful in culture and create a living, organized community rather than a formless, bureaucratic, mass society.[22]

Dawson's respect for the liberal tradition overlapped with his deeply conservative sympathies. Nevertheless, his relationship to political conservatism was subtle. Dawson was never involved more deeply in politics than his brief and unpleasant tenure in 1912 as unpaid private secretary to the Conservative Member of Parliament (MP) for Birmingham East, Arthur Steel-Maitland (1876–1935).[23] In all of his books and articles, he wrote broad-mindedly and never as a propagandist for the Conservative Party. An unpublished lecture to a Conservative group was the nearest he came to such a role, and even then, he argued at the level of broad ideas and culture—not in support of any specific policies or politicians of his day.[24] It is true that when he emerged from the political background, he did so in the company of Conservatives—as when he spoke at a conference in Rome in 1932 against Nazi racialism. He attended that event as part of a British delegation that included Gerard Wallop (Viscount Lymington [1898–1984], the environmentalist and Conservative MP for Basingstoke at the time of the conference) and Charles Petrie (1895–1977), the conservative and Catholic historian. But Dawson's writings always attempted to probe "beyond politics," the title of his 1939 book, as in the following passage from *Religion and the Modern State* (1935):

Technology and the Demise of Liberalism," in *Christianity and Western Civilization: Christopher Dawson's Insights: Can a Culture Survive the Loss of Its Religious Roots?* (San Francisco: Ignatius, 1993), 79–80.

22. Dawson, *The Judgment of the Nations*, 127, 132, 134.

23. Scott, *A Historian and His World*, 57.

24. Christopher Dawson, "Conservatism," STA box 3, folder 38, "Conservativism." I edited this manuscript and published it in *The Political Science Reviewer* 39, no. 1 (2010): 232–62.

Application

It may, I think, even be argued that Communism in Russia, National Socialism in Germany, and Capitalism and Liberal Democracy in the Western countries are really three forms of the same thing, and that they are all moving by different but parallel paths to the same goal, which is the mechanization of human life and the complete subordination of the individual to the state and to the economic process. Of course I do not mean to say that they are all absolutely equivalent, and that we have no right to prefer one to another. But I do believe that a Christian cannot regard any of them as a final solution of the problem of civilization, or even as a tolerable one. Christianity is bound to protest against any social system which claims the whole of man and sets itself up as the final end of human action, for it asserts that man's essential nature transcends all political and economic forms. Civilization is a road by which man travels, not a house for him to dwell in. His true city is elsewhere.[25]

Here Dawson's intellectual asceticism and political detachment are clear, as well as his decidedly Christian stance.

Nevertheless, in his "Conservatism" lecture, he enunciated clear political principles. He argued that a renaissance of conservative principles was more necessary then (1932) than in the past one hundred years. The social and political causes behind the decline of the Liberal Party were not necessarily harmful to conservative principles. He supported the monarchy as representative of the whole British people, and he supported the British Empire as essential to national life. The empire was not purely self-centered, he thought, but in some ways looked out for the needs of the whole in its cultural mission and contribution to world order. Neither liberal individualism nor the "economic absolutism" of socialism "do justice to the complex reality of the facts that are involved in the British imperial system."[26]

Although socialism, deriving its theory from Marx, claimed scientific grounds for its principles, nothing was more unscientific than reducing the complex reality of social life to economic functions and ignoring elements of culture inconsistent with its theory. Conservatism, on the other hand, actually possessed the more scientific view of society because it acknowledged the diversity of social functions. For the conservative, the purpose of political authority was to guard the social

25. Dawson, *Religion and the Modern State*, xv.
26. Christopher Dawson, "Conservatism," *The Political Science Reviewer* 39, no. 1 (2010): 255.

traditions of national life and to encourage the cooperation of different classes and economic interests in the nation.[27]

Socialism, Dawson said, appealed to men's religious instincts, sense of guilt, and desire for social salvation. Socialism sought to replace religion with itself, essentially becoming a state religion.[28] The difficulty was that conservatives had to meet this powerful secular-religious proposal with merely political arguments, for they could not pretend to go beyond the limited political sphere without betraying themselves. They could not counter socialism by creating an alternative political religion because they were bound by their principles "to admit the primacy and independence of the spiritual order"—a nice summary of how Dawson applied his boundary thinking rule to politics. Dawson ended the lecture by calling for intellectual cooperation and organization in support of a renaissance of conservative ideas.[29]

A Cultural Approach to Politics

Dawson approached politics through the lens of culture rather than through overt ideological or party interest. "It is not possible to discuss the modern situation either from the point of view of religion or politics without using the word 'culture.'"[30] This meant politics was part of a wider cultural milieu and that the true dynamics of history are found there—not in political action per se. Thus, one must fight for the true freedom of culture as the space of human creativity and life. Culture is an intermediate zone where diverse people strive for wider interests than those merely of politics, civil or ecclesiastical. The sphere of culture should remain distinct in relation to both state *and church* because it belongs to neither. It has its own laws of life and its own right to self-determination.[31] Dawson defended the proper autonomy of culture well before Catholic ecclesiastical leaders would do the same at the Second Vatican Council.

---

27. Dawson, "Conservatism," 247.
28. Dawson, "Conservatism," 248, 260.
29. Dawson, "Conservatism," 250, 260, 262.
30. Dawson, *The Judgment of the Nations*, 63.
31. Dawson, *Beyond Politics*, 23.

Application

In a 1939 article in *Scrutiny*, Dawson examined the duties of intellectuals such as himself to defend the claims of culture against the claims of politics. The expansion of politics in the all-embracing totalitarian states had destroyed the spiritual freedom of the man of letters, the philosopher, and the religious teacher, he wrote. Intellectuals needed to keep their heads clear and not allow themselves to be confused by the "over-simplification of the issues which has always been the besetting sin of the political partisan."[32] Furthermore,

when it comes to the consideration of the final ends of political action, to the criticism of the ideologies on which the action is based and to the creation of a social consciousness and sense of responsibility which transcend the limits of the political community, it is clear that the thinker and the writer have a more important contribution to make than the man of action or the political orator; and it is their primary function to serve society with intellectual integrity in this sphere rather than to take an active part in party politics or in the actual work of government.[33]

Intellectuals such as Friedrich Nietzsche and Georges Sorel, who had failed to recognize these priorities, had prepared the way for the totalitarian regimes "by their theoretic justification of violence and terrorism." If the intellectuals abandon the "interests of culture and cease to recognize the primacy of spiritual values, we can hardly expect the politician to do otherwise." The intellectual is the servant of wider interests that transcend politics and must defend free criticism, personality, and free spiritual activity. The social responsibilities of the man of letters cannot be identified "with his duty as a citizen or subordinated to the interests of the state of which he is a member. He is bound to think of the interests of culture as a whole and to direct his activities in whatever direction he can serve them best."[34] It was partly because British culture continued to support the intellectual and spiritual freedom to advance arguments such as these that the country was able to resist totalitarianism.

32. Dawson, "The Claims of Politics," 136. *Scrutiny* was a British journal of literary criticism edited by F. R. Leavis that lasted from 1932 to 1953.
33. Dawson, "The Claims of Politics," 138.
34. Dawson, "The Claims of Politics," 139–40.

Dawson's cultural approach to politics did cause misunderstanding, due to his journalism for the Catholic press and his book *Religion and the Modern State* (1935). Some thought he supported, or at least held sympathy for, Italian fascism—a typical Catholic position between the wars. Due to the influence of Hilaire Belloc's "political Catholicism," which deeply influenced English Catholics between the world wars,[35] as well as to English Catholic support of Franco during the 1930s and fear of communism and secularism, there was widespread belief that Catholics supported fascism.[36] Belloc was an anticapitalist and disillusioned with British democracy, believing it was the mere creature of financial power. He met Mussolini in 1924 and hailed him as a great man.[37] In addition, antimodernists like the Catholic intellectual founder of Welsh nationalism, Saunders Lewis, and the Anglo-Catholic architect A. J. Penty, who appeared in chapter 2, felt the appeal of fascism because of its apparent anti-modern stance. The medievalism that attracted them to fascism, however, eventually led them to moderate their enthusiasm for the ideology.[38]

To some readers, Dawson occasionally sounded like these characters. For example, he wrote that fascism derived its vigor from its reaction to the weaknesses of democracy and from the pursuit of patriotism, heroism, and the moral value of violence.[39] "Fascism is a real thing, a spontaneous reaction of Western or Central European society to the new conditions of the post-war epoch."[40] He noted that Catholic social ideals (especially corporatism[41]) of popes Leo XIII and Pius XI "have far more affinity with those of Fascism than with those of ei-

35. James R. Lothian, *The Making and Unmaking of the English Catholic Intellectual Community, 1910–1950* (Notre Dame, Ind.: University of Notre Dame Press, 2009), chap. 1.

36. James Flint, "'Must God Go Fascist?': English Catholic Opinion and the Spanish Civil War," *Church History* LVI (1987): 364–74; Grosvenor, "The British Anti-Moderns and the Medievalist Appeal of European Fascism," 103–15; Kevin L. Morris, "Fascism and British Catholic Writers 1924–1939," *The Chesterton Review* XXV (February/May 1999): 21–51; and Tom Villis, *British Catholics and Fascism: Religious Identity and Political Extremism Between the Wars* (New York: Palgrave Macmillan, 2013), 1.

37. Morris, "Fascism and British Catholic Writers 1924–1939," 22–26.

38. Grosvenor, "The British Anti-Moderns and the Medievalist Appeal of European Fascism," 104, 112.

39. Dawson, *Religion and the Modern State*, 9–10.

40. Dawson, *Religion and the Modern State*, 8.

41. Corporatism is defined as the cooperation of different social and economic groups toward the common good of a society.

ther Liberalism or Socialism."[42] Statements such as this sometimes left readers wondering where Dawson stood.

Reviewers of *Religion and the Modern State,* therefore, thought he sympathized with fascism: "Mr. Dawson seems to me a little too indulgent to Fascism, and not sufficiently alive to the importance of defending the democratic front. He associates democratic self-government with economic laissez-faire too easily and dissociates both economic and political freedom from spiritual liberty too readily."[43] In the *Times Literary Supplement,* he was also viewed as giving a favorable opinion of fascism.[44] There was sufficient ambiguity in his writings of the mid-1930s that he felt compelled to write to the *Catholic Herald* clarifying his views, stating that the final end of fascism (the state) is "irreconcilable with the Catholic ideals of unity and moral order,"[45] and he disallowed the republication of *Religion and the Modern State.*[46]

Nevertheless, even scholars such as historian Bruno P. Schlesinger (1911–2010) misinterpreted the way Dawson applied his cultural mind to fascism. Schlesinger wrote the first doctoral dissertation (University of Notre Dame, 1949) on Dawson, called "Christopher Dawson and the Modern Political Crisis." Schlesinger claimed that Dawson's political thought changed dramatically from before the Second World War (1933 to 1939) to after (1939 to 1949). The first phase of his writings, Schlesinger claimed, revealed antidemocratic, profascist leanings, and in the second, one saw a complete reversal.[47] Schlesinger wrote: "Dawson sees the rise of Fascism against the background of the decay of the nineteenth century order. He sees it as a genuine attempt to solve the problems created by World War I, and as a positive effort to construct a new social order."[48] This was not, in fact, the case.

---

42. Dawson, *Religion and the Modern State,* 135.

43. H. G. Wood, "Religion and State Idols," review of *Religion and the Modern State, Spectator,* August 9, 1935, 231.

44. Harold Martin Stannard, "The Christian and the World," review of *Religion and the Modern State, Times Literary Supplement,* August 22, 1935, 520.

45. Christopher Dawson, "Fascism and the Corporate State," *Catholic Herald,* August 3, 1935, page unknown.

46. Scott, *A Historian and His World,* 123–27.

47. Bruno P. Schlesinger, "Christopher Dawson and the Modern Political Crisis" (PhD diss., University of Notre Dame, 1949), 3.

48. Schlesinger, "Christopher Dawson and the Modern Political Crisis," 8.

The Catholic writer Bernard Wall (1908–1974), who had been in-volved in London's Catholic Worker movement during the 1930s, re-membered that "some people thought that Christopher and I were pro-Fascist. This confusion arose because in the general hysteria of the time . . . Christopher went on calmly disentangling the sociological threads in Europe."[49] Schlesinger picked up on the ambiguity present in Dawson's political writings of the 1930s, but he also mistook Daw-son's sociological perspective for prescriptive utterances. He did not understand that Dawson portrayed fascism as a response to the need for community, a real human need, although fascism was not applaud-ed by Dawson as the solution. In a letter to Schlesinger written on Janu-ary 24, 1950, Dawson defended his views: *Religion and the Modern State* had not departed from his previous ideas, nor did he later depart from his original views. He also noted that Schlesinger had mistaken his ex-position of the case for totalitarianism as his own, and the book was essentially antitotalitarian. Later, after Dawson came to America, the two men reached a deeper understanding of each other and collaborat-ed to create the Christian Culture program at St. Mary's College, Notre Dame, in 1956 (see chapter 8).[50]

The perception of Dawson as having fascist sympathies has contin-ued to this day, as when social science professor Jay P. Corrin mistaken-ly stated that Dawson opposed liberalism and democracy and support-ed fascism as more compatible with Catholicism.[51] Likewise, literary scholar Kevin Morris viewed Dawson as sympathetic to fascism and as failing to denounce it.[52]

In response to Morris' article, Christina Scott, Dawson's daughter and biographer, rightly wrote that Dawson's books *Religion and the Modern State* and *Beyond Politics* were essentially anti-totalitarian and that he stood for the English tradition of liberty against the totalitar-ian menace. She offered a personal example to explain British Cath-

---

49. Bernard Wall, *Headlong into Change: An Autobiography and a Memoir of Ideas Since the Thirties* (London: Harvill, 1969), 89.

50. Scott, *A Historian and His World*, 11, 126.

51. Jay P. Corrin, *Catholic Intellectuals and the Challenge of Democracy* (Notre Dame, Ind.: University of Notre Dame Press, 2002), 381–82. He did acknowledge that Dawson was critical of fascism in fn. 33 on p. 442.

52. Morris, "Fascism and British Catholic Writers 1924–1939," 33, 45.

Application

olic support for Franco, recalling her time in a convent school in the 1930s. She heard firsthand from sister houses in Spain of the atrocities perpetrated on nuns and priests by the Republicans. When Madrid fell to Franco, "we all sang a triumphant *Te Deum*," she wrote. "This was religious, not political, rejoicing." One could support the Nationalist Party as an anti-communist and not be pro-fascist.[53] Even Belloc was much more a critic of British government than he was a supporter of fascism.[54] In this way, the sympathy of British intellectuals for not only fascism but also for communism between the wars must be seen in terms of how they projected their anxieties about British society and their desires for social reform onto political conflicts abroad.[55]

Although there was "failure of the political imagination" in Britain during the mid-1930s to realize the dangers of the fascist movement, and some of Dawson's language in *Religion and the Modern State* may have contributed to that failure, there was a growing use of the word "totalitarianism" to understand fascism and to warn others of its novelty and danger.[56] George Orwell, Ernest Barker, and Dawson all used the concept "totalitarianism" in this way. It was those who *took a position*, eschewing philosophical neutrality, who perceived the danger of fascism, including Orwell, who supported democratic socialism, and Barker and Dawson, who both defended the English tradition of constitutional liberty.

Dawson's cultural interpretation of politics led him to work against the Left-Right divide in the political spectrum because that division served the purposes of totalitarianism. "Right" and "Left" were not familiar terms of political analysis until after the Great War,[57] and Dawson refused to accept such a divide. He was by no means a "man of the

53. Christina Scott, "Christopher Dawson's Reaction to Fascism and Marxism," *The Chesterton Review* 25, no. 3 (1999): 406.

54. Lothian, *The Making and Unmaking of the English Catholic Intellectual Community, 1910–1950*, 63.

55. Overy, *The Morbid Age: Britain Between the Wars*, 270, 288.

56. Peter Lassman, "Responses to Fascism in Britain, 1930–1945: The Emergence of the Concept of Totalitarianism," in *Sociology Responds to Fascism*, ed. Stephen P. Turner and Dirk Käsler (London & New York: Routledge, 1992), 214–16. Christian conservative British politicians such as Stanley Baldwin and Lord Halifax also used the word "totalitarianism" to unmask and oppose political developments on the continent; see Williamson, "Christian Conservatives and the Totalitarian Challenge, 1933–40."

57. Bruce Coleman, "The Conservative Party and the Frustration of the Extreme Right," in *The Failure of Political Extremism in Inter-War Britain*, 50.

Right" supporting fascism. In fact, he highlighted fascism's roots on the Left in the thought of Georges Sorel, "whose ideas had a considerable influence not only on Mussolini but also on Lenin himself."[58] Dawson sought to untangle the influences on the rise of both political extremes. A central point of *Religion and the Modern State*, in fact, was that it was futile to blame a single ideology (whether fascism, democracy, capitalism, or communism) as the root of all evil.

Historian James Chappel argued that confronting totalitarianism during the 1930s significantly influenced Catholic intellectual history. Catholic intellectuals in Germany, France, and Austria accepted political modernity in its distinction between the secular public sphere and the religious private sphere. They gave up the ideal of a "Catholic state" in order to ally with anyone of good will to defend the private sphere of families and associations from the crushing threat of totalitarianism of either right or left. They realized they needed to work with others in support of the secular political project. They shifted from speaking of the "rights of the Church" to "human rights." Chappel wrote: "Through a confrontation with totalitarianism, the Church became modern."[59]

Dawson advocated this in England. The British economist Barbara Ward (1914–1981), who worked with Dawson in the Sword of the Spirit movement, said, "The one thing that Dawson did, for me and others, was to emphasize that there is a great constitutional position between the extreme right and the extreme left." This was important in the 1930s because of the polarity of fascism and communism; "Dawson kept alive the constitutional center with its natural law basis."[60] He did this partly because, according to rule four of his cultural mind ("intellectual asceticism"), he did not view the world ideologically. He interpreted fascism culturally as a political religion (as do many historians today), and thus he saw its danger. This broad-mindedness was one of Dawson's central contributions to interwar Catholic political thought in Britain.

---

58. Dawson, *Religion and the Modern State*, 8.

59. James Chappel, *Catholic Modern: The Challenge of Totalitarianism and the Remaking of the Church* (Cambridge, Ma.: Harvard University Press, 2018), 2–3, 11, 12, 61.

60. Birzer, *Sanctifying the World*, 146. Birzer cited Barbara Ward, "Christian Woman of the World," *Our Sunday Visitor*, May 17, 1959.

Application

The 1932 Rome Conference

Dawson's view of the intellectual as defender of the claims of culture against the total claims of politics led him to an international conference in Rome on the subject of "Europe," held from November 14th to the 20th, 1932. The Royal Academy of Italy invited distinguished leaders of thought to discuss European unity and the position of Europe in the contemporary world. The invitation sent to Dawson acknowledged that Europe was suffering "a historic crisis of capital importance" as a result of the Great War and its aftermath. Despite this crisis, there existed, said the invitation: "a European unity, historic and spiritual in character, that admits of definition and that is the resultant of deep-seated internal affinities and of some thousands of years of joint effort in the most essential branches of human activity, from religion to law, from science to poetry, from economics to art, in a word from spiritual to practical life values."[61] This mult-disciplinary focus on European unity appealed to Dawson's own views. In fact, it supported the argument Dawson advanced that same year in his book *The Making of Europe,* which demonstrated that Europe was formed from the influence of Greece, Rome, Christianity, and indigenous cultures. Dawson decided to attend the conference with his wife, and he went as part of a British delegation of five.[62] Notably, Herman Göring (1893–1946), who had been president of the German *Reichstag* since August 1932 and who would become a top Nazi leader, and Alfred Rosenberg (1893–1946), the Nazi theorist, also attended, as part of the German delegation. "What most of the European delegates did not realise," Scott wrote, "and it was a factor which annoyed Christopher considerably, was that this was no historical or academic conference as they had been led to believe but a 'put-up job' by Mussolini's government to turn events to their own ends." Everywhere

61. STA, box 1a, folder "Invitation to the Royal Academy of Italy's 'Volta' Meeting for the Moral and Historical Sciences" (1932).

62. James Rennell Rodd (1858–1941), who had been the British Ambassador to Rome from 1908 to 1919; Gerard Wallop, the environmentalist and Conservative MP for Basingstoke at the time of the conference; Charles Petrie, the conservative Catholic historian; and Paul Einzig (1897–1973), the economist. Among the outstanding figures from other countries at the conference were the distinguished politician Count Albert Apponyi (1846–1933) from Hungary; Stefan Zweig (1881–1942), the Austrian historical novelist; Louis Bertrand (1866–1941), the French novelist and historian; and Daniel Halévy (1872–1962), the French historian whose work Dawson particularly admired.

the delegates went, they were followed and spied on, but they were also entertained in sumptuous splendor by the government at the Excelsior Hotel. The meetings were formal occasions at which morning dress and top hats were *de rigueur*; for the evening functions, "it was full evening dress, uniforms and decorations for those who had them."[63] Charles Petrie recalled an amusing incident when Göring, whose turn it was to preside, made an announcement regarding the wearing of decorations at an official reception that evening. His French was so poor, however, that no one understood. Playing it safe, everyone arrived that evening with decorations—except Göring.[64]

The opening ceremony, at which inventor Guglielmo Marconi (1874–1937) and Mussolini spoke, was in the Julius Caesar Hall on the Capitol, not far from Santa Maria in Ara Coeli, the place where Dawson had conceived of his life work in 1909 to write the history of culture. The rest of the meetings took place in the Farnese Palace, the great Renaissance structure now serving as the French embassy in Italy. Dawson's lecture was on "Interracial Cooperation as a Factor in European Culture." In it, he traced the complementary role of different races in European history. It was a veiled attack on the racial interpretation of history of figures such as Alfred Rosenberg, who had published the widely read *Myth of the Twentieth Century* in 1930. Rosenberg offered Germans the new faith and the new values of the "racial soul" as recompense for the loss of common vision during the Great War.[65] Dawson, however, attacked the view that the Aryan race was the only creative force in civilization. He said that the "relatively benign Nationalism of the early Romantics paved the way for the fanaticism of the modern pan-racial theorists who subordinate civilization to skull measurements and who infuse an element of racial hatred into the political and economic ri-

---

63. Scott, *A Historian and His World*, 105–6.

64. Charles Petrie, *Chapters of Life* (London: Eyre & Spottiswoode, 1950), 185–86. Petrie recalled another humorous incident at the event: a "long-winded German was getting well into his stride when Lord Rennell suggested that he and I should retire for a drink. When we had done so, he remarked, 'Let me give you a word of advice as an old man to a young one. When Germans talk about things that end in *–ismus*, and Frenchmen about things that end in *–ologie*, it is wisest for an Englishman to withdraw to the bar'" (186). Petrie remembered Dawson as "one of the deepest thinkers of our time" (145).

65. Alfred Rosenberg, *The Myth of the Twentieth Century* (1930), trans. James Whisker, http:// archive.org/details/ TheMythOfThe20thCentury.

Application

valries of European peoples." Dawson continued, with words that must not have pleased the Nazi element in the audience, "It is obvious that these theories do not correspond to cultural facts. Even the national cultures themselves are due to the co-operation of different racial elements, and if we were to subtract from German culture, for example, all the contributions made by men who were not of pure Nordic type, German culture would be incalculably impoverished." He argued that European culture had developed by a continuous process of international and interracial collaboration. The great task of the present age was to find a new basis for such collaboration to continue.[66]

Scott recounted that the highlight of the event was a dinner given by Mussolini on behalf of the Italian government in the Grand Hotel. Dawson's wife, Valery, had the "doubtful honour of being placed next to Göring at the high table and only two places from Mussolini—she also had to submit to having her hand kissed by Göring when they were introduced." Scott continued:

Conversation with him tended to be heavy going; not only was there the language barrier but his mind was evidently more in Berlin than in Rome at that moment. He was constantly leaning across the lady next him on the other side to talk excitedly to Mussolini about some impending event of great importance to him; eventually a telegram arrived for him in the middle of the dinner with the news of Von Papen's resignation as Chancellor of the Reichstag, which meant Hitler's rise to power, and after brief apologies he left to fly back to Berlin. The Austrian Minister, who was also sitting next to Valery, said he hoped Göring's plane would come down in the Alps![67]

The plane did not come down, and the Nazis consolidated their power a few months later.

66. Christopher Dawson, "Interracial Cooperation as a Factor in European Culture," in *Convegno Volta* (Rome: Reale Accademia D'Italia, 1933), 8–9. This essay is obscure, but I found a copy of it in STA, box 1a, folder "Invitation to the Royal Academy of Italy's 'Volta' Meeting for the Moral and Historical Sciences" (1932).
67. Scott, *A Historian and His World*, 106–7.

The Moot: Why Dawson Avoided Meetings

As the sense of crisis deepened after 1938, Dawson became involved in a discussion group called the Moot[68] as the only Catholic member. This was a gathering of leading minds organized by the Protestant missionary and author J. H. Oldham to discuss—two or three times a year—themes such as education, how to counter the threat of totalitarianism, and the re-Christianization of Britain. The Moot brought British and continental scholars together and revealed the strength of the Judeo-Christian-perspective on society and politics in mid-twentieth-century Britain.[69] Participants included the theologian John Baillie (1886–1960), who later encouraged Dawson's Gifford Lectures to successful completion; T. S. Eliot (1888–1965), who published his *Idea of a Christian Society* in 1939 and his *Notes towards the Definition of Culture* in 1948—the latter book drawing from his work within the Moot; the journalist and author John Middleton Murry (1889–1957); Adolf Löwe (1893–1995), a German Jewish refugee sociologist and economist; and Karl Mannheim (1893–1947), the Hungarian-born Jewish sociologist who, like Löwe, was forced out of his academic position at Frankfurt. Mannheim's *Man and Society in an Age of Reconstruction* (1940) had appeared in German in 1935. His thought provided a primary stimulus to the group, and when he died in 1947, the Moot ended. According to the attendance list, Dawson appeared at only three meetings: April 1938, January 1941, and August 1941.[70] Due to the existence of the nearly verbatim records of their exchanges in the Oldham Archive at New College, University of Edinburgh, a "rare kind of chronicle to intellectual debate" concerning totalitarianism was published in 2010, which has opened a rich mine for further study.[71]

There was tension in the group between theology and sociology:

---

68. "Moot" is an Old English word meaning an assembly or meeting-point, OED, "Moot." This group was active from 1938 to 1947.

69. "Moot," entry by Matthew Grimley, ODNB; Birzer, *Sanctifying the World*, 120.

70. Attendance List, E-JHOP, box 12, folder 1.

71. Keith Clements, *Faith on the Frontier: A Life of J. H. Oldham* (Edinburgh: T&T Clark, 1999), chap. XVII; Potts and Turner, "Making Sense of Christopher Dawson," 127; and Keith Clements, ed., *The Moot Papers: Faith, Freedom and Society 1938–1947* (New York: T&T Clark, 2010), 2. See the following for a survey of archival and secondary work connected to the Moot: Jonas Kurlberg, "Resisting Totalitarianism: The Moot and a New Christendom," *Religion Compass* 7, no. 12 (2013): 517–31.

was society a human-made order guided by reason, or was it a spiritual order guided by the Spirit? While Dawson thought sociological remedies could help, he challenged the group to think in theological terms about the need for social transformation guided by the Spirit of God above all else.[72]

Mannheim argued for a "third way" between totalitarianism and *laissez-faire* in a democratic state that would plan much of society and culture.[73] In his response paper, Dawson argued against this position: "The organization of culture means bringing it into the service of social ends and hence of the state." Furthermore, "the remoulding of human nature is a task that far transcends politics, and . . . if the state is entrusted with this task it will inevitably destroy human freedom in a more fundamental way than even the totalitarian states have yet attempted to do." Dawson stood firmly against any attempt by the state to sacrifice the liberties and spiritual values of the older type of culture for the sake of power and immediate success.[74] State control of culture would negate the great inheritance of the past, he wrote:

But what has always given the English system its unique strength and social solidity has been the existence of a social unity behind the monarchy and behind parliament, a unity of which they are the political organs, but which itself transcends politics. It is this unity which makes it possible for our party system to function on a basis of common understanding without dividing the nation into two hostile camps with mutually exclusive ideologies.

The state should serve as a vehicle of the wider and deeper life of the people.[75]

In order to "organize" culture while safeguarding personal freedom, Dawson called for a *party* of culture, a voluntary organization for common ends based on a common vision. This would be an "organization of

72. Potts and Turner, "Making Sense of Christopher Dawson," in *The History of Sociology in Britain*, 128.

73. "Moot," entry by Matthew Grimley, ODNB.

74. Dawson, "Planning and Culture," E-JHOP, box 14, folder 4, paras. 13, 19, and 20. In para. 20, Dawson wrote: "The planning of culture cannot be undertaken in a dictatorial spirit, like a rearmament plan. Since it is a much higher and more difficult task than any economic organisation, it demands greater resources of powers of knowledge and understanding. It must in fact be undertaken in a really religious spirit."

75. Dawson, *Beyond Politics*, 14.

national culture which would not be directly dependent on the State or on any political party." This was necessary because, "What has been lacking hitherto is any satisfactory basis for common action." At the present time in democratic countries, the "realm of culture has become a no-man's-land which is given up to anarchic individualism." Dawson had in mind a nonpolitical party of national culture that could "find room for everyone who is not committed to a totalitarian ideology and who is loyal to the national tradition and to national institutions and ideals." It would function like the Action Française or the Fabian Society—"and though these aspired to direct political action in the last resort, I do not see why this should be the inevitable condition of their existence."[76] Dawson's startling juxtaposition of Action Française (rightwing) and the Fabian Society (leftwing) underscored his point: to draw attention away from *ideological agenda* to *sociological function*. He had in mind a movement of ideas and cultural influence distinct from a political party.

The Moot was no such "party of culture," and he remained on the margins of it. This was not only because of differences in ideas and other commitments but also because he seemed to be cautious about the whole idea of meetings and "group activities" in the first place. "There is also the other point we raised which may be of less importance," Dawson wrote to Oldham, "but which is of even greater practical urgency; I mean this question of 'meeting,' on which you rightly lay such stress, but which seems to me to be in practice stifled and overlaid by 'meetings.'" He continued:

In other words, is not the great question for us to-day whether and how it is possible to avoid the absorption of personal relations by organized group activities. It is of course our old friend the question of Planning and Freedom,

76. Dawson, *Beyond Politics*, 24, 26, 27, 28, 55–56. The Fabian Society, founded in 1884, was an intellectual socialist organization and an important influence on Britain's Labour Party. The Action Française, founded in 1898, was a far-right, nationalist organization supporting monarchism and the restoration of Catholicism as the national religion. It made antirepublicanism and antisemitism respectable in intellectual circles and was condemned in 1926 by Pope Pius XI. The antisemitism of the Action Française would have been repugnant to Dawson. There is no known instance of any antisemitic statements made by him. In fact, in his *Making of Europe* (1932), he described how Christianity clearly derived out of the Jewish tradition—see Dawson, *The Making of Europe*, 34. At the 1932 Rome conference, he forcefully argued against the racial interpretation of history, and in a 1959 lecture at Brandeis University called "On Jewish History," he wrote of the significance of Jewish culture in world history—see www.ewtn.com/library.HOMELIBR/DAWJEWHS.TXT. This was Dawson's last article published during his lifetime—in *Orbis* 10 (Winter 1967): 1247–256.

but it works differently in theory and practice, because the representations of the religious point of view, who in principle should be the defenders of personality, are in practice more completely committed to the supremacy of organization than are the representatives of the secular point of view.[77]

Dawson wanted to do something more real than attend meetings, to be part of a greater *action* that was more open to prophetic inspiration. Therefore, he chose to devote his energies not so much to the Moot as to an actual "party of culture," of a sort, that he would help to create: the Sword of the Spirit movement.

The Sword of the Spirit

Dawson received a letter dated June 27, 1938, from a private secretary of Cardinal Arthur Hinsley (1865–1943), the Archbishop of Westminster. "His Eminence the Cardinal is an admirer of your writings," it said, "and wants to make your acquaintance."[78] They apparently got on well, for after the shock of the fall of France in June 1940, Dawson was appointed by Hinsley to the editorship of *Dublin Review*. Dawson gave the journal a cultural program and not a sectarian one by publishing authors from diverse national, academic, and religious backgrounds, not just Catholics. Dawson's "intellectual bridges" linked anyone who could contribute to the interdisciplinary cause of Christian humanism and European unity.[79] Then, in August, he was also invited by the Car-

77. Dawson to Oldham, April 18, 1942, STA, box 15, folder 80. He had expressed similar concerns in a letter to Oldham dated June 20, 1939, E-JHOP, box 9, folder 2. In a 1942 conversation over dinner with his friend David Jones, Dawson told him that he (Dawson) found that Catholics, "in his experience, since he became a Catholic, were getting far more, not less, 'institutional' (in the bad sense) and mechanical, so to say. That the age of von Hügel, the 'belief' in the Holy Ghost, in the subtlety of where truth resides etc. seemed far away—and a belief in effecting things by organization and formulas etc. etc. (among Catholics) growing rather than lessening. In short, that 'propaganda' is universally dominant in the Church as outside it, and once you yield *interiorly* to the propagandist attitude you're sunk." Letter of David Jones to Harman Grisewood, June 1, 1942, in René Hague, ed., *Dai Greatcoat: A Self-Portrait of David Jones in His Letters* (London: Faber & Faber, 1980), 120 (emphasis in the original).

78. Valentine Elwes to Dawson, June 27, 1938, STA, box 14, folder 169.

79. Writers in the first two numbers edited by Dawson included: Hermann Rauschning (1887–1982), a German and early Nazi who later renounced the ideology and moved to the United States; Stanislas Fumet (1896–1983), a French Catholic writer and critic; Charles Williams (1886–1945), an Anglican poet, novelist, theologian, literary critic, and member of the Inklings; Paul Vignaux (1904–1987), a French historian of medieval philosophy; David Knowles (1896–1974), an En-

dinal to be vice-president of the new movement called the Sword of the Spirit (SOS).

During the 1930s, much of the Catholic press had supported Franco, and Hinsley himself had privately done so.[80] Therefore, the cardinal responded to the dangerous national predicament in the summer of 1940 by trying to counter the fascist image of Catholics. Hinsley wanted to demonstrate that even if a "Latin bloc" of Catholic (and fascist) countries developed in Europe, British Catholics would remain patriotic. He had already used St. Paul's phrase "the sword of the Spirit"[81] in an address broadcast by the BBC on December 10, 1939, about "the battle which goes on in the inmost hearts of men, of that spiritual conflict inside each man resulting in the triumph of good or of evil in the outward world." "I am convinced," he said, "that Britain has engaged in this war in the main for defence of the things of the spirit."[82] In this way, Cardinal Hinsley emerged as a national religious war-leader. Though the Archbishop of Canterbury, Cosmo Gordon Lang (1864–1945), had cosigned a letter to the *Times* with Hinsley supporting Pope Pius XII's "Five Peace Points" in December 1940, Lang did not take on a national role in the war effort. Some clerics remembered all too well the overblown religious rhetoric used to support the Great War in 1914 and 1915.[83] Hinsley did not hesitate, however, and strongly encouraged Catholics to support the government. When SOS was launched in August 1940, it was part of his campaign to state clearly that Catholicism and fascism were not synonymous. SOS was referred to as a "Crusade

---

glish historian and Benedictine monk; Georges Bernanos (1888–1948), a French writer and critic of Vichy; Jacques Maritain (1882–1973), a French Catholic philosopher; A. D. Lindsay (1879–1952), a British academic and peer; Jacob Peter Mayer (1903–1992), a German sociologist and political writer who had fled to England; and Barbara Ward (1914–1981), a British economist. Dawson was ousted from the *Dublin Review* after Hinley's death in 1943 by the editor and devout Catholic Douglas F. Jerrold. Jerrold publicly supported fascism in Italy and Catholic nationalism in Spain; he despised Dawson's broad-minded approach at the *Dublin Review* to include articles by Catholics such as Maritain and Bernanos who did not support Franco.

80. Thomas Moloney, *Westminster, Whitehall and the Vatican: The Role of Cardinal Hinsley, 1935–43* (Tunbridge Wells: Burns & Oates, 1985), chap. 3.

81. Ephesians 6:17.

82. Cardinal Hinsley, "The Sword of the Spirit," *Tablet*, December 16, 1939, 705.

83. Stuart Mews, "The Sword of the Spirit: A Catholic Cultural Crusade of 1940," in *The Church and War*, ed. W. J. Sheils (Oxford: Basil Blackwell, 1983), 410–12. For the joint letter to the editor of the *Times*, see "Foundations of Peace," signed by Cosmo Cantuar, A. Cardinal Hinsley, Walter H. Armstrong, and William Ebor, December 21, 1940, 5.

against Nazi Paganism" (in the *Times*) which attempted "to coordinate and intensify the efforts already being made by the Roman Catholic body in England to fit themselves by prayer, work, and study to contribute as much as they can to the national cause."[84]

Dawson enthusiastically supported SOS from the start. Early in 1941, Hinsley wrote to him: "I have just read your article 'The Sword of the Spirit" in the *Dublin*. It is excellent. I congratulate you, and I thank you heartily." He continued: "You have my full confidence. I desire that you should be the leading spirit and directing light in the movement. Your vote should have a deciding influence at the meetings of the Executive."[85] There was urgency and decisiveness in the Cardinal's tone, and rightly so, for this letter to Dawson was written only two weeks after a major bombing on London by German planes that destroyed hundreds of buildings, but spared St. Paul's cathedral, as recorded in the iconic photo, "St. Paul's Survives."

The Board of SOS, with Hinsley as president and Dawson as vice-president, consisted of the legal scholar Richard O'Sullivan (1888–1963, KC) as chairman and economist Barbara Ward and historian A. C. F. Beales (1905–1974) as joint honorary secretaries. The wealthy convert Manya Harari (1905–1969), future cofounder of Harvill Press, although not a member of the board, was a leading figure as well.[86] Fr. Martin D'Arcy (1888–1976), Jesuit and theologian, served as advisor. Robert Speaight (1904–1976), an actor and literary scholar involved with SOS, described the movement as: "launched by Cardinal Hinsley, animated by Manya Harari, put into operation by Barbara Ward, and intellectually nourished by Christopher Dawson.... Faith was strong in both these remarkable women and Christopher Dawson leaned heavily upon them, as they—for different reasons—leaned upon him."[87]

---

84. "A Crusade Against Nazi Paganism," *Times*, July 22, 1940, 2.

85. Hinsley to Dawson, January 16, 1941, AAW, box "Sword of the Spirit, Hinsley 2/219 + Bo. 1/174," folder "Correspondence Christopher Dawson/Hinsley." Hinsley referred to Christopher Dawson, "The Sword of the Spirit," *Dublin Review* CCVIII (January 1941): 1–11.

86. Scott, *A Historian and His World*, 140.

87. Robert Speaight, *The Property Basket: Recollections of a Divided Life* (London: Collins & Harvill, 1970), 218–219. Harari provided European contacts and was described by Scott as: "A White Russian émigré, half-Jewish by birth and married to an Egyptian financier, she had a certain air of almost Eastern mystery with her long cigarette holder and romantic black cloak which she often wore" (Scott, *A Historian and His World*, 140).

Jacques Maritain (1882–1973) was closely linked as well, and the movement quickly made contact with various national groups exiled in Britain.[88] SOS pamphlets were written by Dawson, and the government's Ministry of Information moved in quickly to assist financially with the early pamphlets written in August 1940. The ministry circulated the fortnightly number of 400,000 pamphlets through Catholic organizations.[89]

Dawson wrote in August for the *Tablet*:

Our great need is unity. . . . The favourite method of causing division and strife is the exploitation of the 'ideological' conflict between Left and Right, which may be extended to cover almost every shade of opinion. If this conflict is developed in an extreme form, it produces a situation like that of the Spanish civil war, in which the nation is divided into two hostile camps, with no common ground between them.

How can Catholics contribute to the national resistance and to national unity? he asked. "There must surely be some relation between the Christian virtues of faith, hope and charity, and the social faith, hope and charity which hold societies together and preserve them from the social vices of faction and treachery and defeatism." Politics are not enough, he said. "If political Parties are the only forces in a nation, they inevitably lead to division and strife. They must be supplemented by another element, which is that of religion." "Thus," he concluded, "Catholics can make a vital contribution to the cause of national unity, not by their political action or by launching Catholic political programmes, but by strengthening the moral basis of unity which underlies political action."[90]

For Dawson, SOS was founded as "a spiritual movement against a spiritual evil. It is a crusade against totalitarianism, not on the political plane, but on the spiritual plane, a crusade to defend man against the anti-human forces that are striving to dominate the world."[91] Those

88. For example, the minutes of a meeting of the executive committee on August 28, 1941, mentioned that in an August 6 meeting, representatives from Poland, Czechoslovakia, Belgium, France, and the Netherlands attended. See AAW, box "Sword of the Spirit, Executive Minutes, 1940–41," folder "Minutes, 1941–42"; see Moloney, *Westminster, Whitehall and the Vatican*, 190, 195.

89. Moloney, *Westminster, Whitehall and the Vatican*, 190.

90. Christopher Dawson, "The Sword of the Spirit," *Tablet*, August 31, 1940, 172. This was reprinted from the second bulletin of the SOS.

91. Christopher Dawson, *The Power of the Spirit* (London, 1943), 3.

forces included "propaganda," especially coming from the totalitarian states. (That was why *study* was important—to defend oneself intellectually.) Such propaganda was an "organization for the creation and control of mass opinion in the interests of power without regard for moral consideration."[92] Dawson saw SOS as countering two extremes. On one hand, there was the realism of the militarist who recognized the problem of Hitler but who viewed resistance as simply making munitions and bombing Germany. This kind of person "believes that it is possible by force alone to destroy the evils that threaten our civilisation." On the other hand, Christians, "who presumably realize the importance of spiritual things, do not always recognise that they have any bearing on the present crisis." Wars come and wars go, these pious idealists think, so the great thing is to cultivate the religious life and go to church as much as possible. "We cannot agree with either, for, though we believe that the spiritual war is different and far more important than the war with Germany, we also believe that there is a relation between them and that the war is an external manifestation of a spiritual disorder, in a different sense to that in which all wars are." One must connect one's religious views to the real world; that was the whole point about the relation between religion and culture studied in chapter 5, and the link between I and FWP from chapter 2. The "demonic" power of National Socialism advanced because Christians retreated and abdicated in and after 1933.[93] "In such a work," he wrote, "it is useless to look for quick results, for our present danger is the result of literally centuries of neglect, during which culture has been secularized and religion gradually pushed out of public life in the private sanctuary of the individual conscience." He continued: "But with the coming of totalitarianism even this last refuge [the individual conscience] is no longer secure. The new powers demand everything."[94] That was why Dawson defended democracy—but not merely the democracy of majority rule. He defended the specific form of self-government that embodied the ideal of personal liberty in representative or parliamentary institutions that derived their strength from the Christian belief in the value of the individual human soul.[95]

92. Christopher Dawson, "Propaganda," *Tablet*, October 5, 1940, 265.
93. Dawson, *The Power of the Spirit*, 6.
94. Dawson, "Propaganda," 266.
95. Dawson, *The Judgment of the Nations*, 15.

Dawson blamed the separation between religion and culture (secularization) as a leading factor in the contemporary situation. Christian disunity since the Age of Reformations had created a "neutral territory which gradually expanded till it came to include almost the whole of social life." The wars of religion led to the eventual exclusion of religion to a private world.[96] For a Christian "who believes in the existence of a divine and universal society all such ideas are blasphemy against Christ the King," he wrote.[97] In this way, in *The Judgment of the Nations* (1942), a book published by Sheed & Ward as a way of supporting the Sword of the Spirit movement, he blamed Christian disunity for the division between religion and culture that led to secularization.[98]

Dawson also included in that book an entire chapter on "The Return to Christian Unity." The greatest step toward Christian unity was an internal and a spiritual one, he wrote. One must purge from the mind the lower motives that contaminate faith. "For in the vast majority of cases the sin of schism does not arise from a conscious intention to separate oneself from the true Church, but from allowing the mind to become so occupied and clouded by instinctive enmities or oppositions that we can no longer see spiritual issues clearly, and our religious attitude becomes determined by forces that are not religious at all." In the history of the church, he wrote, heresy and schism had often derived their main impetus from sociological causes.[99]

One could potentially encourage Christian unity by mutually supporting a common social cause, and that was part of the mission of the Sword of the Spirit. With an interest in greater Christian unity as part of the war effort, the Sword of the Spirit was the first Catholic attempt to found an ecumenical movement in England. Ecumenism lay close to Dawson's concerns, and he was personally a bridge between Anglicans and Catholics during the war: "I saw . . . Dawson a few days ago," David Jones wrote to a friend in June 1942, and "had dinner with him in . . . the 'Mausoleum' in Queen's Gate Terrace—I must say it is a gloomy place. [Dawson] had just had tea with the Archbishop of Canterbury, the Bishop of London and Arthur Cardinal Hinsley, and Miss

96. Dawson, *The Judgment of the Nations*, 70.
97. Dawson, *Religion and the Modern State*, 149.
98. Birzer, *Sanctifying the World*, 197.
99. Dawson, *The Judgment of the Nations*, 178–80.

B[arbara] Ward—what an astonishing party."[100] Dawson was also close friends with George Bell (1883–1958), Anglican Bishop of Chichester, who, apparently, held up Dawson's *Judgment of the Nations* during a speech in the House of Lords and recommended everyone to read it.[101]

Ecumenism was very evident at the two public gatherings of May 10 and 11, 1941, held at the Stoll Theatre in London under the auspices of SOS. The events, presided over by Cardinal Hinsley and the Anglican Archbishop of Canterbury, Cosmo Gordon Lang, were an immense success and aroused considerable enthusiasm.[102] The advertisement for the meetings indicated the topics: "A Christian International Order" and "A Christian Order for Britain." Speakers included Christopher Dawson,[103] Barbara Ward, George Bell, Martin D'Arcy, and the Acting Moderator of the Free Church Federal Council (Dr. Sidney Berry).[104] The coming together of the leaders of three major branches of Christianity on one platform was a "great achievement," Dawson said—as reported in the Seventh Day Adventist magazine (which showed interest from the United States).[105] T. S. Eliot had been invited to speak. In a letter to Beales, however, he explained that he could not attend, but said: "I feel honoured by the invitation to join such a distinguished company: also I have a warm desire to support anything promoted by Christopher Dawson, with whose views I am in cordial sympathy."[106] The list of "platform guests" included Anglican bishops, peers, Catholic ecclesiastical heads, knights, members of Parliament, headmasters, heads of colleges, foreign church representatives, editors, representatives from France, and representatives of various societies and institutions (e.g., the Y.M.C.A.

100. Jones to Harman Grisewood, June 1, 1942, in Hague, *Dai Greatcoat*, 119. The Archbishop of Canterbury from April 1942 to October 1944 was William Temple (1881–1944). The Bishop of London from 1939 to 1945 was Geoffrey Fisher (1887–1972), who succeeded Temple as Archbishop of Canterbury.

101. Scott, *A Historian and His World*, 148.

102. Mews, "The Sword of the Spirit," in *The Church and War*, 424.

103. Dawson was unable to attend due to illness, but his talk was read aloud.

104. "Two Public Meetings" advertisement, AAW, unsorted box "Sword, Stoll Meetings."

105. "Toward a Christian Order," *Present Truth*, vol. 57, no 12 (1941), 2.

106. Eliot to Beales, April 5, 1941, AAW, unsorted box "Sword, Stoll Meetings." Eliot had admired Dawson's work for some time. He wrote to the historian in 1929: "I have recently read some of your work and have had it in my mind some little time to write to you to express my interest. . . . the *Criterion* ought to publish some essay by you and I should be very grateful if you would write to me and make some suggestion" (Eliot to Dawson, STA, box 14, folder 120).

and Catholic Social Action).[107] On May 10, over 2,200 people so filled the theater that over five hundred additional people could not enter.[108] That night, the *Luftwaffe* bombed the city and killed or wounded three thousand people in its final major Blitz attack on London before the German squadrons shifted east in preparation for the attack on Russia. Due to this violence, not quite as many people attended on May 11.[109]

The success of the Stoll meetings opened the possibility of many non-Catholic members joining SOS. Other members of the Catholic hierarchy grew nervous, however, over Hinsley's promise of further ecumenical cooperation and joint recitation of the Lord's Prayer. Others worried that leadership of SOS would pass out of Catholic hands. Therefore, "At the first annual meeting on August 9, 1941, Hinsley, with great regret, and some embarrassment, announced non-catholics were only eligible for associate membership in the Sword of the Spirit and had no voting rights. A parallel non-catholic movement was set up under the title 'Religion and Life'."[110] Hierarchical division, theological controversy over ecumenism, the lack of structural organization within SOS, Hinsley's death in 1943, and the passing of an immediate threat of German invasion contributed to the decline of the movement after only three years. However, Sword of the Spirit, renamed Catholic Institute for International Relations (CIIR), continued until 2017 as an ecumenical organization concerned with international volunteer work and speaking out against human rights abuses.[111]

The Containment of Politics

The breakdown of the relation between religion and culture, Dawson believed, had contributed to the spiritual and psychological void

107. "List of Platform Guests," AAW, unsorted box "Sword, Stoll Meetings."

108. "Report on the Actual Meetings," AAW, unsorted box "Sword, Stoll Meetings, Organisation, 2."

109. Moloney, *Westminster, Whitehall and the Vatican*, 192.

110. Mews, "The Sword of the Spirit," in *The Church and War*, 426–27.

111. See Michael Walsh, *From Sword to Ploughshare: Sword of the Spirit to Catholic Institute for International Relations, 1949–1980* (London: Catholic Institute for International Relations, 1980). CIIR became Progressio in 2006, which then closed in 2017 due to funding issues. Thus ended one of Cardinal Hinsely's greatest legacies, in which Dawson had played an important role by giving intellectual backing to its mission.

into which rushed the totalitarian ideologies seeking to integrate life on the basis of a "secular religion." Modern Christianity had to "become communal and break down the old barriers that separated religion from life," Dawson argued. Far from creating a new theocracy,[112] far from countering secular religion (the ideologies) with a new form of Christian "political religion,"[113] far from creating social programs for renewing society,[114] the church's task "is not to become a competitor with the State in its social action but to find new social means of expression for its spiritual action. The Church remains what she has always been, the organ of the Divine Word and the channel of Divine Grace. It is her mission to transform the world by bringing every side of human existence and every human activity into contact with the sources of supernatural life."[115] The church's mission, as Dawson saw it, was to unite men by what is highest (the fellowship of the Holy Spirit), not by what

112. "Wherever the Church has seemed to dominate the world politically and achieves a victory within the secular sphere, she has had to pay for it in a double measure of temporal and spiritual misfortune. Thus the triumph of the Orthodox Church in the Byzantine Empire was followed first by the loss of the East to Islam and then by the schism with the West. The mediaeval attempt to create a Christian theocracy was followed by the Reformation and the destruction of the religious unity of Western Europe, while the attempt that was made both by the Puritans and by the monarchies of the Counter Reformation to dragoon society into orthodoxy and piety was followed by the incredulity and anticlericalism of the eighteenth century and the secularisation of European culture" (Dawson, *Religion and the Modern State*, 120–21).

113. "It is notorious that ecclesiastics often make the most unscrupulous politicians, as we see in the case of Wolsey, Richelieu, Mazarin, and Alberoni, and in the same way the political parties which adopt religious programmes and claim to represent the cause of God, like the thirteenth century Guelfs, the Holy League in the sixteenth century and the Covenanters and Puritans in the seventeenth, have always distinguished themselves by their fanaticism and violence: in fact by a general lack of all the political virtues. Political religion is an offence alike to religion and to politics: it takes from Caesar what belongs to him of right and fills the temple with the noise and dust of the market place. The only really and specifically Christian politics are the politics of the world to come, and they transform social life not by competing with secular politics on their own ground but by altering the focus of human thought and opening the closed house of secular culture to the free light and air of a larger and more real world" (Dawson, *Religion and the Modern State*, 122–23).

114. "In a sense it is quite true to say that all our troubles are due to the neglect of Christian teaching and that Christianity is the remedy for our social as well as our individual evils. But it is not like a patent medicine that is warranted to cure all diseases. It offers no short cuts to economic prosperity or social stability.... [T]he true social function of religion is not to busy itself with economic or political reforms, but to save civilization from itself by revealing to men the true end of life and the true nature of reality" (Dawson, *Religion and the Modern State*, 121, 125). "The greatest service the Church can render to western civilization at the present time [1939] is to keep her own inheritance intact and not to allow her witness to be obscured by letting herself be used as the instrument of secular powers and politics" (Dawson, *Beyond Politics*, 21).

115. Christopher Dawson, "Church, State and Community," *Tablet*, June 26, 1937, 910.

are lowest common factors, in class interests or physical unity of blood and race. Whence comes the power to unite people and affect culture? Not from the spirit of power so evident in interwar politics, Dawson asserted in 1943, but from the power of the spirit, the Holy Spirit, God himself, active among other Christian denominations, too, and even among non-Christians. Christians, however, uniquely possessed the gift of his power. Only their lack of faith and generosity inhibited the spirit.[116]

The significance of Dawson's wartime work in the *Dublin Review*, the Sword of the Spirit, and *The Judgment of the Nations* was to put him at the center of the Christian response to the Second World War in Britain. The First World War had raised criticism about "progress" and "civilization" and "decline" and "democracy" and "capitalism"; the Second World War returned attention to the *value* of democracy and raised new questions about the relationship between Christianity, culture, and the state for Dawson and other Catholics. With the decline of the political power of the Catholic Church in Europe, what realistic role could it play in society? Before 1940, the typical European Catholic praised the states that claimed explicit Catholic legitimation, such as Austria, Portugal, and Spain. The Fédération Nationale Catholique in France was a good example of mass support for the older ideal of the "Catholic social order." This ideal partly underpinned the enthusiasm many French Catholics later gave to Vichy France (1940–1945), which courted the church in the interest of "moral regeneration."[117] Though there had been voices contrary to the "Catholic state" idea in the interwar years, such as Luigi Sturzo (1871–1959), the Italian Christian Democrat who had been exiled to London in 1924, it was not until *after* 1940 that the typical European Catholic would really accept the merits of democracy.[118] In Britain, Dawson played an important role in this transformation.

The Second World War demonstrated the importance of the West-

---

116. Dawson, *The Power of the Spirit*, 10.

117. James F. McMillan, "Catholicism and Nationalism in France: The Case of the Fédération Nationale Catholique, 1924–39," in *Catholicism in Britain and France Since 1789*, ed. Frank Tallett and Nicholas Atkin (London: Hambledon, 1996), 151–63.

118. Joan E. Keating, "Discrediting the 'Catholic State': British Catholics and the Fall of France," in *Catholicism in Britain and France Since 1789*, 27–28; Adrian Hastings, *A History of English Christianity: 1920–1990*, 3rd ed. (1986; London: SCM, 1991), 372.

ern liberal tradition of limited government, and Dawson's rethinking of
that tradition held significance for British Catholics by moving them
out of Belloc's ideal of political Catholicism. Though sharing in some of
the medievalist atmosphere of the interwar years, Dawson did not look
upon medieval Europe as Belloc and others did for a definite model of
ideal Christian society. Despite his hostility to the Communist forces
during the Spanish Civil War, he ultimately disagreed with "Catholic
imperialists" who sought to defend Christian culture through national
aggrandizement.[119] He also dismissed the ideal of rebuilding "Christendom."[120] Thus, as Joan Keating's work has shown, Dawson's most
important achievement during the Second World War was "suggesting to British Catholics that the way ahead was by accepting a circum-
scribed role in mainstream British life." Inspired by St. Augustine to
deemphasize the role of the state, he sought to justify Catholic action
in the world, with the church as a dynamic moral and social force, not
to justify a certain political order.[121] "He was certainly no fan of the
confessional state. . . . Dawson's importance lies in his championing of
democracy," Keating noted. His role was to underpin the voice of the
See of Westminster with a historical analysis to wean Catholics away
from the confessional state idea. "Dawson was suggesting a role for the
Church in a non-theocratic Britain." Dawson's focus on the distinct *oth-
erness* of the Church suggested choice and the plurality of options in
politics for Catholics.[122] Freedom, in other words, depended on maintaining the proper vertical *and* horizontal orientations of religion. "If
we are to build a Christian order for Britain," he wrote in 1942, "it must
be based on freedom, otherwise it would not be British, but it must
be a Christian freedom, not a freedom of economic materialism and
individual selfishness." This meant a freedom in which the social or-

119. Joan E. Keating, "Roman Catholics, Christian Democracy and the British Labour Movement, 1910–1960" (PhD diss., University of Manchester, 1992), 123–24.

120. "For what we must look for," Dawson wrote, "is not the alliance of the temporal power,
as in the old Christendom, and an external conformity to Christian standards, but a re-ordering
of all the elements of human life and civilization by the power of the Spirit: the birth of a true
community which is neither an inorganic mass of individuals nor a mechanized organization of
power, but a living spiritual order" (Dawson, *The Judgment of the Nations*, 109).

121. Keating, "Roman Catholics, Christian Democracy and the British Labour Movement,
1910–1960," 128, 131.

122. Keating, "Roman Catholics, Christian Democracy and the British Labour Movement,
1910–1960," 151, 152.

der was directed toward spiritual ends and all people have a chance to use their freedom "for the service of God according to [their] own powers and gifts."[123] Dawson's perspectives, built on his critique of totalitarianism and political religion, were a significant contribution to English-speaking Catholics. They helped articulate their experience of pluralistic societies and democratic politics. That experience then proved a powerful influence in the reorientation of the Catholic Church at the Second Vatican Council (1962–1965) toward a more robust defense of religious freedom and other human rights.[124]

Political developments during the interwar years brought into public the Christian and the national and even the polemical Dawson in ways that his temperament and ordinary scholarly interests did not. But he approached politics only *after* having immersed himself in other subjects. He proceeded from cultural studies *to* political studies. He thought "beyond politics." The modern dilemma was firstly a cultural and spiritual dilemma. The problem was how to contain the claims of politics so as to protect the true freedom of culture. Only in the spheres of culture and religion could human beings possess spiritual, intellectual, and psychological certainties and personal meanings. Only by acknowledging the distinctness of those spheres could politics be free to focus on truly political questions and avoid the confusion and amalgamation of political and religious categories that could end nowhere but in totalitarianism.

123. Dawson, *The Judgment of the Nations*, 126.
124. Keating, "Roman Catholics, Christian Democracy and the British Labour Movement, 1910–1960," 151; Jeffrey Paul von Arx, "Catholics and Politics," in *From Without the Flaminian Gate: 150 Years of Roman Catholicism in England and Wales, 1850–2000*, ed. V. Alan McClelland and Michael Hodgetts (London: Darton, Longman & Todd, 1999), 267. Interestingly, theologian John Courtney Murray (1904–1967), who influenced the Second Vatican Council's position on religious freedom, referred to Dawson's work to help distinguish between democracies inspired by the liberal tradition reaching back to the Christian Middle Ages and the modern Jacobin tradition of totalitarian democracy very much at odds with the church. See John Courtney Murray, "The Church and Totalitarian Democracy," *Theological Studies* 14, no. 1 (December 1952): 525–63. The implication of this was that liberal democracy, characterized by government of the people through free institutions, could be compatible with a Catholic world view because it grew out of the Christian democratic tradition itself. In addition, after the Second World War, Catholics and Protestants collaborated to create a significant "Christian democracy" movement that has played an important role in politics in Europe and Latin America ever since.

Chapter 8

Education

The recovery of a Christian culture is therefore the essential educational and religious task.

—Christopher Dawson (1946)

One of the main channels for propagating political religions during the age of the Great War was state controlled education. It is not surprising that Dawon's first serious engagement with the theme of eduction occurred when war came close to home, during the time of German V-1 bombing attacks on London. Launched from across the English Channel in revenge for the Normandy invasion of June 6, 1944, the V-1 flying bombs flew low and sounded like a Model-T engine that would suddenly cut out and plunge to the ground in terrific explosions, indiscriminately killing and maiming thousands of civilians over the following months.

Living a safe distance away in Oxford, Dawson nevertheless participated in the 1944 series of Edward Alleyn (pronounced "Alan") Lectures at Christ's Chapel in Dulwich, just south of London and within the target zone. The chapel dated back to 1616 when a highly talented and generous actor during the age of Shakespeare, Edward Alleyn (1566–1626), built it and the nearby College of God's Gift for poor students. Three hundred years later, the chaplain initiated a lecture series by mostly Anglican scholars, including theologian V. A. Demant (1893–1983) and writer Dorothy Sayers (1893–1957). Their theme was the crisis of contemporary culture, and Dawson gave the third lecture in the

---

Christopher Dawson, "Education and the Crisis of Christian Culture," *Lumen Vitae* 1, no. 2 (1946): 215.

series. He considered this lecture the most important articulation of his educational philosophy and had it republished in Belgium and the United States.

The first wave of seventy-three flying bombs to hit London arrived on June 16, the day of the second lecture in the series by philosopher H. A. Hodges (1905–1976). During one or two of these June lectures, the audience was forced to take refuge under their seats in Christ's Chapel as nearby explosions made the crisis of contemporary culture feel very relevant. An attitude of "carry on regardless" prevailed. On the morning of June 30, the day of Dawson's lecture, five V-1 flying bombs damaged dozens of buildings in Dulwich. Days later, a V1 explosion destroyed the whole south wing of the College, injuring three people, and on July 28, a V-1 severely damaged more college buildings and the chapel, delaying the rest of the lectures for six months.[1]

The bombs reduced whole sections of this venerable educational and charitable institution to ruins—and much of London, as well. This was a veritable "war against culture," Dawson wrote in the published version of his Edward Alleyn lecture. Historian Alan Kramer argued this war against culture was characterized by what he called the "dynamic of destruction," which mobilized cultures for the sake of destroying other cultures in the age of total war: from the burning of Louvain

---

1. For the context of Dawson's Edward Alleyn Lecture, I have relied on the following sources: Brian Green, *Christ's Chapel, Dulwich* (Great Britain: Board of the Incorporated Trustees of the Dulwich Estate, n.d.); C. W. Dugmore, ed., *The Interpretation of the Bible: Edward Alleyn Lectures 1943* (London: Society for Promoting Christian Knowledge, 1944); V. A. Demant, ed., *Our Culture: Its Christian Roots and Present Crisis* (London: Society for Promoting Christian Knowledge, 1947), which contained the original publication of Dawsons's Edward Alleyn Lecture; Peter Reese, *Target London: Bombing the Capital, 1915–2005* (Barnsley, South Yorkshire: Pen & Sword Military, 2011). The online V-1 log of explosions for the Dulwich area was also helpful: http://www.flyingbombs androckets.com/V-1_summary_dulwich.html (accessed February 10, 2017). For Dawson's view on the importance of his Edward Alleyn Lecture, see the reference to his letter to Leo R. Ward in Leo R. Ward, "Dawson on Education in Christian Culture," *Modern Age* 17, no. 1 (1973): 402. For the Belgian reprint, see Dawson, "Education and the Crisis of Christian Culture," 204–15. For the U.S. reprint (shortened version), see Christopher Dawson, "Task for Christian Education," *Catholic World* 165, no. 1 (1947), 463–64. I am grateful to Soraya Cerio of the Edward Alleyn Foundation for sending me the *Order of Services* for Christ's Chapel of God's Gift at Dulwich, Series XI, no. 4, May–July 1944, and to Brian Green for sending me his history, referenced above. The only evidence I have found of Dawson seriously thinking about education before this Edward Alleyn Lecture is the introduction he wrote for Mary Florence Margaret O'Leary, *The Catholic Church and Education* (London: Catholic Book Club, 1943). O'Leary links her book with the Sword of the Spirit movement on p. 111.

Application

Library and the shelling of Rheims Cathedral in 1914 to later German art-looting during the Second World War, the destruction of Warsaw's Old Town, and the indiscriminate bombing of cities and educational institutions such as at Dulwich in 1944. Cultural destruction—the mutilation of memory and identity—occurred not simply as an incidental by-product of combat but from deliberate policy—from the ideas and beliefs in the minds of the actors who carried out the policy.[2]

Thus, educationalists held a large measure of responsibility for the crisis, Dawson said in his 1944 lecture, because they participated in putting those ideas in the minds of the actors. They had given up on the proper ordering and hierarchy of knowledge according to "Divinity, Humanity, and Natural Science," Dawson observed, and could not offer a compelling account of Western culture to their students. Instead, they passed on to the young merely a national and secular identity that masqueraded as an ultimate value, the end-all of their education.

Even highbrow cultural advocates concerned with education, such as Matthew Arnold (1822–1888), had contributed to the fragmentation of knowledge. Their advocacy of "culture" without any "cult" severed the idea of culture from religion and life in the nineteenth century. This marginalized the idea of culture in the twentieth century and left few points of unity in modern education. The resulting disintegration of higher education into independent specialisms, Dawson said in his lecture, is "fatal to any ideal of culture, and if, as is sometimes the case, religious knowledge is treated as one of these independent specialisms, it is even more fatal to religion."

In the ensuing spiritual vacuum, "strange gods" emerged during and after the Great War from the "underworld of culture in the half-light between the old European day and the dark night of total barbarism," Dawson said. The crisis of the period from 1914 to 1944 revealed not only the "bankruptcy of secular humanism" but also the repercussions of the "starvation and frustration of man's spiritual nature." This meant that "civilization can be creative and life-giving only in the proportion that it is spiritualized. Otherwise the increase of power inevitably increases its power for evil—its destructiveness." The task of a renewed

2. Kramer, *Dynamic of Destruction*, 1–5.

Christian education emerged from the rubble of European civilization: to reinterpret the tradition of Christian culture in terms of the new knowledge and to relate the instruments of culture to their true spiritual end.[3]

It is obvious in this 1944 lecture that the idea of culture played an important role in Dawson's approach to his contemporary time and in his educational proposal. What problems did it help him solve? How did he apply his cultural mind to education? Why did he propose his educational ideas most forcefully in the United States rather than in Britain? And what led so many American Catholics to dislike them?

Concern for education emerged out of Dawson's lifelong comparative study of civilizations. The four great civilizations of the world— Western, Islamic, Indian, and Chinese—are really four educational traditions of immense antiquity and persistence, he wrote. Education is the process whereby a society hands on its culture to individuals of the next generation; therefore, the survival of each culture depends on the continuity of its educational tradition.[4]

Dawson applied his cultural mind to education primarily in the United States in response to cultural destruction he saw in Europe, for reasons explained in this chapter. The "Dawson Plan"in education tried to: 1) integrate fragmented knowledge; 2) connect a purely theological or humanistic conception of "Christian culture" to the social sciences and historical reality; 3) ground Great Books, ideas, theology, and philosophy in cultural context, helping to connect faith and life; 4) form students in a moderate cultural relativism to better equip them to face the spreading metaphysical relativism of the time; 5) mediate between tradition and assimilation to the "American way of life"; and 6) restore conversation between religion and culture in a secular age.

American humanities specialists denounced the Dawson Plan for its scope (too broad—students need to focus on the classics) and its methods (too populist—students need to specialize). Some of those influenced by John Henry Newman criticized the aim of the proposal (too

---

3. Christopher Dawson, "The Crisis of Christian Culture: Education," in *Our Culture*, 35–36, 47–48.

4. Christopher Dawson, "Education and the Study of Christian Culture," *Studies* 42, no. 1 (Autumn 1953): 293.

Application

evangelistic—students need to gain knowledge for its own sake). Most American critics targeted the subject of Dawson's proposal, "Christian culture," defined as the Christian way of life, as too narrow. They eschewed the idea of Christian culture partly because, as historian Adam Tate argued, they feared the power of the state and sought to assimilate into modern secular culture for the sake of relevance, and because Dawson failed to win political allies.[5]

Developing these educational ideas of Dawson's and situating them in relation to the critics, I will show in this chapter that educated American Catholic elites opposed Dawson's proposal to study Christian culture due to their religious idealism and their overweening emphasis on theology and philosophy. Parallel to these intellectual and spiritual trends, ordinary Catholics' daily *experience* of Christian culture fundamentally changed in the 1950s. The disintegrating effects of technology in family life, religion, sexuality, and commerce in the new suburbs made Christian culture, as a common way of life, increasingly unthinkable. Intellectual change reinforced sociological change (I→FWP), and vice-versa (FWP→I, the "culture-process" from chapters 2 and 5), to amplify opposition to Christian culture during the 1950s and 1960s.

Utilizing Dawson's own insights into the culture-process, this chapter seeks not only to make sense of the opposition to Dawson's educational ideas but also to elucidate why the loyalty and theological confidence of American Catholic elites in their own distinctive subculture collapsed during the 1960s. Critics came to believe the study of Christian culture involved returning to the "ghetto," intellectually speaking. They wanted greater assimilation to the American way of life, a process put in motion by the Great War, which united most American Catholics around a national cause for the first time and gave birth to a national Catholic hierarchy[6] seeking to improve the position of the faithful in the country. These trends deepened during the 1960s. Theological change paralleled sociological change, as demonstrated through the

5. Adam Tate, "Wrestling with the Modern State: Christopher Dawson and the Background to *The Crisis of Western Education*," *The Political Science Reviewer* LXI, no. 2 (2017): 98–99, 109, 121, 123. For another account, see James F. Hitchcock, "Rehearsal for Deconstruction," *Fellowship of Catholic Scholars Quarterly* 30, no. 4 (Winter 2007): 3–9.

6. The National Catholic War Council (1917) became the current United States Conference of Catholic Bishops.

lives of two Dawson critics, ex-Jesuit Bernard E. McGoldrick (dates unknown) and journalist John Cogley (1916–1976), but *not* in the case of a Dawson supporter, Eugene Kevane (1913–1996), priest and catechist. Dawson's educational ideas provided the tools by which contemporaries could not only have understood these changes but could have responded to them with greater sociological sophistication and discernment toward preserving Christian culture amidst assimilationist pressures. Those pressures eventually resulted in a kind of cultural destruction very different from that produced by German V-1 weapons but that led to much the same result: the gutting of educational institutions, this time through internal secularization by well-meaning and pious educators who suffered from severe sociological naiveté about how cultures work and pass on their identity. They failed to appreciate how difficult it is for people to sustain religious identity without the framework of a supporting culture made tangible through humble, institutional means. Ultimately, through my attempt to apply cultural mind to the problem of why so many Catholics opposed Dawson's educational ideas, I hope to illuminate how the process of Catholic cultural decomposition worked in the late twentieth-century United States.

Nevertheless, as a kind of coda, I will show that Dawson's educational ideas *did* make a small difference in the United States, such as at St. Mary's College in Notre Dame, Indiana. Here the combination of American administrative energy and risk-taking in the person of its president, Sister M. Madeleva Wolff (1887–1964), along with the extraordinary teacher Bruno Schlesinger (1911–2010), created a Christian Culture program as one way to implement Dawson's ideas. That program, in its early years, approached the subject of Christian culture with the sociological sophistication, historical sensitivity, and theological continuity to show-up the weaknesses of the critics and to produce the kinds of fruit in the lives of students that Dawson hoped for through his educational proposals.

Application

Why the United States?

The Second World War marked a moment of intense reflection on education in the English-speaking world. Many wondered how young people could be educated in a way worthy of victory, and how education could help prevent another major war. It seemed that poor education had led the world astray.[7] The German émigré and later economist E. F. Schumacher (1911–1977) wrote in his *Guide for the Perplexed* about how his 1930s education at New College, Oxford, lacked any kind of vision of life or "philosophical map" to the essential questions young people need to face to help them conduct their lives well. So, too, the philosopher and former vice-chancellor of the University of Manchester, Walter Moberly (1881–1974), lamented in the late 1940s about the inability of British university students to acquire a philosophy of life. The supposed "neutrality" of the university is an illusion that hides the vacuum at the center of university life, and the result is a loss of interest in students amid a "chaotic university." He developed these ideas in *The Crisis of the University* (1949), a widely discussed book hailed as the first in England since Newman to seriously consider the philosophy of education. When Dawson met with Moberly in Oxford in 1953, he found him "very sympathetic to this idea of the study of Christian culture."[8] Moberly, a member of the Moot, shared a concern with Dawson to trace the cultural crisis of the time to its educational roots.

Nevertheless, as an outsider to British academic life, Dawson did not look for the renewal he hoped for in Britain. Along with much of the world at the time, right after the Second World War, he looked to the United States for hope. After all, there was a network of hundreds of Catholic colleges and universities there. In addition, Winston Churchill told Americans in March of 1946 that they stood at the "pinnacle of world power" and possessed a grave responsibility to defend what

7. Alan Jacobs, *The Year of Our Lord 1943: Christian Humanism in an Age of Crisis* (New York: Oxford University Press, 2018), xiv–xv.

8. E. F. Schumacher, *A Guide for the Perplexed* (New York: Harper Perennial, 1977), 1; Harold Silver, *Higher Education and Opinion Making in Twentieth-Century England* (London: Woburn, 2003), 105, 106, 114, 117, 119. The quotation is from Christopher Dawson to John J. Mulloy, December 15, 1953, NDA, folder "Dawson: Christian Culture," Letters of Christopher Dawson on Christian Culture, p. 1.

he called "Christian civilization"—perhaps borrowing the phrase from Pope Pius XII (who reigned from 1939 to 1958) who had used it in January in an American magazine. The pope wrote that, "into the hands of America, God has placed the destinies of an afflicted humanity." Even though a younger Dawson had sometimes portrayed the United States negatively as a "standardised type of mass-civilisation," he too now looked westward across the Atlantic with hope. Dawson believed America's greater material resources and system of independent Catholic colleges could serve as organs of cultural renewal. Catholics lacked their own system of university education in England, and the system in place offered few opportunities to study Christian culture—or any coherent vision, as Schumacher and Moberly also realized—in an integrated way. Dawson was not fully cognizant, however, of how the powerful ideology of the American way of life accompanying America's rise to power would fuel resistance to his own educational ideas and draw the very institutions of Catholic higher education that he admired away from their religious and cultural roots.[9]

A second reason Dawson looked to the United States involved the fragmentation of the Catholic intellectual community in England after the Second World War, causing Dawson to feel out of place. The interwar, antiparliamentary, Bellocian synthesis of faith, politics, and history collapsed after the Second World War. Britain's parliamentary system, after all, had won. "The war, in exposing the deficiencies of Bellocianism, had breached the defenses that separated English Catholics from the wider English society" historian James Lothian noted. The distinctive Catholic subculture in England broke down in the subsequent years, foreshadowing eventual developments in the United States. In addition, Dawson saw Catholics in England moving away from spiritual and intellectual revival toward a more materialistic and socially activist spirit. Increasingly, they traded fear of the servile state for ac-

9. Christopher Dawson, "The Place of the Study of Christian Culture in Modern Education," 15, STA, Series VI: Miscellaneous Lectures, box/folder 2/115, "The Place of the Study of Christian Culture in Modern Education Newman Summer School, Oriel College, Oxford, July 1953"; Winston Churchill, "Iron Curtain Speech" (1946), Milestone Documents, https://www.milestone documents.com/documents/view/winston-churchillsthe-sinews-of-peace/text; Christopher Dawson, "The New Leviathan," in *Enquiries into Religion and Culture*, 7; and Pope Pius XII, "Wisdom—Not Weapons of War," *Collier's Weekly*, January 5, 1946, 13.

ceptance of the welfare state and attachment to their subculture for entry into the wider society.[10] Thus, Dawson looked with hope to the United States rather than to England, though the apparent Catholic renaissance in America lacked deep roots and would wither in the face of similar forces of assimilation.

At a personal level, Dawson's attention was also drawn toward the United States through his friendship with the American educationalist John J. Mulloy (1916–1995), who visited him in England in 1953. Mulloy corresponded with Dawson for years and edited the one-volume compendium of Dawson's thought *Dynamics of World History* (1956) that attracted much attention, including from outside Catholic readership. Mulloy did much to popularize Dawson's ideas in the United States.[11]

The fourth reason Dawson looked toward the United States was his awareness of lively interest there in "general education," as represented by the 1945 Harvard report *General Education in a Free Society*, which stood as a critique of specialization and loss of overall vision in education. In his introduction to the report, the president of Harvard, James B. Conant (1893–1978), a chemist who had worked on developing poison gas during the Great War and then witnessed the repercussions of that tragedy, wrote: "Neither the mere acquisition of information nor the development of special skills and talents can give the broad basis of understanding which is essential if our civilization is to be preserved." The liberal and humane tradition of education must inform American education at all levels, he wrote, imparting the wisdom of the ages and

10. Scott, *A Historian and His World*, 174; Lothian, *The Making and Unmaking of the English Catholic Intellectual Community, 1910–1950*, 382; and Bernard Bergonzi, "The English Catholics: Forward from 'The Chesterbelloc,'" *Encounter*, January 1965, 19, 29.

11. After studying Western as well as Chinese, Indian, and Islamic cultures, Mulloy pursued graduate work at Notre Dame before bringing Dawson's ideas to bear in his masterly teaching at the prestigious Philadelphia Central High School. He gave local public lectures on how the history of philosophy and cultural anthropology help reveal God's providence. Their success led to the development of a special Christian culture seminar, which he offered at various schools and universities throughout the United States. Mulloy was ecstatic at the success of *Dynamics*. "In a sense . . . the success of *The Dynamics* among the non-Christian community was a wonderful fulfillment of Dawson's own statement about the Church existing to preach the Gospel not only to the converted, but especially to the *unconverted*—the people most desperately in need of it." See William Doino, Jr., "John J. Mulloy, 1916–1995," EWTN, https://www.ewtn.com/library/HOMELIBR/MULLOY.TXT (accessed May 16, 2017); Dominic A. Aquila, "In Memoriam: John J. Mulloy," Catholic Social Scientists, http://catholicsocialscientists.org/cssr/Archival/1996/1996_277.pdf (accessed May 16, 2017).

the importance of value judgments without which one runs the risk of partial blindness.[12] General education, then, was a philosophy of unity: "unity of knowledge, unity of the curriculum, and unity of education and life." It involved nonspecialized learning, core course requirements, and an interdisciplinary approach.[13] While this movement ultimately failed to take hold, even at Harvard, where it originated, Dawson hoped common concerns such as these would give traction to his own educational ideas.

Finally, Dawson looked to the United States in response to the second vocational moment of his life—the first having occurred in Rome in 1909. The Protestant clergyman Douglas Horton (1891–1968), Dean of Harvard's Divinity School, while travelling in England, met Dawson for lunch at Salisbury on February 21, 1958. He invited him to take up the Stillman Chair for Catholic Studies at Harvard because Chauncy Stillman (1907–1989), heir to a large banking fortune, had converted to Catholicism and endowed the chair. The selection committee did not even need to debate who the first occupant should be: Christopher Dawson. Few other Catholic intellectuals of the day commanded such respect on both sides of the Atlantic Ocean. Normally nervous and hesitant, on this occasion meeting with Horton, Dawson immediately accepted the invitation, explaining to his shocked wife that "it is a call." He felt it his destiny to continue his work for Christian culture in the United States. Wide enthusiasm greeted the public announcement of Dawson's acceptance, and even Protestant students from all over the United States enquired about studying with him.[14]

The Dawson Plan

Christopher and Valery Dawson moved to the United States that year, 1958. When not teaching courses such as Religion and Culture, Catholicism from the Reformation to the Present, and Catholicism and

---

12. *General Education in a Free Society: Report of the Harvard Committee* (Cambridge, Mass.: Harvard University Press, 1945), viii–ix.

13. Gilbert Allardyce, "The Rise and Fall of the Western Civilization Course," *American Historical Review* 87, no. 3 (1982): 698.

14. Scott, *A Historian and His World*, 181, 183–84.

the Development of Western Culture,[15] Dawson wrote for magazines and gave lectures to spread his educational ideas, which he had first introduced in America from afar through various articles written during the early 1950s, particularly in *Commonweal*.[16]

Dawson outlined what became known as the Dawson Plan,[17] which focused on comparative study of Christian culture as the central object of knowledge. "The only true criterion of a Christian culture," he stipulated, "is the degree in which the social way of life is based on the Christian faith." Regardless of how "backward" a society may be, if its members possess a genuine Christian faith, they will possess a Christian culture. The more genuine a faith, the more Christian the culture. So, when using the phrase "Christian culture," he wrote, one must not think of some "ideal pattern of social perfection which can be used as a sort of model or blueprint by which existing societies can be judged." One should think above all about the two-thousand-year-old historical reality of Christianity as a living force spreading across the globe entering into the lives of people and societies and changing them. Where it takes root in good soil, one sees again and again through time the divine creativity bringing about a new spiritual harvest out of the "old soil of human nature and past social tradition."[18]

The Dawson Plan was a cooperative study of Christian culture

15. *Harvard Divinity School: Official Register of the University* (Cambridge, Mass.: Havard University Press, 1958–1961), vol. 55, 59; vol. 56, 60; vol. 57, 59 respectively.

16. Much of the criticism of Dawson's educational ideas emerged in *Commonweal*, too. This was the oldest lay-Catholic magazine in the United States, which emerged in 1924 as part of the "Catholic Renaissance" after the Great War. During wartime, U.S. Catholics for the first time created a national body (the National Catholic Welfare Council, 1919), and some of them, such as George N. Shuster, discovered through their military service in France the deep continuity of Christian life and culture in Europe, broadening their sense of purpose upon returning home. "Though literature and art seem to many of us only trifles, we know at last that they are mighty trifles, like grenades," he wrote a few years before taking over as the managing editor of *Commonweal* (1928 to 1937). The magazine would eventually publish the work of figures such as François Mauriac, Georges Bernanos, Hannah Arendt, G. K. Chesterton, Hilaire Belloc, Jacques Maritain, Dorothy Day, Graham Greene, Emmanuel Mounier, Christopher Dawson, and Christopher Lasch. It would take on a major role in the intellectual life of American Catholics as a forum for internal debate and point of contact with the wider culture for well-educated Catholics. See Philip Gleason, *Contending with Modernity: Catholic Higher Education in the Twentieth Century* (New York: Oxford University Press, 1995), 133, 134.

17. The phrase "Dawson Plan" appeared first, I believe, in Herbert A. Musurillo, "Dawson's Program: A Criticism," *Thought* 30, no. 1 (1955): 176.

18. Dawson, "The Outlook for Christian Culture Today," 127–28.

through philosophical and theological principles, literature, and history (particularly of social ways of life and of institutions). It was thus interdisciplinary in the way the Oxford *Literae Humaniores* degree approached classical culture. Acceptance of Christian faith was not an essential condition for the study of Christian culture.[19] Students would need, however, language preparation[20] and immersion in the three main phases of Christian culture: its origins in the age of the church fathers and the Christian Empire, its medieval development, and its flowering in the vernacular cultures and literatures down to the seventeenth century.[21] Dawson later expanded this timeline of Christian culture into the six ages of the church, each with periods of birth, growth, and retreat, up until the present day. In this way, he dissented from the usual ancient, medieval, modern division he thought lost sight of the multiplicity of Christian cultures (plural) behind the concept of "Christian culture."[22]

Dawson viewed his educational ideas as part of the broader trend to reconsider the nature of general education and of Western civilization after the Second World War. In his view, for good or for ill, the sciences, ideologies, and technologies of Western civilization had transformed the globe since 1500, which Dawson called the "movement of world revolution." Education needed to account for that fact, he held, in order to understand the world as it is today. It is extraordinarily important, he thought, to grasp how it happened that a collection of European cultures came to so alter the rest of the world and so dramatically change the course of human history. That is why the study of Western civilization in education has such import, and it is through study of Christian culture "in its several forms"—not simply medie-

19. "It is perfectly possible in theory to appreciate and to study Western culture as a spiritual whole without being a Christian. That was, after all, the position of many of the great liberal humanitarian historians and sociologists of the nineteenth century" who nevertheless accepted the ethos of Christian culture (Christopher Dawson, *Understanding Europe*, 15).

20. Latin, French, and English, Dawson suggested at first; he did not emphasize these language requirements in later educational writings, probably because they were impractical.

21. Christopher Dawson, "Education and Christian Culture," *Commonweal*, December 4, 1953, 218. This key article, originating as a Newman Association lecture (see footnote 9, above) at Oriel College, Oxford, first introduced the Dawson Plan in the United States and generated ten years of literary discussion.

22. Dawson, *The Historic Reality of Christian Culture*, 58.

THE DAWSON STUDY PLAN

1. *The Basic Theological Principles*
   A. The Incarnation as the center of history and the key to the Christian interpretation of hisory.
   B. The Church as the extension of the Incarnation. The doctrine of the Mystical Body of Christ.
   C. The People of God. The doctrine of the Church as the true Israel, the representative of a specialized historical tradition which it is its mission to renew and transmit.
   D. The City of God. The Augustinian theory of Christian Dualism and of the historical process as developed through the conflict of the opposing spiritual forces.
   E. The Communion of Saints. The Christian conception of an existent society which is not limited to its living members.
   F. The Cult of the Saints: its historic importance as a formative influence on Christian culture and as a principle of integration.
   G. The Holy Places of Christendom: the consecration of place in Christian culture and the institution of pilgrimage.
   H. The Holy Images. Christian art in its relation to culture. Aniconic forms of Christianity. The Reformation and Iconoclasm.
   I. Liturgy and Culture.

2. *The Literary Traditions*
   A. The Bible, the Fathers, the *Acta Sanctorum*, the Latin Christian literature of the Middle Ages.
   B. The relation of the vernacular Christian literatures to this tradition.

3. *Christian Social Institutions*
   A. The Christian family and the Christian state. The Christian tradition of law and the idea of the Law of Nature.
   B. The Christian conception of liberty and authority: personal and corporate rights.
   C. The Christian attitude to wealth and poverty. The service of the poor and institutions arising from it.
   D. Christian education and educational institutions.
   E. The comparative study of Christian institutions as developed by the different national cultures.

(*continues*)

4. *Christian Thought*

A. Hellenism and the Christian tradition. The Platonism of the Greek Fathers. The Augustinian tradition.

B. Saint Thomas and the *philosophia perennis*. Scholasticism and the birth of Western science. Humanism and Christian philosophy.

C. The relation of modern Western philosophies to the Christian tradition. Christian rationalism and the rationalism of the Enlightenment. Christian idealism and the idealism of the Romantic philosophers.

D. Christianity and technology.

5. *Christian History*

A. The conversion of the Roman Empire. The conversion of the barbarians: Celts, Germans, Scandinavians, Slavs.

B. The conversion of the Eastern peoples: Syrians, Armenians, Georgians, Abyssinians.

C. Islam and the decline of Christendom in West Asia and North Africa.

D. The history of monasticism and the religious orders. The religious orders as representing different ways of Christian life or in relation to their particular historical backgrounds.

E. Analogies to the religious orders in Protestantism—Pietism, Methodism, The Brethren, communistic religious societies in the United States.

F. The cultural causes and results of the Reformation.

G. The Counter Reformation and the Baroque culture.

6. *Post-Medieval Social and Economic Developments*

A. The expansion of Western civilization: its Christian and un-Christian aspects.

B. Christian missions and policy toward the natives. Attempts to create a missionary culture—Paraguay, Canada, California.

C. Christianity and the Slave Trade.

D. Christianity and the Humanitarian movement.

E. Christianity and the French Revolution.

F. Christianity and the American Revolution.

G. Christianity and Socialism: Utopian or Marxian.

H. Christian cultural tradition in the United States: a study of American nineteenth century society as the result of the pattern of Free Church competitive enterprise.

Source: Christopher Dawson, "Christian Culture: Its Meaning and its Value," *Jubilee*, May 1956, 38–39. Reproduced with permission of Julian Scott, literary executor of the estate of Christopher Dawson.

val culture—that we are "led to understand Western civilization from within outwards." It would be much more difficult to proceed from outwards to within, to discover the principle of unity in Western civilization by beginning with the centrifugal multiplicity on the outside. Hence, the centrality of Christian culture to his ideas.[23]

Because he believed the study of Christian culture to be the missing link in the survival of Western education, he proposed a curriculum of studies that would help students understand the essential values for which Western civilization stands. Such a program would approach its object—Christian culture—externally as an objective historical study involving one of the world's great civilizations, and from within, as the study of the history of the Christian people, of the ways in which Christianity has expressed itself in human thought and life and institutions through the ages. For educational purposes, both these approaches should be combined.

However, no opportunities for such a synthetic (holistic) study of Christian culture then existed, even in Catholic colleges and universities. Dawson did not clearly enunciate logistics of how institutions could implement his plan, but he believed that seeking self-knowledge through study of Christian culture in its various forms, studied both internally and externally, could serve as the central principle of a robust, liberal arts educational program.[24] It fell to others, such as John J. Mulloy, to work out the details of the Dawson Plan in terms of American academic and institutional structures (see appendix E).

After the first Christian Culture program inspired by his ideas launched at St. Mary's College in 1956, Dawson formulated a more concrete educational proposal in his 1961 book *Crisis of Western Education*. He suggested the subject of Christian culture as the province of a special institute on the graduate level, or as a field of concentration to students in their later years of undergraduate study, as at St. Mary's. In this latter case, their study could parallel vocational and professional preparation, as in Catholic Studies programs today. Either way, Daw-

23. Allardyce, "The Rise and Fall of the Western Civilization Course," 695; Dawson, *The Crisis of Western Education*, 96–98; and Dawson, *The Movement of World Revolution*.

24. Dawson, *The Crisis of Western Education*, 107–8; Dawson, "Education and Christian Culture," 216, 218.

son pointed out, history shows that every educational advance has been prepared "by a preliminary period in which the pioneers work outside the recognized academic cadres."[25]

Objections of the Humanities Specialists

Many administrators, Jesuits, priests, philosophers, liberal reformers, and humanities specialists attacked Dawson's ideas on education—especially the notion of Christian culture. Historians and humanities educators generally supported them. This dichotomy had a lot to do with the failure of his critics to comprehend Dawson's pedagogical purposes or his dual humanistic and socio-historical modes of cultural inquiry.

At the most basic level, critics objected to the unworkability of the plan and its supposed superficiality. John W. Simons, priest and teacher at Overbrook Seminary in Pennsylvania, noted that shifting to the study of Christian culture was a radical proposal, even for Catholic colleges, and that the great barrier was language: translations of works into English from the multiple languages of Christian cultures across the ages simply could not do justice to the richness of the past. "For the response we give to the past, if it is to be a true and sympathetic one, must have a greater immediacy than translation." Herbert Musurillo agreed with him. As a Jesuit priest, classical scholar, and lecturer in the Humanities at Bellarmine College and Fordham University, he had met Dawson while working on a doctorate at Oxford from 1948 to 1951. Nevertheless, he thought the program unmanageable at the undergraduate level because there were too many texts that students would have to study, and most college teachers were not "universal geniuses" capable of soaring over great vistas of literature and history. Poor translations of the great "Christian classics" would vitiate the program from the

25. Dawson, *The Crisis of Western Education*, 118, 119. In an appendix for the first edition of *The Crisis of Western Education* (New York: Sheed & Ward, 1961), John J. Mulloy worked closely with Dawson to sketch out five possible ways of organizing an academic program in Christian culture studies: as a program of graduate study, as an undergraduate upper-division program (e.g., at St. Mary's), as a lower-division fulfillment of liberal arts requirements, as a program spanning the lower and upper divisions of undergraduate study, and as an Honors program. He went on to suggest specific courses for each of these tracks. This has been reprinted herein as Appendix E.

start, which was why "it is clear that the Dawson Plan, for all its good intentions, will not solve" the many defects of contemporary Christian education.[26]

While early on Dawson advocated language study and serious engagement with "classic" texts from Christian history, he did not see these goals as the main thrust of his program. He did not envision an exhaustive, encyclopedic approach to Christian culture but rather a general overview of the main phases of it that would function like Western civilization courses at non-Catholic universities. He did not propose the study of *subjects* in Christian culture through isolated classes, like liturgy, church history, medieval philosophy, Dante, Newman, or Hopkins. Rather, he had in mind educating students in a "comprehensive vision of the whole" as a "cultural study in the sociological and historical sense," he wrote for *Catholic World*. This comprehensive whole would be the context in which to understand such subjects. Christian culture expressed itself not simply in theology but "also in philosophy and literature, in art and music, society and institutions," he noted in "The Challenge of Secularism." One can only completely understand each of these forms of expression in relation to the rest. Thus, "Christian culture" is not the same thing as "medieval culture" or a collection of great texts. It is defined not as some ideal way of life but anthropologically as a real, common way of life, like Islamic or Hindu or Confucian culture, of a largely Christian people attempting to live out their vision amidst the competing claims of non-Christian, secular, and pagan cultures. Under existing curricula, one can study some parts of the whole in detail but never the whole itself, Dawson pointed out, and classical studies has itself become a specialized field in a world of competing specialisms. No wonder the humanities specialists had difficulties with his proposal.[27]

Dawson proposed a *popularization* of material that might horrify

26. John W. Simons, "Putting American Catholics in Touch with the Christian Past," *Commonweal*, May 14, 1954, 136, 137; Herbert A. Musurillo, review of *European Literature and the Latin Middle Ages*, *Thought* 29, no. 114 (1954): 435–39. Musurillo mentions Dawson's educational ideas on p. 436. See also Musurillo, "Dawson's Program: A Criticism," 178, 186; John W. Simons, "Liberal Education as Transmissor of Values: The Proposals of Christopher Dawson," *Thought* 30, no. 1 (1955): 170.

27. Dawson, *The Crisis of Western Education*, 103, 116; Christopher Dawson, "The Study of Christian Culture in the American College," *Catholic World* 183, no. 1095 (1956): 198, 200; and Christopher Dawson, "The Challenge of Secularism," *Catholic World*, 182, no. 1091 (1956): 329.

the specialists but would nonetheless serve an undergraduate audience pedagogically very well. This implied the benefits of working with translated texts overcame the losses. He wanted to undo the separation of humanist culture from the wider society brought about by cultural elites, starting in the nineteenth century with figures such as Matthew Arnold. Their aloofness from common people and common culture—a lack of charity—threw their high "culture" into disrepute. Ever since he began writing during the Great War, Dawson's cultural mind sought to bridge the gap between high culture and the rest of society with a writing style that aimed for the broad, educated audience rather than the academy. He applied the intellectual bridges and asceticism rules of his cultural mind. Specifically, he emphasized popularization in order to overcome the wide gulf between the highly specialized tradition of Catholic scholarship and the culture of the educated layman. The vast resources of Christian culture do few people any good if they are locked up in archives and monasteries. It is that gap between the specialized Christian scholars and the rest of society that had been largely responsible for the secularization of modern culture, he thought.[28]

That is because scholarship alone rarely changes culture. People with creative ability must instigate a broad movement for cultural change to take hold—as did the *philosophes* of the eighteenth century. Dawson envisioned education in American Catholic colleges and universities as contributing to a wider cultural movement, a kind of "reverse-secularization," such as the Oxford Movement (in the 1830s and 1840s), whose influence spread far and wide, even to figures such as Matthew Arnold and John Ruskin, who were only loosely connected to Christianity. This "tends to show the far-reaching effects of a religious movement on culture," he wrote in a 1957 letter to John J. Mulloy.[29]

28. Dawson, "Education and Christian Culture," 220; Dawson, "The Crisis of Christian Culture: Education," 43–44. This point about popularization is central to Dawson's educational ideas. He proposed works of synthesis as the starting point of study, "as I think this is the only way to give a student insight into the material and the problem he is going to study. My own Making of Europe was an attempt to provide such a work for the early medieval period, and there are a number of other books, old and new: Hazard's two books on the Enlightenment, Basil Willey's one on the 17th century, Burckhardt's Renaissance, Huizinga's Waning of the Middle Ages, Troeltsch on Christian Social Teaching, Rostovtzeff's two books on the Roman Empire and on the Hellenistic culture, and Fustel de Coulanges' old book on the ancient city." (Dawson to Mulloy, March 13, 1954, NDA, folder "Dawson: Christian Culture," Letters of Christopher Dawson on Christian Culture, p. 3).

29. John J. Mulloy, August 20, 1953, NDA, folder "Mulloy Conversations with Christopher

Application

Not catching on to Dawson's pedagogical concern to connect with undergraduate students, humanities specialists such as Musurillo proposed impossible lists of obscure but great Catholic texts for undergraduates and then, thinking they understood Dawson's proposal, pronounced it unworkable. They shared the mentality of the *Great Books of the Western World* (1952) series coming out of the University of Chicago in response to the crisis of the West. However, the ahistorical "Great Books" approach was not what Dawson had in mind. He wrote to Mulloy:

It seems to me that the chief danger in the study of Christian culture at present is that it will be treated as a kind of Catholic Great Books course or a Great men course, whereas what it ought to study is how spiritual forces are transmitted and how they change culture, often in unexpected ways. If you can make students see the process, they will apply it themselves in the course of their study, but if you only give them the final product—the great writers—they won't look beyond. A culture as I see it is essentially a network of relations, and it is only by studying a number of personalities that you can trace this network.[30]

In response to the humanities specialists, Dawson noted in *Catholic World,* what is needed is not an encyclopedic knowledge of all the products of Christian culture but a "study of the culture-process itself from its spiritual and theological roots, through its organic historical growth to its cultural fruits. It is this organic relation between theology, history and culture which provides the integrative principle in Catholic higher education."[31]

This call to comprehend the "culture-process" in the quotation above expressed the heart of Dawson's educational proposal. Despite a DPhil degree from Oxford and a PhD from Fordham, however, Musurillo explicitly said he could not understand what Dawson meant by "culture-process." He did not grasp the socio-historical mode of cultur-

Dawson August 18 – September 2, 1953," p. 2; Dawson to Mulloy, July 19, 1957, NDA, folder "Dawson: Christian Culture," Letters of Christopher Dawson on Culture Studies and Catholic Higher Education, p. 12.

30. Dawson to Mulloy, July 19, 1957, NDA, folder "Dawson: Christian Culture," Letters of Christopher Dawson on Culture Studies and Catholic Higher Education, p. 12.

31. Dawson, "The Study of Christian Culture in the American College," 201.

al understanding, so he missed Dawson's description of this process as the interaction of the four cultural categories introduced in chapter 2 (I/FWP) and further discussed in chapter 5. Change one cultural category, and the rest of the culture might change, too. Through this process, one comes to understand, for example, how a new religion enters an old society, thereby changing the life of the people. Out of this culture-process, "a new culture arises which may be transmitted to other societies and may change them also," Dawson wrote.[32] This held for any world-historical culture, Dawson thought, and he wanted students to understand how the culture-process worked in general and in various Christian contexts.

By studying the process of transformation in historical cultures, Dawson hoped to connect past and present by suggesting avenues of cultural transformation in his own age. European Christian culture of the seventeenth century, for example, was essentially a "sacramental culture which embodied religious truth in visible and palpable forms": art, architecture, music, poetry, drama, philosophy, and history. These were all used as "channels for the communication of religious truth." The Christian world of the past "was exceptionally well provided with ways of access to spiritual realities" precisely in those networks often lost in modern secular culture, thereby falling into impoverishment. Today, he continued in a *Catholic World* article, all those channels had been "closed by unbelief or choked by ignorance." The task of Christian education is to recover these lost contacts and to restore relation between religion and modern society in order to form the whole person.[33]

Thus, Dawson viewed education through his cultural mind. Through study of the historic reality of Christian cultures he sought to connect both socio-historical approaches to culture *and* humanistic ones to the curriculum. "If the one aim of education were the complete and harmonious culture of the whole man, then the intellectual faculty would not as at present be favoured at the expense of either physical, artistic or

---

32. Herbert A. Musurillo, "The Problem of Catholic Education: A Reply to Christopher Dawson," *Catholic World* 184, no. 1100 (1956): 95; Musurillo, "Dawson's Program: A Criticism"; and Christopher Dawson, "The Institutional Forms of Christian Culture," *Religion in Life: A Christian Quarterly of Opinion and Discussion* 24, no. 3 (Summer 1955): 379.

33. Dawson, "The Challenge of Secularism," 328–29.

Application

moral development," he wrote. "And for the full enrichment of personality and community together is needed, above all, an education based
on a spiritual tradition," he added. For Dawson, education was not simply "instruction" but *enculturation* into an inheritance, and, as he put
it in his Edward Alleyn lecture—a "discipline of the whole man." This
was simply another way of stating Newman's own composite ideal of the
university principle training the intellect of students and the residential
college principle providing the "formation of mind and heart" through
the personal and communal pursuit of truth, as educational pioneer
Don J. Briel (1947–2018) once summarized.[34]

John Henry Newman versus Christopher Dawson?

Some American critics, however, only focused on the first principle
of Newman, the training of intellect, neglecting the concern for formation in Newman's work as a whole.[35] They recoiled at the evangelical
dimension to the Dawson Plan: to recover contact between religion
and culture in modern society by helping students see the importance
of connecting faith to concrete ways of life.

Newman's *Idea of a University* had a profound role in shaping educational thought and initiatives in America ever since its publication in
1872, especially among Catholics, such as in the founding of the Cath-

34. Christopher Dawson, "The Passing of Industrialism," *Sociological Review* XII (1920): 16;
Dawson, "The Crisis of Christian Culture: Education," 39; Don J. Briel, "The Idea of the University
and the College," in *The University and the Church: Don J. Briel's Essays on Education*, ed. R. Jared
Staudt (Providence, R.I.: Cluny, 2019), 51. See also Mary Katherine Tillman, "The Tension between
Intellectual and Moral Education in the Thought of John Henry Newman," *Thought* 60, no. 238
(September 1985): 322–34.

35. "The University is for theology, law, and medicine, for natural history, for physical science,
and for the sciences generally and their promulgation," Newman wrote; the College is for the "catechetical lecture . . . the formation of character, intellectual and moral, for the cultivation of the
mind, for the improvement of the individual." See John Henry Newman, "Abuses of the Colleges:
Oxford," in *University Sketches*, ed. Michael Tierney (1856; Westminster, Md.: Newman, 1953), 220.
See also John Henry Newman, "Professors and Tutors," in *University Sketches*; John Henry Newman, "Colleges the Corrective of Universities: Oxford," in *University Sketches*. Don Briel wrote to
me that "Newman was indeed close to Dawson" on how dogmatic theology should not primarily
form students. Rather, a kind of "lay theology" in the colleges would do this through a "combination of apologetics, catechetics, and history" (Don Briel to Joseph Stuart, emails from May 27,
2017, and June 8, 2017). Newman essentially talked about forming students through the study of
"Christian culture" without using the phrase in his section on "Elementary Studies" in John Henry
Newman, *The Idea of a University* (1873; Tacoma, Wash.: Cluny Media, 2016), 275–78.

olic University of America (CUA) in 1887 and the establishment, by the early twentieth century, of Newman Clubs to promote pastoral care and socialization of Catholic students on non-Catholic university campuses. These Newman Clubs greatly impressed Dawson. He visited the one attached to the University of Southern Louisiana where its chaplain was doing a great work, he wrote. "One gets the feeling of something that is almost a new vocation, almost a new 'religious order' spreading in America," Dawson told the associate editor of *America* magazine.[36]

Interest in Newman exploded in the 1950s when the Cold War seemed to demand a renewal of humanistic cultural values in the United States. Newman had argued in his *Idea* for the centrality of theology in university studies and that the aim of education is cultivation of the intellect for its own sake, not merely acquisition of information or preparing for a career.[37] To some, Newman's *Idea* ruled out higher education serving any kind of practical purpose. Since Dawson advocated the study of Christian culture partly in order to renew contact between the modern world and Christianity, faith and life, this smacked of an evangelistic "utilitarian value." Critics claimed Dawson failed to respect the nature of the university as spelled out by Newman. For example, one wrote that Dawson's 1953 article in *Commonweal* had done a "distinct disservice to serious reflection on the needs of Catholic education in this country."[38]

Justus George Lawler, a professor of Humanities at Saint Xavier College whose views Dawson considered *avant-garde* among American Catholic educationalists, best enunciated this criticism. Lawler had written the Newman-steeped book *Catholic Dimension in Higher Education* in 1959 and then went on to attack Dawson's *Crisis of Western Education* (1961). He interpreted the Dawson Plan as making Christian culture the synthetic basis of the entire undergraduate curriculum rather than simply a program within an institution—a distinction that Daw-

36. C. J. McNaspy, "A Chat with Christopher Dawson," *America*, October 28, 1961, 121.

37. Philip Gleason, "Newman's *Idea* in the Minds of American Educators," in *Building the Church in America: Studies in Honor of Monsignor Robert F. Trisco on the Occasion of His Seventieth Birthday*, ed. Joseph C. Linck and Raymond J. Kupke (Washington, D.C.: The Catholic University of America Press, 1999), 114, 123.

38. Gleason, "Newman's *Idea* in the Minds of American Educators," 132; Joseph H. McMahon, "Christian Culture," *Commonweal*, January 7, 1955, 382–83.

son was not entirely clear about. As a synthetic basis, Lawler thought, the plan would "destroy the traditional ideal of *universitas* and would be as detrimental to education as to the mission of religion." Dawson was evidently not interested in education as such, Lawler wrote, but in using it as an instrument for safeguarding certain values, as a tool for his own "personal brand of social engineering" by imparting the kind of "historical information" that he favors. Christian education at the service of a vague notion of "Christian culture" is a betrayal of Newman. What is needed in Catholic higher education is the "cultivation of the mind" in the old humanist sense—and not through a program in Christian culture but through a traditional program in *classical* culture. Here Lawler quoted Newman to back up his point and thus joined forces with the critiques of the classical scholars and humanities specialists discussed earlier.[39]

While Dawson did acknowledge that his plan for the study of Christian culture involved a break with an exclusive focus on Greek and Latin classics, he did not attack classical education as such. He advocated classical studies at the high-school level in a letter to Mulloy as preparation for a university education that would enculturate students in Christian culture while also training them for a career. Classical education in the college years was in decline everywhere, Dawson observed, but this did not necessarily imply a decline of liberal education, for the two are distinct. The passing away of the idealization of classical antiquity by humanities scholars since the Renaissance, an idealization that had led many Christian educators to ignore the historical reality of Christian culture, gave an opportunity for educators

39. Justus George Lawler, "*The Crisis of Western Education* [2]," review of *The Crisis of Western Education, Harvard Educational Review* 32, no. 1 (1962): 216, 219; Christopher Dawson, "The Study of Christian Culture," *Thought* 35, no. 1 (1960): 488–89 (Dawson directly engaged Lawler here). See also Justus George Lawler, "*The Crisis of Western Education* [1]," book review, *Theological Studies* 22, no. 3 (September 1, 1961): 504–6; Justus George Lawler, *The Catholic Dimension in Higher Education* (Westminster, Md.: Newman, 1959), 224–25. In *The Catholic Dimension*, Lawler quoted on p. 225 from Newman's *Idea* to reinforce the importance of classical education: "The simple question to be considered is, how best to strengthen, refine, and enrich the intellectual power," Newman wrote: "the perusal of the poets, historians, and philosophers of Greece and Rome will accomplish this purpose, as long as experience has shown; but that the study of the experimental sciences will do the like is proved to us as yet by no experience whatever." After quoting this, Lawler commented that the same could be said of "Christian culture" as of experimental science: its value as a liberal subject is untested. See Newman, *The Idea of a University*, 196–97.

to "exorcise the ghost of this ancient error"—the idealization of classical culture—and "to give the study of Christian culture the place that
it deserves in modern education."[40] The rapidly secularizing modern
world—unprecedented in world history—and the emergence of political religions required a new solution to the problem of education, but
one that would build on the achievements of centuries of Christian humanities education rather than negate them, as Lawler implied. Christian culture, after all, preserved classical culture and indeed connected
it to the modern world as a kind of bridge across the millennia. The
study of Christian culture would necessarily involve a rediscovery of
the classical world.

If Dawson saw his ideas in continuity with humanities classical education, he also saw himself in continuity with Newman. Both attended Trinity College at Oxford, and Dawson's entry into the church came
about in 1914 partly through reading Newman. He wrote a book on the
Oxford Movement in 1933 as the context of Newman's conversion. The
more he reflected on Newman's thought, he wrote, the more the man
seemed relevant to the contemporary situation: "For Newman was the
first Christian thinker in the English-speaking world who fully realised
the nature of modern secularism and the enormous change which
[w]as already in process of development." Besides a lecture for the Newman Association at Oriel College, Oxford (where Newman had been a
Fellow), Dawson also spoke in 1953 at University College, Dublin—the
descendent of the Catholic University of Ireland that Newman helped
establish. In the latter lecture, Dawson noted how the bitter realities
of two world wars had destroyed the faith of Europeans in their own
values. But any "breach in the continuity of the educational tradition
involves a corresponding breach in the continuity of the civilization."
There is a need to recover an appreciation for the tradition of liberal
education in Western culture, and toward that end, he appealed to the
Christian philosophy of history that underlay Newman's whole doctrine on education. "If I understand [him] aright," Dawson wrote, Newman held that Western civilization and the Christian tradition over-

40. Dawson to Mulloy, March 13, 1954, NDA, folder "Dawson: Christian Culture," Letters of
Christopher Dawson on Christian Culture, p. 3; Dawson, "The Study of Christian Culture," 487.

lapped but constituted two distinct realities. However, the West had "provided the natural preparation and foundation for the diffusion of the new spiritual society in which the human race was finally to recover its lost unity." While Newman lacked the global consciousness and moderate cultural relativism of Dawson's anthropologically grounded cultural mind, and tended to absolutize Western civilization, Newman nevertheless prefigured Dawson's proposal to study the relationship between Christianity and the West, revealing a deep affinity between the two men.[41]

John J. Mulloy asked Dawson: "The end of liberal education is, according to Newman, a 'freedom, equitableness, calmness, moderation and wisdom' of intellect. Would Mr. Dawson's proposed curriculum have a like result?" Dawson responded by letter in 1954 that it would,

For Newman in the passage referred to is simply maintaining the value of a liberal University education as against a technical utilitarian one, and consequently the study of Christian Culture would be fully in accordance with his ideas. Indeed it is a study in which he himself was very interested, as we see from his historical essays, etc.; and what distinguishes his theology from that of most of his contemporaries is that he based it firmly on a knowledge of its historical and cultural background.

Newman pondered deeply the connection of theology to history in his *Essay on the Development of Christian Doctrine* (1845). In that work, Mulloy wrote in response to Lawler, Newman "pointed out that the body of revealed truth within the Church develops and becomes more explicit through its contact with the social and historical circumstances which confront it throughout the course of Christian history." Mulloy continued: "The same process which interested Newman from the side of Christian theology [FWP→I] interests Dawson from the opposite side: the historical societies and cultures which Christianity encounters and influences in its journey through history [I→FWP]." Thus, Dawson wrote that the student of Christian culture has three fields of study:

41. Dawson, "Education and the Study of Christian Culture," 293, 297; Christopher Dawson, "Newman and the Sword of the Spirit," *The Sword of the Spirit*, August 1945, 1. Dawson identified sections II and III of Newman's lecture "Christianity and Letters" in *Idea* as an exposition of Newman's philosophy of history. The essay "Newman and the Sword of the Spirit" was reprinted in the *Dawson Newsletter*, Spring-Summer 1991, 12–13.

"(1) The Christian way of life, which is the field of study that he shares with the theologian; (2) the pre-existing or co-existing forms of human culture, which is the field he shares with the anthropologist and the historian; and (3) the interaction of the two which produces the concrete historical reality of Christendom or Christian culture, which is his own specific field of study." The development-of-doctrine-process in Newman was analogous to the culture-process in Dawson.[42]

Furthermore, Dawson did not propose the study of Christian culture in an absolute or exclusive way; he simply wanted to put the subject on the map, to show that it can and should be studied. He wrote to Mulloy in 1955: "Hence what I am concerned with primarily is the *idea* of the study of Christian Culture, like Newman's *Idea of a University*. (When it came to the actual building of the university at Dublin, a whole series of totally different problems turned up with which he was unable to cope—questions of a 'political' order)."[43] An inability to bring about his ideas practically would afflict Dawson, too. That task would await the talents of other figures.

In response to the charge of Dawsonian utilitarianism made by Lawler, Mulloy also quoted the Harvard Report *General Education in a Free Society* on the objectives of higher education, which included the transmission of cultural heritage. All education has a social dimension because it enculturates students into a tradition—not an abstract excellence without relation to anything else, as Lawler implied. The implication of Mulloy's point is that there is no contradiction in Dawson's position. A liberal arts education can serve to renew not only "culture" in the individual, humanistic sense (knowledge for its own sake) but

42. Dawson to Mulloy, August 16, 1954, NDA, folder "Dawson: Christian Culture," Letters of Christopher Dawson on Christian Culture, p. 15; John J. Mulloy, "A Reply," *Harvard Educational Review* 32, no. 1 (1962): 222, 224; and Dawson, "The Study of Christian Culture," 490. Newman wrote of how a *living idea* moves people and enters into "the framework and details of social life, changing public opinion, and strengthening or undermining the foundations of established order. Thus, in time, it will have grown into an ethical code, or into a system of government, or into a theology, or into a ritual, according to its capabilities." Newman's interest here was like Dawson's concern with the culture-process (I→FWP and FWP→I). See John Henry Newman, *An Essay on the Development of Christian Doctrine* (London: Longmans, Green, 1906), 37–38.

43. Dawson to Mulloy, August 16, 1954, NDA, folder "Dawson: Christian Culture," Letters of Christopher Dawson on Christian Culture, p. 15; Dawson to Mulloy, April 13, 1955, NDA, folder "Dawson: Christian Culture," Replies of Christopher Dawson to Proposals for a Specific Curriculum in Christian Culture, p. 2.

also renew it in the communal, socio-historical sense—the common way of life of modern people; indeed, it had done that very thing over the centuries. Dawson did not think of his plan as overtly evangelistic. He desired to see the disinterested study of Christian culture, which is why he hoped that his proposal would find some supporters even in non-Christian institutions. "I think there is a danger," he wrote to Mulloy in 1955, "that the study of Christian Culture might be conducted in too apologetic and sectarian a spirit which would antagonize possible allies in the non-Catholic universities. The danger is that the theological approach may be heavily stressed, and perhaps the historical and literary aspects somewhat neglected in comparison." If Christian culture would be treated in overly theological ways, he thought, it might give an opening to the kind of criticism made by Lawler.[44]

Religious Idealism and the Denial of Christian Culture

Besides humanities specialists and narrow readings of Newman, religious idealism also motivated attacks on Dawson's idea of Christian culture and thereby of his educational proposals. "Religious idealism" approaches religion by deemphasizing the temporal order, material reality, and the connection of religion to culture—an orientation characteristic of Americans. For example, Friedrich von Hügel, the philosopher of religion discussed in chapter 5, once characterized the American Catholics he had met as "rarely enriched and widened by any instinctual understanding of [history]." Religious idealism had emerged from the pietism motivating those waves of religious revivals in the United States since the eighteenth century that had focused religion on private experience and the individual conscience. The pietists held to the primacy of "spirit over letter, [personal] commitment over institution, affect over intellect, laity over clergy, invisible church over visible," historian James Burtchaell (1934–2015) wrote. He identified this movement as a major factor in the loss of Christian identity in American institutions of higher learning in the later twentieth century because of

---

44. Mulloy, "A Reply," 221–22; Dawson to Molloy, February 21, 1955, NDA, folder "Dawson Christian Culture," The Christian Culture Program under Fire: Challenge and Reply. p. 15.

its inability to sustain communal, institutional commitment. Because of religious idealism, "American religion was detached from the objective world which was the domain of business and politics," Dawson said in a lecture in Houston. "This, I believe, has left a permanent mark on the American mind, so that, as several Americans have remarked to me, they find some difficulty in relating the two concepts of religion and civilization since these seem to belong to two quite distinct orders of existence." Through American assimilation since the Great War, religious idealism worked its way into American Catholic culture by the 1950s. This movement made Christian culture largely unthinkable and motivated much of the resistance to Dawson's ideas.[45]

For example, a certain Mr. Edward J. Tully, Jr., from Patchogue, New York (not far from Levittown, the first mass-produced suburb in the United States), wrote to *Commonweal*, wondering exactly why Christian culture holds importance. "I look on religion as (in its creed and code) divinely established, and independent of time and place," he said, "I look on culture as the contradictory of this: as something that is, and that *should* be dependent on time and place." One can disassociate culture from Christianity, Tully continued, as in the case of the Jesuit missionaries in China attempting to disassociate Christianity from European "Christian culture.". Culture is simply relative to time and place and not all that important in relation to unchanging religion.[46]

While culture can never fully embody faith, as Tully rightly implied, surely the attempt by Jesuit missionaries such as Matteo Ricci (1552–1610) to translate Christianity into Chinese culture proved the *importance* of culture, not its irrelevance. In his response to Tully, Dawson wrote that one cannot separate culture from religion—"It is impossible to be a Christian in church and a secularist or a pagan outside." When the Jesuit Alessandro Valignano (1539–1606) wrote in his 1581 missionary directives that, "When preaching the Gospel, we should avoid mixing in European customs not needed for the salvation of souls," he did

45. Friedrich von Hügel to Wilfrid Ward, January 5, 1899, SAA, papers of Wilfrid Ward, ms38347, p. 3; Christopher Dawson, "America and the Secularization of Modern Culture," Smith History Lecture of 1960, *Logos* 3, no. 3 (Summer 2000), 27; and James T. Burtchaell, *The Dying of the Light: The Disengagement of Colleges & Universities from their Christian Churches* (Grand Rapids, Mich.: William B. Eerdmans, 1998), 839.
46. Edward J. Tully, Jr., "Core of the Curriculum," *Commonweal*, October 15, 1954, 38.

not attempt to disassociate Christianity from culture per se. In the case of Ricci in China, in fact, it was precisely certain achievements of European culture that most impressed the Chinese and opened them up to adapting Christianity into their context, such as Western Renaissance painting techniques, world maps, technology, and astronomy, as imported by the Jesuits at the time. If these men know so much about the natural world, then maybe they also know about the supernatural? The Jesuits attempted to inspire Chinese cultural responses to Incarnation *through* examples of European cultural responses to Incarnation—hence the different forms that Christian culture has taken across place and time.[47] There is no such thing as culture-less religion.

Religious idealists also appealed to universal notions such as the "Mystical Body" to downplay the historical realty of Christian culture. Sr. Marie McNichols, a Religious Sister of Mercy with a bachelor-of-arts degree from Saint Xavier College in Chicago, wrote that, "By idealizing a specific culture in a particular geographical location, some historians have implicitly rejected the doctrine of the Mystical Body, which affirms an equality among all Christians and hence among all historical periods." This was true, some historians did do this, but in her critique of Dawson Sr. McNichols urged transcending "the realm of accidentals." Latin, monastic traditions, celibate clergy, architectural style—historians "err by equating these limited cultural traits with a universal Church." Neglecting the fact that religion, no matter how catholic, never exists as a universal abstraction apart from concrete culture, she wrote that the Church does not identify with any one culture; therefore "Christian culture" is a misnomer and an education plan based on it an impossibility.[48]

In addition, religious idealists who also happened to adopt a purely humanistic conception of culture completely misinterpreted Dawson's educational idea. To them, "Christian culture" implied a normative "ideal culture" in which Christianity perfectly expressed itself. Since that has never happened, Christian culture is an illusion and its historical reality relatively unimportant. For example, Justus Lawler wrote that one can

47. Christopher Dawson, "Core of the Curriculum," *Commonweal*, December 3, 1954, 256; Alessandro Valignano, "Missionary Directive," in *Matteo Ricci & the Catholic Mission to China: A Short History with Documents*, ed. R. Po-chia Hsia (1581; Indianapolis, Ind.: Hackett, 2016), 66.

48. Marie Corde McNichols, "Western Culture and the Mystical Body," *Catholic World* 186 (December 1957): 166, 168, 172.

indeed speak of "Islamic culture," but since Christianity is the true religion, it will only fully mesh with the temporal order at the end of time. Christian culture cannot claim a central place in the curriculum until we know which age has preeminent value; otherwise, why study it? In addition, why assume the gospel is less effective today and turn one's attention to the past? wondered James Campbell at Catholic University of America. Herbert Musurillo wrote of the foolishness of thinking of Christian culture as the only one worth studying—an idea Dawson never held. Sister McNichols wrote that "one might well wonder, considering the limitations of the temporal order, whether a Christian culture as such, that is, a pure Christian culture in which theological principles permeate and influence all spheres of social action has ever existed or could possibly exist." Christian culture is a non-subject.[49]

In his scathing review of Dawson's *Crisis of Western Education*, Lawler charged that Dawson's use of the phrase "Christian culture" highlighted the "insular character of his thought." In the present moment, he said, revealing his underlying religious idealism, "it is precisely this identification of Christianity with any specific temporal achievements that seems most likely to inhibit its mission." What about all the failures to live out Christianity? Don't they negate any meaningful concept of Christian culture, he wondered? What about the failure of the medieval world to consider the worth of the individual or all the medieval vulgar literature that lacks any reference to Christianity? A wide chasm between theology and temporal affairs, a separation between theory and practice in Christian history, leads one to wonder whether the term "Christian culture" is the best description for historical realities composed of so many non-Christian forces, he wrote. This is why, from the educator's point of view, Christian culture fails, especially when compared to the traditional study of classical culture, to provide a unified scheme of learning. Dawson's main error involved confusing the natural and the supernatural in his identification of a nominally Christian society with a "Christian society" that can never be realized in history.[50]

49. Lawler, "*The Crisis of Western Education* [1]," 506; James M Campbell, "The Dawson Challenge: A Discussion," *Commonweal*, April 16, 1955, 69; Musurillo, "Dawson's Program: A Criticism," 177; and McNichols, "Western Culture and the Mystical Body," 170.

50. Lawler, "*The Crisis of Western Education* [2]," 218, 219.

Application

Dawson commented that Lawler's purely humanistic view of culture led him to define it as an intellectual ideal—the perfect Christian society. Since such a society has never existed, Lawler was indignant that anyone would insist on finding an example of it in the past. Clarifying this point, and writing in Dawson's defense, Mulloy noted that, "When we speak of Islamic culture or Confucian culture or Christian culture, do we mean that the societies having these cultures have to conform in every way to the ideal norms by which the culture's values are expressed? Or do we mean that these norms and values serve as a kind of goal toward which human activities are directed as an ideal standard or law?" From the anthropological (cultural) point of view, the second is correct. Failing to make this distinction would undergird much of the criticism of "Christian culture" in the Dawson Plan, in which concrete Christian cultures serve as the context within which to consider humanistic ideals and transcendent principles with students.[51]

Hence, Dawson was concerned over what the theologians and philosophers would do with his educational ideas if they tried to implement them, due to their lack of sympathy for the socio-historical sense of culture. "I think both the philosophers and the theologians would turn the subject [Christian culture] into an abstract systematic study of what they consider an ideal Catholic culture should be, so that the study of the actual tradition of Christian culture as a sociological and historical fact or 'phenomenon' would be left on one side," he told Mulloy. Dawson's recommendation to study not more "universals" but rather "determinate cultures in all of their particularity," as Hittinger summarized, prompted him to reflect at length on the proper relation of theology and philosophy to his plan.[52]

The Relation of Theology and Philosophy to Christian Culture

Some objected—not surprisingly—that creating a Christian Culture program would emphasize history too much. From the point of

---

51. Dawson, "The Study of Christian Culture," 489; Mulloy, "A Reply," 223.

52. Dawson to Mulloy, March 13, 1954, NDA, folder "Dawson: Christian Culture," Letters of Christopher Dawson on Christian Culture, p. 3; Russell Hittinger, "Christopher Dawson: A View from the Social Sciences," in *The Catholic Writer*, vol. 2, 38.

view of some Catholics, the *body of truths* needs to be taught, not their genealogy. Theology and philosophy are the real basis of integration in Catholic education, they argued. However, Dawson opposed a kind of theological and philosophical reductionism in thinking about the unity of Catholic higher education. At the same time, he believed the study of Christian culture as an object of knowledge would actually benefit theology and philosophy. It would connect them to the liberal arts, put them in contact with sources outside themselves, and guard them against a pedagogical approach to education prescinding from cultural tradition.

One of these critics was the priest, classical scholar, and dean of the College of Arts and Sciences at the Catholic University of America, James M. Campbell. While recognizing the importance of Dawson's ideas and the fact that "not a few Catholic educators" were seriously considering his proposals, Campbell argued Christian culture could not serve as the core subject matter of the liberal arts. "By 'core' is meant essentially subject matter which lies at the basis of *all* the curricular items and to which students turn sooner or later as a unifying principle." But the only subjects that reach into all fields in that way are theology and philosophy. Christian culture must give way to the master disciplines of theology and philosophy as the core of the curriculum, he argued—not recognizing that everything also has a history, a story of meaningful development, including these two fields. The Jesuit priest and political scientist Robert C. Hartnett agreed with Campbell, as did Justus Lawler. A certain Mr. Charles Stinson, writing from Los Angeles to *Commonweal,* went so far as to relegate Christian culture to irrelevance. What is needed is theology and scripture—not contemplation of the past, as Dawson recommended.[53]

Dawson responded to these views by pointing out that he did not wish to reduce the role of theology in education. The study of Christian culture, however, would guard against theological and philosophical domination of the curriculum. Dawson pointed to the excessive

---

53. Campbell, "The Dawson Challenge: A Discussion," 69, 73, 74; Robert C. Hartnett, "The Dawson Challenge: A Discussion," *Commonweal,* April 16, 1955, 89–90; Lawler, "*The Crisis of Western Education* [2]," 215; and Charles Stinson, "Christian Culture," *Commonweal,* February 4, 1955, 479.

intellectualism of theology and philosophy in the medieval universities that had pushed out other studies, causing the humanist reaction of the Renaissance. In a private letter to Mulloy he wrote that the
"theological-philosophical monopoly" at that time "killed medieval
culture and led to the Reformation," just as the "dictatorship of the
theologians at the Sorbonne was equally fatal to French Catholic culture in the 18th century." Dawson opposed a too-powerful role for these
disciplines as damaging to the liberal arts.[54]

Indeed, philosopher Germain Grisez (1929–2018), educated by Jesuits and Dominicans in philosophy during the early 1950s, remembered
the "decadent scholasticism" of those years. This rationalistic "technical education" in Thomism often lacked any historical context, engagement with contemporary thought, or clear relation even to theology.
It was "supposed to integrate the college curriculum, but the abstract
theses to be memorized by students derived from a problematic situation that antedated the development of modern science and the
emergence of critical historical scholarship." Furthermore, "Theology
courses often were taken seriously by no one." They involved "unreflec-
tive inculcation of religious information." Finally, the practical formation of the day "involved outward conformity to a detailed set of rules
and practices. . . . The freedom of the student was not elicited to make
a commitment to values which might have grounded the practices he
was expected to enact."[55]

Traditionally, Dawson pointed out, theology had served as the
crown of the educational system rather than the foundation, and the
liberal arts possessed an independent origin in the classical world.
"I think the center of the liberal arts course must be humanist rather than theological or metaphysical, as indeed, it always has been,"
Dawson wrote. In a letter to Mulloy: "I was looking up the Council of
Trent the other day and I was rather struck by the way their decree on

54. Dawson to Mulloy, March 15, 1955, NDA, folder "Dawson: Christian Culture," Letters of
Christopher Dawson on Culture Studies and Catholic Higher Education, p. 3; Christopher Daw-
son, "Problems of Christian Culture," *Commonweal*, April 15, 1955, 35; and Christopher Dawson,
"On the Place of Religious Study in Education," *Christian Scholar* 45, no. 1 (1962): 39.

55. Germain Grisez, "American Catholic Higher Education: The Experience Evaluated," in
*Why Should the Catholic University Survive? A Study of the Character and Commitments of Catholic
Higher Education*, ed. George A. Kelly (New York: St. John's University Press, 1973), 43–44.

studies (in the 5th session, I think) put the whole emphasis of Christian education on 'Sacred Scripture and the liberal arts', that is, litterae humaniores, and says nothing about philosophy. Even theology seems identified with Biblical studies. This is rather remarkable as compared with the present practice, which gives philosophy the lion's share."[56]

Dawson suggested two ways to avoid theological and philosophical reductionism. First, as Newman had done from the theological side, connect theology to history (and other social sciences[57]). "In my view and dominating my whole life work," Dawson wrote in response to a question posed during Mulloy's visit in 1953, "the key problem is that of Theology and History. For while philosophy and theology occupy different spheres, theology and history do not, except in so far as history is purely factual or united to special aspects of culture." He continued: "Christian theology is a theology of Incarnation and of the successive stages of revelation—Mosaic, Prophetic and Christian; and each of these stages is not simply a question of new truths, but of events through which the truths are revealed." Dawson called this historical approach "positive theology" concerned with matters of historical or particular facts; it was closely linked to scripture and sacred tradition, and thus exegesis and history. He valued the Baroque period so highly because, he wrote by letter to Mulloy in April of the following year, "it was the creator of positive theology (from Petavius onwards) as it was also of scientific Catholic history. It is only by positive theology that the Catholic can deal with the problems of historical and religious relativism"—because it considered historical context. Perhaps thinking of his Jesuit critics, Dawson noted in another letter that year that his plan did not conflict with their own tradition: "In higher studies the Jesuits were among the pioneers in the study of history, positive theology and oriental studies. The systematic philosophical and theological treatment of higher education is, I think, largely due to neo-Thomist influence and is Dominican rather than Jesuit." In this way, the very history of the

---

56. Dawson to Mulloy, March 15, 1955, NDA, folder "Dawson: Christian Culture," Letters of Christopher Dawson on Culture Studies and Catholic Higher Education, p. 3; Dawson, "Problems of Christian Culture," 35.

57. R. Jared Staudt, "Christopher Dawson on Theology and the Social Sciences," *Logos* 12, no. 3 (Summer 2009): 91–111.

Jesuits subverted some of their objections to his educational ideas—proving his point about the importance of understanding the historic reality of Christian culture.[58]

Dawson's approach to positive theology resembled Newman's "lay theology," which was at once historical, catechetical, and apologetic, designed to prepare lay people for their vocations in the world. Newman excluded academic or dogmatic theology from colleges because "students lacked the philosophical preparation to engage its claims," Newman scholar Don J. Briel wrote, but also because Newman said that he was "professing to contemplate Christian knowledge in what may be called its secular aspect, as it is practically useful in the intercourse of life and in general conversation."[59] Catholic elites in the United States wanted academic theology to be the integrating discipline of the university, Briel wrote to me by email (on May 28, 2017): "That was never Newman's view, or Dawson's. And we see the result, a new gnosticism." (By "Gnosticism," Briel meant the claims of an intellectual elite to special spiritual knowledge downplaying incarnational and cultural expressions.)

The second way to avoid Catholic reductionism was to recognize that the reconciliation among the different disciplines competing for dominance of the liberal arts is found not in the synthetic powers of philosophy but in the lived practice of *worship*. While reaffirming that the study of Christian culture should primarily be historical, the "starting point of education must of course always be religion." By this, Dawson meant that, at the university level, a "theological element" can be introduced through the study of Christian culture and the theological and spiritual literature of a particular age, for example. "In that case the fundamental 'classics' are not St. Thomas and St. Augustine, but the Bible, the Missal, the Breviary and the Acta Sanctorum." Through the tradition

58. Christopher Dawson, "Theology and the Study of Christian Culture," memorandum written on August 22, 1953, in response to questions from Murray the preceding day, NDA, folder "Mulloy Conversations with Christopher Dawson August 18–September 2, 1953"; Dawson to Mulloy, April 22, 1954, NDA, folder "Dawson: Christian Culture," Letters of Christopher Dawson on Christian Culture, p. 11; and Dawson to Mulloy, March 27, 1954, NDA, folder "Dawson: Christian Culture," Letters of Christopher Dawson on Culture Studies and Catholic Higher Education, p. 2.

59. Don J. Briel, "Truth and Theology: A Response to Land O'Lakes," in *The University and the Church*, 119; Newman, *The Idea of a University*, 276.

of Catholic worship, religion "touches the individual psyche" at the core of the education he envisioned. These resources had great potential for educational purposes—because one cannot fully understand a culture without experiencing it. "I learnt more during my school-days from my visits to the Cathedral at Winchester than I did from the hours of religious instruction in school," Dawson wrote. "That great church with its tombs of the Saxon kings and the mediaeval statesmen-bishops gave one a greater sense of the magnitude of the religious element in our culture and the depths of its roots in our national life than anything one could learn from books." Real encounter with culture can profoundly move a person and enculturate one into a community and vision much more effectively than "universal" knowledge pretending to prescind from culture. On this point, he agreed with the view of educational theorist John Dewey (1859–1952) that education should initiate students into the total experience of communal life. The question was, though, which community? Dewey proposed the secular democratic community; Dawson the historical reality of Christian culture.[60]

Dawson expressed surprise over the strictly scholastic and metaphysical tendencies that seemed to dominate American Catholic higher education. "Is there not a danger that this highly abstract treatment of learning will produce some antagonism to Catholic education among the younger generation?" he asked Mulloy in 1954. He found troubling the tendency to prescind from the cultural roots of ideas and institutions. Lack of attention to the historical dimension of Christian culture in Catholic education meant that students, well-grounded in the principles of Thomist theology and ethics, might remain in the sphere of theory and textbooks unless they are "able to make some study of how these doctrines and these ethical values have in fact affected or failed to affect the way of life of Christian men and societies." That effort to live out the faith looked different in the various ages of the past, so a proper historicism (see chapter 3) should characterize the Christian mind.[61]

60. Dawson, "Problems of Christian Culture," 35; Dawson, *Understanding Europe*, 198; Christopher Dawson, "Dealing with the Enlightenment and the Liberal Ideology," *Commonweal*, May 14, 1954, 139; John Dewey, "My Pedagogic Creed," *School Journal* 54, no. 1 (January 1897): 77–80.

61. Dawson to Mulloy, August 4, 1954. NDA, folder "Dawson: Christian Culture," Letters of Christopher Dawson on Culture Studies and Catholic Higher Education, p. 1; Dawson, "The Study of Christian Culture," 488.

Application

Contemporary followers of St. Thomas, he thought, had ignored the diversity of cultures and showed little interest in Chinese and Indian philosophy. He wrote in a 1955 letter to Mulloy: "Thomism may represent the *philosophia perennis* of the Western world, and it may be potentially the *philosophia perennis* of the whole world. But it cannot become so until it has incorporated the philosophical traditions of the rest of the world in the same way that it incorporated the philosophical tradition of Hellenism."[62] Such a historicist view of Thomism as the fruit of Christian culture in the West would educate students in a moderate historical relativism that sought to understand cultures and peoples on their own terms, and compare one tradition of thought in relation to other traditions in their search for truth.

Bringing a sociological viewpoint to the study of Christian culture would keep students grounded. This meant making "institutions, and the processes by which they are built and eventually decay, as a subject for inquiry antecedent to a detailed study of the intellectual and aesthetic artifacts of those institutions," wrote legal scholar Russell Hittinger. "More simply put, and to take one of Dawson's own examples, one should first understand the institution and culture of monasticism and then turn to monastic philosophy, illuminated manuscripts, and the other artifacts of the institution."[63] Cultural artifacts of art and philosophy, focused on by humanistic scholars, should be understood in the wider socio-historical context. The greatest of cultural achievements possess lowly roots in their place and time. Cultural mind embraces both perspectives at once to make culture intelligible. Otherwise, (I) remains separate from the (FWP), leading to fragmentation of life and thought.

Such historical relativism, or "relatedness" of ideas to contexts, Dawson thought, would help to counter the spreading metaphysical relativism of the age. It would gird students against it. Unfortunately, neither theologians, on the one hand, nor sociologists, on the other, seemed to recognize this vital distinction between historical and metaphysical relativism—the first compatible with Christian faith by apply-

62. Christopher Dawson, enclosure "The Relation of Philosophy to Culture," letter to John J. Mulloy, September 7, 1955, NDA box 1, folder 15, "The Dynamic of Culture Change," p. 43.
63. Hittinger, "Christopher Dawson: A View from the Social Sciences," 34–35.

ing the boundary-thinking rule, while the second was not. The failure to make this distinction pushed secular education and Catholic education further and further apart. Catholics reacted to metaphysical relativism by advocating "metaphysical absolutism" in the way they rallied around Thomism, leaving little room for criticism. Students would then have to take the dominant Thomism largely on faith since they would not experience the competition of rival schools of thought—devouring "premise and conclusion together with indiscriminate greediness," as Newman put it. Thus, one was in danger of having a solid and monolithic structure of "infallible knowledge" that included philosophy as well as theology and treated the two as coequal. Catholic education, Dawson wrote, then becomes identified with an authoritarian ideology, like Marxism. The "distinction between theology and ideology becomes blurred. It may not be so in practice, but it may become a real danger unless students have a deep grounding in culture, either literary or historical." Newman had warned how those students who adopt whole sciences on faith eventually, as might be expected, "throw up all they have learned in disgust, having gained nothing really by their anxious labors." The comparative study of Christian culture as a spiritual and material matrix formed through historical contact with other cultures, Dawson proposed, would protect students from such insularity and integrate a curriculum in ways that theology and philosophy by themselves could not.[64]

Making Christian Culture Unthinkable

Besides these criticisms of Dawson's proposals, a wider cultural process was at work in the United States making the whole idea of Christian culture largely unthinkable. The idea of progress, which Dawson had critiqued as incoherent in light of the Great War, reigned

---

64. Dawson, "The Study of Christian Culture," 488, 491; Newman, *The Idea of a University*, 116. In relation to Thomism, Dawson noted that, "I don't see any fundamental contradiction between Thomism and the culture approach," he added. "At least the Aristotelian view of the nature and function of society agrees very well with the anthropological concept of culture, though it is true that the Thomists have tended to concentrate on the Aristotelian metaphysics and have devoted too little attention to his theory of society." See Christopher Dawson, "Christian Culture Study and the College," STA, box 6, folder 75, "Christian Culture Study and the College," pp. 2–3.

supreme. According to this myth, he wrote, science and technology would bring about the "complete transformation of human society, an abrupt passage from corruption to perfection, from darkness to light." The mechanization and uniformity of life increased dramatically after the Second World War. Social planning threatened to create a static and lifeless social order.[65] Dawson's cultural criticism had some merit, for the daily experience of Western people, particularly Americans, fundamentally changed in the 1950s. Technology, suburbia, and urban development involved material changes (FWP) that penetrated the American way of life and made it seem a universalized ideal (I).

As a result of this mid-century culture-process, the attachment of many Catholics to the *particular* migrated during the 1950s toward the *universal*—a process sped up by the new emphasis on universal human rights and by interpretations of the Second Vatican Council in the 1960s. Previously, a "theology of the local"—together with prevailing ways of life—stressed that people came to know God in definite, geographically defined places and through particular means. A wafer of bread or a neighborhood evidenced God's presence. Religion *and* geography defined a parish, which served all the people within its boundaries. This inculcated a strong commitment to place in Catholics and anchored their neighborhoods around churches. This all started to change during the 1950s. Dawson's talk of "Christian culture" seemed a throwback to an older cultural pattern derided as the "ghetto" by the rising Catholic middle class seeking to leave that all behind.[66]

A brief Dawsonian analysis of this culture-process of assimilation as a whole reveals how the categories, introduced in chapter 2, of ideas (I—in the form of religious idealism and theology and philosophy detached from other disciplines) and Folk-Work-Place (FWP—in the form of technological and suburban change) conspired together to dismantle Catholic subculture from within and fuel opposition to the Dawson Plan. What follows is a mere sketch of a complex development.

65. Dawson, *The Judgment of the Nations*, 72, 73; Dawson, *Progress and Religion*, 22.

66. John T. McGreevy, *Parish Boundaries: The Catholic Encounter with Race in the Twentieth-Century Urban North* (Chicago: University of Chicago Press, 1996), 11, 19, 24–25. For the "theology of the local," McGreevy cited, along with other sources, Karl Rahner's "Theology of the Parish," in *The Parish: From Theology to Practice*, ed. Hugo Rahner, trans. Robert Kress (Westminster, Md.: Newman Press, 1958): 23–35.

For decades in U.S. history minority religious groups formed their own distinctive subcultures. Among Catholics, waves of discrimination from the 1830s to the 1850s turned them in on themselves to create their own internal organizations, particularly within the large cities. This formed "a kind of ghetto mentality," Dawson noted, "which separated the Catholics from the rest of American society," and a sense of social and intellectual inferiority took a long time to shake off. But circumstances in the 1950s did not justify such feelings of inferiority, for by then, Catholics constituted the "strongest and the most united religious body on the continent," he noted. The Jewish sociologist of religion William Herberg (1901–1977) agreed, writing in 1955 that the church is heard by "the entire nation, and not merely its own community."[67] The Catholic community possessed clear and distinct "borders," but they were permeable and mediated what it meant to be both "Catholic" and "American."

Those who remembered the 1950s wrote of the centrality of Catholic education to this cultural mediation and the profound, primal sense of identity inculcated through communal habits: "prayers offered, heads ducked in unison, crossings, chants, christenings, grace at meals; beads, altar, incense, candles; nuns in the classroom . . . priests garbed black on the street . . . all things going to a rhythm, memorized, old things always returning, eternal in that sense." Catholicism was a "parallel culture." Lived faith in urban Catholic neighborhoods created dense social networks that connected school, sports, dating, and social and professional (Catholic) organizations. Despite the clericalism, racism, triumphalism, and ahistorical conception of the church prominent in that time, these "plausibility structures"—the sociocultural contexts within which systems of meaning make sense—enculturated a strong sense of identity across generations.[68]

Nevertheless, their sense of inferiority blinded Catholic elites to the value of their subculture. In addition, urban design and the develop-

67. Christopher Dawson, "Documents of American Church History," *America*, April 27, 1957, 134, 135; Will Herberg, *Protestant, Catholic, Jew: An Essay in American Religious Sociology* (New York: Doubleday, 1955), 175.

68. Garry Wills, "Memories of a Catholic Boyhood," in *American Catholic History: A Documentary Reader*, ed. Mark Massa with Catherine Osborne (New York: New York University Press, 2008), 263–64; Kenneth L. Woodward, *Getting Religion: Faith, Culture, and Politics from the Age of Eisenhower to the Era of Obama* (New York: Convergent, 2016), 20–31.

Application

ment of suburbs represented powerful material forces that would undo their geographical and metaphorical boundaries, propelling Catholics toward full assimilation into the American way of life. These changes cut against Dawson's ideas about Christian culture.

In 1954, the U. S. Housing Act laid the basis for urban renewal according to essentially the same principles as those pioneered by Le Corbusier in his Voisin Plan of 1925 to clear away slums. Corbusier had called for the demolition of central Paris in exchange for isolated, freestanding towers, amidst the sense of dramatic break with the past after the Great War. While few took this plan seriously at the time, his principles were partially realized in the suburbs of Paris and in the United States during the 1950s. Journalist Jane Jacobs (1916–2006), author of *The Death and Life of Great American Cities* (1961), already realized by the mid-1950s their disastrous effects as the modernist plan for Harlem unfolded, destroying small businesses and working-class communities. The "so-called slums were generally healthier and more humane than the superblock towers that replaced them," she thought. Catholic social activist Dorothy Day agreed with her. Previously, Day remembered, neighbors would run to see how the others were getting along and offer a bowl of soup or a dish of fresh rolls. This open character contrasted with the closed character of the "ordinary" Americans whose desire for privacy isolated them, "each afraid another would ask something from him." The physical and spiritual world of the immigrants passed away as they sought to conform to the American way of life, often resulting—Day observed—in the loss of their cult, culture, skills, faith, folk songs, costumes, and handcrafts.[69]

In addition, the GI Bill, that profound engine of social change in America written by veterans of the Great War, put higher education and home ownership within the grasp of many. The first mass-produced suburb, by Levitt & Sons, Inc., appeared on Long Island in 1951, followed by Levittown, Pennsylvania (1952–1958) and Lakewood outside of Los Angeles (1953), at a time when eight million Americans moved to the West Coast. Places like these promised a new kind of life, the so-called

69. Michael J. Lewis, "What Jane Jacobs Saw," *First Things*, March 2017, 53; Day, *The Long Loneliness* , 16, 154; Themis Chronopoulos, "Robert Moses and the Visual Dimension of Physical Disorder: Efforts to Demonstrate Urban Blight in the Age of Slum Clearance," *Journal of Planning History* 13, no. 3 (2014): 207–3.

38835

American way of life, and dispersed baby-boomer families, including Catholics, away from urban institutional supports. This population movement, channeled by the Federal-Aid Highway Act of 1956 creating the interstate system, drained the old, inner-city ethnic parishes and local communities of vitality. The comfortable advantages of suburban living, pictured attractively in the 1957 film *Into the Suburbs*, usually "failed to include a strong sense of community and a religious identity centered on church and parochial school," journalist Russell Shaw noted. The sociologist Herbert Gans studied "the Levittowners" and found that the regional, ethnic, and religiously distinctive identities of the largely working-class people moving to the new suburbs declined in favor of the suburban melting pot.[70]

Writer Charles R. Morris noted how the typical Catholic family living in Los Angeles during the 1950s was "headed by a junior aerospace engineer who'd gone to school on the GI Bill, with help from his wife, and who drove to his nonunion job on a new freeway from his tract bungalow, while his wife stayed home and took care of their four kids." These sociological changes toward suburbia and technological culture produced tremendous forces of assimilation and conformity, deepening a process begun among American Catholics during the Great War. They could easily work against personal freedom and vocation, and Dawson identified them as major factors in secularization.[71]

The profound pressure toward conformity did not always lead to happiness, as Betty Friedan (1921–2006) made clear in her book *Feminine Mystique* (1963). Many women experienced an "emptiness," "boredom," and "mental vacuum" in the suburbs as they sought to achieve happiness according the dictates of their cultural surroundings. The poverty of public culture there turned women inward to find meaning in domestic life alone. The open plan of the ranch or split-level home facilitated this, because without true walls or doors, the woman was never separated from her children. In an interesting application of Dawsonian

70. Russell Shaw, *American Church: The Remarkable Rise, Meteoric Fall, and Uncertain Future of Catholicism in America* (San Francisco: Ignatius, 2013), 106; Herbert J. Gans, *The Levittowners: Ways of Life and Politics in a New Suburban Community* (New York: Vintage Books, 1967), vii.

71. Charles R. Morris, *American Catholic: The Saints and Sinners Who Builts America's Most Powerful Church* (New York: Random House, 1997), 259; Dawson, *The Judgment of the Nations*, chap. 6.

boundary thinking to house design, Friedan wrote that, "She can forget her own identity in those noisy open-plan houses. . . . In what is basically one free-flowing room instead of many rooms separated by walls and stairs, continual messes continually need picking up." American society as a whole, she thought, looked increasingly like this one, free-flowing room. There were few places in which to be alone, to think, write, and create culturally, Friedan noted—a lack of "alcoves." "No homogeneous room, of homogeneous height, can serve a group of people well," wrote the authors of one of the bestselling books on architecture. "To give a group a chance to be together, as a group, a room must also give them the chance to be alone, in one's and two's in the same space."[72] Cultures, like large rooms, need small spaces ("subcultures") set aside from the others by permeable boundaries for stable identities to exist.

However, the powerful forces destroying boundaries and "cultural alcoves" increasingly made it difficult for American critics to conceive of what Dawson meant by "Christian culture." In interviews in 1961, he characterized American society as essentially monist, not pluralist. "It is very hard for the individual or the group to maintain separate—pluralist—standards of value or independent ways of life," he said. "I wonder, will the family be able to stand this? Isn't the family becoming outdated?" Businessmen, advertisers, and television experts had created a "conformist society" in which the motel is the symbol of a modern, mechanized civilization—"all the same over the States," burying the old regional differences—"alcoves"—under a uniform network of identical forms. Other sources of this conformity included public education. The First Amendment—originally designed to *protect* religious freedom, had by 1961 morphed into a "bulwark of secularist dogma," Dawson thought, banishing religion from the common school and increasingly from society. The so-called "separation of church and state" had become an article of faith that no loyal American could question. The secular pattern of culture in the minds of many made it difficult to create or even conceive of Christian culture.[73]

72. Betty Friedan, *The Feminine Mystique* (1963; New York: Dell, 1973), 242–57, quoted on 246; Christopher Alexander et al., *A Pattern Language: Towns, Buildings, Construction* (New York: Oxford University Press, 1977), 829.

73. C. J. McNaspy, "Motel Near Walden II," *America*, January 21, 1961, 508, 511; Michael Novak,

Secularization from Within

Two biographies of Dawson critics reveal how certain kinds of assimilation corresponded with a lack of understanding—or even hostility—toward the idea of Christian culture. Bernard E. McGoldrick, a Jesuit priest, wrote to *Commonweal* in 1957 that if the Dawson Plan calls for a "renewal of spirit through the study of such writers as St. Augustine, St. Thomas Aquinas and Dante (and doubtless, it does include them), then let's have them by all means!" But McGoldrick mistakenly thought Dawson's idea of "Christian culture" by-passed "the traditional Graeco-Roman contribution" and therefore would lead students to believe that Christianity has little foundation in natural reason.[74]

Thirteen years later, McGoldrick left the active priesthood and, married to a former nun who had obtained a dispensation from Rome, drove across country to California to take up a position in political science at Fresno State College. Their traumatic decisions to leave priestly functions and the convent induced much soul-searching. "We are not rebelling against the essentials of our faith, but only the accidentals," McGoldrick said in a newspaper interview, including a photo of the smiling couple in their new home. As a graduate of Fordham University and a Jesuit, McGoldrick would have studied theology and philosophy extensively in the 1950s. But his transition to political science in the 1970s and his view of the church through the lens of a "struggle for power" in his later work confirmed Dawson's fear: without grounding in history and a moderate cultural relativism informing an understanding of doctrinal development in the church, would not the tendency toward universalism in American Catholic education in the 1950s cause a reaction among the younger generation, and naiveté about enculturating the next generation? Indeed, it would, as many Catholic elites (Jesuits included) absorbed contemporary psychology's focus on subjective experience and increasingly viewed the Catholic past as irrelevant, at best. It seems that McGoldrick lacked a sense of Christian culture as an historical, lived reality, a sense that might have supported

---

"Professor Dawson Speaks out on Church, State and Religious Education in America," *Jubilee*, April 1961, 27.

74. Bernard E. McGoldrick, "To the Editors," *Commonweal*, February 15, 1957, 513.

a deeper continuity in his own life. Rather, as a common vision disintegrated among Jesuits during the 1960s, individualism intensified, and hundreds left the order. In 1971, McGoldrick became president of the Federation of Christian Ministries, an organization that included other former Jesuits with similar stories to his own. Its members sought to work outside the church's structure to push for greater Catholic assimilation to contemporary culture. McGoldrick "shifted the group's attention from theological considerations to ways of understanding and implementing political change in the church," a document on the history of the organization noted.[75]

Sociological and intellectual changes toward American assimilation characterized "boundaries" as old fashioned and unneeded. The neglect of boundary thinking in cultural and religious identity placed Catholics such as McGoldrick at odds with Christian culture and institutions in the space of ten short years, shedding light on why Dawson's educational ideas received such widespread criticism.

John Cogley is another example. He received Catholic education all the way through, including a Jesuit education in philosophy and Dominican training in theology in Europe. Cogley operated a Catholic Worker "hospitality house" in Chicago, his home city, and then worked as executive editor of *Commonweal* (from 1949 to 1954), remaining a regular columnist until 1964. Assumption University of Windsor awarded him their Christian Culture Award Gold Medal in 1960, but he did not think much of the Dawson Plan, writing that his Jesuit education was a good one, so why change it? Furthermore, with an entirely humanistic understanding of culture, he did not understand Dawson's socio-historical argument, wondering if "there was ever a Christian age in any valid sense." In another piece (1957), he waxed eloquent about the state of Catholicism in America: where is the church in a healthier condition, he asked. The American way of life allowed the system of church and state to work beautifully:

75. Bette Tambling, "Priest, Nun 'Live By Love' As Husband, Wife," *Fresno Bee*, February 16, 1970, 9; James Hitchcock, *The Pope and the Jesuits: John Paul II and the New Order in the Society of Jesus* (New York: National Committee of Catholic Laymen, 1984), iii–iv, 21–24; and Antoinette M. Marold, *Federation of Christian Ministries 45th Anniversary 2013 President's History*, 2013, http://www.federationofchristianministries.org/pdfs/President-Book.pdf.

Stand outside a busy suburban parish church on Sunday morning and watch the crowds coming and going. Enter and count the people approaching the altar. Study the bulging classrooms of parochial schools, the buzzing campuses of Catholic colleges and universities. Take a look at the seminaries, monasteries, convents. Visit the hospitals, orphanages, nursing homes. Try to make a reservation at one of the busy retreat centers. Count up the number of Catholic papers and magazines and follow the activities of American missionaries abroad.

Dawson thought Cogley overstated the situation. As he read various *Commonweal* articles, he discerned in this Cogley piece why so many American Catholics attacked his proposal: "Everything is so good materially with the state of Catholicism in America that it would be a great mistake to criticize the modern secularist culture that has made it possible. Nothing must be done to disturb the smooth working of the concordat." Thinkers such as Cogley "will not recognize that what is at stake is not the dualism of State and Church, but the far more fundamental opposition of Church and World that runs all through the gospels. If Catholicism accepts the secularist culture, it means the surrender of the Church to the World: an act of apostasy."[76]

And apostasy is precisely what happened. Even before Cogley converted to the Episcopal Church in 1973, he had by 1967 completely reversed his earlier pride in the institutions of Catholic culture in America, now writing them off as an "illusion." Catholic universities would face the same fate as the papal states, he argued, for the idea of the church conducting something identifiable, with boundaries, so to speak, as a "Catholic university," will soon seem anachronistic, an embarrassing hangover from the past. Universities must inhabit the modern, secular world of scientific reason and cultural pluralism. "The reality, of course, is that the Church does not serve as the bearer of any actual living culture," he wrote. If the church does not represent any actual, Christian culture, then neither can a university. It is simply a center of independent criticism, as Newman also believed (!), wrote Cogley

---

76. Dawson to Mulloy, September 16, 1957, NDA, folder "Dawson: Christian Culture," The Christian Culture Program Under Fire: Challenge and Reply, p. 20; John Cogley, "Education—and all That," *Commonweal*, April 29, 1955, 104; and John Cogley, "God and Caesar," *Commonweal*, September 6, 1957, 563.

in an odd and highly selective appeal to Newman's thought. In Cogley's view, the individual scholar, not the institution, is the only link between the world and the wisdom of the church—a central pietist assumption.

Cogley overtly described the process of internal secularization affecting himself over the previous ten years. At first, it unnerved him when he realized his secular condition. "For years, I frequently felt misplaced on Sunday morning. Neither the liturgy, the language of the liturgy, nor the sermons I heard seemed to have a vital connection with my daily life." Then came the day he realized he no longer felt at home on Catholic campuses or other church-sponsored intellectual gatherings. When his eldest son left for college, "I found myself quite content that he did not choose a Catholic campus." The son went to Harvard, as Cogley wanted him prepared for the wider world, even at the cost of missing the "classical" Catholic culture of his own upbringing. Cogley's own youthful idealism had sent him into the Catholic Worker movement; his son's idealism sent him to the Peace Corps, with strictly secular concerns. The process of enculturating faith had broken down, and by 1967, Cogley knew it.[77]

This failure occurred partly due to the sociological transformation of American society and the idealist reaction among Catholic liberals in the 1950s against the older Catholic culture, which now, in their view, smacked of the ghetto. The Jesuit historian John Tracy Ellis (1905–1992) wrote in 1955 about American Catholics and what he perceived as their poor intellectual life due to "their frequently self-imposed ghetto mentality" and separation from other Americans. Changing the self-perception of intellectual inferiority served as one reason Douglas Horton invited Dawson to Harvard. The Ellis indictment of Catholicism resonated powerfully with many who took up the cry against the "ghetto" that supposedly impeded Catholic assimilation into American culture—and many of Dawson's *Commonweal* critics saw the Dawson Plan as a return to the ghetto. Speaking of a "Christian culture" would delay Catholic integration; accidentals matter little—it is the spirit and essence of Catholicism that matters.[78]

77. John Cogley, "The Future of an Illusion," *Commonweal*, June 2, 1967, 311, 313, 314.
78. John Tracy Ellis, "American Catholics and the Intellectual Life," in *American Catholic History*, 100. On the Ellis indictment, James Burtchaell noted wryly that Catholics struggled to ap-

In the spirit of this new Gnosticism mentioned by Briel earlier, Sister McNichols had written about the need to transcend the world of accidentals and limited cultural traits such as Latin, monastic traditions, celibate clergy, and architectural style. McGoldrick and Cogley agreed: mere cultural accidentals seemed unimportant in the face of the new lives they pursued. Russell Shaw noted that the infrastructure of Catholic culture—what helped make the faith believable for generations— fell into disfavor with Catholic intellectuals who saw it as a vestige of immature Catholicism. They pressed for the "unmediated integration of Catholics into the secular milieu," Shaw noted. A pervasive secularization from within resulted.[79]

That process profoundly affected Catholic institutions of higher learning. After Russia launched *Sputnik* in 1957, the near mania for educational excellence in the United States swept Catholics along with it. Confidence in their own educational vision declined through the 1950s as Catholic institutions looked to places like Harvard, Columbia, and the University of California for models to emulate. They assumed uncritically the supposed neutrality of those institutions when, in reality, they, too, possessed a worldview and set of values, sometimes in conflict with Christianity. Secular institutions such as these increasingly lost touch with important human questions due to their size, specialization, and secularization, historian C. John Sommerville commented. Imitating them marked the moment of transition when Catholic educators *accepted* modernity rather than *challenge* it, historian Philip Gleason noted.[80]

At Notre Dame, for example, President Theodore Hesburgh (1917–

---

preciate the native strengths of their own system and the weaknesses of the Ivies. "So when John Tracy Ellis (PhD, Catholic University), who … hadn't trained in the major leagues, told [Catholic educational leaders] Catholics had no intellectual life, they believed him, but when Andrew Greeley (PhD, University of Chicago), who *had* got the big diploma, said Ellis was way out of date and that Catholic students were testing quite high for intellectuality, he went on about it for more than fifteen years and they still wouldn't believe him" (Burtchaell, *The Dying of the Light*, 707). Burtchaell cited Philip Gleason, "A Look Back at the Catholic Intellectualism Issue," *U.S. Catholic Historian* 13, no. 4 (Fall 1995): 19–37.

79. Shaw, *American Church*, 81; Joseph A. Varacalli, *Bright Promise, Failed Community: Catholics and the American Public Order* (Lanham, Md.: Lexington Books, 2000), 5.

80. C. John Sommerville, *The Decline of the Secular University: Why the Academy Needs Religion* (New York: Oxford University Press, 2006), 90; Gleason, *Contending with Modernity*, 295, 296, 318.

2015), an admirer of Newman and the Thomistic synthesis, desired to bring Dawson to campus after reading his 1953 article "Education and Christian Culture" in *Commonweal*. Hesburgh liked his idea of Christian culture as a unifying focus for higher education. He wanted Dawson to lead faculty discussions in how to make it a concentration. However, Dawson did not accept the invitation, living in England at the time.

By the early 1960s, the forces of assimilation were causing Hesburgh to lose confidence in the possibilities of the Christian intellectual tradition and the study of Christian culture. "Instead," wrote a biographer, "he settled for making his university more modern and more American" and turned against Newman's ideas. This signal meant that across the university, the desire for intellectual unity and synthesis in the undergraduate curriculum could more easily collapse. By 1961, faculty gave up the fight. From then on, they placed greater emphasis on departmental autonomy and specialized disciplines, moving away from the older idea that Catholic higher education should embody a distinctively Catholic intellectual vision. This move effectively eliminated identifiable centers of Christian culture within which and from which believers could critique and engage the values of secular culture. In their desire to engage pluralism, many Catholics sacrificed the preservation of their own tradition, thus guaranteeing they would eventually have little distinctive to say or contribute to pluralism. The trajectory of much of Catholic higher education, Burtchaell wrote, set by well-meaning institutional leaders who nonetheless suffered from severe self-deception in their desire to emulate secular institutions, aimed at assimilating Catholicism into modern America. They often ended up secularizing their institutions from within, replacing a distinctively Christian culture with the academy and its culture.[81]

This also happened at Catholic University of America, where the case of Eugene Kevane's faithfulness proves the point about how the assimilationist movement represented by McGoldrick and Cogley undergirded opposition to the idea of Christian culture. Kevane (1913–1996), dean of CUA's School of Education (from 1964 to 1968), had devoted his

81. Wilson D. Miscamble, *American Priest: The Ambitious Life and Conflicted Legacy of Notre Dame's Father Ted Hesburgh* (New York: Image, 2019), 98, 379; Burtchaell, *The Dying of the Light*, xi; and Bradley J. Birzer, *Sanctifying the World*, 3, 245.

priesthood to Catholic education and the church. Without education into the tradition of Christian culture, he wrote in 1959 about Dawson's work, student minds will be "ill prepared to withstand the secularizing pressures of the modern environment." He comprehended Dawson's point about cultural education in more than just philosophy and theology. Eight years later, Kevane resisted the assimilationist movement represented at CUA by Fr. Charles Curran, who supported public dissent to Pope Paul VI's encyclical *Humanae Vitae* by Catholic theologians. Kevane spoke against Curran's dissent and thereby sacrificed his academic career, as he was ousted by assimilationist forces in 1968.[82]

Behind-the-scenes administrative changes had fostered a culture of dissent at CUA, but Kevane refused to accept the individualist idea of academic freedom then percolating into institutions of higher learning. In direct contrast to Cogley, then, Kevane argued that an institution can indeed commit itself to a particular religious identity as a corporate body. The desire to use "academic freedom" as a tool to make CUA more accepted and more like other American institutions of higher learning would make it possible to introduce secularization from within, and that secularization would prevent CUA's freedom to be itself and thus stifle authentic pluralism in American society, he predicted. Though he failed to convince his colleagues at the time, Kevane's understanding of "Christian culture," in contrast with his critics, moved him to defend distinctive Catholic cultural and institutional identity. Secularization did not occur so much through the work of godless intellectuals at places like Notre Dame or CUA as through the increasingly pietistic Christians of the mid-twentieth century who individualized and subjectivized faith away from the "mere" accidentals of Christian culture as a historically continuous community.[83]

Hence, one arrives at the place this chapter began: cultural de-

---

82. Eugene Kevane, "Christopher Dawson and Study of Christian Culture," *Catholic Educational Review* 57, no. 1 (1959): 457.

83. Peter M. Mitchell, *The Coup at Catholic University: The 1968 Revolution in American Catholic Education* (San Francisco: Ignatius, 2015), 103–5, 115, 118; Burtchaell, *The Dying of the Light*, 842. Kevane utilized the idea of Christian culture in his later work—and directly linked it to Dawson. See Eugene Kevane, *The Lord of History* (1980; Steubenville, Ohio: Emmaus Road, 2018), 11. After leaving CUA, Kevane went on to work in the area of catechetics and create the *Faith and Life* series, known for its beautiful art and fidelity to church teaching.

struction, not by German V-1 weapons but by ideas and by decisions in which Catholics and other Christians, swept along by sociological changes in postwar America, dismantled their own institutions and local cultures from within.

The Sociological Imperative of Christian Education

Represented by figures such as McGoldrick and Cogley, and institutions like Notre Dame and CUA, intellectual and spiritual changes within American Christian culture followed wider sociological forces toward assimilation. This cultural transformation propelled Dawson to propose the study of Christian culture based on four sociological imperatives: 1) plausibility structures, 2) moderate cultural relativism, 3) permeable boundaries, and 4) cultural consciousness of religion.

First, Christian cultures of the past possessed plausibility structures that made faith make sense to people. The Christian way of life was a "sacramental culture which embodied religious truth in visible and palpable forms": from art to liturgy, from poetry to social institutions—these were all "channels for the communication of religious truth." Today, Dawson noted, all these channels have been closed by unbelief or choked by ignorance. Hence the need to reopen them through education.[84]

Second, moderate cultural relativism: students approaching Christian culture should first read something like Alfred Kroeber's *Anthropology: Culture Patterns and Processes* (1923), Dawson wrote in 1957, so they can see what a culture is, how it forms and changes, and how it should be studied from the socio-historical direction. On this basis, they would approach the study of Christian culture "from the right angle." However, it was a problem to know where to find Catholics who were interested in culture study and who were not averse to the anthropological approach, Dawson complained to Mulloy.[85]

---

84. Dawson, "The Challenge of Secularism," 328.

85. Dawson to Mulloy, March 3, 1955, NDA, folder "Dawson: Christian Culture," Letters of Christopher Dawson on Culture Studies and Catholic Higher Education, p. 9; Dawson, "Education and Christian Culture," 217; and Dawson, "Problems of Christian Culture," 34. Dawson emphasized this point of studying a culture for its own sake: "The other method of taking some question which is of actual interest—like the prevention of war—and studying it through the different periods of history is, I think, unsatisfactory because it makes us study the past in terms of what

From his vantage point in the 1950s, Dawson praised the older gen-eration of anthropologists such as Franz Boas and Ruth Benedict for their cultural relativism, their striving to study a foreign culture for its own sake rather than primarily through the lens of their own cultur-al values. Christian culture students needed such an ability in order to think outside the box of the dominant and unitary American cul-ture. They needed to become aware of the "relativity" of said American culture in order to imagine other ways of life "outside the box," so to speak. The increasingly homogenous culture of the "American way of life" of the United States left "little room" for traditional cultural val-ues in the Christian view—"the supernatural, spiritual authority, God and the soul—in fact, the whole notion of the transcendent," Dawson wrote. Most people, including most Catholics, simply accept the cul-ture around them as culture in the absolute sense, he noted. They sim-ply swim around in the water of the fishbowl, not imagining there is anything else. "This is why the problem of Christian culture is of such paramount importance," Dawson wrote, "for unless Christians are able to defend their cultural traditions they will not be able to survive." Thus, "unless students can learn something of Christian culture as a whole—the world of Christian thought and the Christian way of life and the norms of the Christian community—they are placed in a position of cultural estrangement—the social inferiority of the ghetto without its old self-containedness and self-sufficiency." In response, it is necessary to "show not only the dangers to human values inherent in our modern unitary culture, but also the positive values of the Christian cultural tradition and its universal significance." This is a great challenge, for, "It needs a considerable amount of study and imagination to understand the difference of cultures and the existence and value of other ways of life which diverge from the dominant pattern," Dawson wrote. He noted hopefully, however, that Americans have had exceptional opportunities to understand the diversity of cultures due to their contact with Native

---

interest us, instead of what interested them. One wants to get the student to see a culture as an intelligible whole, with its own form and spirit and its own raison d'etre. The chief obstacle is this obsession with contemporaneity to which you have alluded" (Dawson to Mulloy, March 13, 1954, NDA, folder "Dawson: Christian Culture," Letters of Christopher Dawson on Christian Culture, p. 3).

American peoples from the beginning of their story. Indeed, American anthropologists, partly through their study of Native Americans, had first formulated the concept of *culture* as the fundamental object of scientific social study, as described in chapter 1.[86]

In order to gain awareness of the relativity of culture in the American context, Dawson thought it important for students to examine the ways the Enlightenment movement of the eighteenth century shaped American national culture. He suggested a course covering the two classical moments in America: the age of Jefferson and the age of Emerson. "If these two were studied properly they would give the student a clear objective notion of the Enlightenment and Liberalism in their American forms and would provide a bridge for dealing with the European Enlightenment and European Liberalism."[87] This would historicize the dominant American ideology, aiding students in evaluating points of contact and points of conflict with Christian cultural traditions.

But as America reached a pinnacle of world power after the Second World War and experienced unprecedented prosperity during the 1950s, Americans (even anthropologists!) found it difficult to think outside their own, liberal culture pattern. In an insightful review of Margaret Mead's *New Lives for Old: Manus 1928–1953*, about an island in Papua New Guinea and the cultural effects of having the American army stationed there during the Second World War, Dawson challenged her "change of faith" away from cultural relativism. Mead no longer believed that the function of anthropology was to defend local cultures; rather, it was to integrate them as swiftly as possible into the American way of life as the best of all possible cultures—a disaster for cultural identity, Dawson thought. This was the false universalism of assimilation. Instead, traditional cultural values needed preservation, Dawson believed, even while subordinated to the universal moral values that are the essence of a higher civilization.[88]

---

86. Dawson, *The Crisis of Western Education*, 112, 113.

87. Dawson, "Dealing with the Enlightenment and the Liberal Ideology," 139.

88. Christopher Dawson, "The Impact of Religion on the Modern World," *Commonweal*, January 18, 1957, 412–13. In her introduction to the book, Margaret Mead wrote of waves of foreigners entering America and leaving behind their different ways of life. "As we have learned to change ourselves, so we believe that others can change also, and we believe that they will want to change,

As Dawson applied his cultural mind to the study of Christian culture, a third sociological imperative comes into view: permeable boundaries. In the historic reality of Christian culture, the "I" of Christianity incarnated itself through individual vocations into the particularities of the F, W, and P of various human societies. Over time, this culture-process created a mosaic of subcultures with spatial boundaries, and hence distinct identities. Local traditions and the "mere accidentals" of faith really mattered in the social formation of self. Historic Christian cultures, for all of their particularities, strengths, and weaknesses, constantly interacted with and drew inspiration from other cultures. Dawson showed this, for example, in his *Mongol Mission* (1955), which described the medieval journeys of Franciscan diplomats representing the papacy in Mongolia and China. Permeable boundaries make for a challenging but necessary tension in any healthy subculture: preserving and transmitting faith, on the one hand, and engagement with other cultures, on the other—an inward and an outward movement.[89]

Thus, in the context of homogenous, modern societies, the concept of Christian culture helps one to conceive of a different way of life in which people can find their identities and stand up for who they are. When attitudes, values, beliefs, and habits are highly diffused and mixed up as they are in modern society, "it is almost inevitable that the person who grows up in these conditions will be diffuse and mixed up too," architect and design-theorist Christopher Alexander noted. In ecology, "members of the same species develop distinguishable traits when separated from other members of the species by physical boundaries like a mountain ridge, a valley, a river, a dry strip of land, a cliff, or a significant change in climate or vegetation."[90] In just the same way, differentiation from and within the American way of life might involve

---

that men have only to see a better way of life to reach out for it spontaneously. Our faith includes no forebodings about the effect of destroying old customs. We conceive [of people] as seeing a light and following it freely." See Margaret Mead, *New Lives for Old: Cultural Transformation—Manus, 1928–1953* (1956; New York: William Morrow, 1966), 6.

89. Shaw, *American Church*, 201. One fascinating section in the *Mongol Mission* recounted the theological discussions between Franciscans, Buddhist monks, Muslims, and Nestorians. See Christopher Dawson, ed., *The Mongol Mission: Narratives and Letters of the Franciscan Missionaries in Mongolia and China in the Thirteenth and Fourteenth Centuries* (New York: Sheed & Ward, 1955), 187–201.

90. Alexander, *A Pattern Language*, 46, 47, 78.

not only geographic and cultural boundaries of place but also meta-phorical thresholds where judgment and discernment take place mediating the flow of values, style, and information into local subcultures and institutions. Education as enculturation needed to respect these sociological truths.

The fourth imperative was cultural consciousness of religion through the study of actual, historic Christian cultures. Only this could address the situation of someone like John Cogley, who came to feel religion ceased to have vital connection to his daily life, despite years of Jesuit and Dominican education. In one of his most important statements about education, Dawson wrote:

> The central problem of the Catholic educationalist is a sociological one: how to make students culturally conscious of their religion; otherwise they will be divided personalities—with a Christian faith and a pagan culture which contradict one another. . . . Thus the sociological problem of Christian culture is also the psychological problem of integration and spiritual health. I am convinced that this is the key issue.[91]

Effective teachers of the time, such as Frank O'Malley (1909–1974) at the University of Notre Dame, agreed with this assessment. Recognized as one of the greatest undergraduate teachers the institution ever produced, O'Malley wove together history, literature, and theology in his packed classes. The whole challenge in education is to reconnect culture and cult—"to draw the works of the mind within the world of worship," he wrote in a highly positive commentary on Dawson's educational ideas. The underlying necessity is to form students with a vital possession of the realities of Christian culture.[92] This first happened in a programmatic way right across the street from O'Malley's Notre Dame, at St. Mary's College.

91. Dawson, "Problems of Christian Culture," 36.
92. Frank O'Malley, "The Culture of the Church," *Review of Politics* 16, no. 2 (1954): 146; John W. Meaney, *O'Malley of Notre Dame* (Notre Dame, Ind.: University of Notre Dame Press, 1991), 35, 131, 146. O'Malley's students such as Kenneth Woodward (long-time religion editor at *Newsweek*) remembered him for introducing them to "a lively tradition of Catholic culture—broadly humanistic, rigorously critical, and decisively Incarnational—to which we as students, we came to feel, were the fortunate heirs." Catholicism became something "infinitely more compelling" than a way of belonging—above all, it was a "way of seeing and coming to understand, and I was dazzled by the possibility that the life of the mind could be integrated with the spiritual life of the church," Woodward noted. (Woodward, *Getting Religion*, 32.)

Christian Culture Program at St. Mary's College

Despite widespread criticism, many great figures defended Dawson's ideas on education, including (besides Eugene Kevane and Frank O'Malley, already mentioned) philosopher Frederick Wilhelmsen (1923–1996), intellectual historian Philip Gleason, philosopher Leo Ward (1893–1984), poet and college president Sister M. Madeleva Wolff (1887–1964), historian and educator Bruno Schlesinger, and others.[93] Madeleva and Schlesinger took up Dawson's ideas to create the first actual program in 1956 inspired by the Dawson Plan—called the "Christian Culture Program"—at St. Mary's College in Notre Dame, Indiana. This was a college for women founded in 1844 by the Sisters of the Holy Cross. The achievement of Madeleva and Schlesinger showed for the first time that Dawson's proposal could serve as the basis for a highly popular undergraduate education.

As president of St. Mary's from 1934 to 1961 and author of numerous books, Madeleva exerted considerable influence on Catholic education in the United States. She was a dynamic speaker and writer and a highly cultured woman who reviewed manuscripts by theologian Thomas Merton (1915–1968) before publication, discussed teaching and writing with C. S. Lewis, corresponded with John F. Kennedy (1917–1963), and formed a friendship with actress Helen Hayes (1900–1993). Her many correspondents included Christopher Dawson.

She set out to make St. Mary's a center of Christian culture. The Second World War helped, for, as during the First World War, Americans encountered European culture in the midst of the conflict. Political and religious exiles visited or stayed to teach at St. Mary's, and Madeleva listened and learned from each one. She set about encouraging a culture of beauty on campus through art, music, drama, poetry, architecture, and landscaping. She reformed the curriculum along the

---

93. Frederick D. Wilhelmsen, "Christian Culture," *Commonweal*, March 4, 1955, 583–84; Frederick D. Wilhelmsen, "The Vision of Christopher Dawson," *Commonweal*, January 5, 1958, 355–58; Philip Gleason, "A Practical Experiment in Education: The Study of Christian Culture as the Core of the College Curriculum," *The Chesterton Review* 9, no. 2 (1983): 167–71; Ward, "Dawson on Education in Christian Culture"; O'Malley, "The Culture of the Church," 131–54; Kevane, "Christopher Dawson and Study of Christian Culture," 447–62; and Bruno Schlesinger, "Responses to Dawson's Ideas in the United States," *The Chesterton Review* 9, no. 2 (1983): 171–76.

lines of the medieval Trivium. Freshmen learned correct thinking and writing through the study of literature, composition, and logic.

The ideal of the college as a center of Christian culture gained further clarity with the hiring in 1945 of the young Austrian immigrant and Jewish convert Bruno Schlesinger, then completing his doctoral dissertation on Christopher Dawson at the University of Notre Dame. The culture of Saint Mary's through the 1980s emphasized teaching over scholarship, and Schlesinger was a master teacher. A true Renaissance man, with abiding interests in music, art, philosophy, and history—all connected to a deep, personal faith, Schlesinger embodied the humanities on campus.

Schlesinger proposed the Christian Culture program based on Dawson's ideas that would substitute for the traditional history major. For years, however, it lay quietly on the desk of Sister Maria Renata, head of the history department (she served as president after Madeleva), who opposed it with silence, concerned that it would adversely affect her program. For her part, Madeleva delayed acting against the wishes of a member of her own community. Opposition to the Dawson Plan at the national level was reflected at the local level at St. Mary's: it was a profound challenge to the status quo.

Madeleva was a visionary, however. After intense internal negotiation at St Mary's, Schlesinger credited Dawson's publisher Frank Sheed (1897–1982) with convincing her to move on the idea. Madeleva's own love of medieval culture attracted her to it, too, so she authorized the program as an interdisciplinary major entirely separate from the history department to begin in the fall of 1956. She approved Dawson as adviser to the program, and—after Dawson's move to Harvard in 1958—Schlesinger would consult him during the summers. The program integrated art, literature, history, theology, and philosophy, and was unique among contemporary programs in General Education tried at such universities as Columbia, Princeton, Harvard, and Yale, for it was the only one to examine a civilization from the Christian perspective.

In time, the program became a crown jewel of the institution, supported and enriched by the wider sacramental culture of the institution that Madeleva fostered, and Schlesinger guided the program for decades. Asked why he had stayed at St. Mary's so many years, Schlesinger highlighted a pleasant work environment, congenial colleagues, and "an atmosphere of absolute independence" to develop Dawson's program. "Nobody ever interfered with my work," he said. Best of all, enthusiastic, cooperative, good-humored, and intelligent students helped translate a paper model into living reality. In 1965, however, he changed the name of the program from "Christian Culture" to "Humanistic Studies" because students increasingly interpreted "Christian culture" as romanticizing the past or only about religion. By the late 1970s, new faculty joined the still-popular program, though some of the original vision had disappeared.[94] Bruno taught until 2005, but by then the program had become something very different from the early decades—much to the chagrin of many alumnae who complained to school administrators about the loss of Dawson's vision in its structure.[95]

Nevertheless, in its early days, the Christian Culture program was an integrated curriculum for students at the upper level of the college that could function as a double-major—rather than as a full, four-year curriculum as Dawson had originally envisioned. Electives from other

94. Gail P. Mandell, *Madeleva: A Biography* (Albany: State University of New York Press, 1997), 169, 174–75; Nancy Fallon, "A Talk with Professor Bruno Schlesinger," in *Bruno Schlesinger: A Life in Learning & Letters*, ed. Rick Regan (Lulu.com, 2013), 68. In addition, with the name change to Humanistic Studies in 1965, Schlesinger extensively revised the curriculum in response to a less and less "Catholic" student body. Gail Porter Mandell, who took the endowed Bruno P. Schlesinger Chair in Humanistic Studies after him, wrote to me by email (June 4, 2017): "By the time I joined the program [1978], he had dropped many of the texts he had used in the early days, including those by Dawson (many of which had gone out of print), Southern, and Huizinga, because 'students were no longer up to reading them.' He had dropped the course on 'Early Christian Writers' and almost all of the readings from the fathers of the early church, including 'The Confessions,' and pared back the medieval section of the course to one semester. 'Church, State and Society' [was] gone, as was 'Christianity and American Culture.' Bruno wove the 'Dawsonian' thread through his cultural history courses, he told me, and I believed him then and still do, but to be honest, when younger historians joined the program (including a medievalist), he discouraged them from using any of Dawson's texts as too difficult and refused to let any of us sit in on his classes, to see how he worked his magic. . . . I don't think he lost faith in Dawson's ideas or the educational approach that they spawned, but I do think he may have concluded that passing them on in an increasingly secularized culture (including that at Saint Mary's) was something only he could do." Schlesinger—insecure about his written English—did not write much or leave behind papers. His memory is kept alive by those who knew him, and I am so grateful to Gail Mandell for her personal communication with me about Schlesinger and the program. As of spring 2021, the Humanistic Studies department has produced 1,063 graduates since 1953.

95. Mary Schlesinger to Joseph Stuart, email, April 23, 2020. Mary is Bruno's eldest daughter. In protest against colleagues and administrators excluding Dawson from the curriculum while continuing to claim title to his legacy, Schlesinger absented himself from fiftieth anniversary celebrations in 2006.

departments could count toward a Christian culture degree. Designed
to counter the fragmentation of knowledge that Dawson viewed as
both the result and the cause of specialization and secularization, it
focused on Western civilization from an interdisciplinary perspective,
with Christianity as the core influence, and it included three-credit sequence courses (taught by Schlesinger), two-credit weekly colloquia
(taught by guest lecturers), and two-credit specialty courses (taught in
other departments).[96]

The program proved Dawson's ideas on education could work in
practice, and students loved it. "I think this is the course [of study] you
learn to live life with," one student from a small Illinois coal-mining
town said. Recalling her time in the program fifty years later, Ann Harris Mohun (class of '58) wrote, "I was in the first class and loved the
program dearly. It was, for me, an astonishing academic adventure."
Dawson's works provided the foundation and organizing principle
to focus on the "effect of Christianity on the formation and growth of
Western civilization and its culture," she wrote. But it was not the program on its own that the students cherished; they loved the man who
embodied it. Schlesinger was a master teacher (unlike Dawson). He did

96. Juniors took "Christianity and Culture I: The Making of Europe" as their first sequence
course in the fall semester. This corresponded to a colloquium in which a visiting lecturer presented on a topic ranging from art and literature to the Christian classics from the period under
consideration—in this case, the period of the making of Europe. With Schlesinger present, for the
sake of continuity, students then discussed the lecture, its historical implications, and especially
its significance for the present. Spring-semester juniors took "Christianity and Culture II: Medieval Christendom," followed by "Christianity and Culture III: The Age of Religious Division" and
"Christianity and Culture IV: The Age of Revolutions and World Wars."

Specialty courses also paralleled the sequence courses—so "Early Christian Writers," for
instance, also listed as THE 125, could be taken alongside first semester study of the making of
Europe and Colloquium I. Other special topics courses included "Church, State and Society"
and—as Dawson had recommended—"Christianity and American Culture."

A group of scholars at St. Mary's and Notre Dame taught the colloquia. Grant money helped
create an annual Christian Culture Lecture that brought in distinguished scholars such as Dawson himself, the historian of religion Mircea Eliade (1907–1986), and the historian of theology
Jaroslav Pelikan (1923–2006). See M. Loretta Petit, "Sister M. Madeleva Wolff, C.S.C.," *Catholic Education: A Journal of Inquiry and Practice* 9, no. 3 (March 2006): 326–27; Bruce Cook, "An Answer
for Colleges: The St. Mary's Program," *U.S. Catholic*, November 1965, 25–31. For other accounts of
the St. Mary's program, see Gleason, "A Practical Experiment in Education: The Study of Christian
Culture as the Core of the College Curriculum," 167–71; John Gleason, "The Study of Christian
Culture: A New Approach to General Education," *Educational Record* 40, no. 1 (1959): 155–58. For a
list of courses in the program, see STA, box 2a, *Christian Culture: An Interdepartmental Program
for the Junior and Senior Year* (pamphlet).

not take an encyclopedic approach in his teaching; instead, he took a wide and "popular" approach, in the best sense, as Dawson had recommended. Schlesinger focused on the study of institutions and trends in thought—on culture in the broadest sense, always connecting historical themes to the present. He initiated students into the excitement and wonder of the intellectual life. Gail Porter Mandell, who took the endowed Bruno P. Schlesinger Chair in Humanistic Studies after him, wrote that, "His Socratic method, requiring mental discipline and close attention from students, his keen sense of what he called the 'unifying threads' of culture as well as the 'big picture' of history, his flair for drama, his masterly storytelling, his Puck-ish sense of humor—all that, plus his great personal charm, ensured that students did not forget him nor what he taught them." Schlesinger embodied Christian culture for his students and showed how it initiated them into a great living tradition helping to make sense of the present, as Dawson suggested it would.[97]

Forgetting Dawson

In the end, beyond the classicists, the specialists, and the confused appeals to Newman, and even beyond the religious idealism and cultureless Catholic mentality inspiring resistance to Dawson, may have lurked an academic elitism that simply rejected a "gentleman scholar" with only an Oxford undergraduate degree. Dawson lacked academic credentials. He was shy, self-effacing, and stammered. A polite but superficial engagement by his education critics resulted in failure to really grapple with Dawson's cultural mind.[98]

Lawler and others did not appreciate how Dawson related the two traditions of meaning behind the English word "culture," depending on

97. Cook, "An Answer for Colleges: The St. Mary's Program," 31; Ann Harris Mohun, letter to Prof. Philip Hicks, undated but probably from the summer of 2006. A copy of this letter was sent to me by Mary Schlesinger; Gail P. Mandell, "Reflections on Bruno Schlesinger," in *Bruno Schlesinger: A Life in Learning & Letters*, 73.

98. Gail P. Mandel to Joseph Stuart email, June 4, 2017. Mandell wrote to me that once, during conversations with Schlesinger and Dawson's daughter, Christina Scott, both agreed Dawson's lack of credentials and the fact that his ideas were co-opted by the Catholic "right" (traditionalists) prevented widespread acceptance of his educational ideas in the United States.

context. The etymologies of the word "culture" sometimes intertwined: "The higher the culture, the more important are its intellectual and spiritual elements, so that the two uses of the word *culture* become almost indistinguishable; i.e., classical culture in the humanist sense is a part of the study of Graeco-Roman culture in the sociological or anthropological sense," Dawson wrote. "This no doubt produces great complications, but then the study of higher cultures is inevitably a complicated matter," he concluded.[99] An authentic cultural education connects both socio-historical and humanistic traditions within a normative worldview, thus bridging different kinds of truth. In this way, Dawson's idea of culture directed students and readers toward unity and differentiation without treating Christianity as a unitary ideology or fragmenting it into isolated specialisms.

Boundary thinking about overlapping cultural identities and traditions *could* have helped American Catholics navigate assimilation into the American way of life with greater sociological sophistication and discernment. Undermined by sociological change that increasingly made Christian culture unthinkable, however, critics misunderstood Dawson and then forgot him.

Dawson recognized that radical reform of Christian education might not happen in his lifetime—"for education institutions and curricula are very resistant to change," he wrote.[100] He was right. Not only were his educational ideas about Christian culture neglected, but his entire legacy was submerged for more than two decades after his death in 1970.

What happened? Various explanations have been advanced: the shift in Catholic sensibilities away from tradition after the Second Vatican Council, the move away from broad historical study toward microhistory, the unpopularity (at least in Great Britain) of literary and artistic sources for historical writing, and the fact that Dawson never really fit into an academic department and so could be written off as not belonging anywhere.[101] The sociologists thought of him as an his-

---

99. Dawson, *The Crisis of Western Education*, 114.

100. Dawson, "Christian Culture: Its Meaning and its Value," *Jubilee*, May 1956, 38.

101. E. I. Watkin, "Tribute to Christopher Dawson," *Tablet*, October 4, 1969; Patrick Allitt, *Catholic Converts: British and American Intellectuals Turn to Rome* (Ithaca, N.Y.: Cornell University

torian, while the historians thought of him as a sociologist, his Harvard colleagues wrote.[102] Dawson's lifelong friend E. I. Watkin surmised in 1969 that even those who had once praised Dawson forgot him because they turned away toward religious and cultural avant-gardism, "without the least regard for the 'historical institutional' element in religion and concerned only to establish an impossible order of universal material well-being. Such men are remote from everything for which Dawson stands."[103] As a result, his work was almost completely forgotten until rediscovered around 1990.

Press, 1997), 271–72; Stratford Caldecott and John Morrill, eds., *Eternity in Time: Christopher Dawson and the Catholic Idea of History* (Edinburgh: T&T Clark, 1997), 2; and Scott, *A Historian and His World*, 213.

102. Daniel Callahan et al., "Christopher Dawson: 12 October 1889–25 May 1970," *Harvard Theological Review* LXVI, no. 2 (1973): 168.

103. Watkin, "Tribute to Christopher Dawson," 974.

Conclusion

Recovery of a Cultural Mind

The study of culture shows the same process at work in history that may be seen in detail in the lives of men.

—Christopher Dawson

Twenty years or so after his death in 1970, Christopher Dawson's work was rediscovered for the same reasons it was lost: changes in Catholicism and in historiography. The rediscovery happened through the republication of his books,[1] as well as articles[2] and dissertations[3] about him. There was an effort to mark the centenary of his birth,[4] a release of his first biography in an American edition,[5] and a conference bringing together the first generation of Dawson scholars.[6] New edu-

---

Dawson, "Christian Culture: Its Meaning and Its Value," 40.

1. While a few earlier republications did appear, *The Crisis of Western Education* came out in 1989 by Franciscan University Press, *Religion and the Rise of Western Culture* in 1991 by Image Books, and *Progress and Religion* in 1991 by Sherwood Sugden.

2. Hittinger, "Christopher Dawson: A View from the Social Sciences," 31–47; James Gaston, "Understanding Europe: Christopher Dawson's Vision of the Unity and History of Europe," *European Studies Journal* (1992): 161–64; James Hitchcock, "Christopher Dawson," *The American Scholar* 62, no. 1 (Winter 1993): 111–18; and Paul Costello, *World Historians and Their Goals: Twentieth-Century Answers to Modernism* (DeKalb: Northern Illinois University Press, 1993), ch. 6.

3. The first dissertations on Dawson since his death included Cesar Corcuera Garcia, "Religion and Culture in Christopher Dawson" (PhD diss., Universidad de Navarra, 1990); Joan E. Keating, "Roman Catholics, Christian Democracy and the British Labour Movement, 1910–1960" (PhD diss., University of Manchester, 1992); and Adam Schwartz, "The Third Spring" (PhD diss., Northwestern University, 1996 [published in 2005]).

4. John J. Mulloy gave a lecture at the Franciscan University of Steubenville in 1989 marking the centenary of Dawson's birth. Mulloy's prediction that "the future flourishing of Dawson's influence will probably be in America rather than in Great Britain" has proven correct. See John J. Mulloy, "The Influence of America on Christopher Dawson," *The Wanderer*, November 23, 1989, 6.

5. Scott, *A Historian and His World*. St. Mary's College awarded Christina Scott, daughter of Christopher Dawson, an honorary doctorate in 1993 for this biography and for her work as literary executor.

6. The Wethersfield Institute sponsored a Dawson conference in New York City on October 15,

cational programs inspired by his work appeared. The literary scholar R. V. Young praised the republication of Dawson's *Crisis of Western Education* in 1989 as "more likely to find responsive readers and make a substantial impact now than when it was first issued in 1961." Two years later, the controversial Rembert Weakland, Archbishop of Milwaukee, wrote how Dawson's work remained "a classic" in the area of cultural analysis. Historian James Hitchcock noted, also in the early 1990s, how Dawson was ahead of his time in calling for a marriage of history and the social sciences, including anthropology, "showing in his own work how it might in fact be accomplished."[7]

If changes in Catholicism and in the culture of history writing during the 1970s and 1980s obscured Dawson's legacy, changes in those same areas uncovered it after 1990. Examining both in turn will reveal why Dawson is still read in the twenty-first century and the importance of further recovering his cultural mind.

Catholicism and Culture in the Age of Pope John Paul II

The Second Vatican Council marked the end of the "Constantinian epoch," papal biographer George Weigel wrote, when the Catholic Church possessed a state and an army and supported specific political parties. After that watershed event, John Paul II (who reigned from 1978 to 2005) shifted from a "church of power" model to a "church of culture." Church leaders still operated certain levers of diplomacy and political influence, naturally, but emphasis changed. As a poet and philosopher, John Paul established the Pontifical Council for Culture in 1982, and he left rich contributions to intellectuals, scientists, and artists. Those close to the pope remembered how he loved to repeat the phrase: "Faith must become culture." One of his great legacies, in fact, was pointing to "a more profound way of understanding the rapport

1993, that brought together some first-generation Dawson scholars, including philosopher Joseph Koterski, literary scholar Robert V. Young, historian James Hitchcock, philosopher Russell Hittinger, and historian Glenn Olsen. See *Christianity and Western Civilization: Christopher Dawson's Insights* (San Francisco: Ignatius, 1995).

7. R. V. Young, "The Continuing Crisis," in *The Crisis of Western Education* (Steubenville, Ohio: Franciscan University Press, 1989), ix; Rembert G. Weakland, foreword, in *Religion and the Rise of Western Culture* (1950; New York: Image, 1991), i; and Hitchcock, "Christopher Dawson," 111.

between faith and culture."[8] He did this through both his actions[9] and his writings, and these efforts set a tone favorable for recovering Dawson's work after 1990.

For example, John Paul's concern for culture pervaded his apostolic constitution *Ex corde Ecclesiae* (*From the Heart of the Church*) (1990). The document regarded the mission and religious identity of Catholic colleges and universities, and its title referred to the fact that the first universities were born "from the heart of the Church," as at Bologna, Paris, and Oxford. It was read in the United States as a criticism of the way Catholic institutions there had assimilated to the wider culture of American higher education during the previous decades. In the face of powerful cultural trends away from institutional religious identity, *Ex corde Ecclesiae* "altered the conversation" about Catholic higher education and offered a rich vision of enculturation akin to Dawson's.[10] In ways consistent with its nature as a university, a Catholic university should not be afraid to give institutional witness to Christ and contribute to the church's work of evangelization. Accordingly, new college-level, Christian-culture type programs appeared,[11] partly

8. George Weigel, "John Paul II and the Priority of Culture," *First Things*, February 1998, 12, https://www.firstthings.com/article/1998/02/001-john-paul-ii-and-the-priority-of-culture; Joaquin Navarro-Valls, "Faith Must Become Culture: John Paul II's Legacy to Intellectuals and Scientists," 2011, http://inters.org/faith-must-become-culture.

9. Historians recognize that John Paul played an important role in the peaceful collapse of communism in western Eurasia from 1989 to 1991. The pope showed how culture trumped politics by his actions in Poland during the preceding decade, preaching there courageously and inspiring heroic, collective action. He "was an intellectual with deep convictions about the integrity and power of popular piety and the traditions of Polish culture," George Weigel wrote. See George Weigel, *The End and the Beginning: Pope John Paul II—The Victory of Freedom, the Last Years, the Legacy* (New York: Doubleday, 2010), 186; Paul Kengor, *A Pope and a President: John Paul II, Ronald Reagan, and the Extraordinary Untold Story of the 20th Century* (Wilmington, Del.: ISI Books, 2017).

10. Jason King, "After *Ex corde Ecclesiae*," *Journal of Moral Theology* 4, no. 2 (2015): 168, 173.

11. The Humanities and Catholic Culture program (HCC) started in 1990 at Franciscan University of Steubenville and Catholic Studies started in 1993 at the University of St. Thomas in St. Paul, Minnesota. James Gaston, Stephen Krason, and Michael Healy started HCC with the goal of teaching key themes found in Dawson's work. Gaston provided the vision and administration of the program, and in an interview said Dawson pioneered certain ideas about how to integrate learning in a way no one else had ever brought together. "Culture is not only in the ancient world or in foreign lands," Gaston said; "we must also apply anthropological insights to our own modern culture. Culture is real and it is *in me*. Dawson's focus on the Incarnation of Jesus Christ and its implications is the key" (phone interview, August 1, 2021). I had the privilege of studying in the HCC program (from 1998 to 2001) under James Gaston. This profoundly shaped me, and thus this book. Gaston brought Dawson's insights to bear on the subject of religion and culture throughout his teaching and writing; see, for example, James Gaston, "Catholic Culture: What Is It and Why

Conclusion

inspired by Dawson's work and the same evangelistic spirit of renewal found in *Ex corde Ecclesiae*. "What is needed," Dawson wrote in 1956, "is nothing less than a radical reform of Christian education: an intellectual revolution which will restore the internal unity of Christian culture."[12] It was something like this the author of this document seemed to have in mind.

Ex corde Ecclesiae used the word "culture" fifty-seven times and also the phrase "Christian culture" to convey the vital role institutions of higher learning play in the dialog between the church and the modern world and in forming students. The dual usages of the culture idea (the socio-historical and the humanistic views) pervade the document, as they do Dawson's work. For example, "the dialogue of the Church with the cultures of our times" (plural—socio-historical) is juxtaposed with: "There is only one culture: that of man, by man and for man" (singular—humanistic).[13] The complexity of culture demanded these two perspectives, for there is something particular and local about it, and at the same time something universal based on a common humanity. As demonstrated in the previous chapters, Dawson's cultural mind coordinated these two modes according to the four rules of his interdisciplinary logic.

The complexity of culture demands interdisciplinary approaches, and all during the 1990s, scholars in Britain and America demanded these due to growing dissatisfaction with purely disciplinary knowledge. The separation of fields reinforced the isolation of science from society, faith from reason, and business from humanities. This contemporary concern is reflected in *Ex corde Ecclesiae*: "While each discipline is taught systematically and according to its own methods, interdisciplinary studies, assisted by a careful and thorough study of philosophy

Should We Care About It?" *Lay Witness*, November/December 2012, 4–8. Together, Gaston and I tried to bring a "Dawsonian" perspective to economic development in North Dakota and the Ohio River Valley: see Joseph T. Stuart and James Gaston, "Holy Oil?" *360 Review*, Fall 2015, 88–97. As of spring 2021, the HCC program has graduated about 550 majors since it began, including about forty-five students who are now Catholic priests and about forty-three who are now Catholic nuns. As Gaston told me: "It's been a stunning and incredibly rewarding career" (email September 1, 2021).

12. Dawson, "Christian Culture: Its Meaning and Its Value," 38.

13. Pope John Paul II, *Ex Corde Ecclesiae* (1990), §3, http://www.vatican.va/content/john-paul-ii/en/apost_constitutions/documents/hf_jp-ii_apc_15081990_ex-corde-ecclesiae.html.

and theology, enable students to acquire an organic vision of reality and to develop a continuing desire for intellectual progress." But the document envisioned a more radical kind of interdisciplinary thinking than offered by most contemporary critics: the challenge for the Catholic university was to unite "by intellectual effort" two orders of reality: human knowledge and divine revelation. This effort involved the integration of knowledge while respecting the proper autonomy, integrity, and methods of each discipline. A "vital interaction" of two distinct levels of truth leads to a more comprehensive understanding of what it means to be human, the document noted.[14]

As we have seen, Dawson's model of interdisciplinary and even transdisciplinary thinking, involving his four rules of cultural mind, demonstrated just such an "intellectual effort" bringing together the "vital interaction" of spiritual and physical reality called for in John Paul's document. Some of Dawson's contemporary critics, however, denounced his efforts to do this. In a review of *Dynamics of World History* for the *Journal of Modern History*, the world historian William H. McNeill (1917–2016) admitted Dawson was "occasionally brilliant" but added that "Dawson the sociologist and Dawson the Catholic often seem to speak a rather different language." "As a sociologist, for example," McNeill continued, "he can contemplate either the 'complete secularization of Western culture' or 'the coming of a new religion' or 'the revival of the old religion with which the culture was formerly associated' as apparently equally possible courses for the future." Since Dawson believed the "sociologist is dependent on the data furnished by theology or the science of religion," it "seems that Dawson the Catholic, armed with 'the science of religion,' should have no difficulty in coming to the rescue of Dawson the sociologist and deciding which of his three choices for the future is the only possible one."[15] This was a problem of "intellectual jurisdiction," McNeill wrote. Both sociology and theology claim a certain universality; "Can a man keep a foot in both camps, as Dawson does, without intellectual inconsistency? And, if so, on what principle does one draw the line, beyond which the one or the other

---

14. Pope John Paul II, *Ex Corde Ecclesiae* (1990), §1, 16–17, 20.

15. William H. McNeill, review of *Dynamics of World History*, *Journal of Modern History* XXIX (1957): 257, 258.

discipline may not exercise jurisdiction. This Dawson never makes clear," he concluded.[16] The classical scholar Peter Morris Green agreed with McNeill about Dawson's supposed dualism:

One can speak without inconsistency of the two halves of Mr. Dawson's mind, since he so frequently declares that the two aspects of human culture they represent must, somehow, be combined, yet seldom achieves a wholly satisfactory synthesis in the event. This gives a subtly schizoid quality to some of his best work. "What we need," he writes, "is a scientific sociology which . . . must recognize at once the determination of natural conditions and the freedom of spiritual forces, and must show how the social process embraces both these factors in a vital union like that of the human organism." Is such an ideal . . . possible even on its own terms? It seems doubtful.[17]

Both critics discounted Dawson's boundary thinking and the metaphysical line he drew between the objects of knowledge in sociology and theology. It seemed to them Dawson's religious and sociological sides either conflicted or failed to integrate. His was a false intellectual architecture because it either (1) violated boundary thinking by suffocating his social science in his Catholicism, or (2) violated intellectual bridges by only pretending sociology connects to theology.

Another way to look at the "two halves of Mr. Dawson's mind," however, and the problem of "intellectual jurisdiction," would be to see in his bifurcated view of reality a crucial metaphysical distinction between materiality and spirituality. Each side required different methods to understand it. Dawson's was no simplistic dualism, however. If theology and philosophy could directly access unseen reality, then psychology, history, and the other social sciences could *indirectly point at it*. In other words, Dawson "managed to make his views of history relevant to those who were not believers simply by demonstrating religion's cultural and historical importance," Hitchcock wrote. Whether an illusion or not, religion was indubitably, as an empirical fact, the engine that has in large part propelled human societies throughout

16. McNeill, review of *Dynamics of World History*, 257–58. McNeill referred to Dawson's "Prevision in Religion" from *Dynamics of World History*, 95–107.

17. Peter Morris Green, "God and History," review of *The Dynamics of World History*, Times Literary Supplement, Dec. 27, 1957, 782.

world history. Dawson gently gestured at spiritual reality using empirical methods—the facts of the social sciences. He attempted to cross McNeill's and Green's dualistic divide not directly but in the good manner of English reserve. He tried "to say matter in terms of spirit," as the poet Robert Frost (1874–1963) once said, "or spirit in terms of matter, to make the final unity. That is the greatest attempt that ever failed. We stop just short there. But it is the height of poetry, the height of all thinking."[18] That was the point of Dawson's cultural mind: the attempt to reach for the whole as an interpenetrating reality, to create imperfectly an extensive intellectual architecture while trying to respect the boundaries of disciplines.

Dawson utilized the rules of his cultural mind as a kind of logic of interdisciplinarity to both understand and communicate incarnational reality to a wide audience. Perhaps Dawson's most stimulating quality, even his critic Green acknowledged, was "ranging freely through a whole complex of allied disciplines, correlating them into a living whole." He was "never for a moment unaware of the immense, unquenchable variety of human life and human experience." McNeill stated that while "explicit affirmation of a theological faith is relatively rare among historians today," this "introduces a distinctive . . . note into Dawson's work."[19]

In Dawson's cultural mind, there was space for the meeting of very different kinds of minds, and his ecumenism built bridges. His subtle evangelization *through his research*, as *Ex corde Ecclesiae* later encouraged, sought to meet modern people where they are at. His "apostolate of study" (quoted in chapter 1) often put explicitly Catholic values in the background because he knew empirical findings hold much greater sway than theology and philosophy to the modern mind. Thus, as one commentator on *Ex corde Ecclesiae* noted, there is a need to develop methodologies and research programs in the social sciences congruent with the philosophical assumptions about the person defended by the magisterium. This "smart evangelization" could involve both critique of assumptions motivating existing social science research and investi-

18. Robert Frost, "Education by Poetry," 1931, http://moodyap.pbworks.com/f/frost.Education ByPoetry.pdf.

19. Green, "God and History," 782; McNeill, review of *Dynamics of World History*, 257.

gation into human actions conducive to authentic human flourishing. History may be one of the best areas for the encounter between modern people and religion to take place, historian Wilfred McClay wrote, because no one is required to accept or reject any particular truth claim. One can simply appreciate the profound importance of religion in history and culture, bridging between believers and unbelievers.[20]

As an historian, Dawson's engagement with the social sciences represented an important moment in the Catholic intellectual tradition, dominated as it is by excellence in literature, philosophy, and theology—from G. K. Chesterton to Jacques Maritain and Hans Urs von Balthasar (1905–1988). The "Catholic Renaissance" represented by these figures, however, was an "incomplete intellectual response to modernity," Hittinger wrote. Catholics failed to deal with the sociological point of view. This was where Dawson stood almost alone. In notes for a 1934 lecture he typed (as quoted in chapter 2): "Need for Catholic study of sociology, since the main assault on Christianity has based itself on sociological theories (Rousseau, Comte, Marx and others)." Dawson's engagement with the social sciences gained him respect outside the world of Christian scholarship. "Today," Hittinger wrote in 1991, "any prospect for another renaissance of Catholic thought will require a more direct reckoning with the social sciences—both for their diagnostic power and for the reminder that all the important things have sociological feet."[21]

Dawson and the Renewal of Christian Education

Inspired by Dawson, *Ex corde Ecclesiae*, and John Henry Newman and other figures of the Catholic Renaissance largely forgotten during the baby-boomer generation, a small group of faculty members at the University of St. Thomas in St. Paul, Minnesota, decided to do something about the formation of undergraduate students in the early 1990s. Spurred by a failed attempt to better integrate the core curriculum at

20. Brian Simboli, "*Ex corde Ecclesiae*, Social Science, and the Public Square," *The Catholic Social Science Review* 17, no. 1 (2012): 323, 324; Wilfred M. McClay, "Teaching Religion in American Schools and Colleges: Some Thoughts for the 21st Century," *Historically Speaking* 3, no. 2 (2001): 17.

21. Hittinger, "Christopher Dawson: A View from the Social Sciences," 33, 46.

St. Thomas, they formed the first Catholic Studies program. This has since become the model for dozens of other programs around the country and the world. They also created the Center for Catholic Studies to advance "conversation about the historical and contemporary implications of the impact of the Incarnation of Christ on thought and culture."[22]

Don J. Briel,[23] theologian and educational pioneer, emerged as the central figure inaugurating the interdisciplinary Catholic Studies program and the Center for Catholic Studies. He lamented that only fragments of knowledge pervaded university systems in specialized disciplines, while few opportunities existed to bring them together into a meaningful whole. He and his colleagues wanted to form students in a habit of mind to see things in relationship to each other. They could then better make sound judgments amid the contemporary world.

George Weigel noted that Briel's inauguration of this program was one of the most significant events in the history of Catholic higher education in America since the Second World War. That was because Briel reconceived the relationship between university and church in ways mutually reinforcing faith and reason in the proclamation of the Gospel. Briel's two "intellectual heroes"—John Henry Newman and Christopher Dawson—helped him do it. Like them, "Briel took what was best in Enlightenment and post-Enlightenment thought, and then married it to the perennial truths he had found in the biblical, classical, and medieval worlds."[24] Having written his doctoral dissertation on Newman, Briel took from him the need for a community of learning within the university oriented toward personal formation. Dawson offered a "depth to Catholic Studies' interdisciplinary approach to Catholicism," R. Jared Staudt wrote, "with his articulation of an organic study of Christian culture in all of its dimensions." Thus, Briel's work, Weigel noted, "aimed at nothing less than creating, in 21st century cir-

22. Center for Catholic Studies, https://www.stthomas.edu/cathstudies/ (accessed April 6, 2020); R. Jared Staudt, introduction, in *The University and the Church: Don J. Briel's Essays on Education*, ed. R. Jared Staudt (Providence, R.I.: Cluny Media, 2019), xix–xxxv. As of spring 2021, the Catholic Studies program at St. Thomas counted 1,500 graduates, including 165 priests and six religious.
23. "Don Briel: A Life of Purpose and Joy," https://www.youtube.com/watch?v=Xz7qiSeElSc.
24. George Weigel, foreword, in *The University and the Church*, i.

cumstances, the 'idea of a university' that animated" these two English-men.[25] To forward that goal, Briel oversaw the acquisition of the Christopher Dawson Collection in 1998, including Dawson's personal library of nearly five thousand volumes, manuscripts, and public correspondence. He also served as general editor for the republication project of Dawson's works at the Catholic University of American Press from 2001 until his death in 2018.

Many factors contributed to Briel's work, but Dawson aided his cultural diagnosis of the contemporary situation to which his Catholic Studies project tried to respond in creative ways. The "technological culture" of the modern world instrumentalized life without a spiritual foundation and thus fragmented disciplines. Students found themselves immersed in the "unitary culture" of the secular world, little realizing the existence of other ways of life, Briel diagnosed, drawing from Dawson.[26] Students could gain a newfound sense of the cultural relativity of modern (American) culture by travel—hence the Bernardi Campus in Rome inaugurated by Briel in 2000. Or they could gain it by studying historical Christian cultures as coherent ways of life through theology, philosophy, music, art, literature, society, and institutions—viewed together, and viewed as interacting with pre-, non-, and post-Christian cultures, as Dawson modeled. Understanding the culture-process, students might then negotiate a bicultural identity if they chose—"modern" *and* "Christian." Implicitly, Catholic Studies sought to form students with cultural minds they could then apply to their own lives and contexts, to experience life "forming new wholes."[27]

The "true revolutionary" in American Catholic higher education in recent decades was Don Briel, Weigel concluded, for he "enlivened an approach to higher education and the New Evangelization as no one else has done."[28] Dawson helped him do it.

25. Staudt, introduction, in *The University and the Church*, xxvii; George Weigel, foreword, in *Renewal of Catholic Higher Education: Essays on Catholic Studies in Honor of Don J. Briel*, ed. Matthew T. Gerlach (Bismarck, N.D.: University of Mary Press, 2017), 2.

26. Don J. Briel, "The University Needs the Church," in *The University and the Church*, 104; Don Briel, "Renewing the University in a Tragic Culture," in *The University and the Church*, 125.

27. Don J. Briel, "Catholic Studies at the University of St. Thomas," in *The University and the Church*, 168; Don J. Briel, "A Reflection on Catholic Studies after Twenty Years," in *The University and the Church*, 220, 221.

28. Weigel, foreword, in *Renewal of Catholic Higher Education*, 2.

Another example of how Dawson's cultural mind has inspired educational renewal in the spirit of *Ex corde Ecclesiae* comes from twenty-first-century Australia. Australian culture—in its Western variety, as distinct from its aboriginal cultures—was secular from the beginning. It was unlike the United States in this regard, and religious people had to adapt. The Catholics there developed a major system of their own primary and secondary schools, as in the United States, but no Catholic universities until the early 1990s. That lack may have spared Australian Catholics "from the ideological and 'identity' disputes that plagued Catholic higher education in the States in the 1960s and later," one commentator noted.[29] Dawson's ideas were able to percolate without the resistance they experienced in the United States. Their spread eventually led to several initiatives across the country and in nearby Tasmania.[30]

One of them is Campion College, founded near Sydney in 2006 as Australia's first liberal arts college. Two major influences there included American institutional models and the "seminal importance" of Dawson's work, Karl Schmude wrote. Schmude is not only a biographer of Dawson but a Founding Fellow of Campion College whose vision guided implementation. In his *Campion Book: The Ideal of a Liberal Arts Education in the Light of Faith and Reason*, it is possible to see how Dawson influenced the college. Just as for Briel, Dawson provided Schmude with cultural diagnosis and inspiration toward creative response.[31]

As a young man in the late 1960s, Schmude delved into Dawson's *Crisis of Western Education*. He was "immediately captivated by Dawson's understanding of culture and the centrality of education as the transmitter of culture," he wrote. Only through the medium of culture can faith spread to embrace a whole people, "rather than simply a devout elite," he noted. "I was struck by Dawson's insight that, if ordinary people do not develop an appreciation of Christian culture, the Chris-

29. Karl Schmude to Joseph Stuart, email January 10, 2020.
30. See fn. 8 in the introduction.
31. Karl Schmude, *Christopher Dawson: A Biographical Introduction* (Hobart, Tasmania: Christopher Dawson Centre for Cultural Studies, 2014); Karl Schmude, *The Campion Book: The Ideal of a Liberal Arts Education in the Light of Faith and Reason* (Sydney: Campion College, 2014), 4, https://www.campion.edu.au/about-campion/.

tian way of life through its various expressions over time, they would largely surrender their distinctive identity in the face of a pervasively secularist society," Schmude commented. A Catholic educational response to these cultural conditions was needed. The most exciting part of *Crisis*, Schmude recalled, was the outline of courses John J. Mulloy provided at the end of the first edition (reprinted in appendix E). "These represented a clear and concrete form of Dawson's ideas."[32]

The movement to start a new liberal arts college in Australia gathered support during the 1990s. Then, a refurbished seminary opened its doors as Campion College in 2006, with Mulloy's interpretation of the Dawson Plan serving as a foundation for the interdisciplinary curriculum in history, literature, philosophy, and theology. "Christian culture" was the unifying principle and synthetic object of study. While trying to avoid sectarianism, triumphalism, and defensiveness, the mission of Campion in its founding document was to cultivate a "cultural perspective"—like what I call "cultural mind"—in students to leaven the wider secular culture as future leaders.[33]

In these ways, changes in Catholicism after 1990 aided the process of recovering Dawson's ideas. Dawson helped inspire the kinds of educational reform called for by *Ex corde Ecclesiae*, even if the Catholic Studies movement sometimes lacks the historical and intellectually ecumenical orientation of Dawson's original plan for the study of Christian culture schematized in chapter 8.

Dawson and the Possibilities of Cultural History

Besides changes within Catholicism during the 1990s bringing greater attention to culture and education and thus to Dawson's work, the "cultural turn" on the historiographical landscape of the decade also made his work compelling again. The preceding arguments in this book demonstrated how a fruitful approach to Dawson's achievement and his relevance consists in studying the underlying logic by which he

32. Karl Schmude to Joseph Stuart, email December 24, 2016.

33. Schmude, *The Campion Book*, 6, 9, 24. As of spring 2021, Campion College has graduated about three hundred students, including two ordained Catholic priests, four seminarians, two Benedictine monks, and four nuns (Karl Schmude to Joseph Stuart, email, September 8, 2021).

worked. I call that logic his cultural mind, which coordinated the two modes of the science of culture (the socio-historical and the humanistic) depending on the problem at hand. This involved the four rules of intellectual architecture, boundary thinking, intellectual bridges, and intellectual asceticism. The "new" cultural history flourishing in academia since 1990 offers various points of contact with Dawson's cultural mind, demonstrating his continued relevance to the historian's craft today.

The rise of cultural history was influenced by at least three intellectual currents converging after the 1970s: cultural anthropology's concern with questions of cultural meaning and identity, partly churned up by the psychological impact of globalization; the linguistic turn, showing how reality is shaped by language; and postmodernism's doubts about so-called "Enlightenment" rationalism, due to the realization that *thinking* always takes place against the background of culture. Human minds do not exist apart from time, place, and micro power-relations. Cultural history represented a change in focus away from mining facts or describing the laws of historical causation to interpretive explorations of meaning in cultures, including religious meaning. Different peoples construct the meaning of events, artifacts, and essential human questions in different ways. "This is an understanding of history that celebrates plurality within human societies and therefore embraces many different views of culture," one historian wrote.[34] In one of my own areas of interest, the cultural history of the Great War, cultural historians have tried to understand the conflict as a "whole," "to capture the spirit of an age,"[35] and to see how it mobilized, destroyed, and changed culture.[36] The "cultural turn" in many disciplines and subfields of history has made Dawson's work seem insightful once again for three reasons.

First, Dawson proposed an alliance between history and the other social sciences. Here he was more an "interpretive theorist" than

34. Alan Gordon, "Introduction: The New Cultural History and Urban History: Intersections," *Urban History Review/Revue d'histoire urbaine* 33, no. 1 (Fall 2004): 3.

35. Modris Eksteins, *Rites of Spring: The Great War and the Birth of the Modern Age* (Toronto: Lester & Orpen Dennys, 1989), xiv; Stuart, "The War to Start All Wars," 22–29.

36. Kramer, *Dynamic of Destruction;* Stuart, "North Dakota and the Cultural History of the Great War," 3–17.

Conclusion

a statistician, putting him closer to the cultural history of the 1990s than to the social history of the 1960s and 1970s. This is evident in the cultural relativism he adopted. He realized early in his career the profound significance of modern anthropology in undermining rationalism (chapter 1). As anthropologist Clifford Geertz (1926–2006) wrote, many eighteenth-century thinkers tended to view man as a "naked reasoner" who only appears as he is "when he took his cultural costumes off." By the 1920s, Geertz continued, anthropology substituted for this the "transfigured animal that appeared when he put them on." In other words, culture is the "womb" in which "virtually all of our thinking is formed," Hittinger wrote. For Dawson, what seemed "primitive" beliefs could not simply be dismissed as absurd because they were different. Rather, they possessed deep meaning within their respective cultures. Contact with the universal is made *in* and *through* culture, not by prescinding from it in a traditionless body of knowledge—a point philosopher Alasdair MacIntyre later made, as quoted in the introduction. "Dawson saw perhaps sooner than anyone else," Hitchcock noted, "how cultural relativism, in principle, undermined the supremacy of the Enlightenment by forcing modern Westerners to acknowledge their culture as merely different from those of the past, not necessarily superior."[37] Dawson's cultural relativism (as distinct from metaphysical relativism), as well as his non-Eurocentric approach to European cultures, offers a point of contact with contemporary cultural history.

Second, in his engagement with the social sciences, Dawson's cultural mind repairs conceptual incoherence surrounding the idea of culture in his day and ours. The problem, sociologist Christian Smith wrote, is that many of the best culture scholars today "define and conceptualize 'culture' in ways that make the definitions and conceptualizations of many of their fellow culture scholars impossible." Smith identified at least eleven distinct views—culture defined as human practices, as mental representations of the world, as meanings, as ideas and beliefs, as an aspect of social reality, and as a vision of reality—to

37. Hitchcock, "Christopher Dawson," 111, 112; Clifford Geertz, "The Impact of the Concept of Culture on the Concept of Man," in *The Interpretations of Cultures* (New York: Basic Books, 1973), 38; and Hittinger, "Christopher Dawson: A View from the Social Sciences," 36.

list just some of them. But an objective "practice" is a very different kind of thing than a subjective "idea" or a "belief."[38]

Sociologist Victoria E. Bonnell and historian Lyn Hunt also commented on this vagueness. Is culture "an aspect of life, like society or politics, or a way of defining a certain set of beliefs and practices?" they asked. "If it permeates every other aspect of life, ... then how can it be isolated for analysis in a meaningful way?" Indeed, sociologist Margaret S. Archer wrote, "There is no ready fund of analytical terms for designating the components of the cultural realm."[39] Few scholars agree about the basic nature of one of the foundational concepts in social science.

Dawson's simple definition of culture as a common way of life, however, and the rules of his cultural mind, help repair this problem. Because he adopted the methodological holism of anthropology (chapter 1), he refused to separate the inner life of ideas and meanings from outer actions. Therefore, cultures as whole ways of life automatically reconcile intellectualist and behaviorist perspectives—avoiding the pitfall that even great anthropologists like Clifford Geertz have fallen into by treating culture too much in terms of subjective emotions.[40] Culture constitutes *both* I (ideas, meanings, beliefs, emotions) *and* FWP (social, economic, and environmental factors, from Geddesian sociology)—as shown in chapter 2. The culture-process is the dynamic interaction of these categories, over time (chapters 3–5). Dawson's idea of culture joins the subjective to the objective realms of reality because it is centered on the human person.

In addition, while other social categories like class, race, and gender now appear fluid, Dawson's stable and universal categories I/FWP can provide a firm basis for cultural analysis. Geographer Jared Diamond, for example, in effect used FWP in his Pulitzer-Prize-winning *Guns, Germs, and Steel: The Fates of Human Societies* (1997) to explain the development of world history.[41] As quoted in chapter 2, sociologist Lewis

38. Smith, "The Conceptual Incoherence of 'Culture' in American Sociology," 400.

39. Victoria E. Bonnell and Lynn Hunt, eds., *Beyond the Cultural Turn: New Directions in the Study of Society and Culture* (Los Angeles: University of California Press, 1999), 11–12; Margaret S. Archer, *Culture and Agency: The Place of Culture in Social Theory*, rev. ed. (Cambridge: Cambridge University Press, 1996), 1.

40. Daniel L. Pals, *Seven Theories of Religion* (New York: Oxford University Press, 1996), 263.

41. Diamond called them "categories of cultural differences," not Folk, Work, and Place. Nevertheless, in effect, he utilized FWP as the structural basis of his book. Rightly criticized by McNeill for

Conclusion

Mumford noted FWP proved "highly useful as a check to keep one from leaving out data that . . . less rigorous categories might let one neglect." Dawson's innovation was to add I. Ernst Breisach wrote that, in the work of great cultural historians, like Emmanuel Le Roy Ladurie, Robert Darnton, and Natalie Zemon Davis, "the nonconstructed elements in the human condition [I/FWP elements] . . . constituted anchors for the narratives that limited the range of constructing narratives. Indeed, they have proved to be a defense against a pure subjectivism" in cultural history.[42] Thus, the formula I/FWP protects culture scholars from neglecting one factor or another in trying to explain human affairs holistically and from falling into idealism and subjectivism.

There *is* a "ready fund of analytical terms for designating the components of the cultural realm" —in response to Archer above, all of which (I/FWP) can be analyzed through various disciplines (see appendix C). In response to Bonnell and Hunt: culture does permeate every aspect of life, but it is more a "gathering concept" than an analytical one. One analyzes "culture" not by studying it per se but by studying its components (I/FWP) and *bringing them together*. As quoted in chapter 1, anthropologist Eric Wolf wrote: "It is precisely the shapeless, all-encompassing quality of the concept that allows us to draw together . . . material relations to the world, social organization, and configurations of ideas. Using 'culture,' therefore, we can bring together what might otherwise be kept separate." Dawson's idea of culture is not so much a direct subject of research—although it can be. It is, through the operation of his rules, more an itinerary for *coordinating research* in consideration of the whole, human picture.

The importance of coordinating research by means of an idea of culture like Dawson's is seen in the struggles of contemporary "borderlands history." This is a microfield influenced by the cultural turn and maturing during the first decade of the twenty-first century. Bor-

---

neglecting how "conscious purposes and shared meanings" often propel human beings to modify their historical environments (the "I" factor), Diamond nevertheless showed clearly how sociological, economic, and environmental factors shaped cultural development on different Polynesian islands. These are "essentially the same categories that emerged everywhere else in the world," Diamond wrote, and explained the development of world history. See Diamond, *Guns, Germs, and Steel*, 65; William H. McNeill, "History Upside Down," *New York Review of Books*, May 15, 1997, 50.

42. Breisach, *Historiography: Ancient, Medieval, & Modern*, 427.

derlands history examines the edges of empires and nations where indigenous and immigrant peoples mix and pass through, creating unstable identities and unexpected contingencies. Some historians view the idea of borderlands history as a metaphor for cultural encounters in general. The hope is to reconceptualize history apart from nation states and political structures. However, as noted by two historians, despite continental-wide perspectives and research into the languages, archives, and historiographies of multiple nations and empires, older politically structured narratives continue to assert themselves in the field. They wrote: "If the purpose of borderlands history is to perforate and expose historical currents between historical spaces, then how might one encapsulate that history without simply pouring it back into its former containers?"[43] They had no answer to this question.

Their question, however, is precisely the one that historians faced after the Great War when they looked for alternatives to "nations" in their restructuring of historiography (chapter 4). As demonstrated, Dawson's history of culture and boundary thinking pointed the way forward. Making culture the central object of knowledge in historical study avoided political straitjackets, opened up new kinds of sources, and turned attention to encounters between cultures and their environments as the engines of historical change. All of this not only coordinated specialized socio-historical researches with each other but it also aligned them to broad and meaningful humanistic kinds of questions through Dawson's rule of intellectual architecture. From this point of view, focusing on "Latin American culture" or "Native American culture" or even "Christian culture" on the North American continent would necessarily cross national borders between Mexico and the American Southwest, for example, aligning borderlands history away from political "containers" into cultural ones.

In addition to cultural relativism and definitional clarity, Cambridge historian John Morrill summarized well the third reason Dawson's books catch the mood of the present day. "Unlike many scholars more fashionable at [his] time, his method and his palette have a strong contemporary feel to them," Morrill wrote in 1997. This is be-

---

43. Hämäläinen and Truett, "On Borderlands," 339–340.

cause of Dawson's sensitive reading of literary texts. Though he did not utilize today's critical techniques, "the sheer breadth, attentiveness and retentiveness of his reading means that his own writings achieve much the same effect unselfconsciously."[44]

In other words, Dawson anticipated certain elements of the linguistic turn in historiography arising after his death and flowering in the cultural history of the 1990s. This interdisciplinary influence from philosophy and language-study deemphasized the objectivity of history in favor of the ways the past is constructed by the historian. Besides tangible documents and archeological evidence, for example, intangible values, ideas, and representations can also serve as historical sources. Dawson's wide engagement with different kinds of sources, as well as his cultural relativism, meant he paid attention to subjective perception and—later in his career—to the importance of language in the making of culture. "The word," he wrote, "not the sword or the spade, is the power that has created human culture," Dawson wrote in 1967. "Language is the organ of social tradition and the means of social communication, and these are the two main factors which make human culture possible."[45] Language certainly signified reality, however. Dawson's philosophical realism differentiated him from postmodernists who deny any historical reality beyond that constructed by texts.

It is unsurprising, then, that in 2015, historian Herman Paul discovered indirect evidence of Hayden White (1928–2018) borrowing his notion of "metahistory" from Christopher Dawson. White was an extremely influential theorist of the literary nature of historical discourse who helped pioneer the linguistic turn in modern historiography, and hence postmodernism. His *Metahistory: The Historical Imagination in Nineteenth-Century Europe* (1973) argued for the existence of a "precritically accepted paradigm of what a distinctively 'historical' explanation should be." White continued: "This paradigm functions as the 'metahistorical' element in all historical works that are more comprehensive in scope than the monograph or the archival report." Paul showed that White did not create the term "metahistory." Rather, White positioned

44. Caldecott and Morrill, eds., *Eternity in Time: Christopher Dawson and the Catholic Idea of History*, 3, 4.
45. Dawson, *The Formation of Christendom*, 33, 34.

himself within a well-established, predominantly European-based, religiously inspired metahistorical discourse about how one's presuppositions concerning the historical process inevitably shape one's historical writing. In this sense, metahistory was the "prearchival mind" introduced in chapter 4 to describe the universal quality Ranke brought to his research. Dawson viewed historical reason as the coordination of a faith or a vision (prearchival beliefs, judgments, assumptions, and insights) *with* empirical facts. Paul wrote, "It seems likely, on the basis of indirect evidence, that White borrowed his notion of 'metahistory' from Christopher Dawson."[46]

The "indirect evidence" included a lengthy essay White wrote about Dawson's work,[47] and similarities in their conception of metahistory. Paul wrote how Dawson argued (as White did later) that historians are not only *unable* to escape metahistory but that they *need* metahistory as the very foundation of their work. The mastery of research techniques will not produce great history, Dawson commented, any more than a mastery of metrical technique will produce great poetry: "For this something more is necessary—intuitive understanding, creative imagination, and finally a universal vision transcending the relative limitations of the particular field of historical study." Compare these to White's own words, who postulated a "deep level of consciousness" on which historians choose conceptual strategies by which to explain or represent their data: "On this level, I believe, the historian performs an essentially *poetic* act." Paul concluded: "The similarity between White's and Dawson's views on metahistory is striking."[48]

---

46. White, *Metahistory*, ix; Paul, "Metahistory," 24.

47. Hayden White, "Religion, Culture and Western Civilization in Christopher Dawson's Idea of History," 247–287. White cited Dawson's essay "The Problem of Metahistory" (1951) on his third page. White wrote: "Dawson has worked with amazing consistency towards the formulation of a philosophy of history which could accommodate both the findings of modern social sciences such as anthropology and the presuppositions of Thomism. In a sense, Dawson's life work may be seen as an attempt to construct a philosophy of history which will unite in a single system the modern concept of secular progress with the medieval notion, first stated clearly in St. Augustine, of history as Heilsgeschichte or history of salvation" (249). He ultimately condemned Dawson's work, however, as "monist," as reducing history to religion: "It may be said that instead of succeeding in enclosing within a single system the faith of St. Augustine and the reason of the modern age, Dawson has merely restated the traditional subservience of the latter to the former which must always result from any attempt at synthesis of this sort" (285–286, fn. 67).

48. Paul, "Metahistory," 25, 26; White, *Metahistory*, x; Dawson, "The Problem of Metahistory," in *Dynamics of World History*, 309–310.

Conclusion

Dawson's concern for the literary dimension in historiography, however, was balanced by the rules of his cultural mind. He had more confidence than White did, for example, in history as a science and the possibility of knowledge about reality, thus avoiding White's tendency toward literary reductionism.

Both Dawson and White occupied minority historiographical positions vis-à-vis the majority empiricist consensus, one as a Catholic and one who sometimes adopted a Marxian framework. This gave them critical detachment from the presuppositions and rules defined by the dominant historiographical community. Writing history based on their *own* presuppositions could be just as legitimate, they believed. If all scholarship rests on precritical assumptions, then all types of interpretations are possible—including religious and cultural ones, which were the entire basis of Dawson's lifework. After all, any science of society, White held, must be conducted on the basis of *some* assumptions about what a good society might be. This did not suggest, however, that all interpretations or assumptions are equal: for example, the *fact* of the Holocaust is beyond dispute, historian Daniel Woolf summarized a distinction White made, but the Holocaust's *meaning* might shift as it is viewed from different perspectives over time.[49]

The interpretive freedom advanced under the aegis of the new cultural history has created historiographical space for Dawson's works. Writers are more aware in the twenty-first century, I think, that they, in fact, construct their historical narratives based on some fundamental view of reality, on what they deem as most important in life. As writer David Foster Wallace said in his 2005 Kenyon College commencement speech: "Everybody worships." The only choice is *what* to worship. "When we read, or teach, or write history, we are discerning a story line," wrote historian Mike Aquilina. "We are saying that certain events are directly related to other events. We say that events proceed in a particular manner until they reach a particular end, and that they resolve themselves in a particular way." Historians must choose principles by which to interpret the past. For example, some select economics or military

49. Bonnell and Hunt, *Beyond the Cultural Turn*, 24; Paul, "Metahistory," 27; and Daniel Woolf, *A Concise History of History: Global Historiography from Antiquity to the Present* (New York: Cambridge University Press, 2019), 271.

events, Aquilina noted. Such a choice might imply a metaphysical belief, he continued—that what matters most is power, wealth, and pleasure in this world. Wallace said: worship money or things, and "you never feel you have enough"; worship power, and "you will need ever more power over others to numb you to your own fear"; worship intellect, and "you will end up feeling stupid." The cults of our culture shape not only our daily lives but even our view of the past. "But if there is a God—and most people believe there is—then God's view of things should not be merely incidental or personal," Aquilina wrote.[50] Without a doubt, God's view is mysterious. However, interpreting such a view of history *sub specie aeternitatis* is at least as legitimate as any other view.

Despite promising developments in cultural history, its practitioners today often disagree about the definition of culture, neglect appropriate methods of studying culture, and fragment the field even further through the loss of the holism that used to inspire earlier cultural history, historian Peter Burke wrote.[51] As shown, however, Dawson offered insight into all these problems. He took large views across time and space—the *longue durée* also adopted by the French *Annales* school. Dawson's cultural relativism, his clear definition of culture and its universal categories, and his sympathy for the "linguistic turn" in the construction of historical narratives offer points of contact with contemporary concerns. In addition, Dawson's approach to culture as a common way of life of a particular people, as well as the rules of his cultural mind that I have excavated beneath the surface of his texts, connect history to other fields of knowledge. Dawson's history of culture is not lost in subjectivism and endless analysis of change but is capable of connecting to permanent things, normative outlooks, and life-guiding values. This feature of change-and-continuity will be increasingly important in a globalized age as deracinated postmoderns struggle more than ever to form stable, often bicultural identities. In sum, Dawson's cultural mind provides impetus toward writing new histories of culture sensitive to these problems.[52]

50. Wallace, "2005 Kenyon Commencement Address"; Mike Aquilina, *The Church and the Roman Empire*, 301–490 (Notre Dame, Ind.: Ave Maria, 2019), xii.
51. Burke, *What Is Cultural History?* 115–17.
52. For my own attempt at a "Dawsonian" approach to the eighteenth century aimed at a

Conclusion

As we have seen, Dawson substituted "culture" for "state" as his primary collective entity around which to shape historical narratives. This meant he decentered politics in favor of an interdisciplinary history wide and deep enough to throw light on the human quest for meaning. He accordingly drew evidence out of the past far beyond the standard political documents. Spiritual treatises, art, and archeological finds all revealed the life of cultures. Because Dawson pursued cultural understanding in both socio-historical and humanistic modes, he asked compelling questions about the past and pushed his answers as far as the evidence would take him.

Dawson responded to the cultural fragmentation of the Age of the Great War by means of his cultural mind. He sought to repair the separation of values from truth, religion from culture, ideas from material reality, technology from ecology, past from present, faith from reason, and education from life by way of his integrated view of culture as a common way of life. But the four rules of his interdisciplinary logic demanded smart integration: the analytical demands of boundary thinking checked the synthetic thrust of intellectual architecture and intellectual bridges. Then, in turn, his intellectual asceticism and charity led him to popularization in the best sense: connecting the history of culture to a general audience rather than just other academics. In this way, he tried to recreate the past in order to influence the making of the future.

general audience, see Joseph T. Stuart, *Rethinking the Enlightenment: Faith in the Age of Reason* (Manchester, N.H.: Sophia Institute, 2020).

APPENDIX A: THE GEDDES-LE
PLAY FORMULA

Biology shows how life results from functional interactions between organisms and their environments. Among human populations, Patrick Geddes used the categories FWP—Folk (Organism), Work (Function), Place (Environment)—to communicate this idea. He created a sociological synthesis of life, coordinating anthropology, economics, and geography.

I created this diagram based on a paper Geddes submitted for the 1922 Oxford Conference on the Correlation of the Social Sciences, initiated by the Sociological Society.[1]

The arrows indicate mutual influence. A new technology (W) entering a culture, for example, affects both social ways of life (F) and the way a society relates to its environment (P). Geddes intended these arrows to demonstrate an interrelation between these categories yet leave analytic isolation in place when required. He did not intend to create rigid subject and departmental boundaries.[2]

SOCIOLOGY
The comprehensive study of social life

FOLK
organism
(Anthropology)
↑↓
WORK
function
(Economics)
↑↓
PLACE
environment
(Geography)

Geddes was concerned about the fracturing of knowledge and the resulting poverty of mind, hence his attempt at a synthesis of life. Geography, economics, and anthropology were commonly studied apart, he lamented, in separate programs, institutes, and learned societies. He desired, on the other hand, to bring them into living unison: "Place, studied without work or folk, is a matter of atlases and maps. . . . Folk, without place and work, are dead: and hence Anthropological collections and books are too much of mere skulls and

1. Patrick Geddes, "A Proposed Co-Ordination of the Social Sciences," *Sociological Review* XVI (1924): 54–65.

2. John Scott and Ray Bromley, *Envisioning Sociology: Victor Branford, Patrick Geddes, and the Quest for Social Reconstruction* (New York: State University of New York Press, 2013), 213.

_*Appendix A*

weapons. So, too, Economics, the science of work, when apart from definite place and definite folk, comes down to abstractions."[3]

Dawson referred to this schema, FWP, as the "Geddes-Le Play formula"[4] but he added a fourth element—"I" for ideas (see appendix C). With this addition, I/FWP guided Dawson's analytical approach to cultures as common ways of life.

3. Patrick Geddes, "The Mapping of Life," *Sociological Review* XVI, no. 3 (1924): 194.

4. Christopher Dawson, "Prevision in Religion," in *Dynamics of World History*, ed. John J. Mulloy (1956; Wilmington, Del.: ISI Books, 2002), 98.

APPENDIX B: THE SPIRITUAL SIDE OF SOCIAL LIFE ACCORDING TO PATRICK GEDDES

Patrick Geddes recognized the importance of spiritual and creative forces (psychology, or Ps) in shaping the material factors of social life. Thus, the essential problem was how to coordinate the temporal (FWP) and spiritual (Ps) "hemispheres" of reality. One could read Place-Work-Folk, he wrote, "forwards with the materialists, the determinists [as PWFPs], who trace the influence of environment on economic conditions and of these on social institutions. But we must also read the formula in reverse order [PsFWP] with thinkers of the more spiritual schools, who see the ideals of life reacting on labour and on environment."[1] Reading PsFWP both ways would link biology to the social sciences, psychology, and the humanities. Thus, for Geddes, sociology was not value-free. It was committed to truth and to a vision of authentic social renewal.[2]

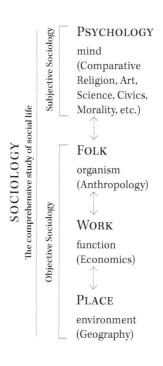

Sociology had to combine study of the material foundations of culture (FWP) with the higher cultural values (Ps). Both Geddes and Dawson believed this. "If we isolate society from its material body and its cultural soul, we have nothing left but an abstraction," Dawson wrote. Geddes' attempt to relate the

1. Victor Branford and Patrick Geddes, *The Coming Polity: A Study in Reconstruction* (London: Williams and Norgate, 1917), 202.
2. Scott and Bromley, *Envisioning Sociology*, 82, 87.

mental side of social life to FWP, however, was generally thought to be unsuccessful. He admitted that though the psychology of religion, doctrine, myth, and emotions are all essential to a complete sociology, psychology as such lacked a unified method: "So too it is with morals, with philosophy, sciences, mathematics; their psychology has not yet related itself to our simple unification [FWP], or its elements to theirs. And so again with imagination, poetry, and the arts. To all these and more our sociology must seek to come: but *how*, from conceptions so simple and so elemental as Place, Work, and Folk?"[3]

Dawson would answer that question by adding the fourth category "Ideas." A central problem for Geddes was that he did not fully differentiate metaphysically the spiritual and intellectual side of human nature. Spiritual and intellectual realities needed to be interpreted from within the social environment, Dawson believed, but also and primarily from *their own viewpoint* through their own disciplines of theology and philosophy. One could not view them simply as derivatives of something else, such as psychology. "The intrusion of these qualitatively distinct categories or orders of being [material and spiritual] into the sociological field is a great stumbling-block in the social sciences,"[4] Dawson wrote. Geddes stumbled. Despite his language about temporal and spiritual hemispheres, he did not, in fact, have a capacious and methodologically differentiated enough understanding of the spiritual dimension. Hence, Dawson modified Psychology/FWP to Ideas/FWP (see appendix C).

3. Christopher Dawson, "Sociology as a Science," in *Dynamics of World History*, ed. John J. Mulloy (1956; Wilmington, Del.: ISI Books, 2002), 25; Geddes, "A Proposed Co-Ordination of the Social Sciences," 62.

4. Christopher Dawson, "Sociology as a Science," in *Dynamics of World History*, 25.

APPENDIX C: DAWSON'S SCIENCE OF CULTURE

Influenced by Patrick Geddes and the Sociological Society, Christopher Dawson adopted the Geddes-Le Play formula (see appendix A) into his science of culture but added a fourth category: Ideas (I). Thus, simple and complex cultures are all shaped by four factors: the intellectual factor (I), the sociological factor (F), the economic factor (W), and the geographical or ecological factor (P). A (permeable) line in the schema below distinguishes the intellectual element from the material elements, indicating metaphysical differentiation but also influence in both directions. Thus, the vertical arrows indicate what Dawson called the "culture-process" by which a culture is open to change. "Any material change which transforms the external conditions of life will also change the cultural way of life and thus produce a new religious attitude. And likewise any spiritual change which transforms men's views of reality will tend to change their way of life and thus produce a new form of culture," Dawson wrote.[1] Note in the I/FWP schema that Dawson thought of sociology as a subsidiary field under a comprehensive science of culture, not as the master discipline as did Geddes.

The "I" in this schema represents three levels of human psychology in Dawson's work, as also discussed in chapter 5. He wrote:

There is, first, the subrational life of unconscious instinct and impulse which plays such a large part in human life and especially the life of the masses. Secondly, there is the level of conscious voluntary effort and rational activity which is the sphere of culture, par excellence. And, finally, there is the superrational level of spiritual experience which is the sphere not only of religion but of the highest creative forces of cultural achievement—the intuitions of the artist, the poet, and the philosopher—and also of certain forms of scientific intuition which seems to transcend the sphere of rational calculation and research.[2]

1. Christopher Dawson, *Religion and Culture* (1948; Washington D.C.: The Catholic University of America Press, 2013), 45.

2. Christopher Dawson, "American Education and Christian Culture," *American Benedictine Review* 9, no. 1 (1958): 12–13.

Appendix C

open to transcendent	Elements of Cultural Life	Representative Disciplines
I ideas ↑↓	Ideas { intellectus / ratio / subrational instinct religious vision, culture as a moral and linguistic order	Theology Philosophy Psychology/Intellectual Hist. Comparative Religion
F folk ↑↓	Social Organism state, nation, church, folk music, custom, etc.	Sociology/Anthropology Social History Literary Studies Political Science
W work ↑↓	Economic Function industry, trade, fishing, technology, agriculture, etc.	Socioeconomics Economics History of Technology
P place	Environment rivers, soil, climate, region, cityscape, etc.	Human Ecology Geography Environmental History Geology

(left margin: Culture as a common way of life)
(right margin: Culture as an object of knowlege)

Dawson did not use the words *intellectus* and *ratio* (see schema, middle column) to distinguish between the higher and middle levels of human psychology (I borrow the terms from Josef Pieper[3] because they are succinct), but he did so distinguish between those two levels. Critical reason, as important as it is, does not create spiritual unity or cultural consensus about the meaning of life, Dawson wrote. Historically, the dynamic element in primitive culture was not found in rational enquiry but in the "sphere of direct religious experience" and the "intuition of pure being."[4] It is in this highest level of human psychology that "a culture finds its focus and its common spiritual ends, and it is also the source of the higher moral values which are accepted not merely as rules imposed by society for its own welfare but as a sacred law which finds its tribu-

3. *Ratio*: the power of discursive, logical thought—searching, examining, abstracting, defining, and drawing conclusions. *Intellectus*: understanding through the simple vision of truth—not active but receptive, conceiving within that which it sees and touching, as the Greeks thought, on the order of the pure spirits. "The faculty of mind, man's knowledge, is both of these things in one, according to antiquity and the Middle Ages, simultaneously *ratio* and *intellectus*; and the process of knowing is the action of the two together." See Josef Pieper, *Leisure the Basis of Culture* (San Francisco: Ignatius, 2009), 28–29.

4. Christopher Dawson, *Progress and Religion: An Historical Enquiry* (1929; Washington, D.C.: The Catholic University of America Press, 2001), 76, 176.

nal in the human heart and the individual conscience."[5] The existence of this highest level of human psychology means a culture is never a deterministic order but is constantly open to the unpredictable influence of the transcendent through receptive and creative human minds: "The influence of the exceptional man—we may even say of the genius—whether as organizer, teacher, or seer, is to be observed among savages no less than in advanced civilizations."[6]

The most vital changes in human life come from within, so the study of culture in Dawson's work necessitated accounting for both human interiority (I) *and* the outer world of FWP. One of the reasons for conceptual incoherence in twentieth- and twenty-first-century theories about culture, sociologist Christian Smith noted, is the desire to evade human subjectivity and all its complexity—the "I" in the schema, focusing on the external manifestations of culture. He wrote, however, that any "more coherent and fruitful account of culture will have to take subjectivity entirely seriously, however methodologically difficult that is."[7] In other words, there is a need to put the human person, mind and body, at the center of culture, as Dawson did.

Because Dawson located the human person at the center of his cultural analysis, he did not create a false dichotomy between culture and society as happened in sociology after his time. That dichotomy views culture simply as intangible ideas, on the one hand (studied by humanities scholars), and society as hard facts and definite social institutions, on the other (studied by social scientists). Never the twain shall meet, splitting the I from the FWP. Dawson did not follow these intellectual grooves, however, for culture "represents the whole complex of life and thought," he wrote. Thus, "culture and society are interdependent aspects of a single reality," he noted, "neither of which can exist without the other." Indeed, more recently, Christian Smith expressed this same view: "every social system, structure, and institution is always and necessarily constituted and defined by cultural rules or schemas that make it more or less meaningful and legitimate; and every cultural rule or schema depends on systems of material and nonmaterial resources to be sustained. Thus, society apart from culture...is like the body without a living spirit." In Aristotelian terms, Dawson concluded, "every culture is the form of a society and every society is the matter of a culture"—though a culture normally includes a number of independent social units. Societies (e.g., of ants) can exist among animals without cultural form, but that is not possible among humans.[8]

5. Dawson, "American Education and Christian Culture," 14.

6. Dawson, *Progress and Religion*, 66; Christopher Dawson, "Rationalism and Intellectualism: The Religious Elements in the Rationalist Tradition," in *Enquiries into Religion and Culture* (1933; Washington, D.C.: The Catholic University of America Press, 2009), 114–28.

7. Christian Smith, "The Conceptual Incoherence of 'Culture' in American Sociology," *The American Sociologist* 47, no. 4 (2016): 411.

8. Christopher Dawson, *The Formation of Christendom* (New York: Sheed & Ward, 1967), 36,

Appendix C

Culture is a kind of "middle earth." Angels, for example, are not part of culture, they are above culture, so to speak—though they might have influence in culture and culture might portray them in art or treatises. Nature is also not part of culture, for it is below it, so to speak—though nature becomes cultural when "tended" by humans.

One of the roots of the word culture, in fact, is tending or "cultivating," so the idea of culture really rests on a metaphor: the tending of natural growth.[9] Culture is not a forest growing up naturally; rather, it is artificial because human minds and spirits reshape nature according to its possibilities. This distinction between nature and culture is common to many human societies, such as the Yanomamo, a large tribe of tropical South America: the things of their village and garden are "of the village" (culture), and all other things are "of the forest" (nature).[10] The village is made of natural things (trees, leaves), but they become cultural through the transformation of human effort—hence the need for academic disciplines such as human ecology, geography, and geology in the science of culture *to the extent that they illuminate what it means to be human*. What is not part of culture is what is not directly connected to the human.

At the same time, however, a culture is "never conceived as a purely man-made order,"[11] for humans rely on powers both above and below them. Thus, the culture scholar ultimately must grapple with both theology *and* geology, and everything in between—as schematized in the "Representative Disciplines" column of the I/FWP schema representing Dawson's science of culture.

In the author's interpretation of Dawson's work, I/FWP was the basis of the intellectual architecture supporting his cultural mind. These categories helped him to maintain a unified vision of the factors shaping culture and to respect the limits of the disciplines needed to study it (boundary thinking). In effect, these interrelated categories applied John Henry Newman's "philosophical habit of mind" to cultural studies—the habit of "viewing many things at once as one whole, of referring them severally to their true place in the universal system, of understanding their respective values, and determining their mutual dependence."[12]

40; Christian Smith, *Moral, Believing Animals: Human Personhood and Culture* (New York: Oxford University Press, 2003), 20, 21; and Dawson, *Religion and Culture*, 35.

9. Raymond Williams, *Culture & Society: 1780–1950* (1958; New York: Columbia University Press, 1983), 335; OED, senses 2, 3, and 4.

10. Napoleon A. Chagnon, *Yanomamo*, 5th ed. (1968; Belmont, Calif.: Wadsworth, 1997), 55.

11. Dawson, *Religion and Culture*, 43.

12. John Henry Newman, *The Idea of a University* (1873; Tacoma, Wash.: Cluny Media, 2016), 108.

APPENDIX D: POLITICAL RELIGION

Christopher Dawson saw ideology—even democratic ideology rooted in the sacredness of the people—as a functional substitute for religion yet capable of arousing genuinely religious emotions:

An ideology in the modern sense of the word is very different from faith, although it is intended to fulfill the same sociological functions. It is the work of man, an instrument by which the conscious political will attempts to mould the social tradition to its purpose. But faith looks beyond the world of man and his works; it introduces man to a higher and more universal range of reality than the finite and temporal world to which the state and the economic order belong. And thereby it introduces into human life an element of spiritual freedom which may have a creative and transforming influence on man's social culture and historical destiny as well as on his inner personal experience.[1]

Religious Faith		Ideology	
Traditional Culture secularization →	Nazism	Communism	Nationalism and Fascism
<u>I</u>	<u>F</u>	<u>W</u>	<u>P</u>
F	I	I	I
W	W	F	F
P	P	P	W

1. Christopher Dawson, *Religion and the Rise of Western Culture* (1950; New York: Doubleday/Image Books, 1991), 14.

Appendix D

The modern ideologies, however, sacralize F (race), W (working class, the proletariat), and P (nation or state)—worldly realities rather than transcendent ones, which are the proper objects of religion. FWP are, in effect, "consecrated to themselves and elevated into substitutes for the ends to which they were formerly subjected"—hence, they are placed at the top of the ideology columns above. This sacralization is, however, a temporary state of affairs, Dawson predicted, dependent on an inherited stock of religious emotion.[2]

Instead of uniting people as Christianity did by what is highest, Dawson wrote—"by faith in Christ and the fellowship of the Holy Spirit"—the political religions unifying the world "appeal to the lowest common factors—to class interest, or the physical unity of blood and race, so that they cast out the devils of selfishness and avarice only to enthrone the prince of this world and the powers of darkness."[3]

2. Dawson, "Prevision in Religion," 103–4.
3. Christopher Dawson, *Beyond Politics* (London: Sheed & Ward, 1939), 109–10.

APPENDIX E: SPECIFIC PROGRAMS FOR THE STUDY OF CHRISTIAN CULTURE

John J. Mulloy

In discussing the proposals which Christopher Dawson advances in the present volume for the study of Christian culture, one of the first matters to be considered is how these proposals might be realized within the actual structure of the college or university curriculum. Professor Dawson's own consideration of this problem is given in the following passage from Chapter XI above [in *The Crisis of Western Education*]:

It is a question of adjustment which must be solved in different ways in different places according to the needs and opportunities of the particular society and institution.

The situation is not unlike that which the non-Catholic colleges have to face in so far as they try to combine a general study of "Western civilization" with the special studies of the particular student, and the same methods can be applied to the study of Christian culture. Moreover, it might be possible to give different courses in Christian culture appropriate to the different studies being taken; thus, the course could be orientated towards either literature, history, art, the classics, philosophy or theology or education. Alternatively, we can conceive the study of Christian culture as the province of a special institute on the graduate level. Or it might be offered as a field of concentration to the student in his later years of undergraduate study. In this case, it could be co-ordinated with the student's vocational preparation so as to lead, for example, to teaching on the secondary or collegiate level or to postgraduate studies in law.[1]

This appendix first appeared in Christopher Dawson's *The Crisis of Western Education* (New York: Sheed & Ward, 1961), 205–37. Bloomsbury Publishing—which inherited Sheed & Ward—was unable to find a record of this publication, but Bloomsbury affirmed it had no objection to reprinting it. All footnotes appeared in the original document although I have modified to past tense the biographical information about John J. Mulloy, which appears at the end of this appendix.

1. Attention should be called to the fact that, although Professor Dawson has had Catholic education primarily in mind in his advocacy of Christian culture studies, he also hopes to encourage consideration of his proposals in terms of the goals sought by the non-Catholic colleges and universities, whether these be denominational or non-sectarian. Consequently, most of the courses mentioned in this Note are intended for use, not only by Catholic colleges, but by any college program of liberal studies, which recognizes the affinity between Christianity and the Western humanist tradition.

Appendix E

Based upon Professor Dawson's suggestions which we have just quoted and looking to the programs of general or liberal education already in existence in American colleges and universities,[2] there are at least five different ways in which a formal program in Christian culture studies might be inaugurated (as distinguished from the informal leavening of existing courses by insights and ideas related to the Christian culture concept):

1. A program of Graduate Study (which might be related to a graduate institute).
2. An Upper Division field of concentration.
3. A Lower Division fulfillment of liberal education requirements.
4. A program spanning the Lower and Upper Divisions of the college.
5. An Honors program.

What would be the actual courses that might be given on each of these five levels for incorporation of Christian culture study into the college or university? Accepting the fact that all blueprints of this nature are subject to variation and revision in terms of the actual circumstances and resources of the college or university, I nevertheless think it will serve to stimulate thought upon the matter and serve as a basis for later action, if certain definite course offerings are specifically set down and described.[3] Some of these courses are already in existence and have been given on one or more occasions; others are simply blueprints which need to be subjected to experiment and trial. Others again have been given, but on a more condensed basis than is here suggested. All of them, however, are derived from the ideas concerning the relationship between Christianity and culture which Christopher Dawson discusses in the present volume, and which indeed have formed the integrating principle of his work over the last thirty-five years.[4]

1. The Program of Graduate Study

This program, which might possibly be administered through a graduate institute of Christian culture, would offer courses which would be counted for graduate credit towards the master's or the doctor's degree in any one of

2. See *General Education: An Account and an Appraisal*, by Lewis Mayhew (New York, Harper, 1960), for a description of these programs.

3. While recognizing the validity of Professor Dawson's observation that "the planning of the curriculum must be a co-operative task," with "the whole subject being discussed by a committee of experts," I believe that, in order to arrive at that stage, a preliminary statement of the different means for realization of Christian culture needs to be provided.

4. See *The Dynamics of World History* for a compendium of these ideas, and such recent books as *The Movement of World Revolution* and *The Historic Reality of Christian* Culture for their application to the present cultural crisis.

a number of disciplines, either of the humanities or the social sciences or in philosophical or theological studies. The custom which prevails at most graduate schools of allowing or encouraging the student to take one or more minors to support his major field of study might here be employed to permit the student to add a certain number of Christian culture courses in fulfillment of his requirements for a minor. As a means of developing an understanding of the interdisciplinary dimensions of the study of Christian culture, and providing a broader view of its unifying effects, it seems advisable that a student take the Christian culture courses in some discipline not too closely related to that of his major field.

Suggested Course Offerings

The Theological Foundations of Christian Culture. A consideration of the relation between theology and Christian culture through the study of such subjects as: the Incarnation as the center of human history; the Church as the extension of the Incarnation in time; the Church as the representative of a specialized historical tradition which it has a mission to renew and transmit; the Augustinian conception of the historical process as developing through the conflict of opposing spiritual forces; the Communion of Saints as a bond of historical continuity between past, present and future generations; the doctrine of the End of History and the Last Things.

The Historical Development of Revelation. A study of the Jewish-Christian tradition, here seen historically and dynamically as the development of the spiritual tradition of the Old and New Testaments, which contain the sacred history of the Peoples of God—the old and the new Israel.

Christian Social Institutions. The Christian family and the Christian state. The Christian tradition of law and the idea of the Law of Nature. The Christian conception of liberty and authority and of personal and corporate rights. The Christian attitude toward wealth and poverty: the service of the poor and the institutions arising from it. Christian education and educational institutions. The comparative study of Christian institutions as developed by the different national cultures.

The Study of Christian Thought. Hellenism and the Christian tradition: the Platonism of the Greek Fathers; the Augustinian tradition. St. Thomas and the *Philosophia Perennis.* Scholasticism and the birth of Western science. Humanism and Christian philosophy. The relation of modern Western philosophies to the Christian tradition. Christian rationalism and the rationalism of the Enlightenment. Christian idealism and the idealism of the Romantic philosophers. Christianity and technology.

Christianity and Comparative Culture. The chief approaches which anthropology affords for the study of a culture and its institutions and values. The extension of these approaches to the study of civilizations, with particular reference to the comparative study of the civilization of Christendom and that of one of the Oriental religion cultures.

Christianity and the Open Society. The meaning of such terms as "open" and "closed" in relation to society and culture, and the questions raised concerning these issues by Bergson and Toynbee. A consideration of the critiques of modern mass culture by sociologists and humanists in their relation to the issue of an open society. Christianity and the transcendence of religious values and their effect upon society and culture. A consideration of the relevance of the Christian conception of culture to the modern criticisms of mass society.

Christianity and Church-State Relationships. A study of the changing relationship between Church and State in the historical development of Christian culture: attitudes concerning Church and State in the early Church, in the Byzantine empire, in medieval Europe after Gregory VII, and the different conceptions and practices in this matter of post-Reformation Catholicism, Lutheranism, Calvinism, Anglicanism, and the sects. A consideration of the different ways in which the French Revolution and the American Constitution have affected the development of Church-State relationships.

The Missionary Expansion of Christianity. A study of the expansion of Christianity throughout the centuries with reference to those factors which have helped or hindered its spread to new peoples. Comparison of the main features of the expansion of Catholicism in the sixteenth and seventeenth centuries with the missionary activities of Protestantism in the nineteenth and twentieth centuries.

The Protestant Sects and Their Influence upon Culture. A consideration of the Protestant sects as different ways of religious life, and their sociological analogy to the religious Orders in Catholic Christendom. The interaction between the ideals of the sects and the cultural forces with which they came into contact, and the effects of this on the formation of social ideals and patterns in England and America. A comparison of the relation of the sects to cultural development in Russia with that in England and the United States.

Prophecy and Culture Change. A consideration of the nature of prophetic testimony and its significance for the conditions of modern culture. A study of the effect upon Western culture of such prophetic figures as St. Augustine, St. Odo of Cluny, Gregory VII, St. Bernard, Martin Luther, George Fox, John Wesley, Kierkegaard, Newman, and in the secular sphere, Rousseau and Karl Marx.

Christianity and the Development of Western Science. The character of Western culture, and the influence of Christianity and of science upon its formation. The significance of the technological development of science in Western culture and its relation to the ethos of Western Christianity. A study of the interaction between scientific and Christian attitudes in certain key figures in the history of scientific development: Roger Bacon, Francis Bacon, Copernicus, Galileo, Descartes, Newton, Locke, etc.

Christianity and Conceptions of World History. A discussion of the different views of world history held by certain key figures from the Enlightenment to the present and their evaluation and critique in terms of the Christian understanding of history. The Rationalist and the Romantic conceptions of history. Hegel, Marx, Burckhardt, Nietzsche, Spengler and Toynbee are among those studied in the development of historical consciousness since the eighteenth century. A consideration of Dawson's view of the development of world history as an example of the interaction between the Christian conception of history and the fruits of modern historical knowledge.

The Prophets of Literature and the Culture of Christendom. An examination of the developing social crisis and the separation of religion from culture since the French Revolution, as seen in the thought of such men as Novalis, de Maistre, Lamennais, Kierkegaard, Dostoievski, Newman, Ruskin, Carlyle, Arnold, Pater, Henry Adams, Santayana. A study of their attitudes toward the Christian culture of the past in relation to the cultural situation of their own time.

The Six Ages of Christian Culture. A consideration of the main themes that give each age its specific character and cultural outlook. The permanent contribution of each age to the subsequent development of Christian culture. The pattern of historical development followed by each age in its rise and decline.

For a more intensive examination of the historical development of Christian culture, courses might be provided on one or several of the six periods of its history:

The Early Church and the Rise of Christian Culture
Byzantine Culture and the Age of the Fathers
The Formation of Western Christendom
Medieval Christendom and the Gothic Culture
Divided Christendom and the European National Cultures
Secularized Christendom and the Age of Revolution

The Ecumenical Councils and the Development of Doctrine. The conception of doctrinal development, with special reference to its analysis by Cardinal Newman. The Ecumenical Councils as the focus for the encounter of certain historical and cultural factors which require the response of an explication of doctrine and thus set the conditions for doctrinal development. The problems faced by certain selected councils as examples of the process by which the development of doctrine takes place. A consideration of the interaction between transcendental and historical factors in the development of the Church's teaching.

The Problem of Christian Unity. A consideration of the meaning of the unity of the Church and the different interpretations placed upon it. Problems to Christian unity resulting from the historical heritage of divided Christendom. The impact of developments in secular history upon the division of Christendom, both before and after the French Revolution. The development of the ecumenical movement within Protestantism and its influence upon Protestant attitudes toward the Catholic Church and its tradition.

2. The Upper Division Field of Concentration

This program would constitute a major field of study for the student in his junior and senior years. It would be advisable to arrange the Christian culture studies in such a way that the student in the program would pursue a double major: one in a regularly established discipline, such as History, English, Foreign Languages, Education, Sociology, Philosophy, etc., and one in the interdepartmental discipline of Christian culture.

As an example of the Upper Division field of concentration we give below the courses developed at St. Mary's College, Notre Dame, Indiana, under the chairmanship of Dr. Bruno Schlesinger. This program has been in successful operation for the past five years. The core courses are those in Christianity and Culture (4 terms) and in the Colloquia (4 terms). The other four courses constitute exploration in depth of particular subjects from a Christian culture standpoint. Depending on the resources of the particular college or university, one or more the courses mentioned above as part of a graduate program might be either added to this group of courses or used in place of some of them.

Courses of Study

Christianity and Culture I: The Making of Europe. The formation of Christian culture in both East and West down to the eleventh century. 3 sem. hrs.

Christianity and Culture II: Medieval Christendom. The maturity of Christendom in the age of St. Thomas and Dante and the growth of Gothic culture to the fifteenth century. 3 sem. hrs.

Christianity and Culture III: The Age of Religious Division. The expansion and disintegration of Christendom to the eighteenth century; Humanism, Baroque Culture, the Enlightenment. 3 sem. hrs.

Christianity and Culture IV: The Age of Revolutions and World Wars. World ascendancy of secularized Western Culture; internal and external forces of disintegration. Nationalism, Communism and the Totalitarian State. 3 sem. hrs.

Colloquium I: Christian Classics. The study and discussion of works, such as St. Augustine's *Confessions* and *The City of God*; the Rule of St. Benedict; Bede's *Ecclesiastical History*; *The Song of Roland*; the Legends and Lauds of St. Francis of Assisi; Latin Hymns and Sequences; and Byzantine Art. 2 sem. hrs.

Colloquium II: Christian Classics. The study and discussion of works, such as St. Thomas Aquinas' *On Kingship,* Joinville's *Life of St. Louis,* Dante's *Divine Comedy,* Langland's *Piers Plowman,* Chaucer's *Canterbury Tales; Revelations of Divine Love,* by St. Juliana of Norwich; the Trial of Joan of Arc; *Everyman;* Romanesque and Gothic Art. 2 sem. hrs.

Colloquium III: Significant Books of Divided Christendom. The study and discussion of works, such as Erasmus' *Colloquies,* St. Thomas More's *Utopia,* St. Teresa's *Life,* Hooker's *Laws of Ecclesiastical Polity;* Poems by Donne, Herbert, Crashaw and Vaughan; Milton's *Paradise Lost,* Calderon's *Life is a Dream,* Pascal's *Pensées,* Fénelon's *Letters,* Swift's *Argument against Abolishing Christianity,* Pope's *Essay on Man;* Renaissance and Baroque Art.

Colloquium IV: Significant Books of Divided Christendom. Burke's *Reflections on the Revolution in France,* Goethe's *Faust* (Part One), Newman's *Idea of a University,* Orestes Brownson's *Essays,* Hawthorne's *The Scarlet Letter,* Kierkegaard's *Fear and Trembling,* Marx and Engels' *The Communist Manifesto,* Dostoievski's *The Possessed,* Ibsen's *The Master Builder,* G. M. Hopkins' *Poems,* Eloy's *Pilgrim of the Absolute,* Chesterton's Essays, Mauriac's *Vipers' Tangle,* T. S. Eliot's *Murder in the Cathedral;* Nineteenth Century Art and Contemporary Art.

Early Christian Writers. An introduction to the writings of St. Clement of Rome, St. Ignatius of Antioch, Tertullian, Origen, St. Athanasius, St. Jerome and St. John Chrysostom. 2 sem. hrs.

History of Christian Philosophy. An introduction to the history of philosophical ideas in the Middle Ages from St. Augustine to William of Ockham. 2 sem. hrs.

Church, State and Society. An examination of the impact of Christianity upon such social institutions as the family, slavery, property, the state, and an introduction to the enduring problems raised by the claims of Church and State. 2 sem. hrs.

Christianity and American Culture. A study of the roots of American culture in Christianity and in the Enlightenment from colonial times to the present, with special emphasis upon the age of Jefferson and the age of Emerson. 2 sem. hrs.

Beginning with the academic year 1960–61 there has been added to the curriculum a course of lectures on the Oriental religion cultures, given in a two-year cycle by visiting lecturers from the University of Chicago and other outside sources. The first year's lectures deal with Chinese and Islamic cultures, the second year with the religion cultures deriving their inspiration from Indian sources, such as Hinduism and Buddhism.[5]

---

5. For another account of the Saint Mary's College program, see the article by Mr. John P. Gleason in Section II of this appendix [not included here—JS].

Appendix E

3. The Lower Division Program in Liberal Education

The Lower Division program is set up to provide the student with a general education in the freshman and sophomore years, before he enters upon his specialized studies in the later years of college. This type of program is the one most commonly used in American colleges and universities for the presentation of the Western cultural heritage; the Columbia University curriculum in Contemporary Civilization is possibly the earliest and best-known of these programs.

For the adequate study of Christian culture, a Lower Division program should involve four semesters of cultural history. Their presentation would be primarily the responsibility of the department of History, but it would also enlist the aid, through consultation and special lectures, of members of other departments such as Sociology, Literature, Foreign Languages, Classics, Art, Music, etc. Since the six periods of Christian culture delineated by Mr. Dawson would have to be presented in four semesters, it would require a shorter treatment of some periods compared with others. It is possible that it might be found preferable to handle the first two periods of Christian culture during the first semester, under the general heading Christianity and the Ancient World, and the two medieval periods in the second semester (Christianity and the Medieval World), which would then allow a semester for each of the two periods—that of Divided Christendom, 1500–1750, and that of the Age of Revolution, 1750 to the present—dealing with Christianity in the modern world. However, should there be greater interest and more faculty resources available for the ancient and medieval sequences, then it might well be preferable to provide the more detailed treatment in the opposite direction from the emphasis on the modern periods.

In addition to the four periods of cultural history, a two-semester course in English Literature in the sophomore year could be established so as to co-ordinate with study of Christian culture since the Renaissance being given by the History department during this same sophomore year. This would allow both Literature and History to benefit from the sharper focus in clarity of perception and understanding which each subject would gain from the reinforcement provided by the other.

Moreover, as forming part of the reading list for freshman students in English, it might be possible to introduce the students to certain works which would enable them to grasp the nature of Christian culture and its achievements. Such works might well take on a deeper significance for the student because of his concomitant study of the historical development of Christian culture in his history courses of that year. As an illustration of the type of reading that might be done along this line, we would suggest the following specific examples. (The faculty of each particular college would best be able to judge which and how many of these works might be found suitable for the level of the student at their institution. Of course, if this Lower Division program is made part of an Honors program, the quality of work expected of the student would be correspondingly higher.)

Dawson, "St. Augustine and His Age" (in *A Monument to St. Augustine*, ed. by Martin D'Arcy); Chesterton, *The Ballad of the White Horse*; T. S. Eliot, *Murder in the Cathedral*; *The Little Flowers of St. Francis*; Dante, *The Divine Comedy* (the Inferno and the last ten cantos of the Paradiso); Undset, *The Bridal Wreath* (the first volume of the Kristin Lavransdatter trilogy) or *The Axe* (the first volume of the Master of Hestviken tetralogy); H. F. M. Prescott, *The Man on a Donkey*; Péguy, *Men and Saints*; Chesterton, *Orthodoxy*; Greene, *The Power and the Glory*; Koestler, *Darkness at Noon*; Dawson, *The Movement of World Revolution*.

Finally, it would help the student to realize the historical source of the Christian cultural tradition and how its roots extend far back into ancient history if the freshman course in Religion were so arranged as to provide a view of the historical development of Revelation, through the successive stages of Jewish history to its eventual culmination in the Gospel and the new religious community of the Church. Of the first part of this program, the study of the Old Testament, Christopher Dawson has written: "The study of the Old Testament is especially valuable from the cultural angle, and it gives one a starting point on the Christian view of history, which is unintelligible without a good knowledge of the Old Testament. . . . If we wish to find the roots of the Christian interpretation of history, we must go back behind the Fathers, behind the New Testament, behind even the Hebrew prophets to the very foundation of the religion of Israel."[6]

If the biblical-historical approach to the Religion program were carried over into the second year, the first term might deal with the establishment of the first Christian communities and the development of Christian teaching as seen in the Acts of the Apostles and in selections from St. Paul's Epistles; while the second term might study the liturgy as manifesting the continuity between the Old and New Testaments and exhibiting the full historical scope of the Christian mystery of man's redemption. It would thus serve as a recapitulation of the sacred history which had been studied in the preceding terms and would make the student aware of the form in which that history was being communicated to future generations of Christians to the end of time.

---

6. The first part of this passage is from a letter addressed by Professor Dawson to the present writer; the second is from *The Dynamics of World History*, p. 252.

Appendix E

Suggested Course Offerings: Theology Courses

Israel and the Scriptures. A study of the successive stages of revelation—Mosaic, Prophetic and Christian—each of these stages involving not simply a question of new truths, but of events through which the truths are revealed. In the first term's work the study of this development in the Old Testament, the prehistory of the Incarnation, as seen in such events as the calling of Abraham, the covenant between God and Israel at Sinai, the history of the Chosen People, and the successive revelations by the Prophets as to the nature of the Kingdom of God.

The Gospel and the Kingdom. In this second term's work, a study of the Incarnation as the fruit of history, the dispensation of the fullness of time. The Gospel as the fulfillment of the heritage of Jewish prophecy concerning the Messiah and the restoration of Israel, but also the beginning of a new world order which would renew all things through the action of the historical person of Jesus. An examination of the twofold character of the Kingdom portrayed in the Gospel: internal and spiritual, a leaven in the heart of man which is in the process of creating a new humanity; and external and cosmic, the universal Kingdom of the Son of Man, the consummation of human history, which is as yet present only in embryo in the womb of the old order.

The Apostolic Church. The establishment and spread of the early Christian communities in the Graeco-Roman world, as narrated in the Acts of the Apostles. The development of the Christian Revelation in St. Paul's Epistles, and the relation of this development to the challenges presented to St. Paul in his apostolate to the Gentiles. The principal themes of St. Paul's teaching.

The Liturgy and Sacred History. The liturgy as the recapitulation of the mystery of Divine Providence in bringing to fulfillment the Incarnation and Redemption in "the fullness of time." A study of the liturgy as based on a sacred history and presenting this in an historical cycle in which the whole story of human creation and redemption is progressively unfolded, as the revelation of the Divine purpose on earth and in time. The close inner relation and counterpoint between the movement in the Old Testament and in the New, as seen especially in the Advent and Paschal liturgy.

Each of these courses might be either two or three semester hours.

Cultural History

Christianity and the Ancient World. A study of the process of interpenetration between the Christian tradition and Gentile culture in the early Christian Church (before Constantine) and in the Byzantine Empire down to the opening of the seventh century. The interaction between Hebraic, Oriental, Greek and Roman cultural elements in the first six centuries of the Christian era, and the manner in which Christianity served to integrate these elements in a new religious culture. A comparison and contrast of the main features of Christian culture during the first three centuries of Primitive Christianity with that of Patristic Christianity in the following period, which saw the conversion of the Roman-Hellenistic world and the rise of Byzantine culture.

Christianity and the Medieval World. A study of the interpenetration of barbarian culture by the higher cultural tradition which Christianity brought to Northern Europe from the Mediterranean world. The mutual influences by which the barbarians were Christianized and Christian culture incorporated certain barbarian institutions and social patterns in its new cultural synthesis. A comparison of the key features and social organs of Christian society during two successive periods or phases of the history of the medieval world: the predominantly rural culture of Northern Europe during the first five centuries of Christianization (the period of the Formation of Western Christendom), and the mixed feudal and urban culture which resulted from the renewed contact of medieval Europe with Greek learning in the eleventh and the twelfth centuries, leading to the flowering of Gothic culture in the second half of the medieval millennium.

Christianity and the Modern World. An examination of the changes in Christian culture brought about by two different developments in two successive periods of modern history: (1) the expansion of Christian culture and the division of Christendom in the period from the Renaissance to the Enlightenment; (2) the Revolution and its social and political consequences in the period from the eighteenth to the twentieth centuries. A comparison of the new forms of Christian culture developed in Protestant and Catholic Europe in response to the challenge of the Renaissance and the Reformation with the impact of the European revolution upon these forms in the last century and a half.

Note: If the first two sequences in the cultural history are each given in one semester, so that two semesters are allowed for the third member of the sequence, Christianity and the Modern World, then it is suggested that some provision might be made for giving to cultural history in the freshman year four semester hours each term instead of three. This would permit more adequate attention to be given to each of the first two sequences and would afford opportunity for some attention to the literature in which the process of cultural transformation could be seen taking place. Thus, in the first of these sequences, Christianity and the Ancient World, an extra semester hour each week should make it easier for the student to learn some of the representative ideas of Plato, Cicero and Marcus Aurelius, in selected passages from their work, and see their relationship to the thought of the first Christian centuries. (Ernest Barker's volume, *From Alexander to Constantine* [Oxford, 1956], is most helpful for a study of certain aspects of this development, although it stops short of the great age of the Fathers of the Church.) Thus, for example, ideas concerning the soul and its future might be compared in Plato (see the Livingstone edited volume of Plato in the World's Classics series) with those in Tertullian's *Testimony of the Soul*; or the relation between man and God in Marcus Aurelius's *Meditations* with the new conception to be found in St. Augustine's *Confessions*. And there are many other examples of the way in which the literature of the period illustrates the nature of the social and spiritual change taking place as Christianity gradually replaces Hellenic philosophy and *paideia* as the accepted religion of the ancient world. (Werner Jaeger's brief volume on *Humanism and Theology* is rich with insights on the change in values which was taking place, although he tends to stress the continuity with the past more than some other writers are likely to do.)

For the course on Christianity and the Medieval World, the student should be expected to read such works (or significant parts thereof) as Bede's *Ecclesiastical History*, Joinville's *Life of St. Louis*, the Franciscan missionary narratives found in *The Mongol Mission* (in The Makers of Christendom series), selections from *Piers Plowman*, and the Prologue to *The Canterbury Tales*. And, if *The Divine Comedy* and *The Little Flowers of St. Francis* are not read as part of the reading list in freshman Literature, then they should certainly be included here.

In addition to this, a certain time should be set aside for the use of either filmstrips or film slides showing the different styles of architecture and sculpture of the different periods of the Christian cultural development, as well as how styles were affected by variations from one country to another (e.g., differences between Roman basilicas and Byzantine churches, between Romanesque and Gothic, Renaissance and colonial Baroque, colonial styles in Mexico and in the Spanish missions contrasted with those of colonial New England, modern church architecture in Europe and in the United States, etc.).

Filmstrips or film slides (in color) should also be used to show the different schools and masters of painting from the Byzantine era down to the present, with special reference to their reflection of cultural values and attitudes and the influence of both Christianity and secular cultural currents upon them.[7]

For these reasons, an additional hour for the course each of the two semesters of the freshman year would be highly desirable if an adequate account is to be given of the first four periods of Christian culture (that is, on the premise that these will be covered in the first two semesters of the four available in a Lower Division program).

As an example of what is available in filmstrips and film slides from just

---

7. For a general survey of material available for these purposes, see Edgar Dale's *Audio-Visual Methods in Teaching* (1954), and more specific guides such as Milton Brooke and Henry J. Dubester's *Guide to Color Prints* (1953), William Chapman's *Films on Art* (1952), and UNESCO's *Films on Art* (1950). (These are cited by Patrick D. Hazard in his article in *Contemporary Literary Scholarship* [1958], ed. by L. Leary.)

one publisher, the following items from the Herbert E. Budek Company of Hackensack, N.J., may be cited: *In color:* Ten sets of Italian paintings of different schools, 35 to 40 frames each; six sets of Flemish paintings of different schools, 30 to 35 frames each; six sets of Mosaics and Frescoes in Italian Church Buildings, 35 frames each; one set on the Mission Churches of New Mexico, 32 frames; two sets on the paintings of Rouault, 33 frames each. *In black and white:* The History of Western Art, comprising 30 sets of filmstrips and film slides, including such subjects as: (1) Greek Art, 2 sets of 40 frames each; (2) Early Christian, Byzantine and Migration Art, one set of 40 frames; (3) Architecture and Sculpture of the Early and the Late Middle Ages, 2 sets of 40 frames each; (4) Illuminated Manuscripts, one set of 40 frames; (5) Architecture, Sculpture, and Painting of the Renaissance, 3 sets of 40 frames each; (6) Architecture, Sculpture and Painting of the Baroque, 2 sets of 40 frames each; (7) The Cathedrals at Reims and Chartres, 2 sets of 40 frames each; (8) Architectural Styles: Romanesque, Gothic, Renaissance, Baroque, 1 set of 60 frames; (9) Impressionism and The Art of the Twentieth Century, 2 sets of 35 frames each. In addition, there are two other black and white series available: twelve sets dealing with the History of American Art, from 1600 to 1930; and five sets dealing with Italian Architecture, from the Florentine Renaissance to the eighteenth century.

Literature Courses—Sophomore Year

Literature and the Baroque Culture. A reading and discussion of certain selected works from the Renaissance to the eighteenth century. The focus will be on the coexistence of two contrasting influences on the culture of this period: the luxuriance and fantasy and passion of the Baroque spirit, and the sobriety and dedication and moral earnestness of the Protestant ethos, and their eventual replacement by the rationalism of the Enlightenment. Representative works that might be chosen for study include: Marlowe's *Dr. Faustus,* Shakespeare's *Macbeth* or *Antony and Cleopatra;* John Donne: selected sermons and poems; Cervantes' *Don Quixote* (Part One), Pascal's *Pensées,* Milton's *Paradise Lost* (first four books) and *Samson Agonistes;* Camoens' *Lusiads,* Bunyan's *Pilgrim's Progress,* Defoe's *Robinson Crusoe;* Jonathan Edwards: selections; Dryden's *The Hind and the Panther,* Pope's *Essay on Man.*

Literature and Modern Culture. A reading and discussion of selected works which represent the main streams of cultural development since the eighteenth century. A focus for most of the works selected should be found in one or another of three principal features of the cultural situation of this period: (1) the revolutionary attitude toward the established order of thought and social organization, which resulted from the Enlightenment and the French Revolution and produced reactions as various as Novalis' *Europe or Christendom,* Marx's *The Communist Manifesto,* and Nietzsche's *The Antichrist;* (2) the increasing isolation of the individual consciousness from the new technical society that was developing in the nineteenth and twentieth centuries: Freud's work (see, for example, *Civilization and Its Discontents*) and the parallel to his thought in modern poetry and fiction suggest possible selections for inclusion under this heading; (3) the effect upon the religious conscience of the growing secularization of society. (For example, Kierkegaard's *Attack upon "Christendom,"* Newman's conflict with the Liberalism of his age, Matthew Arnold's criticism of Philistine values, as also the thought of the other Victorian "prophets," all have their origins in this cultural situation.)

4. The Program Spanning the Lower and Upper Division

In this type of program, there would be time to devote one semester to each of the six periods of Christian culture and at the same time provide an exploration of the historical roots of the Christian tradition in the Old and New Testaments. Thus the freshman year would permit the Religion department of the college or university to present two historically oriented courses on the Scriptures, along the lines described for the Lower Division program; and if faculty resources and curricular arrangements permitted, this might be continued into the sophomore year with a study of the Apostolic Church and the Liturgy, also as described above. This second year might be made optional for the student, so that he might choose either this or some other approach to the study of Religion in the denominational college. Thus the courses which could be offered would include (see the titles under the Lower Division program for content and approach):

> Freshman Year: Israel and the Scriptures
>   The Gospel and the Kingdom
> Sophomore Year: The Apostolic Church
>   The Liturgy and the Christian Mystery

Beginning with the first term of the sophomore year, the student would be introduced to the study of Christian culture in itself, and he would thenceforth take one course in Christian culture (covering each of the six periods) each term until he had concluded his senior year. This would allow for a more leisurely approach to the subject and would give the student an opportunity to engage in more outside reading in connection with the course being taken. For this reason it should be possible to have key works of literature read in connection with the course rather than having them form part of a separate literature course related to Christian culture. However, two supplementary arrangements should be considered as a means of providing the student with a maximum of communication with Christian culture insights and understandings:

Christian Culture by John J. Mulloy

1. During the freshman year, as part of his reading list, the student might be required to read a certain number of books related to the historical development of Christian culture, which would at the same time afford him a rewarding esthetic experience. The choice might be made from the following works: T. S. Eliot, *Murder in the Cathedral*; G. K. Chesterton, *The Ballad of the White Horse* or *Orthodoxy* (or both, if the student became interested in Chesterton's thought); Sigrid Undset, *The Bridal Wreath* (first volume of Kristin Lavransdatter) or *The Axe* (first volume of The Master of Hestviken); Péguy, *Men and Saints* (a selection from his prose and poetry); Christopher Dawson, *The Movement of World Revolution*. There are, of course, numerous other volumes which might be used for the purpose in place of those which are here suggested.

2. For those who have found the Christian culture program a means of integration of their college work, there might be offered in the senior year a choice of either one or both of the courses in Literature—we have listed above for the Lower Division program (Literature and the Baroque Culture, Literature and Modern Culture), or a course in different conceptions of world history held by key thinkers since the eighteenth century (see in the list of courses under the graduate program the one entitled Christianity and Conceptions of World History). For those electing to take the Literature course(s) in the senior year, a more mature level of work and exploration of underlying ideas might be expected than from sophomore students taking it in the Lower Division program, and it might serve also as a basis for a senior essay.

The courses in cultural history would include the following:

The Ancient World and the Rise of Christian Culture. An examination of the chief elements in the culture of the ancient world in the first century B.C. A study of the development of the Christian Church and its influence upon culture during the first three centuries. Christianity's gradual penetration of the dominant urban Roman-Hellenistic culture, reaching its full development in the first half of the third century—the age of Clement and Origen in the East and of Tertullian and Cyprian in the West. A consideration of the main influences that moulded Christian culture during this period: the Bible and its tradition, martyrdom and ideals of Christian spirituality, the Christian conception of history, the Church as the new Israel, etc.

Byzantine Culture and the Age of the Fathers. A study of Byzantine culture from the fourth to the sixth centuries as the translation into Christian terms of the Hellenistic culture of the later Roman Empire. The fourth-century Fathers in East and West and the classical age of Christian thought. The Oriental origins of monasticism, its influence on Byzantine culture and its spread to Western Europe. Byzantine culture as the synthesis of Oriental and Hellenic elements. The flowering of Christian art and architecture and liturgical poetry, reaching its climax in the age of Justinian. Imperial patterns of Church-State relations and their effect upon the Oriental peoples of the Empire. Expansion of Christianity in the Orient. The coming of Islam, and its effects.

The Formation of Western Christendom. A study of the transplantation of Christianity from the civilized world of the Mediterranean to the barbarian world of Northern Europe. The change from urban to rural patterns of culture, and the key importance of monasticism in the new culture. The adaptation of barbarian institutions to Christian purposes. The creation of a Christian-barbarian culture through the mutual interpenetration of its two constitutive elements. The cultural achievements and missionary activities of the Celtic and Anglo-Saxon peoples. The Carolingian renaissance and the foundations of later medieval culture. The Viking and Magyar invasions and the conversion of Northern and Eastern Europe.

Medieval Christendom and the Gothic Culture. A study of the development of medieval culture from the eleventh to the fifteenth century. The creative centuries of Gothic culture as resulting from the union of the dynamic force of the monastic reforming movement with the universal spiritual leadership of the Papacy. The decline of medieval culture when the alliance of these two forces was severed early in the fourteenth century. Expressions of the creative unity of medieval culture in such developments as the Crusading movement and the Cistercian reform, the rise of the communes and the creation of the medieval universities, scholastic philosophy and the poetry of Dante, Gothic architecture and art and the establishment of new forms of monasticism in the Franciscan and Dominican Orders. Medieval culture in the fourteenth and fifteenth centuries as gradually disintegrating the imposing synthesis of the classical age, but producing its own specific cultural achievements: the mysticism of the Rhineland and the Low Countries, the scientific movement in the universities, the rise of national states and parliaments, the poetry of Chaucer and Langland, the art of Burgundy and Flanders, and the development of new styles of Gothic architecture for civic and religious purposes.

Divided Christendom and the Expansion of Western Culture. A study of the response of Western Christendom from the sixteenth to the eighteenth century to the challenges presented by the Protestant Reformation, the new lay culture of the Renaissance, the Turkish conquest of Eastern Europe, and the widening of geographical horizons in Asia and the Americas. The emergence of new patterns of religious culture in Protestant and Catholic Europe, the development of a new form of Christian humanist culture and education, the great expansion of missionary activity by Catholic Europe, and the formation of the new Baroque culture through the fusion of the humanist Renaissance with the Catholic Revival. Widespread influence of the Baroque in Europe and the Americas. The transplantation of Christian culture, in both its Catholic and Protestant forms, to the Americas. The rise of modern science and the international channels for its communication. The retreat of the Baroque culture before the rationalist culture of the Enlightenment.

Secularized Christendom and the Age of Revolution. A study of the rise of revolutionary ideologies and new forms of secularized culture in Europe, and their spread to other parts of the world. The effects of this development upon Catholic and Protestant culture areas and the differing character of their response. Topics to be studied will include: The Enlightenment and the European Revolution. The Impact of Liberalism on Protestant and Catholic Europe. The Industrial Revolution and the World Expansion of Western Culture. The Rise of the United States and New Patterns of Church-State Relations. Christian Missionary Expansion in Asia, Africa and Oceania. Nationalism and the Two World Wars. The Rise of Communism and the Totalitarian State. The Scientific Revolution and the Rise of Mass Culture. The Conflict between Christianity and Secularized Culture. Oriental Nationalism and the Shift in the Balance of World Power. Movements toward World Unity and the Ecumenical Problems of Christian Culture.

5. Honors Program

In accordance with current practice in Honors programs now in existence at American colleges and universities, the student should begin this program in the freshman year and have an opportunity to carry it through to its completion in the senior year. A senior essay should be required, based upon work in a seminar course in the senior year, in which the student would attempt to tie together in the perspective of an integrated view of reality the liberal arts studies he had pursued throughout his college curriculum.

The basic courses in cultural history should be given to the student in the freshman and sophomore year along the lines of the Lower Division program—which provides for a consideration of the interaction between Christianity and culture in three different social milieu—the ancient world, the medieval world, and the modern world. Alternatively, it might be thought preferable to have three years allotted to the study of the cultural development, in which case the required courses would end with the junior year and each of the six periods of Christian culture would have one term allotted to its study.

In the junior and senior years, the student should have the opportunity to take courses in two or more subject fields which would provide exploration in depth of some significant area, problem or historical development viewed from the Christian culture standpoint. At least two of these should be in addition to the seminar course upon which the senior essay is based.

Depending upon the faculty resources available for the Honors program at a particular college or university, the following courses might be found suitable for presentation on this Upper Division level.

Appendix E

1. One of the more specific courses we have listed above in the St. Mary's College Upper Division program: e.g., Ancient Christian Writers; Church, State and Society; Christianity and American Culture.

2. In universities with graduate divisions, the graduate courses listed above under the first of the alternatives suggested—the Graduate Program in Christian Culture Study—might be made available to undergraduate Honors students in the junior and senior years.

3. Courses in particular disciplines that show a cultural-historical orientation and involve understandings related to more than one departmental field. Examples of these, which might also be found helpful as the basis for the senior seminar, are as follows:

Greek Religious Thought and Early Christianity. A study of the religious orientation of Hellenic philosophy from the time of Socrates and Plato down to that of Marcus Aurelius and Plotinus, and the relationship of this tradition to the thought of the Fathers of the Church. An examination of the way in which the Hellenic tradition influenced Christian thought and at the same time was transformed into something new in the process of doing so.

Aspects of the History of Science. A study of the characteristics of scientific thought and the cultural factors that affected it in three different periods: the Hellenistic age, Europe in the thirteenth and fourteenth centuries, and the rise of modern science in the seventeenth century. Through this, an examination of the relationship of science to the Hellenic and Christian traditions.

The Unity of Philosophical Experience. A study of the philosophical challenge confronting the thinkers of three different periods in the development of Western philosophy: the medieval, the Cartesian, and the modern. A consideration of the responses made by the thinkers of each period and how the solutions arrived at in the historical development of each period suggest a certain unity that characterizes man's philosophic quest.

Christianity and the Renaissance. A study of the effects upon the Renaissance conception of man and the world of the converging influences of Christianity and classical humanism, and of how these affected the most characteristic developments of the period. An examination of the equilibrium between the two forces in the ethos of the Baroque culture and literature. Selections from Petrarch, Marsilio Ficino, Pope Pius II, Pico della Mirandola, Leonardo da Vinci, Erasmus, Leonardo Bruni, Thomas More, Cervantes, Campanella, John Donne, etc.

Spiritual Values and Mass Culture. A comparison of the critique of bourgeois culture in the Victorian period with the twentieth-century criticism of mass culture. Selections from Matthew Arnold and T. S. Eliot (both prose and poetry), and from Ruskin, Riesman, MacDonald, Dawson, Fromm.

Psychology and Comparative Culture. A study of the relationship between psychology, religion and culture, as expressed in the thought of certain key thinkers (e.g., Freud, Jung, William James, Max Weber, Erich Fromm, Bergson, Dawson), and as supported by the evidence of historical societies, both primitive and advanced, and of different periods in the development of Western culture.

The Religion Cultures of the Orient. A comparative study of the ethos and effects upon culture of each of the great world religions of the Orient—Confucianism, Hinduism, Buddhism, Islam. The particular values, institutions, and directions of cultural achievement characteristic of the different Oriental religion cultures. Points of similarity and contrast with Christianity, in both its Eastern and Western forms, and its effects upon cultural development.

Biographical Note

John J. Mulloy was the editor of the synthesis volume of Christopher Dawson's thought, *The Dynamics of World History*, and carried on with Dawson a continuing discussion about the implications of the Christian Culture proposals for the college and university curriculum. Mulloy taught modern European history at Central High School in Philadelphia, lectured in cultural anthropology at La Salle College, and served as chairman of the Committee on Religion in a Free Society, sponsored by the Philadelphia chapter of the National Conference of Christians and Jews for the furtherance of the dialogue and interreligious understanding.

In development of the ideas which he here sets forth for specific programs of Christian culture study, Mulloy gave graduate courses and conducted faculty seminar discussions in Christian Culture and in the Philosophy of History at Gonzaga University (Spokane, Washington); Rosemont College (Rosemont, Pennsylvania—near Philadelphia); Saint Mary-of-the-Woods College (near Terre Haute, Indiana); Mount St. Mary's College (Los Angeles, California); and St. Norbert College (West De Pere, Wisconsin—near Green Bay). He also served as organizer and general chairman of the Symposium on Christian Culture, co-sponsored by Rosemont College and Villanova University in the summer of 1959. This symposium brought together for panel discussions of Christian culture, Christopher Dawson and faculty representatives from different colleges and universities in the Eastern part of the United States

WORKS CITED

Sources Contemporary to Dawson or Earlier (before c. 1970)

(Note: Author names in the *Times Literary Supplement* did not originally appear with the anonymous reviews.)

"The Age of the Gods." Review of *The Age of the Gods. Dublin Review* CLXXXII (April 1928): 286–99.

"Communist Party Directive." In *Revolutionary Russia: A History in Documents,* edited by Robert Weinberg and Laurie Bernstein, 98–99. 1923; New York: New York University Press, 2011.

"A Crusade Against Nazi Paganism." *Times,* July 22, 1940, 2.

The Ethics of Birth Control. London: Macmillan, 1926.

General Education in a Free Society: Report of the Harvard Committee. Cambridge, Mass.: Harvard University Press, 1945.

Harvard Divinity School: Official Register of the University. Cambridge, Mass.: Havard University Press, 1958–1961.

Humanist Manifesto. 1933. http://americanhumanist.org/about/manifesto1.html.

"LePlay House." *Sociological Review* XII (1920): 1.

"Rig Veda." https://www.milestonedocuments.com/documents/view/rig-veda/text. Accessed December 17, 2019.

"Toward a Christian Order." *Present Truth* 57, no 12 (1941): 2–3, 7.

"War Cabinet, 1917." In *British Government 1914–1953: Select Documents*, edited by G. H. L. Le May, 229–32. London: Mathuen, 1955.

Acton, John E. E. D. (Lord). *A Lecture on the Study of History.* London and New York: Macmillan, 1895.

———. "Letter to Contributors to the *Cambridge Modern History*." In *Essays in the Liberal Interpretation of History*, edited by William H. McNeill, 396–99. Chicago and London: University of Chicago Press, 1967.

———. "The Massacre of St. Bartholomew." In *Essays in the Study and Writing of History*, edited by J. Rufus Fears, 198–240. Indianapolis, Ind.: LibertyClassics, 1986.

———. "Review of Philp's *History of Progress in Great Britain*." In *Essays in the Study and Writing of History*, edited by J. Rufus Fears, 31–33. Indianapolis, Ind.: LibertyClassics, 1986.

Alzog, John. *Manual of Universal Church History.* Vol. 1. Translated by F. J. Pabisch and Thos. S. Byrne. Cincinnati, Ohio: Robert Clarke, 1874.

Baillie, John. *The Belief in Progress.* London: Oxford University Press, 1950.

Barker, Ernest. *Age and Youth: Memories of Three Universities & Father of the Man.* London: Oxford University Press, 1953.

Works Cited

———. *The Dominican Order and Convocation: A Study of the Growth of Representation in the Church During the Thirteenth Century*. Oxford: Clarendon, 1913.

Barnes, Harry Elmer. Review of *Dynamics of World History*. *American Historical Review* LXIII (1957): 77–79.

Becker, Carl L. *The Heavenly City of the Eighteenth-Century Philosophers*. New Haven, Conn.: Yale University Press, 1932.

Belloc, Hilaire. *Characters of the Reformation*. London: Sheed & Ward, 1936.

———. "The Entry into the Dark Ages." Review of *The Cambridge Mediaeval History*, vol. 1. *Dublin Review* CLI (1912): 357–69.

———. *Europe and the Faith*. London: Constable, 1920.

———. "Mr. Belloc on the Middle Ages." *Tablet*, February 4, 1922.

———. "On a Method of Writing History." *Dublin Review* CXLIX (1911): 143–55.

———. "A Page of Gibbon." *Dublin Review* CLIX (1916): 361–76.

———. "Professor Bury's *History of Freedom of Thought*." *Dublin Review* CLIV (1914): 149–71.

———. *Robespierre: A Study*. 1901; London: Nisbet, 1927.

Bergonzi, Bernard. "The English Catholics: Forward from 'the Chesterbelloc.'" *Encounter* XXIV, January 1965, 19–30.

Binding, Karl, and Alfred Hoche. *Allowing the Destruction of Life Unworthy of Life: Its Measure and Form*. Translated by Christina Modak. 1920; Greenwood, Wisc.: Suzeteo Enterprises, 2015.

Blake, William. "Auguries of Innocence." 1863. Poetry Lovers Page. http://www.poetryloverspage.com/poets/blake/ to_see_world.html.

Boas, Franz. "The Methods of Ethnology." *American Anthropologist* 22, no. 4 (October/December 1920): 316–17.

Branford, Victor. Review of *Progress and Religion*. *Sociological Review* XXI (1929): 361–62.

———. and Patrick Geddes. *The Coming Polity: A Study in Reconstruction*. London: Williams and Norgate, 1917.

Bremond, Henri. *A Literary History of Religious Thought in France: From the Wars of Religion Down to Our Own Times*. Translated by K. L. Montgomery. London: Society for Promoting Christian Knowledge, 1928.

Brinton, Crane. Review of *Dynamics of World History*. *Speculum* XXXIII (1958): 272.

Brittain, Vera. "Modern Europe Adrift." Review of *Progress and Religion*. *Time and Tide* X (1929): 592–93.

Brunner, Emil. *Eternal Hope*. Translated by Harold Knight. London: Lutterworth, 1954.

Bruun, Geoffrey. "Why Civilizations Rise and Decline." *New York Times*, January 25, 1959, BR 26.

Buckle, H. T. *History of Civilization in England*. Vol. 1. London: J. W. Parker & Son, 1857.

Bury, J. B. "Cleopatra's Nose." In *Selected Essays of J. B. Bury*, edited by Harold Temperley, 60–69. Cambridge: Cambridge University Press, 1930.

———. "Darwinism and History." In *Selected Essays of J. B. Bury*, edited by Harold Temperley, 23–42. Cambridge: Cambridge University Press, 1930.

———. *A History of Freedom of Thought*. London: Williams & Norgate, 1913.

———. *The Idea of Progress: An Inquiry into Its Origin and Growth*. London: Macmillan, 1920.

———. *An Inaugural Lecture, Delivered in the Divinity School Cambridge on January 26, 1903.* Cambridge: Cambridge University Press, 1903.

———. "A Letter on the Writing of History." In *Selected Essays of J. B. Bury*, edited by Harold Temperley, 70–71. Cambridge: Cambridge University Press, 1930.

Butler, Abbot. "Friedrich von Hügel." *Tablet*, February 14, 1925, 201–2.

Butterfield, Herbert. *Lord Acton*. London: G. Philip & Son, 1948.

———. *Man on His Past: The Study of the History of Historical Scholarship.* Boston: Beacon, 1960.

———. "Religion's Part in History." Review of *The Dividing of Christendom*; *The Gods of Revolution. Times Literary Supplement*, July 28, 1972, 881–82.

Calverton, V. F. *The Bankruptcy of Marriage*. New York: Macaulay, 1928.

Campbell, James M. "The Dawson Challenge: A Discussion." *Commonweal*, April 16, 1955, 66, 68–70, 73–74.

Carlyle, Thomas. *On Heroes, Hero-Worship and the Heroic in History*. 1841; London: Chapman & Hall, 1888.

Chesterton, G. K. *A Short History of England*. 1917; London: Chatto & Windus, 1924.

Childe, V. Gordon. Review of *The Age of the Gods. Antiquity* II (1928): 485–86.

Churchill, Winston. "Hitler and His Choice." In *Great Contemporaries*, edited by James W. Muller, 251–58. 1937; Wilmington, Del.: ISI Books, 2012.

———. "Iron Curtain Speech." Milestone Documents, March 5, 1946. https://www.milestonedocuments.com/documents/view/winston-churchillsthe-sinews-of-peace/text.

———. "King George V." In *Great Contemporaries*, edited by James W. Muller, 251–58. 1937; Wilmington, Del.: ISI Books, 2012.

Cogley, John. "Education—and All That." *Commonweal*, April 29, 1955, 104.

———. "The Future of an Illusion." *Commonweal*, June 2, 1967, 310–16.

———. "God and Caesar." *Commonweal*, September 6, 1957, 563.

Cole, G. D. G., and Margaret Cole. *A Guide to Modern Politics*. New York: Alfred A. Knopf, 1934.

Collingwood, R. G. *An Autobiography*. 1939; Oxford: Clarendon, 1978.

Cook, Bruce. "An Answer for Colleges: The St. Mary's Program." *U.S. Catholic*, November 1965, 25–31.

Crombie, John. Letter to his mother, March 2, 1917. In *World War I & European Society: A Sourcebook*, edited by Marilyn Shevin-Coetzee and Frans Coetzee, 201. Lexington, Mass.: D. C. Heath, 1995.

Dawson, Christopher. *The Age of the Gods: A Study in the Origins of Culture in Prehistoric Europe and the Ancient East*. 1928; Washington, D.C.: The Catholic University of America Press, 2012.

———. "America and the Secularization of Modern Culture." *Logos* 3, no. 3 (Summer 2000): 23–34.

———. "Arnold Toynbee and the Study of History." In *Dynamics of World History*, edited by John J. Mulloy, 405–18. 1956; Wilmington, Del.: ISI Books, 2002.

———. "St. Augustine and His Age." In *Enquiries into Religion and Culture*, 164–213. 1933; Washington, D.C.: The Catholic University of America Press, 2009.

———. *Beyond Politics*. London: Sheed & Ward, 1939.

Works Cited

——. "The Catholic Tradition and the Modern State." *Catholic Review* 1916, 24–35.

——. "The Challenge of Secularism." *Catholic World* 182, no. 1091 (February 1956): 326–30.

——. "Christian Culture: Its Meaning and Its Value." *Jubilee*, May 1956, 37–40.

——. "Christianity and Sex." In *Enquiries into Religion and Culture*, 214–40. 1933; Washington, D.C.: The Catholic University of America Press, 2009.

——. "Christianity and the Idea of Progress." *Dublin Review* CLXXX (1927): 19–39.

——. *Christianity and the New Age*. London: Sheed & Ward, 1931.

——. "The Christian View of History." In *Dynamics of World History*, edited by John J. Mulloy, 245–62. 1956; Wilmington, Del.: ISI Books, 2002.

——. "Church, State and Community." *Tablet*, June 26, 1937, 909–10.

——. "Civilisation and Morals; or, The Ethical Basis of Social Progress." *Sociological Review* XVII (1925): 174–81.

——. "The Claims of Politics." *Scrutiny* VIII, no. 2 (1939): 136–41.

——. "Conservatism." 1932. Edited by Joseph T. Stuart. *The Political Science Reviewer* 39, no. 1 (2010): 232–62.

——. "The Crisis of Christian Culture: Education." In *Our Culture: Its Christian Roots and Present Crisis*, edited by V. A. Demant, 35–49. London: Society for Promoting Christian Knowledge, 1947.

——. "The Crisis of the West." *Dublin Review* CLXXXI (1927): 261–77.

——. *The Crisis of Western Education*. 1961; Washington, D.C.: The Catholic University of America Press, 2010.

——. "Cycles of Civilisation." In *Enquiries into Religion and Culture*, 55–77. 1933; Washington, D.C.: The Catholic University of America Press, 2009.

——. "The Dark Mirror." *Dublin Review* CLXXXVII (1930): 177–200.

——. "Dealing with the Enlightenment and the Liberal Ideology." *Commonweal*, May 14, 1954, 138–39.

——. *The Dividing of Christendom*. Garden City, N.Y.: Image Books, 1965.

——. "Documents of American Church History." *America*, April 27, 1957, 32–36.

——. *Dynamics of World History*. Edited by John J. Mulloy. 1956; Wilmington, Del.: ISI Books, 2002.

——. "Editorial Note." *Dublin Review* CCVII (October 1940): 129–31.

——. "Education and Christian Culture." *Commonweal*, December 4, 1953, 216–20.

——. "Education and the Crisis of Christian Culture" *Lumen Vitae* 1, no. 2 (1946): 204–14.

——. "Education and the State." *Commonweal*, January 27, 1957, 423–27.

——. "Education and the Study of Christian Culture." *Studies* 42, no.1 (Autumn 1953): 293.

——. "Edward Gibbon." *Proceedings of the British Academy* XX (1934): 1592-80.

——. "Edward Gibbon and the Fall of Rome." In *Dynamics of World History*, edited by John J. Mulloy, 341–67. 1956; Wilmington, Del.: ISI Books, 2002.

——. "The End of an Age." *Criterion* IX, no. 1 (April 1930): 386–401.

——. *Enquiries into Religion and Culture*. 1933; Washington, D.C.: The Catholic University of America Press, 2009.

——. "European Democracy and the New Economic Forces." *Sociological Review* XXII (1930): 32–42.

——. "Fascism and the Corporate State." *Catholic Herald*, August 3, 1935.

——. *The Formation of Christendom*. New York: Sheed & Ward, 1967.

_____. "Future of Christian Culture." *Commonweal*, March 19, 1954, 595–98.

——. "The Future of National Government." *Dublin Review* CXCVI (1935): 236–51.

——. *The Gods of Revolution*. London: Sidgwick & Jackson, 1972.

——. "He Gave ... His Whole Self." *Sociological Review* XXIV (1932): 24.

——. "Herr Spengler and the Life of Civilisations." *Sociological Review* XIV (1922): 194–201.

——. *The Historic Reality of Christian Culture: A Way to the Renewal of Human Life*. London: Routledge & Kegan Paul, 1960.

——. "History and the Christian Revelation." In *Dynamics of World History*, edited by John J. Mulloy, 263–73. 1956; Wilmington, Del.: ISI Books, 2002.

——. "Hitler's 'Mein Kampf.'" *Tablet*, March 25, 1939, 373–74.

——. "The Impact of Religion on the Modern World." *Commonweal*, January 18, 1957, 412–13.

——. "The Institutional Forms of Christian Culture." *Religion in Life: A Christian Quarterly of Opinion and Discussion* 24, no. 3 (Summer 1955): 373–80.

——. "Interracial Cooperation as a Factor in European Culture." In *Convegno Volta*. Rome: Reale Accademia D'Italia, 1933, 5–10.

——. "Islamic Mysticism." *Dublin Review* CLXXXVI (1930): 34–61.

——. "On Jewish History." 1959. www.ewtn.com/library.HOMELIBR/DAWJEWHS. TXT.

——. *The Judgment of the Nations*. 1942; Washington, D.C.: The Catholic University of America Press, 2011.

——. "The Kingdom of God and History." In *Dynamics of World History*, edited by John J. Mulloy, 283–99. 1956; Wilmington, Del.: ISI Books, 2002.

——. "The Life of Civilisations." *Sociological Review* XIV (1922): 51–68.

——. *The Making of Europe: An Introduction to the History of European Unity*. 1932; Washington, D.C.: The Catholic University of America Press, 2003.

——. *Medieval Essays*. 1954; Washington, D.C.: The Catholic University of America Press, 2002.

——. "Memories of a Victorian Childhood." In *A Historian and His World: A Life of Christopher Dawson*, by Christina Scott, 221–39. 1984; New Brunswick, N.J.: Transaction, 1992.

——. *The Modern Dilemma: The Problem of European Unity*. London: Sheed & Ward, 1932.

——. *The Movement Towards Christian Unity in the Nineteenth Century*. Latrobe, Pa.: Saint Vincent Archabbey, 2006.

——. *The Mongol Mission: Narratives and Letters of the Franciscan Missionaries in Mongolia and China in the Thirteenth and Fourteenth Centuries*. New York: Sheed & Ward, 1955.

——. *The Movement of World Revolution*. 1959; Washington D.C., The Catholic University of America Press, 2013.

——. "Mystery of China." *Sociological Review* XIX (1927): 297–303.

——. "The Nature and Destiny of Man." In *Enquiries into Religion and Culture*, 256–86. 1933; Washington, D. C.: The Catholic University of America Press, 2009.

——. "The New Leviathan." *Dublin Review* CLXXXV (1929): 88–102.

——. "Newman and the Sword of the Spirit." *The Sword of the Spirit*, August 1945, 1–2.

——. "On the Development of Sociology in Relation to the Theory of Progress." *Sociological Review* XIII (1921): 75–83.

——. "The Outlook for Christian Culture Today." *Cross Currents* 5, no. 1 (Spring 1955): 127–36.

Works Cited

———. "The Passing of Industrialism." *Sociological Review* XII (1920): 6–17.

———. "On the Place of Religious Study in Education." *Christian Scholar* 45, no. 1 (1962): 37–43.

———. "The Politics of Hegel." *Dublin Review* CCXII (1943): 97–107.

———. *The Power of the Spirit (Sword of the Spirit* pamphlet). London, 1943.

———. "Prevision in Religion." In *Dynamics of World History*, edited by John J. Mulloy, 95–107. 1956; Wilmington, Del.: ISI Books, 2002.

———. "Problems of Christian Culture." *Commonweal*, April 15, 1955, 34–36.

———. "The Problem of Metahistory." In *Dynamics of World History*, edited by John J. Mulloy, 303–10. 1957; Wilmington, Del.: ISI Books, 2002.

———. "The Problem of Wealth." *Spectator*, October 17, 1931, 485–86.

———. "Progress and Decay in Ancient and Modern Civilization." In *Dynamics of World History*, edited by John J. Mulloy, 57–70. 1956; Wilmington, Del.: ISI Books, 2002.

———. *Progress and Religion: An Historical Enquiry.* 1929; Washington, D.C.: The Catholic University of America Press, 2001.

———. "Propaganda." *Tablet*, October 5, 1940, 265–66.

———. "Rationalism and Intellectualism: The Religious Elements in the Rationalist Tradition." In *Enquiries into Religion and Culture*, 114–28. 1933; Washington, D.C.: The Catholic University of America Press, 2009.

———. "Religion." In *Chamber's Encyclopedia* XI: 591–93. London: George Newnes, 1950.

———. *Religion and Culture.* 1948; Washington, D.C.: The Catholic University of America Press, 2013.

———. "Religion and Primitive Culture." *Sociological Review* XVII (1925): 105–19.

———. "Religion and the Life of Civilization." In *Religions of the Empire: A Conference on Some Living Religions with the Empire*, edited by William Loftus Hare, 455–69. New York: Macmillan, 1925.

———. *Religion and the Modern State.* New York: Sheed & Ward, 1935.

———. *Religion and the Rise of Western Culture.* 1950; New York: Doubleday/Image Books, 1991.

———. "Religion in an Age of Revolution." *Tablet*, October 24, 1936, 549–51.

———. "Religious Enthusiasm." Review of *Enthusiasm* by Ronald Knox. *Month* (new series) V (1951): 7–14.

———. "The Revolt of the East and the Catholic Tradition." *Dublin Review* CLXXXIII (July 1928): 1–14.

———. "A Scheme of British Culture Periods, and of their Relation to European Cultural Developments." *Sociological Review* XVI (1924): 117–19.

———. "The Significance of Bolshevism." In *Enquiries into Religion and Culture*, 17–26. 1933; Washington, D.C.: The Catholic University of America Press, 2009, 17–26.

———. Review of *Small Houses of the Late Georgian Period: 1750–1820. Sociological Review* XVI (1924): 76.

———. "Sociology and the Theory of Progress." In *Dynamics of World History*, edited by John J. Mulloy, 35–45. 1956; Wilmington, Del.: ISI Books, 2002.

———. "Sociology as a Science." In *Science Today: The Scientific Outlook on World Problems Explained by Leading Exponents of Modern Scientific Thought*, edited by J. G. Crowther and Sir J. Arthur Thomson, 151–72. London: Eyre & Spottiswoode, 1934.

——. "Sociology as a Science." In *Dynamics of World History*, edited by John J. Mulloy, 13–33. 1956; Wilmington, Del.: ISI Books, 2002.

——. "Spain and Europe," *Catholic Times* [London], March 12, 1937.

——. Letter to the Editor. *Spectator*, September 27, 1957, 398.

——. *The Spirit of the Oxford Movement*. 1933; London: Saint Austin, 2001.

——. "The Study of Christian Culture." *Thought* 35, no. 1 (1960): 485–93.

——. "The Study of Christian Culture as a Means of Education." *Lumen Vitae* 5, no. 1 (January 1950): 175.

——. "The Study of Christian Culture in the American College." *Catholic World* 183, no. 1095 (1956): 197–201.

——. "The Sword of the Spirit." *Dublin Review* CCVIII (January 1941): 1–11.

——. "The Sword of the Spirit." *Tablet*, August 31, 1940.

——. "Task for Christian Education." *Catholic World* 165, no. 1 (1947): 463–64.

——. "T. S. Eliot on the Meaning of Culture." In *Dynamics of World History*, edited by John J. Mulloy, 109–15. 1956; Wilmington, Del.: ISI Books, 2002.

——. *Understanding Europe*. 1952; Washington D.C.: The Catholic University of America Press, 2009.

——. "Why I Am a Catholic." *Catholic Times* [London], May 21, 1926, 10–11.

——. "William Langland (1333–1399): *The Vision of Piers Plowman*." In *The English Way: Studies in English Sanctity from St. Bede to Newman*, edited by Maisie Ward, 159–94. London: Sheed & Ward, 1933.

——. "The World Crisis and the English Tradition." In *Dynamics of World History*, edited by John J. Mulloy, 225–36. 1956; Wilmington, Del.: ISI Books, 2002.

——. and Alexander Farquharson. "The Beginnings of Rome." *Sociological Review* XV (1923): Part I: 132–47; Part II: 296–311.

De la Bedoyere, Michael. "An Introduction to Catholic Sociology." *Dublin Review* CXCIII (1933): 31–45.

De Man, Henry. *The Remaking of a Mind: A Soldier's Thoughts on War and Resurrection*. New York: Charles Scribner's Sons, 1919.

Demant, V. A., ed. *Our Culture: Its Christian Roots and Present Crisis*. London: Society for Promoting Christian Knowledge, 1947.

——. *Theology of Society: More Essays in Christian Polity*. London: Faber & Faber, 1947.

Dewey, John. "My Pedagogic Creed." *School Journal* 54, no. 1 (January 1897): 77–80.

Digby, Kenelm. *Godefridus*. London: Bernard Quaritch, 1877.

Doyle, Sir Arthur Conan. "My Religion." In *My Religion*, 27–33. London: Hutchinson, 1925.

Dugmore, C. W., ed. *The Interpretation of the Bible: Edward Alleyn Lectures, 1943*. London: Society for Promoting Christian Knowledge, 1944.

Durkheim, Émile. *The Elementary Forms of Religious Life*. Translated by Carol Cosman. 1912; Oxford: Oxford University Press, 2001.

Eckermann, Johann P. *Conversations of Goethe with Eckermann and Soret*. Translated by John Oxenford. London: Smith, Elder, 1850.

Eliot, T. S. *Notes Towards the Definition of Culture*. New York: Harcourt, Brace, 1949.

——. "The Waste Land." 1922. Poetry Foundation, https://www.poetryfoundation.org/poems/47311/the-waste-land.

Works Cited

Ellwood, Charles A. *The Reconstruction of Religion: A Sociological View*. New York: Macmillan, 1922.

_____. "The Social Problem and the Present War." *Sociological Review* VIII (1915): 1–14.

Farquharson, Alexander. "The Oxford Conference on the Correlation of the Social Sciences: An Appreciation of the Discussions, with Abstracts of the Papers Read." *Sociological Review* XV (1923): 48–64.

Fisher, H. A. L. "European Unity." Review of *The Making of Europe*. *English Review* LV (1932): 97–99.

———. *A History of Europe*. London: Edward Arnold, 1936.

Fitzgerald, F. Scott. *The Great Gatsby*. 1925; Oxford: Oxford University Press, 1998.

Fliche, Augustin. *Le Moyen Age* VII (1936): 142–44.

Forde, C. Daryll. Review of *The Age of the Gods*. *American Anthropologist* (new series) XXXIV, no. 2 (1932): 340–41.

Frankl, Viktor E. *Man's Search for Meaning: An Introduction to Logotherapy*. 1946; New York: Pocket Books, 1963.

Frazer, James George. *The Golden Bough*. 1922; New York: Macmillan, 1950.

Freud, Sigmund. "Totem and Taboo." In *The Basic Writings of Sigmund Freud*, translated by A. A. Brill, 807–930. New York: Modern Library, 1938.

Friedan, Betty. *The Feminine Mystique*. 1963; New York: Dell, 1977.

Frost, Robert. "Education by Poetry." 1931. http://moodyap.pbworks.com/f/frost.EducationByPoetry.pdf.

Fueloep-Miller, René. *The Mind and Face of Bolshevism*. 1926; New York: Harper Torchbooks, 1965.

Gans, Herbert J. *The Levittowners: Ways of Life and Politics in a New Suburban Community*. New York: Vintage Books, 1967.

Geddes, Patrick, and J. Arthur Thomson. *Biology*. London: Williams & Northgate, 1925.

Gibbon, Edward. *Memoirs of My Life and Writings*. 1796. Project Gutenberg, http://www.gutenberg.org/files/6031/6031-h.htm.

———. *The Decline and Fall of the Roman Empire*. 1776–1789. https://www.ourcivilisation.com/smartboard/shop/gibbone/rome/volume1/chap31.htm.

Gillespie, James Edward. *American Historical Review* 38, no. 4 (July 1933): 785–86.

Gilson, Étienne. *The Unity of Philosophical Experience*. 1937; San Francisco: Ignatius, 1964.

Gleason, John. "The Study of Christian Culture: A New Approach to General Education." *Educational Record* 40, no. 1 (1959): 155–58.

Green, J. R. *A Short History of the English People*. Revised ed. New York: American Book, 1874.

Green, Peter Morris. "God and History." *Times Literary Supplement*, December 27, 1957, 781–82.

Guthrie, Keith. "The Modern Dilemma." Review of *Religion and Culture*. *Spectator*, December 10, 1948, 784, 786.

Halphen, Louis. "Histoire de France." *Revue historique* CLXXI, no. 1 (1933): 143–61.

Harnack, Adolf. *History of Dogma*. Vol. 1. Boston: Roberts Brothers, 1897.

Hartnett, Robert C. "The Dawson Challenge: A Discussion." *Commonweal*, April 16, 1955, 74, 76, 88–90.

Hearnshaw, F. J. C., ed. *Mediæval Contributions to Modern Civilization*. New York: Barnes & Noble, 1921.

Works Cited

Herberg, Will. *Protestant, Catholic, Jew: An Essay in American Religious Sociology*. New York: Doubleday, 1955.

Herbertson, Dorothy. *The Life of Frédéric Le Play*. Edited by Victor Branford and Alexander Farquharson. Ledbury: Le Play House, 1950.

Herodotus. *The Essential Herodotus*. Translated by William A. Johnson. New York: Oxford University Press, 2017.

Hill, Christopher. "The Church, Marx and History." *Spectator*, September 20, 1957, 370.

———. Letter to the Editor. *Spectator*, October 11, 1957, 479.

Hinsley, Cardinal. "The Sword of the Spirit." *Tablet*, December 16, 1939, 705–6.

Hitler, Adolf. *Mein Kampf*. Vol. 1. http://www.hitler.org/writings/Mein_Kampf/ index.html. Accessed January 9, 2020.

Hobhouse, L. T. *Development and Purpose: An Essay towards a Philosophy of Evolution*. Revised ed. 1913; London: Macmillan, 1927.

———. *Mind in Evolution*. 3rd ed. 1901; London: Macmillan, 1926.

———. *Social Development: Its Nature and Conditions*. London: George Allen & Unwin, 1924.

Hobson, J. A., and Morris Ginsberg. *L. T. Hobhouse: His Life and Work*. 1924; London: Routledge/Thoemmes, 1996.

Hügel, Friedrich von. Letter to William James, May 10, 1909. In *Downside Review* XCVIII (1980): 214–36.

Husserl, Edmund. *The Crisis of European Sciences and Transcendental Phenomenology*. Translated by David Carr. 1936; Evanston, Ill.: Northwestern University Press, 1970.

Huxley, Aldous. "Light on the Dark Ages." Review of *The Making of Europe*. *Spectator*, August 20, 1932, 235.

Inge, W. R. "The Idea of Progress." In *Outspoken Essays*. London: Longmans, Green, 1922, 158–83.

James, William. *The Varieties of Religious Experience*. New York: Random House Modern Library, 1902.

———. *The Will to Believe: And Other Essays in Popular Philosophy*. London: Longmans, Green, 1896.

Joad, C. E. M. "Forward to Christendom." Review of *The Judgment of the Nations*. *New Statesman and Nation*, August 28, 1943, 141–42.

Kevane, Eugene. "Christopher Dawson and the Study of Christian Culture." *Catholic Educational Review* 57, no. 1 (1959): 447–62.

———. *The Lord of History*. 1980; Steubenville, Ohio: Emmaus Road, 2018.

Knowles, David. "Christopher Dawson." *Tablet*, June 6, 1970, 558.

Kochan, Lionel. *Acton on History*. Port Washington, N.Y.: Kennikat, 1954.

Kölmel, W. *Stimmen der Zeit* CXXX, 1936.

Lawler, Justus George. *The Catholic Dimension in Higher Education*. Westminster, Md.: Newman, 1959.

———. "*The Crisis of Western Education* [1]." *Theological Studies* 22, no. 3 (1961): 504–6.

———. "*The Crisis of Western Education* [2]." *Harvard Educational Review* 32, no.1 (1962): 214–20.

Lowie, Robert H. *Culture and Ethnology*. New York: Basic Books, 1966.

Löwith, Karl. *Meaning in History*. Chicago: University of Chicago Press, 1949.

Works Cited

MacDougall, Hugh A. *The Acton-Newman Relations: The Dilemma of Christian Liberalism.* New York: Fordham University Press, 1962.

Malinowski, Bronislaw. *Argonauts of the Western Pacific: An Account of Native Enterprise and Adventure in the Archipelagoes of Melanesian New Guinea.* London: George Routledge & Sons, 1922.

———. *Sex and Repression in Savage Society.* London: Kegan Paul, Trench, Trubner, 1927.

Martin, William Oliver. *The Order and Integration of Knowledge.* Ann Arbor: University of Michigan Press, 1957.

Mathew, Gervase. "Religion in History." Review of *Religion and the Rise of Western Culture. Times Literary Supplement,* April 7, 1950, Religious Book Section, vii.

McGoldrick, Bernard E. "To the Editors." *Commonweal,* February 15, 1957, 513.

McMahon, Joseph H. "Christian Culture." *Commonweal,* January 7, 1955, 382–83.

McNaspy, C. J. "A Chat with Christopher Dawson." *America.* October 28, 1961, 120–22.

———. "Motel near Walden II." *America,* January 21, 1961, 508, 511.

McNeill, William H. *Journal of Modern History* XXIX (1957): 257–58.

McNichols, Marie Corde. "Western Culture and the Mystical Body." *Catholic World* 186 (December 1957): 166–72.

Mead, Margaret. *New Lives for Old: Cultural Transformation—Manus, 1928–1953.* 1956; New York: William Morrow, 1966.

Mill, John Stuart. *On Liberty.* 1859; Indianapolis, Ind.: Hackett, 1978.

Miller, Perry. *The New England Mind: The Seventeenth Century.* Cambridge, Mass.: Harvard University Press, 1954.

Mills, C. Wright. *The Sociological Imagination.* New York: Oxford University Press, 1959.

Moss, H. St. L. B. Review of *The Making of Europe. History* XVIII (1933): 250–53.

Mulloy, John J. "A Reply." *Harvard Educational Review* 32, no. 1 (1962): 220–25.

Murray, Gilbert. "Religio Grammatici: The Religion of a 'Man of Letters.'" In *Essays and Addresses,* 11–30. London: George Allen and Unwin, 1922.

Murray, John Courtney. "The Church and Totalitarian Democracy." *Theological Studies* 14, no. 1 (December 1952): 525–63.

Mussolini, Benito. "The Doctrine of Fascism." 1932. Milestone Documents. http://www .milestonedocuments.com/documents/view/benito-mussolinisthe-doctrine-of-fascism/text.

———. *My Autobiography.* Translated by Richard Washburn Child. 1928; London: Hutchinson, 1939.

Musurillo, Herbert A. "Dawson's Program: A Criticism." *Thought* 30, no. 2 (Summer 1955): 174–87.

———. "The Problem of Catholic Education: A Reply to Christopher Dawson." *Catholic World* 184, no. 1100 (November 1956): 94–98.

Newman, John Henry. "Abuses of the Colleges: Oxford." In *University Sketches,* edited by Michael Tierney, 220–30. 1856; Westminster, Md.: Newman, 1953.

———. "Colleges the Corrective of Universities: Oxford." In *University Sketches,* edited by Michael Tierney, 206–19. 1856; Westminster, Md.: Newman, 1953.

———. *An Essay on the Development of Christian Doctrine.* 1845; London: Longmans, Green, 1906.

———. *The Idea of a University.* 1873; Tacoma, Wash.: Cluny Media, 2016.

———. "Professors and Tutors." In *University Sketches*, edited by Michael Tierney, 172–84. 1856; Westminster, Md.: Newman, 1953.

Niebuhr, Reinhold. *Faith and History: A Comparison of Christian and Modern Views of History*. London: Nisbet, 1949.

Novak, Frank G., Jr., ed. *Lewis Mumford and Patrick Geddes: The Correspondence*. 1915–1932; London: Routledge, 1995.

Novak, Michael. "Professor Dawson Speaks out on Church, State, and Religious Education in America." *Jubilee*, April 1961, 27.

O'Connor, Flannery. *Mystery and Manners*. Edited by Sally and Robert Fitzgerald. New York: Farrar Strauss and Giroux, 1969.

O'Connor, J. Arthur. "The Issues of Catholic Sociology." *Dublin Review* CXCIV (1934): 101–16.

O'Doherty, John Francis. *Irish Ecclesiastical Record* XLIV (1934): 553–55.

O'Leary, Mary Florence Margaret. *The Catholic Church and Education*. London: Catholic Book Club, 1943.

O'Malley, Frank. "The Culture of the Church." *Review of Politics* 16, no. 2 (1954): 131–54.

Otto, Rudolf. *The Idea of the Holy*. Translated by John W. Harvey. 2nd ed. 1923; Oxford: Oxford University Press, 1958.

Park, Robert E. Review of *Enquiries into Religion and Culture*. *American Journal of Sociology* XLI (1935): 109–11.

Paul VI, Pope. *Gaudium et Spes*. Pastoral Constitution. Vatican. December 7, 1965. http://www.vatican.va/archive/hist_councils/ii_vatican_council/documents/vat-ii_const_19651207_gaudium-et-spes_en.html.

Paul, Herbert, ed. *Letters of Lord Acton to Mary Gladstone, Daughter of the Right Hon. W. E. Gladstone*. London: George Allen, 1904.

Petrie, Charles. *Chapters of Life*. London: Eyre & Spottiswoode, 1950.

Pieper, Josef. *Leisure the Basis of Culture*. 1952; San Francisco: Ignatius, 2009.

Pius XI, Pope. *Divini Redemptoris*. Encyclical Letter. Vatican. March 19, 1937. http://www.vatican.va/content/pius-xi/en/encyclicals/documents/hf_p-xi_enc_19370319_divini-redemptoris.html.

Pius XII, Pope. "Wisdom—Not Weapons of War." *Collier's Weekly*, January 5, 1946, 11–13.

Pollard, A. F. "A School of Historical Research." *Contemporary Review* CXVIII (1920): 507–13.

Powicke, F. M. *Journal of Ecclesiastical History* II (1951): 109–12.

Rahner, Karl. "Theology of the Parish." In *The Parish: From Theology to Practice*, edited by Hugo Rahner, translated by Robert Kress. Westminster, Md.: Newman Press, 1958.

Ranke, Leopold von. "On the Character of Historical Science." In *The Theory and Practice of History*, edited by George G. Iggers, 8–16. New York: Routledge, 2011.

———. "On the Relations of History and Philosophy." In *The Theory and Practice of History*, edited by George G. Iggers, 5–7. New York: Routledge, 2011.

———. "Preface to the First Edition of *Histories of the Latin and Germanic Peoples*." In *The Theory and Practice of History*, edited by George G. Iggers, 85–87. New York: Routledge, 2011.

Ratcliffe, S. K. "S. H. Swinny." *Sociological Review* XV (1923): 274–77.

Reckitt, M. B. "The Idea of Christendom in Relation to Modern Society." In *The Return of Christendom*, 1–27. New York: Macmillan, 1922.

Works Cited

Rilke, Rainer Maria. *Wartime Letters of Rainer Maria Rilke.* Translated by M. D. Herter Norton. New York: W. W. Norton, 1940.

Rosenberg, Alfred. *The Myth of the Twentieth Century.* 1930. Translated by James Whisker. http://archive.org/details/TheMythOfThe20thCentury.

Russell, Bertrand. *The Practice and Theory of Bolshevism.* London: George Allen & Unwin, 1920.

Sandeman, George. "A Gardener of Paradise." Review of *Town Planning Towards City Development. Sociological Review* XII (1920): 58–63.

Schlesinger, Bruno P. "Christopher Dawson and the Modern Political Crisis." PhD diss., University of Notre Dame, 1949.

Schmitt, Carl. *The Necessity of Politics.* London: Sheed & Ward, 1931.

Sertillanges, A. G. *The Intellectual Life: Its Spirit, Conditions, Methods.* 1921; Washington, D.C.: The Catholic University of America Press, 1998.

Shaw, George Bernard. "Fabianism in Action." *Times,* August 13, 1931, 6.

Shevin-Coetzee, Merilyn, and and Frans Coetzee, eds. *World War I & European Society.* Lexington, Mass.: D. C. Heath, 1995.

Simons, John W. "Liberal Education as Transmissor of Values: The Proposals of Christopher Dawson." *Thought* 30, no. 2 (1955): 165–73.

———. "Putting American Catholics in Touch with the Christian Past." *Commonweal,* May 14, 1954, 135–38.

Smith, J. A. "Progress as an Ideal of Action." In *Progress and History,* edited by F. S. Marvin, 295–314. London: Oxford University Press, 1916.

Speaight, Robert. *The Property Basket: Recollections of a Divided Life.* London: Collins & Harvill, 1970.

Spender, Stephen. *Forward from Liberalism.* London: Victor Gollancz, 1937.

Spengler, Oswald. *The Decline of the West.* Abridged ed. 1918, 1922; New York: Modern Library, 1962.

Stannard, Harold Martin. "The Christian and the World." Review of *Religion and the Modern State. Times Literary Supplement,* August 22, 1935, 520.

Stinson, Charles. "Christian Culture." *Commonweal,* February 4, 1955, 478–79.

Stocking, George W. "Matthew Arnold, E. B. Tylor, and the Uses of Invention." *American Anthropologist* (new series) 65, no. 4 (August 1963): 795.

———. "Franz Boas and the Culture Concept in Historical Perspective." *American Anthropologist* (new series) 68, no. 4 (August 1966): 871.

Stone, Marla. *The Fascist Revolution in Italy: A Brief History with Documents.* Boston: Bedford/St. Martin's, 2013.

Stubbs, William. *The Constitutional History of England: In Its Origin and Development.* 6th ed. Oxford: Clarendon, 1903.

Stuart, Joseph T. "Yorkshire Days in Edwardian England: E. I. Watkin's Diary and His Friendship with Christopher Dawson." *Yorkshire Archaeological Journal* 84, no. 1 (2012): 205–23.

Tambling, Bette. "Priest, Nun 'Live by Love' as Husband, Wife." *Fresno Bee,* February 16, 1970, 9.

Tawney, R. H. *The Acquisitive Society.* London: G. Bell & Sons, 1921.

———. "The Study of Economic History." *Economica* XIII (1933): 1–21.

——. "Tract for the Times." Review of *The Judgment of the Nations. Manchester Guardian*, March 24, 1943, 3.

Taylor, A. J. P. *English History 1914–1945.* New York: Oxford University Press, 1965.

Taylor, Rachel Annand. Review of *Progress and Religion. Sociological Review* XXII (1930): 52–65.

Thomson, J. Arthur. "Biological Contributions to Sociology." *Sociological Review* XV (1923): 85–96.

Tocqueville, Alexis de. *The Ancien Régime and the Revolution.* 1856; New York: Penguin Books, 2008.

——. *Democracy in America.* 2 vols. New York: Vintage Books, 1972.

Trevelyan, G. M. "The Present Position of History." In *Clio, A Muse, and other Essays,* 177–96. London: Longmans, 1930.

——. *The War and the European Revolution in Relation to History.* London: University of London Press, 1920.

Trevor-Roper, H. R. Review of *Religion and the Rise of Western Culture. New Statesman and Nation,* March 11, 1950, 276–77.

Troeltsch, Ernst. *The Social Teaching of the Christian Churches.* Vol. 1. Translated by Olive Wyon. 1912; Louisville, Ky.: Westminster/John Knox, 1992.

Tully, Jr., Edward J. "Core of the Curriculum." *Commonweal,* October 15, 1954, 38 .

Tylor, Edward. *Primitive Culture.* 1871; New York: Harper & Row, 1958.

Voegelin, Eric. *The Political Religions.* Edited by Manfred Henningsen. Translated by Virginia Ann Schildauer. London: University of Missouri Press, 2000.

Von Hügel, Baron Friedrich. *The Mystical Element of Religion as Studied in Saint Catherine of Genoa and Her Friends.* 2 vols. 1908; London: J. M. Dent & Sons, 1961.

Wagner, Fritz. "Church History and Secular History as Reflected by Newton and His Time." *History and Theory* VIII (1969): 97–111.

Wall, Bernard. *Headlong into Change: An Autobiography and a Memoir of Ideas Since the Thirties.* London: Harvill, 1969.

Walpole, Hugh. "My Religion." In *My Religion.* London, Hutchinson, 1925.

Ward, Barbara. *New York Times,* March 29, 1959, BR7.

Ward, Maisie. *Unfinished Business.* New York: Sheed & Ward, 1964.

Watkin, E. I. "Tribute to Christopher Dawson." *Tablet,* October 4, 1969, 974.

Webb, Sidney, and Beatrice Webb. *Soviet Communism: A New Civilisation?* 2 vols. New York: Charles Scribner's Sons, 1936.

Weber, Max. "'Objectivity' in the Social Sciences and Social Policy." In *Philosophy of the Social Sciences: A Reader,* edited by Maurice Natanson, 355–418. New York: Random House, 1963.

——. *The Protestant Ethic and the Spirit of Capitalism.* Translated by Talcott Parsons. 1904–1905; Mineola, N.Y.: Dover, 2003.

Wells, H. G. *The Outline of History: Being a Plain History of Life and Mankind.* London: George Newnes, 1920.

White, Hayden. "Collingwood and Toynbee: Transitions in English Historical Thought." *English Miscellany* VIII (1957): 147–78.

——. *Metahistory: The Historical Imagination in Nineteenth-Century Europe.* Baltimore: Johns Hopkins University Press, 1973.

Works Cited

———. "Religion, Culture and Western Civilization in Christopher Dawson's Idea of History." *English Miscellany* IX (1958): 247–87.

———. Review of *Les Moines Blanc: Historie de l'Ordre Cistercien*. Speculum 34, no. 2 (April 1959): 304–8.

Whitehead, Alfred North. *Religion in the Making*. New York: Macmillan, 1926.

———. *Science and the Modern World*. 1925; New York: Free Press, 1953.

Wilhelmsen, Frederick D. "Christian Culture." *Commonweal*, March 4, 1955, 583–84.

———. "The Vision of Christopher Dawson." *Commonweal*, January 5, 1958, 355–58.

Williams, Raymond. *Culture and Society 1780–1950*. London: Chatto & Windus, 1958.

Wissler, Clark. *Man and Culture*. New York: Thomas Y. Crowell, 1923.

Wood, H. G. "Religion and State Idols." Review of *Religion and the Modern State. Spectator*, August 9, 1935, 231.

Yeats, W. B. "The Second Coming." 1920. https://www.poetryfoundation.org/poems/43290/the-second-coming.

Secondary Sources (after c. 1970)

The Catholic Intellectual Tradition: A Conversation at Boston College. The Church in the 21st Century Center, Boston College. 2010. https://dlib.bc.edu/islandora/object/bc-ir:101053/datastream/PDF/view.

"Center for Catholic Studies." University of St. Thomas. https://www.stthomas.edu/cathstudies/. Accessed April 6, 2020.

"New Evangelization and Culture." Mother of the Americas Institute: A Think Tank for the New Evangelization. https://mainstitute.org/tutorials/new-evangelization-and-culture. Accessed November 19, 2019.

Acton, Lord. "The Massacre of St. Bartholomew." In *Essays in the Study and Writing of History*, edited by J. Rufus Fears, 198–240. Indianapolis, Ind.: LibertyClassics, 1986.

Adair-Toteff, Christopher. "Max Weber's Mysticism." *Archives Européennes de Sociologie* XLIII (2002): 339–53.

Adams, James Luther. "Letter from Friedrich von Hügel to William James." *Downside Review* XCVIII (1980): 214–36.

———. "The Sacred and the Secular: Friedrich von Hügel." In *The Prophethood of All Believers*, edited by George K. Beach, 61–70. Boston: Beacon, 1986.

Aikman, David. *Jesus in Beijing: How Christianity Is Transforming China and Changing the Global Balance of Power*. Washington, D.C.: Regnery, 2003.

Akyol, Mustafa. *Islam without Extremes: A Muslim Case for Liberty*. New York: W. W. Norton, 2011.

Alexander, Christopher, Sarah Ishikawa, and Murray Silverstein. *A Pattern Language: Towns, Buildings, Construction*. New York: Oxford University Press, 1977.

Alexander, Michael. *Medievalism: The Middle Ages in Modern England*. New Haven, Conn.: Yale University Press, 2007.

Allardyce, Gilbert. "The Rise and Fall of the Western Civilization Course." *American Historical Review* 87, no. 3 (1982): 695–725.

Allitt, Patrick. *Catholic Converts: British and American Intellectuals Turn to Rome*. Ithaca, N.Y.: Cornell University Press, 1997.

Works Cited

Anderson, Benedict. *Imagined Communities: Reflections on the Origin and Spread of Nationalism*. 1983; London: Verso, 1991.

Aquilina, Mike. *The Church and the Roman Empire, 301–490*. Notre Dame, Ind.: Ave Maria, 2019.

Archer, Margaret S. *Culture and Agency: The Place of Culture in Social Theory*. Revised ed. Cambridge: Cambridge University Press, 1996.

Arx, Jeffrey Paul von. "Catholics and Politics." In *From without the Flaminian Gate: 150 Years of Roman Catholicism in England and Wales, 1850–2000*, edited by V. Alan McClelland and Michael Hodgetts, 245–71. London: Darton, Longman & Todd, 1999.

Atkinson, B. J. "Historiography." In *The Twentieth Century Mind: History, Ideas, and Literature in Britain*, edited by C. B. Cox and A. E. Dyson, 100–112. Oxford: Oxford University Press, 1972.

Atran, Scott. "The Devoted Actor: Unconditional Commitment and Intractable Conflict Across Cultures." *Current Anthropology* 57, no. 13 (June 2016): 192–203.

Aquila, Dominic A. "In Memoriam: John J. Mulloy." Catholic Social Scientists. http://catholicsocialscientists.org/cssr/Archival/1996/1996_277.pdf. Accessed May 16, 2017.

Bailey, Garrick, and James Peoples. *Essentials of Cultural Anthropology*, 3rd ed. Belmont, Calif.: Wadsworth Cengage Learning, 2014.

Barmann, Lawrence F. *Baron Friedrich von Hügel and the Modernist Crisis in England*. Cambridge: Cambridge University Press, 1972.

———. *The Letters of Baron von Hügel and Professor Norman Kemp Smith*. Edited by Lawrence Barmann. New York: Fordham University Press, 1981.

———. "The Modernist as Mystic." In *Catholicism Contending with Modernity: Roman Catholic Modernism and Anti-Modernism in Historical Context*, edited by Darrell Jodock, 215–47. Cambridge: Cambridge University Press, 2000.

Barrett, Stanley R., Sean Stokholm, and Jeanette Burke. "The Idea of Power and the Power of Ideas: A Review Essay." *American Anthropologist* 103, no. 2 (2001): 468–80.

Barry, Andrew, Georgina Born, and Gisa Weszkalnys. "Logics of Interdisciplinarity." *Economy and Society* 37, no. 1 (2008): 20–49.

Bashkow, Ira. "A Neo-Boasian Conception of Cultural Boundaries." *American Anthropologist* CVI (2004): 443–58.

Bentley, Michael, ed. *Modern Historiography: An Introduction*. London: Routledge, 1999.

———. *Modernizing England's Past: English Historiography in the Age of Modernism 1870–1970*. Cambridge: Cambridge University Press, 2005.

Bevir, Mark. *The Logic of the History of Ideas*. Cambridge: Cambridge University Press, 1999.

Birzer, Bradley J. *Sanctifying the World: The Augustinian Life and Mind of Christopher Dawson*. Front Royal, Va.: Christendom Press, 2007.

Blakely, Jason. *We Built Reality: How Social Science Infiltrated Culture, Politics, and Power*. New York: Oxford University Press, 2020.

Bonnell, Victoria E., and Lynn Hunt, eds. *Beyond the Cultural Turn: New Directions in the Study of Society and Culture*. Los Angeles: University of California Press, 1999.

Bregni, Marco. "The Facts Speak for Themselves." *Traces* XI, no. 4 (2009): 16–19.

Breisach, Ernst. *Historiography: Ancient, Medieval, and Modern*. 3rd ed. Chicago: University of Chicago Press, 2007.

Brewer, John D. "Sociology and Theology Reconsidered: Religious Sociology and the Sociology of Religion in Britain." *History of the Human Sciences* XX (2007): 7–28.

Works Cited

Briel, Don J. "Catholic Studies at the University of St. Thomas." In *The University and the Church: Don J. Briel's Essays on Education*, edited by R. Jared Staudt, 167–88. Providence, R.I.: Cluny Media, 2019.

———. "The Idea of the University and the College." In *The University and the Church: Don J. Briel's Essays on Education*, edited by R. Jared Staudt, 33–57. Providence, R.I.: Cluny Media, 2019.

———. "A Reflection on Catholic Studies after Twenty Years." In *The University and the Church: Don J. Briel's Essays on Education*, edited by R. Jared Staudt, 209–30. Providence, R.I.: Cluny Media, 2019.

———. "Renewing the University in a Tragic Culture." In *The University and the Church: Don J. Briel's Essays on Education,* edited by R. Jared Staudt, 123–44. Providence, R.I.: Cluny Media, 2019.

———. "Truth and Theology: A Response to Land O'Lakes." In *The University and the Church: Don J. Briel's Essays on Education*, edited by R. Jared Staudt, 109–21. Providence, R.I.: Cluny Media, 2019.

———. "The University Needs the Church." In *The University and the Church: Don J. Briel's Essays on Education,* edited by R. Jared Staudt, 87–107. Providence, R.I.: Cluny Media, 2019.

Brooke, Michael Z. *Le Play: Engineer and Social Scientist: The Life and Work of Frédéric Le Play*. London: Longman, 1970.

Brown, Peter. *The Rise of Western Christendom: Triumph and Diversity, A.D. 200–1000*. Oxford: Blackwell, 2003.

Burke, Peter. *The French Historical Revolution: The* Annales *School, 1929–89*. Stanford, Calif.: Stanford University Press, 1990.

———. *What Is Cultural History?* Cambridge: Polity, 2008.

Burleigh, Michael. *Earthly Powers: The Clash of Religion and Politics in Europe, from the French Revolution to the Great War*. New York: Harper Perennial, 2005.

———. *Sacred Causes: The Clash of Religion and Politics, from the Great War to the War on Terror*. New York: Harper Perennial, 2007.

Burrow, John W. "Intellectual History in English Academic Life: Reflections on a Revolution." In *Advances in Intellectual History*, edited by Richard Whatmore and Brian Young, 8–24. Houndmills: Palgrave Macmillan, 2006.

Burtchaell, James T. *The Dying of the Light: The Disengagement of Colleges & Universities from Their Christian Churches*. Grand Rapids, Mich.: William B. Eerdmans, 1998.

Byerly, Carol R. *Fever of War: The Influenza Epidemic in the U.S. Army During World War I*. New York: New York University Press, 2005.

Caldecott, Stratford, and John Morrill, eds. *Eternity in Time: Christopher Dawson and the Catholic Idea of History*. Edinburgh: T&T Clark, 1997.

Callahan, Daniel, Mildred Horton, Francis Rogers, Bernard Swain, and George H. Williams. "Christopher Dawson: 12 October 1889–25 May 1970." *Harvard Theological Review* LXVI, no. 2 (1973): 161–76.

Cannadine, David. *G. M. Trevelyan: A Life in History*. London: Penguin Books, 1992.

Cervantes, Fernando. "Progress and Tradition: Christopher Dawson and Contemporary Thought." *Logos* II (Spring 1999): 84–108.

Chadwick, Owen. *Acton and History*. Cambridge: Cambridge University Press, 1998.

Chagnon, Napoleon A. *Yanomamo*, 5th ed. 1968; USA: Wadsworth, 1997.

Chappel, James. *Catholic Modern: The Challenge of Totalitarianism and the Remaking of the Church*. Cambridge, Ma.: Harvard University Press, 218.

Chronopoulos, Themis. "Robert Moses and the Visual Dimension of Physical Disorder: Efforts to Demonstrate Urban Blight in the Age of Slum Clearance." *Journal of Planning History* 13, no. 3 (2014): 207–233.

Clements, Keith. *Faith on the Frontier: A Life of J. H. Oldham*. Edinburgh: T&T Clark, 1999.

Cloud, Henry, and John Townsend. *Boundaries in Marriage: Understanding the Choices That Make or Break Loving Relationships*. Grand Rapids, Mich.: Zondervan, 1999.

Coetzee, Frans, and Marilyn Shervin-Coetzee. *World War I and European Society*. Lexington, Mass.: D.C. Heath, 1995.

Collini, Stefan. *Liberalism and Sociology: L. T. Hobhouse and Political Argument in England, 1880–1914*. Cambridge: Cambridge University Press, 1979.

Corrin, Jay P. *Catholic Intellectuals and the Challenge of Democracy*. Notre Dame, Ind.: University of Notre Dame Press, 2002.

Costello, Paul. *World Historians and Their Goals: Twentieth-Century Answers to Modernism*. DeKalb: Northern Illinois University Press, 1993.

Cracraft, Joel. "The Scientific Response to Creationism." *Science, Technology, & Human Values* 7, no. 40 (1982): 79–85.

Day, Dorothy. *The Long Loneliness*. 1952; New York: HarperOne, 1980.

Deane, Seamus F. "Lord Acton and Edmund Burke." *Journal of the History of Ideas* XXXIII (1972): 325–35.

Dewald, Jonathan. "'A La Table De Magny': Nineteenth-Century French Men of Letters and the Sources of Modern Historical Thought." *American Historical Review* 108, no. 4 (2003): 1009–33.

Diamond, Jared. *Guns, Germs, and Steel: The Fates of Human Societies*. New York: W. W. Norton, 1999.

Doino, Jr., William. "John J. Mulloy, 1916–1995." EWTN. htps://www.ewtn.com/library/HOMELIBR/MULLOY.TXT. Accessed May 16, 2017.

Drake, Tim. "The Year of Benedict." *National Catholic Register*, January 4–10, 2009, 1.

Dreuzy, Agnes de. *The Holy See and the Emergence of the Modern Middle East: Benedict XV's Diplomacy in Greater Syria (1914–1922)*. Washington D.C.: The Catholic Univeristy of America Press, 2016.

Eksteins, Modris. *Rites of Spring: The Great War and the Birth of the Modern Age*. Toronto: Lester & Orpen Dennys, 1989.

Ellis, John Tracy. "American Catholics and the Intellectual Life." In *American Catholic History: A Documentary Reader*, edited by Mark Massa and Catherine Osborne, 95–101. 1955; New York: New York University Press, 2008.

Evans, David F. T. "Le Play House and the Regional Survey Movement in British Sociology 1920–1955." Unpublished M.Phil thesis, City of Birmingham Polytechnic, March 1986. http://www.dfte.co.uk/ios.

Evans, Richard J. *Cosmopolitan Islanders: British Historians and the European Continent*. Cambridge: Cambridge University Press, 2009.

———. "Nazism, Christianity and Political Religion: A Debate." *Journal of Contemporary History* 42, no. 1 (2007): 5–7.

Works Cited

Fallon, Nancy. "A Talk with Professor Bruno Schlesinger." In *Bruno Schlesinger: A Life in Learning & Letters*, edited by Rick Regan, 65–70. Self-published, Lulu.com, 2013.

Ferguson, Niall. *Civilization: The West and the Rest*. New York: Penguin, 2011.

Fink, Carole. *Marc Bloch: A Life in History*. Cambridge: Cambridge University Press, 1989.

Flint, James. "'Must God Go Fascist?': English Catholic Opinion and the Spanish Civil War." *Church History* LVI (1987): 364–74.

Foster, Paul. "The Making of Europe." *The Chesterton Review* IX (May 1983): 137–42.

Fussell, Paul. *The Great War and Modern Memory*. 1975; Oxford: Oxford University Press, 2000.

Gamble, Richard M. *The War for Righteousness: Progressive Christianity, the Great War, and the Rise of the Messianic Nation*. Wilmington, Del.: ISI Books, 2003.

Gaston, James. "Catholic Culture: What Is It and Why Should We Care About It?" *Lay Witness*, November/December 2012, 4–8.

———. "Understanding Europe: Christopher Dawson's Vision of the Unity and History of Europe." *European Studies Journal* (1992): 161–64.

Geertz, Clifford. "The Impact of the Concept of Culture on the Concept of Man." In *The Interpretations of Cultures*, 33–54. New York: Basic Books, 1973.

Gentile, Emilio. *Politics as Religion*. Translated by George Staunton. Princeton, N.J.: Princeton University Press, 2006.

———. "The Sacralization of Politics: Definitions, Interpretations and Reflections on the Question of Secular Religion and Totalitarianism." *Totalitarian Movements and Political Religions* I (2000): 18–55.

Gilbert, Martin. *A History of the Twentieth Century*. Vol. 1, *1900–1933*. New York: William Morrow, 1997.

———. *The Somme: Heroism and Horror in the First World War*. New York: Henry Holt, 2006.

Girouard, Mark. *The Return of Camelot: Chivalry and the English Gentleman*. New Haven, Conn.: Yale, 1981.

Gleason, Philip. *Contending with Modernity: Catholic Higher Education in the Twentieth Century*. New York: Oxford University Press, 1995.

———. "A Look Back at the Catholic Intellectualism Issue." *U.S. Catholic Historian* 13, no. 1, (Winter 1995): 19–37.

———. "A Practical Experiment in Education: The Study of Christian Culture as the Core of the College Curriculum." *The Chesterton Review* 9, no. 2 (1983): 167–71.

———. "Newman's *Idea* in the Minds of American Educators." In *Building the Church in America: Studies in Honor of Monsignor Robert F. Trisco on the Occasion of His Seventieth Birthday*, edited by Joseph C. Linck and Raymond J. Kupke, 113–39. Washington, D.C.: The Catholic University of America Press, 1999.

Goffin, Magdalen. *The Watkin Path, an Approach to Belief: The Life of E. I. Watkin*. Brighton, Sussex: Academic Press, 2006.

Goldman, Lawrence. "Victorian Social Science: From Singular to Plural." In *The Organisation of Knowledge in Victorian Britain*, edited by Martin Daunton, 87–114. Oxford: Oxford University Press, 2005.

Goldstein, Doris S. "J. B. Bury's Philosophy of History: A Reappraisal." *American Historical Review* LXXXII (1977): 896–919.

Gordon, Alan. "Introduction: The New Cultural History and Urban History: Intersections." *Urban History Review/Revue d'histoire urbaine* 33, no. 1 (Fall 2004): 3–7.

Grafton, Anthony. "How the Historian Found His Muse: Ranke's Path to the Footnote." In *The Modern Historiography Reader: Western Sources*, edited by Adam Budd, 178–83. New York: Routledge, 2009.

Green, Anna, and Kathleen Troup. *The Houses of History: A Critical Reader in Twentieth-Century History and Theory.* Manchester: Manchester University Press, 1999.

Green, Jay D. *Christian Historiography: Five Rival Versions.* Waco, Tex.: Baylor University Press, 2015.

Gregor, A. James. *Totalitarianism and Political Religion: An Intellectual History.* Stanford, Calif.: Stanford University Press, 2012.

Grisez, Germain. "American Catholic Higher Education: The Experience Evaluated." In *Why Should the Catholic University Survive? A Study of the Character and Commitments of Catholic Higher Education*, edited by George A. Kelly, 41–55. New York: St. John's University Press, 1973.

Grosvenor, Peter C. "The British Anti-Moderns and the Medievalist Appeal of European Fascism." *The Chesterton Review* XXV (February/May 1999): 103–15.

Habib, Khalil M. "Christianity and Western Civilization: An Introduction to Christopher Dawson's *Religion and the Rise of Western Culture.*" *The Political Science Reviewer* 41, no. 2 (2017): 164–89.

Hague, René, ed. *Dai Greatcoat: A Self-Portrait of David Jones in His Letters.* London: Faber & Faber, 1980.

Halliday, R. J. "The Sociological Movement, the Sociological Society and the Genesis of Academic Sociology in Britain." *Sociological Review* (new series) VI (1968): 377–98.

Hämäläinen, Pekka, and Samuel Truett. "On Borderlands." *Journal of American History* 98, no. 2 (September 2011): 338–61.

Hamid, Tawfik. *Inside Jihad: How Radical Islam Works, Why It Should Terrify Us, How to Defeat It.* Mountain Lake Park, Md.: Mountain Lake, 2015.

Hannam, James. *The Genesis of Science: How the Christian Middle Ages Launched the Scientific Revolution.* Washington D. C.: Regnery, 2011.

Hastings, Adrian. *A History of English Christianity: 1920–1990*, 3rd ed. 1986; London: SCM, 1991.

Herman, Arthur. *The Idea of Decline in Western History.* New York: Free Press, 1997.

Hitchcock, James. "Christopher Dawson." *The American Scholar* 62, no.1 (Winter 1993): 111–118.

———. *The Pope and the Jesuits: John Paul II and the New Order in the Society of Jesus.* New York: National Committee of Catholic Laymen, 1984.

———. "Rehearsal for Deconstruction." *Fellowship of Catholic Scholars Quarterly* 30, no. 4 (Winter 2007): 3–9.

Hittinger, Russell. "Christopher Dawson: A View from the Social Sciences." In *The Catholic Writer*, vol. 2, edited by Ralph McInerny, 31–47. San Francisco: Ignatius, 1991.

———. "Christopher Dawson on Technology and the Demise of Liberalism." In *Christianity and Western Civilization: Christopher Dawson's Insights: Can a Culture Survive the Loss of Its Religious Roots?*, 73–95. San Francisco: Ignatius, 1993.

Works Cited

———. "The Metahistorical Vision of Christopher Dawson." In *The Dynamic Character of Christian Culture*, edited by Peter J. Cataldo, 1–56. New York: University Press of America, 1984.

———. "The Two Cities and the Modern World: A Dawsonian Assessment." *Modern Age* XXVIII (1984): 193–202.

Hürten, Heinz. "Waldemar Gurian and the Develoment of the Concept of Totalitarianism." In *Totalitarianism and Political Religions*. Vol. 1, *Concepts for the Comparison of Dictatorships*, edited by Hans Maier, 42–52. New York: Routledge, 1996.

Iggers, George G. *The German Conception of History: The National Tradition of Historical Thought from Herder to the Present*. Middletown, Conn.: Wesleyan University Press, 1983.

———. "Historicism: The History and Meaning of the Term." *Journal of the History of Ideas* 56, no. 1 (1995): 129–52.

———. *Historiography in the Twentieth Century: From Scientific Objectivity to the Postmodern Challenge*. Middletown, Conn.: Wesleyan University Press, 1997.

———. Introduction. In *The Theory and Practice of History*, edited by Georg G. Iggers, xi–xlv. New York: Routledge, 2011.

———. and Q. Edward Wang. *A Global History of Modern Historiography*. Harlow: Pearson/Longman, 2008.

Jacobs, Alan. *The Year of Our Lord 1943: Christian Humanism in an Age of Crisis*. New York: Oxford University Press, 2018.

Jankovic, Ivan. "Monstrous Modernity: Western Roots of Islamic Radicalism." *360 Review*, Summer/Fall 2019, 78–89.

Jiping, Zuo. "Political Religion: The Case of the Cultural Revolution in China." *Sociological Analysis* 52, no. 1 (1991): 99–110.

John Paul II, Pope. "Address to the Italian National Congress of the Ecclesial Movement for Cultural Commitment." January 16, 1982. *L'Osservatore Romano*, English edition, June 28, 1982, 1–8.

———. *Ex Corde Ecclesiae*. Apostolic Constitution. August 15, 1990. http://www.vatican .va/content/john-paul-ii/en/apost_constitutions/documents/hf_jp-ii_apc_15081990_ ex-corde-ecclesiae.html.

Kahn, Joseph, and Daniel J. Wakin. "Western Classical Music, Made and Loved in China." *New York Times*, April 2, 2007. http://www.nytimes.com/2007/04/02/world/asia/ 02iht-china.html?pagewanted=all&_r=0.

Keating, Joan E. "Discrediting the 'Catholic State': British Catholics and the Fall of France." In *Catholicism in Britain and France Since 1789*, edited by Frank Tallett and Nicholas Atkin, 27–42. London: Hambledon, 1996.

———. "Roman Catholics, Christian Democracy and the British Labour Movement, 1910–1960." PhD diss., University of Manchester, 1992.

Kengor, Paul. *A Pope and a President: John Paul II, Ronald Reagan, and the Extraordinary Untold Story of the 20th Century*. Wilmington, Del.: ISI Books, 2017.

Kennedy, Arthur. "Christopher Dawson's Influence on Bernard Longergan's Project of 'Introducing History into Theology.'" *Logos* 15, no. 2 (Spring 2012): 138–64.

Kerr, Fergus. *Theology after Wittgenstein*. Oxford: Basil Blackwell, 1986.

King, Jason. "After Ex Corde Ecclesiae." *Journal of Moral Theology* 4, no. 2 (2015): 167–91.

Kinlaw, Jeffrey. "Troeltsch and the Problem of Theological Normativity." In *The Anthem*

Companion to Ernst Troeltsch, edited by Christopher Adair-Toteff, 105–25. London: Anthem, 2018.

Knasas, John F. X. "Aquinas' Natural Law Versus Ethical and Cultural Pluralism." In *Religion and Culture in Dialogue: East and West Perspectives*, edited by Jānis Tālivaldis Ozoliņš, 77–92. Switzerland: Springer, 2016.

———. "Tracey Rowland's 'Augustinian Thomist' Interpretation of Culture." *Angelicum* 86, no. 1 (2009): 689–700.

Knowles, David. "Christopher Dawson." *Tablet*, June 6, 1970, 558.

Kramer, Alan. *Dynamic of Destruction: Culture and Mass Killing in the First World War.* New York: Oxford University Press, 2007.

Küklick, Henrika. "Islands in the Pacific: Darwinian Biogeography and British Anthropology." *American Ethnologist* 23, no. 3 (August 1996): 611–26.

Kurlberg, Jonas. "Resisting Totalitarianism: The Moot and a New Christendom." *Religion Compass* 7, no. 12 (2013): 517–31.

Kurtz, Angela Astoria. "God, Not Caesar: Revisiting National Socialism as 'Political Religion.'" *History of European Ideas* 35, no. 2 (2009): 236–52.

Larsen, Timothy. *The Slain God: Anthropologists and the Christian Faith.* Oxford: Oxford University Press, 2014.

Lassman, Peter. "Responses to Fascism in Britain, 1930–1945: The Emergence of the Concept of Totalitarianism." In *Sociology Responds to Fascism*, edited by Stephen P. Turner and Dirk Käsler. London & New York: Routledge, 1992.

Layton, Colleen, Tawny Pruitt, and Kim Cekola, eds. *The Economics of Place: The Value of Building Communities Around People.* Ann Arbor: Michigan Municipal League, 2011.

Lewis, Michael J. "What Jane Jacobs Saw." *First Things*, March 2017, 51–56.

Lindbeck, George A. *The Nature of Doctrine: Religion and Theology in a Postliberal Age.* Philadelphia: Westminster, 1984.

Lindberg, David. *The Beginnings of Western Science.* 2nd ed. Chicago: University of Chicago Press, 2007.

Lothian, James R. *The Making and Unmaking of the English Catholic Intellectual Community, 1910–1950.* Notre Dame, Ind.: University of Notre Dame Press, 2009.

MacIntyre, Alasdair. *After Virtue: A Study in Moral Theory.* 3rd ed. Notre Dame, Ind.: University of Notre Dame Press, 2007.

Maier, Hans. "Concepts for the Comparison of Dictatorships: 'Totalitarianism' and 'Political Religions.'" In *Totalitarianism and Political Religions*, edited by Hans Maier, 199–215. New York: Routledge, 1996.

———. "Political Religion: a Concept and Its Limitations." *Totalitarian Movements and Political Religions* VIII (2007): 5–16.

Mandell, Gail P. *Madeleva: A Biography.* Albany: State University of New York Press, 1997.

———. "Reflections on Bruno Schlesinger." In *Bruno Schlesinger: A Life in Learning & Letters*, edited by Rick Regan, 71–76. Self-published, Lulu.com, 2013.

Mann, Charles C. "Birth of Religion: The World's First Temple." *National Geographic* 219, no. 6 (June 2011): 39–59.

Marks, Robert S. *The Origins of the Modern World: A Global and Environmental Narrative from the Fifteenth to the Twenty-First Century.* 4th ed. Lanham, Md.: Rowman & Littlefield, 2020.

Works Cited

Marold, Antoinette M. "Federation of Christian Ministries 45th Anniversary 2013 President's History." 2013. http://www.federationofchristianministries.org/pdfs/President-Book.pdf.

Mazzotti, Massimo. *The World of Maria Gaetana Agnesi, Mathematician of God*. Baltimore: Johns Hopkins University Press, 2007.

McCarthy, John P. "Hilaire Belloc and Catholic History." *Thought* LXVII (1992): 62–73.

McClay, Wilfred M. "Teaching Religion in American Schools and Colleges: Some Thoughts for the 21st Century." *Historically Speaking* 3, no. 2 (2001): 13–17.

McGrath, Alister E. *The Open Secret: A New Vision for Natural Theology*. Oxford: Blackwell, 2008.

McGreevy, John T. *Parish Boundaries: The Catholic Encounter with Race in the Twentieth-Century Urban North*. Chicago: University of Chicago Press, 1996.

McMillan, James F. "Catholicism and Nationalism in France: The Case of the Fédération Nationale Catholique, 1924–39." In *Catholicism in Britain and France Since 1789*, edited by Frank Tallett and Nicholas Atkin, 151–63. London: Hambledon, 1996.

———. "Writing the Spiritual History of the First World War." In *Religie: Godsdienst En Geweld in De Twintigste Eeuw*, edited by Madelon de Keizer, 47–71. Zutphen: Walburg, 2006.

McNeill, William H. "History Upside Down." *The New York Review of Books*, May 15, 1997, 48–50.

Meaney, John W. *O'Malley of Notre Dame*. Notre Dame, Ind.: University of Notre Dame Press, 1991.

Meller, Helen. *Patrick Geddes: Social Evolutionist and City Planner*. London and New York: Routledge, 1990.

Mews, Stuart. "The Sword of the Spirit: A Catholic Cultural Crusade of 1940." In *The Church and War*, edited by W. J. Sheils, 409–30. Oxford: Basil Blackwell, 1983.

Mills, C. Wright. *The Sociological Imagination*. New York: Oxford University Press, 1959.

Miscamble, Wilson D. *American Priest: The Ambitious Life and Conflicted Legacy of Notre Dame's Father Ted Hesburgh*. New York: Image, 2019.

Mitchell, Peter M. *The Coup at Catholic University: The 1968 Revolution in American Catholic Education*. San Francisco: Ignatius Press, 2015.

Mitchell, Philip I. "Civilization Sickness and the Suspended Middle: R. G. Collingwood, Christopher Dawson, and Historical Judgment." *Logos* 21, no. 3 (Summer 2018): 85–113.

Moeller, Robert G. *The Nazi State and German Society: A Brief History with Documents*. Boston: Bedford/St. Martin's, 2010.

Mokyr, Joel. *A Culture of Growth: The Origins of the Modern Economy*. Princeton, N.J.: Princeton University Press, 2017.

Moloney, Thomas. *Westminster, Whitehall and the Vatican: The Role of Cardinal Hinsley, 1935–43*. Tunbridge Wells: Burns & Oates, 1985.

Monaghan, John, and Peter Just. *Social & Cultural Anthropology: A Very Short Introduction*. Oxford: Oxford University Press, 2000.

Morris, Charles R. *American Catholic: The Saints and Sinners Who Built America's Most Powerful Church*. New York: Random House, 1997.

Morris, Kevin L. "Fascism and British Catholic Writers 1924–1939." *The Chesterton Review* XXV (February/May 1999): 82–95.

Morris, Randall C. "Whitehead and the New Liberals on Social Progress." *Journal of the History of Ideas* LI (1990): 75–92.

Mosse, George L. "Fascism and the French Revolution." *Journal of Contemporary History* 24, no. 1 (1989): 5–26.

Mulloy, Clement A. "The Impact of the West on World History: The Contrasting Methods and Views of Jared Diamond and Christopher Dawson." *Catholic Social Science Review* 15 (2010): 137–52.

Mulloy, John J. "The Influence of America on Christopher Dawson." *The Wanderer*, November 23, 1989, 6.

Murawiec, Laurent. *The Mind of Jihad*. New York: Cambridge University Press, 2008.

Nagel, Thomas. *Mind and Cosmos: Why the Materialist Neo-Darwinian Conception of Nature Is Almost Certainly False*. New York: Oxford, 2012.

Navarro-Valls, Joaquin. "Faith Must Become Culture: John Paul II's Legacy to Intellectuals and Scientists." 2011. http://inters.org/faith-must-become-culture.

Nicolson, Juliet. *The Great Silence: Britain from the Shadow of the First World War to the Dawn of the Jazz Age*. New York: Grove, 2009.

Niebuhr, Reinhold. "What's a Mote to One is a Beam to Another." Review of *The Historic Reality of Christian Culture*. *New York Times*, March 13, 1960, BR 18.

Olsen, Glenn W. "Why We Need Christopher Dawson." *Communio* 35 (Spring 2008): 115–44.

O'Neil, Mary, and Simon Akhtar, eds. *On Freud's "The Future of an Illusion."* London: Karnac Books, 2009.

Overy, Richard. *The Morbid Age: Britain Between the Wars*. London: Allen Lane, 2009.

Pals, Daniel L. *Eight Theories of Religion*, 2nd ed. Oxford: Oxford University Press, 2006.

———. *Seven Theories of Religion*. New York: Oxford University Press, 1996.

———. *Introducing Religion: Readings from the Classic Theorists*. Oxford: Oxford University Press, 2009.

———. "Is Religion a *Sui Generis* Phenomenon?" *Journal of the American Academy of Religion* LV (1987): 259–82.

———. "Reductionism and Belief: An Appraisal of Recent Attacks on the Doctrine of Irreducible Religion." *Journal of Religion* LXVI (1986): 18–36.

Paul, Herman. "Metahistory: Notes Towards a Genealogy." *Práticas da História* 1, no. 1 (2015): 17–31.

Petersen, Jens. "The History of the Concept of Totalitarianism in Italy." In *Totalitarianism and Political Religions*, edited by Hans Maier, 3–21. New York: Routledge, 1996.

Petit, M. Loretta. "Sister M. Madeleva Wolff, C.S.C." *Catholic Education: A Journal of Inquiry and Practice* 9, no. 3 (March 2006): 320–33.

Pinkerton, Roy M., and William J. Windram. *Mylne's Court: Three Hundred Years of Lawmarket Heritage*. Edinburgh: University of Edinburgh Information Office, 1983.

Pipes, Richard. *A Concise History of the Russian Revolution*. New York: Alfred A. Knopf, 1995.

Polke, Christian. "Troeltsch's Personalism." In *The Anthem Companion to Ernst Troeltsch*, edited by Christopher Adair-Toteff, 71–82. London: Anthem, 2018.

Potts, Garrett, and Stephen P. Turner. "Making Sense of Christopher Dawson." In *The History of Sociology in Britain: New Research and Revaluation*, edited by Plamena Panayotova, 103–36. Cham: Palgrave Macmillan, 2019.

Works Cited

Pugh, Martin. *We Danced All Night: A Social History of Britain Between the Wars*. London: Vintage Books, 2008.

Quinn, Dermot. "Christopher Dawson and Historical Imagination." *The Chesterton Review* XXVI, no. 4 (2000): 484.

———. Introduction. In *Dynamics of World History*, edited by John J. Mulloy. 1956; Wilmington, Del.: ISI Books, 2002.

Radu, Mattei Ion, "Dawson and Communism: How Much did He Get Right?" *The Political Science Reviewer* 41, no. 2 (2017): 276–302.

Raftis, James Ambrose. "The Development of Christopher Dawson's Thought." *The Chesterton Review* IX (1983): 115–35.

Ratzinger, Joseph. *Truth and Tolerance*. San Francisco: Ignatius, 2004.

Reese, Peter. *Target London: Bombing the Capital, 1915–2005*. Barnsley, South Yorkshire: Pen & Sword Military, 2011.

Reno, R. R. "Thinking Critically about Critical Thinking." *First Things*, June-July 2011, 7.

Renwick, Chris. *British Sociology's Lost Biological Roots: A History of Futures Past*. New York: Palgrave Macmillan, 2012.

Reuth, Ralf Georg. *Goebbels*. Translated by Krishna Winston. New York: Harcourt Brace, 1993.

Rhein, Jacob D. "How Dawson Read *The City of God*." *Logos* 17, no. 1 (Winter 2014): 36–62.

Ripperger, Chad. "The Sixth Generation." *Latin Mass*, Summer 2012, 34–38.

Risjord, Mark W. "Ethnography and Culture." In *Philosophy of Anthropology and Sociology*, edited by Stephen P. Turner and Mark W. Risjord, 399–428. Amsterdam: North-Holland, 2007.

Robertson, David G. "Conspiracy Theories and the Study of Alternative and Emergent Religions." *Nova Religio: The Journal of Alternative and Emergent Religions* 19, no. 2 (2015): 5–16.

Rodden, John. *Every Intellectual's Big Brother: George Orwell's Literary Siblings*. Austin: University of Texas Press, 2006.

Rowland, Tracey. *Culture and the Thomist Tradition: After Vatican II*. New York: Routledge, 2003.

Royal, Robert. *A Deeper Vision: The Catholic Intellectual Tradition in the Twentieth Century*. San Francisco: Ignatius, 2015.

Rue, Loyal D. Review of *Religion and World History*. *Church History* 45, no. 1 (1976): 126.

Schama, Simon. "Flaubert in the Trenches." *The New Yorker* 72, April 1, 1996, 96–99.

Schlesinger, Bruno. "Responses to Dawson's Idea in the United States." *The Chesterton Review* 9, no. 2 (1983): 171–176.

Schmude, Karl. *The Campion Book: The Ideal of a Liberal Arts Education in the Light of Faith and Reason*. Sydney: Campion College, 2014. https://www.campion.edu.au/about-campion/.

———. *Christopher Dawson: A Biographical Introduction*. Hobart (Tasmania): Christopher Dawson Centre for Cultural Studies, 2014.

Schoeman, Roy H. *Salvation Is from the Jews: The Role of Judaism in Salvation History from Abraham to the Second Coming*. San Francisco: Ignatius, 2003.

Schumacher, E. F. *A Guide for the Perplexed*. New York: Harper Perennial, 1977.

Schwartz, Adam. "Confronting the 'Totalitarian Antichrist': Christopher Dawson and Totalitarianism." *Catholic Historical Review* 89, no. 3 (July 2003): 464–88.

———. "'I Thought the Church and I Wanted the Same Thing': Opposition to Twentieth-Century Liturgical Change in the Thought of Graham Greene, Christopher Dawson, and David Jones." *Logos* I (1998): 36–65.

———. *The Third Spring: G. K. Chesterton, Graham Greene, Christopher Dawson, and David Jones*. Washington, D.C.: The Catholic University of America Press, 2005.

Scott, Christina. "Christopher Dawson's Reaction to Fascism and Marxism." *The Chesterton Review* 25, no. 3 (1999): 406.

———. *A Historian and His World: A Life of Christopher Dawson*. 1984; New Brunswick, N.J.: Transaction, 1992.

Scott, John. *British Social Theory: Recovering Lost Traditions Before 1950*. London: SAGE, 2018.

Scott, John, and Ray Bromley. *Envisioning Sociology: Victor Bradford, Patrick Geddes, and the Quest for Social Reconstruction*. New York: State University of New York Press, 2013.

Scott, John, and Christopher T. Husbands. "Victor Branford and the Building of British Sociology." *Sociological Review* LV (2007): 460–84.

Scott, Julian. "The Life and Times of Christopher Dawson." *The Political Science Reviewer* 41, no. 2 (December 2017): 141–63.

Shannon, Christopher, and Christopher Blum. *The Past as Pilgrimage: Narrative, Tradition and the Renewal of Catholic History*. Front Royal, Va.: Christendom Press, 2014.

Shapiro, Barbara. *A Culture of Fact: England, 1550–1720*. Ithaca, N.Y.: Cornell University Press, 2000.

Shaw, Russell. *American Church: The Remarkable Rise, Meteoric Fall, and Uncertain Future of Catholicism in America*. San Francisco: Ignatius, 2013.

Silver, Harold. *Higher Education and Opinion Making in Twentieth-Century England*. London: Woburn, 2003.

Simboli, Brian. "*Ex Corde Ecclesiae*, Social Science, and the Public Square." *The Catholic Social Science Review* 17, no. 1 (2012): 323–36.

Skinner, Quentin. "Interpretation and the Understanding of Speech Acts." In *Visions of Politics*, vol. 1, 103–27. Cambridge: Cambridge University Press, 2002.

———. "Meaning and Understanding in the History of Ideas." In *Visions of Politics*, vol. 1, 57–89. Cambridge: Cambridge University Press, 2002.

Slee, Peter. *Learning and a Liberal Education: The Study of Modern History in the Universities of Oxford, Cambridge and Manchester 1800–1914*. Manchester: Manchester University Press, 1986.

Smith, Christian. "The Conceptual Incoherence of 'Culture' in American Sociology." *The American Sociologist* 47, no. 4 (2016): 388–415.

———. *Moral, Believing Animals: Human Personhood and Culture*. New York: Oxford University Press, 2003.

Soffer, Reba N. *Discipline and Power: The University, History, and the Making of an English Elite, 1870–1930*. Stanford, Calif.: Stanford University Press, 1994.

———. "Why Do Disciplines Fail? The Strange Case of British Sociology." *English Historical Review* XCVII (1982): 767–802.

Sommerville, C. John. *The Decline of the Secular University: Why the Academy Needs Religion*. New York: Oxford University Press, 2006.

Stafford, William. "This Once Happy Country: Nostalgia for Pre-Modern Society." In *The*

Works Cited

Imagined Past: History and Nostalgia, edited by Christopher and Malcolm Chase Shaw, 33–46. Manchester: Manchester University Press, 1989.

Stanley, Matthew. *Practical Mystic: Religion, Science, and A. S. Eddington*. Chicago: Chicago University Press, 2007.

Stanlis, Peter J. *Robert Frost: The Poet as Philosopher*. Wilmington, Del.: ISI Books, 2007.

Stapleton, Julia. *Englishness and the Study of Politics: The Social and Political Thought of Ernest Barker*. Cambridge: Cambridge University Press, 1994.

———. "Resisting the Centre at the Extremes: 'English' Liberalism in the Political Thought of Interwar Britain." *British Journal of Politics and International Relations* 1, no. 3 (1999): 271–88.

Staudt, R. Jared. "Christopher Dawson on Theology and the Social Sciences." *Logos* 12, no. 3 (Summer 2009): 91–111.

———. Introduction. In *The University and the Church: Don J. Briel's Essays on Education*, edited by R. Jared Staudt, xix–xxxv. Providence, R.I.: Cluny Media, 2019.

———. ed. *The University and the Church: Don J. Briel's Essays on Education*. Providence, R.I.: Cluny Media, 2019.

Stone, Marla. *The Fascist Revolution in Italy: A Brief History with Documents*. Boston: Bedford/St. Martin's, 2013.

Stuart, Joseph T. "Bourgeois or Baroque?" September 28, 2017. https://voegelinview.com/-bourgeois-or-baroque/.

———. "Catholic Studies and the Science of Culture." In *Renewal of Catholic Higher Education: Essays on Catholic Studies in Honor of Don J. Briel*, edited by Matthew T. Gerlach, 182–99. Bismarck, N.D.: University of Mary Press, 2017.

———. "Christopher Dawson and the Idea of Progress." *Logos* 14, no. 4 (2011): 74–91.

———. "At the Heart of the World: Reflections on Mandan History & Culture." *360 Review*, Spring/Summer 2017, 6–15.

———. and James Gaston. "Holy Oil?" *360 Review*, Fall 2015, 88–97.

———. "North Dakota and the Cultural History of the Great War." *North Dakota History* 83, no. 2 (2018): 3–17.

———. "The Question of Human Progress in Britain after the Great War." *Britain and the World* I (2008): 53–78.

———. *Rethinking the Enlightenment: Faith in the Age of Reason*. Manchester, N.H.: Sophia Institute, 2020.

———. "The War to Start All Wars: The Great War & Its 100-Year Legacy." *360 Review*, Summer/Fall 2019, 22–29.

———. "Yorkshire Days in Edwardian England: E. I. Watkin's Diary and His Friendship with Christopher Dawson." *Yorkshire Archaeological Journal* 84, no. 1 (2012): 205–23.

Sydenham, M. J. Review of *The Gods of Revolution*. *Canadian Historical Review* LIV (1973): 434–35.

Sykes, S. W. "Theology." In *The Twentieth-Century Mind: History, Ideas, and Literature in Britain*, edited by C. B. Cox and A. E. Dyson, 146–170. Oxford: Oxford University Press, 1972.

Tate, Adam. "Wrestling with the Modern State: Christopher Dawson and the Background to *The Crisis of Western Education*." *The Political Science Reviewer* 40, no. 1 (2017): 98–123.

Taylor, Brian. "The Anglican Clergy and the Early Development of British Sociology." *The Sociological Review* XLII (1994): 438–51.

Taylor, Charles. *A Catholic Modernity?* Marianist Award Lectures, Book 10. Dayton, Ohio: University of Dayton, 1996. http://ecommons.udayton.edu/uscc_marianist_award/10/.

———. *A Secular Age.* Cambridge, Mass.: Belknap/Harvard University Press, 2007.

———. *Varieties of Religion Today: William James Revisited.* Cambridge, Mass.: Harvard University Press, 2002.

Taylor, W. David O. "Beauty as Love: Hans Urs Von Balthasar's Theological Aesthetics." *Transpositions.* 2012. http://www.transpositions.co.uk/beauty-as-love-hans-urs-von-balthasars-theological-aesthetics/.

Thornhill, John. *The Road All Peoples Travel: Christopher Dawson's Interpretation of Cultural Developments That Ultimately Produced Our Western Civilization.* Self-published, FeedAReed.com, 2018.

Thorpe, Andrew, ed. *The Failure of Political Extremism in Inter-War Britain.* Exeter: University of Exeter, 1989.

Tillman, Mary Katherine. "The Tension Between Intellectual and Moral Education in the Thought of John Henry Newman." *Thought* 60, no. 238 (September 1985): 322–34.

Tocqueville, Alexis de. *Democracy in America.* 2 vols. New York: Vintage Books, 1972.

Toynbee, Arnold. *A Study of History.* Vol. 12, *Reconsiderations.* London: Oxford University Press, 1961.

———. *A Study of History.* Revised ed. London: Oxford University Press, 1972.

Trepanier, Lee. "Culture and History in Eric Voegelin and Christopher Dawson." *The Political Science Reviewer* 41, no. 2 (December 2017): 211–42.

Turner, Stephen P. "Religion and British Sociology: The Power and Necessity of the Spiritual." In *The Palgrave Handbook of Sociology in Britain,* edited by John Holmwood and John Scott, 97–122. New York: Palgrave Macmillan, 2014.

Valignano, Alessandro. "Missionary Directive." In *Matteo Ricci & the Catholic Mission to China: A Short History with Documents,* edited by R. Po-chia Hsia. 1581; Indianapolis, Ind.: Hackett, 2016.

Varacalli, Joseph A. *Bright Promise, Failed Community: Catholics and the American Public Order.* Lanham, Md.: Lexington Books, 2000.

Vickery, John B. *The Literary Impact of* The Golden Bough. Princeton, N.J.: Princeton University Press, 1973.

Villis, Tom. *British Catholics and Fascism: Religious Identity and Political Extremism Between the Wars.* New York: Palgrave Macmillan, 2013.

Wagar, W. Warren. *Good Tidings: The Belief in Progress from Darwin to Marcuse.* Bloomington: Indiana University Press, 1972.

———. "Modern Views of the Origins of the Idea of Progress." *Journal of the History of Ideas* XXVIII (1967): 55–70.

Wallace, David Foster. "2005 Kenyon Commencement Address." May 21, 2005. https://web.ics.purdue.edu/~drkelly/DFWKenyonAddress2005.pdf.

Walsh, Michael. *From Sword to Ploughshare: Sword of the Spirit to Catholic Institute for International Relations, 1949–1980.* London: Catholic Institute for International Relations, 1980.

Ward, Leo R. "Dawson and Education in Christian Culture." *Modern Age* 17, no. 1 (1973): 402.

Weakland, Rembert G. Foreword. In *Religion and the Rise of Western Culture,* by Christopher Dawson, i–ii. 1950; New York: Image, 1991.

Works Cited

Weigel, George. *The End and the Beginning: Pope John Paul II—the Victory of Freedom, the Last Years, the Legacy.* New York: Doubleday, 2010.

———. Foreword. In *Renewal of Catholic Higher Education: Essays on Catholic Studies in Honor of Don J. Briel,* edited by Matthew T. Gerlach, 1–2. Bismarck, N.D.: University of Mary Press, 2017.

———. Foreword. In *The University and the Church: Don J. Briel's Essays on Education,* edited by R. Jared Staudt, i–iii. Providence, R.I.: Cluny Media, 2019.

———. "John Paul II and the Priority of Culture." *First Things,* February 1998, 19–25.

Weinstein, David. "The New Liberalism of L. T. Hobhouse and the Reenvisioning of Nineteenth-Century Utilitarianism." *Journal of the History of Ideas* LVII (1996): 487–507.

Williams, Raymond. *Keywords: A Vocabulary of Culture and Society.* London: Fontana/Croom Helm, 1976.

Williamson, Philip. "Christian Conservatives and the Totalitarian Challenge, 1933–40." *English Historical Review* CXV (2000): 607–42.

Wills, Garry. "Memories of a Catholic Boyhood." In *American Catholic History: A Documentary Reader,* edited by Mark Massa and Catherine Osborne, 263–71. New York: New York University Press, 2008.

Wilson, A. N. *Hilaire Belloc.* 1984; London: Gibson Square Books, 2003.

Winter, Jay M. "Spiritualism and the First World War." In *Religion and Irreligion in Victorian Society,* edited by R. W. Davis and R. J. Halmstadter, 185–200. London: Routledge, 1992.

Winthrop, Delba. "Tocqueville's *Old Regime*: Political History." *Review of Politics* 43, no. 1 (1981): 88–111.

Witham, Larry. *The Measure of God: Our Century-Long Struggle to Reconcile Science & Religion.* San Francisco: HarperSanFrancisco, 2005.

Woodruff, Douglas. "Christopher Dawson." *Tablet,* June 6, 1970, 558–59.

Woodward, Kenneth L. *Getting Religion: Faith, Culture, and Politics from the Age of Eisenhower to the Era of Obama.* New York: Convergent, 2016.

Woolf, Daniel. *A Concise History of History: Global Historiography from Antiquity to the Present.* New York: Cambridge University Press, 2019.

Young, R. V. "The Continuing Crisis." In *The Crisis of Western Education,* ix–xxiii. Steubenville, Ohio: Franciscan University Press, 1989.

Zmirak, John. "Christopher Dawson's Economic Blindness." April 14, 2014. https://isi.org/-intercollegiate-review/christopher-dawsons-economic-blindness/.

INDEX

Index

Index

Index

Federal-Aid Highway Act (1956), 339
Fédération Nationale Catholique, 295
Federation of Christian Ministries, 342
Fertile Crescent, 35
Final Solution, 62
Firth, Charles, 150, 152
Fisher, Geoffrey, 292
Fisher, H. A. L., 40, 159, 180
Fitzgerald, F. Scott, 135
Five-Year Plan, Russia, 255
Fleury, Claude, 97
Fliche, Augustin, 40
FWP (Folk-Work-Place formula): and the American way of life, 336–37; "categories of cultural differences," 376; in comparative religion, 219; connection to biology, 91; consecrated by religion, 219; and Darwin, 91, 376; and Diamond, 375–76; Dawson's innovation, 91, 376; failure to account for the time factor, 107; and Geddes, 91, 383; as "Geddes-Le Play formula," 384; and geographic region, 92; Hobhouse criticism of, 98–99; and Le Play, 89; and Mumford, 92, 376; and political religion, 244; and psychology, 99–102, 385–86; and OFE (organism, function, environment), 91; and sacralization, 244, 391–92; schema, 383; separated from the (I) factor, 334, 337; and social renewal, 93; and suburbia, 336. *See also* I/FWP
Forde, C. Daryll, 5, 37
formal object (of study), 11
Forster, E. M., 268
Foster, Paul, 97
Foucault, Michel, 112
Fox, George, 193, 396
fragmentation, 6, 9–13, 26–29, 57–63, 235, 300–301, 305, 334, 356, 369, 382
Franciscan University of Steubenville, Ohio, 2, 361, 363
Franco-Prussian War, 172
Franco, Francisco, 275, 278, 287
Frankfurt School, 111
Frankfurt, Germany, 283
Frankl, Viktor, 253
Frazer, James, 31, 37, 183, 187, 190–93, 198, 209, 211–12
freedom of association, 271
French Revolution: causes of, 221, 229; Christianity and, 311, 396, 397, 398; compared to the Fronde, 230; Dawson's view on, 250, 251; as historical moment, 44, 48, 97, 100;

and ideologies, 231–32, 243, 405; and the Jacobins, 237, 249; in relation to the Great War, 51; as a spiritual revolution, 45; de Tocqueville on, 47, 235
Fresno State College, California, 341
Freud, Sigmund: criticism of James, 206; and Dawson, 187, 200, 202, 211; and the Great War, 51; ideologies, 72; influence, 406; and rationalism, 199; as reductionist thinker, 31, 183; and religion, 190, 198, 209, 411
Friedan, Betty, 339–40
Fronde, 230
Frost, Robert, 367
Fueloep-Miller, René, 247
Fumet, Stanislas, 286

Gallican Church, 231
Galton, Francis, 81
Gaspari, Alcide de, 38
Gasquet, Francis, 165
Gaston, James, 2, 363–64
Geddes, Patrick: and civic processes, 102; and Dawson, 86, 99, 101, 103; and environmental sociology, 88, 90–92, 94, 105–107, 375; and Hobhouse, 81, 98; influence, 78, 82–83, 85; Le Play formula, 199, 219, 383, 384–87; and Mumford, 87; and psychology, 385–86; and religion, 100; and sociology, 79–80
Geertz, Clifford, 374–75
Gell, Edith, 80
general education, 306–307, 309, 323–24, 354, 375, 400
Geneva, 83, 85, 104
George V, 267
ghetto, 302, 336–37, 344, 349
GI Bill, 338–39
Gibbon, Edward, 27, 52, 122–23, 169
Gifford Lectures, 20, 186–87, 192, 196, 214, 224, 247, 283
Gifford, Adam, 188
Gilson, Etienne, 4, 186
Ginsberg, Morris, 84–85
Girl Guides, 267
G. K. Chesterton Institute, Seton Hall University, New Jersey, 2
Gladstone, William and Mary, 228–29
Glasgow, University of, 186
globalization, 68, 241, 245, 373
Gnosticism, 332, 345
Göbekli Tepe, 36
Goebbels, Joseph, 246–47
Goethe, Johann Wolfgang von, 218

Index

Gooch, G. P., 155, 166
Göring, Herman, 280–82
Gothic culture, 97, 156, 397–99, 403–405, 408
Grand Hotel, Rome, 282
Great Books program, 301, 316
Great War (1914–1918): and Belloc, 173; and
 culture, 66, 68–70, 72–73, 325; and crisis
 of humanity, 63; and cultural assimilation
 to the American way of life, 302; cultural
 history of, 57–63, 373; and Dawson, 19, 28,
 31, 46, 54, 57–58, 110, 121, 141, 148, 238, 240,
 255, 315, 336; and expansion of politics,
 237–41; and Germany, 59, 62, 64; and GI
 Bill, 339; historical event, 26, 27, 33, 56, 81,
 82, 194; and historiography, 139–43; and
 Hitler, 258; legacies, 58–63; and Mussolini,
 257; and political religion, 238, 243, 254–58;
 and Power, 146; questions following, 29,
 145; and religion, 184–85; and "Right" and
 "Left," 278; and sex, 60, 73–74; spiritual results of, 255–56; and Trevelyan, 142–43; and
 Wagner, 181; and world history, 145–47
Greece, 38, 113, 120, 134, 280, 320
Green, J. R., 143, 149
Green, T. H., 81
Griffiths, Bede, 186
Gurian, Waldemar, 247

Haeusser, Ludwig Christian, 256
Halévy, Daniel, 280
Halifax, Lord, 268, 278
Halphen, Louis, 4, 40
Harari, Manya, 288
Harnack, Adolf von, 124–25, 128–29
Harvard Divinity School, 21
Harvard University, Massachusetts, 1, 32, 206,
 213, 307, 344–46, 354, 359
Harvill Press, 288
Hayes, Helen, 353
Hegel, Georg Wilhelm Friedrich, 124, 253, 397
Heidegger, Martin, 129
Hellenic civilization, 14, 315, 403, 407, 410
Hellenism, 311, 334, 395
Herberg, William, 337
Herbertson, Dorothy, 89
Herder, Johan Gottfried, 64
Herodotus, 69
Hesburgh, Theodore, 345–46
Hetherington, H. J., 86
High Middle Age, 39
higher education, 300, 305, 316, 319–20, 323,
 329, 331–33, 338, 346–47, 363, 369–71

Hill, Christopher, 5
Himalayas, 220
Hinduism, 186, 216, 399, 411
Hinsley, Cardinal Arthur, 286–88, 291–93
historicism: and Boas, 65; and the Christian
 mind, 334, 350; crisis in, 64, 123, 125; and
 Dawson, 30, 122–32, 333–34; different meanings, 64–65; in Germany, 122–32; Gibbon's
 lack of, 122–23; and Harnack, 124–25; as
 philosophy of history, 122; and Ranke, 122;
 and relativism, 125–26; and the socio-
 historical mode of cultural study, 64–65;
 and Troeltsch, 125–27; and Weber, 127–28
historicist nexus (eternity-in-time), 122,
 125–26, 137, 175, 179, 374
historiography: alternatives to national, 144;
 Annales school, 137, 140–41, 178–79, 381;
 Belloc on, 174; British, 135, 138, 142, 154,
 182; Dawson on, 149, 166, 180–83, 188, 361,
 377–78, 380, 382; French, 141; German, 64;
 twentieth-century, 136–37, 139; Western, 2
History and Theory (journal), 181
History (journal), 40
Hitler, Adolf, 31, 237, 239, 245–47, 255–60, 262,
 282, 290
Hobhouse, L. T., 79–82, 85, 97–99, 102–103, 105,
 111, 115, 210
Hoche, Alfred, 62
Hodges, H. A., 299
Holocaust, 253, 380
"the holy" (Otto), 195, 214
Holy Land, 219
Holy Spirit, 223–24, 295, 392
Horton, Douglas, 307, 344
House of Lords, 292
Hughes, Philip, 165
Huguenots, 221
Huitzilopochtli, Aztec god, 239
Hulme, T. E., 20
Humanae Vitae, 347
humanism: Christian, 286, 311, 395, 398; classi-
 cal, 410; and Dawson, 20, 300; theological,
 137
Humanist Manifesto, 20
humanistic mode (of the science of culture):
 and comparative religion, 225–26; in
 containment of politics, 265; in *Ex corde
 Ecclesiae*, 364; and culture as a moral order,
 8–9, 72–76; Dawson's youthful experience
 of, 55–57; described, 7–9, 56–57; and
 education, 300, 313, 318; and idealism (religious), 326–28; and Lawler, 320, 327–28;

Index

Index

Index

Index

Tylor, Edward, 64–65, 68–69
Tyrrell, George, 204

unconscious (psychology), 198–200
United States Conference of Catholic Bishops, 302
University College, London, 37
University College of the South West, England, 86
University College, Dublin, 321
University of Chicago, 316, 399
University of Notre Dame, 345–46, 352, 354
University of Strasbourg, 140
University of Southern Louisiana, 319
universalism, 65, 224–27, 333, 336, 341, 349–51
Ur, Sumerian city of, 35
U.S. Housing Act, 338
utilitarianism, 251, 323

V-weapons, 298–99, 303
vacuum (spiritual), 31, 177, 237, 251–55, 262, 300–301
Valignano, Alessandro, 325–26
verstehen (interpretive understanding), 7, 128
Vignaux, Paul, 286
Vincennes, France, 229
vocation, spirit of, 271
Voegelin, Eric, 1, 242
Voisin Plan, 338
Volk, 64
Voltaire, 114
Von Hügel, Friedrich: on American Catholics, 324; and Bremond, 179; and Dawson, 31, 151, 183, 195–96, 205–206, 214, 231, 286; elements of religion (experientialism, intellectualism, institutionalism), 184, 203–208, 230–31, 359; and intellectual bridges, 228; and Gifford Lectures, 183, 187; and James, 206–207; modernist, 24; and Otto, 208; personal faith, 203–205

Wagner, Fritz, 181–82
Wall, Bernard, 277
Wallace, David Foster, 217, 380–81
Wallop, Gerard, 271, 280
Walpole, Hugh, 185
Ward, Barbara, 4, 279, 287, 288, 292
Ward, Leo, 299, 353
Ward, Maisie, 21, 144
wars of religion, 291
Watkin, Edward Ingram, 51, 54–58, 247, 359
Webb, Beatrice and Sidney, 261
Weber, Max, 7, 47, 80, 127–29, 195, 209, 214, 411
Weimar Republic, 260
Wells, H. G., 34, 111, 116, 145–46, 169, 191
Werfel, Franz, 242
Wesley, John, 231, 396
Western civilization, 32, 43, 69, 121, 145, 239, 294, 309, 312, 314, 321–22, 356, 393
whig historiography, 141–44, 149, 154
White, Andrew Dickson, 114
White, Hayden, 165, 172, 175, 378, 379, 380
White, Martin, 81
Whitefield, George, 231
wholly other (Otto), 195
Whitehead, Alfred North, 114, 185
Wilhelmsen, Frederick, 353
Williams, Charles, 286
Williams, Raymond, 96, 225
Wilson, Woodrow, 139, 239
Wissler, Clark, 67–68, 70
Wittgenstein, Ludwig, 129, 192
Wolf, Eric, 67, 376
Wolff, Sister M. Madeleva, 303, 353
Woodruff, Douglas, 4
world history, 145–49, 376, 397, 407

Yeats, W. B., 62

Zweig, Stefan, 280

{ 454 }